A History of Irish Republicanism
in Dundee *c*1840 to 1985

PRAISE FOR
IRISH REPUBLICANISM IN DUNDEE c1840 to 1985

'In *Irish Republicanism in Dundee c1840 to 1985*, Rút Nic Foirbeis offers a compelling account, scrupulously researched, of the role played by this historically radical Scottish city in the struggle for Irish independence across 150 years of political transformation. Dubbed 'Yes City' in the wake of the Scottish Independence Referendum of 2014, Dundee was a crucible of revolutionary activism from the famine to the hunger strikers, saying Yes to independence across the water, and No to Anglo-British hegemony. This book maps out in fascinating detail the myriad ways in which activists and agitators from a diverse immigrant community contributed to Irish republican resistance to the British imperial monarchy. Through a painstaking narrative that embraces complexity rather than seeking clear lines of development Nic Foirbeis points the way to a deeper understanding of Irish-Scottish relations and a fuller appreciation of Dundee's place in a shared history shadowed by colonialism and conflict.'

Willy Maley, editor of *Scotland and the Easter Rising*

'In this extremely well-researched and thoroughly absorbing account of Dundee's radical republican tradition, Rút Nic Foirbeis, herself a radical Republican activist, has provided a much needed and very welcome addition to the corpus of Irish Republican history and the vital support networks which existed among the Irish diaspora and their allies for the long struggle for Irish national self-determination. From the mid-nineteenth through to the mid-twentieth century Rút charts the unbroken line of Dundee radicals and Republicans who never lost faith in or contact with the Irish Republican struggle. We owe them a huge debt of gratitude for their commitment and owe Rút our gratitude and thanks for bringing their story in from the shadows. A must-read for all serious students of Irish history and radical Republicanism.'

Jake MacSiacais, former Republican prisoner, Irish language activist and former Blanketman

'This well-researched book makes an invaluable contribution to our understanding of the Irish in Scotland. A misconception has long existed that the impact of Irish migration was largely confined to the west of Scotland and Edinburgh. Rút Nic Foirbeis has corrected that error by detailing the history of that community in Dundee. She skillfully illustrates the influence these migrants and their descendants had on the political and social life of that city. Two themes dominate. Their engagement with the labour movement and their role in the centuries old issue surrounding Irish independence. In respect to the latter, this book excels, detailing every significant phase and participant. Moreover, while never ignoring the fractious nature of radical politics, Nic Foirbeis illustrates the permanence of transformative activism in her native city. Cause for thought, surely, when contemplating the ongoing campaign for Scotland's independence. A book that simply must be read.'

> **Tommy McKearney, former Republican prisoner and hunger striker, trade union organiser and author of *The Provisional IRA: From Insurrection to Parliament***

'In this pioneering study the author charts the role played by the Irish in Dundee during a turbulent period in Irish history when momentous changes took place. Included among the topics covered are the rise of the Fenian movement, the War of Independence, and successive campaigns for Irish freedom up to the most recent phase of the struggle in the north of Ireland. Nic Foirbeis has drawn on an impressive range of sources to provide the first detailed local study of how an Irish community in Scotland reacted to the momentous political events in the period covered.'

> **Stephen Coyle, editor of *'We Will Rise Again': Ireland, Scotland and the Easter Rising***

'This is not only an important contribution to our understanding of the history of Dundee, but also of the political struggles within and on behalf of the Irish diaspora. Throughout, the central narrative thread detailing the cause for Ireland is well told, while the complex and changing relationship between social class and nationalist interests within the diaspora communities is given due recognition. There is great attention to historical detail that speaks to the author's scholarship, while a strong historical narrative is maintained. Nic Foirbeis rightly pays particular attention not just to class but also to gender with nuance and insight and the women activists are especially well drawn. It is a cracking read while still presenting a wealth of evidence. It should also annoy all the right people.'

Graham Smith, Professor of Oral History, University of Newcastle

'The Scots/Irish nexus is rooted in a common Gaelic heritage. This history encompasses a shared language as well as shared mythologies and faith systems from the Fianna to Colmcille and Knox. Over millennia, waves of migration moved people in both directions across the sea of Moyle. This movement is central to both unionist and nationalist biographies and yet it remains under-researched. Moreover, the politics of this nexus have tended to receive even less attention – despite the centrality of James Connolly to both Irish and Scottish radical traditions. Rút Nic Foirbeis corrects this in forensic detail in terms of the experience of one city, Dundee. But her analysis also addresses the key issues of Irish solidarity in Scotland and Britain. (Reminding us *inter alia* of the value of a *cois tine* praxis – combining politics and craic!) The book brilliantly fulfils her commitment to 'weave Irish threads into the rich tapestry of Scottish radical history.'

Robbie McVeigh, author of *Ireland, Colonialism, and the Unfinished Revolution: Anois Ar Theacht an tSamhraidh*

A History of Irish Republicanism in Dundee

c1840 to 1985

Rút Nic Foirbeis

A History of Irish Republicanism in Dundee, c1840 to 1985 – Rút Nic Foirbeis

Copyright © 2024. All rights reserved.

The right of Rút Nic Foirbeis to be identified as the author of the Work has been asserted in accordance with the Copyright, Designs & Patents Act 1988.

This first edition published and copyright 2024 by Tippermuir Books Ltd, Perth, Scotland.

mail@tippermuirbooks.co.uk – www.tippermuirbooks.co.uk

No part of this publication may be reproduced or used in any form or by any means without written permission from the Publisher except for review purposes. All rights whatsoever in this book are reserved.

ISBN 978-1-913836-27-6 (paperback).

A CIP catalogue record for this book is available from the British Library.

Project coordination and editorial by Paul S Philippou.
Cover design by Matthew Mackie.
Editorial support: Ajay Close and Steve Zajda.

Co-founders and publishers of Tippermuir Books:
Rob Hands, Matthew Mackie and Paul S Philippou.

Text design, layout, and artwork by Bernard Chandler [graffik].
Text set in Adobe Garamond Pro 10.5pt on 14pt.

Printed and bound by Ashford Colour Press.

*This book is dedicated to
John Milton Malone (1953–2017)*

About the Author

Rút Nic Foirbeis is an independent working-class historian who was born and raised in Dundee where she continues to live. In 2003, she was awarded a PhD from the University of Dundee for her thesis on 'Patterns of Cultural Production in Dundee c1850–c1900'. An Irish solidarity activist since her early youth, she subsequently became involved in, amongst other progressive causes, the Dundee Nablus Twinning Association, Tayside for Justice in Palestine and the Radical Independence Campaign. In late middle age, she remains committed to the causes of destroying the capitalist system and establishing an independent Scottish socialist republic. She is currently striving to improve her technique on the tin whistle.

Acknowledgements

This book could not have been written without the help of many people. I would like to express my gratitude to all those who took the time to talk to me and answer my questions. I reserve a special thanks to Michael Taylor who, despite facing the challenge of serious illness, took time to discuss his recollections of Irish solidarity campaigning in Dundee and to search through his collection of newspapers and photographs. I am also indebted to the participants in various campaigns and related activities for the small but significant details that helped me to construct a fuller picture of events. I would also like to thank the friends, relatives and former associates of some of the protagonists in this story for sharing their personal memories and family histories. Of the many archivists and librarians who responded to my requests for information, I wish to thank the staffs of National Library of Ireland; the Irish National Archives; the Irish Military Archives; the National Library of Scotland; the National Records of Scotland; the Linen Hall Library, Belfast; the Mitchell Library, Glasgow; the Local History Department of Dundee Central Library; the A K Bell Library, Perth; Dundee Archive and Record Centre; and Dundee University Archives. I would especially like to credit Gerry Kavanagh of the National Library of Ireland, who it was my good fortune to meet at a critical point in my research, and the late Gregory O'Connell of the National Archives of Ireland, who guided me to the sources which enabled me to put names, and at least one face, to Dundee's Fenians. I would like to thank all friends and relatives, comrades and collaborators for their kind words of encouragement and support. I am especially indebted to Stephen Coyle, Willy Maley, Tommy McKearney, Jake MacSiacais and Graham Smith who read the final draft, offered valuable feedback and kept me right on the finer details. I have also benefitted greatly from conversations with Tony Cox, Mary Henderson, Steve Keenan, Lucy and John Keaveney and Margaret Ward. I would like to acknowledge the support of Paul Philippou and the team at Tippermuir Books for having faith in this project and seeing it through to publication. Special thanks are due to my son, Pádraig Durnin, for helping me to access resources which would have been otherwise difficult for an independent researcher operating outside the academic sector, and for boosting my confidence in moments of self-doubt. Thanks are also due to my mother, Marion Forbes, who in her tenth decade, continues to be a source of candid advice and illuminating observations. Finally, alongside the generations of Irish Republican activists whose stories remain untold, I dedicate this to John Malone who had the foresight to record his recollections while the memory was still vivid.

CONTENTS

Preface 1

Chapter 1   Radicals, Republicans and Repealers 1841–58 13

Chapter 2   Fenians 1859–69 50

Chapter 3   A New Departure: Constitutionalism,
             Compromise and Collaboration 1870–79 105

Chapter 4   The Land for the People 1879–89 133

Chapter 5   Celtic Twilight, Socialist Dawn 1890–1908 194

Chapter 6   A New Militancy 1909–16 240

Chapter 7   Revolution 1916–23 291

Chapter 8   A Partitioned Politics 1923–69 394

Chapter 9   A Legacy Reclaimed 1970–85 436

Epilogue 516

Select Bibliography 520

Select Index 532

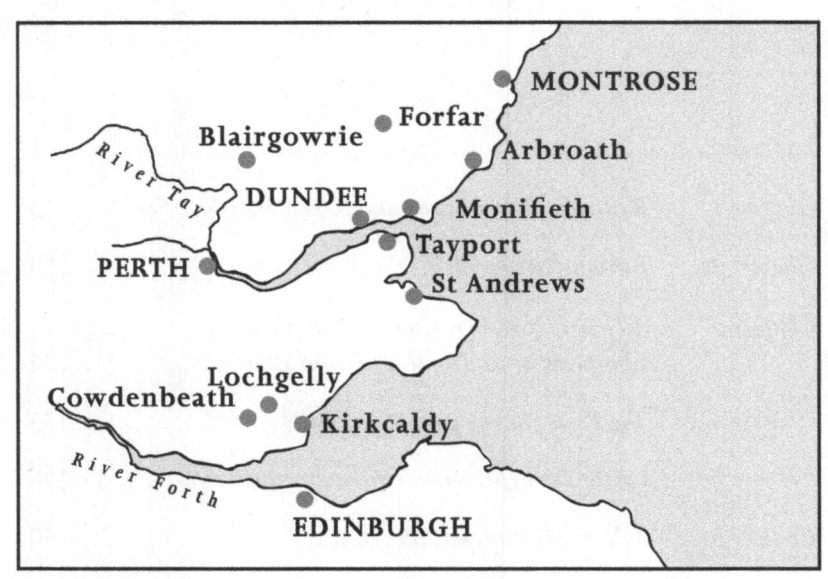
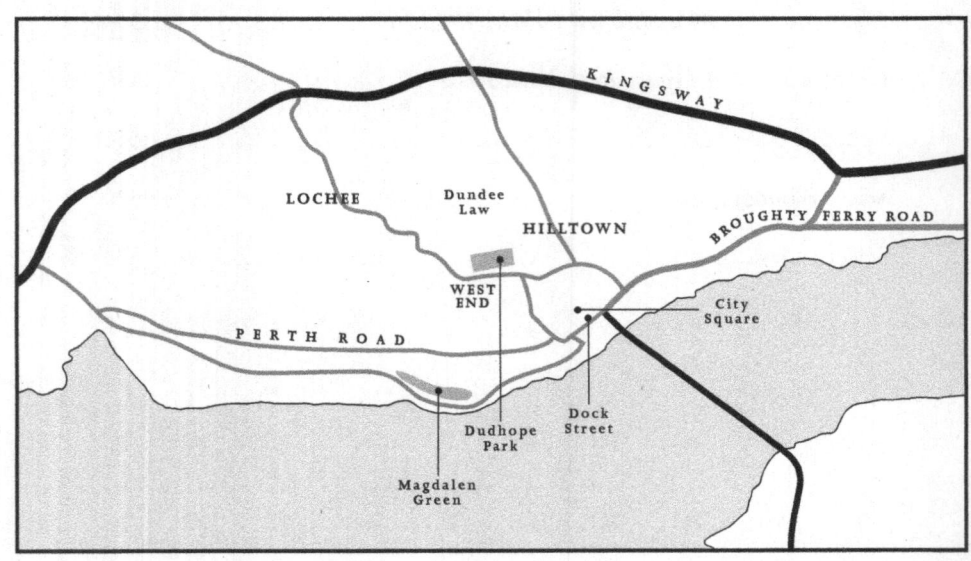

PREFACE

THIS IS the story of the struggle to establish an Irish Republic, and how it manifested itself in a support for physical force Irish republicanism in the Scottish town of Dundee from the early 1840s up until 1985. Since the IRA ceasefire of 1997 and signing of the Good Friday Agreement in 1998, there has been an upsurge in the study of physical force republicanism, particularly of the last phase of the long, protracted campaign to end British rule and establish a united Ireland. It is fair to say that, with the suspension of military hostilities, this formerly pariah subject now meets the criteria of being 'safe' and fertile territory for historical study. In turn, the number of studies on physical force Irish republicanism has escalated exponentially throughout what has been labelled, somewhat contentiously, as 'the Decade of Centenaries' of 'the Revolutionary Period' in Ireland's history.[1] Yet, amidst the growing body of literature focusing on various parts of Ireland and the diaspora, there has been no intensive examination of Irish republicanism in Dundee in its totality. For a town so intrinsically Irish in its DNA, with a long reputation of being a 'radical toun', this may seem like a strange oversight. At the same time, the fact that Dundee was frequently overlooked, ignored and forgotten by leading figures within the Irish national movement, and consequently by historians of it, is an integral part of the story.

In the Scottish context, the story of Irish republicanism in Dundee and north-east Scotland is perhaps less spectacular than that of other parts of the country. In terms of the 1916–23 period, it has been overshadowed by Glasgow and the west, where, for example, the Coatbridge-born schoolteacher turned Irish revolutionary sharpshooter, Margaret Skinnider, has been rememorised and restored to her rightful place as a key player in the 1916 Easter Rising and the consequent struggle for Irish national and social liberation; and dramatic incidents such as the 'Smashing of the Van' – the daring attempt by the Glasgow IRA to rescue Sligo Brigade leader, Frank Carty, from a prison van in broad daylight on a busy main street in May 1921 – have been celebrated in song and story. Edinburgh too has elicited attention, mainly through being the birthplace and early political stomping ground of James Connolly, the most revered socialist republican thinker and organiser in Irish history. Yet, Connolly's period of residence in Dundee, during which he took his first tentative steps into the socialist movement and into a life of social and political activism which culminated in an armed uprising against British imperial rule in Ireland, has remained largely unexamined. Taking in a longer sweep of history, Máirtín Ó Catháin's study on Irish republicanism in Scotland from 1858 to 1916 offers a broad perspective on republican activity in Scotland. However, as the bulk of activity took place in and around Glasgow (and the sources reflect this), the study naturally focuses on that area. Nevertheless, the numerous references to Dundee, as well as other parts of the country, hint at a hidden seam of activity which invites detailed local scholarship.[2]

It is also important to state what this is not. It is not a history of 'the Irish in Dundee'. The impact of Irish immigration on the political and cultural life of the city has been well covered by other authors. In particular, William Walker and Richard McCready have examined the influence of Dundee's large Irish-Catholic population on constitutional politics and labour organisation, in the course of which both have touched on the Irish community's support for the Republican movement in the 1916–22 period. Nevertheless, up until now, there has been no investigation into the full extent and distinctive nature of support for Irish republicanism in Dundee.[3]

Furthermore, the tendency to define 'the Irish', in Dundee, or anywhere else, as a single amorphous entity can result in assumptions being made of a homogeneous Irish psychology which fails to account for the diverse range of attitudes and opinions which existed within the diaspora. Many people of Irish birth or descent chose at some point to relinquish their Irish identity and the national, political and religious allegiances which often accompanied it, while other people of mixed Scotch-Irish parentage or no Irish heritage at all became fervent Irish republicans. Likewise, advanced nationalists of Irish origin also embraced the Scottish radical tradition as a part of their common Celtic heritage and working-class identity. Indeed, while the Irish community was the mainstay of militant Irish republicanism, support for an Irish Republic was not exclusive to it. Thus, this study also feeds into a wider history of working-class political struggle.

I was initially drawn to this subject by my own involvement in Irish solidarity campaigning in Dundee in the 1980s, which led me, initially, to investigate the campaigns that preceded it, then to question, and ultimately seek to redress the relative absence of Dundee from the wider historical record. Accordingly, this project has had long gestation. In the winter of 1988/89, I found myself at the end of a fixed period of employment at the Community Programme-funded Dundee Oral History Project.[4] My awareness of the potential of grassroots history had been raised. However, the prospect of developing it had been curtailed and I was looking for a new focus. At the same time, a chance meeting with an old campaigner, John Malone, who was nearing the end of a government-sponsored Work Start programme, elicited the information that he had started to record his recollections of involvement in the Irish solidarity campaign in Dundee in the late 1970s and early 1980s. Over the course of that winter, he passed his 'scribbles' to me for grammatical improvements and further suggestions, which I added in pencil, then typed out and returned along with the original manuscript. Some weeks later, the old black notebook in which the manuscript was written was returned in the post with a note bidding me to keep it. I packed it away at the back of a drawer and got on with my life. In due course, I went on to do a college course, which led to university and a history degree – including a dissertation on the topic of social mobility in the Irish community in Dundee in the late nineteenth century, then a postgraduate diploma in librarianship and a doctorate on cultural activity, also in late nineteenth-century Dundee.

Fast forward to 2016. For some time, I had been struggling to cope with a chronic pain condition. Resolving to foreswear prescription medication due to its enervating side effects, I turned to my GP, who referred me to a pain clinic, which led in turn to attendance on a pain management course and a session with a counsellor. With the help of the latter, I hoped to acquire techniques that would enable me to reprogramme my overactive nervous system and alleviate the litany of debilitating conditions that stemmed from it. It was a complex issue, he admitted, and beyond the realms of his experience. He suggested another approach – to think of an activity that would absorb my attention, and make a point of doing it every day, if only for a few minutes. I thanked him and left. I had already thought of something – within the realms of my experience and capabilities, I hoped – the process of historical research. I recalled the moments when, beavering through a box of files in some archive or library, or, more often than not, flipping through my pile of disconnected notes and photocopies in the dead of the night, my eyes would alight on a name, a phrase or some other detail, which confirmed an instinct, generated an idea, or blew a long-held theory out of the water.

I walked home, consciously, by a deliberately circuitous route. It took me from the clinic on Hawkhill, down through the streets, lanes and wynds that cut across Brook Street, beneath which ran the path of the Scouring Burn, the ancient water course that once sprang up from the eastern slopes of Balgay Hill and flowed down through the town into the River Tay and out to the North Sea. I was keenly aware of where I was walking. Almost a century ago, at the height of Irish War of Independence, Brook Street had been at the heart of the Dundee IRA gunrunning operation. I decided there and then to revisit an earlier inquiry into the Dundee gunrunning trial of 1921 – a key incident in Dundee folk history with which many of the city's older inhabitants, and a few of its younger ones, were vaguely familiar. I set myself the task of conducting a deeper, more forensic study which covered the details of the incident, the wider historical context in which it occurred, and the motives of the people involved. In time, this developed into a larger study of Irish republicanism in Dundee during the 'Tan' and Civil Wars.[5] Rewardingly, embedded within the source material were the traces of a deep-rooted support for militant Irish republicanism going back two or more generations. Thus, what started as a study of one campaign in one period evolved, organically, into a history of Irish republicanism in Dundee which extended back to the radical Land League of the 1880s, the Fenian campaign of the 1860s, and the Young Ireland and physical force Chartist movements of the 1840s, the latter two of which had drawn inspiration from the revolutionary republican ideals and endeavours of the United Irishmen, United Scotsmen and other fraternal organisations of the 1790s.

I resolved to gather information on each phase of activity, to compile a chronology of events which others could possibly draw upon and use as a basis for further study. I considered finishing at the end of the 'Civil War' in 1923. Upon reaching that point, however, I was aware that I had failed to address the most recent phase of the struggle, and the event that had triggered my involvement in the first place – the hunger strike of 1981. Sadly, John Malone died in 2017, and his memoir of that crucial period had been lost in the course of a house move. I decided to press ahead by reconstructing what I had already committed to memory and seeking the recollections of other people involved. Then, just when I had given up hope of ever seeing it again, the manuscript turned up – wrapped, appropriately, in a green scarf in a dusty red suitcase. Written five to ten years after the campaign it recounted; it was close enough to events to have a clear memory of them but far enough away to have a measure of perspective. Besides providing a useful memory trigger, it has served as a valuable source by which to compare and contrast other peoples' versions of events.

This study has presented a number of challenges, both practical and personal. Chief amongst the former is the nature of the source material. Personal recollections of Irish republican activity were often composed and recorded several decades later, increasing the potential for interference and displacement by subsequent memories and events, or the suppression of uncomfortable truths and unfashionable opinions which cut against the prevailing political and ideological narratives. Moreover, official records on physical force Irish republicanism in Dundee are notoriously thin on the ground. Much activity involved organisations whose effective functioning made them necessarily secretive and resistant to keeping paper records, all of which calls for a more forensic analysis of other sources. For example, the activities of the Irish Republican Brotherhood were often hidden behind a raft of cover organisations whose activities were often reported in the local and Irish national press.

Besides occasional private papers and military service pension records, the main primary sources consulted have been police and government records and newspapers. While references to Dundee in the former two are minimal, the city had the advantage of having a newspaper industry which, in the second half of the nineteenth century, was one of the most advanced in the British Isles. The expansion of the provincial press in the late 1850s also coincided with the growth of Irish national sentiment and of the burgeoning Fenian Movement whose shrewd organisers were quick to recognise the power of the press and use it to promote their cultural activities and political opinions. The presence of two newspaper publishing houses in the one town also stimulated a fierce competition which cut across the political biases of editors and proprietors to produce a high standard of journalism. Besides attracting experienced staff from further afield, the Dundee newspapers were also the training ground for aspiring local journalists and writers, many of whom went on to greater things. A pertinent example here is William Cruikshanks, the son of a jute production overseer, who began his career with one or other of the Dundee newspaper firms at the turn of the century. Within ten years, Cruikshanks had procured a job as editor of the Dublin-based *Weekly Irish Times*, a post which he went on to hold for over thirty years. Under his editorship, the first post-Easter Rising edition of the *Irish Times*, published in May 1916 and containing over three weeks of news, became the biggest selling edition of any newspaper in Dublin's history. The following year, Cruikshanks went on compile the *Sinn Féin Rebellion Handbook*, a 308-page compendium of detailed information relating to the Easter Rising, which remains a valuable resource for historians today.

This study has been motivated by my origins and upbringing in Dundee, and my own political views. While this brings its insights, it also presents another more personal challenge. As stated, I also come with experience of involvement in Irish solidarity campaigning at the tail end of the period under study and my opinions of what transpired during that time. That considered, I have endeavoured to stand back and give due consideration to the perspectives of others, many of whom were and are old comrades with whom I did not always agree. I have also endeavoured throughout to interrogate and corroborate all the sources at my disposal to the best of my abilities.

The long time period allows me to chart the peaks and troughs of Irish and other radical activity in Dundee against a wider historical backdrop; to identity the points at which the interweaving strands of radicalism, nationalism, republicanism and socialism converged and diverged; to examine the dynamic tensions within and between the Irish national and other radical movements, and the critical moments at which national and social interests coalesced into a single struggle.

The first chapter starts with a brief description of the nature of Irish immigration to Dundee and a look at early manifestations of radical protest, before going on to consider the relationship between the physical force Chartist and Irish Repeal movements. Chapter 2 notes how the drive to revive the Irish national spirit after the quelling of the Young Ireland Rebellion and the upheaval of An Gorta Mór found expression in support for cultural initiatives such as the McManus Sword Testimonial and National Brotherhood of St Patrick, which latter organisation became a conduit for the Irish Republican Brotherhood (IRB – the Fenians). It looks at the distinctive nature of the IRB in Dundee, and notes how support for a secular Irish republic was demonstrated in active participation in the aborted Irish insurrection of 1866 and, subsequently, the fund-raising effort for the Fenian prisoners. Chapter 3 examines the tentative alliance between physical force and constitutional nationalism as militant nationalists initiated, infiltrated and attempted to subvert the emerging Home Rule Movement. As the recurring spectre of famine, poverty and eviction gave rise to a protracted Land War, it also looks at how Dundee's militant nationalists were instrumental in initiating the next major campaign in the town, the Irish National Land League. Chapter 4 looks at the prodigious achievements of the Land League in Dundee and, notably, as radically minded women such as Anna Parnell took the lead in the national organisation, the Ladies' Land League. It considers the various offshoots and legacies of the Land League, including the Irish National League, the Irish National Foresters, the Scottish Land Reform League and the emerging socialist movement. It also examines James Connolly's period of residence in Dundee and the chain of events that led him to join the socialist movement at that particular time. Chapter 5 goes on to look at the impact of the Parnell/Irish Parliamentary Party split on grassroots Irish nationalism and to examine the complex and precarious relationship between Irish kindred organisations and the socialist movement. As an older generation of militant Irish nationalists died off or moved on, it considers how efforts to promote the Gaelic League, which was pivotal in nurturing a new generation of militant Irish Republicans in the west of Scotland, was met with limited success in Dundee. It also considers how the strong influence of the Liberal-supporting United Irish League in Dundee contributed to Winston Churchill, being elected MP for the burgh for fourteen years. Chapter 6 looks at the upsurge in industrial and suffragette militancy in the years immediately preceding the First World War. It considers how the deeply rooted notion of working-class solidarity in struggle was manifested in an escalating number of sympathetic strikes and a support for the victims of the Dublin Lockout of 1913 which belied the economic status of Dundee's poorly paid textile workforce. It also looks at how the actions of militant suffragettes, many of whom had Dundee connections, impacted on the escalating struggle for Irish self-determination. As one chapter ends with the negative response of Dundee's Irish Home Rulers to the Easter Rising, so the next one begins with the change in attitudes following the execution of its leaders, before going on to survey the most intensive phase of militant Irish Republican activity in Scotland's history, the Tan and Civil Wars. It examines Dundee's prolific record in the area of arms procurement, and the key protagonists involved. It also considers the wider base of support for the Irish Republican project, giving due attention to the communist and unemployed workers' movements and advanced Scottish nationalists. Chapter 8 looks at the decline in popular support for Irish republicanism following the end of the Civil War. It considers how of the Church of Scotland's 1923 report on 'The Menace of the Irish Race to Our Scottish Nationality' gave rise to a huge wave of anti-Irish sectarianism which reached its height in the 1920s and 30s but continued to influence attitudes for several decades afterwards. It notes that while Dundee escaped the worst aspects of anti-Irish prejudice, anxiety about creating division amongst Dundee's working-class population led to the partitioning of socialist and labour politics from Irish ones to the detriment of both traditions. The final chapter takes us up to the most recent phase of the struggle, focusing largely on the campaign to regain political status for Irish Republican prisoners from the early days of the blanket protest to the period directly after the hunger strikes. It examines how a renewed consciousness of their Irish heritage by a younger generation of Dundonians combined with an awareness of the conflict in Ireland to produce the first consciously pro-Republican Irish solidarity campaign in the city for over fifty years. As a corollary of this, it considers the often tense and torturous relationship with the London-based Troops Out Movement and other sections of the British left.

Much of the last chapter draws on the aforementioned memoir of John Malone, parts of which I have incorporated into the text. His candid, unvarnished account, coming at the end of a long chronological study, provides a dynamic counterbalance to my own attempts to create a more nuanced, inter-subjective narrative. Nevertheless, even here I am aware that total objectivity is neither attainable nor desirable and it behoves me to state, at the outset, that this history has been written from a broadly pro-Republican socialist perspective. Given the long historical sweep and tight geographical focus, it has also been necessary to restrict the material and condense the narrative in areas that would benefit from further consideration. Ultimately, the decision about what to include and prioritise has been largely mine. I am aware that, inevitably, there will be errors and omissions, and that some may disagree with my interpretation. My only hope is that this will stimulate others to explore in greater detail some of the issues merely hinted at here, bringing their own experience and insight.

Rút Nic Foirbeis
October 2023

Endnotes to Preface

1. Areas of contention include where the decade of centenaries begins and, more importantly, ends; whether the course of events deserve the definition of revolution, and consequently counter-revolution; and the imposition of a temporal boundary on a longer revolutionary process which extends further back and remains unfinished.

2. For example, *Mackie Rooney, Margaret Skinnider, 1916 Heroine: The Monaghan Connection* (Monaghan: The Margaret Skinnider Appreciation Society, 2016), pp40–41; Kirsty Lusk, 'Short Skirts, Strong Boots and a Revolver', in Kirsty Lusk and Willy Maley (eds), *Scotland and the Easter Rising* (Edinburgh: Luath Press, 1916); Maggie Chetty, 'Margaret Skinnider; A Modest Revolutionary', in Stephen Coyle and Máirtín Ó Catháin (eds), *We Will Rise Again* (Glasgow: 1916 Centenary Committee (Scotland), 2018); 'Margaret Skinnider – Rebel Heart', play by Maggie Chetty, performed as a rehearsed reading in Glasgow in May 2016, rewritten by Cat Hepburn for a Scottish tour in the spring of 2024; Mary McAuliffe, *Margaret Skinnider* (Dublin: University College Dublin Press, 2020); Stephen Coyle, *High Noon on High Street* (Glasgow: Clydeside Press, 2008); Máirtín Ó Catháin, *Irish Republicanism in Scotland: Fenians in Exile, 1858–1916* (Dublin: Irish Academic Press, 2007). Research undertaken by Stephen Coyle of the 1916 Centenary Committee (Scotland), continues to add significantly to our knowledge of Irish republicanism in Scotland, and, particularly of the key role of Scottish operatives in the struggle for full Irish independence in the 1913–23 period.

3. William M Walker's chapter on 'The Irish in Dundee', in *Juteopolis: Dundee and its Textile Workers, 1885–1923* (Edinburgh: John Donald, 1979) and Richard B McCready, 'The Social and Political Impact of the Irish in Dundee, c1845–1922' (Unpublished PhD thesis, University of Dundee, 2002). The topic has also been covered by Brian King, *Undiscovered Dundee* (Edinburgh: Black & White Publishing, 2011). More recently, interest generated by the decade of the centenaries, together with Dundee's famed reputation as a 'women's town' with a large Irish population, has stimulated postgraduate research, for example, Niamh Coffey on women in Irish politics in Dundee.

4. The Dundee Oral History Project (DOHP), initiated in 1984 and founded a year later, was staffed by a workforce drawn exclusively from the ranks of the long-term unemployed, none of whom, with the exception of the project's founder, Graham Smith, had any qualifications or background in academic history. The low wages, which were marginally above the unemployment benefits of the time, served to discourage the involvement of most academic historians. Despite efforts to procure funding from other sources, the DOHP folded in February 1989, when the Community Programme and other job creation schemes (initiated by the Thatcher governments to reduce the unemployment figures and encourage private enterprise) were finally wound down.

5   Shorthand for the 'Black and Tan War', otherwise known as the War of Independence, which latter term is disputed by anti-Treaty Republicans as full independence did not result. The preferred term, 'Tan War' is also inaccurate as it excludes the Royal Irish Constabulary (RIC) and the unionist militias in Ulster. The term 'Civil War' is similarly disputed with some historians preferring the term 'counter-revolution'. (John O'Neill, 'Terminology: 'Tan War' or 'War of Independence'?', The Treason Felony Blog. https://treasonfelony.wordpress.com/2015/11/29/terminology-tan-war-or-war-of-independence/, accessed 19 May 2023; John M Regan, *The Irish Counter-revolution 1921–1936: Treatyite Politics and Settlement in Independent Ireland* (Dublin: Gill & Macmillan, 1999). See also endnote 1, above.

CHAPTER 1

Radicals, Republicans and Repealers 1841–58

Too glorious has our struggle been
To sink so soon benighted
'Twas not a shout for Blue or Green,
But one and all united.[1]

*Ar scáth a cheile a mhaireann na daoine.
Under each other's shadow is how people survive.*

IRISH PROVERB

BY THE 1840s, Irish immigration to Dundee was well established.[2] Close trading links between the Dundee textile industry and the Irish domestic linen industry had generated immigration from the counties of south-west Ulster and the bordering counties of north-east Connacht since the 1820s. As the dual economy of handloom weaving and potato cultivation grew increasingly precarious, many Irish families saw the expanding Dundee textile industry as providing a work structure into which they could integrate.[3] By 1841, around 5,000 of Dundee's population were Irish-born, and the census of that year reveals a substantial number of Irish households clustered together in densely populated areas of the town such as the Hilltown and the Overgate. The preponderance within the 1841 census of male handloom weavers, flax dressers, female flax spinners and the occasional female millworker indicates the presence of a family industry in transition as the textile industry developed. Most had come from close-knit rural communities where poverty and religious persecution had produced a culture of economic and social interdependency. Their counties of origin – Cavan, Monaghan, Fermanagh, Leitrim and Sligo – had been the heartlands of Ribbonism, the secret, oath-bound societies rooted in the late eighteenth-century Defender movement which carried forth longstanding grievances of poor Catholic tenant farmers against sectarian land laws, and perpetuated resentment towards rack-renting landlords, the Orange Order and other manifestations of Protestant privilege and British rule. This was expressed in attacks on landlords and their agents, intimidation and ostracisation of collaborators and informers, and a defiant Catholic nationalism.[4]

The Ribbon tradition was subsequently transported and recalibrated to a new urban environment where it manifested itself in a vigorous sense of kinship, an ethic of self-help, and, on the pretext that offence is the best defence, in violent clashes with Orange elements.[5] By 1839–41, police intelligence in Scotland had identified numerous Ribbon societies in and around Glasgow and Edinburgh, but not, it appears, in Dundee.[6] On 12 July 1841, nevertheless, a large group of Irish Catholics laid siege to a meeting of the Irish Protestant Association that had gathered in the Masons' Hall, Overgate, to celebrate the anniversary of King William III crossing the Boyne. As the crowd grew more numerous and the atmosphere increasingly febrile, the Provost and Superintendent of Police, hastened to the hall where they directed the Protestant party to disperse in groups of two and three under police escort. Once outside, however, the crowd pursued them along the street throwing missiles at the police, who succeeded in apprehending one of the ringleaders, Patrick Redding, a handloom weaver of Maxwelltown (Hilltown).[7]

After four days in the Old Jail, Redding appeared before the police court and was fined £5, which considerable sum – equivalent then to three months' wages[8] – was raised over the course of the day by, as the Tory *Northern Warder* claimed, 'the Roman Catholics'.[9] The behaviour displayed – from the organised targeting of a conspicuously Orange celebration held by the more privileged Irish-Protestant community, and the assailing of the police authorities, to the financial assistance and social solidarity offered to one of their number – contain all the hallmarks of a Ribbon Society, working in alliance with radical Chartists with whom Dundee's Irish handloom weavers had established political links.

Both elements were doubtless aware that the Irish Protestant Association was no benign social club but had been founded, in Glasgow in 1835, to combat the growing support amongst Scots Radicals for the emancipatory politics of Daniel O'Connell, and the lessening hostility towards his Irish-Catholic compatriots who had settled in the country.[10] In this instance, it was perceived as the conduit by which the Orange Order, having effectively colonised the west and south-west of Scotland and formed lodges in Edinburgh, was seeking to extend its influence to the north-east. Dundee's Irish-Catholics and their Chartist allies were having none of it, however, and this show of violent opposition and working-class solidarity inhibited the ability of the Orange Order to organise in the town for many years to come.[11]

The Irish population was also becoming involved in other forms of nationalist and radical protest. 1840 saw the relaunching of O'Connell's campaign to Repeal the Union between Ireland and Britain. O'Connell had launched the campaign in the early 1830s. However, while there had been considerable enthusiasm for the idea amongst the Irish working class, and limited support from radical politicians, there was nothing approaching a concerted grassroots campaign.[12] Indeed, when O'Connell visited Scotland in September 1835, the delegation which travelled from Dundee to Edinburgh to greet him (O'Connell came no further north) consisted of three Liberal town councillors; and while one, William Christie, presented an address calling for the 'speedy and effectual reform of the House of Lords', one of O'Connell's pet causes, he made no reference to Repeal of the Union.[13]

In 1842, the second petition of the National Charter Association added Repeal to its original Six Points.[14] The petition, which was drafted by the English Chartists' Convention, caused a rift amongst Scottish Chartists. At a meeting of their Central Committee in January, the delegates were split evenly between two competing resolutions: from anti-Repealer, James Jack of Balfron, Stirlingshire, who recommended they reject the draft petition and adopt another one 'without embracing any question of detail', and from pro-Repealer John McCrea, of Beath, Ayrshire, who urged they adopt the national petition 'without alteration or amendment'. The petition was rejected on the casting vote of the chair, John Duncan of Dundee, who voted for Jack's motion, possibly due to his belief that the strength of the movement lay in its capacity to accommodate a wide range of opinion on all but the most fundamental points of the Charter.[15] This position was subsequently challenged, however, as local Chartist groups accused delegates of ignoring their instructions to support the petition, and by January, most Scottish Chartists were effectively behind it.[16]

Chartist groups continued to exercise a strong local autonomy, however, and for the small band of handloom weavers and artisans who comprised the Dundee Chartist Council, strategy and tactics were largely determined by the town's occupational structure and works' culture. The link between industrial and political action appears to have been stronger in Dundee than anywhere else in Scotland. From the early stages of the movement, Dundee's Chartists had identified in the Irish population – with whom many of them shared the common occupation of handloom weaving – an untapped source of industrial and political strength. In January 1838, the organisers of a Chartist demonstration from the High Street to Magdalen Green circulated handbills soliciting the support of Irishmen residing in the town, not, as the notoriously antagonistic Tory *Dundee Courier* was wont to claim, out of a desperate attempt to 'swell the mob' by appealing to the lowest sub-section of 'the great unwashed' but because, in a society rife with anti-Irish, anti-Catholic prejudice, they put worker solidarity above differences of religion or nationality. Encouraged by appeals to popular national sentiment, or as the *Courier* put it, 'a dose of claptrap expressions to gull the ignorant natives of the Emerald Isle', the Irish 'turned out in considerable numbers', 'decently dressed and respectable in appearance', motivated, as were others, by a rumour that the Irish demagogue, Feargus O'Connor, was to make an appearance.[17]

The livelihoods of native Scots and immigrant Irish handloom weavers were equally threatened by the transition to power-loom weaving, and when trade depression struck in 1841–2, the handloom weavers were amongst the hardest hit. The Chartist strikes of August 1842 occurred on the back of a dispute over the allocation of relief payments and a protest demonstration in which unemployed workers had marched, behind a black flag depicting a human skeleton and a call to support the People's Charter, on the Town House, to urge the Council's Relief Committee to provide 'permanent support for the starving unemployed' so as 'not to compel the people…to acts of desperation'.[18] After their appeals were ignored, many struggling workers turned to the Chartists for leadership. On Tuesday, 16 August, a meeting called by the Dundee Trades Democratic Suffrage Association was thick with inflammatory rhetoric as hackler Thomas Henderson declared that 'class legislation was the sole cause of all evils'; the pastor of Dundee Chartist Church, John Duncan, condemned the magistrates for their treatment of the unemployed and urged the meeting 'to rise with determination and power'; and leading physical force Chartist, John Mitchell, called on 'those in employment to demand their employers raise wages to 1839 levels, [if necessary], to take steps to compel them'.[19]

The following Friday, a conference of around a hundred delegates from 53 workplaces agreed to strike 'for an indefinite period' for the People's Charter and higher wages, and on Saturday evening, an estimated 8,000 to 14,000 people gathered on Magdalen Green to show their support.[20] The calls to action would undoubtedly have appealed to the anti-establishment Ribbon element within the beleaguered handloom weaving community. Here, the long tradition of radicalism amongst the weavers and flax dressers (hacklers), and the support of a significant number of Dundee Chartists for the physical force Chartism of Feargus O'Connor, were key motivating factors.[21]

The strike protests began on Monday, 22 August, and continued the following day with a 4,000-strong demonstration on Magdalen Green from where around 2,000 people marched northwards to the mills and factories of Hawkhill and Scouringburn. There they were joined by several disaffected workers, including a number of young women who placed themselves at the head of the procession and 'marched in warlike array', calling their workmates to join them. The strikers were confronted by a wall of brawny policemen and special constables armed with batons and 'huge pine-polished treenails'. Having been advised against retaliation, and at any rate unprepared for it, the strikers circumvented the forces of law and order until they reached the Lochee Road where Sheriff Henderson read the Riot Act and the police raised placards ordering the demonstrators to disperse. Still, they held their ground. Finally, as violence threatened to break out in the ranks, and obstructed from proceeding to the town centre, the marchers pressed north-westwards to the spinning mills of Lochee, then eastwards to Fair Muir, where, after being joined by another 400 strikers and briefed by John Mitchell, the procession regrouped and headed for Forfar, whose sizeable community of handloom weavers and Chartists had declared their intention to join the strike the day before.[22] At this point, the marchers abandoned instructions to 'respect property' and eschew physical force, and helped themselves to food from the fields and armed themselves with sticks cut from trees. They arrived in Forfar early the next day, and after remaining to address local supporters, made their way back to Dundee where a number of the leaders, including Duncan, were arrested.[23] The case came to trial at the High Court in Edinburgh in January 1843, when weaver James Graham, flax-dressers John Scott and Peter Bennett, and mechanic John Penny were sentenced to four months' imprisonment.[24] Despite attempts of critics to play down its importance, the Dundee Chartist strike procession of 1842 was the arguably most significant event of this type to take place in Scotland at that time.[25] That said, the forces ranked against them were too powerful, and, as the Dundee Chartists subsequently noted, the machinery was prepared.'[26]

The Chartist movement subsided precisely as the Repeal agitation was gaining momentum. By the summer of 1843 most Scottish towns with large Irish populations had their Repealers, all of whom had held meetings and contributed to the Repeal Fund.[27] On 23 January, the 'Repealers of Dundee' made their first 'small but willing' subscription of £3, which sender William Duffy trusted 'will show our countrymen at home that we are resolved to do as we much as we can in these trying and distressing times which are truly lamentable in this, as well as other manufacturing towns'.[28] The following April, Duffy forwarded a further £7, accrediting 'the poor Irish here [who] are determined to work hard this great Repeal year'. Over the next few months, the money received from Dundee continued to grow. At a meeting of the National Repeal Association in Dublin on 19 June, William O'Neill Daunt, MP for Mallow, acknowledged receipt of £8 10s from the Treasurer of the Dundee Repealers, Dr Edward Brennan, bringing the total received from the town to £20.[29] In August, John O'Connell, son of Daniel, acknowledged receipt of a further £10 3s comprising the subscriptions of Scotch Presbyterians, Irish Protestants and Catholics, and one shilling from the Reverend John Gillan, 'a young Irish clergyman, who had recently gone to [Dundee] and written him a letter describing the state in which he found the poor Irish on his arrival'. It was,' O'Connell stated, 'owing to his exertions [that] so large a sum had been sent from that locality'.[30] Gillan was admitted as a Volunteer (£10 subscriber), as were Mr McElroy, a handloom weaver of the Scouringburn, and Surgeon Brennan. O'Connell added that 'everyone whose family had subscribed to the fund might claim a similar honour'.[31]

CHAPTER 1 – RADICALS, REPUBLICANS AND REPEALERS 1841–58

As a young Irish doctor who lived in the West Port, at the foot of the Hawkhill, Edward Brennan was in a prime position to witness the hardships endured by the Irish community which he served, and to appreciate that their 'small but willing' contribution to the Repeal Fund was a sacrifice they could ill-afford, and for which they expected to receive something in return. Brennan was also aware that it was the misfortune of the Irish in Scotland, and especially in Dundee, to be overlooked by the gentleman leaders of the National Repeal Association, and to have their efforts overshadowed by the larger contributions received from bigger, more affluent urban centres. Many subscribers, no doubt, had not forgotten how Dundee had been omitted from O'Connell's Scottish tour in 1835; still, they remained unquestioningly loyal to the man and the cause.

In September Brennan travelled to Dublin to deliver the message in person, and to submit the latest instalment of repeal rent, a modest £3 10s, which, he told a packed meeting of the Loyal National Repeal Association (LNRA), brought the total received from Dundee to almost £40: 'a large sum' when they considered that it came from that portion of the population composed principally of the Irish labouring class, most of whom could trace their present condition to the effect of the Union. They were, however, 'unwilling to leave the glory of the redemption of their country to the people of Ireland alone', and when 'the day of redemption arrived' and their native parliament was restored, 'they expected to participate in the benefits resulting from it'.[32]

Popular enthusiasm for Repeal waned after October, however, when O'Connell pre-empted the threats of the Conservative Peel government to repress what looked set to be the largest of his 'monster' repeal meetings to date at Clontarf, by calling it off at the last minute.[33] This triggered a rift in the Association between O'Connell supporters on the one side and the idealistic Young Ireland group, led by the founders of *The Nation* newspaper, on the other.[34] Nevertheless, Daniel O'Connell's arrest and conviction on a charge of conspiracy triggered a new wave of popular sympathy. The conviction was later quashed, and on 17 September 1844, over a thousand people gathered in Bell Street Hall, Dundee, to celebrate O'Connell's release and to promote the Repeal cause. George O'Farrell, Head Repeal Inspector for the town, presided, and the broad range of speakers included Catholic clergymen John Gillan, Stephen Keenan and

John MacPherson; and Repealers Augustine Burke – who denounced absentee landlordism as one of the prime causes of Ireland's distress – and Samuel McKinney, who spoke on the Repeal martyrs, as O'Connell and his fellow prisoners had been dubbed.[35]

By this time, Edward Brennan had stepped down to focus on his medical career and the needs of his growing young family. He was succeeded by John Coogan, in the post of Secretary, and John Toner (Treasurer), who, along with Repeal Wardens Patrick O'Neill and William Sweeney, continued to recruit more new members, a significant number of whom were married women who managed household budgets and contributed on their families' behalf. The majority were of modest means – for example, when Bridget Sanna was proposed as a member by Brennan in January 1843, she was a 57-year-old domestic servant living in Hawkhill with her weaver husband John and youngest son James, also a weaver. Similarly, when Mary Costello was signed up by Coogan in August 1844, she lived in the Hilltown with her handloom weaver husband Henry and three young daughters, the eldest two of whom were millworkers.[36]

Around this time, a resurgence in Ribbonism in its north-central Irish heartlands had given rise to fears amongst the LNRA leadership that it would spread abroad and infiltrate the 'Movement'. The fear was not without foundation: on 21 January, the central executive voted to expel two Repealers from Airdrie, Bernard Kane and Peter Short, 'who had avowed themselves Ribbonmen'.[37] A committee 'to enquire and check the progress of Ribbonism' was formed, and a fortnight later, Maurice O'Connell reported that 'they were already receiving considerable information on the subject'. Amongst this was a letter from Dundee Repeal Wardens Coogan and Toner, enclosing the latest subscription and stating that there was 'no Ribbonism in Dundee'.[38]

Of all the Dundee Repealers, Coogan and Toner were amongst the least likely to belong to a Ribbon Society, or to have need of one. At the time, Coogan, who was born in Edinburgh, or at least claimed be, was a young upwardly mobile proprietor of a draper's shop in the Greenmarket with aspirations to involvement in civic and cultural life.[39] By 1845, he was a subscriber to the Dundee Public Library, of which he subsequently became a committee member. He later went on to become Convenor of the Rate Payers of the Third Ward, and, along with Head Repeal Warden,

George O'Farrell, a member of the Parochial Board. Unlike Airdrie, which was a stronghold of Orangeism in which Irish Catholics formed a vulnerable and defensive minority, Dundee's Irish Catholics formed a large and increasingly confident one, suffered less prejudice and, for the most part, enjoyed good relations with the indigenous Scots community. At any rate, Coogan's Irish political allegiances and Catholic faith does not appear have inhibited his business interests nor his civic ambitions.[40]

Coogan was of a different economic class and social background to most of the Irish families who subscribed to the Repeal Association. He would have had little experience of Ribbonism, which he likely saw as the last vestiges of a rural Irish past. Toner, who owned a furniture shop in Reform Street in the town centre, and O'Farrell, the proprietor of a pawnbroker's shop in nearby Lindsay Street, were likely of a similar mind. At the same time, it seems a contradiction in terms that members of a secret society would break their oath and reveal its existence and in this respect the Airdrie Ribbonmen's behaviour seems incongruous or downright careless. Still, as a shrewd political operator working within the Irish community, Coogan is unlikely to have been oblivious to the presence of former Ribbonmen in his midst. Unlike the gentlemen leaders of the Repeal Association, however, he does not appear to have been anxious about it. Coogan and Toner's denials of Ribbonism may also have been an attempt to ingratiate themselves with the gentlemen of Repeal Association by presenting their hitherto overlooked district in a favourable light. However, this was no intent to deceive. The fact was that Ribbonism in Dundee had been dissipating since 1841 when the large Irish-Catholic community had, with the assistance of Scots Presbyterian radicals, thwarted the attempts of the Orange Order to promote their supremacist ideology amongst Irish Protestants on their turf. Indeed, the Dundee Repealers boasted a number of Scots Presbyterians and Irish Protestants amongst their subscribers, and the potential was there to recruit many more.

So attractive was this prospect to the LNRA leadership that when organiser William O'Neill Daunt embarked on a five-week 'missionary' tour of Scotland in the summer of 1845, he began it in Dundee, before proceeding to Aberdeen, Edinburgh, Glasgow and Greenock. The meeting, which took place in Bell Street Hall on 25 June, was meticulously stage-managed to promote social harmony, encourage peaceful agitation and convince non-aligned Scots of the merits the Irish cause. The *Dundee Advertiser* noted that the hall was 'beautifully decorated with evergreens bearing various inscriptions', the focal point being a crown-shaped cake ornamented with roses surmounted by an arch wreathed with shamrocks, in the centre of which was depicted the word 'Repeal'. At 5s 2s 6d, the tickets were beyond the means of the poorest Scots and Irish families; nevertheless, they quickly sold out, and long before Daunt's arrival, the hall was 'crowded to suffocation with native Irish and [indigenous Scots] townsmen wishing to hear what might be said on the subject'.[41]

Above all, the meeting was remarkable for the large number of Catholic clergymen on the platform, half of whom (Mackay, Macpherson and Gordon) were Scottish, and the other half (Gillan, Keane and Keenan) Irish. On this occasion, the Scots took centre stage. The Reverend James Mackay of Perth who presided, stated that he 'came forth as a Catholic clergyman, Voluntary and a Repealer', but especially as a Scotsman, to affirm that 'Irishmen had been too long deprived the management of their affairs', and that a 'Parliament in London was not the same as a Parliament on College Green'. John MacPherson of Dundee stressed the necessity of extra-parliamentary agitation and urged them to 'be of one mind...unite heart and soul...persevere and 'do Ireland a service'. He stopped short of advocating physical force, however. The Reverend Gordon of Arbroath was more circumspect. Observing that 'there were many Scotsmen who [felt] the same sense of injustice and oppression to Ireland as the Irish themselves', he insisted that, 'Our victory must be one of peace'.[42]

Daunt, who was received with great cheering, proceeded to appeal to Scottish pride, patriotism and common sense. 'Scotland', he claimed, 'had improved *in spite* of the Union of 1707 than because of it', which he ascribed to 'the personal and intellectual qualities of Scotchmen themselves, and to the admirable situation of the country for commerce'. 'Scotland', he continued:

> had got nothing from the Union that she could not have got without it. It was said that the Union gave her peace. Was there peace in 1715? Was there peace in 1745? Was there peace during the long interval between those years; whilst, if an appeal to arms did not actually take place, yet the sword was trembling at the side of every man, and longing to spring from the scabbard?[43]

'Whatever the merits and demerits of the Scottish Union', he concluded, 'no argument in favour of the Irish Union could be drawn from its results'.[44]

In the short term, Daunt's mission appears to have paid off. The Dundee meeting yielded £10 – the tour itself raised a total of £68 9d – and attracted a 'large admixture' of Scots to, as well as sustaining Irish enthusiasm for, the Repeal cause. Significantly, Daunt's tour of Scotland occurred against a background of growing unrest in Ireland. Just three weeks previously, O'Connell had told a meeting of the LNRA executive that Ribbonism and Mollie Maguire-ism were 'fearfully on the increase in the counties of Leitrim, Cavan and Fermanagh', and that 'the spirit of infernal machination was spreading abroad'.[45] The majority of Irish immigrants to Scotland, and to Dundee especially, had come from these troubled counties, and more were still arriving. In this light, the visit of Daunt – who was O'Connell's protégé and former secretary – can be seen as an attempt to steer recent Irish immigrants away from secret societies and physical force. Here, the role of the Catholic clergy, as the moral influencers of the Irish community, was instrumental. Indeed, the Reverend Gordon had concluded the clergymen's speeches by advising against the spilling of blood, as 'nothing could weaken the cause [of Ireland] more'.[46]

The harmonious mood of the Dundee meeting masked growing tensions within the Repeal movement which came to a head in July 1846 when the Young Irelanders, led by Thomas Meagher, withdrew from the LNRA following O'Connell's insistence that they reject the option to pursue their political goals by force of arms. While the majority of the Association and the Catholic clergy remained faithful to O'Connell, a significant number of grassroots supporters, including the Dundee Repealers, hitched their colours to the Young Ireland mast. On 7 January, William Sweeney, Repeal Warden of the William Smith O'Brien Ward, Dundee, wrote to the editor of *The Nation*, Charles Gavan Duffy, proclaiming their 'unqualified dissent from the manifesto of Mr O'Connell and his son John', and giving their reasons:

> When we find a popular leader turning around upon a number of patriotic gentlemen, and declaring that they are violating the law – the law that says Irishmen must be ruled by Englishmen – we cannot restrain our indignation... To see a popular leader,

who, for the last forty years, never ceased instilling into the minds of the people that English prime ministers never missed an opportunity to crush and oppress the Irish people, that they are full of deceit and lying, devoid of every principle, that they have always violated faith with the Irish people; to see Mr O'Connell adduce a man of this description [Prime Minister Lord John Russell] as evidence against *The Nation*! It is well known that during the monster meetings Lord John declared that they must be put down. Let Mr O'Connell commence holding monster meetings like those of '43, and see if the Whigs will countenance them.[47]

Sweeney concluded by urging Duffy and his confederates to continue promoting advanced nationalist principles in the belief that a more honourable and independently minded population would result.

These events were overtaken by a far more cataclysmic one, as a combination of ecological disaster and the consequences of years of British misrule – not least the laissez-faire policies of the new Whig government – conspired to produce An Gorta Mór (The Great Hunger or Famine), in which the population of Ireland were subjected to mass starvation, disease, destitution and, ultimately, displacement. Separated from their famine-stricken homeland, the uncompromising Repealers of Dundee continued to support the political body which best spoke to their nationalist ideals and aspirations – the Irish Confederation, the organisational wing of Young Ireland, which was formed in January 1847. When the Confederation issued instructions for the formation of clubs in England and Scotland later that autumn, they felt compelled to comply. However, in a town where the majority of those inclined to do so were poor, they faced a severe handicap.[48]

Within days of the instructions being issued, 'Quaero' of Dundee wrote to Gavan Duffy asking if it was 'absolutely necessary that persons desirous of forming a Confederate Club should first become (in a pecuniary sense) members of the Irish Confederation'. Explaining that he already had 'the expenses of procuring and furnishing a place of meeting sufficient for twenty poor men', he suggested a policy of 'getting them clubbed first', following which 'they will consult each other, and send their aid freely'. In reply, Gavan Duffy stuck firmly to the official line that the Clubs were 'integral parts of the Confederation', whose fundamental duty was 'to strengthen the central body with funds and sympathy that it may be able to act with authority and success'.[49]

Undeterred by the failure to accommodate their hardships, the Dundee Repealers pressed ahead, and two months later William Sweeney submitted the sum of £1 2s, 'the subscription of sixteen determined haters of the Act of Union, which has been the cause of their exile, and which still subjects them and their children to the scoffs and taunts of the strangers amongst whom, reluctantly, they have been forced to seek for that subsistence denied them by the laws in their own country'. All of them, Sweeney stated, professed 'full confidence in the intelligence and integrity of the Confederation's leaders', and swore to aid them 'by every constitutional means, to restore independence to their country'.[50]

Dundee Subscribers to the Irish Confederation, December 1847

John Coogan, ex-Repeal Warden	5s
Augustine Burke	2s
Patrick O'Neill, ex-Repeal Warden	2s
John Cassidy	1s
William Donoghue	1s
Peter Golden, sen.	1s
Peter Golden, jun.	1s
John Mangan	1s
Patrick Mulgrew	1s
John Quinn	1s
William Sweeney, ex-Repeal Warden	1s
James Tierney	1s
Dennis Tierney	1s
Patrick Tracy	1s
John Ward	1s
James Watton	1s

The Dundee Confederates also responded to the central body's request for comprehensive information on the economic, social and political position of the Irish inhabitants, and principal manufactures of the town, reflecting the Confederation's preoccupation with promoting Irish trade, commerce and manufactures, and their desire to encourage 'men of property'.[51] Priorities were, however, changing.[52] The French Revolution of January 1848 demonstrated the efficacy of physical force and resulted in a greater support for Young Ireland to whom the horrors of the An Gorta Mór and the ideas of James Fintan Lalor on land reform had given a harder, more radical edge.

The revolutionary ferment in Europe also stimulated a revival of Chartism and saw the forging of fraternal links between Irish Repealers and Chartists in Scotland, England and Wales. The cause of Ireland topped the agenda at the National Chartists' Convention in London in April 1848 which preceded the presentation of their third petition to Parliament. *The Nation* opined that one of the most interesting features of the Convention lay in 'the indications the delegates gave of English [*sic*] sympathy with the Irish'. Significantly, the first to express it was the Dundee delegate and key player in the Dundee Chartist strike of 1842, James Graham, who conveyed his conviction that 'the people of Dundee [would] indignantly resist any attempt to coerce the Irish'. Leading Glasgow Chartist James Adams concurred that his 'constituents [would] not stand idly by should the government proceed to bloodshed in our sister country', while James Cummings reported that 'the men of Edinburgh were determined to stand by Ireland in the event of having to struggle with desperate power'.[53] Delegates from England and Wales made similar assertions.

Fraternity was the order of the day. The spring of 1848 saw the forging of alliances between Chartists and Repealers across the country.[54] Whereas in Dundee it was previously the Chartists who had targeted the Irish population, this time the call came, somewhat controversially, from the Repealers, at a Chartist meeting in the Thistle Hall on 10 April, when one of four named speakers – an Irishman named Hugh O'Neill[55] – stated that he had been authorised to call on the meeting to express the sympathy of the Repealers towards the Chartists. At this point a member of the audience interjected that O'Neill was 'not a residenter in Dundee' and had no authority from 'any body of Irishmen in the town to make such a declaration', whereupon O'Neill withdrew. Whether this indicates a difference of opinion between the Dundee Confederates and other more moderate Repealers in different parts of the country – O'Neill's speech was interrupted by frequent cries of 'pikes, pikes' – or simply the desire of Dundee Irishmen to mark their own territory, O'Neill had overstepped the mark.[56] The invitation stood, however, and the following evening, John McCrae, who had succeeded John Duncan as pastor of Dundee Chartist Church, was the key speaker at a joint meeting of Repealers and Chartists hosted by the Dundee Confederate Club and chaired by its President William Sweeney. On behalf of the Repealers, Samuel McKinney, an Irish weaver from the Hilltown, extended 'the right hand of fellowship' to 'the lovers of liberty...in their struggle to obtain the equality of rights and principles of the People's Charter', concluding that after ten to fifteen years of petitioning with no result, it was 'now time to lay aside talking and act'. If the Repealers were advocating physical force, they had an enthusiastic ally in John McCrea who, on behalf of the Chartists, expressed the warmest sympathy with Confederation leaders John Mitchel, Thomas Meagher and William Smith O'Brien, who had been arrested for sedition twenty days before, and pledged to support 'their endeavours to forward the cause of freedom in Ireland and the world'.[57]

The radical Ayrshire preacher proceeded to state his own record on the matter. He had dined with O'Connell in Kilmarnock during the latter's tour of Scotland in 1835, when he had urged him to endorse collaborative action between Irish Repealers and Scottish Chartists (which O'Connell had pointedly failed to do) and he had brought the issue of Repeal before his own body (at the Scottish Chartists' Convention in January 1842, when he was voted down). In addition, he had petitioned against the Irish Coercion Bill in 1846.[58]

McCrea turned to the condition of Ireland, citing 'the history of Robert Emmet, [which] shows the treatment the friends of the people experience' under British laws which allow a 'ruthless soldiery...to enter the cabin of the peasant...drag out the "inmates" and reduce their dwelling to ashes'. The scenario was familiar to many of Dundee's Irish immigrants who had lived at the sharp edge of Ireland's sectarian land laws and needed little convincing of the need for physical force to combat them. McCrea, however, was aware that Scots Protestants in his audience may have perceived things differently.

> He thought he heard some good Christian say 'Oh! But the Irish commit murders! Do they not shoot their landlords?' God forbid he should plead the cause of the murderer [but] he would look upon the man who blew out one's brains with a pistol as an angel of mercy in comparison with the person who subjected hundreds and thousands of individuals to a lingering death by cold and starvation, or exposed them to perish by disease on a foreign shore. Were they not aware that Archdeacon Ryder was charged with the murder of nine persons at Rathcormac, and that a jury brought a true bill of wilful murder against him? Had Archdeacon Ryder been brought to trial for his crime? No; instead of this he had received £500 out of the millions which was wrung from the pockets of the people of England and Scotland.[59]

Having evoked the memory of the Republican martyr Emmet, McCrea now marshalled the Scots Covenanters to buttress his case:

> Again, the people of this country complained of the Irish resorting to physical force for the redress of their grievances. Scotchmen, least of all, should complain of using physical force. Did not their forefathers do so to vindicate their rights? In former times, the minister took the sword in one hand and the Bible in the other. The sword was taken, not for aggression, but for resisting the attacks of the Bloody Claverhouse and his party. Cameron and Cargill did not think it improper to defend themselves, and Airdmoss and Bothwell Bridge were the fields on which they and their party asserted their religious liberty. Were they ashamed of what their ancestors had done? (Cries of 'No, no!') Men of their opinions put the bloody Archbishop to death and he would say that there were few belonging to Establishment or Dissenters who did not approve of the deeds done on Magus Moor (Cheers).[60]

McCrea, who professed to a long and deep interest in Irish affairs, was keenly attuned to the historic connections and parallels which ran between the two nations. He would have been aware that, fifty years before, Scots-Irish Covenanters had sworn allegiance to the United Irishmen, and possibly of the key role in that movement of the recently deceased James 'Jemmy' Hope in mobilising working-class support for the 1798 Rebellion. Hope, a humble linen weaver whose Covenanter grandfather had emigrated from Scotland to escape religious persecution, had been raised in the radical Presbyterian tradition, and his political beliefs, particularly his conception of a radical Irish nationalism were a logical extension of his religious faith.[61] Whether McCrea was aware of the contribution of Hope and the Irish Covenanters towards the Irish liberation struggle or not, the actions and subsequent martyrdom of the radical Scots Covenanters continued to exert a strong hold on the popular imagination, and the lesson was a pertinent and persuasive one.

McCrae then called the meeting to be unanimous in asserting their rights and in supporting those who were 'persecuted for vindicating the liberties of the people', following which it fell to Irish weaver and Secretary of the Dundee Confederate Club, Patrick Mulgrew, to propose setting up a defence fund for Mitchel, Meagher and O'Brien. Finally, McCrea proposed that those on the platform shake hands as a token of fraternity between Scotland and Ireland and bid all the 'Scotchmen' and Irishmen in the hall do the same. The *Dundee Advertiser* reported that 'fraternisation took place amidst vociferous cheering', concluding with three cheers each for the French Revolution, the National Convention, the People's Charter and the Repeal of the Union.[62]

It was an important symbolic statement designed by McCrea to alleviate any lingering distrust and pave the way for joint action between the Repealers and the Chartists. Apart from sharing a common interest in overthrowing the government, however, the policy of joint or coordinated action was dictated by more practical concerns: Dundee's Repealer-Chartist alliance consisted primarily of low-paid workers, mainly weavers, who were motivated, not only by common economic and political interests, but by a real practical need to pool resources and consolidate numbers.

As a member of the Chartist National Executive and the leading proponent of physical force operating in Scotland at the time, McCrea would have been instrumental in conceiving and expediting a military strategy, the first stage of which was to establish a 'National Guard' across four districts, with headquarters in Edinburgh, Dundee, Glasgow and Aberdeen, under the command of a publicly elected Brigadier-General, 'to whom all subordinate officers and privates must yield implicit obligation'.[63]

Over the next month, National Guards were formed in Edinburgh and Aberdeen. On 8 May, the Glasgow Repealers voiced sympathy with the idea, with leading Repealer James Daly advocating the acquisition of arms.[64] On 15 May, a public meeting called by the Dundee Chartists approved a proposition by local organisers William Davidson, seconded by William Donovan, to form a National Guard in Dundee, following which Brigadier-General Mackay of Edinburgh exhorted those present to enrol in it with the assurance that there would be no fear in wanting arms as 'there were certain speculative gun makers in Birmingham who would give them six months credit'. Enthusiasm waned somewhat after Mackay declared that he was 'not a Chartist, Whig or Tory, but a Conservative Republican of the school of Robespierre', which revelation was met with 'considerable disapprobation' that continued as the relentless questioning of Mackay, by one individual, as to what would happen if the National Guard became unable to cope with Her Majesty's forces elicited accusations of 'Spy!' and 'Traitor!' from the conflicted audience. Despite any reservations, however, the plan went ahead and a Brigadier-General, Secretary and Treasurer were duly elected.

On 5 June, the Chartists and Confederates held another joint meeting to protest against the sentencing of John Mitchel to fourteen years' penal servitude with transportation under the new Treason Felony Act. A resolution condemning the government and sympathising with Mitchel was moved by Chartists Davidson and Imrie, whose 'comparatively temperate speeches' contrasted with that of an unidentified young Irishman, who after revealing his intimate acquaintance with Meagher, Mitchel, O'Brien and other leading Young Irelanders, roused the audience with talk of guns, pikes and pistols, and concluded by asking if they were prepared to support the Irish in their struggles, to which the answer was a resounding 'Yes'. Unlike the previous meeting, there was total consensus on the matter.[65]

The unidentified Young Irelander was one of several speakers to address a demonstration on Magdalen Green, which coincided with a similar joint meeting on Glasgow Green, on Monday, 12 June. On this occasion he adopted a more diplomatic tone, as, from the back of a cart upon which was displayed a tri-coloured flag of blue, white and green surmounted by a pike, he moved a moderate resolution disapproving Lord John Russell's opposition to the People's Charter and pledging the 3,000-strong crowd to agitate for it until it became law. As he proceeded to advise they prepare for a blood sacrifice, however, he was reined in by the chairman, James Graham, who had been reinstated as Dundee's permanent delegate to the National Convention, after being sacked and replaced by McCrea, due to his cautious attitude to physical force.[66] Graham, whose experience of the Chartist Strike appears to have engendered an anxiety about overt displays of militancy, urged the crowd 'not to form a procession or do anything to injure property or disturb the peace' thus to 'show the public [and the magistrates] that working people could meet in their thousands and disperse as peaceably as the higher or middle classes'.[67] Here, Graham's stance differed from that of McCrea, who had recently decamped to the English metropolis as Secretary of the five-man Chartist National Executive alongside leading proponents of physical force, Peter McDouall, Ernest Jones, John Leach (who was responsible for liaising with the Confederates in Ireland) and Samuel Kidd (trade unions), to co-ordinate preparations for the imminent insurrection.[68]

Graham was not present at the following evening's meeting in Bell Street Hall to develop plans for recruiting to the Dundee National Guard, where the 'talented young Irishman', who steadfastly refused to give his name, was billed as the main speaker. The chair was taken by weaver John Robertson, who opened the proceedings by pointing to the pike atop the tri-coloured flag at the front of the platform and bidding everyone present to procure one 'as a curiosity'.[69] The appearance of a green, white and blue tricolour surmounted by a pike at these meetings is deeply significant. The flag displayed at the Glasgow demonstration – surmounted by the red cap of liberty – had been the red, white and blue tricolour of the French Republic. A green, white and blue tricolour is reputed to have been adopted by the United Irishmen in the 1790s to acknowledge the allying Presbyterian-Covenanter and native Irish-Catholic traditions. Still, the flag most commonly associated with the Irish Republic remained the green flag with the gold harp. On 7 March 1848, however, Thomas Meagher had hoisted the new green, white and orange tricolour of the Irish Republic above the Wolfe Tone Confederate Club in Waterford City, which he followed up on 15 April by presenting a similar flag 'of the finest French silk', surmounted by 'the Irish pike', to the trades and citizens of Dublin. Stating that the symbolism needed little explanation, Meagher emphasised that 'the white in the centre signifies the lasting truce between the "Orange and the "Green", that 'between the folds, the hands of the Irish Protestant and the Irish Catholic may be clasped in heroic brotherhood'.[70] While the symbolism of the Dundee flag was likely influenced by the French and Irish ones, in the light of McCrea's speech at the launch of the Chartist-Repealer alliance on 11 April, the colours took on a deeper historic meaning. Green can be interpreted as representing the radical Repealers, i.e., Young Ireland and the Irish revolutionary tradition in general. Blue, which signified liberty in the French flag, was the colour of Scotland, simultaneously, the flag of the radical Covenanters, and, as McCrea had emphasised, the religious and civil liberties they had fought to uphold, which had been carried forth by the Scottish radicals, and appropriated by a new generation of Scottish Chartists.[71] The colour white, as with the Irish and French flags, represented the peace and equality which bonded the peoples together.

While the concept of a 'Blue-Green' alliance had retained its currency amongst radical Chartists and Irish Repealers in many parts of Scotland, there is no other record of a blue, white and green tricolour surmounted by a pike being displayed anywhere else in the country at this time, and it seems likely that the flag and pike were 'got up' by Dundee's own radical alliance to express their credo and promote their campaign. [72]

The appearance of the Young Irelander on the platform was the cue for 'uproarious approbation' from a thin but strongly partisan audience who hung onto his every word as he confided that at sixteen years of age he had knelt at the grave of Robert Emmett and prayed that he might be enabled to free his country from a tyrannical government. He then proceeded to develop his plan for a National Guard, which, the *Courier* observed, was 'nothing else but a copy of [that] propounded by Mitchel and other fire-eating gentry'. As such, it was met with the wholehearted approval of the 'beardless youths' who formed the majority of his audience.[73]

The identity of the enigmatic young Irishman was never revealed, and his mission to Dundee remains shrouded in mystery. He had already mentioned his connections with the Young Ireland leadership; was it possible he was acting on instructions to procure arms and gather recruits for an insurrection in Ireland? He appears to have been aware that he was being watched, not least by the *Dundee Courier*, who tried unsuccessfully to obtain his name, and advised the local authorities to 'keep an eye' on him.[74] Around two weeks later, the authorities in Glasgow 'discovered', presumably on the word of a spy or informer, the small-scale manufacture of pikes 'on speculation for the Irish market' by three blacksmiths in the Anderston district.[75] The fact that the anonymous Young Irelander's visit pre-dated that of Confederate leader, Thomas D'Arcy McGee, who visited 'four of the principal towns in Scotland' in the last week in July, when he attended meetings of Confederate clubs, instituted committees, and obtained 'a list of nearly 400 men, pretty well-equipped, ready for the risk', suggests that other less prominent emissaries had gone ahead to prepare the ground.[76] The plan was to land an expeditionary force in Sligo to trigger a series of local uprisings in the north-west, and draw off British forces from strategic locations in the south-east upon which they were most focused. Despite the eagerness of the Dundee Confederates to participate in such a scheme, it is unlikely that McGee made it any further north than Edinburgh from where he was forced to flee on Friday, 28 July when it became known that his cover had been blown by a former Dublin resident who recognised him on the streets of Glasgow.[77] By this time, the situation was escalating rapidly as the ramping up of repressive legislation precipitated a premature strike in County Tipperary to which the Glasgow authorities responded by mobilising the military and placing them on standby.[78] Just two to three days earlier, police authorities in Edinburgh, Glasgow and Greenock had taken the precaution of apprehending key Chartist conspirators on charges of sedition.[79]

In contrast with their counterparts in the central belt of Scotland, the authorities in Dundee remained relatively unperturbed. Despite the promptings of the Tory *Courier*, who carried reports of public meetings promoting, setting up and recruiting to the National Guard, advocating the procurement of pikes and guns, and vowing 'to support the Irish in their struggles', neither Dundee's Irish Repealers nor physical force Chartists were considered dangerous enough to pose a significant threat. Compared to the prejudice which attached itself to the Irish population in the west of Scotland, Dundee's authorities and major employers endeavoured to promote a positive image of the Irish population as hardworking, law-abiding and an asset to the economy. Insofar as the Chartists were concerned, the re-appointment of James Graham as Dundee representative on the National Convention was taken as confirmation that the conciliatory, moral force element had the upper hand, despite the differences of opinion in the ranks.[80] Moreover, the fact that attendance at fraternal meetings in Dundee, as elsewhere in Scotland, was diminishing, plus the belief that the large crowds at open-air meetings were attracted by curiosity not intent, served to reassure the authorities that there was little need to take precautionary measures. Neither was it necessary. As Martin Mitchell noted with the west of Scotland, there is no evidence of any real insurrectionary activity in or around Dundee in this period.[81] Indeed, all the talk of pikes, pistols and insurrectionary expeditions came to nought as the suppression of the rebellion in Ireland 'put an end to the daring scheme of the Scottish Confederates'.[82]

In London, where the Chartists had been preparing for a coordinated insurrection at the heart of the British establishment, plans also fell through. In mid-July, the Secretary of the National Executive, John McCrea, revealed that there were no funds with which to carry on the agitation (although it is not unlikely that communications had been intercepted and he simply didn't receive the money sent).[83]

Over the next few weeks, several conspiracies in England were thwarted and their organisers, including Ayrshire militant Peter McDouall and Confederate link man James Leach, were arrested, the latter alongside the Manchester delegate to the National Convention, Dan Donovan, and other members of the Manchester Confederate Club.[84] McCrea appears to have gone to ground before resurfacing in Dundee in January 1849, where he established a Chartist school.[85]

In many ways, the scheme was doomed to failure. There was little attempt at concealment. Indeed, the open method of agitation ensured that every step of the campaign, and the identity and movements of its key organisers, were known to the government who had little difficulty in quelling the Irish rebellion and averting a sympathetic Chartist one. On 8 August, the *Dundee Advertiser* wrote:

•

CHAPTER 1 – RADICALS, REPUBLICANS AND REPEALERS 1841–58

> The Irish rebellion is making no farther progress, nor is it likely to for some time to come. It seems to be agreed that the attempt must be abandoned, and the proposal now is to wait until the present alarm has subsided, and the Government off their guard. The open and advised speaking will not do. Rebels and co-conspirators must revert to their old secret means if they would have a chance of even a temporary or local triumph.[86]

Interestingly, while the Dundee Repealers had taken great pains to deny the existence of Ribbon Societies to the 'gentlemen' of O'Connell's Loyal National Repeal Association, the failure of the rising appeared to vindicate secret conspiratorial methods of organisation. When the rebels resumed their campaign for national liberation over a decade later, it would be expedited through the 'old secret means'.

Meanwhile, the majority of Irish and native Scots inclined to support an Irish uprising and/or the overthrow of the British government, had more pressing concerns. In Dundee, most were members of a precarious, dying trade or were low-paid mill workers who lacked the means to purchase a pike-head, let alone a gun, even at good rates of credit. The Irish immigrants who flocked to the town in the wake of An Gorta Mór were lumbering through what Francis Sheehy Skeffington termed the 'deathly post-famine trance' – the debilitating disorientation of hunger, disease, grief, poverty and displacement – to contemplate resistance of any form.[87]

As the Great Hunger provided the catalyst for global emigration, Dundee, like other industrial centres in Britain, experienced a massive influx of immigrant families. Between 1841 and 1851, the number of Irish-born people in the town trebled to 15,000; 20 per cent of the total population, the highest percentage of Irish-born citizens in any town in Scotland, England or Wales.[88] Although work was plentiful, subsistence wages meant that the whole household worked to ensure basic survival, and the slightest drop in income resulted in destitution.

The worst year of the Famine, 'Black 47', saw the death rate in Dundee reach its highest figure for nine years – 2641 compared to 1526 the year before – of which, the Irish-born constituted 20 per cent compared to 5 per cent in 1840.[89] The majority succumbed to typhus fever, the biggest single cause of mortality overall. The *Dundee Advertiser* also noted the presence of a form of disease 'not usually known in the town, a combination of scurvy and dyssentry [sic]', which had 'proven so destructive to the poor Irish', noting its cause as the 'want of nourishing food...aggravated by destitution'.[90] Contemporary reports indicate that around a third of patients admitted to Dundee Infirmary suffering from infectious diseases were Irish, that many were admitted in rags, and that, of those who recovered, some were prevented from being discharged through want of clothes while others were discharged 'a good deal destitute in food and clothing'. As the pandemic subsided elsewhere, however, the *Courier* noted that 'typhus fever continues to prevail to an unusual extent' in certain locations in Dundee of which 'the Scouringburn is entitled to a bad pre-eminence'.[91] In January 1848, the death rate there from typhus alone was averaging fifteen per day, which grim statistic earned the worst infected area, around Horsewater Wynd, Malcolm's Pend and Henderson's Wynd, the unenviable title of the 'Valley of Death'.

In an observational account which appeared in the *Dundee Courier* in July 1849, five months after it was conducted, the anonymous author took his readers on a sensory journey through the area which, he established 'is principally inhabited by poor Irish families who work in the surrounding mills'.[92] Starting at Henderson's Wynd – 'of the three above-mentioned lanes, the worst' – he contrasted, by recourse to an older companion's memories of Dundee in times past – the 'green kailyard of other days' lovingly maintained by the former Scots residents, with the bare patch of ground which the 'the potato-loving migrants from the sister island' have allowed to go to waste. He registered the solitary wooden posts – remnants of garden fences which the poverty-stricken inhabitants had torn down for firewood – and the small windows of the 'once holy-looking dwellings, now broken and patched with brown paper or 'filled with the remains of old trousers or "pob" from the mill'. Inuring himself to the 'pestiferous atmosphere of the "Valley of Death"', he approached an open door through which he was bid welcome by an old Irishwoman sitting by a 'cold cheerless fire struggling for life amongst the a few cinders'. He surveyed the 'bare, damp walls', the 'cold mud floor', and the total lack of furniture besides the beds – 'square boxes of unwrought wood, covered with rags, black with smoke and dust', and a large stool upon which he and his companion sat while the woman told her tragic story.

It transpired that she was a widow from County Leitrim, in 'one of the prettiest parts of all Ireland', who came to Dundee in November 1846. Her husband had been a small farmer:

> We kept cows and pigs, and lived comfortably an' easy for many years. Afther he died I kept up the farm, but the rot came among the praties, the cows died, an' the pigs took the maisles; in less than three years after I had closed the eyes of my poor Teddy, I was turned out of my little farm without a pound note in the world. Everything [was] seized by the landlord for the rint. I have two sons in Ameriky but whether they are dead or alive goes agin me to tell. There was none of my neighbours were able to help me. I could not stay longer there, an', with the few shillings I had, I begged my way to Belfast, where I took a passage to Scotland, an' here I am, keepin' this house for mill girls, an' thankful to God for his mercy on my poor self.[93]

Her doleful comment – 'Had my poor Teddy had been alive, it's not in this strange country I would be seeking my bread' – spoken through silent tears, tells of her grief at being separated from her roots in a familiar rural landscape, from her husband's grave by 'the ould abbey of Dromahair', and from her sons in America, who she is resigned to never seeing again.[94] The 'cold cheerless fire, struggling for life among the cinders', provides a metaphor for her cheerless existence – deprived of her livelihood, friends and family, she draws emotional solace and material sustenance from her young female boarders, many of whom, like herself, were struggling for survival in an unfamiliar urban environment. In a society where fear of the workhouse was omnipresent, many widows perceived Dundee as a place where a respectable living could be made by taking in lodgers, and over the course of the next two decades, many such Irish landladies became the trusted guardians of young Irish girls, whose families could rest assured that their daughters were being cared for in a family environment.[95]

The widow's tale of a life turned upside down by 'The Great Calamity' – the combined consequences of unjust land laws, ecological disaster, displacement and poverty – was not untypical. However, while the author noted 'many such could be heard by those who have left their beautiful country', his sympathy for the 'poor woman' and her compatriots is superficial and contrived. The anonymous author was in fact local bookseller and aspiring writer, James Myles, a former moral force Chartist who espoused a philosophy of self and social improvement rooted in Protestant Christianity, and a belief in the city as the bastion of opportunity and social progress. Besides his antipathy towards physical force Chartism, Myles was, by definition, antagonistic towards the mainly Catholic Irish who cleaved to their rural customs and religious faith, and blamed the most recent 'famine' migrants for 'adding to the weight of demi-civilization, to the descending state of morals, and to the already unbearable weight of the poor laws'.[96]

Taking his leave of the cailleach and Henderson's Wynd, Myles turned into the shop of a grocer and spirit dealer on the Scouringburn, where a 'tall gaunt-looking individual, apparently, by his clothes a weaver or mill worker', pleaded for credit on a penny bread roll, and a ragged child presented a bowl and handkerchief for a bawbee's (tuppence) worth of brose meal, a bawbee red herring and a penny Bannock.[97] 'The stinted purchases of the poor', he conjectured,

> are an attempt to be economical; they have an idea they are saving money by getting the very smallest quality of goods at one time. To purchase a whole week's provisions at once and thereby incur the necessity of laying out the sum of five to six shillings has, in their eyes such an appearance of extravagance that they cannot bring themselves to the custom, even though they might save a few pence on articles sold cheaper in large quantities than in trifles. A strange idea seems to float in their minds that that twenty-four halfpenny worth make more than a shillings' worth, and that they must be gainers by twenty-four turns of the scale – never taking into account the probability of the grocer's attention to his own interests, and to the fact that what often costs a shilling in halfpenny worth's, may be purchased at tenpence when bought at once.[98]

Here, Myles failed to recognise the evidence of his own eyes which indicated that the poorest section of the working class, of which Dundee's recent Irish immigrants were included, were in no condition to play the capitalist system, nor indeed to combat it. Most lived from day to day – if they were lucky enough to get work, they were forced to endure long hours, low wages, dear food, and cramped, squalid living conditions in the most pestilent parts of the town. In January 1848, the *Dundee Advertiser* noted of such areas, 'fever is a constant and deadly resident, defying all professional skill and all domestic precautions. Want of water, of proper ventilation, and unwholesome effluvia consequent thereon, keep [typhus] alive, and prepare the way for [other diseases] equally formidable. The inhabitants of these districts can never be said to be in good health'.[99]

Given the circumstances in which many had been forced to leave their former homes, adaptation to a new environment was accompanied by an aggressive territorialism and, in many cases, a lingering enmity towards the forces of law and order. In January 1850, the Police Commissioners acted on reports of gangs of youths – the majority of whom were Irish – roaming the streets armed with clubs, sticks and stones, by stepping up patrols in the areas most affected.[100] However, the intervention of two police officers into a street fight between a half-dozen Irishmen in the Scouringburn on the evening of Monday, 25 January escalated into a full-blown riot after the officers, attempting to quell it, were approached by the 'ringleader', Patrick Flanagan, who continued to challenge them. After a short scuffle, Flanagan and another Irishman, Patrick Prior, were huckled into temporary custody in an adjacent grocer's shop upon which a gathering crowd proceeded to lay siege, attacking it with stones and sticks and smashing the windows. By this time, the Superintendent of Police had arrived on the scene with 'the whole disposable police force' who charged the 'mob'. However, rather than dispersing, the crowd, which by now had increased to several thousands and consisted, as the *Advertiser* noted, 'almost entirely of Irish', resorted to 'a more dangerous and deadly form of warfare' as 'large stones and other heavy missiles' were flung from windows, lanes and closes upon the invading force who found themselves 'assailed in every direction', not least by a large number of women bearing stones in their aprons.[101]

The riot, which the *Advertiser* noted, presented 'a very dangerous appearance', was eventually 'put down' around two hours later after several of the participants had been taken into custody. Over the course of the next week a total of fifteen Irishmen, mostly weavers and millworkers, appeared before the police courts where it was reported that six of the officers and watchmen who had assisted in the 'suppression' had been rendered unfit for duty, and all others on the spot had received an injury 'more or less'.[102] All cases were remitted to the Criminal Court where Flanagan was sentenced to twelve months in Perth Penitentiary for mobbing and rioting, breach of the peace and assault; Prior, Philip Diamond, Patrick Mulligan and Patrick Reilly to nine months in Dundee Jail, Bell Street, for the same; and another nine men to sixty days for mobbing and rioting.[103] It was not the end of the matter, however. In the early hours of Sunday morning, two watchmen patrolling the west end of the Perth Road were viciously assaulted by six to eight men wearing 'dresses', which the concussed victims recalled as resembling those worn by sailors. On this occasion, due to their remoteness from the police office, the watchmen were unable to procure assistance and the men escaped into the night. However, the *Advertiser* conveyed the general presumption that they were connected 'in some way or other' with the riot in the Scouringburn. Indeed, the fact that all of the perpetrators were armed with shillelaghs and wearing 'dresses' or long white shirts, suggests that the Ribbon or Mollie Maguire element that had resurfaced in the past five years, most notably in the counties of Ireland from where the majority of town's famine immigrants came, was present in Dundee.

The Great Hunger of the late 1840s was followed by the Great Clearances of the 1850s when around five million acres of land was bought over by Irish land speculators or 'gombeen men' who set about consolidating small tillage farms into larger, more profitable grazing ranches, evicting hundreds of thousands of families in the process.[104] In a bid to find work and escape the proselytising conditions of the workhouse, many families sought exile in large centres of production across the Irish Sea. Dundee, in particular, saw a large and steady stream of Irish incomers. The areas of most heavy settlement were the Scouringburn, which had more spinning-mills and factories than any other part of the town, and the manufacturing village of Lochee, the location of the jute manufacturing firm of Cox Brothers.

The upturn in trade from the mid-1850s onwards saw a large inflow of Irish women to Dundee to take up work in the growing number of large-scale centres of production such as Logie Works in the Scouringburn, the first and biggest jute and flax spinning works in Dundee, and one of the largest employers of female labour in the north-east of Scotland, and the ever-expanding Camperdown Works in Lochee, at its height the largest centre of jute production in the world. By the end of the decade, around half of the textile workforce was Irish-born, the vast majority being women who outnumbered Irish men by three to two. The 1850s and 1860s also saw a new generation of children born to Irish parents and given the ratio of Irish women to men and the higher rate of intermarriage, children of Scots-Irish parentage. Thus, the Irish influence over the next generation of Dundonians was far more likely to be a female one (mothers, grandmothers and aunts). These years also saw an increase in all-female households, containing groups of young Irish sisters, widows and an increasing number of older unattached working women.

Still, many immigrants were forced to apply for Poor Relief, and the Liff and Benvie Poor Register of 1854–65 reveals a disproportionately high number of Irish paupers. The most common applicants were women: women with young children, widows unable to support their families, women who had been deserted by their husbands, and unmarried mothers. In an effort to keep the poor rates down, there were several instances of paupers being forcibly repatriated, and while this was more common in Glasgow and the west of Scotland, it did occur in Dundee where paupers were being repatriated well into the 1860s. In places with longer established Irish communities, such as Dundee, however, it was carried out less brutally.[105] Nevertheless, while a few immigrants, usually elderly men, requested to be sent back, the Liff and Benvie Poor Register cites many examples of vulnerable young mothers, one of a baby of eleven days, being sent back by warrant.[106] Many more immigrants were refused relief, despite meeting the legal and residential qualifications, and were forced to fall back on their own community, and on the charity of the Catholic Church.

Throughout the second half of the nineteenth century, the Catholic Church played an important role in administering both spiritual and material relief to the Irish poor, and this appears to have been reciprocated by a staunch loyalty from the Irish community. While weekly pledges may have discouraged the poorest from attending, the Church appears to have developed to accommodate them, for example, by holding 'Poor Masses', where people could gather to worship in their working clothes without attracting unwelcome attention. The Catholic Church also provided a meeting-place where useful information could be exchanged, and by introducing new immigrants to the community, it acted as a link between the old world and the new, as well as providing a structure upon which much Irish political activity would be organised. For the moment though, most immigrants were still reeling in the aftershock of the Great Hunger and were too focused on the business of self-preservation to turn their attention to politics.

Despite the difficulties, these fallow years were instrumental in shaping the conditions and attitudes which would characterise political nationalism in Dundee in the years to come. Memories of the Great Hunger and, most pointedly, resentment at being uprooted from a familiar rural landscape and transplanted to a hostile urban one, altered the way in which many Irish people perceived the world and, consequently, the struggle for national independence. Common origins in a rural community, with its culture of interdependence and self-reliance, also combined with recent experience of urban poverty to strengthen the bonds of kinship. Added to this, the established links with Dundee's fraternity of political radicals, of which many earlier Irish immigrants could claim to be an intrinsic part, and the relative lack of sectarianism amongst the poorest members of the Scottish working class, who suffered the same appalling wages and living conditions, served to engender a wider sense of working-class solidarity and, ultimately, to encourage sympathy for and identification with the Irish cause.

Meanwhile, although wage rates remained chronically low, and the few extra pennies earned from increased hours of labour made minimal difference to the lives of individuals, the aggregate growth in income of the working-class population had a significant impact on the Irish community, coinciding as it did with a revival of the nationalist movement in Ireland and a growing national sentiment in the Irish nation abroad. Thus, when the Irish Republican movement re-emerged in Dundee at the beginning of the next decade, that cohesive working-class community was at its very heart.

Endnotes to Chapter 1

1. From 'Better Thoughts', by 'A Belfast Man', published in *The Nation*, 17 October 1846.
2. T M Devine (ed), *Irish Immigrants and Scottish Society in the Nineteenth and Twentieth Centuries* (Edinburgh: John Donald, 1991), p5.
3. Brenda Collins, 'Proto-industrialisation and pre-Famine Emigration', *Social History*, 2:2 (1982), pp127–46.
4. For a full and detailed study of Ribbonism, see Kyle Hughes and Donald MacRaild, *Ribbon Societies in Nineteenth-Century Ireland and Its Diaspora: The Persistence of Tradition* (Liverpool: LUP, 2021).
5. James E Handley, *The Irish in Scotland* (Cork: Cork University Press, 1943), p145.
6. See, for example, Máirtín Ó Catháin, 'Bullet Moulders and Blackthorn Men: A Comparative Study of Irish Nationalist Secret Societies in mid-nineteenth century Scotland and Ulster', in R J Morris and Liam Kennedy (eds), *Ireland and Scotland: Order and Disorder* (Edinburgh: John Donald, 2005), pp152–61.
7. *Northern Warder*, 13 July 1841.
8. Report of Royal Commission on Hand-loom weavers, 1841.
9. *Northern Warder*, 20 July 1841.
10. Handley, *The Irish in Scotland*, p137.
11. Although the Dundee Orange Order grew during 1870, it remained relatively small and discreet in comparison with Glasgow and the west. A J Cox, *Empire and Industry* (Edinburgh: Routledge, 2013), p17.
12. Gearóid Ó Tuathaigh, *Ireland Before the Famine, 1789–1848* (Dublin and London: Gill & Macmillan, 1972), p164.
13. *Northern Whig*, 21 July 1835.
14. The 1842 petition also called for the disestablishment of the Anglican Church, Repeal of the New [English] Poor Law, freedom of assembly, the release of the prisoners arrested in the Newport Rising of November 1839, no taxation without representation, and a reduction in working hours, cuts in costs of the monarchy, the army and the police. Malcolm Chase, *Chartism: A New History* (Manchester: MUP, 1970), p316.
15. *The Chartist Circular*, 29 January 1842, 2, 123, pp510–11.
16. Signatories to the second petition increased from 1,280,000 in 1839 to 3,220,000. However, numbers decreased in Glasgow and Lanarkshire, and specifically Paisley, where the signatures dropped from 15,000 to 2,000. (Chase, *Chartism: A New History*).
17. *Dundee Courier*, 30 January 1838.
18. *Dundee Warder*, 9 August 1842.

19 *Dundee Warder*, 23 August 1842.

20 The figure of 14,000 was quoted by the Chartists on the platform; 8,000 was claimed by the *Dundee Warder*.

21 Other Chartist leaders, notably John Duncan, continued to emphasise peaceful protest and moral persuasion. James Myles, a moral force Chartist with strong anti-Irish anti-Catholic views, was intensely critical of the physical force turn of the Dundee Chartist Council, led by John Mitchell, which he later described as 'the skep where the honey of the rump of O'Connor democracy was collected, and around which fluttered demagogues, drones and fools'. James Myles, *Rambles in Forfarshire or Sketches of Town and Country* (Dundee, 1850), p68.

22 It was around this time that Forfar handloom weaver and Chartist sympathiser, David Shaw, composed 'The Wark o' the Weavers', which was performed at weavers' society and Chartist meetings as an assertion of the dignity of the craft. Robert Ford, *Vagabond Songs and Ballads of Scotland* (Paisley: A Gardner, 1904).

23 *Northern Warder*, 30 August 1842.

24 *Northern Warder* 24 January 1843. The case against Duncan was never concluded. Broken by his imprisonment, he was released on bail, whereafter his health continued to deteriorate, and he died in an Edinburgh Lunatic Asylum on 11 January 1845. *Northern Star*, 22 January 1845.

25 Myles, *Rambles in Forfarshire*, pp66–70. Myles' representation of the march to Forfar as 'The Pilgrimage of Folly' was later adopted by Peter Carmichael, senior partner of Baxter Brothers. *The Dundee Textile Industry, 1790–1885, from the papers of Peter Carmichael of Arthurstone*. (Scottish History Society, 1969), p93.

26 *Dundee Herald*, quoted in the *Bradford Observer*, 1 July 1843.

27 Martin Mitchell, *The Irish in the West of Scotland, 1797–1848: Trade Unions, Strikes and Political Movements* (Edinburgh: John Donald, 1998), p232.

28 *Freeman's Journal*, 2 March 1843.

29 *Freeman's Journal*, 20 June 1843.

30 *Freeman's Journal*, 8 August 1843.

31 *The Nation*, 12 August 1843.

32 *The Nation*, 23 July 1843.

33 These massive gatherings, which were held in sites of historical significance across Ireland in 1842–43, were the key tactic by which O'Connell and his supporters sought to mobilise the maximum popular support for Irish self-rule, and pressurise the British government into granting their demands. The most recent meeting, held at the Hill of Tara (the seat of the ancient High Kings of Ireland) on 15 August 1843, was reputed to have attracted around 800,000 people. Gary Owens, 'Hedge Schools of Politics: O'Connell's Monster Meetings' *History Ireland*, 2:1 (Spring 1994), pp5–40.

34 *The Nation* was founded on 15 January 1842 by Charles Gavan Duffy, Thomas Davis and John Blake Dillon, 'to direct the popular mind and the sympathies

Chapter 1 – Radicals, Republicans and Repealers 1841–58

of educated men to the great end of nationality', to foster a spirit of nationality which would 'not only raise our people from their poverty, by securing to them the blessings of a domestic legislature, but inflame and purify them with a lofty and heroic love of country'. Prospectus of *The Nation*, written by Thomas Davis.

35 *Dundee Courier*, 20 July 1844.
36 *The Nation*, 21 January 1843, 17 August 1844; Census of Scotland, 1841, 1851.
37 *The Nation*, 26 January 1844.
38 *The Nation*, 16 November 1844.
39 The 1851 census lists Coogan's birthplace as Edinburgh. That same year, Dundee poet, William McGonagall, whom the 1841 census lists as being born in Ireland, declared his birthplace as Edinburgh, a fiction he maintained for the rest of his life.
40 Nor indeed his marriage prospects. In 1849, Coogan married Margaret Coupar, the daughter of a wealthy Protestant farming family in St Andrew's RC Cathedral.
41 *Dundee Advertiser*, 1 July 1845.
42 *The Nation*, 19 July 1845.
43 *The Nation*, 2 August 1845.
44 *Dundee Advertiser*, 1 July 1845.
45 *Sligo Champion*, 7 June 1845. The Irish press also reported that Leitrim and Monaghan were in 'a very disturbed state, the Mollie Maguires being active in crime', and noted the widespread belief amongst the peasantry that government agents were behind a series of recent 'outrages' in County Monaghan. *Dublin Evening Post*, 7 June 1845.
46 *Dundee Advertiser*, 1 July 1845.
47 *The Nation*, 17 October 1846.
48 *The Nation*, 9 October 1847. The instructions stipulated that members of a Club must also be members of the Irish Confederation, that subscriptions be sent at least once a month and that meetings must not be held in public houses. It also prohibited sectarian discussions, membership of other political groups and societies, adding that any member who seeks to establish, or professes a connection with any other club or society would cease to be a member.
49 *The Nation*, 16 January 1847.
50 *The Nation*, 18 December 1847.
51 *The Nation*, 15 January 1848.
52 Gearóid Ó Tuathaigh, *Ireland Before the Famine*, pp198–200.
53 *The Nation*, 15 April 1848.
54 Mitchell, *The Irish in the West of Scotland*, p246.
55 Possibly Hugh O'Neill, who had chaired a fraternal meeting in Hamilton, four days before.
56 *Dundee Courier*, 11 April 1848.

57 *Dundee Advertiser*, 14 April 1848.
58 Peel's Coercion Bill of May 1846, which was blocked in the House of Lords, leading, in part, to Peel's resignation the following month.
59 William Ryder, Anglican Archdeacon of Cloyne, County Cork. McCrea was referring to the Rathcormac/Gortroe massacre of 18 December 1834, when a 100-strong militia opened fire on 250 anti-tithe protestors defending the cottage of the widow Johanna Ryan – where Ryder had come to distrain the sum of forty shillings – killing nine outright and mortally wounding eleven more.
60 Radical Presbyterian preachers, Richard Cameron and Donald Cargill, who claimed the right to independent worship, were opposed to the Episcopalian (top down) form of Church governance, and disowned the King's authority as the head of the established church. Cameron was killed in a skirmish with government at Aird's Moss, Ayrshire on 22 July 1680 and Cargill was executed in Edinburgh on 27 July 1891 for declaring an open case for rebellion in pursuit of 'the overthrow of the kingdom of darkness and whatever is contrary to the Kingdom of Christ'. The 'Bloody Archbishop', James Sharp, Primate of Scotland, was killed in an ambush by Covenanters on Magus Moor in May 1679. Thomas Johnson, *History of the Working Classes in Scotland*, 1920, (Glasgow: Unity Publishing, 1946), p95.
61 Unlike those with whom he organised – Henry Joy McCracken, Robert Emmett and Thomas Russell – Hope's humble status enabled him to evade capture and execution. Regarded as the most radical and egalitarian of the United Irishmen, his ideas on class relations and on the ownership and distribution of land prefigured James Fintan Lalor and Michael Davitt, and, in turn, influenced James Connolly, to whom Hope was a hero. John Newsinger (ed), *United Irishman – The autobiography of James Hope* (London: Merlin Press, 2001); Mary McNeill, *The Life and Times of Mary McCracken* (Belfast: Blackstaff Press, 1988), pp94–95.
62 *Dundee Advertiser*, 14 April 1848.
63 The National Guard in smaller towns and villages would be commanded by a colonel, captain, lieutenant on ensign, according to their numbers. *Dundee Advertiser*, 19 May 1848.
64 Despite the apparent enthusiasm of the Glasgow Repealers, no National Guards were formed in the west of Scotland. Mitchell, *The Irish in the West of Scotland*, p247.
65 *Dundee Advertiser*, 7 June 1848.
66 Graham had written a letter advising against taking up arms against Her Majesty's government, rather recommending the 'every man provide himself with arms, not for aggressive purposes, but to protect his wife, family and children' and 'to give their demands more weight', i.e., pressurise the government into granting the Charter without blood being spilt. *Dundee Advertiser*, 2 May 1848.
67 *Dundee Advertiser*, 14 June 1848; *Dundee Courier*, 14 June 1848.

68 R Challinor, 'Peter Murray McDouall and 'Physical Force Chartism', *International Socialism*, 2:21 (1981); John Denvir, *The Irish in Britain* (London, 1897), p146.

69 *Dundee Advertiser*, 16 June 1848.

70 Meagher also emphasised that, 'If this flag be destined to fan the flames of war, let England behold once more, on the white centre, the RED HAND that struck her down from the hills of Ulster'. *United Irishman*, 22 April 1848.

71 At the first Chartist procession in Scotland, from Glasgow Green to Parkhead and back, on 21 May 1838, a group of marchers from the Strathaven Weavers' Society carried the tattered blue Saltire borne by the Covenanters at the Battle of Drumclog in 1679. Chase, *Chartism: A New History*, p5.

72 The nearest contemporary reference is that of a green, white and blue horizontal tricolour designed by English craftsman, writer and moral force Chartist, William James Linton, as the flag of an English Republic, which appeared in the frontispiece of his largely self-penned journal, *The English Republic*, in 1851. While Linton's flag was possibly derived from a sunburst tricolour flag devised by the Welsh Chartist, Hugh Williams, with whom Linton was acquainted, Linton himself was hostile to nationalism, and believed that Ireland (as well as Scotland and Wales) should fall in behind the democratic struggle in England, which he equated with Britain. Linton's journal had a limited distribution, however; and the blue, white and green tricolour in Dundee predated it by two and half years. Moreover, Linton's Anglocentric views, and his description of the colour white as representing cliffs of Albion, would have been anathema to Irish republicans and most radical Scottish Chartists. W J Linton, 'Our Tricolour', *The English Republic*, 1 (1851), p35, quoted in Alexander Roob, 'Radical Landscapes – William James Linton's Art of Graphic Macchia', Melton Prior Institute (2011) https://meltonpriorinstitut.org/pages/textarchive.php5?view=text &ID=99&language=English, accessed 19 May 2023; Flags of Reform in 19th century Wales, https://www.crwflags.com/fotw/gb_charw.html, accessed 19 May 2023.

73 *Dundee Courier*, 16 June 1848.

74 *Dundee Courier*, 13 June 1848.

75 Mitchell, *The Irish in the West of Scotland*, p248; *Dundee Advertiser*, 4 July 1848.

76 Denvir, *The Irish in Britain*, pp143–44.

77 Denvir, *The Irish in Britain*, p145. McGee returned to Ireland, via Carlisle and Liverpool, from where he fled to North America where he relaunched *The Nation*, suppressed in Ireland, as a patriotic emigrant newspaper. He later moved to Canada where he stood for the Confederated Parliament, in which he became Minister of Agriculture in 1865. By this, time, McGee had renounced physical force republicanism, was a staunch defender of the British Dominion, a loyal supporter of the Queen, and an outspoken critic of the Fenian Brotherhood. He was assassinated by a Fenian sympathiser in April 1868.

78 Mitchell, *The Irish in the West of Scotland*, p256, n107.

79 The Scots Chartists arrested were James Cumming, Henry Rankin and proprietor-editor of the Scottish Chartist and pro-Repeal newspaper, the *North British Express*, Archibald Walker, who were arrested in Edinburgh on Wednesday, 26 July; Glasgow editor of the *North British Express*, James Smith, who was arrested in Glasgow on Thursday, 27 July; and bookseller Robert Burnett, and Secretary of the Greenock Arms Club, Andrew Neilson, who were arrested in Greenock, also on the 27th. *Greenock Advertiser*, 28 July 1848; *Glasgow Herald*, 31 July 1848.

80 Nevertheless, Graham's views cannot be so easily reduced. The fact that he supported the aims of the Irish Confederates and expressed a genuine sympathy with Mitchel and the Irish leaders in their fate, while stopping short of openly promoting their physical force methods, partly explains why the large Irish element were prepared to support him. Ironically, Graham was expelled from the Dundee Chartist ranks after a showdown with Feargus O'Connor in Bell Street Hall, in which he attempted to expose O'Connor's failure to support the Irish Confederates. The audience, blindsided by O'Connor's celebrity and swayed by his rhetoric, took O'Connor's side. *Dundee Advertiser*, 1 November 1848; *Dundee Courier*, November 1848; *Northern Star*, 4 November 1848.

81 Mitchell, *The Irish in the West of Scotland*, p248.

82 Denvir, *The Irish in Britain*, p146.

83 *London Standard*, 15 July 1848.

84 *Dundee Advertiser*, 22 August 1848; Denvir, *The Irish in Britain*, p149.

85 McCrea's school was visited by Feargus O'Connor when he returned to Dundee to promote his Land Scheme in late January. O'Connor's Dundee meeting was reported to have been well-attended, particularly by the Irish. However, little was heard of the Chartists or the Irish Repealers after this. *Northern Star*, 4 November 1848; C A Whatley, 'The case of James Myles, the 'Factory Boy' and mid-Victorian Dundee', in Louise Miskell, Christopher A Whatley and Bob Harris (eds), *Victorian Dundee, Image and Realities* (East Linton: Tuckwell Press, 2000), p82.

86 *Dundee Advertiser*, 8 August 1848.

87 Francis Sheehy Skeffington, *Michael Davitt*, 1908 (London: McGibbon and McKee, 1967), p63.

88 Brenda Collins, 'The Origins of Irish Immigration to Scotland', in Devine, *Irish Immigrants and Scottish Society in the Nineteenth and Twentieth Centuries*, p6.

89 Mortality figures for 1847, *Dundee Advertiser*, 22 January 1848.

90 *Dundee Advertiser*, 4 May 1847.

91 *Dundee Courier*, January 1848.

92 *Dundee Courier*, 18 July 1849.

93 *Dundee Courier*, 18 July 1849.

94 Dromahair (Droim Dhá Thiar – Ridge of the Two Demons), in North West Leitrim at the foot of the Sleeping Giant mountain range, was the capital of the medieval Gaelic Kingdom of Breifne c700–1565, which comprised counties Leitrim and Cavan, and extended to Kells in County Meath. It was later divided into East Breifne (Cavan) and West Breifne (Leitrim). Creevelea (Craobh Liath) Abbey, was founded by the Franciscan order in 1508, forcibly vacated by Henry VIII's army in in the 1560s, dissolved in 1598, reoccupied by the Franciscans in 1613, forcibly vacated by Cromwell's troops in 1642, and finally dissolved in 1650.

95 B Collins, 'Irish Emigration to Dundee and Paisley in the First Half of the Nineteenth Century', in J M Goldstrom and L Clarkson (eds), *Irish Population, Economy and Society* (Oxford: Clarendon Press, 1981), p21.

96 *Dundee Courier*, 18 July 1849.

97 A bawbee was a Scottish sixpence.

98 Myles's serialised accounts of Dundee street life, which appeared in the *Dundee Courier* in 1849, were subsequently re-edited and published as *Rambles in Forfarshire or Sketches in Town and Country* in 1850. Ironically, for someone so 'infected' with anti-Irish prejudice, Myles died of typhus in March 1851, at the age of 32.

99 *Dundee Advertiser*, January 1848. The typhus epidemic was followed by Asiatic cholera which hit the town in January 1849, peaking in July 'most severely…in localities known as being particularly unhealthy, and almost invariably the seat of typhus when it prevailed'. Report of the General Board of Health on the epidemic cholera of 1848 and 1849, p115–16.

100 *Dundee Advertiser*, 11 January 1850.

101 *Dundee Advertiser*, 1 March 1850.

102 *Dundee Advertiser*, 1 March 1850.

103 *Dundee Advertiser*, 17 April 1850; *Dundee Advertiser*, 19 April 1850.

104 F S L Lyons, *Ireland Since the Famine* (London: Fontana Press, 1973), p26; Sheehy Skeffington, *Michael Davitt*, p18.

105 J E Handley, *The Irish in Modern Scotland*, (Cork: Cork University Press, 1947), p208.

106 Liff and Benvie Poor Register, 1854–65.

CHAPTER 2

Fenians
1859–69

They have had their mead of praise in English pelf,
They fought for English glory and for self,
They've encouraged absenteeism and rack-rents,
For which they've got their bronze and granite monuments.
But thou, brave chieftain of the Celt and Gaul,
Whose name made despots run and legions fall,
To thee with lightning speed the message wings,
Thrice welcome true descendant of old Ireland.1

Down with all faction old,
Concert and action bold,
This is the creed of the Fenian men![2]

ON 15 AUGUST 1859, Patrick McNally of Dundee wrote a letter to *The Irishman* enclosing the sum of 7s 4d – the first instalment from a group of subscribers to the MacMahon Sword Testimonial. The MacMahon Testimonial had been initiated in July by *The Nation* and its younger contemporary, *The Irishman*,[3] with the aim of commissioning a 'Sword of Honour' to be presented to the nearest living descendant of the last King of Ireland, Murtagh O'Brien, the great-grandson of Brian Boru. The prospective recipient was ascertained – from documents procured in post-Revolutionary Paris by the Irish antiquarian, Chevalier O'Gorman – to be Patrice MacMahon, the Marshal Duc de Magenta of Maguien, Burgundy, whose enterprising Irish-born grandfather had gained access to the higher ranks of the French aristocracy by tendering proof of an ancient royal bloodline stretching back to O'Brien's son, Mahon.[4] On 4 June 1859, MacMahon led French troops to victory against the Austrian army at the Battle of Magenta in Lombardy, for which Napoleon III awarded him his eponymous title.[5] In an article initiating the campaign, *The Irishman* explained its reasoning:

> We care little for Kings or nobles... nor shall we ever be willing to concede our republican rights of perfect individual equality which we all hope one day to establish for ever for our long down-trodden people. But we do so passionately forever *reverence* whatever connects itself with the ancient Irish Laws and Customs and Government... Aye, even in the midst of our degradation, we feel a longing... to be as living links with the past, when the day shall come for that revival of ancient Nationality in which Ireland has never ceased to believe with all the certainty of Fate.[6]

The MacMahon Sword Testimonial was part of a broader drive on the part of the Irish national movement to revive the national spirit after the long decade of displacement and demoralisation which followed the Great Hunger and the quelling of the Young Ireland Rebellion of 1848. Indeed, another descendent of King Murtagh O'Brien was former leader of the Rebellion, William Smith O'Brien, who, after a period of imprisonment in Van Diemen's Land, had returned to Ireland to co-found the Ossianic Society with the aim of reviving the poetry and prose of Óisin, son of Fionn Mac Cumhall, and one of the Fianna warriors of ancient Irish mythology. The legend of the sleeping Fianna warrior, destined to rise up and defend Ireland in her hour of greatest need, had inspired the formation of the Irish Revolutionary (subsequently Republican) Brotherhood, the American Fenian Brotherhood and the Phoenix National and Literary Society, and provided names for the latter two. The concept of a symbolic sword placed in the hands of a battle-hardened descendant of Ireland's warrior kings also captured the imagination of a wide Irish audience who responded with donations and messages of support from all over Ireland and centres of Irish settlement in England, Scotland, Wales and the Isle of Man.

Patrick McNally, who had been forced off his small Irish farm by the landlord's battering ram in the wave of evictions following the Great Hunger, appreciated the symbolism and the potential of the initiative. On behalf of the Dundee subscribers, he congratulated *The Irishman* and

The Nation for propounding 'so noble and national an idea' and trusted that a committee be formed '*forthwith...* to give it every aspect of a *National* movement'. But above all, he warned, 'Let Parliamentarian jugglers and West British flunkeys have nothing to do with it or your gallant efforts will be brought to nought; if not to disrepute'. Here, McNally affirmed the aversion of many his compatriots to constitutional politics and to the toadying politicians who had failed to counter the repressive land policy that lay at the heart of British injustice in Ireland, and which had driven hundreds of thousands into exile. 'Consider when that flashing sword will be wielded, on some other soil – by and by – by the arm of that gallant warrior to avenge the wrongs of other oppressed races', McNally fancied. The image was metaphorical (although whether McNally intended it to be taken as such is unclear): the placing of a sword in the hands of a modern-day general symbolising the return to physical force, by which methods, steered by high-minded patriots and supported by the Irish nation at home and abroad, Ireland would ultimately shake off the bonds of oppression. McNally went on to propose that Young Ireland leader William Smith O'Brien be prevailed upon to lead a deputation to present the Sword as it would give the exercise a greater significance. 'If he thinks well enough', McNally concluded, 'I am sure he is brave enough to undertake it'.[7]

While O'Brien may have been brave enough, he did not think well of the idea, describing MacMahon as 'the agent of a military despot' who 'has neither done or suffered in the cause of Ireland', and fearing that the presentation encouraged the belief that he would be welcome in Ireland at the head of a French army.[8] Nevertheless, while O'Brien and his former comrade, John Mitchel, considered the MacMahon Sword an impolitic and superficial scheme, the idea resonated with the Irish public, and in December the subscription list was closed, the target having been long exceeded.[9]

The Sword, sheathed in its green and gold scabbard, was eventually presented to MacMahon in Paris in September 1860 by a deputation headed by John Mitchel (who was prevailed upon to do the honours, and agreed, despite his reservations), editor-owner of *The Nation*, T D Sullivan, Paris-based Irish Republican and unofficial Irish ambassador, John Patrick Leonard (who later hosted Fenian leaders in Paris and facilitated

John Devoy's military training in the Foreign Legion) and independent nationalist MP for Tipperary, Daniel O'Donoghue, in his capacity as Chairman of the committee.

The MacMahon Sword movement was a short-lived episode, but it was a significant one. It accommodated a wide spectrum of nationalist ideas, and as such contained many inherent contradictions, not least being the fact that its subject was a political conservative who went on to become the Governor of Algiers, second President of France, and led the Versailles Army which put down the revolutionary Paris Commune in 1871. William Smith O'Brien's criticisms were not unjustified. Nevertheless, for the first time since the Repeal agitation of the 1840s, the MacMahon Sword provided a national project in which the ordinary Irish immigrant population could play an active and influential part. The earlier Irish immigrants to Dundee who had participated in the Repeal movement had been augmented by the new wave of post-famine immigrants who, by the beginning of the 1860s, had found their feet, formed new social and economic networks and were now looking for a new outlet for national, cultural and political expression. At the same time, the revival of the national movement in Ireland, presented them with a new type of organisation.

The National Brotherhood of St Patrick

The National Brotherhood of St Patrick (NBSP) was founded in Dublin on 17 March 1861, and spread quickly throughout Ireland, and those parts of Scotland, England and Wales with large Irish communities. The Irish in Dundee were amongst the first to join – in early May, the Central Committee in Marlborough Street, Dublin, received a request for membership cards from Daniel Hannah of 156 Scouringburn.[10] Within a few weeks, Dundee, with its population of 90,417, had two branches, based in the Hilltown and Scouringburn areas, alongside Liverpool (340,900) and Dublin (c410,000). London, with its population of 2,803,000, had three.[11] While the character of each branch was determined by local conditions and priorities for which it was permitted to make its own byelaws, the raison d'être – to promote 'fidelity to the principle of [Irish] Nationality' – remained common to all. After some initial tension between the two Dundee branches, and some practical advice from *The Irishman* that they 'work in harmony' or 'better be repressed at once', the branches rallied together under one association centrally based in Pullar's Close in the Murraygate, focusing on the single purpose of raising funds for the obsequies of the exiled Young Ireland leader Terence Bellew McManus, who died in San Francisco on 15 January 1861.[12]

The funeral arrangements of McManus, undertaken by the American Fenian Brotherhood and the Irish Republican Brotherhood (IRB), involved an extended ten-month procession from San Francisco to New York and Cork to Dublin. Over 100,000 people turned out to witness McManus's final journey to Glasnevin Cemetery on 10 November where Father Patrick Lavelle defied the directive of the Archbishop of Dublin, Paul Cullen, and pushed himself forward to the graveside to perform the funeral rites and deliver the eulogy, thus upstaging Colonel Smyth who IRB chief, James Stephens, had drafted in to give the oration, and sealing his reputation as a Fenian sympathiser to Irish Republicans the world over.

McManus's funeral was widely reported in the press, and in terms of propaganda, fundraising and recruitment, played a huge part in the revival of the Republican movement. Indeed, the successful appropriation of McManus's funeral by the Fenian movement in 1861 provided the template for that of exiled Fenian leader, Jeremiah O'Donovan Rossa, 54 years later, at which the words spoken by Patrick Pearse, 'They have left us our Fenian dead, and while Ireland holds these graves, Ireland unfree will never be at peace', imitated those written by Stephens in 1861, 'Yesterday that sarcophagus was the symbol of Erin's grave. Tomorrow it will be her resurrection'.[13]

Having proven they could 'unite in cordial brotherhood', and with the increased numbers drawn in by the McManus funeral, the Dundee NBSP once more branched out. Sunday, 10 November saw the re-establishment of the Scouringburn, now West Port, branch at 8 Henderson's Wynd. A branch was also formed in Lochee. The officers of these branches comprised an eclectic body of advanced nationalists including Samuel McKinney, John McElroy, Patrick and James McNally, Peter and Philip Clarke, Peter Martin, Thomas Morrison, Daniel Hannah and Owen Walsh. McKinney brought his previous experience of involvement in the Repeal movement and of having helped to co-ordinate joint activity between Irish Repealers and Scottish Chartists in 1848. McElroy, a weaver of 17 Henderson's Wynd, was President of the first NBSP branch and chaired most Irish political meetings in the town thereafter; the McNallys and the Clarkes filled the interchanging officer roles in the Hilltown and West Port branches; and Peter Martin presided over the Lochee branch. Hannah, President of the West Port branch, also as acted as night school tutor and unofficial press officer. A 31-year-old carpet weaver living in the Scouringburn with his wife Eliza and two young children, Hannah was articulate, highly literate and a ferociously independent thinker, as was Owen Walsh, a Hilltown-resident sheet weaver, who first appeared on the NBSP officer boards as Secretary of the Hilltown branch in Rosebank Street, in April 1863.[14]

Following the funeral of McManus, the Dundee Brotherhood reached agreement on the establishment of reading rooms as a means to raising the literacy level and national consciousness of Dundee's large working-class Irish community. While historian of Dundee's Irish textile workers, William Walker, has argued that the Dundee NBSP's preoccupation with reading rooms was not particularly Irish or nationalistic, a closer examination reveals the project to be politically driven, and the NBSP itself to be increasingly Republican minded. Indeed, while the growth of reading rooms in nineteenth-century Scottish urban society may have had its origins in the Scottish Enlightenment and seemed to be, as Townend notes of Ireland, 'inextricably linked to everything that Irish nationalism was not', the objectives of the NBSP reading rooms resembled those of the proto-Fenian Phoenix National and Literary Society, founded by O'Donovan Rossa and other militant nationalists in 1856, which had gone on to merge with the IRB and its American auxiliary, the Fenian Brotherhood, in 1858.[15] Within its name and its mission statement, the Phoenix National and Literary Society linked Enlightenment principles of rational debate and critical thinking with Irish nationalist ideas of regeneration, liberation and self-determination. Asserting that 'to be free, a nation must be enlightened', the Phoenix Society aimed, ostensibly,

> to place within the reach of its members... a national literature of the purest and best description; to afford them with every useful information connected with the past and a knowledge of

what they are entitled to for the future, so that they may ponder on their present degraded position, contrast it with that of variously other nations inferior to Ireland in extent, population and resources; and make it their constant aim and labour to regain those rights which have been, and are, forcibly and unjustly held.[16]

Such a route to enlightenment could not occur without raising the literacy level of Dundee's large Irish working-class population first. To this end, the Dundee NBSP set up basic reading rooms in 'convenient' locations, presided over by Morrison (Central), Peter Clarke (Dundee Hilltown) and Hannah (West Port). Hannah, in particular, was a vigorous proponent of secular education for the working classes free from clerical interference, in which he was supported by his colleagues whose concept of patriotism owed more to their class than their religion, and who otherwise had little allegiance to a priesthood drawn from the Scottish (Highland) elite. Moreover, unlike the Glasgow NBSP, whose leading officers, bookseller James Walsh and medical practitioner Dr John Tynan, were chary of alienating the Catholic clergy, their proletarian Dundee equivalents reflected the position of the Dublin General Council which promoted a secular, anti-clerical perspective of Irish identity.[17]

The position of the Dundee NBSP was further reinforced when two local clergymen, the Reverend Archibald Mcdonald of St Mary's Forebank and his co-adjutant, Robert Clapperton, attempted to undermine it. The Dundee priests were likely taking their lead from James Gillis, Vicar-Apostolic of the Eastern District of Scotland, who in November 1860 had pronounced Ribbonism to be the bane of Catholic Christianity in Scotland, and Paul Cullen, Archbishop of Dublin, who in late 1861 had spoken out against the involvement of secret societies in the NBSP.[18]

All this was brought to the attention of the wider public through a letter entitled 'The Roman Catholic Clergy versus the Reading Rooms', which appeared in the *People's Journal*, the weekly newspaper of the respectable, literate working classes, in January 1862.[19] In the long and detailed letter, the enigmatically named 'Hibernicus' related how a number of Irish working men had endeavoured to ameliorate 'the moral degradation of their fellow-countrymen' by establishing the reading rooms, of which the 600–700 members and large number of casual visitors was taken as proof that 'the seed [had] not fallen upon a barren soil, and that the poor Irish artisan, even the "navvy" unlettered as he is, is capable of a higher culture and even of nobler deeds than Fair Muir rowdying and midnight brawling from street to street, and from corner to corner of our adopted town'.[20] Yet, he stated, rather than offering their sympathy and respect, the Roman Catholic clergy 'launch[ed] forth thunders against us – some of [them] going so far as to threaten "cudgelling in the streets" the leading members of our institution!' Hibernicus claimed that these 'respected and reverend gentlemen' had condemned the reading rooms because they were 'not under their immediate control' and were 'of a secular and educational tendency'. Explaining that 'our rules forbid the discussion of religious topics or sectarian differences of opinion', he contended that 'some leisure time may be as usefully spent in "secular" reading as the recital of certain formal "Novenas" in a bending posture', and was 'more congenial to the acquired habits of our street-going fellow-countrymen', whom, he stated, 'we wish to reclaim and who could never be prevailed to appear in rags in the company of their better clad brethren of the pious fraternity'.[21]

Consequently, the priests had accused them of being 'men of a questionable moral character' and admitting 'bad, sinful, irreligious characters' as members. His parting shot – 'Let him who is without sin cast the first stone' – provoked a terse response from McDonald and Clapperton in which they accused the *People's Journal* of defaming their characters by printing Hibernicus's letter, which, they claimed, should have been titled 'The Roman Catholic Clergy versus the Reading Rooms *under the cloak of Ribbon Societies*'.[22]

A furious debate between members of the NBSP and defenders of the clergy ensued, with President of the West Port branch, Daniel Hannah, accusing McDonald and Clapperton of founding their allegations on 'the false assertions of mean persons who think they are saving their souls by telling lies on their neighbours', and challenging 'any man, lay or clerical', to prove that the NBSP was a secret society. 'The National Brotherhood of St Patrick is a Political Association, having as its object the political welfare of Ireland', he asserted, before proceeding to list the achievements of the West Port night school in raising the literacy level of the working men of the community. However, he noted:

> No sooner was it observed...that we were getting strong in numbers, that our influence was beginning to be felt around us than the cry of Ribbonism, of conspirators and ruffians was raised against us...We were told that we were Ribbonmen and could not deny it; the priest had said it and who knew better... They had us nearly believing that we were Ribbonmen without our knowledge; that perhaps we were initiated in our sleep, and I think we would have put up with it in silence were it not for 'Hibernicus' who gave it the light of day. [23]

To which one supporter of the clergy, pen-named 'Candour', responded, 'The chief object of [Mr Hannah's Association] is not to teach Irishmen to read and write but to keep alive, if possible, the spirit of political faction, which in this country can never bear good results'. 'The Catholic clergymen of Dundee', he reasoned, 'had perfectly justifiable grounds for endeavouring to suppress [it]'.[24]

Others were even more perturbed by the strong anti-clerical turn within the Dundee NBSP. The mouthpiece of the Irish-Catholic community in Scotland, the Glasgow-based *Free Press,* dubbed Hibernicus 'a pretended Catholic...we hope...not an Irishman', whose criticisms of Catholic clergymen and mocking of religious devotions in a Protestant publication exhibited 'all the worst evils which might be expected to arise from seditious re-unions of unlettered men'.[25] 'You can be a Jew, a pagan or even a profligate and still drape yourself in the banner of St Patrick!', wrote one Dundee correspondent, who signed himself 'Incog.[nito], a member of the Library connected with the Living Rosary and the Blessed Virgin'. Describing the Dundee Brotherhood as 'the dregs of the shebeen and a few pot orators', he claimed, somewhat fancifully, that a recent meeting he had attended consisted of a paganistic ritual involving the smoking of narcotic weed and the dancing of Irish jigs until a state of collective 'spiritual enlightenment' had been reached, at which point the chairman, who had gained a hypnotic power over his 'pupils', proceeded to malign the clergy and valorise 'our learned "Hibernicus"' who had 'come forward like a man' and told them to 'mind their own business'.[26]

A flurry of critical correspondence was followed by another letter from Hibernicus regretting that he had awoken 'not the latent intelligence, but the blatant bigotry of many of my countrymen', and noting, 'I have yet to learn if the Presbyterian clergymen of Dundee or any zealot of their congregations have "thundered" against the Working Men's Colleges'.²⁷ Nevertheless, he noted, 'Tis the result of thunder generally to purify the air. A larger number have joined us. What we want in "prestige", we have in courage and self-reliance, [without which] vigour of character – so essential to individuals and nations cannot exist'. And so Hibernicus concluded artfully:

> As this Association is formed for no secret or sectarian design, for the advancement of our own moral and social welfare, we therefore solicit the assistance of all Irishmen, no matter to what denomination they may belong, to come forward and aid in securing those blessings.

Ironically, whether 'propagating sedition' was the underlying aim of the Dundee NBSP, by conflating the reading rooms with Ribbon Societies, the clergymen and their conservative allies inadvertently created the situation they were anxious to prevent – the radicalisation of the Reading Rooms. The priests' 'thunderings' and the ensuing debate in the press made the NBSP all the more attractive to Ribbon sympathisers – it weeded out the timid members and left a more defiant, rebellious body of men whose growing literacy and knowledge of Irish affairs conspired to provide their radical nationalism with a new political edge. 'A Connaught Man' of St Peter's Street wrote:

> I am not a Ribbonman, but a member of the Reading Rooms, from which I have already derived great benefit. I find in the Irish newspapers of last week, ten men arrested in Donegal accused of being connected with a Ribbon Society. [It caused] a great sensation in the north of Ireland, and I suppose that Messrs McDonald and Co. consider this a most suitable time for manifesting their loyalty by accusing the Reading Rooms of being cloaks for Ribbonism...

If any such evidence existed, he stated, they would be justified in arresting every one of the 700 men and boys 'who devote their weekly pence to the purchase of books for their own improvement in the very real way... recommended by Dr McHale [the Archbishop of Tuam] Father Lavelle [and] fifty other worthy Catholic clergymen'.[28]

In contrast with the Catholic clergy in Dundee, the NBSP recognised the power of the press, and were astute enough to cultivate a cordial relationship with local and Irish newspapers – notably the Liberal *Dundee Advertiser* and the NBSP-supporting *Irishman* – which helped to ensure their reports and letters were gratefully accepted and fairly published. On 15 February, the *Advertiser* published a letter which had been 'put in their hands' by Thomas Morrison, Peter Clarke and Daniel Hannah, from 'the celebrated Father Lavelle', in which he urged them to 'bear up against [their opponents] like men', and announced his intention to visit Scotland 'when I will scatter to the "four winds" every calumny piled up against you and your organisation'.[29] Interestingly, three days prior to penning this letter to Morrison *et al*, Lavelle delivered a lecture in the Dublin Rotunda on 'The Rights of Catholics to Revolt against Unjust Governments', in which he confided to the audience that he 'carefully avoided making any expression which could be called seditious or treasonable as he had no desire to be "locked up" in Newgate'.[30] *The Irishman*, which also published Lavelle's letter to the Dundee NBSP, lauded the 'patriotic Irishmen and humble Irish working men of Dundee', and contrasted the sage advice of 'the good Irish '*Sogarth*'' – to 'follow their priests in all things spiritual [but to] remember that their political opinions are their own' – with the sanctimonious proscriptions of the 'two Scotch priests' in Dundee, 'who, no doubt, would join Lord John Russell, in fighting to death against "Repeal of the Union"'.

Thus emboldened, Hannah informed the *Dundee Advertiser*, 'The National Brotherhood of St Patrick is not a sectarian Society, and "Candour" and others of your correspondents are compelled to admit this'. Citing as proof the NBSP's National President, Thomas Neilson Underwood, a Presbyterian lawyer, and its Secretary, D H Hays, a former Lieutenant in the Papal Brigade, he maintained, 'It is a political society [and] surely we have the liberty to choose our own political opinion'. 'It will not do for the clergy to call us Ribbonmen', he insisted. 'We are nothing of the sort. Perhaps there are such men among us, but we don't know of them; and if we did, they would be expelled.'[31]

CHAPTER 2 – FENIANS 1859–69

Hannah was perhaps disingenuous in denying all knowledge of Ribbonmen in his midst. He, however, was not so impolitic as to incriminate himself or his comrades. He was, nevertheless, correct in insisting that the NBSP was a distinctly different organisation from the oath-bound Ribbon Societies of the north and midlands of Ireland whose purpose was to protect poor tenant farmers from rack renting landlords and, more contentiously, to assert their territorial claims as Irish-Catholics in violent confrontations with the Orange Order. As noted in the previous chapter, Dundee almost certainly had its share of Ribbonmen, a number of whom likely became members of the NBSP or casual users of the reading rooms, although whether they defined themselves as 'Ribbonmen' at this point is questionable. The NBSP, however, was a new development altogether, which gave the rural Irish exile meaning and purpose within their adopted urban environment and suffused the tradition of popular Catholic resistance with a broader, more advanced concept of Irish nationalism.

St Patrick's Day 1862 saw the three combined branches of the Dundee and Lochee NBSP toasting their success in the Camperdown Hall, the Overgate, with speeches on 'Ireland a Nation' by Thomas Morrison, 'The Irish at Home and Abroad' by Francis Fitzgerald of the Glasgow Association and 'The National Brotherhood of St Patrick' by Thomas Donegan. Songs and recitations included 'The Green Above the Red', 'The Irish Soldier of Freedom', 'Young Donald of Dundee', 'The Dear Little Shamrock' and 'The Isle of Saints'.[32] In early June, Fitzgerald delivered an extended version of his address which charted an unbroken chain of Irish resistance to foreign oppression, from Brian Boru's victory over the Vikings at Clontarf through to the United Irishmen, the Young Ireland Movement, the Irish post-famine exodus and the contemporary role of the Irish Brigade in the ongoing 'struggle for American Union' under General Thomas Meagher. It was their first proper lecture on Irish politics and, as Secretary of the West Port branch Peter Clarke noted, the audience 'listened…with breathless attention, interrupted only by frequent bursts of applause'.[33]

Despite the enthusiasm of some of its members, not all Dundee Irishmen were lining up to join the NBSP. In late October, the Secretary of Central branch, John McElroy, submitted the second of two donations to *The Irishman*'s Indemnity Fund[34] along with an appeal to 'our countrymen in Dundee' to sign up ahead of the following week's branch elections where they could exercise their vote and influence the policies of the organisation. McElroy pointed to the example of Irishmen in Glasgow, Liverpool and Birkenhead, and 'the heart of the Saxon metropolis', who had 'come forward in their thousands and rallied round the National cause'. 'Will it now be said that you, the Irishmen of Dundee, are less patriotic than they are?' he asked. 'Come one, come all, no matter what be your creed or class; within our halls you will find cordial union, based on devotion to the independence of our country, among us.'[35]

While it was perhaps unrealistic for the officers of the Dundee NBSP to compare their adopted town, with its population of around 20,000 Irish-born, less than a third of whom were adult men, with the much larger population centres of Glasgow, Liverpool/Birkenhead and London, it gives an indication of the intensity of their patriotism and the loftiness of their ambitions. It is possible that some reluctant Dundee Irishmen buckled under pressure from the Catholic Church, which was exerted though employers, family members and other figures in the Irish community. For other disaffected Irishmen who frequented the reading rooms but failed to join the NBSP, it may have been that while reading rooms and lectures provided a forum to examine and express radical nationalist ideas, they did not provide a practical structure by which these ideas could be politically or militarily realised. The cost of membership may have been a further disincentive. Whatever the reasons, we can assume the NBSP got their answer, for by March 1863 the problem appears to have been resolved. It was noted that the St Patrick's Day festival in the Camperdown Hall was the largest and most enthusiastic assembly the building had ever held. The hall was decorated with portraits of Irish patriots, and the opening speech: 'The Political Exiles', and the songs and recitations: 'Soldier of Irish Liberty', 'Burning for the Fray', 'The Downfall of Poland' and 'O'Donnell Abu' indicate a sympathy for physical force nationalism. Dundee also appears to have been the only Scottish centre to send a telegram to the NBSP's celebrations in Dublin – which received similar dispatches from Leicester, London and Manchester – the reply to which was received with great cheers several hours later. [36]

The increasingly militant turn of the Dundee NBSP over the following year can be partially attributed to Owen Walsh, a young factory weaver from the Hilltown, who was elected Secretary of the Central branch in

Rosebank Street in May 1863.[37] An intelligent strategist and strong Fenian sympathiser, Walsh may also have consciously shaped and articulated the opinions of the hitherto reticent Dundee Irishmen who were also 'burning for the fray', and following his own radical agenda through to its logical conclusion.

By 1864, the NBSP in Ireland was under IRB control, and it is likely that Dundee, which mirrored Dublin in its secular nationalist agenda, was moving in the same direction, while continuing to use the NBSP as a convenient (and legal) front for public meetings, and, simultaneously, a structure for IRB recruitment. In February, NBSP Secretary and cofounder, Christopher Clinton Hoey, began his tour of Scotland with a two-part lecture on 'the Rights of Ireland' in the Thistle Hall, Dundee. The *Advertiser* reported that the attendance numbered about 200, all of whom 'with the exception of five or six women', were 'Irishmen of the working classes', which Owen Walsh, promptly begged them to correct to '300 Irishmen and upwards of a hundred other classes'.[38] For Walsh and his Fenian-sympathising countrymen, the acknowledgement of the non-Irish attendees was vitally important. Firstly, it exemplified the Fenian ideal of an inclusive, secular Republic, the ethos of which had a local precedent in the joint activity between Irish Catholic Repealers and Scots Presbyterian Chartists in 1848, and it is likely that Walsh was mindful of the progressive Dundee Scots who had joined ranks with the Dundee Irish sixteen years before. Moreover, it challenged the persistent assumption of the local press that all attendees of Irish meetings were Irish. Underpinning this was the fact that, while Dundee's Irish immigrants continued to cherish and nurture their Irish identity, they were tentatively laying claim to a new Scottish one.

Hoey's lectures were otherwise favourably reported. Indeed, unlike the Catholic clergy, the *People's Journal* took them at face value, praising the 'fullness of information, force, ease of expression and earnestness' of Hoey's discourse, and noting that he 'vindicated himself from all possible suspicion of interested motive'.[39] The only sour note in Hoey's visit came in a short letter from Irish grocer, John Green, publicly dissociating himself from the unauthorised inclusion of an advert for his shop on the handbills for Hoey's lectures, which Hoey suspected had been 'written under certain pressure'.[40] Indeed, Green was a leading member of the Catholic Young

Men's Association, a branch of which had been formed in the town to counter the allure of the NBSP's reading rooms.

Hoey's visit was followed by another in May from the Reverend David Bell, an Ulster Presbyterian minister and leading officer in the NBSP and IRB, whose espousal of Republican ideas in the United Irish Presbyterian tradition appealed to Scots Protestants as well as Irish Catholics. Indeed, Walsh's acknowledgement of the one hundred plus 'non-Irish' attendees at Hoey's lectures suggests that some were already sympathetic, although whether Bell, who very likely enrolled several members of the NBSP into the IRB, ever recruited any Scots Protestants is unknown.

Father Lavelle

The biggest single factor in advancing the cause of militant Irish nationalism in Scotland, however, was the visit of Father Patrick Lavelle, 'the patriot priest of Partry', whose politically tinged fundraising for those of his homeless parishioners evicted by proselytising landlord, Anglican Bishop Thomas Plunkett, had led to Lavelle being perceived as the personification of Irish resistance to British injustice. This was especially so in Dundee, where Lavelle had come to the aid of the NBSP in its battle against a hostile Scottish clergy, at a time when the main Irish-Catholic newspaper in Scotland, the *Free Press*, had been critical and unsupportive. Indeed, Moran's comment that Lavelle's letter writing to local newspapers, especially in Scotland, added an important geographical dimension to his own conflict with Archbishop Cullen of Dublin, gains in significance given that Lavelle's public intervention in the Dundee conflict predates his own with Cullen which became public in May 1862.[41]

Lavelle visited Dundee on two occasions, in June and July 1864, accompanied by Augustus Henry Keane, on a tour in support of the *Free Press* and his own charitable fund. Under Keane's stewardship, the *Free Press* had published several articles broadly sympathetic to the Fenians and critical of the Highland-dominated Catholic clergy, who had taken out several libel actions against the newspaper. As the *Free Press* had supported Lavelle and the Fenians, so the militant Irish nationalists of Dundee, who had been waging their own war of words with the local clergy for over two years, naturally threw their weight behind the *Free Press*, which had finally come around to their view. In June 1864, Owen Walsh, who ran a newspaper agency from his home at 41 Hilltown, became one of three Dundee agents for the newspaper, alongside Donegal-born weaver Patrick Higgins of East Henderson's Wynd, another Fenian sympathiser and possible IRB man, and Daniel Neely of Scouringburn.[42]

Hundreds had to be turned away from Lavelle's first meeting in the Union Hall, which, the *Dundee Courier* reported, was packed with an enthusiastic crowd 'composed principally of the lower working classes'. Lavelle's description of the evictions in Partry struck a chord with many members of the audience who, little over a decade after An Gorta Mór, had direct experience of eviction, hunger and displacement. For the chairman, Patrick McNally, 'once a respectable farmer in Ireland, but a victim to the crowbar system', the memory was painfully raw and the sense of injustice still rankled. McNally praised Lavelle's fight against Bishop Plunkett, a 'formidable enemy' in 'the double-capacity of Irish Landlord with irresponsible power and pillar of the bloated Church Establishment', and proposed that they pledge, along with their fellow exiles in America, Australia and Britain, to help liquidate the debt incurred by Father Lavelle in 'saving his poor people from proselytism and starvation'. Deeming Lavelle to exemplify 'the true priest and patriot [and] exponent of truly Irish National feeling', he further proposed they continue to 'support him in his charitable and patriotic endeavours, no matter by whom he be assailed, whether open enemies or covered foes'.[43]

McNally was seconded by veteran Repeal activist, Samuel McKinney, who emphasised their intention to meet 'charity on the one hand [with] justice on the other'. The meeting ended with loud cheers for the speakers and for Lavelle's Bishop, John McHale of Tuam, 'the Lion of the fold of Judah', who, in contrast to Archbishop Cullen of Dublin, had encouraged Lavelle in his mission. Significantly, there were no reports of the meeting in the *Dundee Advertiser*, which, in a change to its even-handed reporting of local Irish affairs, had in the past few weeks been representing views sympathetic to the Catholic clergy. For example, on 17 May the *Advertiser* stated that the clergy 'deserve the good wishes of all loyal subjects for banishing from this town the Brotherhood of St Patrick and placing in its stead a good loyal society – namely the Catholic Young Men's Society'.[44] This elicited a blistering response from Daniel Hannah:

I do not envy the Irishman who gets the name loyal from you. To be loyal in that sense of the word – namely loyal to the British Government – is to be a traitor to his home and kindred, sit on packed juries if wanted, return a verdict for the Crown, if guilty or not; to swear away the life of his nearest relative... to cast away his conscience – that is, if he has got one. Reynolds of '98 was a 'loyal' subject; Jemmy O'Brien was another; Sullivan 'Goula' of '59 was the same; Sadler the suicide and Keogh the 'perjurer' were two more. If the members of the 'CYMS' think it proper to accept your praise, and by doing so claim relationship with the above-named persons, I have no objection but I do not envy their choice.[45]

A week after Lavelle's talk, the *Advertiser* quoted from a Papal prescript recently read from the altars of Dundee's Catholic churches, accusing Father Lavelle of 'giving countenance to certain newly named societies... claimed by the prelates of Ireland to be pernicious', and commanding his Bishop to suspend him immediately.[46] Lavelle responded by denying knowledge of the prescript – the business of which was, in any case, between him and his Bishop – denying all connections with secret societies, and accusing the *Advertiser* of entering into a secret alliance with members of the Catholic clergy. Lavelle highlighted the disingenuous conduct of the latter by explaining that, when in Dundee, he had called upon the most senior of them (McDonald), to be told he was 'sick in bed' – yet he had been seen in town an hour later denying that Lavelle had visited him. Lavelle also alluded to the acrimonious relationship with high-ranking members of the Irish Catholic clergy who were, he stated, 'in the telling lines of your immortal Burns, "Bought and sold for English gold, Such a parcel of rogues in a nation"'. Lavelle's warning to the *Advertiser*, to withdraw the libellous statement and apologise, or he would seek redress elsewhere, had the desired effect. The *Advertiser* promptly complied, with the assurance that there was no 'secret alliance', their reporter had simply been following up a lead, and adding that, in their opinion, there was nothing wrong with secret societies, the Freemasons being an example of a perfectly good one.[47]

To Dundee's militant Irish nationalists, the consequences of the priests' condemnations and the ensuing publicity were delightfully predictable.

An open meeting to discuss whether they were to be prevented from relieving their starving relations at home 'by men who had no sympathy with them or their afflicted country', once more saw the Union Hall crowded to the doors. A reporter for the Tory *Dundee Courier*, which had gamely stepped onto territory vacated by its rival, seemed pleased to have his preconceptions about the Irish working class amply disproven. The proceedings were conducted with the 'utmost decorum from start to finish', he noted, focusing on the humbling image of a plate by the door, which 'brimmed over with coppers' long before the meeting started.⁴⁸

John McElroy, presiding, began the proceedings by stating 'they were not aristocrats, nor shopcrats, nor any kind of crats but they were honest men', and proceeded to warn 'a certain gentleman' – presumably the Reverend McDonald, who, in view of the libel actions by the Catholic clergy against the *Free Press*, the *Courier* was careful not to name – who had called the NBSP 'rascals and vagabonds... that [he] should better take care, as they had reputations to protect as well as him'. Daniel Hannah stated that 'as poor Irishmen working for their daily bread', they could not divest themselves of their natural antagonism towards 'men who were strangers to them in everything but religion'. The link between the Irish priest and the Irish people, he posited, had been forged by persecution.⁴⁹ In that same tradition, Father Lavelle had responded to the needs of the persecuted Irish people, and it was beholden to the Irish people, including the working-class Irishmen and Irishwomen of Dundee – the women, Hannah stressed, were *not* in the Brotherhood of St Patrick – to fulfil their part of the bargain. The brimming plate of coppers, Hannah declared, represented 'the blood and sinew' of the Irish working class, yet those 'who had made a little money', the 'shopcrats' as McElroy termed them, distanced themselves, and the clergy had told him he should be 'sent to the Bridewell' after he collected £12. Owen Walsh proposed that it was the duty of every Irishman in Dundee to support Lavelle's cause and that 'any man who strives to prevent us from fulfilling this duty is an enemy to the Irish poor, an enemy to humanity and an enemy to the sacred principles of religion'. Seconding Walsh's resolution was C Kenny, a laconic physical force Republican, who regretted that he had to attend a meeting to defend the obligation to support people who had been impoverished by a bad system of government. 'There were 1,500,000 acres of uncultivated land in

Ireland', Kenny asserted bluntly, and 'if Ireland got justice 'charity would not be needed'. One point, however, rang through all the speeches – the truest supporters of the oppressed Irish people and, consequently, of Ireland's fight for national independence, were the poorest working class.

In the tradition of the radical priest, rooted in the community as well in the political sense, Lavelle was aware of the dynamics of this mutually binding relationship, and the obligations it demanded of him. Failure to fulfil these obligations could lead to the collective body of Irish expatriates, who were the mainstay of his support, withdrawing their obligations to him, as indeed they had in the case of the Scottish clergy in everything bar religion. A notable exception was Father Davidson of St Mary's, Lochee, who acted in the interests of his working-class parishioners, and took his moral authority from the community he served rather from his clerical superiors. Scottish priest Davidson had recommended Lavelle's cause and defended the *Free Press* amidst the Catholic hierarchy's condemnations of both. In return, he was rewarded with the loyalty of the Irish working class in Lochee and Dundee, and the eulogistic praise of Lavelle himself. Indeed, a report by Owen Walsh of Lavelle's tribute to Davidson noted that his name 'was received with such a burst of enthusiastic applause as never fell to my lot to witness. The cheering and waving of handkerchiefs on the part of the ladies was renewed again and again, and lasted for lasted several minutes with unabated energy'.[50] Davidson was later removed from his post.

Lavelle returned twelve days later to a standing ovation in Dundee's largest hall, the Corn Exchange (later re-named the Kinnaird Hall), expressing an 'overpowering sense of gratitude' at the second demonstration in his favour, 'or rather in favour of the undying principle which was his pride to advise – the cause of creed and country'. Referring to a recent statement by the Bishop of Orleans,[51] that Irishmen formed the principal part of the British Army, Lavelle stated that 'the Irish had shed their blood for strangers' but had got nothing in return but 'stripes and insults'. Lavelle's comment that he 'hoped the day would come, and was not far distant, when Irish soldiers would find battles to fight for themselves', put the religious seal of approval on armed insurrection, and the audience responded with 'tumultuous cheering'. Despite the insurrectionary rhetoric, however, Lavelle denied he was a revolutionist 'in the sense the word was used against him', stating that 'the only revolution he wished was to make Ireland great, glorious and free – depriving no man of his just rights, but giving to the Irish people a portion at least of those rights of which they had been plundered'. If to 'proclaim Ireland's right to self-government, even absolute independence' was heresy, he declared, then he was a heretic, at which point several members of the audience shouted that they too were heretics, and one 'stalwart Irishman' left his seat, approached the platform, knelt and asked for Lavelle's blessing.[52]

Alongside Lavelle on the platform were *Free Press* proprietor, A H Keane, and members of the Dundee Lavelle Committee, most of whom were former officers of the NBSP and Fenian activists and sympathisers, including Chairman McElroy, Walsh, McNally, Morrison, Patrick Higgins, Arthur Vincent of Lochee and C Kenny, who led the cheers. Kenny's final words, that he hoped he would 'yet see Ireland restored and the national banner flying above the College Green', provided a potent image which was repeated and reworked by Irish nationalists of all stripes over the next half century. At a farewell reception in Lamb's Hotel two days later, Daniel Hannah thanked Lavelle for doing 'his duty as an Irish priest and patriot' and 'consigning to his native earth that great, that pure and sincere patriot, Thomas Bellew McManus'. If, Hannah continued, Lavelle's patriotic and humanistic endeavours had earned him 'the hatred of bad men', they had earned him 'the gratitude of the poor, and the admiration of every honest man', including the Irish of Dundee, who would, he promised Lavelle, 'sustain you against your enemies, no matter who or what they may be'. Lavelle replied that the knowledge that the sentiments expressed and the contributions to his fund came from 'the honest, hardworking people of Dundee' – the rich, 'who could have easily sent £100 without their right hand knowing what their left hand was doing, had not sent 100 farthings' – had given him 'a stimulus to persevere in his endeavour to write the wrongs of Ireland'. Lavelle was then presented with £75, which he announced, would be sufficient to pay off the balance of the money he had borrowed.[53]

As the most high-profile Irish cleric of the time, Lavelle combined the pull of celebrity with the authority and influence of a priest, and his visits to Scotland helped secure a solid base of support for the Fenian movement. Moreover, in its objective of moving beyond famine relief to paying tenants' debts and buying land back, and in its exploitation of networks throughout the hugely expanded Irish diaspora, Lavelle's Poor of Partry Fund presaged the Land League. For the moment, however, the conclusion of the campaign completed the transformation of the loose collection of advanced nationalists grouped in and around the NBSP into a cohesive, confident body of physical force Irish Republicans, many of whom were now members of the IRB.

The Irish Republican Brotherhood

Around early December, Walsh contacted O'Donovan Rossa – presently in Edinburgh combining his honeymoon with an assessment of IRB forces in Scotland – with a request to review the IRB in Dundee. Disappointingly, Rossa declined due to lack of time, hastening onwards to inspect troops in Glasgow and the West before returning to Ireland for Christmas. Dundee's remote east coast location often resulted in it being overlooked by Irish nationalist leaders, a reality to which Irish Republicans in the district resigned themselves, possibly with some degree of resentment, but which Republicans on both sides of the Irish Sea later worked to their advantage as it gave them greater autonomy to pursue their own, often more radical agendas, and to bypass 'official' channels which were not necessarily the most effective ones. Denied their meeting with Rossa, the Dundee IRB made the most of every other opportunity that presented itself.

On 7 November, C Clinton Hoey returned to Dundee to address a large meeting of Irishmen and Irishwomen in the Thistle Hall. Hoey was in town, ostensibly, to promote the Irish National Association of Scotland (INA), the brainchild of A H Keane, which had been established in Glasgow in September to encourage Irish Catholics in Scotland to come together in 'union and harmony' to elevate themselves socially, politically and religiously through the creation of a broad range of mutual improvement structures.[54] However, no sooner had Hoey stated that 'it would be a shame if the Irishmen of Dundee could not... form a grand institution as in other towns', than the radical nationalists moved in to take control, with James Clarke asserting that as '[they had] been the only representatives of national opinion in the town, all that [did] not wish to... assist [them]... we shall consider unworthy of the name Irishman'. Following a second resolution by Walsh, the meeting unanimously approved the appointment of a committee to 'take immediate steps to enrol their countrymen into an

Irish National Organisation, with the object of opening a reading room and establishing a public library'. A provisional committee was appointed with McElroy as Chairman and Walsh as Secretary, and including Kenny, Morrison, James Clarke, Arthur Vincent, John Sweeney and James Hennessy – all committed Fenians or Fenian sympathisers. A third and final resolution from Morrison affirmed, 'We reserve to ourselves the right of judging the fittest way we may elevate ourselves, and thereby render us the better able to aid our country and countrymen at home', stating emphatically, 'we hereby altogether ignore all clerical influence in our political affairs'.[55]

On 20 December, Walsh issued a report on the establishment of the Dundee Irish National Institute (DINI) and the opening of its reading rooms in Pullar's Close in the Murraygate. Unlike the general self-help aims of the INA, which recommended a library stock of Irish national, Catholic general and periodical literature, Walsh stated that they intended to procure a quantity of 'truly national' literature, pending which they had stocked the reading rooms with 'a good supply of the leading national journals', including the *Free Press*, *The Irishman* and the New York Fenian newspaper, the *Irish People*.

While the Institute's rules and regulations stated its general object as 'social and political elevation', its members were obliged to 'endeavour in every way that lies in their power to assist their countrymen at home associated for the same object, which includes the independence of Ireland'. The sixth rule stated that 'the Institute shall act in cooperation or under guidance, (if advisable) with a general association in Ireland at any time', but only where its 'principles of action should be identical with theirs', whereupon '[the Dundee Institute] shall render it whatever practical support that lies in its power'. Unlike the INA, which promoted itself expressly as a Catholic Institution, 'no questions were put...as to religion or class', the only qualifications for membership being 'a sincere and practical love for Ireland'.[56] The language was rigorously official, (no doubt to forestall the accusations of secret society involvement that had pursued the NBSP); nevertheless, the use of phrases such as 'practical love for Ireland', 'practical support' and 'principles of action' hinted at a more militant purpose. Indeed, it is worth noting, that while the DINI issued a letter to the *Dundee Advertiser* requesting that 'those who do not wish to come forward and assist us... throw no insults by saying the [the Institute] is secret or illegal... it is neither'; unlike the INA, which 'absolutely and WITHOUT EQUIVOCATION repudiate[d] the use of all SECRET SIGNS, OATHS, VOWS and PASSWORDS of every description', the Dundee Institute's list of rules contained no such prohibition.[57] Signing the report were the newly elected office bearers: President John McElroy, Vice-President James Clarke, Treasurer John McGuigan, Secretary John Sweeney, and Honorary Secretary Owen Walsh.[58]

The radical agenda of the Dundee group did not go unobserved by moral force nationalists elsewhere. The following month, the DINI's constitution was the subject of an address in the *Free Press* by 'Sacerdos Hibernicus'(Irish priest),[59] who found much to praise, but ultimately pointed to 'the fact that 'your first resolution comprises "the independence of Ireland", which is the avowed object of certain secret societies', of which he advised the DINI to 'wash [its] hands, abide by the principle of the great O'Connell, *moral force*', employ constitutional means, and 'let the spirit of obedience to your church be the guiding star of your progress'.[60]

If this was an artful attempt to draw Dundee's physical force nationalists into line, it failed to move the DINI. Walsh responded by assuring 'Sacerdos' that 'the Institute [would] never be guilty of any act that will damage the character of Irishmen'. However, he added, 'We also wish it to be understood that we do not believe in the moral force doctrine, for we firmly believe that no country can ever gain its independence except by force of arms'. At the same time, he continued, 'we do not forget that a down-trodden nation requires to be organised both socially and mentally, before making a grand stand'.[61]

Accordingly, Walsh and his comrades, who had conceived the DINI as a recruiting tool for the IRB, saw the Institute as providing the mental and social training which would complement the military preparation for the planned rebellion, and bolster a future Irish Republic. Appropriately, Walsh bookended his report by logging the steady increase in enrolments and reporting that a subscription for the library had raised £35.

1865 had been designated by IRB leader James Stephens as 'the year of action', and the next few months saw a ramping up in organisation building and drill training. O'Donovan Rossa's inspection had revealed the need to improve the military skills of Scottish troops, to which end Edward Coyne,

IRB Centre for Callan in County Kilkenny, was despatched to Scotland in February. Little is known of Coyne's visit, although it is highly likely that, on this occasion, Dundee was not overlooked. Of some significance in the choice of Coyne as an IRB envoy, is the fact that his brother Philip was a key link to the Fenian Brotherhood in New York, and that Phil Coyne had considerable military experience himself, having joined the Confederate Army while resident in St. Louis, in the pursuit, no doubt, of skills and weaponry. Following defeat by the Union Army, Coyne had been taken prisoner of war, released at the request of the Fenian Brotherhood and, in August 1864, brought over to Ireland to train troops, advise on preparations for the rebellion, and relay plans back to the Head of the Fenian Brotherhood, John O'Mahoney, on his return to New York in December.[62]

As Head of the Dundee IRB, Walsh had the shorthand title of 'A', equivalent to Colonel, and was responsible for initiating the military training of the men in his circle. While Kenny and possibly James Clarke were 'Bs' (Captains) and tasked with training 'Cs' (Sergeants), the IRB command structure at local level was often more flexible than the rule book dictated.[63] At this point, the DINI appears to have served its purpose as a recruiting tool, for by mid-March, reports of its official activities dry up altogether.[64] On 17 April, having left his military command in the capable hands of Kenny, and his newspaper agency in the control of his wife Susan, Walsh departed for Glasgow where, after catching up with 'friends', visiting the sights, and attending Confession at St Andrew's Church, he boarded the *SS United Kingdom* on 22 April and set sail for New York.[65]

In the first of a series of commentaries sent to Peter McCorry, editor of the *Free Press* ad fellow IRB man, Walsh reported that the majority of his 600 fellow passengers were Irish, and the majority of the young men 'belonged to that society which John Bull wants to question the American government about'. Suggesting he could tell a great deal more about 'that noble organisation' if McCorry would print it, Walsh instead chose to give an account of 'the treatment of the 'mere Irish' on board the *United Kingdom*, where passengers in cramped steerage compartments were forced to clamber across piles of luggage to reach the tiny space their meagre income afforded – a berth measuring five to six feet by sixteen inches, in which they were forced to eat and sleep four-abreast, in which a child had suffocated by its mother's side, whereafter its body was 'put in a wooden box and thrown overboard to feed the hungry sharks'. It takes little imagination to see that Walsh was presenting an allegory of the condition of Ireland under British rule. As the living conditions of the Irish passengers on board the *United Kingdom* evoked those of slaves from British colonial Africa, so the people of Ireland were in a state of bondage to a British Imperial government that denied them their right to land and freedom. As the innocent child was fed to the hungry sharks, so the people of Ireland who worked and lived on the land were fodder for the landlord class who extorted the fruits of their labour on pain of eviction, exile and untimely death.

On 10 May, the *United Kingdom* dropped anchor in New York. Unlike many of his fellow passengers who were forced to remain at the immigrant station of Castle Garden until they procured work, Walsh took up residence at 1 Graham Street in East Brooklyn from where, fifteen days later, he described the bleak economic conditions which impacted on all, but especially Irish immigrants:

> Irishmen, when they come here and have no trade, may go idle for months; ay and die of starvation on the streets, if they have no friends to take them by the hand. I have been in conversation with men that are here for years, and are idle for the last six weeks and cannot get work. I have been in many towns in my lifetime, but I never saw so many going about idle as in the streets of New York. I see men going about half-naked, and women going barefooted, with very scanty clothing on their body.[66]

If it had ever been, as the *Free Press* represented it, Walsh's intention to emigrate – which, given his position as head of the Dundee IRB at this important juncture seems extremely doubtful – he was clearly having second thoughts. What is evident, however, is that Walsh was a man of extraordinary drive, dedication and ability who, possibly through impatience at his area being overlooked and neglected by the Dublin leadership, had travelled to the centre of military operations on a dual mission to advance his knowledge of the campaign and to engage in Fenian propaganda. This appears to have been with the approval, encouragement and financial support of his Dundee comrades in the first instance, and McCorry of the *Free Press*, who was also a leading member of the IRB in Scotland, in the second. Indeed, given his journalistic talents and his experience as a newspaper agent specialising in Irish nationalist publications, it is not unlikely that Walsh was also covering his expenses by contributing to other sympathetic journals, such as the *Irish People*, the *New York Herald* and/or the *Boston Pilot*, anonymously or under an assumed name.

Having demonstrated that America offered no freedom worth having, Walsh urged his fellow Irishmen to 'let nothing tempt you to come [here], for the day is not far distant when your own dear land will bid defiance to the Saxon yoke'. 'There are', he continued, 'hundreds, ay, thousands waiting patiently for the word to take up arms against the common foe'. Advising McCorry to publish 'a true account of the great Fenian organisation' from the *New York Herald*, Walsh proceeded to give a description of John O'Mahoney, whom he 'had the pleasure of seeing', probably at the congress of the of the Central Council of the Fenian Brotherhood held at the organisation's Headquarters at 22 Duane Street between 12 and 16 June:

> He is a tall, stout, robust-looking man, close shaven, with a large moustache and long shining hair down to his shoulders; something like our ancient chieftains. He is daily labouring to organise his countrymen at home and abroad, and in full hope of his success.[67]

For his part, Walsh left little doubt about his allegiance and his ultimate intentions:

> All Irishmen want here is the power to arise, when they get the command to cross the Atlantic… It is the opinion of many here that an opportunity will come very soon; and we are prepared. There are thousands of our returned veterans anxiously waiting for the order to pack up and sail, and all of them have their equipments complete. Every man, as he gets his discharge, gets leave to bring his arms with him, and they are bound to keep them in good repair for the coming fray.

And declaring that 'we may soon give [John Bull] sport enough', he rallied others round the flag with rousing Fenian verse:

> So come, Brothers, all unite with us – come join us one and all;
> United we must conquer, but divided we must fall.
> Our flag shall be respected, not trampled in the dust;
> The harp and sunburst shall not come down, though traitors say they must.
> Thank God we have a Colonel to his country ever true;
> We stand by John O'Mahoney as Brothers all should do.[68]

Back home, preparations for the anticipated rebellion were continuing apace. A visit to Scotland by James Stephens in May, and another by Thomas Clarke Luby in July, which took in Dundee and towns outside of Glasgow and Edinburgh, led to the formation of IRB circles in Perth and Blairgowrie amongst other places.[69] If Stephens is to be believed, by late 1865, the IRB had around 80,000 members in Ireland, Scotland, England and Wales of which Mairtín Ó Catháin estimates approximately 2,500 were in and around Glasgow and 1,500 in Edinburgh. The figure for Dundee, derived from Walker's estimate of 3,000, is at best speculative, but if anywhere near close, would make Dundee the largest single hub of Fenianism in Scotland.[70]

As Walsh despatched his report to the *Free Press* in late June, a number of experienced Fenian officers were already making their way across the Atlantic to accelerate preparations for the rising. Plans suffered a setback in September with the suppression of the *Irish People* and the arrest of IRB leaders, including Luby and O'Donovan Rossa, followed by Stephens in November, and were further hampered by the split in the American Fenians in October. Nevertheless, with Stephens sprung from Richmond Jail, Dublin, on 24 November, a date was finally set for 1 January 1866 at the latest and, on the second week of December, messengers were sent across the Irish Sea notifying all those who had the means to make their way over.

On receiving the order, Michael McLaughlin, who appears to have been the IRB's chief military organiser for Scotland, hastened to confirm arrangements with the Military Council in Ireland, before returning to drill his own troops in Glasgow, and setting off on a whistle-stop tour of IRB circles sweeping from Edinburgh, Dalkeith, Dunfermline, Dundee, Blairgowrie, Perth, Coatbridge, Port Glasgow, Greenock and Dumbarton. Writing in the *United Irishman* 22 years later, McLauchlin failed to recall the numbers mobilised, but remained heartened by the spirit and determination of the men involved, calling out across the years and the miles to 'C.K.' (Kenny) of Dundee, 'wishing him to know he is remembered by the shores of the Pacific by his old friend Mac, for he gallantly responded with his men when duty called'.[71]

The lack of a record makes it practically impossible to calculate how many men were mobilised, and especially in which areas. John Devoy noted that the response was 'very general' and made a vague estimate of several thousand in total from Scotland, England and Wales. In the last week of December 1865, however, a letter sent from Dundee to Moneymore, County Derry, found its way into the hands of the Irish Constabulary, in which the writer informed his sibling that 70 men who were 'determined, as it is phrased in certain quarters, to free Ireland' had left Dundee on Friday, 15 December, followed by another 300 a week later. The writer, who confided 'you may depend on this for truth', urged the recipient 'to write and tell [him] everything about Ireland' as 'we have good work here about it', and advised the locals 'not to be sleeping' as 'you will meet a heavy trial, so had better look out for yourselves'.[72]

The first 70 men left for Glasgow from where, after joining forces with McLaughlin's troops, they travelled to locations on the north coast of Ireland, dispersing into smaller groups across Sligo, Leitrim, Roscommon and Mayo, the native counties of many, and where some had friends and relatives who could supply them with information, as the above letter indicates. The other 300 made their way to Derry and Belfast a week later in much the same manner.

As the interception of the Dundee letter also indicates, the British authorities, who had been assiduously monitoring Fenian activity for some time, had got wind of the plans, and at the end of December, the rebellion was postponed pending further instructions. The police were already on the lookout for suspicious activity however, so when the large group of unfamiliar men who had arrived in Sligo town around 27 December on the pretext of visiting friends or representing themselves as stonecutters looking for work – the unblemished hands of some told a different story – were still in the district two weeks later, two dozen fully-armed police constables headed by County-Inspector J Stoker, Sub-Inspector Neynoe and two Head Constables, swooped on their lodgings in Pound (High) Street and Quay Street at around 4.30 am, rounded them up and marched them off to the police barracks. The men, who appeared to have a common understanding, offered little resistance, with exception of 'a Yankee-looking individual [who] protested most bitterly against this violation of his personal rights'. Of the 21 arrested, the majority were from various parts of Scotland, including James Clarke, Hugh Devlin, shopkeeper John McGuigan, and labourer Patrick Curran from Dundee. The prisoners were detained for five days, long enough for a thorough search of their clothing, their lodgings and the premises of the Dominican Friary to yield 'no treasonable documents' or other incriminating evidence, bar a little shot in the pockets of one and a few caps in those of another. With the Habeas Corpus Act still in place, the authorities had no option but to release all 21, which they did, in small batches at thirty-minute intervals for fear of triggering a riot – hundreds of people had gathered outside the jail in anticipation of a mass exodus – to the intermittent cheers of a sympathetic crowd.[73]

And so, released on a bond of good behaviour and ordered to leave the country, some joined the increasing number of undetected Fenians who were drifting back home after the postponement. Others went to ground, including Clarke and McGuigan, who were recaptured collecting letters at the post office in Dromahair, Country Leitrim, on 9 March.[74] Irish Constabulary records note that Clarke's letter contained a postal order from Dundee for £2 8s to be cashed at Drumkeeran, and that he was carrying a map of part of Ireland, suggesting that Clarke was responsible for disbursing subsistence payments to the men of his division who were still in the area. Clarke and McGuigan, who had no other money or visible means of support, were promptly conveyed to Manorhamilton Bridewell and detained for further examination, following which the Crown Prosecutor and Chief Inspector recommended that Clarke be detained in Carrick-on-Shannon Jail until 10 August. The Chief Inspector recommended the same for McGuigan. However, the receipt of a memorial from several inhabitants of Dundee, including a Catholic priest, swearing Clarke 'innocent of all connection with Fenianism', helped to procure his early release on 20 May.⁷⁵ Unlike Michael McLaughlin who had been released from three month's detention and effectively deported to America the day before, Clarke was permitted to return to Dundee, where he became involved, perhaps guardedly at first, in the State Prisoner support fund.⁷⁶

Clarke was not the last Fenian prisoner to be returned to Dundee. According to Irish Constabulary files, Charles Conlon was one of the men under the control of William Byrne of Dundee, who had been sent to Ireland for drill training. Unfortunately for Conlon, his arrival in Ireland coincided with the suspension of Habeas Corpus on 17 February, and, in the ensuing round up of suspected Fenians, he was picked up in Castlerea, County Roscommon, on 25 February and thrown in Roscommon Gaol. Devoy's description of the men from England and Scotland as a 'sturdy, stalwart lot', mostly young and unattached, many of whom had been trained in the army, navy, militia and volunteers, and who were 'ready for immediate action, and fit for any work', is exemplified in Conlon. Born near Cookstown in County Tyrone in c1845, Conlon had moved to Dundee where he obtained work as a shoemaker, become acquainted with Irish cultural circles and was recruited into the IRB. As well as joining the IRB, Conlon joined the Royal Perthshire Rifle Militia – the auxiliary arm of the 73rd Perthshire Regiment of Foot – presumably with the intention of learning something of the craft of warfare without joining the British Army. Nevertheless, John Devoy, who was responsible for IRB recruitment in the British Army, noted that by the end of 1865, 15,000 of regular 'British' troops were in fact sworn Fenians. Devoy commended the Highland regiments, which contained a large number of Scots-born Irishmen who had, naturally, enlisted on their home turf, and singled out the 73rd Regiment who, in their tartan trousers and Glengarry caps, had all the appearance of a Scotch, i.e., British Army regiment but was in fact a 'crack Fenian' one in which the IRB had over 300 men. Significantly, the 73rd were one of the regiments sent to replace the disaffected Irish ones in the middle of February 1866, which coincided directly with Conlon's arrival in the country. Devoy recalled that it was the men from Scotland who introduced him to Flynn, the IRB Centre within the regiment in Dublin, who Devoy introduced to local Fenians.⁷⁷ Whether the deployment of the 73rd in Ireland had a bearing on the decision to send Conlon and other Perthshire Rifle Militia men over and was part of a plan to co-ordinate activity is unknown. In any case, Conlon stuck to the line that he had been 'sent to Castlerea for drill teaching, he being a Militia man', which seems incongruous, considering the men had been mobilised and ready for action six weeks before. Nevertheless, it was a line the authorities were prepared to accept, and Conlon, well-disciplined in the art of concealment and deception, was destined to play the fall guy, the upshot being, that on 10 March, he was formally arrested and lodged in Roscommon Gaol where he remained incarcerated for another six months. A memorial from Dundee precipitated an order for his release on 12 September. However, by this time, funds were severely depleted by subsistence payments, and the Resident Magistrate reported that the prisoner was unable to get bail. Conlon was finally released on 1 October, on the condition that he return to Scotland.[78] Meanwhile, Clarke, McGuigan and the other men who had slipped through the net, were already back home – Clarke putting his experience as IRB paymaster and Fenian felon to good use as Treasurer of the State Prisoner campaign, alongside Daniel Hannah as Secretary.

The State Prisoner Campaign

The postponed insurrection of New Year 1866, and the ensuing round up of Fenian insurgents had a chastening effect on those IRB members and supporters who had invested their time, energy and money in the enterprise, and who were now wary of informers in their ranks and reluctant to place their faith in Stephen's leadership. The same lack of trust did not attach itself to women, namely to the similarly disenchanted Ladies' Committee, formed by the female relatives of prominent prisoners to take responsibility for the State Prisoners and their dependants. Under the stewardship of Letitia Fraser Luby and Mary Jane Irwin O'Donovan Rossa, the Ladies' Committee publicised the plight of the families of imprisoned Fenians, and encouraged the formation of local committees to raise funds for the provision of meals and legal representation for the prisoners and weekly payments for their dependants.[79] While committees were established in seven English towns, Dundee appears to have been the only Scottish centre to have formed one, an appeal issued in *The Irishman* eliciting a response from 'J.W.' that 'Dundee has not been forgetful – it merely wanted to be assured of a good beginning'.[80]

A series of contributions gathered in Dundee and Lochee followed, but tailed off in late May, around the time of Clarke and McGuigan's release from jail. The men returned to Dundee, likely disappointed at the failure of their mission but with a greater appreciation of the importance of prisoner solidarity and support. Clarke had good reason to be grateful to his compatriots in Dundee who had kept him in funds whilst 'on the run' and to the Ladies' Committee who had sustained him whilst in prison. Denied the opportunity for military action, he channelled his energies into the State Prisoner campaign, and, assisted by Daniel Hannah, reorganised the committee along military lines, recruiting volunteers to take responsibility for conducting collections within circles of sympathisers. In early September, the committee sent its first instalment of £2 10s to Letitia Luby, via *The Irishman*, along with a heartfelt appeal to 'the Irish people', 'but above all… to the good *Irish women* of Dundee – those women, who in virtue and goodness are the representation of our mothers, who have not become degenerate, nor contracted the cold, unnatural and selfish habits of the people among whom we live'.[81]

While Clarke and Hannah presented an idealised view of Irish women as immutable paragons of virtue and exemplars of Irish values, it spoke to the experience of Clarke and the other Fenian insurgents that women had not sold them out. Admittedly, women were not admitted to IRB circles, but (as Devoy later testified) as couriers, confidantes and companions, they had neither informed, embezzled nor done anything else to undermine the movement.[82] Clarke and Hannah also understood the importance of encouragement, accountability and acknowledgment – elements lacking in Stephens' leadership of the IRB and the military campaign, but a point of principle with the Ladies' Committee. Donations were accompanied by a catalogue of subscribers, whose colourful pseudonyms disguised their real identities but alluded to their origins, occupations and political allegiances, which Hannah requested that Mrs Luby forward to *The Irishman* for publication. Subscription lists give a tantalising glimpse of the many female supporters – many giving their real names, others feminine pseudonyms, others possibly lurking behind pseudonyms of indeterminate gender. The majority of named collectors were still men. The final list, however, showed the duo of Mrs Mooney and Rose Regan to be the second most prolific after seasoned collector Philip Reilly. Amongst the men who chose to give their real names was grocer-stationer John Green, now agent for *The Irishman*, who contributed 2s 6d. The majority of contributions, however, were of sixpence (listed) and lesser sums (unlisted), for which information Hannah invited interested parties to 'apply to the Secretary's book'. The largest single contribution received by the Ladies' Committee that year came from America – the unique Fenian Sisterhood of New York and Brooklyn sending £448, the proceeds of a special bazaar. However, it would be fatuous to rank the £448 raised in New York – the nerve centre of Fenianism and the largest centre of Irish population in the world – with the modest sums raised in a similar time period in a small Scottish town with a poor working-class population. There were no bazaars in Dundee, mainly as the town's Fenians had nothing to sell.

Pseudonyms of Dundee Subscribers to the Ladies' Committee

A Ballinaforth Man	A Lover of Liberty
Blessington	Man from Ireland
A Canny Scot	Napoleon III
Charity	One who loves the country
A Clare Boy	A Pensioner
A Clonmore Bird	A Policeman
A Croppy	A Policeman's Wife
A Daughter of Erin	Porter
A Donegal Man	Rory of the Hill
A Friend to the Cause	Rose of Erin
Grand Shawnee Boy	Sarsfield
A Hater	Shamrock
Ireland	Sharp Steel
An Irish Girl	Sunburst
I Love Erin	Sweet Voice
A James Street Man	Three Militia Men
The Late Man from Ireland	A True hearted Irishman
A Lover	Tuam
A Lover of the Green	Two Good Girls
A Lover of Ireland	A Yank's Sweetheart

In December 1866, the Dundee committee concluded its business, for reasons unstated, having raised a total of £17 6d. In another heartfelt statement, Clarke and Hannah thanked the collectors and subscribers for their prompt response to the appeal, and for having helped to alleviate, 'even to a trifling extent, the sufferings of our unhappy kindred'.[83] The National Ladies' Committee concluded their propaganda campaign in 1869, and distribution of funds in 1872, by which time the job of supporting prisoners and their dependants had been assumed by the Amnesty Association and other committees. Why the Dundee campaign wound up when it did is unclear. Perhaps the organisers wished to turn their attention to other, military matters. Nevertheless, the State Prisoner campaign demonstrated the capacity for fund-raising amongst the local Irish population which belied their economic status, and, more specifically, demonstrated how small donations from large numbers could be channelled effectively into political solidarity and support. It also set a precedent and provided a model for prisoner support work in the town across the following decades.

Meanwhile, the local authorities and the press were oblivious to the Fenians in their midst, or at least anxious to play down their existence. In January 1866, the *Dundee Advertiser* prefaced a discreet paragraph on the Sligo arrests with the headline, 'Alleged Dundee Fenians Arrested at Sligo', and while Home Office reports stated that Dundee, with its large Irish population, was the one place most likely to be selected for Fenian operations, the *Advertiser* continued to insist that 'Fenianism, if it exists at all in Dundee... is very limited and very weak in character'.[84] The arrival of a detachment of soldiers at the under-serviced barracks at Dudhope Castle, in Dundee's Barrack Park, on 21 February was to be welcomed, the *Advertiser* stated, as Dundee was finally getting the degree of military protection commensurate to the taxes its citizens paid, although it did speculate obliquely that their arrival 'must not be unconnected with the present Fenian disturbances'.[85]

Earlier that month, the *Advertiser* received a press release, also sent to 'several other parties', from 'The Cabalistic Society of Fenians in Dundee', announcing a demonstration in the High Street at 4 pm on 10 February when 'the "Fenian Creed" will be propounded and the ultimate proceedings of the Brotherhood determined', which rounded off with the verse:

On the 'Devil's Punch Bowl' our flag will be raised;
So 'strike-strike-strike' for the good and the true;
To do and die on Killarney's lakes,
In paddling our own canoe.

Denouncing it as an 'unwarrantable and foolish canard', for which 'no foundation whatever' exists, the *Advertiser* nevertheless chose to publish the statement verbatim under the headline, 'The Irish Republic – Fenian demonstration', no doubt to the satisfaction of its author(s).[86] Indeed, such material was grist to the mill for the newspaper industry and, while the *Advertiser* may have denied its existence in Dundee, Fenianism ran riot through the pages of the local and national press in a wave of articles on rumoured risings, reported sightings of Fenian frigates, and descriptions of 'Fenian Fire' and how to make it. Thus, while the staid Tory *Courier* prided itself on its rational and dignified reporting, it also sought to steal a march on its rivals by exploiting the market for sensational Fenian scare stories, often through metafictional techniques.

For example, a report of a rumoured Fenian raid off the coast of Shetland, which appeared in the *Scotsman* in August 1866, provided the inspiration for a piece of creative journalism in which a supposed witness, described as 'A', recounted how he *had* just sat down to read the *Scotsman* when, disturbed by the boom of gunfire, he looked out to see three ships in the distance, the largest flying a green flag bearing images of the stars and stripes and an eagle with a harp in its claw surmounted by a white shamrock. Realising that resistance was 'impolitic', he despatched a messenger across the hills to Lerwick to raise the alarm as he scurried to hide his valuables, all the while twenty Fenians armed with cutlasses and pistols tramped up to his door. The author greeted the leader and bade him direct his men to the kitchen while, up in the drawing room, the leader 'did justice to [A's] finest viands over a glass of his North Port whisky' and perused the contents of his small library, taking a particular interest in a *History of Montrose* which he placed in his pocket. He was about to do the same with the author's prized copy of Burns' poems when, mercifully, a shout from a servant woke him from his slumbers – it was all a dream! The 'gunfire' had been the sound of his snoring, and 'All the noise, like that of the *Scotsman*, was of my own making'.[87] Thus, the *Dundee Courier* took a wry swipe at its Edinburgh rival.

In September 1867, the discovery of a document containing plans for a mass gathering of Fenians at Sheriffmuir and a series of raids on armouries in Stirling, Perth and Dundee, inspired a semi-spoof report from the *Advertiser*:

> Rendezvous on Sherrifmuir !
> Dundee to take part in Struggle!!
> Two additional constables called out!!

The report went on to reveal that 'alarming intelligence that Stirling, Perth and Dundee were to be sacked and pillaged by the Fenian Brotherhood' had led to the appointment of 'two first class Constables', possibly 'armed with batons' and shiny new helmets with which they would, no doubt, 'strike terror into the hearts of the invisible brotherhood'. Having lured in readers with mock-sensational headlines, the *Advertiser* went on to report, more soberly, the consternation caused by the 'document' which had been found in a pocketbook at Stirling Station along with an American coin and a list of American hotel addresses. While this looked suspiciously like a plant, the fact that the Stirling police had encountered a body of Irishmen drilling in Raploch the previous year meant the authorities were taking no chances. Security at Stirling Castle was doubled, the Stirlingshire Militia brought under arms, and a telegram was sent to the Police Superintendent at Perth, and the Commandant of the 4th Hussars, presently stationed at the Cavalry Barracks. The Royal Perth Rifle Militia were also armed and 'held in readiness'.[88]

The convergence of fact and fiction within much sensational journalism presented the Fenians and their supporters with a diversionary tactic which proved increasingly useful as the focus of activity shifted from organising expeditions to Ireland to participating in operations on local territory. While the Scottish press dismissed the Stirling incident as a malicious hoax, the fact that it 'had the air of probability about it' served to unsettle the authorities and divert their resources from elsewhere. While John Devoy later opined that the IRB failed to maximise this potential to keep the British Army tied up 'at home' and thus give Ireland time to 'get her insurgent army into shape', it is likely that in some areas, Dundee especially, the reinforcement of the barracks and arming of the local militia, was the aim in itself. As the abortive arms raid on Chester Castle on 11 February 1867 was largely the initiative of one man (Captain John McCafferty), it is possible that a number of minor actions, including the generation of 'Fenian scares', were initiated by local IRB men to draw arms into their area where they could be obtained, if not by outside raids on barracks and armouries, then by collaborating with the soldiers and staff within.[89]

In addition to being 'honeycombed with Fenianism', as Devoy put it, the rank and file of the British Army contained a number of native Scots who were neither unsympathetic to the Irish cause nor loyal to the British authorities, while others who had taken the Queen's shilling and were living on a soldier's pittance would have been easily bribed into participating in or turning a blind eye to the insider trading of arms. Dundee's Fenians were well-situated for such an enterprise. The military garrison at Dudhope Castle was fringed by areas of high Irish settlement – from Dudhope Street extending to the Hilltown in the east, Lochee Road and Scouringburn to the south, and Upper Pleasance extending to Lochee in the west – all areas where Dundee's Fenians and their sympathisers lived, worked and operated.

By the beginning of 1867, the IRB was gradually reorganising under the direction of a dynamic body of ex-American army officers led by Colonel Thomas J Kelly. A new date for the insurrection was set for 5 March, to which the raid on Chester Castle on 11 February had been geared. While the subsequent lack of arms and the work of spies and informers ultimately doomed that Rebellion to disaster, the IRB, who had already overcome more than one failure, dusted themselves off and prepared for another opportunity. On 22 March, the *Advertiser* reported a 'rumour' that a 'Head Centre' – probably Captain James Murphy, the Cork-born American Civil war veteran who had taken responsibility for organising Scotland[90] – had gone from Dundee to the 'strictly Scotch' and 'decidedly loyal' city of Aberdeen to advise on the seizing of a Volunteer armoury on the night of Tuesday, 19 March. The information, conveyed an anonymous letter, led to the posting of a party of armed Volunteers and military to the armoury and the barracks overnight, however nothing transpired. 'Aberdeen doesn't contain 300 of an Irish population [and] most of them are decent and respectable citizens as need be wished', the *Advertiser* reported; nevertheless, the authorities remained on the alert. The Aberdeen 'rumour' had barely been 'scotched' when rumours of 'threatened disturbances' in Dundee precipitated the arrival of 40 soldiers who were witnessed marching in broad daylight from the railway station to the barracks on the afternoon of Wednesday, 20 March. Meanwhile, stories abounded of 'bodies of men having been seen on roads near the city, and as likely to seize on the powder magazine and attack the barracks'.[91] IRB manoeuvres were also taking place in other parts of Scotland – just three days later, six men were arrested after being captured drilling near Mossend and Airdrie.[92] Unlike their colleagues on the West Coast, however, the Dundee police were not inclined to investigate sightings on their patch, which the *Advertiser*, helpfully, dismissed as having no foundation.

In the rapidly changing urban environment of the mid-nineteenth century, the police were still making the transition from a part-time volunteer body to a full-time professionally trained force. This was proving particularly challenging in Dundee where the overwhelming dependence on coarse textile production, which was highly susceptible to the boom-and-bust cycle of war markets, and the large non-tax paying working-class population had resulted in a straitened public purse which left the Police Commissioners ill-equipped to deal with the growing weight of tasks and responsibilities laid upon them. On top of lighting, paving, sanitation, the fire brigade, hackney carriages, and the police establishment itself, which included the court, the prison and the police force, the 'Fenian outbreaks' were the last unwelcome nuisance, and, despite intelligence from the Home Office suggesting otherwise, the local authorities dealt with it by continuing to insist that Dundee did not have a 'problem', in which they were dutifully supported by the local press.

The 'smashing of the van' incident in Manchester on 18 September, where the successful attempt to liberate Thomas J Kelly and Timothy Deasy from a prison van resulted in the unintended death of a police sergeant, served to remind the British government that the Fenians, who they presumed defeated in March, were very much alive and bolder than ever. In October, the War Office issued a circular to all Commanding Officers of Volunteer Corps regarding the safety of armouries, following which the *Courier* reported that the local police authority, who now believed that 'Fenianism [had] only been Scotched and not killed', had put the powder magazine under strict surveillance.[93]

The explosion at Clerkenwell Prison on 13 December[94] – where an excessive amount of gunpowder used to breach the perimeter wall destroyed the tenements opposite killing twelve people – led the *Advertiser* to put its liberal spin to one side and concede:

> hitherto Dundee was supposed to be pretty free from a rebellious spirit, whether among the Scotch or Irish, [but] at a time when treason is so rife the authorities cannot be too vigilant in providing against every possible danger.

It also disclosed that while many may have considered vague rumours of an intended Fenian outbreak at Broughty Ferry to be 'old wives' fables', the government, 'having been appraised', had sent twelve artillery men from Woolwich Barracks to reinforce the garrison at Broughty Castle with more due to arrive that day. For this at least, the local authorities were to be relieved of the burden of responsibility.

More disturbing was the news that, the previous day, local wool merchant David Scott of Dudhope Street had received an anonymous note bearing the warning, 'Beware. Your house is to be blown up by Fenians'. While the *Advertiser* speculated that it was 'probably intended as a hoax', the fact that the gunpowder magazine in Barrack Park was situated 'almost opposite' Scott's house was a major cause of concern to him and other residents who the *Advertiser* sought tentatively to reassure.[95] Within two days, however, the *Advertiser* proclaimed 'Dundee Free from Fenianism', and denounced the threatening note and the letting off of 'squibs' in the vicinity of the powder magazine as a 'foolish hoax' which brought 'groundless suspicion' on the local Irish population who had displayed 'excellent and exemplary conduct during the recent excitement'. An investigation into the matter appeared to consist of consulting local employers and possibly priests, the former of whom confirmed the Irish workforce to be 'a hard-working, peaceable, well-disposed class' amongst whom 'Fenianism is not in favour', for which the latter claimed the credit.[96] Indeed, the controversial executions of Allen, Larkin and O'Brien (the Manchester Martyrs) on 23 November had re-activated the British establishment's deep-rooted fear of the mob; namely, that a riot by the Irish population in Manchester would trigger riots in other towns and cities which would escalate into widespread unrest and threaten to destabilise the social order. That it had not was attributed in the first instance, to the advice of Manchester priests to their flocks to stay away from the execution site, and of the Catholic clergy to steer clear of Fenianism in general. Indeed, the *Advertiser* noted:

> in a town where we have upwards of 20,000 resident Irish, it is only just that we express our obligation to their religious teachers for exerting their influence on the side of law and order, and discouraging the pernicious movement and the few Fenian agents who have at different times visited Dundee.[97]

These views were strongly in line with the thinking of Dundee's Liberal civic authorities who viewed religious intolerance and extreme political radicalism as equal obstructions in their mission to create an inclusive, cohesive community in which religious, ethnic and class identities were subordinated to an overarching civic one. Accordingly, Dundee's civic fathers and their allies in the Liberal press, sought to recast the Irish community as the town's adoptive children, and privileged the figures of authority 'intimately connected' with them – churchmen, the business class and the local police, to know the minds and speak the minds of 'the Irish population of Dundee' better than they did themselves. This also applied to the working-class population in general, whose candid accounts of irregular goings-on were dismissed as unsubstantiated spurious nonsense.

This benign picture of the Irish population – particularly as national press hysteria over the perceived Fenian threat whipped up hostility towards Irish immigrants – can partly be attributed to the earlier work of IRB men, such as Owen Walsh, in cultivating a positive relationship with the local press, through which Dundee's advanced nationalists had simultaneously expounded Irish Republican principles and promoted an image of themselves as 'honourable men' working within a compassionate, self-reliant community, who had proven themselves to be worthy citizens of their adopted town.

It is with no small measure of irony then that, in March 1868, as the national panic over Fenian attacks was waning, an attempt was made to blow up Dundee's powder magazine, which if it had succeeded would have proven to be more devastating and certainly more spectacular, than the explosion at Clerkenwell. The 'plot' came to light around noon on Thursday, 5 March when the keeper of the magazine, Michael Waters, accompanied by the military guard and Robert Gow, who had been sent to obtain a quantity of gunpowder for his father's gun and fishing tackle business, entered the outer door of the building to find a partially-burned wad of flax attached to a small piece of grey woollen cloth placed at the bottom of the inner wooden door, which, along with the wooden floor, showed signs of extensive fire damage. The quantity of ashes gathered afterwards established that the fire had lasted for 'several minutes at least', but not long enough to communicate with the gunpowder. Had it done so, the *Advertiser* noted, 'about three tons of gunpowder would have ignited… in all likelihood reducing the Barracks and the buildings in the immediate neighbourhood to ruins, and carrying inevitable death to some, if not to hundreds'.[98]

The powder magazine, on the western periphery of the Barrack Square, on rising ground overlooking the town to the south, stored the stock of gunpowder for the trades, not only of Dundee, but for the counties of Fife, Forfarshire and Perthshire, an estimated three to seven tons of it.[99] As it took a grossly miscalculated 'several hundred pounds' of gunpowder to cause the deaths of twelve people and around £15,000 worth of damage at Clerkenwell, the consequences of an explosion involving hundreds of times that amount would certainly have been devastating. The Tory *Courier*, seizing a stick to beat the Liberal authorities, carped:

> While other towns were kept in a state of alarm with regards to the doings of the Brotherhood, the good burghers of Dundee hugged themselves to the belief that they at least were secure from 'diabolical plots' and murderous attempts against the lives of Her Majesty's lieges. Now they find the foul thing (or something very like it) at their doors.[100]

While agreeing that it was evidence of a 'diabolical design' or 'infernal plot', neither the press nor the authorities observed that the attempt was made exactly one year to the day after the ill-fated Fenian Rising. With the brief exception of the *Courier*, Dundee press reports on the incident –

which were unquestioningly reprised in newspapers on both sides of the Irish Sea – made no reference to Fenianism whatsoever. Indeed, even the *Courier* subsequently reviewed the idea that it had its 'origins in Fenian machinations', albeit by recourse to crude racial stereotypes. 'Had the Fenians taken any hand in the matter', it opined,

> the secret would have 'exploded' ere this. It is not in the Hibernian nature to keep things in the dark for any length of time. Irishmen (and we say this in their honour) have always been unsuccessful conspirators, and we believe this has in great means been owing to the peculiarity in their constitution which renders it impossible for them to 'love the darkness' even though their deeds may be evil.[101]

An investigation immediately ensued in which the police authorities strove to absolve themselves of responsibility – Waters, who had initially been arrested (on the orders of a Colour-Sergeant) and released by conflicted or insubordinate soldiers twice in succession, was deemed to be beyond reproach and 'worthy of the confidence that [had] all along been placed in him'.[102] Subsequently, two police constables attested to the Police Court that a soldier they had arrested on a charge of riotous conduct a fortnight before had threatened to 'blow up the bloody powder magazine' if not released, while another had said he 'would do for the police'. The day after the attempted explosion, the same two soldiers had deserted, and it was revealed that another who had left the Barracks the previous Wednesday hadn't been seen since. The finger of suspicion having been pointed at the absconding soldiers, the civil authorities could safely pass the buck. Meanwhile, despite speculation of a cast of a key having been made, an examination of the military witnesses by Captain White of the 42nd Highlanders (Black Watch), 'shed no light on the matter', while a police interrogation of five soldiers arrested for their part in the earlier 'disturbance' revealed 'nothing of interest'.[103] The picture presented by the military here, as beset by incompetence, indiscipline, insubordination and disaffection, is consistent with Devoy's observation that, as well as being 'honeycombed with Fenianism', the British Army was 'hopelessly deficient and inefficient' in its administration and organisation.[104] Although the

42nd Highlanders, of which 150 were said to be stationed at the barracks, drew its recruits from the local counties of Fife, Perthshire and Forfarshire, the possibility that some of these recruits may have been Fenians with links to the local Irish population, is not one that Dundee's local authorities were prepared to consider.

Significantly, it was around this time that Donegal-born Patrick Higgins, procured a job as a night watchman, presumably to offset his original declining trade as a handloom carpet weaver. From his home at 6 East Henderson's Wynd (neighbouring the NBSP's West Port Reading Rooms for which he helped provide the furniture), Higgins had acted as an agent for the *Free Press*, sold tickets for Lavelle fund-raising concerts, and – although the responsibilities of a growing family probably prevented him from joining Kenny's men in Ireland in 1865–6 – continued working quietly behind the scenes for the Irish Republican cause. While it is unknown where Higgins' watch was based in 1868, the fact that Henderson's Wynd was situated directly opposite the barracks on the south side of the Lochee Road presents intriguing possibilities and opportunities; for example, to obtain casts of keys to pass on and make duplicates – the piece of flax tow used in in the process of carpet weaving wrapped in the scrap of grey flannel cloth from which military clothing was made providing a fittingly utilitarian metaphor for the collaborative relationship which existed between Fenians in the British Army and those in the local Irish community.[105]

That no suspicion fell on the Irish population was possibly because Dundee's Fenians – the ordinary weavers, factory hands, occasional shopkeeper and trusty night watchman, with their mingling, melding Irish-Scots accents, were far removed from the image of the battle-hardened Yankee desperados perpetuated in the popular press. Indeed, the *Advertiser* had earlier claimed that Fenianism was not even Irish, but 'a foreign importation from America used to extract money from dupes on both sides of the Atlantic'.[106] However, it was far greater a credit to the internal discipline of the IRB in Dundee, and in Scotland in general – a legacy of the enduring Ribbon tradition with its pervasive codes of secrecy and deep-rooted contempt for anyone who dared to breach them. That informers were shunned, and literally branded, in certain cases, as traitors, is illustrated in the following account given by Scottish IRB commander,

Peter McCorry, to the American Fenian Brotherhood:

> From Dundee to Newcastle-on-Tyne, every seat of manufacture is crammed with Fenians; and I am proud to say that discretion has preserved every one of them from all efforts that English or Scots law could make to incriminate them. We had one informer there...whose deeds of darkness were none the less because the world has not heard of them. He visited London at the time I was defending poor Michael Barrett, and though not publicly examined, yet he came from Glasgow in company with detectives and police officials. The last time I saw him, his face bore marks of some kind as if he had been badly beaten. Had Coryden, Nagel, Massey and Mullany sprung up in Glasgow or any other part of Scotland, they might have given evidence for once against their comrades, but certainly not twice![107]

McCorry was writing six months after the trial of Glasgow-based Fenian, Michael Barrett, whose execution on 26 May precipitated the exodus of several senior IRB figures to America, McCorry included. His comrade and confidante, Owen Walsh, also appears to have made his emigration permanent.[108] Despite these losses, by the end of 1868, the IRB in Scotland remained strong in number and spirit. McCorry, who stated that his knowledge came from personal inspection, put the number of Fenians in Scotland at '10,000 men, well-drilled, partially armed, and all abiding their time faithfully and discreetly, keeping together like one man, and impregnable in their devotion to their country's cause'.[109]

On 24 April 1868, the IRB Supreme Council issued a 'Message to the Irish People' attributing the failures of January 1866 and March 1867 to divisions in the American organisation, owing to which the army in Ireland, England and Scotland had been '[mis]represented to be almost complete in equipment', hence supplies dispatched to Ireland 'almost wholly inadequate'. 'Arm Ireland and Ireland is free' became the mission to which the IRB applied itself.[110] A new generation was moving up through the ranks, including Michael Davitt, who was appointed arms procurement officer for Scotland and the North of England some time in 1869. On 14 December, Davitt travelled to Dundee, consequently writing to fellow agent, Arthur Forrester, that he had left the place 'all right' – an IRB codeword, in this case indicating that he had conducted a successful transaction, either acquiring or delivering a quantity of arms or receiving a tidy sum of money with which to buy them.[111] Ironically, the letter, which sheds a rare light on the capacity of Dundee's Irish Republicans to deliver the goods when called upon, was thick with coded references, most notably to sales of a 'pen' which sealed Davitt's fate when the letter was used to incriminate him in a 'Fenian' conspiracy resulting in a fifteen-year jail sentence for treason-felony in May 1870.[112]

Davitt's visit occurred ten days after a fund-raising concert held under the auspices of the newly formed Dundee branch of the Amnesty Association. Founded in Dublin in June 1869 by leading Fenian, John 'Amnesty' Nolan, the Amnesty Association had built on the work of the State Prisoner campaign hitherto conducted by the Ladies' Committee; and, unlike the moderate Amnesty Committee from which it arose and eventually split, aimed to intensify pressure on the British government to grant an unconditional amnesty to all Irish political prisoners. While its aims were acceptable to constitutional nationalists, for Dundee's physical force nationalists, the Amnesty Association provided an opportunity to discreetly manoeuvre themselves into positions of influence and control over much-needed funds (in a town the size and socio-economic consistency of Dundee, this was extremely important). It also provided an opportunity to influence, if not altogether radicalise the moderate nationalists within it. For example, the first President of the Dundee branch, John Green, had been a leading figure in the formative years of the Catholic Young Men's Society and had initially dissociated himself from militant nationalism following pressure from the clergy. In the intervening years, Green appears to have modified his position, becoming an agent for *The Irishman* and the *Free Press* after the latter, and those selling it, had been condemned by the Catholic clergy. It is possible that Green was simply protecting his business interests by pandering to the political ones of the community in which he remained all his life (his home and stationer's shop were in the Scouringburn), but if so, he appears to have advanced his own political views in the process. Influential members of the Dundee Amnesty Association included veteran Repealer and Young Ireland supporter, Samuel McKinney (named McKenna in press reports), and Secretary

Daniel Hannah, who was later joined by seasoned front-men of IRB cover groups of the past decade, Thomas Morrison and James Hennessy. These practical and independently minded Irish Republicans were accustomed to making the most of every opportunity and adapting their tactics to meet the needs of the moment, and the proximity of the Amnesty fundraiser on 4 December 1869 to Davitt's productive visit ten days later suggests a level of creative accounting whereby a percentage of money raised through official campaigns such as the Amnesty Association was directed into the purchase of arms.

The Amnesty concert, which was widely advertised in the press and on bills posted throughout the town appealing to 'all patriotic Irishmen and liberal Scotchmen to give their generous support to [the] occasion', attracted an audience of over 2,000 people composed principally of young men, teenage boys and, in a now constant feature of Irish events in Dundee, a large number of women. Following a disastrous Glasgow Amnesty meeting which had its platform of constitutional nationalists rushed by Fenians, invitations to Glasgow speakers were withdrawn on the advice of John 'Amnesty' Nolan, and the speeches of the Dundee committee condensed and pushed down the programme. Thus, while Hannah's double resolution that the Irish population of Dundee throw their weight behind the demand to free the political prisoners, and to regard any government which refused or delayed this 'as *hostile*, therefore unfit to govern Ireland in the spirit of justice and fair play', was enthusiastically passed, the highlight of the evening was Lochee singer James Kearney's opening rendition of 'God Save Ireland', which was repeated at the end of the evening to the cheering and tramping of a well-versed audience A large green board bearing the slogan was hung in front of the Kinnaird Hall's centrepiece organ, and a hired troupe of green-clad performers from McFarland's Music Hall 'acquitted themselves creditably', with reports noting that 'anything bearing to the state of Ireland was received three times three'.[113] If the organisers were uneasy about the inclusion of the Fenian anthem in the programme, it is possibly because they were aware that the army and police had been placed on standby in the event of a disturbance arising from the 'Fenian entertainment', as the event had been dubbed, and feared that passions aroused by the song might spill over on to the streets. The committee were under pressure to avoid, and perhaps reverse, the negative publicity which had arisen from the Glasgow demonstration, to make as much money as discreetly as possible, and to present a positive image to the press which would appeal to sympathetic Scots. They need not have worried. *The Irishman* noted that 'the meeting was conducted in the same orderly manner that all Irish events in Dundee are, [with] not as much as one hitch', and that 'the committee were laughing in their sleeves at the extreme precautions taken by the authorities'.[114]

The Scots in the audience, and the local press also took it with a liberal dose of good spirit. The *Courier*, which reaffirmed Dundee's pride in 'the orderly disposition of our Irish fellow-townsmen' during the recent Fenian 'incendiarism', stated that the overall impression was of an event 'overflowing with Irish feeling', similar to the intense expressions of patriotism witnessed at a gathering of expatriate Scotchmen at a dinner at the London Scottish Hospital the previous week. Noting that 'Scotchmen appear in London streets in plaid and bonnet', who would never dream of doing so in Edinburgh', the *Courier* reasoned:

> We are not disposed to attach very great importance to the ribbons, or the 'God Save Ireland' of the Kinnaird Hall last Saturday...We are not to conclude...from some excited talk and still more excited singing...that the Irishmen of Dundee are about to enter on a course of sedition.[115]

While the *Courier* was happy to accommodate benign expressions of Irish nationalism, the songs and speeches provoked the ire of one self-styled 'True Briton' who pronounced the former 'idiotic doggerel' which 'would scarcely pass muster in a third-rate tap room.' Of the latter, he proffered:

> The Irishman steals from his neighbour and robs his landlord in the name of liberty [but] has a very dim perception of the meaning of the word...Let them understand that forbearance is past, and their shouts, vapourings and national songs will wither and die. Before fully accomplishing fully this object, the national press of Dublin must be totally suppressed with no hope of resurrection.[116]

This elicited a swift response from 'A True Celt' who, taking care to

Chapter 2 – Fenians 1859–69

thank the *Courier* for its 'generous and partial article', observed:

> It is no doubt very galling to a would-be True Briton to see such a large orderly meeting giving vent to Irish national principles in Dundee…What a pity we cannot be brought to show our tolerance… by crushing the national press of Ireland or walking knee deep in the blood of our fellow men who differ with us in religion &c.

Explaining that the 'stamping out process' had been tried for 300 years by the British' with no effect beyond embittering the Irish people and creating a more vigorous resistance, 'A True Celt' claimed that 'any person putting forth such a fiendish idea in the nineteenth century' required the 'special guardianship of his friends, and removal to an institution that is situated in the east end of Dundee' – a reference to the Lunatic Asylum in Albert Street, then on the north-eastern fringes of the town. While favouring mental therapy, he nevertheless warned him 'not to test the want of courage in an Irishman [as] he might find it very disagreeable…even if he had a truncheon'.[117] Another letter, purporting to be from 'One of the Fenian Brotherhood, Dundee Branch', put it more bluntly:

> If your correspondent writes any more epistles of a like nature he will be as well to make all necessary arrangements for his funeral. The Fenian Brotherhood do not believe in discussing their principles in the columns of Dundee newspapers – indeed I may say that they disapprove of discussions altogether. We know the secret of our power, which does not consist in argument. If we are to gain our object, the revolver must be exercised much more than it has yet been. We have every confidence that in a short time the British Government will be glad to give up Ireland. Irishmen will then have the land to themselves. Everyone not born in the country will be forcibly expelled. May that happy day soon arrive. God Save Ireland![118]

The letter put the secret, conspiratorial and physical force tradition of the movement in Dundee in a Ribbon-tied nutshell. Indeed, if the 'Fenian

Brother' was as he claimed, one senses that he had already said too much, especially to a twenty-first-century perspective, where talk of forcible expulsions of the non-Irish-born smacks of ethnic cleansing and xenophobia. However, the lack of large-scale immigration to Ireland in the nineteenth century meant that most poor Irish tenant farmers and labourers had little experience or perception of non-indigenous inhabitants beyond rack-renting English landlords and advantaged Protestant Planters, many of whom sought to safeguard and maintain their economic privileges through membership of the Orange Order. Indeed, 'A True Celt' wrote, 'If 'A True Briton' would style himself "A True Orangeman", I would be better able to understand him. [His] are the opinions of a goodly number of bigoted, brutal, debauched Irish landlords'.[119]

While the identity of 'A True Celt' (and the other correspondents) is unknown, the statement that '[I decline] to drag my religion through the columns of a newspaper, as the matter of dispute is political', recalls earlier comments by, and possibly points to, Daniel Hannah. Nevertheless, the distinction between secular and religious spheres – most recently enshrined in the Fenian Proclamation's separation of Church and State – was a key principle espoused by other deep-thinking Irish Republicans. The rhetoric is also indicative of Paisley-born James Ward, a discreet IRB operator who had settled in Dundee at least by the time of his marriage to Catherine Devine in 1868. Significantly, the final sentence of 'A True Celt's' letter, not only spoke to the prominence of the land issue in the minds of the exiled Irish population and its central importance to notions of national independence, but also prefigured Ward's involvement with the Land League in the 1880s. His words, 'So long as these opinions are held by [A True Briton's] class, and so long as the law protects them in their inhumanity to man, so long will the agrarian war continue, and the newspapers chronicle now and again another "landlord shot"', were to echo across the decade to An Gorta Beag of 1879 – the year of famine and fury, the formation of the Irish National Land League, and the beginning of the Land War.

Endnotes to Chapter 2

1. *The Irishman*, 17 September 1859.
2. 'The Fenian Men', [Fifth verse], as published in the *Free Press*, 27 August 1864.
3. The Dublin-based newspaper was established in 1858 to cater for the growing Irish immigrant market in England, Scotland and Wales.
4. The French monarchical convention of '*monter dans les carrosses du Roi*' ('to ride in the King's carriage') by which a family offering perfect legal proof of noble lineage going back before 1400 had a right to claim, and be granted, admission to the French aristocracy and the honours of the court.
5. And for which a new purple-red dye, invented and patented by French chemist François-Emmanuel Verguin, was also named
6. *The Irishman*, 23 July 1859.
7. *The Irishman*, 20 August 1859.
8. *The Irish American*, reprinted *The Irishman*, 8 December 1860.
9. William Dillon, *Life of John Mitchel Volume 1*, (1888), pp137–38; *The Irishman*, 22 October 1859.
10. *The Irishman*, 18 May 1861.
11. *The Irishman*, 22 June 1861.
12. *The Irishman*, 14 September 1861; 5 October 1861.
13. Gerard Moran, 'The Radical Priest of Partry: Patrick Lavelle (1825–1886)' in Gerard Moran (ed), *Irish Radical Priests, 1660–1970* (Dublin: Four Courts Press, 1998), pp111–30; Shane Kenna, *Jeremiah O'Donovan Rossa: Unrepentant Fenian* (Sallins, County Kildare: Merrion Press, 2015), p44.
14. *The Irishman*, 16 November 1861, 5 October 1861; Census of Scotland, 1861: *Irishman*, April 1863.
15. Paul Townend, '"Academies of Irish Nationality": The Reading Room and Irish National Movements, 1838–1905', in Laurence W McBride (ed), *Reading Irish Histories: Texts, Contexts and Memory* (Dublin: Four Courts Press, 2003), p27.
16. Manifesto of the Phoenix National and Literary Society, quoted in Shane Kenna, *Jeremiah O'Donovan Rossa: Unrepentant Fenian* (Sallins, County Kildare: Merrion Press, 2015), p17.
17. For more on the NBSP in Glasgow, see Terence McBride, 'Ribbonmen and Radicals: the cultivation of Irishness and the promotion of active citizenship in mid-Victorian Glasgow', *Irish Studies Review*, 23:1 (2015), pp15–32.
18. McBride, 'Ribbonmen and Radicals', pp18–19.
19. Established in 1858 by John Leng, the Liberal proprietor of the *Dundee Advertiser*.
20. Fair Muir, at the top of the Hilltown, was the site of Dundee's annual summer fairs, which were renowned occasions of heavy drinking and rowdy behaviour.
21. *People's Journal*, 18 January 1862.

22 *Dundee Advertiser*, 22 January 1862.
23 The identity of Hibernicus has been the subject of speculation by historians. William Walker suggests it was Hannah (Hannah himself, on behalf of the NBSP, denied all knowledge of Hibernicus's identity), while Terence McBride has suggested it was Owen Walsh. McBride, 'Ribbonmen and Radicals', p30, n73.
24 *Dundee Advertiser*, 1 February 1862.
25 *Free Press*, 1 February 1862. At this point, the *Free Press* saw Irish national identity as essentially Catholic, was strongly pro-clergy and naturally suspicious of perceived Protestant proselytism within the NBSP.
26 *Free Press*, 8 February 1862.
27 The Working Men's Reading and News Rooms, of which there were five, in addition to another five Working Men's News and Coffee Rooms, operating in Dundee at the time.
28 *Dundee Advertiser*, 29 January 1862.
29 *Dundee Advertiser*, 15 February 1862.
30 *The Nation*, 8 February 1862.
31 *Dundee Advertiser*, 18 February 1862.
32 *The Irishman*, 12 April 1862.
33 *The Irishman*, 7 June 1862.
34 The *Irishman* Indemnity Fund was set up to help pay the legal expenses of the paper's editor, Charles Holland, who had been threatened with a libel action for publishing an excoriating article about an Armagh landlord. Unlike the pro-clergy *Free Press*, the *Irishman* provided a forum for advanced nationalist opinion, and had recently published a letter by Father Lavelle condemning Archbishop Cullen's pastoral against the Fenians. The *Irishman*'s defence of Republican principles in the face of clerical opposition resonated with the NBSP in Dundee who rallied round with a total of £3 9s 6d collected from 81 subscribers. At the top of the list was Thomas Morrison (the possible organiser of the collection), who contributed the grand sum of 2s 6d, as did John McElroy and Patrick and James McNally. Other shilling and sixpenny subscribers included Edward Kilboyne, Edward Barrett and Joseph Clifford (former subscribers to the MacMahon Testimonial), William Sweeney, Samuel McKinney, Owen Walsh, Peter and Philip Clarke, Mesdames McElroy, Menzie, Ogilvie, and Warnock, Nancy McCaffery, Bridget Neary, Jane Pollard and Helen Breen.
35 *The Irishman*, 1 November 1862.
36 *The Irishman*, 11 April 1863.
37 Walsh, who was born in Ireland *c*1839, had emigrated to Dundee while a child, with his father Edward, also a weaver, most likely during An Gorta Mór, His mother, Catherine McManus, had died, possibly as a result of hunger and disease, following which his father remarried. Walsh's younger half-brother, James, was born in Dundee in 1852.

38 *Dundee Advertiser*, 23, 24 February 1864.

39 *People's Journal*, 5 March 1964.

40 Green stated that he asked for the notice to be withdrawn, to which Hoey replied that he was 'not so *green*' as to fail to see who had forced his hand. (*Dundee Advertiser*, 29 February 1864; *Dundee Courier*, 1 March 1864).

41 Moran, 'The Radical Priest of Partry', p119.

42 *Free Press*, June 1864.

43 *Dundee Courier*, 14 June 1864; *Free Press*, 16 June 1864.

44 *Dundee Advertiser*, 17 May 1864.

45 *Dundee Advertiser*, 24 May 1864. Thomas Reynolds and Jeremy O'Brien, who informed against the United Irishmen in 1798; Daniel O'Sullivan 'Goula', principal informer in the Phoenix Society trials of 1859; and John Sadleir and William Keogh, who broke their pledges as members of the Independent Irish Party not to take government office in 1852. Financier Sadleir committed suicide in 1856 after the failure of several fraudulent financial schemes, and lawyer Keogh, who was appointed Attorney-General for Ireland in 1855, presided over the Fenian/*Irish People* trials in 1865–66, handing out savage sentences to O'Donovan Rossa and the other IRB leaders involved.

46 *Dundee Advertiser*, 21 June 1864.

47 *Dundee Advertiser*, 25 June 1864.

48 *Dundee Courier*, 24 June 1864.

49 Hannah, self-schooled in the history of Irish resistance, likely had in mind Father Nicolas Sheehy of Clogheen, Tipperary, who was brutally executed by the British in 1766 for his involvement in agrarian protest in support of his oppressed parishioners; and Fathers Murphy of Boolavogue and Manus Sweeney of Newport, Mayo, local leaders in the 1798 Rebellion, who met a similar fate.

50 *Free Press*, 19 June 1864.

51 Monsignor Félix Dupanloup, who had conducted an eloquent and powerful defence of Lavelle.

52 *Dundee Advertiser*, 5 July 1864, 9 July 1864.

53 *Dundee Advertiser*, 7 July 1864.

54 *Free Press*, 13 August 17 September 1864.

55 *Free Press*, 19 November 1864.

56 *Free Press*, 29 December 1864.

57 *Free Press*, 17 September 1864.

58 *Dundee Advertiser*, 21 December 1864.

59 Considered by many to be the editor of *Free Press*, Peter McCorry (who was also Honorary Secretary of the INA at the time), although he vociferously denied it. For example, when critic of the Irish Catholic clergy, the Reverend Father Duncan

McNab of Airdrie suggested 'Sacerdos' was a concoction of the *Free Press*, McCorry stated he would write to him demanding an apology for his slanders, and informing him of Sacerdos' identity privately. *Free Press*, 7 January 1865.

60 *Free Press*, 14 January 1865.
61 *Free Press*, 28 January 1865.
62 John Devoy, *Recollections of an Irish Rebel*, 1842–1928, (1929), p30; National Archives of Ireland [hereafter NAI], Fenian papers, CSO/ICR/15; Seán Ó Lúing, *O'Donnobhain Rosa Volume 1*, (Baile Atha Cliath: Sairseal & Dill, 1969), p155.
63 The military command structure of the IRB cell system was as follows: The Centre, 'A', trained the 'Bs' who then trained the 'Cs' who trained the rank and file. However, local conditions a degree of flexibility and local autonomy existed, with some 'Bs' taking on the duties of 'As' etc. Ó Lúing, *Fremantle Mission* (Tralee, County Kerry: Anvil Books, 1965), p6.
64 The last reference to the DINI is a notice in the *Free Press* of 4 March 1865 calling the committee to a meeting to finalise arrangements for St Patrick's Day.
65 Walsh submitted a verbatim report of a post-Confessional dialogue between himself and Father Vassal of St Andrews, Glasgow, in which the priest grilled him over his support of the *Free Press*, and denied him absolution for refusing to write to his wife 'command[ing] her to stop selling it', and challenging his authority on political matters. *Free Press*, 29 April 1965.
66 *Free Press*, 27 May 1865.
67 *Free Press*, 17 June 1865. A report in the *Boston Pilot* explained that the Fenian Brotherhood's congresses were composed of representatives chosen from its several circles who proposed and voted on resolutions concerning principles and policy.
68 *Free Press*, 15 July 1865.
69 Seán Ó'Lúing, *Fremantle Mission*, (Tralee, County Kerry: Anvil Books, 1965), p14.
70 Devoy, *Recollections*, p33; Máirtín Ó Catháin, *Irish Republicanism in Scotland, 1858–1916* (Dublin: Irish Academic Press, 2000), p47; W M Walker, 'Irish Immigrants in Scotland: their priests, politics and parochial life', *Historical Journal*, 15:4 (1972), p655, n28.
71 Ó Lúing, *Fremantle Mission*, p14.
72 *Belfast Newsletter*, 3 January 1866.
73 *Sligo Chronicle*, 13 January 1866; *Dublin Daily Express*, 19 January 1866.
74 *Irish Times*, 14 March 1866.
75 NAI, Fenian papers, CSO/ICR/10.
76 McLaughlin was prohibited from going to Scotland, England and Wales, and was escorted from the gaol to the boat for America. Ó Catháin, *Irish Republicanism in Scotland*, p56.

CHAPTER 2 – FENIANS 1859–69

77 Devoy, *Recollections*, p191. The Royal Perthshire Rifle Militia amalgamated with the 73rd and 42nd Foot Regiments to form the Black Watch in 1881.
78 NAI, Fenian papers, CSO/ICR/10. The return address given by Conlon was Simpson's land, Rose Street – just off Rosebank Street, which was well-known to Dundee Fenians as the former meeting place of the Hilltown branch of the NBSP.
79 Eva O'Cathesir, *Soldiers of Liberty: A Study of Fenianism, 1858–1908* (Dublin: The Lilliput Press, 2018), pp204–6.
80 *The Irishman*, March 1866.
81 *The Irishman*, 13 September 1866.
82 'Not one woman betrayed a secret, proved false in the trust reposed in her, or by any carelessness or indiscretion was responsible for any injury to the cause.' Devoy, *Recollections*, p113.
83 *The Irishman*, 22 December 1866.
84 *Dundee Advertiser*, 16 January 1866; Public Record Office [hereafter PRO], Home Office Papers, letter from Lord Advocate to Home Secretary, 10 February 1866, HO/45/7799.
85 *Dundee Advertiser*, 23 February 1866.
86 *Dundee Advertiser*, 10 February 1866.
87 *Dundee Courier*, 21 August 1866.
88 *Dundee Advertiser*, 22 September 1867.
89 Devoy, *Recollections*, p114.
90 Ó Catháin, *Irish Republicanism in Scotland*, p55.
91 *Dundee Advertiser*, 22 March 1867.
92 *Free Press*, 30 March 1867.
93 *Dundee Courier*, 17 October 1867.
94 Carried out by the London IRB in an attempt to rescue leading Fenian Ricard O'Sullivan Burke, who was there awaiting trial.
95 *Dundee Advertiser*, 28 December 1867.
96 *Dundee Advertiser*, 30 December 1867.
97 *Dundee Advertiser*, 24 November 1867.
98 *Dundee Advertiser*, 5 March 1868.
99 The variance in estimates, which was reflected in newspaper reports throughout the British Isles, can be explained by the fact that that no inventory appears to have been kept. Dundee's Police Commissioners were also unaware who was responsible for the gunpowder for the areas outside the town.
100 *Dundee Courier*, 6 March 1868.
101 *Dundee Courier*, 7 March 1868.
102 *Dundee Advertiser*, 6 March 1868.

103 *Dundee Courier*, 10 March 1868.

104 Devoy, *Recollections*, p115.

105 In January 1862, Daniel Hannah wrote that furniture for the NBSP's reading rooms had been supplied by the neighbours. Higgins' influence extended across three generations – he had four daughters, and four sons, at least one of whom may have been in the British Army. During the Irish War of Independence, a grandson in the British Army passed guns to his cousins, Lena and Catherine McDonald, who were gunrunners for the IRA. See Chapter 7.

106 *Dundee Advertiser*, 30 December 1867.

107 *Flag of Ireland*, 14 November 1868. John Joseph Coryden, who betrayed the raid on Chester Castle; Pierce Nagle, who testified against the IRB leaders in the *Irish People* trial; Godfrey Massey, who betrayed the Fenian Rising of March 1867; and Patrick Mullany who implicated Barrett in the Clerkenwell explosion. Ó Catháin concludes that McCorry was probably nominee to the Supreme Council around this time. Ó Catháin, *Irish Republicanism*, p66.

108 Ó Catháin speculates that Walsh may have been one of the senior officers attending an IRB convention in Manchester in July/August 1867. *Irish Republicanism*, p61. No documentary evidence, however, exists to indicate that Walsh returned to Scotland after his trip to America in 1865. McCorry later took over from John O'Mahoney as the editor of the *Irish People* in New York.

109 *Flag of Ireland*, 14 November 1868.

110 Message from the Supreme Council of the Irish Republic to the Irish People, Dublin.

111 On the use of 'all right' as an IRB password, see Ó Lúing, *Freemantle Mission*, pp106, 111.

112 T W Moody, 'Michael Davitt and the 'Pen' Letter', Irish Historical Studies, 4:15 (1945), pp224–53.

113 *Dundee Courier*, 9 December 1869.

114 *The Irishman*, 4 December 1869, 11 December 1869.

115 *Dundee Courier*, 8 December 1869.

116 *Dundee Courier*, 9 December 1869.

117 *Dundee Courier*, 10 December 1869, 13 December 1869.

118 *Dundee Courier*, 15 December 1869.

119 *Dundee Courier*, 13 December 1869.

CHAPTER 3

A New Departure: Constitutionalism, Compromise and Collaboration 1870–79

Over a torn and distracted country – a country agitated by dissension and weakened by distrust – we raised the banner on which we emblazoned the magic words, 'Home Rule'.[1]

THE POSITIVE OUTCOME of Michael Davitt's visit, and the success of the Fenian-flavoured Amnesty concert, revealed a local movement that was confident, optimistic, financially healthy and strongly independent. Davitt's arrest in May 1870, however, brought to light the problems of a larger national movement that was compromised by informers and infiltrated by police spies – a situation which Dundee, in its relative isolation, had avoided. From his prison cell, Davitt could ponder on the irony that the culture of secrecy – considered necessary to prevent a repetition of 1848, where the open revolutionary organisation of the Young Ireland movement had made it an open target for the British authorities – was a double-edged sword that had ultimately cut against them. While Davitt praised the courage and dependability of the majority of Fenians, he noted that the larger the movement became, the greater the chances of 'unsteady or disreputable elements' entering the ranks who could be enticed into committing acts of treachery.[2] Moreover, the secrecy of the organisation had made it difficult to estimate how far the failure of the rebellion was due to a lack of support on the ground, or, as Anna Parnell put it, 'how far the Irish people, as a whole, were responsible for its ineffectiveness'.[3] Almost half a century later, and a decade after Anna's and Davitt's assessment of it, the oft-dubbed 'premature' Fenian Rebellion of March 1867 was reconceived by IRB leaders as an important object lesson in justifying the insurrection of Easter 1916 – better to act and fail, than to wait for the right moment – which, in turn, led V I Lenin to comment, 'Whoever expects a "pure" revolution will never live to see it'.[4] In the wake of the failures and betrayals of the Fenian organisation, however, there was a widespread feeling that 'the last thing done had left them in a bad position for any more doing'.[5]

With the arrest of its leaders and key operatives and the interception of arms shipments, Dundee's Fenians poured their energies into the Amnesty Association, which, thanks to government perceptions that the Fenians no longer posed a significant threat, was achieving most of its aims.[6] By early 1871, a large number of Fenian prisoners, including all the prominent leaders, had been released. By autumn, Dundee's Amnesty Associates were focused on raising money for the legal defence of Robert Kelly, presently on trial for the murder of police spy, Thomas Talbot, in Dublin.[7] However, with no military or mass popular campaign to rally around, their supporters were becoming demotivated. On 31 October, the committee of the Kelly Defence Fund appealed for collectors in the Catholic parishes of St Mary's, St Andrew's and St Joseph's to 'come forward and make themselves known' at the weekly meetings held at Peter McGuire's in Dudhope Street.[8] Lamenting that 'we would not have made this appeal had it not been for the apathy displayed by the whole of St Mary's Parish, east of Dens Road and Bucklemaker Wynd', Secretary Thomas Morrison reminded the slackers of their duty to 'promote, collect and acknowledge sums received in the [Irish] national newspapers'. Morrison's comment, 'We consider them the proper parties to represent us to the people, and to look after due acknowledgement of their respective sums', and that 'any parties… collecting funds in our name… do not [have] our sanction', also hints at an element of misrepresentation and misappropriation of funds.[9]

Notwithstanding, Dundee's canny Fenians were adept at exploiting every opportunity, and by 1872 a new one had arisen. The Parliamentary Reform Act of 1867 (1868 in Scotland), and the introduction of the secret ballot in 1872, gave a new incentive to constitutional politics, and to the establishment of a Home Rule League to complement the new political party formed by Isaac Butt, the Orange convert to Irish nationalism who had acted as the defence lawyer for several Fenians, most recently Robert Kelly.[10] On 14 January 1872, the advanced nationalists ranked around Morrison called 'the Irishmen of Dundee' to the recently-opened Larch Street schoolroom to debate the question of Home Rule, with a view to establishing a branch of the League. The first proposition, by O'Hara, that it was the duty of Irishmen in Dundee 'to cooperate with their brethren in Ireland, England and Scotland in gaining for Ireland the benefit of her native parliament', was vigorously supported by Morrison, who proposed that they elect a local committee to assist the central one in Dublin in achieving that aim. However, Morrison's proviso that 'Ireland is holding the hand of fellowship to England at present, and if she refused, their differences would only be settled by the sword,' spoke for the Fenian position that their cooperation with the constitutionalists remained conditional.[11]

The motion was carried, and on 12 February 1872 the Dundee Home Rule Association was inaugurated at a packed meeting in the Thistle Hall. Chairman Francis Hagan directed the elections, adhering to a committee structure laid out by Morrison, who seconded Hagan's nomination of James Hennessy, the former chair of the Fenian-controlled Dundee Irish National Institute, as President. Hagan was elected Treasurer, however, both Morrison and Daniel Hannah, arguably the Provisional Committee's most experienced and articulate members, declined nominations. The result was a committee composed of the small business class, the majority of whom were on the electoral register.

Committee of the Dundee Home Rule Association, February 1872[12]

President: James Hennessy, grocer
Secretary: Thaddeus Clancy, draper
Treasurer: Francis Hagan, grocer
Vice President: John Gallacher, draper
Vice President: Andrew Higgins, spirit dealer

John Bradley, funeral undertaker
John Brady, mill foreman
Michael Coyle, spirit merchant
Peter Daniel, grocer
Daniel Flanagan, grocer
James Kelly, mill foreman
William McAuley, grocer

Hugh McCaffrey, cabinet maker
Michael McDonald, spirit merchant
Alex McLauchlan, milliner and draper
Bernard McManus, grocer
Lawrence Phin, grocer and spirit dealer
Michael O'Rourke, joiner
Patrick Redding, grocer and spirit dealer
Edward Rowan, pawnbroker
Patrick Flynn
Francis Hughes
Patrick Traynor
Morgan

Within that class, nevertheless, were shades of difference. Thaddeus Clancy, for example, whose shop was located in the Scouringburn, lived in West Wynd off the Perth Road; and Edward Rowan owned a pawn shop in the Overgate but lived four miles away in the more salubrious setting of Broughty Ferry. At the other end of the scale, grocer Daniel Flanagan continued to live and work at his shop in Polepark Road. Also making an appearance on the committee was former handloom weaver, road labourer and leader of the anti-Orange riot of 12 July 1841, Patrick Redding, who after several attempts of applying and being rejected due to 'unsuitability', had finally obtained a licence for his spirit dealer's shop on the Hilltown.[13]

In declining a nomination for Vice-President, retiring Treasurer Hannah confided that it had been 'a distinct understanding in the Provisional Committee that certain members should not be proposed in consequence of some of their previous affairs in Dundee', adding that he personally was 'not prepared to yield to certain authorities [to whom] they owed no allegiance in political matters'. This cryptic reference to the clergy drew cries of 'Sit down' and hisses, to which Hannah retorted, 'I know of only two animals which hissed – the goose and the serpent, and I am sorry to think that Irishmen should be either', concluding that he hoped 'they would pursue this Home Rule movement to the end', but very much doubted it.[14]

That Morrison and Hannah, who had been at the forefront of advanced Irish nationalism in Dundee for over a decade, initiated the debate on

Home Rule, and helped set up an association in which they had no intention of taking a leading role, suggests they were possibly acting on the recommendations of the IRB Supreme Council, certain members of whom had assured the leaders of the Home Rule Association at its inauguration in Dublin that they would not intervene. However, the Supreme Council was divided on the issue, and, despite any reservations Dundee's Fenians may have had about the limitations of Home Rule, the effectiveness of constitutional methods, and the conservatism of some HRA committee members, the apathy in the organisation following the cessation of military operations meant that the IRB in Dundee were more concerned with rallying the national spirit and keeping the movement alive. Thus, the planting of figures such as Hennessy (whose former presidential status in the Dundee Irish National Institute suggests that he too was a sworn Fenian) in key management positions, can be seen as an attempt by the IRB to maintain a presence and keep their bases covered. From the perspective of the Home Rule movement, figures such as Morrison and Hannah had the organisational experience, working-class support and Irish republican clout that Thaddeus Clancy and the various 'shopcrats' on the committee lacked. Within the large working-class Irish community, Morrison in particular was known and trusted, and his endorsement of the Home Rule Association would have been an instrumental factor in bringing newly enfranchised voters on board.

In time, Hannah's scepticism proved to be well-founded. Nevertheless, the HRA got off to a resounding start with the endorsement of two of the founders of the Home Rule movement in Ireland, A M Sullivan, editor of *The Nation*, and John Martin MP, who addressed a St Patrick's celebration in the Thistle Hall on 19 March, alongside the leader of the Home Rule movement in Scotland, John Ferguson. While Sullivan attributed the woeful state of Ireland to bad English governance, Martin nevertheless declared that Home Rule did not preclude allegiance to the British Crown and encouraged all those who had the franchise to use it to advance Ireland's 'prosperity and happiness'. In supporting O'Hara's restated motion, Ferguson commended the conversion of the *Glasgow Herald* to Home Rule, and quoting an article, concluded, to loud cheers, that 'it was not long since they were called rebels, Fenians and all sorts of bad names for arguing this way'.[15] The meeting, which was chaired by

Hennessy with strong Fenian input, concluded with a pledge by the exclusively male audience to give the Dundee branch of the Home Rule Association their 'earnest and active support', and a final three cheers for O'Donovan Rossa. The HRA followed up by inviting the 'Father of Federalism', Catholic clergyman Thaddeus O'Malley, to address a public meeting in the city. A longstanding Christian Socialist, in 1848, O'Malley had put his head above the parapet when he urged the Irish people to follow the example of the Paris workers and take up arms against the monarchist government. O'Malley also advocated religious conciliation, secular education and 'the complete and absolute divorce of connection between Irish Church and Irish State'.[16] Unlike the Fenians, however, he had espoused a Federalist Union as the solution to Ireland's grievances. Now in his 75th year, O'Malley's theories found new favour in the Home Rule movement whose Dundee promoters he counselled to 'make no parade' about his visit, as the majority of the Irish in Dundee were already in full sympathy, but rather to 'direct their efforts to bringing to the meeting as many Scotch citizens and Conservative Irish as possible'.[17]

The meeting in the Kinnaird Hall was attended by a 'respectable audience of ladies and gentlemen', the ladies being admitted after several complaints about the last meeting. Ferguson, presiding, noted the progress of the Home Rule movement, which, he declared, now had so many advocates, 'the only danger was to discriminate the true Home Ruler from the false – the peoples' day had come, they now wanted the peoples' men'. O'Malley, who was accompanied by Church of Ireland cleric, Professor Joseph Galbraith of Trinity College, Dublin, and Belfast Presbyterian, the Reverend Isaac Nelson, stated that his chief purpose in coming all the way to 'Bonnie Dundee' was to convince the Scottish people that Home Rule 'was not merely an Irish question, [but] had a Scottish and English interest and more than a large imperial [one]'. Unfortunately, O'Malley's equation of federalism as 'bringing the greatest happiness to the greater number', failed to factor in the millions of other British colonial subjects, or to fully appreciate the different relationships of Scotland and Ireland to the British State, and the different experiences of their respective populations under British rule. While both nations may have, as O'Malley put it, 'laboured under disadvantages' within the Union, the Scottish elite had traded national sovereignty for the status of junior partner in the British State and a stake in Empire. Scotland retained control of her key institutions (education and legal systems) and had developed an advanced industrial economy from which the growing urban population derived a comparatively stable livelihood. By contrast, the experience of Ireland was that of a colony – reliant on a transitioning agricultural economy, the prime role of which was to supply the British market, regardless of the needs and conditions of the predominantly Catholic peasant population – a fact of which O'Malley, despite all his crusading rhetoric, was acutely aware. 'There was', he told his audience, 'really no government in Ireland at all; it was absolutely bastard Caesarism, a vacillating regime, not daring to take in hand vigorously any of its afflictions'. 'The present state of government', he noted 'implied a nominal loss…of five million acres', which an independent Parliament in Dublin would 'buy up…and sell in suitable lots to that class now steadily fading away in Ireland, and likewise in [Scotland] – a sturdy peasantry'.[18]

O'Malley's description of a country blighted by bad English government was familiar to the majority of Dundee's Irish population whose support for Home Rule was taken for granted. Converting the mainly Protestant Scots, however, involved overcoming another set of obstacles, to which Nelson alluded in his reference to local Free Church minister, William Knight, who had been threatened with proscription for conducting a joint service with a Unitarian.[19] Ultimately, it fell to the radical Presbyterian Nelson to claim for Home Rule the sympathy of 'all true Scotchmen', to drive home the symbolic lesson of the three clergymen of the Catholic, Episcopal and Presbyterian Churches appearing on the same platform, and to celebrate their association in 'promoting a movement which they believed would advance the welfare and prosperity of their beloved country'.[20]

In 1873, the IRB reconvened in Dublin after a four year hiatus, resolving in its new constitution to 'lend its support to every movement calculated to advance the cause of Irish independence, consistently with the preservation of its own integrity'.[21] This effectively gave the green light for a more direct association with the Home Rule movement which may have given greater cause for celebration at Dundee's St Patrick's Day event which was hosted by the Home Rule Confederation.[22] 'God Save Ireland' and 'Irishmen! Never Forget 'tis a Foreigner's Farm; Your Own Little Isle', proclaimed two of the banners, possibly made by members of the largely female audience. Two women, Mary Hennessy and Agnes Clancy, even made it on to the platform alongside their husbands, James and Thaddeus; HRC Vice-President John Green, guest speaker, R P Blennerhasset, MP for Kerry; and chairman John Ferguson, who began in predictable style by declaring that St Patrick's Day recalled a glorious past when Ireland could boast a nation of warriors 'who did not need to ask permission to carry a gun or pistol'. The applause had barely died down when Ferguson declared he was ashamed to learn that, of the 4,000 Dundee Irishmen eligible to vote, very few were on the electoral roll. 'It was easy to go along to large meetings like this and cheer', he levelled, but they must 'become electors and work in a practical manner' to gain the 'respect of the citizens of England and Scotland' and 'turn the tide' towards the Irish Parliamentary Party (IPP) and the wider Home Rule movement. Having guilt-tripped the audience into supporting Home Rule, Ferguson immediately turned to flatter the Fenians and reconcile their supporters with constitutionalism, and also to reassure the more conservative elements. The Home Rule Association, he told them, had been 'branded, because its members had been Fenians', yet the Prime Minister, Gladstone, had said that the Fenian ranks contained 'the cream of the Irish race'.

> The glory of the Home Rule Association was that it had diverted that cream of the race from an illegitimate conspiracy into a legitimate and constitutional agitation for the repeal of the nation's grievances. Home Rule didn't mean separation. It only meant union on a federal basis…The present condition of Ireland weakened Queen Victoria's throne, and today England dare not fire a shot against a first-class nation. She knew well that Ireland was a reluctant rebel at her rear, and while engaged in a serious foreign conflict she might find Ireland with uplifted hand ready to stab her in the back.[23]

It was a deft piece of rhetoric calculated to appeal to Fenians and Federalists alike, the last sentence in particular serving to reassure the former that supporting constitutional methods did not rule out at return to physical force at a later date.

CHAPTER 3 – CONSTITUTIONALISM, COMPROMISE AND COLLABORATION 1870–79

There is an obvious irony in that Ferguson's advice on becoming electors did not apply to the majority of his audience. Moreover, the large presence of women at Home Rule meetings did not necessarily imply their greater support for constitutionalism – the applause which met Ferguson's references to guns, pistols and armed rebels at England's back rather suggests the opposite – but was more likely a reflection of the dearth of public spaces where women could engage (albeit passively) in political debate. Despite their undoubted influence in the domestic sphere, membership of Irish political networks, from the IRB to the HRC, was confined to men, and it was not until the formation of the Ladies' Land League in 1881 that women had a fully participative political organisation in their own right.

The next public meeting in the town, an address by Isaac Butt, on New Year's Day 1874, again attracted a large female attendance, many of whom had taken their seats shortly after the doors opened at 5 pm. Despite the slow turnout – a consequence of it being the traditional Scottish holiday when the working class could indulge in some welcome rest or revelry – Butt's high profile succeeded in drawing a capacity audience who greeted the speaker with great cheering and waving of hats. Lawyer Butt, who stated that his chief object was 'to place before the Scottish people, deliberately and fairly, the demands of the Irish population', proceeded to posit the argument that 'Ireland was under a system of coercion unparalleled in any civilised country', providing supporting examples, and ending with the question – 'Was that not a system of coercion?' His appeal to Scottish common sense concluded, Butt made a direct appeal to Irish passions, urging them 'to strain every nerve... to secure that great object they had in view; for, compared with the prosperity and liberty of the land of their birth, of the dear old land of their mothers, of the land where their childhood had passed, everything sank into insignificance'.[24]

By manipulating strong emotional connections – to mother and motherland, lost childhood and lost liberty, and projecting the final crowning image of an Irish Parliament 'in the old house on College Green' – Butt encouraged any reluctant Irish nationalists to shelve their doubts and throw their electoral muscle behind the campaign for Home Rule. While Butt had to chivvy the Irishmen of Dundee to exert their political leverage, however, astute local politicians were quick off the mark in cultivating the Irish vote. For example, in a message to the meeting, Councillor Frank Henderson declared himself 'exceedingly sorry and very much disappointed' that a prior engagement had denied him 'the privilege of seeing one who is in so many ways as distinguished and worthy' as Mr Butt. In the event, the two parliamentary candidates endorsed and elected later that February, James Yeaman and Edward Jenkins, were two of only three Scottish MPs who had pledged to support Home Rule.[25]

This result, which attested to the power of the Irish vote, gave a huge boost to the Irish community. The following St Patrick's Day, two celebrations were held in Dundee on the same night: a genteel event by the Catholic clergy in the Kinnaird Hall, which employed professional musicians, and a more dynamic one in the Thistle Hall by 'the national party', as a reporter chose to describe the collective group of Amnesty Associates, Home Rulers and Fenians organised under the convenient umbrella of the Dundee Home Rule Confederation.

It having been agreed that all proceeds from the latter meeting would go to the families of political prisoners, Chairman Hennessy launched into a passionate address on the 'continued incarceration of a few poor Irishmen for the cause of patriotism'. (Dundee had not forgotten Michael Davitt.) Hennessy was supported on the left and right, literally and politically, by members of the broad-based Home Rule council. The toast, 'The Irish at Home' was proposed by canny Fenian Patrick Higgins, followed by 'The Day We Celebrate' by the prodigious Dr Patrick Letters. Thereafter, 'Our Countrymen in British Dungeons' by Thaddeus Clancy, 'The Irish in exile' by the adaptable Francis Hagan and 'The Success of Home Rule' by conservative nationalist Michael Farrell. The interweaving and overlapping of national narratives – from St Patrick to Home Rule to Fenian prisoners – plus the opportunity to engage in patriotic singing (led by local amateurs) and dancing – created a bonding atmosphere which made it their most successful St Patrick's Day celebration to date. Indeed, while noting the attempts by the Catholic clergy to undermine the Home Rule Movement, there was a delicious irony in the fact that, in that establishing its own separate St Patrick's Day event, the Catholic clergy were appropriating a tradition initiated in 1858 by the proto-Fenian National Brotherhood of St Patrick whose Dundee branch they had denounced as a Ribbon front. Over the next decade, St Patrick's Day was to become a contested area amongst those who claimed to speak on behalf of the Irish population.²⁶ For the moment, however, the Fenian-supporting *Flag of Ireland* proclaimed that 'the celebration in Dundee is a signal triumph of the national party', adding that 'the Irish people of Dundee have reason to feel satisfied in that the united causes of nationality, political independence and amnesty continue with time and persecution to advance and to prosper in their hour'.²⁷

It did not take long for the old divisions to re-emerge. The Home Rule Movement, never a solid single body, soon found itself flanked by the Catholic clergy on the one side and the 'Nationalists', a broad euphemism for the Fenians, on the other. While the Scottish Catholic hierarchy was anxious to discourage Irish identification with the politics of the old country, they perceived in the extension of the franchise an opportunity to raise the profile of the Catholic Church in Scotland, and possibly to gain status and influence within the British establishment, which was not incompatible with the Federalist policy of Home Rule. They were, however, aware of alternative opinion which threatened to undermine their influence, particularly within in the more radical elements of Home Rule movement.

Steering the Irish working class away from such influences was a key objective of the St Joseph's Catholic Union – an adjunct of the Catholic Young Men's Society – which opened its meeting rooms in Larch Street in October 1873.²⁸ Amongst various priests present, Father Clapperton of St Andrew's informed members that the Union embodied 'a powerful electoral organisation which will not fail to make its mark – as the Catholic body has done – when the time comes', while parish priest, Father Joseph Holder, warned members against 'that fulsome system of adulation to which working men were at present by designing agitators and unscrupulous writers'.²⁹ Ironically, in 'claiming for himself the title [of 'working man'], Holder deigned to reappropriate the right to act as their political as well as 'spiritual director'.

On the other hand, Dundee's unrepentant Fenians remained unconvinced by the Home Rule movement's broad front approach. The influence of the clergy on office-bearers, Thaddeus Clancy and John Green, who were also prominent members of the CYMS, had already seen off the radical Republican, Daniel Hannah. The '82 Repeal Clubs (named after the year, 1782, when Ireland gained legislative independence) of P J Smyth provided a less compromising front, and when the clubs emerged in Glasgow at the beginning of 1875, Dundee appears to have been quick to follow, thanks in part to Thomas Morrison, Secretary of the Amnesty Association. Indeed, on 24 May, the co-ordinating St Patrick's Club in Capel Street, Dublin, acknowledged the Dundee (John Mitchel), along with the Birkenhead (Repeal) and Liverpool (Robert Emmet) clubs, 'for their praiseworthy efforts in the cause of '82'.[30]

Nevertheless, Dundee's '82 clubbists maintained a comradely relationship with their IRB fellows who chose, for strategic and other reasons, to remain in the Home Rule Confederation.[31] The centenary of O'Connell's birth in August, commemorated by Republicans, Home Rulers and Federalists, saw a large deputation from Dundee travelling to Dublin attend the main 'monster' demonstration, including current HRA office-bearers Hennessy, Farrell and Matthew McKenna. Simultaneously, the Supreme Council of the IRB arranged to facilitate members who wished to attend, and the fact that the Dundee delegation participated in an Amnesty demonstration protesting against the continued incarceration of political prisoners, and an Amnesty Association meeting at Glasnevin afterwards, suggests that there was more than one purpose to their visit.

At around 10 am on Friday, 6 August, the 50,000-strong Amnesty group gathered at Beresford Place from where, led by a horse-drawn carriage conveying a large black banner bearing the words 'Amnesty', 'Remember the Prisoners Still in Chains' and 'God Save Ireland', they proceeded to Kingsbridge Station, the assembly point for the main demonstration. Behind a second carriage bearing IRB members John O'Connor Power, Joseph Biggar and Captain John Kirwan,[32] and the black-uniformed 'Martyrs Band', marched the huge Liverpool contingent accompanied by the Dundee men carrying their banner, embossed with the words, 'God Save Ireland', which *The Irishman* described as 'very tasteful'. Around the left arms of all were the fastened the white ribbons of the Amnesty Association. At Kingsbridge Station, the Amnesty group placed themselves at the head of the procession, whereupon twenty to thirty horsemen dashed up and cut the horses' reins, preventing the march from proceeding. The action was later condemned, *The Irishman* reporting it, erroneously, as an unanticipated and unnecessarily violent protest at the

Amnesty Association being denied a place in the main procession; '[having] resolved to take part, they naturally considered to take up a place at the head would be less disruptive', it claimed defensively.[33] In truth, it was an IRB operation to sabotage the procession in protest at the choice of ex-Lord Chancellor of Ireland, Thomas O'Hagan, to deliver the address on behalf of the nation.[34]

While some of the Dundee men may have participated in IRB or Amnesty Association business under cover of attending the O'Connell centenary commemoration, back at home, the Catholic clergy took advantage of their absence to exert their control over the Home Rule movement.

At a centenary celebration in the Kinnaird Hall, Father McManus, presiding, informed the audience of the half-empty hall – which CYMS member William McVeigh attributed to an ongoing strike in the town – that he had planned on attending the event in Dublin but had been denied the pleasure. Father Holder portrayed Ireland's historic struggle against tyranny in terms of a defence of the Catholic faith, while Father O'Carroll emphasised O'Connell's Catholicism. Solicitor Thomas Fay, who cautioned the audience not to rush into 'premature rebellion' or 'rash measures', reminded them that there was an organisation which in its 'essential principles' carried out O'Connell's ideas, and urged them to become Home Rulers and 'to ask, not for a repeal of the Union, [but] for Home Rule, until rebellion shall seem to be a better measure'. 'If they went this way', he counselled, 'they would deserve to celebrate O'Connell's centenary, and then only would "God Save Ireland"'.[35] Thus, having reduced the father of the Repeal movement to a Catholic Home Ruler, and enrolled the popular Fenian slogan into a more benign cause, the Catholic clergy and their conservative allies attempted to draw the Irish working class away from the militant nationalism of the '82 Clubs and to temper the radical turn in the Home Rule movement.

While the Catholic clergy in Dundee were careful to avoid criticising named groups or individuals – perhaps mindful of how Macdonald's and Clapperton's condemnation of the NBSP's Reading Rooms had directed independently minded Dundee Irishmen to the association, and consequently to the IRB – two of their confreres in Glasgow, Fathers Bernard Tracy and Jeremiah Buckley, chose the occasion of an O'Connell centenary meeting at Pollokshaws to launch a smear campaign against the leader of the Glasgow Home Rule Association, John Ferguson. Amongst other things, Tracy, who conducted his campaign through press and pulpit, alleged that the Belfast-born Protestant's 'patriotism' was motivated by 'trade', in other words, a desire to gain contracts for his printing firm, and suggested that he was guilty of financial impropriety for drawing his travel expenses from branch funds.

Ferguson did the honourable thing and resigned, rallying the Glasgow HRA to his defence. Despite his promotion of federalism, Ferguson was generally respected amongst advanced nationalists as a social progressive, a radical Home Ruler, and an 'honourable man'. He was also extremely astute, and his resignation had the desired effect of unifying the fragmentary Home Rule Confederation. The HRA in Dundee, 'Catholic to a man', passed a resolution expressing their 'deepest sympathy... on account of the unmerited insults cast at [Ferguson] by two clergymen of our Church', and placing their 'unbounded confidence' in his leadership. Hennessy also announced that the deputation to the O'Connell centenary would not be charging the branch for their expenses, although the committee had resolved to pay them. A further resolution, proposed by Thaddeus Clancy, spoke for the consensus that 'from lessons learned practically in times past in Dundee, [it is] our firm conviction that sectarianism is the most damaging principle that could be introduced into Irish politics'.[36] Following a unanimous vote of confidence by the Glasgow HRA, endorsed by Dundee and other branches, Ferguson was reinstated.

Over the next few months, the HRA in Dundee, particularly those members of the IRB who had opted to give Home Rule a fair trial, directed their efforts into combatting the clergy's attempts to turn the movement in a more conservative direction, and possibly to reverse the drift to the '82 Clubs. Indeed, in September the HRA deferred consideration of contesting the School Board election until after St Patrick's Day, 'having their hands full' with the 'opposition meeting' planned by the clergy in the Kinnaird Hall. St Patrick's Day 1876 saw three celebrations in Dundee: by the Catholic clergy, the HRA, and the 'Nationalists', who had begun recruiting members for a new '82 Club, to be named the Red Hand Repeal Club, in early March.[37] The HRA event took place in the Thistle Hall, which was decorated with banners reflecting a broad range of sentiments, ranging from the portentous 'Success to Home Rule – United We Stand, Divided We Fall', the forthright 'Give Us Our Rights' and 'Set the Prisoners Free', and the enduring 'God Save Ireland', to the short-lived 'Friendship with England'. In a show of non-sectarianism and conciliation, guest speaker Captain Kirwan combatted objections to Protestants taking an active part in the Home Rule movement, declaring that if he had to choose between the interests of English [sic] and Irish Catholics on the one hand and the religious and civil freedoms of the Irish people on the other, he would choose the latter. Chairman Matthew McKenna, mindful of the following day's press reports, assured a wider audience that Home Rule did not imply a change in the settlement of property or the establishment of a religious ascendancy: 'If their Scotch friends understood them as they should, they would not consider them so revolutionary as imagined'. Conversely, McKenna also broached the issue at the heart of revolutionary Irish nationalism – the devasting human impact of the transformation of the land to a capitalist agricultural economy. 'Somebody had told him that Ireland [was] yearly improving', McKenna related, yet the fact that 'more cattle, sheep etc. [were] yearly exported... only show[ed] that Ireland [was] being turned into a sheep walk'.[38] Within three years, this very issue was to erupt in a bitter and protracted land war.

The following April, McKenna told a meeting in Lochee that the recent differences which had arisen in connection with their body had been made '"all right" – they were now all united and at peace', the coded language suggesting that the Fenian reformers within the Home Rule movement had dissuaded some of their disaffected comrades from going over to the new '82 Club, or that they had subverted the Dundee Home Rule Association and were hoping to do the same in Lochee. However, McKenna's revelation of advanced plans to form a branch of the HRA in the suburb triggered a heated discussion during which Lochee men Davis and Roche asserted that one already existed (of which Edward Roche, a Fenian, was President), that all was 'in working order', and they resented the Dundee deputation coming in to dictate to their men. Fortunately, quick-thinking Hennessy saved the day by proposing that the meeting ratify the election of the existing officers, and the evening ended in a convivial manner with congratulations being exchanged all round.[39]

The positive mood was not to last. Besides the nationalists' opposition to British federalism, the failure of parliamentarianism to achieve even a modicum of Home Rule was becoming increasingly evident. On 20 August, acting on reports of the damage being done to the organisation and concluding they were no closer to advancing their revolutionary aims than three years earlier, the IRB Supreme Council voted to end its agreement with the Home Rule movement, and instructed all its members to withdraw from active cooperation within six months. The IRB was divided on the issue, however, and while many members chose to cut their formal ties with the movement, others such as Hennessy and Roche had the Dundee and Lochee Associations where they wanted them for all practical purposes and remained in position a while longer while paring back their involvement in the promotion of the movement itself.

Indeed, practical considerations appear to have forged a local arrangement whereby influential middle-class IRB men such as Hennessy and Roche worked the Home Rule Association to keep the prisoner issue in the public eye by placing it on the agenda of every public meeting, and to maximise funds by exploiting the comparatively greater wealth of the businessmen in it. This was bolstered by common membership of the Amnesty Association, which Dundee branch included Fenians Thomas Morrison and James Hennessy, young cosmopolitan nationalist Thomas Flanagan and moderate Home Rulers Matthew McKenna and Thaddeus Clancy. The amount of money raised by the Dundee Amnesty Association is unknown. However, recognition of their contribution is indicated by the place of honour allotted to them at the mass Amnesty procession in Dublin in August 1875.

One of Hennessy's last official roles in the HRA was to chair a meeting endorsing Thaddeus Clancy as a candidate in the Eighth (Hawkhill/ Scouringburn) Ward in the municipal elections of November 1876. While Clancy was one of the strongest-polling Home Rule candidates in Scotland, his 479 votes were insufficient to defeat the sitting candidate Hugh Ballingall (742).[40] Nevertheless, the *Courier* commended Clancy as 'very good candidate [who] had a 'deal of prejudice to contend with, [being regarded] as the representative of an alien idea' which, they opined, lost him many votes. The *Courier's* anti-Home Rule prejudice was offset on this occasion by its antipathy towards Dundee's Liberal 'clique' of which it claimed Ballingall was 'not the most uncompromising supporter'. The *Courier* advised that if Clancy were to stand at a future date he would find greater favour, providing, it implied, he focused less on Irish politics and more on local issues. The prospect of such a scenario had already led one Dundee 'Nationalist' to protest via the Irish national press that Home Rule was being downgraded to the horse-dealings of local government. The cryptically-named 'Phoenix' criticised the tactic of 'turning Home Rulers into ward politicians, which if not checked, will cause much dissension amongst Irishmen', and advised the Home Rule executive to 'discountenance this part of their programme'.[41] Phoenix also alluded to the dishonourable conduct of Clancy, who had written to Ballingall stating that he would not stand against him, but had later declared when pressed that 'he considered the [written] pledge a very small matter'. 'If pledges are small matters made only to be broken', Phoenix insisted, 'why did the Home Rulers condemn Mr Yeaman MP for breaking his to them, [and] what is the use of seeking pledges at all from representatives?'[42] Indeed, when Yeaman had violated his election pledge to support Home Rule and an amnesty for Irish political prisoners, the Dundee Home Rule-Nationalist combine withdrew their support, pinning their hopes on Edward Jenkins, an English upper-class politician in the carpetbagging mould. When Jenkins also violated the pledge, Ferguson's warning about the danger of 'false Home Rulers' and political opportunists jumping on the bandwagon, appeared to have come to pass.[43]

On 16 November, the *Courier* noted 'the Nationalists are proving too many and too strong for [the Home Rule movement]. There have long been symptoms that it would be so, and they are becoming more and more distinctly developed'. It pointed to the 'Nationalist' take-over of a Home Rule meeting in Glasgow to be addressed by Captain Kirwan, who, ironically, was preparing to announce his resignation from the Home Rule Confederation, citing its dismal prospects and the failure of its parliamentary representatives to do their duty.[44] The *Courier*, however, posited 'a better explanation':

> The Home Rule Party is a revolutionary party, but they have always aimed at doing things by halves, and now they are discovering that they must yield to the 'whole hog' men. Nor is this a bad change for the maintenance of the unity and the institutions of the State. It is desirable that the revolutionists

should speak out plainly and fully, which the Irish Nationalists most certainly do; for one consequence of that is to strengthen the cause of those who are loyally and patriotically opposed to revolutions.[45]

Unlike the previous three years, St Patrick's Day of 1877 was marked by a single event in the Kinnaird Hall organised by the Home Rule Confederation, whose Lochee arm roped in the Camperdown Works' band to lead a march around the principal streets of Lochee and Dundee. While the garrulous ex-MP for Galway and self-proclaimed originator of the obstructionist tactic, Frank Hugh O'Donnell, was given an enthusiastic reception, the most significant part of the meeting was the passing of resolutions by 'the Irishmen of Dundee' withdrawing support from their pledge-breaking MPs and vowing to use their influence to prevent the return of any candidate opposed to granting Home Rule to Ireland, and also 'to defeat any member of the present government seeking to represent this borough, or any other', opposed to the release of the political prisoners.[46] The transition from supporting their parliamentary representatives to seeking to undermine any parliamentarian opposed to their aims, was welcomed by many militant nationalists who saw it as a vindication of their tactics, as they did the shift to a new, more aggressive form of parliamentarianism, branded by Daniel O'Donoghue, the pro-establishment MP for Tralee, as 'Fenianism in a new form'.[47]

On 23 September, the Dundee HRC arranged a meeting in the Thistle Hall, to be addressed by two of the most prominent parliamentary obstructionists, John O'Connor Power and Charles Stewart Parnell. A concerted push on ticket sales procured a full house; those hoping to hear the charismatic Parnell's fighting talk were left feeling short-changed when the chairman, James O'Kane, produced a telegram announcing he had been 'detained in Belfast'. Parnell had travelled to that city the previous day after addressing meetings in Greenock, Paisley and two particularly testing ones in Dumbarton and Hamilton, where he had been assailed by a group of hostile 'nationalists' led by Limerick Fenian John Daly, who accused O'Connor Power of being a coward (in his absence, at the Dumbarton meeting) and a traitor (to his face, in Hamilton).[48] O'Connor Power, having been thus rudely alerted to nationalist sensitivities, yet desperate to draw supporters back into the foundering Home Rule movement, used the Dundee meeting to salvage his reputation and talk up the policy of obstruction: 'if it meant resistance to bad measures [or] was likely to be effectual in depriving a tyrannical Government of its power', he effused, 'he would make no apology for being an Irish obstructionist'. Confiding that the Home Rule Party would be powerless without local organisations, he urged the Irishmen of Dundee to enrol in the Home Rule Confederation and support the policy which would '[retrieve] the inalienable rights of the Irish people'. The meeting concluded with an affirmation of the 'signal failure of the conciliation policy', an approval and endorsement of the 'vigorous and energetic... Biggar Parnell [one]', and the customary rendition of 'God Save Ireland'. There was, however, no clamour to join the Home Rule Confederation.[49]

On 7 November, the Dundee HRA called a meeting in the Albion Hall, Overgate, with the aim of uniting 'the Irishmen [of] Dundee and Lochee [of] all shades of Irish national opinion' into one political party with the objects of promoting self-government for Ireland, increasing Irish representation on all local governing bodies, and countering anti-Irish propaganda in the local press.[50] While the 400-strong meeting, which included a specially invited audience of 'intelligent' and influential Irishmen, got as far as appointing a committee to convene meetings in nine municipal wards with a view to assessing and mobilising the Irish electoral strengths of each, there was, however, a distinct lack of engagement at grassroots level.

The HRA's plans, devised by Vice-President Dr Patrick Letters, failed to consider key considerations. Besides the political differences that existed between Republicans and Home Rulers, there were inherent practical limitations. Although some upward mobility had occurred in the 1860s and early 1870s, the majority of Dundee's 35,000-strong Irish population remained in low-paid, semi- or unskilled jobs and did not meet the qualifications for the franchise. Doubtless those independently minded members of the skilled working class who did, and certainly the radical nationalists amongst them, would have hackled at being treated as voting fodder by middle-class Home Rulers, as they may also have done at Letters' presumption that the Home Rule movement 'had no more devoted supporters than men whose opinions were sometimes called extreme'.[51]

Women, who formed the majority of the Irish population, and were proportionately represented at Irish political demonstrations, were excluded entirely from the HRA's plans and rhetoric. While Letters' plans formed the organisational structure for the Irish National League from the mid-1880s, and the United Irish League (UIL) from 1898 through to the 1910s, for the moment, the majority of working-class Irishmen and Irishwomen appeared to have no desire to commit to a local Irish party which offered them no meaningful role beyond being cheerleaders for place-hunting 'shopcrats' and publicans, or to support a parliamentary one which had proven so ineffective in dealing with the deteriorating economic situation in Ireland, a deep-rooted situation by which the course of their own lives had been greatly determined.

In December, an appeal on behalf of the families of the last political prisoners, citing the exhausted fund of the central committee in Cork, elicited a £10 donation from an *ad hoc* Dundee committee headed by Fenians Thomas Morrison, Patrick McCann and William McArdle.[52] The language used – 'The wife of the Political prisoner that sacrifices all that is dear to him for Motherland, should be the Nation's care – the child of the Martyr is the Nation's orphan' – endorsed the view that the political prisoners were living martyrs to the cause, and spoke to the concerns, as well as encouraging the support of women. While the accompanying letter apologised for the small amount, it nevertheless acknowledged 'the liberal contribution' of the Dundee Irishmen and Irishwomen 'who so generously supported us at a time when England's decaying trade has greatly influenced that matter'. After the boom years of the 1860s and early 1870s, the Dundee textile industry had entered a period of depression, and the resultant under- and unemployment and dropping wage rates had hit the working-class population particularly hard. In a positive and perhaps not unrelated development, however, Morrison *et al* also took the opportunity to inform 'their scattered brethren' that 'the Nationalists of Dundee are up and doing'.[53]

The release of the last political prisoners in January 1878 marked the end of the one issue upon which the Fenians and Home Rulers were agreed, and, for the last few members of the IRB conducting amnesty work within the Home Rule Confederation, their main reason for being there. By St Patrick's Day 1878, the IRB were in control of a political agenda in which they appear to have had significant popular support. By contrast, the Home Rule movement had imploded, and the HRC reduced to the status of a gentlemen's club whose highpoint in 1878 was helping to organise an exclusive banquet to celebrate the installation of the first Bishop of the restored Vatican See of Dunkeld, George Rigg. Home Rule was not on the agenda and the *Courier* noted that toasts to the Pope and the Queen were 'warmly responded to'.[54]

When the IRB organised their St Patrick's Day celebration in a packed Thistle Hall on 18 March 1878, Home Rule was certainly not on the agenda, nor indeed on that of the Catholic clergy's parallel meeting in the Kinnaird Hall. The main speaker at the former was staunch anti-Home Ruler John Daly, formerly of the Amnesty Association, with whom Dundee's Fenian-driven Amnesty branch had likely conducted business. Indeed, Edward Fox Coyne, the peripatetic physical force Fenian who presided, had lived in the town at the time of the Association's formation, and had met and married his Dundee-born wife, jute spinner Margaret McKenzie, there.[55] An anonymous 'Home Ruler' was the first to dispute the *Courier*'s report of the 'Nationalist' event which placed the office bearers of the HRC on the platform alongside their most vociferous critic and the editor of *The Irishman*, John O'Connor. '[That] would have been impossible', he lamented, 'as, unfortunately, the Dundee branch of the said Association is at present in a disorganised condition'.[56] Likewise, Coyne, who was well-acquainted with Irish nationalist circles in Dundee, corrected *The Irishman*, which had reproduced the *Courier*'s report:

> There was not a gentleman on the platform who has ever been identified with Home Rule in Dundee except one, and [he] has withdrawn from that body several months ago. The gentlemen on the platform have far holier hopes of the consummation of the struggle their fathers have maintained for seven centuries than to now patch up a dishonourable compromise with England in the hour of her decline, and of Ireland's approaching opportunity.[57]

Here, Coyne was echoing Daly who, in alluding to Britain's imperial anxieties over the Balkans, had stated, in an oft-repeated dictum, that 'England granted concessions [only] when she was in dread of losing some territory or being invaded. She was not far from that difficulty at present, and that difficulty was Ireland's opportunity'.[58] In sentiments reflecting the slogans adorning the wall – 'the Blood of the Patriot is the Seed of Liberty' and 'Remember Emmett' – Daly called on Ireland's sons 'to prepare to give freedom to her daughters and to show their preparedness to die in defence of Ireland's liberties and independence'.[59] How Dundee's doughty 'Irish daughters' – who may have possessed a desire to do the job themselves – felt about being assigned the role of defenceless victims is unknown. The sustained applause which met Daly's call to action suggests they were accustomed to the antiquated tropes of nationalist rhetoric and recognised a cue when they heard one.

Daly's visit came hard on the heels of an inspection tour of the seven IRB provinces (Scotland included) by Revolutionary Director Dr William Carroll of Clan na Gael, who kickstarted a process of reorganisation and reconciliation which concluded in the summer of 1879 with a tour by John Devoy.[60] Throughout this period, Dundee appears to have remained indifferent to the conflict which arose between Edinburgh and the Scottish District Headquarters in Glasgow, allegedly over control of district funds, but possibly due to personal antagonisms, or the traditional rivalry which existed between Scotland's two largest cities.[61] By July 1879, the officers of every circle in every district had been replaced or re-elected and arms trafficking and training re-established. Heading the Dundee circle was Edward (Ned) Lynam, a 24-year-old factory worker of Blackness Road, who was elected President of the Dundee '98 Club on 3 August 1879. The original '98 Club, founded in Dublin to organise celebrations for the centenary of Robert Emmet's birth the year before, had inspired the establishment of similar clubs throughout Ireland and the diaspora. As the name suggests, their ostensible function was the commemoration of key events in the long struggle for Irish freedom, and of figures of patriotic resistance who has fallen in the fight.[62] Like the '82 Clubs before them they also functioned as a cover for IRB activity. Indeed, the Dundee '98 Club incorporated the name and the membership of the John Mitchel '82 Club, including veteran campaigners Thomas Morrison and Patrick McCann, plus a new generation of second-generation Dundee Irishmen, including G McKay, James Devine and James Peter Casey, all of whom who adhered to the physical force tradition. From its reading rooms at

48 Wellgate, the Dundee '98 Club sought to replicate the 'mental preparation' function of the Dundee Irish National Institute (of which McCann had been a committee member) and to improve the calibre of its members by exposing them to nationalist poetry and prose, and information on political developments in Ireland. The first meeting on 3 August included a recitation of Emmet's speech from the dock by McKay, followed by readings from *The Irishman* and the *Irish World* from Lynam and Devine.[63] In 1876, the latter New York-based publication of Patrick Ward had launched a Skirmishing Fund to finance a bombing campaign in Great Britain (from which, unlike later campaigns, Scotland was not to be excluded), and was now moving in an increasingly socially radical direction, changing its name to the *Irish World and American Industrial Liberator* in 1878, and publishing articles promoting land reform and the nascent Irish National Land League.[64]

Before the Land League came into being, key preoccupations and patterns of activity had emerged within the sphere of Irish republicanism in Dundee. Central to these was the notion of fundraising as a practical means supporting the struggle for Irish independence and the people most severely impacted by British rule in Ireland, and, specifically, by their resistance to it. The fact that fundraising was a mundane, diffuse and unremarkable activity, and that its real purpose was often hidden under the guise of legal and 'safe' causes, has possibly resulted in it being under-researched in favour of more sensational military and controversial political activity, records of which are more widely available and easier to fathom. Nevertheless, it was one of the most enduring areas of Irish solidarity work throughout the Irish diaspora, and one in which the Irish population of Dundee punched well above its numerical weight.

Fundraising for causes directly and indirectly related to Ireland's national rights stretched back to the Repeal and Young Ireland movements, through the MacMahon Sword Testimonial, *The Irishman* Indemnity Fund and Father Patrick Lavelle's fund for the poor of Partry – of which the latter spawned further campaigns for the *Free Press* Defence and the Lavelle Sustainment Funds. Although the Lavelle campaign was relatively short-lived, through its interrelated committees, Dundee's advanced Irish nationalists gained valuable experience of raising and managing money and moving it discreetly across different fronts. Besides the subsequent *sub rosa* funding of insurrectionary expeditions and arms purchases, Dundee's Irish republicans were also the driving force behind legal campaigns such as the State Prisoner Fund, the Amnesty Association and other related funds to support political prisoners and their dependants, including, most recently in 1878–9, the most revered and persecuted ex-prisoner of all, O'Donovan Rossa.[65]

Underpinning these endeavours was the concept of economic solidarity, whereby a common experience of hardship merged with a collective memory of dispossession and displacement to generate a deep affinity with those currently struggling under and against British rule in Ireland. The strength of fundraising operations lay in their grassroots organisation through which experienced and trusted administrators co-ordinated a network of collectors across different areas of the town, who took responsibility for organising penny collections within smaller social networks. Here, the participation and contributions of Dundee's large constituency of Irishwomen was encouraged and valued.

Nevertheless, the '98 Club, like the IRB, remained a male affair, and while its public preoccupations of commemorating dead Irish martyrs and supporting living ones drew on the sympathies and amassed copper coins of the Irish community, that alone did little to develop a mass political consciousness or to encourage a deeper political involvement on the part of the Irish working class, the majority of whom were too overwhelmed by their own economic travails and domestic woes to give much more than a rousing cheer for the bold Robert Emmett or the doughty O'Donovan Rossa.

As the worst Irish harvest since An Gorta Mór threw the festering issue that lay at the heart of British injustice in Ireland into sharp relief, a popular resistance movement emerged which gave a new impetus to the struggle for national independence. That issue was the ownership of the land, and the movement was the Irish National Land League.

Endnotes to Chapter 3

1. Address by Isaac Butt to a conference of the Irish Home Rule League, Dublin Rotunda, 18 November 1873.
2. Michael Davitt, *The Fall of Feudalism in Ireland: Or the Story of the Land League Revolution* (London and New York: Harper and Row, 1904), pp111–12.
3. Anna Parnell [1907] and Dana Hearne (ed), *The Tale of a Great Sham* (Dublin: Arlen House, 1986), p39.
4. V I Lenin, *Imperialism, the Highest Stage of Capitalism* (1916).
5. Parnell, *Tale of a Great Sham*, p38.
6. Likewise, the passage of the Land Bill of 1870 was a concession to Irish nationalists to encourage constitutionalism and forestall a return to armed resistance.
7. RIC agent, Talbot, had died on the operating table after surgeon, Sir William Stokes, botched a procedure to remove a bullet from his neck. Kelly's lawyer, Isaac Butt, succeeded in getting Kelly acquitted. He was, however, later jailed for killing another man.
8. Dudhope Street, to the east of Barrack Park, was at the interface of the three parishes, which organisational districts were adopted as they provided a ready-made structure with which Dundee's mainly Catholic Irish nationalists were familiar. The area around Dudhope Street also housed a significant number of Irish (mainly Anglican) Protestants who had come to Dundee to find work in the wake of the Great Hunger.
9. *The Irishman*, 4 November 1871.
10. The 1868 (Scotland) Act extended the vote to all male householders and male lodgers paying £10 a year and gave Scotland seven extra Scottish seats in the House of Commons, making Dundee a two-seat constituency and Glasgow a three-seat one. The Ballot Act of 1872 curtailed the bribery, intimidation and coercion conducted by Irish landlords and their agents.
11. *Dundee Courier*, 15 January 1872.
12. *Dundee Courier*, 13 February 1872.
13. *Dundee Courier*, 13 February 1872; Dundee Directory, 1871–72; Dundee Electoral Register, 1871–72.
14. *Dundee Courier*, 13 February 1872. Thaddeus Clancy, with whom Hannah clearly had differences, insisted that they 'could never go wrong if they moved with their clergymen'.
15. *The Herald* later claimed that the excerpt read by Ferguson: 'What we want is that the affairs of England, Scotland, Ireland and Wales should be left to these countries', did not appear in its columns. *Glasgow Herald*, 20 March 1872.
16. Fergus A D'Arcy, 'Federalist, Social Radical and Anti-Sectarian: Thaddeus O'Malley (1797–1877)', in Moran, Radical Irish Priests, pp91–110.

17   *Dundee Courier*, 14 September 1872.
18   *Dundee Courier*, 20 September 1872.
19   In his defence, Knight stated he was following his 'highest convictions of duty', and had broken no Church law, upon which point the Dundee Free Church Presbytery were forced to drop proceedings against him. *Dundee Courier*, 16 July 1872. In early 1874, Knight left the Free Church and joined the Church of Scotland, taking his congregation with him. In 1876, he become Professor of Moral Philosophy at St Andrew's University, eventually joining the Episcopal Church in 1879.
20   *Dundee Courier*, 20 September 1872.
21   Ó Broin speculates that the Convention, which was attended by representatives from all seven provinces and districts, including Scotland, met 'around St Patrick's day'; however, the exact date is unknown. León Ó Broin, *Revolutionary Underground: The Story of the Irish Republican Brotherhood, 1858–1924* (Dublin: Gill & Macmillan, 1976), pp7, 11.
22   The Home Rule Confederation of Great Britain was founded in Manchester in January 1873.
23   *Dundee Courier*, 19 March 1873.
24   *Dundee Courier*, 2 January 1874.
25   The other being James Fortescue Harrison, Liberal MP for Kilmarnock. Of the 23 Home Rule-supporting MPs in England, the majority were in the north-east, including Morpeth, Gateshead, Tyneside and the two Newcastle seats. Like the three in Wales, Cardiff, Flint and Merthyr Tydfil, most of these constituencies had a high Irish and working-class population and radical tradition or, in the case of Chelsea, a radically minded MP in the person of Radical Liberal, Charles Dilke, who was also a staunch republican.
26   See R McCready, 'St Patrick's Day in Dundee, 1850–1900', in Frank Ferguson and James McConnell (eds), *Ireland and Scotland in the Nineteenth Century* (Dublin: Four Courts Press, 2009), pp134–46.
27   *Flag of Ireland*, 25 March 1874.
28   The rules of St Joseph's Catholic Union state that the post of Spiritual Director was held by the parish priest who had a veto on all proceedings. DPL, LC, 187 (3), Rules of St Joseph's Catholic Union, 22 September 1874.
29   'Opening of St Joseph's Catholic Union Rooms', *Dundee Advertiser*, 16 October 1873.
30   *Irishman*, 29 May 1875.
31   Ó Catháin identifies the IRB at this stage as encompassing three elements: traditionalists, reformists and Ribbonmen. Ó Catháin, *Irish Republicanism in Scotland*, p93.
32   Power and Biggar, Irish Party MPs for Mayo and Cavan respectively, pioneered the tactic of parliamentary obstructionism which Biggar is credited with devising. Kirwan was General Secretary of the Home Rule Confederation.

Chapter 3 – Constitutionalism, Compromise and Collaboration 1870–79

33 *Irishman*, 14 August 1875.
34 The action was deemed counter-productive, and the IRB men involved were disciplined. Ó Broin, *Revolutionary Underground*, p13.
35 *Northern Warder*, 10 August 1875.
36 *The Irishman*, 28 August 1875.
37 *The Irishman*, 6 March 1876.
38 *Dundee Courier*, 18 March 1876; *Flag of Ireland*, 25 March 1876.
39 *Dundee Courier*, 20 April 1876.
40 Home Rule candidates Arthur Skivington in Greenock and Patrick Shields in Paisley also polled well, but failed to win seats. Ó Catháin, *Irish Republicanism in Scotland*, p100.
41 *Dundee Courier*, 10 November 1876.
42 *Flag of Ireland*, 21 October 1876; *The Irishman*, 28 October 1876. The identity of Phoenix is unknown. However, his criticism of the HRA's failure to acknowledge its collection of money for a testimonial to Isaac Butt, suggests it may have been Secretary of the Amnesty Association, Thomas Morrison.
43 *Dundee Courier*, 9 December 1875.
44 Kirwan resigned at the end of November and moved to Canada two weeks later. *The Nation*, 9 December 1876.
45 *Dundee Courier*, 16 November 1876.
46 *The Irishman*, 24 March 1877.
47 Letter from Daniel O'Donoghue MP to Cardinal Cullen, 6 August 1877, Cardinal Cullen papers, 329/3.
48 According to *The Irishman*, O'Connor Power had not been invited to the Dumbarton meeting.
49 *The Irishman*, 29 September 1877.
50 *The Irishman*, 17 November 1877.
51 *The Irishman*, 17 November 1877.
52 *The Irishman*, 22 December 1877.
53 *The Irishman*, 26 January 1878.
54 *Dundee Courier*, 6 August 1878.
55 Edward and Margaret, who both lived in Blackness Road, were married at St Joseph's Chapel on 30 July 1869, when they were aged 22 and 19 respectively and Edward Coyne was working as a shoemaker. The couple then moved, along with their growing family, to India, then Stirling, and then to Glasgow where Coyne was presently based. Marriage record for Edward Fox Coyne and Margaret McKenzie; Census of Scotland, 1881.
56 *Dundee Courier*, 21 March 1878.
57 *The Irishman*, 6 April 1878.

58 The conclusion of the Russo-Turkish War in Russia's favour in February 1878, and the annexation of former Ottoman territories, led to speculation that Britain would go to war against Russia in defence of its imperial, i.e., trading and other economic interests. The conflict was resolved by the Treaty of Berlin in July 1878.

59 *Dundee Courier*, 19 March 1878. Coyne went on to be associated with the hard-militant Irish National Invincibles, and Daly to be falsely implicated in a dynamiting conspiracy for which he was imprisoned alongside future leader of the 1916 Easter Rising, Thomas Clarke, who Daly's niece, Kathleen, later married.

60 Ó Broin, *Revolutionary Underground*, pp22–23. The Revolutionary Directory was established in 1877 to coordinate organisation between the IRB and American-based Clan na Gael, of which latter organisation Carroll was a key member.

61 William O'Brien and Desmond Ryan (eds), *Devoy's Post Bag*, Volume1 (Dublin: C J Fallon, 1948), p257.

62 Guy Beiner, *Forgetful Remembrance: Social Forgetting and Vernacular Historiography of a Rebellion in Ulster* (Oxford: OUP, 2018), p352.

63 *The Irishman*, 19 August 1879.

64 Paul Bew, *Land and the National Question in Ireland, 1858–82* (Dublin: Gill & Macmillan, 1978), p48; Niall Whelehan, *The Dynamiters: Irish Nationalism and Political Violence in the Wider World, 1867–1900* (Cambridge: Cambridge University Press, 2012), p71.

65 The O'Donovan Rossa Testimonial arose out of an appeal in the *Irish World* in August 1878 detailing the destitute condition of Rossa and his family, and reporting the formation of an interim committee 'to receive subscriptions until more definite steps can be taken'. On the other side of the Atlantic, Rossa's old comrade, IRB Head Centre, Charles Kickham, issued a printed address to 'the Irish People' urging the establishment of local committees to organise collections, following which committees were formed in Dundee, Glasgow, Hamilton and Partick, as well as Liverpool, Sheffield, and other centres of Irish population. *Irish World*, 21 August 1878; *Irishman*, 2 November 1878.

CHAPTER 4

The Land for the People
1879–89

Oh! By the God who made us all – the seigneur and the serf –
Rise up! And swear, to hold this day your own green Irish turf;
Rise up! And plant your feet as men where now you crawl as slaves,
And make your harvest fields your camps, or make of them your graves.[1]

To the women of Ireland – Courage! The Ladies' Land League is still undaunted, cool, and defiant. We await the arrival of the enemy. Seven months have passed away since Michael Davitt called upon the women of Ireland to take their places besides those of their brethren in the struggle for the regeneration of their country. Now it is on you, women of Ireland, that the fate of your country depends. Instruct the people to respect and obey the teaching of our imprisoned leaders, Davitt, Dillon and Parnell. To the breach! To the breach! If one of your members be arrested, let another, ay, even the very children, be taught to take your places. Fill up the gap. Our reasons are inexhaustible. The cause of right, the cause of justice, faith and fatherland, is on our side. Remember Limerick. God save Ireland.[2]

THE IRISH NATIONAL LAND LEAGUE was a pivotal movement in Irish history, coming out of a long tradition of agrarian protest and community defence, but also marking a turning point in modern social and political struggle. Its key principles – that the poor tenant farmers of Ireland should not have to pay unfair rents, and that those who lived and worked on the land had the right to own it – struck a chord with Dundee's large Irish population, the majority of whom had ended up there as a consequence of a rapacious British land policy which had changed little since An Gorta Mór.[3] For many amongst them, the famine was an enduring and potent memory, and the knowledge that they may well have been in the same situation as the present generation of Irish tenant farmers had they not been driven out in the first place, aroused a strong sense of kinship and solidarity. Initially, hunger, poverty and displacement had left them ill-prepared to fight back. By the time An Gorta Beag (The Little Hunger or Famine) hit at the end of the 1870s, they had the motivation, the knowledge, and, for those who had been involved with the Fenian and Home Rule movements, the political grounding and organisational experience to effectively support and participate in the Land League's campaign of resistance. Moreover, despite their radically contrasting rural and urban environments, the fact the vast majority of Dundee's large Irish working-class population were employed in the low-waged textile industry and lived in cramped, poorly sanitised housing, enabled them to relate directly to the fight waged by their rural compatriots against rack-renting landlords.

While having a precedent in the Tenant Right League of the early 1850s, the Land League itself originated in the founding of a Tenants' Defence Association in Castlebar, County Mayo, on 26 October 1878, and took off after a monster meeting in Irishtown, County Mayo, on 20 April 1879, organised by the recently-liberated Michael Davitt. The Irish National Land League was officially established in Dublin on 21 October 1879, with the charismatic Charles Stewart Parnell (prospective leader of the Home Rule Party following the death of Isaac Butt in May) as President, and Davitt, Andrew Kettle and Thomas Brennan as joint Secretaries, representing, collaboratively, the League's dual strategy of political advocacy and mass civil action.

The Land League made its debut amongst Dundee's Irish community at a Manchester Martyrs commemoration on 24 November 1879, an event organised by the town's advanced nationalists (Fenians) which included members of the '98 Club. As keynote speaker, Michael Davitt was scheduled to give an address on the land question. When he was re-arrested, on 19 November, however, along with Land League activists James Daly and J B Killen, the demand for tickets rocketed. A protest demonstration was promptly organised, which an estimated 20,000 people turned out to support as it wended its way, to the accompaniment of the Emmett, St Patrick's and Lochee Flute Bands, from Larch Street (to which muster point the Lochee band had already led several hundred people, flanked by 1,200 more) down the Scouringburn, West Port, Nethergate and High Street to the Kinnaird Hall, where an estimated 2,000–3,000 people, a 'considerable portion' of whom were women, crammed themselves into the 1800-capacity venue. Commemorative banners proclaiming, 'Remember Allan, Larkin and O'Brien', 'Remember Emmett' and 'God Save Ireland' adorned the walls alongside large placards addressing the issue of the moment – 'Down with Tyrant Landlords'; 'Davitt, Daly and Killen, our sympathy is with you'; and 'Our indignation against the authors of their arrest'. John Torley of Duntocher, Head Centre of the IRB in Scotland, presided, while John Ferguson of the Home Rule Confederation and Land League Executive stood in for Davitt. Although the meeting was organised by Irish Republicans – who, unlike the Home Rulers, had maintained a popular base in Dundee throughout the previous decade – the platform spanned the spectrum of Irish nationalist opinion, from former office bearers of the Home Rule Confederation, Thaddeus Clancy and John Green to cosmopolitan nationalist, Thomas Flanagan, and to the more militantly-minded members of the '98 Club and Irish Republican Brotherhood, Thomas Morrison and J P Casey.[4]

The presence of Morrison in the proceedings was significant. Now in his early fifties, Morrison had been at the forefront of practically every advanced Irish nationalist grouping in the town, from the National Brotherhood of St Patrick to the Amnesty Association (where he had succeeded his associate, Daniel Hannah, as Secretary) and thereafter of the Kelly Defence Fund. In 1872, Morrison had served on the first (Provisional) Committee of the Dundee Home Rule Association, which, having helped inaugurate, promote and set on course, he had left to align himself with the pro-republican John Mitchel '82 Club. Indeed, the fact that the only apparent gap in his record as an administrator of pro-republican and IRB cover groups in Dundee occurred during a period of residence in Arbroath in the late 1860s, does not rule out the possibility that he may have been discreetly coordinating activity in outlying districts.

As a result of his long experience and commitment, Morrison had gained considerable standing in Irish nationalist circles and the respect of the working-class community in which he lived and worked. He may have lacked the bold eloquence or the military nous of his former associates, Hannah and Owen Walsh, however, with Walsh in America and Hannah off the scene, the plain-speaking, hard-grafting Morrison was the most senior, and as far as Dundee's working-class Irish constituency were concerned, trustworthy Fenian operator still standing.[5] Now, as Honorary Secretary of the '98 Club, he had taken a lead role in organising Dundee's first commemoration of the Manchester Martyrs, and the unofficial launch of the Land League. By their willingness to facilitate the meeting, and thus initiate the Land League in Dundee, we can assume that Morrison and the Dundee IRB had been inducted in the New Departure initiative,[6] possibly by one of its principal architects, John Devoy, on his inspection tour earlier that summer, and almost certainly by Torley in the run up to the event.

Opening the meeting, Torley expressed his pride that so many of his countrymen had turned out 'to honour the memory of the dead… the brave men who…were judicially murdered in Manchester, and offered their lives as a holocaust on the altar of their country's liberty', but also 'to honour the living…the brave men who were suffering in Sligo Prison for the same crime as Allen, Larkin and O'Brien died.' Having equated the jailed Land League leaders to the Manchester Martyrs, Torley placed the Irish land question in the broader historical context of revolutionary republicanism:

> Late eighteenth-century France had been ground down by a system of land tyranny similar to what exists in Ireland, but in one night the people rose, and thrones and landlords were swept away before the might of an outraged people. I know that excesses were committed…but when we think of the wrongs to which the people were subjected…there is no student of history, no lover of the brotherhood of mankind but must glory in the French Revolution. Well, history repeats itself. What happened in France might happen in Ireland…Let us hope that landlordism may be abolished without the guillotine, but it must disappear and Mr Davitt's programme must be realised.[7]

The first resolution, introduced by Daniel Logue, expressed the desire to aid Davitt, Daly and Killen by 'every constitutional means in our power', which former President of the O'Donovan Rossa Testimonial Committee, Thomas Flanagan, took 'great pleasure in seconding', confident in the knowledge that if it involved raising money to support Irish patriots in English jails, the people of Dundee would deliver. Morrison, backed by J P Casey, spoke to their indignation at the arrests of Davitt, Daly and Killen 'for speaking out freely and unreservedly on the land question', by which action, he opined, to loud cries of acclamation, the government intended 'to cause a state of terror and goad the Irish people into a premature revolution'. Finally, Home Ruler John Green, backed by Ferguson, chimed in with the statement 'that the great social evil in Ireland is the system of land tenure', and demanded reform.

Despite disagreements on the precise meaning of Irish freedom and how best to achieve it, on the land question, the Irish in Dundee presented a united front. Interest in the Land League thereafter intensified. The first Dundee branch, presided over by Peter Morris, assisted by Daniel Logue, with Thomas Morrison as Secretary, was established at the beginning of 1880.[8] While the Land League in Dundee remained independent of other Irish associations, its branch committees, like many others in Scotland, were largely, though not totally, dominated by the upwardly-mobile middle-class members of the Home Rule Club, presumably because of their higher educational level and range of social and professional contacts. The first public meeting called by the Dundee Land League, in St Joseph's Union Rooms, Larch Street on 14 March, targeted Irish householders, and concerned the typically Home Rule preoccupation of evaluating the Irish-friendly credentials of candidates standing in the upcoming parliamentary elections, after which the meeting agreed, with due protocol, to delegate office bearers of the League to confer with those of the Home Rule Confederation on the matter.[9] A subsequent meeting, held a few days later in the Albion Hall, took little time to resolve to support ex-MP George Armitstead and Councillor Frank Henderson due to their 'very liberal views to remedy grievances in Ireland'.[10]

However, what little was left of the practically moribund Home Rule Confederation was quickly subsumed into the Land League. As the Land War intensified and resistance to evictions was met with an increasingly brutal response, an increasing number of working-class Dundee Irishmen and Irishwomen attended League meetings, spoke out in support of the tenant farmers, and joined the League in their droves. By February 1881, there were four branches in and around Dundee: the West End (which had been the first Dundee branch), Central, Lochee and St Mary's (East End), which met weekly in Larch Street schoolroom, Tay Street Hall, and the church halls of St Mary's Lochee and St Mary's Forebank respectively.[11]

The fund-raising activities of the Land League were also supported by the local Catholic clergy. Significantly, one of the largest single donations to a collection submitted on 3 February, came from the town's most senior Catholic cleric, the Reverend Robert Clapperton, who appears to have learned from his experience of the Father Lavelle campaign for the poor of Partry seventeen years earlier.[12] On this occasion, Clapperton's donation of £1 was matched by three of his confrères, Phelan, Connor and Harris, and Presbyterian minister John McCheyne.[13] Like the Lavelle fund, however, most of the contributions made over the course of the Land League's history in Dundee were of small amounts gathered regularly from family or household and workplace groups.

If the committees were dominated by known Home Rulers, the branch memberships were not. At a meeting of the Dundee Central branch on 6 February 1881, several 'unnamed gentlemen' commented strongly on the rearrest of Davitt three days before (after the parole on his earlier jail term was revoked) the mere mention of whose name elicited massive cheering and stalled the meeting for several minutes.[14] Davitt's Fenian credentials and his connection to Dundee in this capacity were well-known in nationalist circles. During his eight years in prison, however, Davitt had reviewed his belief in physical force as the sole route to Irish national independence, and shortly after his release, he had joined with Clan na Gael leader John Devoy in subscribing to the New Departure initiative.[15] Nevertheless, while IRB hardliners remained critical of Davitt's and Devoy's rapprochement with constitutional nationalism, they saw nothing to object to in the aims and the tactics of the Land League and, in Dundee as in Glasgow, threw their weight wholeheartedly behind it.[16] To the average Dundee-Irish Fenian sympathiser, less conversant with the internal political wranglings of the IRB, Davitt continued to embody the physical force tradition, and his return to action at the helm of the Land League gave rise to a wave of eager recruits, motivated, no doubt, by a desire to be connected to the action.

The meeting of the Dundee Central branch was 'one of the largest and most enthusiastic yet held' to date, and concluded with the enrolment of several new members and a call to arrange a monster meeting in conjunction with other branches of the League. Simultaneously, half a mile up the road at Larch Street, the President of the West End branch, Thomas Flanagan, was praising the tenant farmers who by their actions 'had driven the landlords and their allies from the field of argument and forced them to fall back on brute force', exposing the fact 'that their cause cannot stand when tested by the principle of abstract justice'.[17]

Thomas 'Tim' Flanagan was the youngest child and only son of Irish-born grocer Daniel Flanagan who had been elected to the first committee of the Dundee Home Rule Association in February 1872. Born in 1856 in Polepark, where his father had his shop, he was too young to have been involved in the IRB at the height of the Fenian activity in the mid-1860s. As a vociferous supporter of Irish national independence, however, he wasted no opportunity to argue the case in a number of organisations of an Irish or otherwise political stamp. Not surprisingly, the younger Flanagan joined the Home Rule Association and quickly become one of its most outspoken members. Nor did his involvement in Home Rule politics exclude a support for physical force tactics or membership of groups which espoused them. In his first publicly-reported speech, at the Dundee HRA's St Patrick's Day celebration in 1876, the twenty-year-old Flanagan moved a resolution advocating the release of Fenian prisoners – the principal objective of the Amnesty Association in which many Fenians were active. As someone who played the field of Irish nationalist politics, he naturally threw himself into the Land League agitation.

The combative rhetoric expressed at branch meetings of the Land League in Dundee indicates the presence of a constituency who were not content to be mere cheerleaders for the Irish Home Rule MPs whose obstructionist tactics, however vigorous and determined, only served to delay the inevitable passage of more repressive legislation. Rather it points to a greater affinity with the people at the sharp edge of that legislation, and a partiality for the direct resistance tactics of the Land League. Significantly, while the name of Fenian felon Davitt was conflated with the Land League, the name of Parliamentarian Parnell was rarely mentioned. This contrasted with a public meeting held in the Thistle Hall the previous December at which T P O'Connor, MP for Galway, portrayed

Parnell as the personification of the Land League, and lauded him above his imprisoned colleague Davitt. Nevertheless, it was O'Connor's references to the actions of the landlords which drew the loudest, angriest interjections from the audience.[18]

Throughout the spring of 1881, however, branch meetings of the Land League reflected the leadership's preoccupation with parliamentary strategy, as the Home Rule-dominated officer boards focused on mobilising the Irish vote. At a meeting of the West End branch, Secretary James Coogan stated his aim 'to have as many Irishmen [as possible] on the [electoral] roll as it would not be long until they were called to exercise that right'. Michael Farrell, Treasurer of the St Mary's branch and the Home Rule Club, urged members to become voters as that was 'the only way they could be of practical use to their country'. How the older Fenian element and younger patriotic spirits felt about being assigned this limited role in determining Ireland's future can only be imagined. Farrell was not popular amongst rank-and-file nationalists, and his opposition to Labour elements in the United Irish League was a source of friction some twenty years later. Even cosmopolitan nationalist Thomas Flanagan appeared to toe the moderate line, calling for 'settlement of the land question on principles that would secure the occupier his rights without infringing on the rights of the landlord [as] the Irish peoples' sense of justice would permit them to demand no more'. As Flanagan was doubtless aware, the rights of the British-backed landlord class and the Irish tenant farmers were fundamentally incompatible, so the possibility that he may have been consciously playing down Irish national aspirations, particularly advanced Republican ones, in order to attract support from the wider Scottish population seems confirmed by branch officer Laurence Phin's concluding comment that he hoped 'to see soon a similar agitation against landlords in Scotland and England'.[19]

Unlike many of their compatriots in the west of Scotland who experienced far more open hostility, by the 1880s, Irish immigrants to Dundee had on the whole gained the acceptance of the native population. The overwhelming dependence on a war-driven jute economy, with its precarious cycle of high demand, overproduction and slump, created a common experience of full employment or under- and unemployment where there was little competition between workers, placing most of them

Chapter 4 – The Land For The People 1879–89

in the same economic boat. That fact that a large percentage of the Irish workforce were young single women, and rates of intermarriage were relatively high, further eased the process of assimilation, helping to mould Irish and Scots identities into a distinctive Dundee one. While there continued to be occasional colourful incidents of Scots-Irish tension, usually focused on St Patrick's Day, by the 1880s, expressions of outright anti-Irish prejudice were relatively rare. Exceptional incidents, such as the desecration of a crucifix in the grounds of St Mary's RC Church in Lochee in April 1883, were deemed all the more newsworthy, spawning graphic reports in the (mainly non-Liberal) press. This furtive act of vandalism, which was likely the work of one or two isolated Protestant iconoclasts, must be placed against the large and confident Irish-Catholic community who dared to erect a twenty-foot figure of Christ on the cross, in a highly visible spot facing Lochee High Street, in the first place.[20]

In a series of letters which appeared in the *Dundee Courier* in May 1881, a Lochee resident, writing under the pseudonym of 'A Scotchman', seized on the meetings of the Lochee Land League to vent his racist bigoted opinions. Arguing that 'these Sunday afternoon political rabbles [were as] offensive to the people of Lochee [as] the Land League agitation is an insult to the people of Great Britain', he called for the Coercion Act to be extended to Great Britain to put 'this blackguard agitation' down. He opined that land reform would be a profitless waste of time as Irish farmers were 'a set of lazy good-for-nothing vagabonds…the highest ambition of which was [to own] a pig, a cow, a donkey and a bit of land' to 'squat' upon. 'Pat [is] particularly fond of a pig', he mused, recalling the 'old days' when 'pigs were kept in the true Irish fashion in Dundee, three storeys from the ground'.[21]

'A Scotchman's' comments prompted an immediate reply from Land League activist, James Ward, who informed him that their meetings were perfectly legal, as indeed were any other political meetings held 'within the bounds of decency and decorum'. As for extending the Coercion Act to Great Britain, Ward advanced a broader historical perspective. 'Scotchmen as a class love their liberty', he declared. 'They cherish it and have fought for it on different occasions, and I am very much misled if the class he represents would like to see the Coercion Act put into force in Scotland, more especially in Lochee. They would rise to a man to oppose such a measure'. Ward was clearly familiar with the independent Lochee spirit. Finally, refusing to address the correspondent by his chosen pseudonym, Ward, himself a Scots-born Irishman, advised his 'anti-Irish friend' to 'attend to his own education and learn more refined language before picking up his pen to comment on any class of society'.[22]

Unsurprisingly, Ward's rebuke provoked 'A Scotchman' into penning two more outpourings of anti-Irish bile in which he reduced 'their highest aim' to 'eating, drinking, counting their beads and reciting paternosters', proposed the government send 'hundreds of thousands' of Irish people to the colonies, and advocated a boycott of all things Irish, starting with 'bundl[ing] everyone of Irish extraction out of Camperdown Linen Works' and 'dispensing with Irish labourers altogether as long as these blackguard meetings are held'. That this last policy would have severely restricted the functioning of Camperdown Works – at that time, the largest centre of jute production in the world – with economic consequences extending far beyond the Irish population of Lochee, had apparently not occurred to him. 'Who is James Ward? He might give his address,' asked the anonymous 'Scotchman', before stating that his main object was to 'bring some intelligent Irishmen out to defend the policy of the Land League', and offering to 'take a night against any Irishman' – with the exception of Ward who, 'as representative of the clan, won't do', in any public hall in Lochee – but not St Mary's, as 'a hearing would not be got there'.[23]

'A Scotchman's' rants were a source of much mirth to those who read them, and generated some opportunistic publicity for the Lochee Land League, whose Secretary James Martin responded that there was 'no necessity to defend the policy of the Land League until [it] has been attacked, which it hasn't yet by any of your correspondents'. Identifying 'A Scotchman's' comments as 'a humorous bit of raving', Martin wryly commented, 'if [he] wants to exhibit himself on a public platform I shall be only too happy to give him any assistance in my power [as] I am quite sure that the people of Lochee would be delighted to see him go through his performance'.[24] As a twenty-year-old factory worker, who lived in Whorterbank, Lochee, with his 40-year-old mother, an Irish-born widow, and three younger siblings, Martin was well placed to speak confidently on the opinions of his generation, class and community. And who indeed was James Ward? No ordinary member of the Land League, it seems, but very possibly a key member of the IRB. Born in Paisley of Irish parents in 1842, Ward had come to Dundee sometime in the 1860s. By 1881, he was living at 14 Court Street, in the north-east end of the town with his 70-year-old Irish-born aunt, his Leith-born wife, and their three young daughters, and working as a railway ticket inspector – a job which allowed him to traverse the country without attracting undue attention.[25] However, while Ward kept any IRB involvement under wraps, he made no attempt to disguise his political opinions, name or address.

Unlike Martin and Ward, 'A Scotchman' did not reveal his, other than giving his address as 1 High Street, Lochee, which was probably false. Ignorant as he may have been, he was not so naïve as to recognise that his views were unpopular in the community in which he lived. Interestingly, these letters appeared a few months after the emergence of the Anti-Land League Association in the west of Scotland, of which the writer may have been a supporter.[26] Despite some fevered activity, mainly postering, in Glasgow in the early months of 1881, the Anti-Land League received little traction in Dundee, and the opinions of obvious sympathisers such as 'A Scotchman' were not taken seriously by the local Land League.

In the wider local context, the intolerant views expressed by 'A Scotchman' cut against the image of an inclusive civic community the Liberal city fathers and the local press wished to present. Unlike the various reports and editorials on the Land League which appeared in national British newspapers such as the *Times*, the Dundee press reported on local Land League activity with relative objectivity, and on occasions sympathetically. That branch and public meetings were regularly reported at length in the *Advertiser,* the *Courier* and their sister publications, indicates that a good relationship existed between Land League activists and the press – perhaps a legacy of the groundwork of the shrewd tacticians of the National Brotherhood of St Patrick in the early 1860s. The general attitude of indigenous Scots Dundonians to the Land League is harder to ascertain. The absence of a significant Orange element, and the common socio-economic experience of Dundee's large working-class population contributed towards a sense of fellowship and neighbourliness which may have encouraged working-class Scots to see the Land League as a just cause. For the majority of the population, however, their day-to-day battles were centred on their own turf, and what didn't affect them directly was unlikely to prevail in their thoughts. While some working-class Scots undoubtedly sympathised with the plight and fight of Ireland's tenant farmers, the concept of an international working-class struggle which manifested itself in practical political activism had not yet developed. In short, the Land League was seen as an 'Irish' issue.

By the late summer of 1881, the Land War was escalating; but the broader working-class support craved by the Land League in Dundee was still not forthcoming. At a meeting of the West End branch on 22 August, a clearly frustrated Thomas Flanagan ditched the moderate rhetoric and launched into a full-blown attack on 'the landlord class' which

> had opposed the extension of the franchise, trades unionism, co-operative societies, and, in fact, anything that would tend to raise the working classes socially and politically. For these reasons, [he could] not see how any Englishman or Scotchman could support a system which had been proved by past events to be so selfish and bad. Irishmen wished to live in harmony with Englishmen and Scotchmen [and] cherished no ill feeling towards them; on the [contrary], they would rather assist them in [taking on their] landlords, and for that reason would expect sympathy in the contest against Irish landlords. But if they scorned the assistance proffered by Irishmen, they would be scorned in return.[27]

Here Flanagan demonstrated a perception of being engaged in a wider struggle where the cause of the beleaguered tenant farmers in Ireland was equivalent to the cause of the working class in England and Scotland. Consequently, he expressed a willingness on the part of 'Irishmen' to enter into a working-class alliance in order to take on the ruling, i.e., 'landlord' class and overturn an evil system, and accordingly, a frustration at the failure of the English and Scottish working class to make common cause and catch on to the real issues at stake.

The Ladies' Land League

One the most significant features of the Land League agitation was the large-scale involvement of women at the forefront of the movement. This was by no means the first time that women had been actively involved in Irish resistance campaigns. Veteran Fenian John Devoy recalled that 'although they took no oath, the women were the keepers of important secrets, travelled from point to point bearing important messages, and were the chief agents in keeping the organisation alive in Ireland'.[28] This lesson was not lost on Michael Davitt, co-founder of the Ladies' Land League, who recalled his reasoning:

> No better allies than women could be found for such a task. They are in certain emergencies, more dangerous to despotism than men. They have more courage, through having less scruples, when and where their better instincts are appealed to by a militant cause in a fight against a mean foe.[29]

The statements of Devoy and Davitt have a hint of the attitude, prevalent in Victorian society, which conceived of women as the morally superior guardians of the domestic sphere, the 'angels in the home'. Davitt continued, 'The fight was to save the homes of Ireland – the sacred, domestic domain of woman's moral superiority in civilised society'. Yet, when seen through the filter of their experience, both men had witnessed a movement that had been wrecked by informers, by men whose egos, carelessness or cowardice, i.e., 'moral weakness', had cost them their liberty and undermined the cause of Irish independence. Women had been at the heart of prisoner support and amnesty agitation, which in due course had helped to secure the release of the Fenian prisoners, and ultimately of Davitt on a 'ticket of leave'. This had led to the view that, to Davitt's mind at least, women were more trustworthy, therefore better fitted than men to take responsibility for the most critical work of the Land League.

The idea of a separate women's organisation, initially to boost the Famine Relief Fund of the Land League, was conceived by the US-domiciled Fanny Parnell, on whose initiative the American Ladies' Land League was founded in New York on 15 October 1880.[30] Complementing the main organisation, the Ladies' Land League took on responsibility for the fundraising, accounting, administration and correspondence of the National Land League, in doing so creating a network of local fundraisers and activists throughout the American-Irish diaspora and Ireland, to where her younger sister, Anna, was dispatched to direct operations. These 'ancillary' tasks were of critical importance in building a widespread and effective campaign, and providing direct assistance to the families of tenant farmers made homeless and destitute through eviction or their resistance to it. The astute Fanny Parnell also envisaged an Irish Ladies' Land League which would provide a caretaker leadership in the likely event of the men being arrested. Davitt agreed with her, and, ignoring the initial scepticism of Fanny's brother Charles and the other male leaders, asked Anna to set it up, which she duly did on 31 January 1881, preceding Davitt's arrest by five days.[31]

Around this time, the increasing presence of women began to be reported at the Land League's public meetings in Dundee. At a 'monster' anti-coercion meeting on 1 March 1881, the outcome of a proposal at the Central branch three weeks earlier, a local reporter (clearly incapable of finding a non-gendered pronoun) noted that, of the 3,000-4,000 'Dundee Irishmen' packed into the makeshift premises of Cooke's Circus in the Nethergate, 'a goodly number [were] ladies'. No women were on the platform, however, which included the President of the Dundee Central Executive of the Land League, Henry O'Gorman, various officers of the Dundee, Perth and Arbroath branches, President of the Land League in Glasgow, John Ferguson, and the ostensible editor of the *Brooklyn Standard*, James J O'Donnell, a leading Irish-American Fenian who was touring Scotland on IRB business.[32]

While the speeches focused largely on constitutional politics, the banners hung on all sides of the hall, from 'God Save Ireland', 'Give us our Rights', 'Success to Home Rule', depictions of St Patrick and the name of Parnell, spanned the breadth of Irish nationalist activity in Dundee over the past two decades, from the St Patrick's Day celebrations (initiated by the eponymous Irish National Brotherhood) and the Home Rule agitation to the Manchester Martyrs commemorations, and now, the Land League. The 'goodly number' of Dundee Irishwomen indicates that women were asserting their presence, conspicuously if not vocally, in the public affairs of the latter.

In early 1881, the main emphasis of the National Land League was on political strategy, which at grassroots level, meant marshalling the expatriate Irish vote. Women, of course, were excluded from this narrative, as were all lodgers, itinerant workers and people living on poor relief.

Universal male suffrage was still not realised, and the percentage of men in Dundee eligible to vote in General Elections was lower than in other Scottish urban centres.[33] The women's suffrage movement had barely got off the ground, and besides using their moral influence to encourage men to 'use their votes wisely', there appeared little place for women in such a scenario.

Over the course of the summer, however, there developed a divergence of opinion within the Land League, and a growing tension between those who favoured grassroots resistance and those who placed their faith in parliamentary action. Class and gender were undoubted factors in determining peoples' inclinations. That the Ladies' Land League chose to align with the extreme, direct-action wing is not surprising, but can also be attributed to the influence of Anna Parnell, who had a much more radical outlook than her parliamentarian brother and, increasingly, of her closest and most trusted ally, Davitt. While moderate Land Leaguers patiently pinned their hopes on the British Parliament, which they believed would eventually be pressed, persuaded and compromised into passing an acceptable measure of land reform, those on the extreme, agrarian wing, came to believe that that the Land War would be won by upping pressure on the landlords, initially, by withholding rent, 'to the point of a bayonet', and latterly, by 'letting the farms go', leaving the landlords with the expense of auction and conveyancing fees, and the onus of reinstating the original tenants when others refused.[34]

Under the directorship of Anna Parnell and her colleagues on the twelve-woman Executive, the Land League was transformed into a military operation. Every week Anna received hundreds of letters, all of which were answered personally. Because of their support work, which involved compiling intelligence files on every land estate in Ireland, the Ladies' Land League became acutely aware of the situation on the ground, the needs of the communities, the urgent need for action and the importance of an effective support network.[35] Moreover, as the committee in Dublin handled all of the correspondence of the INLL, they were aware of how essential the work of the branches was in sustaining the campaign.

In the summer of 1881, Anna sent a letter around all branches of the INLL in Scotland and England, urging them to set up branches of the Ladies' Land League. Wasting no time, the Lochee branch called a preliminary meeting in St Mary's Hall on Friday, 5 August. A large attendance was noted, the only men present being the parish priest, Father Peter Butti, and James Martin, Secretary of the men's branch, who opened the meeting by reading the letter from Anna Parnell 'desiring the Irishwomen of Lochee to cooperate together and form an association for the furtherance of Ireland's rights'. A discussion followed, in which several of the women took part, and the speed with which provisional office bearers were elected – Lucy Paterson as President, Catherine Hopper as Secretary, and Mary McCarron as Treasurer – indicates that a structure of sorts was already in place.[36] Five days later, the Lochee branch of the Irish National Ladies' Land League was officially inaugurated. Unlike the meetings of the men's branches, the ladies' meetings were regarded as a 'private' affair and were rarely reported by the local press. Nevertheless, a discreetly-placed sentence in the *Evening Telegraph* two weeks later noted that the Lochee LLL had remitted £6, the first instalment of subscriptions to the central executive in Dublin, which, if the recommended membership fee of one shilling was adhered to, suggests that around 120 women had signed up.[37]

Irish women activists faced the double prejudice of anti-Irish, anti-Catholic bigotry from outside of the Irish community, and sexist attitudes from within and without it, not to mention the third obstacle of class prejudice, as the majority of Dundee's Irish immigrants were from working-class backgrounds. These prejudices often militated against each other, and while it would be an oversimplification to say one cancelled another out, in the case of Irish immigrant women, it often disguised it or deflected it sideways. For example, the formation of the Lochee LLL provoked the latest in a series of anti-Irish diatribes from one familiar Lochee correspondent to the Dundee press, who opined that 'Irishmen, and those living in Lochee especially, are rank cowards [for] for mixing up their sisters and daughters' with the murderous robbers of the Land League, 'a movement which', he blustered, 'is a disgrace to the civilization of the nineteenth century'. 'Justice for Ireland', as he signed himself on this occasion, asserted that the ladies' branch was a front for the men's, which, he claimed, had been dissolved to enable the feeble Lochee Irishmen to hide behind their women's petticoats. In his own racist view, this was typical of the Irish male character and only served to prove that the Irish were unfit for self-government. The women did even not merit the attention of his prejudice. That dubious right was reserved for the Lochee Irishmen to whom the full force of his bigotry was directed. Women, Irish or otherwise, were deemed incapable of knowing their own minds, let alone organising themselves.[38]

Once again, James Ward responded by informing him that not only was the men's branch 'prospering daily, with recruits filling up its ranks until it is a barrier to any foe', but that 'for the ladies to form a society of their own, in combination with the male society, [was] an honour to themselves and a step in their advancement, and a retort in full to the charge of cowardice'.[39] As the sole man in a household which contained three generations of women, Ward knew more than most that courage and ability were not determined by a person's gender, and he may well have spoken from his ambitions for his daughters, the eldest of whom, eleven-year-old Joan, was working as a 'half-timer' in a local jute mill.[40]

At the end of August, Anna Parnell embarked on a tour of Scotland and England, taking in Glasgow (where she had called Gladstone a 'wretched, hypocritical, bloodthirsty miscreant'), Edinburgh and Greenock, before arriving in Dundee on Monday, 5 September. Her reputation had preceded her, as had reports of her uncompromising rhetoric which had discomfited moderate Home Rulers and put the young John Redmond, considered at the time to be a reasonably advanced and outspoken Home Rule MP, in the shade.[41] Five days earlier in Edinburgh's Cowgate, she had explained to a highly partisan audience that Gladstone and Chief Secretary for Ireland, William Forster (commonly known as 'Buckshot'), were doing such a good job of alerting Irish people to 'the folly and wickedness of believing in English statesmen and English working reforms' that even 'the most ardent follower of dynamite' could see there was no advantage in shooting them. 'All English governments, past present and future, Whig, Tory, Radical, Catholic or Protestant,' she emphasised, 'had been, and would be, treacherous, cruel and murderous'.[42]

After several months of listening to moderate Land Leaguers pontificate on a parliamentary strategy in which they were consigned to the role of election fodder or overlooked altogether, Anna's fighting talk was exactly what Dundee's young working-class, and especially female, Land League supporters wanted to hear. Long before her arrival, the Kinnaird Hall was crowded to over-capacity by an audience composed largely of women and young men. When Anna finally arrived, an hour late, she was received with deafening cheers, the waving of hats and handkerchiefs, and the musical accompaniment of Handel's 'See the Conquering Hero Comes' played by the St Mary's and St Patrick's Flute Bands, who had paraded the streets for the past hour playing Irish airs. Anna was led to the platform by Thomas Flanagan, accompanied by the Secretary of the Glasgow Land League, Edward McHugh, Father Thomas Crumley of St Joseph's, Father John Docherty of St Mary's Lochee, Father Francis Beurms, ex-Lochee now Montrose, former President of the Lochee Home Rule Association, now of the Lochee Land League, and Edward Roche, as well as representatives of the Dundee men's branches.

Roche, chairing, delivered the first address. They were, he said, 'called together on an important occasion. Their countrymen at home were in the midst of a mighty struggle with a power that [was] oppressing them as with a weighty load – the grinding merciless power of the landlords. The aim of the Land League [was] to destroy that power. And to strengthen the Land League [was] the aim of [the] meeting'. And, he insisted, 'there was not a town where [Miss Parnell] was held in more esteem by her countrymen and women than Dundee'.

The newly appointed President of the Lochee LLL, Jane Keenan, then stepped up to the platform to deliver a very different type of address:

> 'Ceud Mile Failte', is the greeting we of the Ladies Land League hail your presence here tonight. Our Irish hearts grow warmer still, and thrill with love and patriotism for beloved Erin on beholding you who have done so much for her homeless children, for her imprisoned martyrs. The ballroom and the chase and pursuits which attract other noble young ladies fail to allure you. Like a true sister of charity, you take your stand by the poor and the oppressed, bringing peace and comfort to many a well-nigh broken heart. May you and your noble-hearted brother live to see your mission crowned with success: to see Ireland free, happy and prosperous. Then as now shall every Irish heart, whether at home or abroad, cry out in transports of gratitude: God bless the Parnell family![43]

It is interesting to compare the rousing language of Edward Roche's address, which talks of strengthening a 'mighty struggle' and 'destroying' a 'merciless, grinding power', with the passive, nurturing terms of Jane Keenan's, which speaks of 'love and patriotism', 'homeless children', 'imprisoned martyrs', 'broken hearts', and 'sisters of charity', and refers to the domestic unit of the Parnell family. The quaint, stilted language suggests that Jane Keenan was unaccustomed to speaking at mass political meetings, and perhaps wary of being seen to be too controversial – not without good reason, as, unlike Anna Parnell, she was not a 'noble young lady' with a modest allowance from her eldest brother John's estate, but a 24-year-old infant teacher living in Camperdown Street, Lochee, with her elderly widowed father, an Irish-born weaver. More importantly, her employers were sitting on the platform. (Father Beurms had been the manager of St Mary's RC School, Lochee, at the time of her appointment two years earlier.) Despite the highly sentimental tone, however, these effusive expressions of sisterly gratitude were perfectly sincere. In Anna Parnell, a new generation of patriotically-minded Irish immigrant women, who had up until now been confined to the background, had a real-life role model beyond the long-suffering Mother Ireland or the ethereal Hibernia of poetic imagination.

Not surprisingly, the press was fascinated by this unusual, non-conformist woman, and devoted inches of column space to her appearance, demeanour and speech. Where the *Edinburgh Daily News* had dubbed her the Ladies' Land League's 'brunette champion', the *Dundee Courier* described her as 'sharp, active and intelligent-looking', of medium height, slim build, attired in black and about 30 (she was 29). Unlike an earlier second-hand report of Anna's 'screaming little speech' at Glasgow, it was noted that she spoke slowly and distinctly, apologising for her late arrival, and cheerfully observing that 'ladies were considerably in the majority'.[44] The social niceties dispensed with, Anna revealed why Dundee was so important to the Irish National Land League. 'This town,' she said, 'was the first town in Scotland to send the League in Ireland help, and no matter what other cities in Scotland might boast of, they in Dundee would always know it because they had her word for it'. Here Anna spoke with authority. As a Secretary of the Ladies' Executive in Dublin, she had responsibility for handling the correspondence of the Land League, including donations. Moreover, through their organisational network, Anna and her colleagues had gathered an extensive knowledge of the economic conditions and prevailing mood in the areas in which they worked, as well the strengths, weaknesses and political allegiances of local activists.

She congratulated the Dundee Land Leaguers for providing a 'proper kind of chairman' in Roche, unlike the organisers of the previous meeting in Greenock who, possibly seeking to ingratiate themselves with local Liberal politicians, had invited the Provost to do the honours. Taking fright at Anna's candid rhetoric, Provost D Campbell had written a precautionary letter warning her off any 'violent and unbecoming language' and 'unseemly clamour' as it would alienate the people of England and Scotland from their Irish brethren and jeopardise support for the Land Act before it had been given a fair trial.[45] To the loud acclamation of her Dundee audience, Anna declared that she 'did not know that the alienation of the English and Scotch people could be any greater', stating, by way of example, that if English government in India resulted in an influx of immigrant workers, cutting the wages of English workers in half and keeping them at starvation point, they would surely place the blame on the government and not the immigrants. This was the result of English government in Ireland, she argued, 'yet the English working people not only tolerate it, but a good many of them give their lives to keep it up'. Her intention in reading from the Provost's letter, she explained, was to demonstrate the danger of allowing people holding elected positions to use them for political ends. They in Dundee would surely understand that she had done the people of Greenock a favour by driving the Provost away.

Her purpose in being there, however, was to lay bare the human cost of British policy in Ireland; to describe the brutal attacks by police and soldiers on evicted tenant farmers, which had created the need for greater resistance by the communities affected and for a better informed, co-ordinated support from the Irish population at home and abroad. Anna related her experience of arriving to address a meeting at Limerick Junction where a posse of police disembarking from her train had charged the crowd with fixed bayonets stabbing a man who offered Anna his hand, and forcing the crowd to flee, whereupon the townspeople had come to their aid by throwing missiles. 'The people', she said, 'have taken to defending themselves'. In an effort to counter the negative propaganda and general failure of the British press to cover the Land War, Anna suggested that 'they might insist some newspaper in Scotland give the truth'. To help expedite this, she revealed her own plans:

> to establish a regular chronicle of all the illegal and cruel actions carried out on the part of the Magistrates and others in Ireland [so] it would be in their power to circulate a real statement of the case between Gladstone's government and the people of Ireland...To make the names of the men responsible – Clifford Lloyd, Richard Eaton, T O Plunkett, Hamilton, County Inspector Smith etc., household names in every Irish home in England, Scotland and America.[46]

Here, however, Anna prioritised those at the blunt end of the stick. By presenting a litany of the victims, their names, ages and the extent of their injuries, Anna personalised the struggle and drove it home. Quinn, who met his death at the butt end of a rifle for being too near to the police. O'Keefe, whose skull was fractured when he would not leave his own field. Maloney, clubbed to death for doing the same. An unnamed grandmother in her seventies, whose back was broken by police, and her seven-year-old granddaughter, who was shot when she ran to help. These should all be circulated, Anna concluded, at which the audience rose to their feet in a wave of loud prolonged cheering and energetic hat waving.

Despite the overwhelmingly enthusiastic response, Anna did not trust to mass shows of emotion and had little taste for the atmosphere of the mass political meeting, knowing well that the passion whipped up in the meeting hall often evaporated in the cold light of day and did not necessarily translate to activism on the ground. Unlike the grandstanding speeches of many of her Land League colleagues, Anna made no attempt to pull upon the heart strings of the audience by romantic references to the old country, but rather trusted to hard facts, hard graft and tight organisation. Experience had taught her that that smaller groups were more conducive to freedom of expression and constructive dialogue. As the meeting closed with the obligatory three cheers for the speaker, Anna descended from the platform to be assailed by a crowd of women, some already members, others who signed up on the spot, after which she held a private conference with the women of the audience, the proceedings of which were, unfortunately, not reported.

Interestingly, in the months following Anna's speech, in which she encouraged the audience to 'insist some Scottish newspaper give the truth', reports of the Land War began to appear in the Dundee press, ratcheting up significantly after the Land League in Ireland was outlawed in October. The Liberal newspapers carried numerous reports on the suppression of the Land League, the arrests of local secretaries and presidents of Land League branches, and instances of communities rallying round throughout Ireland. These included the arrests of C P O'Sullivan of the Cork Land League, a prominent Fenian in 1866, who advocated payment of 'No Rent' as a preliminary to physical force, of Father McHale, curate at Crossmolina, County Mayo, for holding Land League meetings in his church; of J M Walls, the acting editor of the *Roscommon Herald*, and of three men in Buttevant, County Cork, for hooting at the police. It also reported the stories of the 200 Land Leaguers in Loughrea, County Galway, who, with horses and carts drew home the turf of their imprisoned Secretary, John Sweeney and of Father Conway of Skreen, County Sligo, suspended by his Bishop for his advanced Land League views, whereupon his parishioners boarded the church door and posted a notice proclaiming that no priest but Father Conway shall say Mass there.[47] Not to be outdone, the *Dundee Courier* reported the arrests of ex-Fenian prisoner, William Stack, and reporter of the *Wexford People*, Hugh Mahon; convictions on the property of Lord Bantry in County Cork, where four of the tenants were women; and a torchlit procession in Derry where several thousand people accompanied two Land Leaguers convicted at the petty sessions for using 'illegal language'. The *Courier* also carried a detailed report of the inquest of Mary Deane of Belmullet, County Mayo (who died after her windpipe was pierced by a gunshot wound), where the evidence of two witnesses who had seen Police Constable Sullivan step out of the ranks and shoot her, and the jury's verdict of wilful murder, were brushed off by the Crown Solicitor who 'advised' that it would be quashed in the Queen's Bench.[48] Significantly, this local upsurge in factual reporting on the Land War occurred precisely as the LLL in Ireland took on the publishing and distribution of the INLL's weekly newspaper, *United Ireland*, (after its editorial staff were thrown in jail) in which Anna, as pledged, was incorporating a chronicle of incidents, which Dundee's canny Land League supporters may have been feeding to their carefully cultivated contacts in the local press.[49]

Between September 1881 and January 1382, the number of LLL branches in Ireland, Scotland and England increased from 64 to around 500, including a new Dundee (St Andrew's) branch established at the time of Anna's visit.[50] Indeed, Anna's tour had a tremendous impact, not only on her target audience of women, who were inspired with a new faith in their abilities and the confidence to express their support for Land League publicly, but also on a number of working-class and physical force Republicans, who were encouraged by her uncompromising language, practical approach and radical outlook.

When the *Evening Telegraph* quoted correspondence from 'A Daughter of Scotia', criticising Anna's 'diatribes against Gladstone and the Government', and advising the Ladies' Land League to 'find a more useful field for their labours [than] agitating ignorant minds', 'A Daughter of Erin' responded by pointing out that Gladstone was responsible for the Coercion Act which had damaged the prospects of countless Irishmen by throwing them in jail, adding that there was 'no more useful work any lady could be involved in' than giving relief to evicted tenants and prisoners' dependants. But for the noble work of Miss Parnell and the Ladies' Land League, she explained, there would be many more Irish people in that unfortunate position.[51]

The arrests and imprisonment of the male Land League leaders and the outlawing of the INLL in October, which the British government reckoned, by the same sexist logic, would decapitate the movement, propelled the LLL to the front of the campaign where they proceeded to 'block evictions with more energy, determination and boldness than ever', making a mockery of the assumption that an organisation 'reduced to fighting behind petticoats and pinafores' would be incapable of commanding the loyalty of its male members in a time of crisis.[52] Behind the misogynistic language, at least the women attracted notoriety in their own right. In late October, the *Courier* noted that, where 'in the past twelve or eighteen months, women had been put forward, sometimes in a rather cowardly way by the men, to beard and defy the bailiffs and process servers', now:

there was but a step between these infuriated females using their tongues and using weapons of a more forcible kind. Women carried away with excitement were almost sure, before all was done, to call in the aid of stones, sticks, turf, or whatever else came convenient to their hands. Equally, as a matter of course, this would lead to the police charging the viragoes and giving them a taste of the physical force which they had been applying to guardians of the peace.[53]

As evidence of the 'acrid and malignant' ways in which the women were challenging the government's endeavours 'to maintain the law and protect the law-abiding people of Ireland', that is to say the landlords, the *Courier* cited an incident in Loughrea, County Galway, where, it noted, the women of the Land League 'captured' some 400 children, 'equipped them with banners, and sent them out in procession to the streets to march and sing "God Save Ireland"' 'It was', the *Courier* added, 'pitiable that parents should so far forget themselves and their duty towards their innocent offspring to allow them to be used as tools to carry out the spite of scolds driven wild by chagrin at having their fangs drawn and their leading males lodged in prison'. Nevertheless, the *Courier* trusted that with a sufficient balance of caution and firmness, 'this phase of Irish difficulty' would be overcome.

In the days and weeks following the proclamation of the INLL and arrest of its leaders, the LLL office was bombarded with requests for information, as well as donations and membership fees from prospective male, and Ladies' and Children's branches. Anna responded to the latter by sending materials for the children, who the Ladies' League were helping to encourage and educate. However, far from 'capturing' children and manipulating their young minds, the drive and enthusiasm often came from the young people themselves. An unidentified boys' branch declared themselves ready to help 'fill the breach', if not quite step into Parnell's shoes, writing to Anna, 'as yet we can only learn; but we have pledged ourselves to have no other political teachers than Parnell, Dillon, Davitt and their comrades [and] we are determined to make our boys' league worthy of [them] both by the number and the characters of our members'. The Cashel Boys' branch, founded a day after the proclamation of the Land League, sent 8s 6d towards the Prisoners' Sustenance Fund, noting 'it will serve to show how we despise the orders of Buckshot (Forster)'. Elsewhere, a letter from C Mathias of Eton College enclosed a postal order for 8s 2d, the sum of 'this week's collection'. Over the next two months, several more children's, juvenile and boys' branches sprang up throughout Ireland.[54]

With the moderate moral force men out of the way, the physical force men also entered the fray. The seizure of arms and documents related to the Fenian and Land League movements in Bradford in November, and of a large cache of arms in Dublin in early December, revived memories of the dynamite scares of the 1860s.[55] To the eyes of the British ruling class, the convergence of an army of intemperate-tongued, uncontrollable women, defiant children and teams of Fenian dynamitards hell-bent on waging a war of terror on the British establishment, was symptomatic of an irrational disordered world. To the radical-leaning Ladies' Land League and the neo-Fenians, operating from the perspective of the oppressed Irish and working-class populations, theirs was a legitimate revolutionary response to an unequal, brutish society. The British government's tactic of decapitating the INLL, predicated as it was on assumptions of top-down patriarchal power, had seriously backfired. Far from killing off the agitation, it had shifted the locus of control from the male leaders in Parliament, via the radical stewardship of Anna and the LLL, on to the Irish people, with profound, potentially revolutionary implications for the struggle for national independence.

Having thus failed to deal with 'this phase of Irish difficulty', the government finally outlawed the Irish LLL, under legislation aimed at curbing prostitution, on 16 December, an action the *Dundee Courier* considered entirely justified as 'the women had unsexed themselves by indulging in unwomanly language and engaging in proceedings which interfere with the public peace'. The *Courier* assured its readers that in treating these 'patriots in petticoats' (women's clothing figured prominently in disparaging reports of the LLL), in exactly the same fashion as male 'suspects', they, and their followers, would be scared into submission.[56]

As so often is the case with British repression in Ireland, however, the reverse proved true. The suppression of the Irish LLL was met with continued defiance in Ireland and a hastily organised speaking tour of the major Scottish and English cities. A blitz of street postering was sufficient to fill Glasgow's City Hall on the 20 December, and the following night, a mixed audience, which Chairman Edward Roche deemed 'very satisfactory' and highly creditable for a day's notice, crowded into Dundee's Thistle Hall to hear addresses from Marguerite Moore of the Dublin LLL, and two eminent Belfast-based Land Leaguers, Harold Rylett, an English Unitarian minister, who the *Dundee Courier* presumed to be a Catholic priest (which it later corrected), and Charles Dempsey, editor of the *Ulster Examiner*.

Significantly, as in Glasgow, the platform party included women – Catherine Hopper and Mary McCarron of the Lochee and Mary Gray, Ellen Stewart and Annie Darcy of the St Andrew's Ladies' branches – alongside the President of the Dundee Central Executive, Thomas Smith, and officers of the various Dundee and Lochee men's branches. The speakers were less restrained than in Glasgow, where Chairman John Ferguson had dampened the mood somewhat by prefacing Marguerite Moore's speech with a long discussion of local branch politics.[57] By contrast, Roche once again proved true to Anna Parnell's designation of 'a proper Chairman', and, after passing one all-encompassing resolution condemning government coercion, press hostility and the cowardly conduct towards the Ladies' Land League, gave Mrs Moore the floor.[58]

After evoking an Irish landscape blotted by evictions, emigrant ships and imprisoned martyrs, Marguerite confirmed that repression was breeding resistance: 'But for coercion the Land League would not have the power it has today'. To repeated shouts of affirmation, howls of laughter and calls for vengeance, she went on to mock 'Coercion Bill' Gladstone and lambast 'Buckshot' Forster, 'that charitable-hearted Quaker', who 'would give the jail to the women of Ireland'. Nevertheless, she stated that 'they would gaily go, because they knew that the clang of the prison door behind them rang the death knell of the buckshot Government'. In conclusion, she reiterated Anna Parnell's warning against working within the British political establishment, as Liberal and Conservative were Beelzebub and Lucifer as far as Ireland was concerned. Instead, she urged them instead to 'stick to the principles of the Land League', which, judging by the enthusiastic response, the audience were wont to do.

Nevertheless, the tension between the constitutionalists, who advocated political pressure, and the radical Land Leaguers, who favoured direct action in pursuit of their goals, was evident in Roche's counsel to hold off shooting Forster, as someone had suggested, as they would need him (and the other Liberals) to help fight any future Tory government. His appeal to the audience to register their votes met with no discernible response from the, as yet, disenfranchised working-class men, the women, and the large percentage of youths who formed a major part of the audience.[59] The appeals for people to join the Land League, and particularly the Ladies' League, and to support the political prisoners, were immediately responded to. By the beginning of 1882, the St Mary's branch, covering the East Central end of the town, joined the 500 branches of the LLL now in existence. The fund-raising also continued apace. On 14 March, the Central Executive of the Dundee Land League announced that the Irishmen (*sic*) of Dundee and Lochee had sent £92 2s to the Political Prisoners' Sustenance Fund to provide food for the Land League internees.[60]

Marguerite Moore was scheduled to make a return visit in April when, less than a fortnight before, she was arrested and jailed, along with twelve other LLL activists, and sentenced to six months for continuing to mobilise resistance to evictions. The meeting, in the Kinnaird Hall, went ahead with Chairman Thomas Smith reading Moore's apology from Tullaghmore Jail, and her confident assertion that 'her absence in the circumstances would appeal as eloquently to the hearts of the people as any address she could give'. Smith sympathised with Moore in her sufferings, stating that 'the ladies in Ireland had done their duty nobly and shown to the world they had the courage and patriotism their ancestors once displayed on the battlements of Limerick'. Still, although women formed the majority of the 500-strong audience, no member of the LLL appeared on the platform alongside Smith, John Ferguson, and nine other representatives of the men's branches.

As the Land League's most senior representative in Scotland, Ferguson reiterated Anna Parnell's recognition of the remarkable fund-raising achievements of Dundee and Lochee, which were widely acknowledged as the work of their Ladies' branches. Ferguson noted that these achievements were made all the more remarkable, when 'considering that all the things Dundee had' [or, more properly, had not], it had 'eclipsed all other branches on this side of the water'. A resolution by Thomas Flanagan congratulated the ladies of Dundee and Lochee on 'their great energy and activity' in raising the sum of £200 for the LLL in Ireland 'to help them succour men, women and children evicted by tyrannical landlords', and called on every Irishwoman in Dundee and Lochee to become members.

Here, was a local and wider recognition that this was no modest achievement. Despite the persistent tag of 'ladies' charity', Anna Parnell, Marguerite Moore and others clearly distinguished between acts of upper-class philanthropy and predominantly working-class Irish solidarity. In terms of the latter, and especially in the case of Dundee and Lochee, the money had been hard come by, representing the hard graft and mass sacrifice of a community who had little to spare. Raised in a mutual spirit of self-reliance and solidarity with the aims of the Land League, it was all the more valuable and meaningful because of it. There was also an appreciation on the part of the radical wing of the Land League, to which the Ladies were aligned, that this type of support was the life's blood of the campaign, essential to its continuance and survival. Without it, the movement would collapse.

The remarkable achievements of the local Irish community contrasted with the abysmal performance of those parliamentary representatives in whom Dundee's predominantly Home Rule-supporting INLL branch officers had placed their faith, and endeavoured to invest other peoples' votes. James O'Kane, President of the St Mary's men's branch, declared that 'there was not an Irishman or Irishwoman present who was not against the so-called Liberal government which held power in England and ruled Ireland in so despotic a manner'. John Kennedy of the West End branch proposed 'we stigmatise as recreants and cowards the Irish MPs who have supported the Coercion Government'. The angriest words, however, came from Roche, who less than four months earlier had urged 'Irishmen' to throw their electoral weight behind the Liberal Party for Ireland's sake. 'Moderate Home Rulers', he said, 'were the most frothy of patriots, [and] some were the most cruel rack-renters. The Land League had drawn them out of their shell and shown them to be recreants'.[61]

On this occasion, it was Ferguson who seemed out of sympathy with the meeting in advising them to prepare 'in a constitutional way... to exercise their electoral privileges at the next election' where their policy would be to 'mass themselves on the flanks of both [parties] in an independent position' in readiness for the repeal of the Parliamentary Reform Act when the 'men of Dundee would be true to the position nurtured by their leaders'. Yet, while there was no obvious enthusiasm for his words – a heckler still calling for 'buckshot' to deal with Forster – Ferguson was broadly mapping out the route the Irish national movement would eventually follow.

Tensions between the parliamentarians and the grassroots activists came to a head on 2 May in the conclusion of the Kilmainham Agreement between Parnell and Gladstone, when Parnell undertook to withdraw the No Rent Manifesto, to 'slow down' the Land League agitation and to support the Liberals on their programme of ameliorative reform legislation in exchange for the release of the political prisoners and the cancellation of rent arrears up to £30. At a stroke, Parnell negated all the advantages gained by the Land League, and became party to its pacification, and to the pacification of Ireland, a retrogressive move to which the principal leaders, such as Davitt and Dillon, and much of the membership were opposed. They had little time to absorb this, however, when the Irish National Invincibles responded by assassinating, not the much-reviled Forster, but his conciliatory successor, Lord Frederick Cavendish, and the hated Under Secretary Thomas Henry Burke, in Phoenix Park on 6 May. The assassinations caused confusion in the ranks, with many rushing to publicly distance themselves from any association with the act or its perpetrators. On 8 May, a joint meeting of the Catholics of St Mary's and the Dundee East End branch of the Land League passed a resolution expressing their 'deep sorrow, indignation and abhorrence of the cowardly atrocious murder' of Cavendish and Burke:

> We grieve to think that the stigma of a crime which has not, and cannot have, any support or sympathy from the people of Ireland should, on the eve of what seemed a brighter future, endanger the liberties and good fame of our people and country. We earnestly hope that all Irishmen leave nothing undone to bring the perpetrators of so foul a crime to justice and thereby wipe out the stain cast upon the name of our much maligned and beloved country.[62]

What the Land League supporters who had earlier called for bloody vengeance on Forster and other agents of British oppression made of this pathetic condemnation of their avenging countrymen, and particularly of the exhortation that 'all Irishmen leave nothing undone' to hand them over to the British justice system and a certain death sentence, is not recorded. Indeed, this is precisely what happened when the leader of the Invincibles, James Carey, turned Queen's evidence, leading five of his comrades to the gallows in May-June 1883, and securing his own death by an avenger's bullet several weeks later.[63] Whether these appeals by moderate Irish nationalists were a factor in Carey's decision can only be imagined. It is not unlikely that their authors were taking their lead from respected Land League leaders, notably Davitt, who had publicly repudiated the act, most likely to avoid charges of complicity and discourage a further repressive backlash against the Irish people.[64] The nervous, overly earnest tone of the St Mary's statement betrays a similar anxiety, and suggests it was a deliberate tactic to counter anti-Irish sentiment amongst those elements of the wider community who failed to distinguish between Land Leaguers, Fenians, Home Rulers and, in some cases, Irish-Catholics. Indeed, the co-authoring of the resolution by the 'Catholics of St Mary's' suggests the restraining hand of the clergy behind it. Significantly, there were no similar resolutions from the Dundee Executive of the Land League or the longer established West End and independently minded Lochee branches. Interestingly, amongst those later reputed to have been associated with the Invincibles was ex-West End resident and hard-line Fenian Edward Fox Coyne, who had relocated to Dublin in 1881/2.[65] Unsurprisingly, there was no comment whatsoever from the Ladies' branches, the business of which was invariably reported second hand through male spokesmen or journalists, if at all. While the achievements of the women were publicly lauded, unlike their sisters in Ireland, their opinions remained in the private sphere.

Legacies of the Land League

The Kilmainham Treaty marked the end of the most intensive phase of the Land War, and resulted in the downgrading, and eventual dissolution of the Ladies 'Land League in August 1882, amidst Parnell's accusations of irresponsible and extravagant overspending and an atmosphere of intense bitterness. This effectively put an end to the fundraising at which the LLL, and especially its Dundee and Lochee branches, had excelled.[66] Later that autumn, Davitt attempted to revive the Land League agitation within the wider structure of the Irish National League (INL), the political machine for the IPP, which launched its programme in Dublin on 17 October. However, while Davitt continued to campaign for radical land reform, the Liberal *Dundee Advertiser* reported:

> [he] has declared his allegiance to Parnell [who], for the moment, has triumphed. The moderate party are in the ascendant, and [they are] strong enough to command the adhesion of the revolutionists. The programme itself is a confession of Mr Parnell's predominance. There is nothing revolutionary in it nor in the speeches that supported it.[67]

Moreover, unlike the Land League, the INL was a male affair, with an executive dominated by parliamentarians who conceived of it as their party machine. Women were not admitted, and there was no complementary women's organisation. Not until the 1900s, under its successor organisation, the United Irish League, were women again actively encouraged to enter the sphere of Irish politics.

The Irish National League

If it was good enough for Davitt, however, it was good enough for the Irishmen of Dundee and Lochee, who packed into the Kinnaird Hall two weeks later to hear Davitt promote his vision for the Land League and the Irish Party's new programme. Davitt, who had promptly embarked on a tour of Scotland and English centres, explained the difference between Parnell's plan for peasant proprietorship, where 'the land would pass from one class of landlords to another class of tenant farmers', and his own plan for nationalisation where 'the land would be held in trust for the people [and] reasonable rents go towards payment of rates and taxes falling on the industrial classes'. He claimed that 'Scotch people, when they grasped the question and saw that it was really a contest between national right and legalised justice, would fight for it heart and soul on even more radical grounds than was done in Ireland', and expressed his belief that 'the final blow would be given against landlordism in England'. Here, Davitt's views closely resembled those of Karl Marx who believed that the first blow against capitalism would be struck by a politically conscious working class in the most advanced industrial societies. In the meantime, Davitt announced his intention to accelerate the advancement of the Irish artisan class by establishing working men's reading rooms and mechanics' institutes in Irish towns and cities 'to fit them for the struggle of life and inculcate educative thought, which was absolutely essential in Ireland if they were to successfully combat the enemy against which they were fighting'.[68]

Although Davitt's programme of land nationalisation differed fundamentally from Parnell's plans for peasant proprietorship, Davitt repeatedly denied that there was a split in the national movement, reassuring a large meeting of Irishmen in Glasgow City Hall on 25 October, that 'differences of opinion' did not imply 'differences of principles' as he and Parnell were united on the same objective.[69] Whether Davitt actually believed his own rhetoric is hard to say – 22 years later he described the supplanting of the Land League as a counter-revolution, 'the overthrowing of an idea, and the enthronement of a man' – however, it was a line he was prepared to spin at the time, and one which his Dundee audience were prepared to accept, as indicated by their unanimous decision 'to support the national programme adopted by our leaders'.

Yet, Davitt held no office in the INL and, despite his impassioned attempts to popularise land nationalisation, a resolution, introduced by Thomas Smith and Edward Roche, calling on tenant farmers 'to give their labourers a comfortable house and at least half an acre of land, as advocated by the leaders of their Irish people', suggests that Dundee's Irish nationalists had chosen to place their faith in 'the uncrowned King of Ireland', Parnell, most likely through an abstract concept of nationalism which idealised ties of kinship and led them to trust that the better off 'class of tenant farmers' (who, after all, were not foreign landlords) would willingly hand over a 'fair share' of their gains to the poor, landless labourers.

Davitt began his speech at the Kinnaird Hall, Dundee, by stating that 'the Land League [was] dead, and... it [had] taken its sting with it', to which a voice in the crowd responded, 'But it has left many orphans'. The INL, the counter-revolution to the Land League, was promoted as its legitimate successor, and there is a strange irony in that it was born out of a retrogressive move by Parnell to divert the leadership of the semi-revolutionary grassroots movement back into his own hands, and under centralised parliamentary control. Despite Davitt's insistence that land reform was the principal plank of the Irish Party's new programme, within a few months, Parnell had dropped it to focus solely on the pursuit of a limited measure of Home Rule, and – with the exception of the 1885 General Election when they supported the Tories – an alignment with the Liberal Party, which dominated Irish politics and especially Irish politics in Dundee, for the next three decades.

It is perhaps due to the longstanding allegiance of the Dundee-Irish towards Davitt, and his endorsement of Parnell's leadership, that the INL took a firm hold in the town. Unlike their measured support for the Land League, the INL also enjoyed the unequivocal support of the Catholic clergy – a large demonstration addressed by Joseph Biggar on September 1884 (in anticipation of the passing of the Third Reform Act on 6 December), boasted ten priests from six parishes across Dundee, Arbroath and Montrose – the object being, as Biggar stated, to 'bring the whole Irish people into line in support of the cause in which they were all engaged'.[70] Ex-officers of the local Land League branches, including James O'Kane, Thomas Flanagan and Edward Roche, were equally prominent in the activities of the INL. Flanagan, who also joined the Liberal Association and became a member of the Dundee Parliament,[71] played a vocal part in municipal politics and was a 'noted heckler' at election meetings. Similarly, the ever-dutiful Edward Roche took an active part in the political life of the Third (Lochee) Ward.[72]

The Scottish Land Reform Movement

The Irish Land League also had a direct influence on the Scottish movement for land reform. While the Crofters' Revolt in Skye in 1881 may have been the predictable result of a long and burgeoning resentment at the injustice of high rents, evictions and general lack of tenants' rights, the escalation of resistance at that particular time indicates that the Scottish crofters had drawn courage and inspiration from the Irish campaign, which had revealed the need for a similar organisation in Scotland. Ironically, the collapse of the Irish Land League occurred when attempts to build links with Scottish radicals and land reform campaigners were beginning to pay off.[73] At Davitt's meeting in Dundee in November 1882, Chairman James

O'Kane, former President of the East End branch of the Land League, read a message from the Reverend David Macrae, the minister of Gilfillan Memorial Church, stressing 'the need for thorough and radical land reform in Ireland, Scotland and England'.

Macrae went on to organise the Scottish leg of a speaking tour by American land reform ideologue, Henry George, whose influential book, *Progress and Poverty* (1879) had stimulated an interest in land reform philosophy. The tour commenced on 1 February 1884, at the Newsome's Circus in Dundee, and culminated in the establishment of the Scottish Land Restoration League (SLRL) in Glasgow 24 days later. Branches of the SLRL were subsequently formed in Glasgow, Greenock and Edinburgh, but not, despite initial enthusiasm for the idea and Macrae's influential presence, in Dundee.[74] Over the next two years, Macrae developed a strong relationship with Davitt, and when Davitt next spoke in Dundee, at the Kinnaird Hall in 1885, he expressed his 'great indebtedness' to Macrae 'for what he had done in connection with Ireland'. For his part, Macrae proclaimed Davitt 'one of Ireland's most noble patriots,' and claimed he 'would rather sit in prison with [him] for the peoples' rights [and] the peoples' good, than in the palace with the King [sic]'. In a speech which Davitt pronounced as 'splendid', Macrae went on to praise the 'resolute determination' of the Irish leaders, who 'with the Irish people behind them' were endeavouring to rescue their country from 'the despotism of an alien government and alien institutions'. Looking to the future, he predicted:

> The day may come when even Scotland – if a wiser policy is not adopted with regard to her national interests and her national honour – may make the same demand as Ireland; may have to insist that if her interests are not attended to in the Imperial Parliament, they shall be relegated to a national Parliament... But if Scottish honour or Scottish interests may one day call for this, Irish national sentiment, which is a nobler and mightier force than even self-interest, demands it. Are we then advocates for separation? No, but we are advocates for national rights and national honour. We want confederation or union, but a union founded on justice and fair play – a union, not based on compulsion

but on free choice; a union accomplished not by destruction of one nationality, but a weaving together of two or more nationalities, mutually respecting and strengthening each other.⁷⁵

How far Land League founder Davitt appears to have yielded to the constitutional line was also evident when he stated that any expectations of land reform were 'hopeless' until MPs were paid, praised Parnell for 'faithfully and fearlessly' representing the Irish people and expressed his hope that the next Prime Minister of England would have the good sense to appoint a Prime Minister of a devolved Irish parliament in Dublin, which was 'all the Irish people ever wanted'. However, his comment that 'if Ireland were given total separation, she would only get what she was justly entitled to', appeared to reveal his true desires, suggesting that he was tailoring his words to suit the audience which included local councillors, Protestant clergymen and non-Irish supporters of Scottish land reform alongside his loyal Irish support base. Nevertheless, while Macrae's speech may have sounded more radical from a developing Scottish nationalist perspective as Davitt's sounded compromisingly conservative from an advanced Irish one, Macrae's vision for Scotland did not extend to total separation and was, at this point, unashamedly federalist and, essentially, pro-imperialist.⁷⁶

Also on the platform was the President of the SLRL, William Forsyth, one of five candidates standing in Glasgow constituencies in the forthcoming General Election, in tandem with the Crofters' Party in the Highlands. Despite strong rural support for the crofters, however, the SLRL was proving less relevant to the urban working class who, native Scots or Scots-Irish, had themselves been displaced from the land a generation or more earlier. Radical socialists initially attracted by George's programme for land reform were also critical of its limitations, primarily the failure to transfer ideas about the redistribution of land to the redistribution of capital, which had led Karl Marx to dismiss it as 'capitalism's last ditch'.⁷⁷ A pivotal development here, in the Scottish urban context, was the coming to Edinburgh in 1884 of exiled Viennese socialist and member of Hyndman's Social Democratic Federation (SDF), Andreas Scheu. Scheu quickly identified that the SDF, whose London branch had already fractured due to Hyndman's dictatorial style of leadership, 'had failed in Scotland because it neglected local sympathy for crofter agitation and the Irish Land League'. Along with Monaghan-born John Lincoln Mahon, Scheu set about building an Edinburgh branch drawing from former Irish Land League activists and members of the SLRL, and co-founded the Scottish Land and Labour League as a radical socialist alternative to the latter. The existence of an organisation which infused contemporary socialist ideas with the spirit of the Land League, drew a younger generation of working-class Irish-Scots, such ex-Vice President of the Edinburgh Land League, John Leslie, John Connolly, and ultimately Connolly's younger brother, the future Irish revolutionary leader James, like moths to a flame.[78]

While the coming together of these radical strands at this particular time led to Edinburgh becoming the seed bed of socialism in Scotland, Dundee, which had been so prolific in the Land League agitation, lacked a similar cosmopolitan dynamic. Unlike Edinburgh, it did not have the intellectual tradition or community of ideas – a legacy of the Scottish Enlightenment – and it was too small and geographically remote to attract political refugees of the calibre of Scheu and former Mayor of the Paris Commune, Léo Meillet. Within the Irish community, the INL, with its central objective of Home Rule, and its conditional support for the Liberal Party, remained the dominant political force in a field of other, ostensibly apolitical, associations.

The Irish National Foresters

Meanwhile, other radical Land Leaguers found an outlet more suited to their immediate social needs and wider nationalist aspirations in the Irish National Foresters (INF) – ostensibly a benefit society which provided sickness and death payments to its members and their dependants, but which simultaneously offered material support and allegiance to the Republican movement. The latter function was also fulfilled by the Ancient Order of Hibernians (AOH), with which there was considerable overlap in membership, as there was to a lesser extent with the INL.

The failure of Liberal parliamentarians to progress Gladstone's Home Rule Bill, and the eventual return to power of the staunchly Unionist Salisbury government in 1886 – despite the election of two 'approved' Gladstoneite candidates in Dundee – precipitated the collapse of the

INL.⁷⁹ By contrast, the INF, which established its first branch in Dundee, the Sarsfield No. 53, in March 1884, experienced a marked upsurge in membership. From the start, the INF was controlled by the IRB who launched the organisation in Dundee and quickly manoeuvred themselves into positions of leadership – a shrewd piece of strategising from J P Casey, who chaired the first meeting, and senior organiser James Ward, who took on the title of Chief Ranger (CR), and subsequently District CR for the East of Scotland a year later. By the autumn of 1888, the INF had four branches in Dundee and Lochee – the Sarsfield being joined by the William O'Brien (East End) and Father Mathew (Lochee) branches in October and November 1887, and the C S Parnell (West End) in September 1888.⁸⁰ Ward retreated into the background to be succeeded as District CR for the East of Scotland by former CR of the Father Mathew branch, Edward Roche, and as CR of the Sarsfield branch by his fellow railway worker and likely protégé, James Slaven, while Roche was deputised in both posts by another ex-Lochee Land Leaguer, John Paterson.⁸¹

Besides its function as a financial support network for the Irish community, which spared them the indignity of applying to the parochial board for relief, the INF preserved and encouraged a distinct sense of Irish identity and kinship, and provided an outlet for collective cultural expression, which made it particularly attractive to Dundee's pervasive Ribbon element. The importance attached to the symbols and slogans of Irish nationality was illustrated by the purchase, on the occasion of the first anniversary of the Sarsfield branch of a bespoke banner on which was painted, by William Doyle of the Irish Academy of Art, a representation of Jacobite commander Patrick Sarsfield fighting off the Williamite forces at the Siege of Limerick on one side, and the mottos 'Erin Go Brath' and 'Ceud Mile Failte' on the other. Interestingly, the £70 purchase also suggests that, even in the wake of a trade depression, the branch had sufficient funds to meet the claims upon it. Unlike the Sarsfield branch, which started with 40 men 'in the worst of times', the C S Parnell was instituted 'under the most favourable of circumstances', having already enrolled 73 members prior to the official inauguration on 15 September, many of whom had transferred from other over-weighted branches. That afternoon, a 'considerable' number of people converged on Albert Square from where the three INF branches – who had marched there from their respective headquarters in full regalia of sashes, hats and feathers – were marshalled into processional order behind the Camperdown Works' brass band and the Sarsfield banner, whereupon they paraded through the principal streets and up to Larch Street Hall, where the members were ceremoniously initiated and office bearers elected. Interestingly, despite the 'imposing appearance' and martial music of the Foresters, these regimented displays of Irish identity attracted little opposition from non-Irish observers – although the distinction between Scotch and Irish in the context of the Dundee crowd was not always clear – who appreciated the life and colour they brought to the city streets.[82]

While Paul Kane of the Sarsfield branch boasted that the work of the INF was 'conducted by working men, [and] showed what working men could do towards improving their conditions when united', the bywords were self-help and sociability, not socialism, and there was little in the way of political education or activism.[83] Notwithstanding, the proscription of the INL in Ireland, the imprisonment of William O'Brien MP, and the opening of the Parnell Commission, which dragged the IPP and INL leader through the mire for his alleged links with militant Fenianism, rallied support for the INL in Britain, evidenced in the naming of two new Dundee INF branches in honour of the men, alongside the revived East and West End branches of the INL. Indeed, the formation of the Parnell INF was preceded five weeks earlier by an anti-coercion demonstration called by the INL, many of whose key members, such as Roche, Flanagan and Casey, were prominent in the INF. Hitherto, the INL's preoccupation with the pursuit of Home Rule by constitutional means had drawn attention away from the Land War, which continued regardless as a series of bad harvests and an increase in evictions gave way to a new wave of resistance by way of the 'Plan of Campaign'.[84] In response, the Chief Secretary for Ireland, Arthur Balfour, emboldened by his earlier attack on the Highland Land League, drove through the Criminal Law and Procedure (Ireland) Act of 1887, which, by the summer of 1888, had resulted in the imprisonment of several prominent land campaigners, the most recent of which, that of John Dillon, generated a series of protests by Irish nationalists and sympathetic radicals across the country. The reintroduction of coercion kicked the life back into the INL in Dundee, whose target membership had hitherto found the milieu of the Foresters and other fraternal societies such as the AOH to be more hospitable to their experience of being Irish, male and working class than the tedious round of dry political meetings.

On Saturday, 11 August 1888, the massed forces of the INL – whose St Andrew's, Lochee, A M Sullivan and Michael Davitt branches, which corresponded, respectfully, with the Sarsfield, Father Mathew, William O'Brien and embryonic C S Parnell INF – assembled at their common headquarters and marched in processional order to the Magdalen Green where an estimated crowd of 6,000-8,000 (a large proportion of which, the *Scotsman* stated deprecatingly, were women and children) had gathered in the dreich evening air to listen to two hours of anti-government pro-Home Rule speeches. Councillor William Stephenson opened by reminding them that the Magdalen Green had been 'consecrated by the memory' of radical reform campaigner, George Kinloch, and 'other kindred spirits who had fought the battle of freedom in their day', and urged them to 'do everything in their power' to bring [these] principles to the fore. Supporting Stephenson in condemning the Coercion Act and calling for Dillon's release was Scottish land campaigner and Home Ruler, the Reverend David Macrae, who predicted, to the cheers of the Scottish and Irish contingents, that 'Home Rule for Ireland was coming, and Home Rule for Scotland also, and when Scotland got it she would have to thank Ireland for fighting the first of the battle'. The principal speaker, John Deasy, MP for West Mayo, somewhat overcome by the large show of sympathy, explained that if were to speak in Ireland as he did here, he would likely be, as Dillon had been, thrown in jail. His visit to Scotland, he stated, had convinced him that the Scottish people would, at the next General Election, 'hurl the Tory government from power' returning Gladstone to present his Home Rule Bill to the Queen. President of the St Andrew's INL, Thomas Flanagan, began by reading messages of support from Dundee's two MPs, and concluded with another from the (Irish) National League in Dublin thanking 'the men of Dundee for their noble protest', which it 'hoped would be repeated in every town in Scotland, England and Ireland'.[85]

*

The Socialist Movement

Support also came from the Dundee Radical Association, whose President, James Aimer, and Secretary, John Ogilvy, were afforded a place on the platform. Over the course of next few months, the Dundee Radicals passed a series of strongly-worded resolutions denouncing the government's policy on Ireland, the most forceful of which, proposed and seconded by members of the SDF, Alex Taylor and Joseph Carr, condemned the sentence of six month's hard labour meted out to West Kerry MP and editor of the *Kerry Sentinel*, Edward Harrington (the brother of Timothy) for publishing the proceedings of a proscribed National League meeting. In the resolution, copies of which were sent to Irish MPs Harrington, Parnell, T D Sullivan, T P O'Connor, Tim Healy and the Mayor of Dublin, Thomas Sexton, the DRA stated that it 'now fully realised the insulting cause of the inborn hatred of Irishmen to English misgovernment'; declared that it would 'forcibly and violently resist such iniquitous maladministration if attempted in this country'; and concluded that 'it [was] now a momentous question for the Radicals of Britain to consider whether or not they shall at once adopt other than the ordinary methods to hurl from power a tyrannical Tory government that has shamelessly perverted law and justice, and outraged the feelings of every true lover of liberty'.[86]

Despite contemplating the use of physical force to overthrow the Tory government, however, the Dundee Radicals did not go the length of proposing a revolutionary alternative, but rather continued to rally around the Liberal flag. Indeed, while Dundee had branches of the SDF and the Scottish Land and Labour League by 1888, one of the founders of the Socialist League, William Morris, noted the difficulties its organisers faced, as 'ordinary party politics run high in Dundee and the Radicals have not got further than the Gladstoneite programme, if it can be called a programme'.[87] Moreover, what Scheu and Mahon had identified and sought to resolve in Edinburgh, the less advanced socialist movement in Dundee seemed incapable of achieving, and the large working-class Irish community, whose socio-economic status would naturally have led them to support socialist ideas, continued to stick to their own trusted networks where they were not expected to compromise their identity. A rare exception here was Edward De Courcey of the West End (Michael Davitt) branch of the INL, who, as a result of collaborating with the Dundee

Radicals in the run up to the 1886 general election appears to have shifted his focus to the burgeoning socialist movement. Indeed, early Scottish Labour activist David Lowe recalled that De Courcey was one of a small group of SDF activists operating out of the Overgate Hall when he moved to Dundee in February 1888.[88] Nevertheless, De Courcey's first recorded appearance on a platform was at a meeting in Tay Street Hall on 14 June 1886 alongside organiser of the INL in Scotland, Owen Kiernan, officers of the Dundee INL and four Catholic priests, when his proposal that they work with 'Scotch Radicals' to secure the election of two Gladstonian candidates, was passed unanimously.[89] Irish-born De Courcey, who may have come to Dundee to infiltrate and radicalise the INL (despite his uncommon surname, information on his origins and prior movements is elusive) was, however, not typical of the most of his INL colleagues.

Despite the difficulties of operating in a Liberal environment, the socialists were gaining ground, and their ideas were finding favour with radicals such as John Ogilvy and John Duncan who straddled memberships of the Dundee Radical Association with the SDF and the Socialist League. Ogilvy appears to have joined the latter after a public lecture by William Morris in March 1888, on which occasion Morris was subjected to a barrage of questions regarding his views on physical force, namely, whether socialists were prepared to accomplish their objectives by 'bloody revolution' (Morris replied that he favoured constitutional means); on the maintenance of large standing armies (Morris believed socialism meant the extinction of nationalities, but until that was accomplished, every citizen would be liable for military service); and, given that former revolutions had been accomplished by 'individual men making victims of themselves for the cause', whether factory owner Morris should practise what he preached and renounce his business or at least stop paying his men by piecework, which was 'condemned by socialists'. (Morris didn't think it was fair to bring a man's circumstances against him, in any case, he didn't see how he could.)[90]

Regardless of Morris's insipid answers, the fact that the Dundee socialists went on to champion the Plan of Campaign and endorse the use of physical force, if necessary, made them all the more attractive to a new generation of working-class Scots-born Irish, and a number of advanced Irish nationalists, De Courcey included. This occurred in the midst of an uncertain alliance between physical force and constitutional Irish nationalists, the latter of whom had reconciled themselves with Gladstone and the Liberal Party in the hope they would carry a Home Rule Bill through Parliament. In short, a new generation of Scots-born Irishmen and Irishwomen was concluding that they were more likely to find an outlet for revolutionary ideas and action, or at least a more robust strategy towards the British government, in the socialist movement than in anything the Irish nationalists were currently offering. From the perspective of those Irish organisations, however, was the fear that identification with the socialist movement would lead their fellow Irishmen to spurn their kindred organisations and ultimately their Irish identity, a view which was substantiated by the common conception that becoming a socialist meant (as Morris's comments may have led some to believe) subverting all vestiges of national identity. These conflicting allegiances, which may have inhibited Dundee's Irish community from aligning themselves directly with the socialist movement, briefly clashed in the spring of 1889, with significant consequences.

The 'Free Speech' Campaign of 1889

The tradition of open-air Sunday meetings, as conducted by socialists in particular, is considered to have been instigated by John Duncan, an early member of the SDF in Dundee.[91] By 1889, the SDF had two branches operating in the city, the No. 1 and the Central, the latter of which appears also to have accommodated the Socialist League. By the spring of 1889, Duncan's political associate, James Robertson, had been speaking at the High Street/Overgate corner most Sundays for two years without incident until the appearance, on 10 March, of David McCulloch (mis-named in the local press as McCutcheon), who had undertaken a speaking tour of Scottish cities on behalf of the Glasgow Socialist League.[92] According to the *Courier*, McCulloch 'evidently said something which did not please the crowd', and 'the well-known process of hustling was brought to bear on him', forcing him to take refuge up a nearby close, at which point the police intervened and escorted him to Bell Street Police Station for his own safety, where he was detained until the crowd had dispersed.[93]

The attack on McCulloch aroused the concern of socialists throughout Scotland who, over the next few days, debated the matter in the local press. In a letter to the *Courier*, prefaced by the heading, 'James [*sic*, it was John] Leslie and James Robertson state that the orator McCutcheon is not a socialist', a correspondent of the pseudonym 'Vigilante' wrote: 'The orator is not a Socialist, as I well know, by experience in this and other cities in Scotland. He might be more correctly termed a simple Luddite[94] ...The bulk of his ideas run counter to what are generally advocated by Socialists, but in the main he has been fairly treated with courtesy by them all over the world'. Affirming the 'lecturer' to be a reputable man who did not 'grasp the coppers out of a greasy till', the author complained, 'It will be a matter of regret for him, as it is humiliating to me, to know that these meetings have been made to subserve the purposes of a gang of men outside the democratic movement entirely'. Turning their attention to the attack, the author claimed that 'the men who led it on' were, 'in addition to being avowed anti-Socialists, simply and solely concerned [with] putting down movements of men who dare to oppose their views, and do not chime with their hobby of Home Rule', before going on to liken them to 'the 'Molly Maguires, Kellys and Jesse Jameses', which suggests that the AOH, with which the Mollies were historically linked, may have been involved.[95] Indeed, the harassment of socialist street orators by pro-Home Rule 'roughs' was possibly an attempt by Ribbon elements within the AOH and INF to undermine the political competition, and McCulloch, a respectful non-confrontational speaker and identifiable non-Irish outsider, was an easy target.

As well as rousing the ire of Scotland's socialists, the incident also aroused the omnipresent fear of the authorities that unchecked rowdiness would degenerate into wider social disorder, which led the Dundee magistrates to issue a proclamation banning open-air Sunday meetings from all streets in the immediate vicinity of the High Street/Overgate corner. However, the knee jerk response of the magistrates, which had its origins in the centuries-old concern with maintaining public order, and the more recent desire to construct a positive civic image, occurred within the context of current Irish coercion legislation. The socialists, who perceived the ban as an insidious attack on civil liberties, immediately challenged it, applying for a licence which the Chief Constable rejected. The following Sunday afternoon, around forty men and youths, led by James Robertson who carried – ironically for St Patrick's Day – a red flag, marched from the Socialists' Hall in the Overgate through the Murraygate and Wellgate to Robertson's home turf of the Hilltown, where he announced to a rapidly growing crowd the intention to test the ban the following Sunday. Later that day, Robertson addressed another meeting in in the West Port, and a crowd of a thousand in Commercial Street in the evening.[96] Over the next week, copies of the following poster were printed, posted and, on Saturday, 23 March, pasted on to placards, which a number of men carried through the city streets.

DOWN WITH COERCION IN DUNDEE

Indignation meeting in Albert Square on Sunday first at 12 o'clock – speakers from Glasgow and Edinburgh &c. are expected to be present – in order to test the validity of the Magistrates' proclamation. A procession will be formed and will proceed by Reform Street to the West End of the High Street when a second meeting will be held and resolutions proposed condemning the proclamation as unduly restricting the liberty of the people and calculated to lead to a breach of public order. Men of Dundee, show by your presence and sympathy that you are not to tolerate coercion in any shape or form in the suppression of any public meeting!

The use of the term 'coercion' – rather than 'freedom of speech' – evoked the long litany of Irish coercion legislation, the most recent of which, Balfour's notorious Criminal Law and Procedure Act (commonly known as the Perpetual Crimes Act) was placed permanently on the statute book. For the organisers of the demonstration, it was an astute choice of wording guaranteed to win Irish support. For the previous decade, anti-coercion had been at the heart of Irish nationalist activism, and the call to resist coercion on their own turf, would have been sufficient to rally the support of former land leaguers to whom resisting coercion was a principle, if not an active duty.

Thus, it is with some irony that the rousting of McCulloch by aggressive Home Rule supporters, which precipitated the magistrates' ban, triggered a chain of events that united warring socialists, anarchists, Irish nationalists and other groups and individuals who resented the abuse of authority, under one oppositional banner, which on this occasion, as the campaign was initiated by the socialists, happened to be red. At twenty minutes to twelve on 24 March, the proclaimed area was, in the words of a *Courier* reporter, 'one seething mass of humanity', as 'a steady march of persons from all directions' converged on Albert Square, and every onlooking window was occupied by spectators. At twelve o'clock, Robertson left the Overgate Hall, and ceremoniously carrying his chair high above his head, waded his way through the crowd to the High School gates, where, upon mounting his chair, he proceeded to contrast the position of the Irish population in Dundee with that of their countrymen in Ireland under the present Coercion Bill. 'They were there', he said,

> to show their indignation against the introduction of coercion in Scotland [as] they had had enough of this damnable tyranny in Ireland to put up with it in Dundee.... If they allowed the proclamation of the Magistrates to go forth in the present instance untested, they would give their Tory friends a text at their next Primrose meeting. They would say 'There is coercion in Dundee, and the people of Dundee are quite well satisfied with it and why not the people of Ireland?' That was the point from which they ought to look at the question.[97]

Robertson turned to the reality of life for the working class in Dundee, where men were idle for three or four months in the year, and 'on account of the hardships thrust upon them...go home and give the baby the suckling bottle leaving their wives to go and earn 9s 6d a week at the mills'.

Robert Hutcheson of the Edinburgh SDF ascended the chair to launch a verbal attack on the Dundee magistrates, and the capitalists and their 'rag sellers', of which latter agency the *Courier* disparaged Robertson's bid to 'win the support of the Irish' by suggesting that the shouts of approval from the crowd were 'ironic'. As an experienced street orator, however, Robertson would have been familiar with the political opinions of the Dundee Irish element, and knew what to say to bring them on side.

Robertson lived in James Street on the Hilltown, which in the late 1880s, retained a large number of Irish-headed households, and it is hard to believe that the socialist agitator, who was struggling to raise a large family on a tailor's wage, would been insensitive to the concerns and allegiances of his neighbours. Indeed, any 'ironic' backchat was more likely to have been prompted by Robertson's vainglorious self-comparison with the outspoken land campaigner and renowned orator, William O'Brien.

In all, an estimated 20,000-30,000 people turned out to defy the ban, marching down Reform Street to the High Street where an emboldened Robertson took up his stance at the Overgate corner and was promptly surrounded by a cordon of police and arrested, along with seventeen-year-old rivet heater, Richard Simpson, and 47-year-old James Connor, an ostensibly politically-unaffiliated yarn dyer, who the local press presumed to categorise as a Socialist speaker. In fact, Connor was a senior member of the William O'Brien branch of the INF and possibly a Fenian. Hutcheson was arrested later in the day coming out of the Post Office, having gone there to telegraph John Leslie in Edinburgh and SDF Headquarters in London. After a night in the cells and a farcical court hearing, Simpson was dismissed, and the other three were released, pending trial. John Leslie, who had hastened to Dundee from Edinburgh, was on hand to direct the hundred-strong crowd to the Socialists' Hall in the Overgate where Robertson effused about his brief experience as a political prisoner, the most objectionable part of which appears to have been having his socialist papers confiscated.[98]

In a somewhat reductive view, Walker has interpreted this colourful burst of popular protest as 'street circus', which it undoubtedly was. However, this did not detract from the political message but rather emphasised it in the eyes of the crowd, particularly some of its younger elements, who embraced the opportunity to participate in the drama and appear to have revelled in it. A *Courier* reporter observed that, during the short march from Albert Square to the High Street, a gallus youth who had been carried in the speaker's chair, enjoyed the experience so thoroughly that he had to be persuaded to vacate his 'throne'.[99] The performative aspects of political culture were also intrinsic to the INF whose conscientiously choreographed processions, with their colourful banners, imposing regalia and lively music, contained all the elements of street theatre. Indeed, by adopting as wide a range of idioms as possible, the political message could be conveyed to a wider working-class audience who were, as Walker himself noted, too worn down by hard work and poverty to turn to politics and rather 'sought [relief] in entertainment.[100]

Within a few days of the Dundee arrests, even the 'capitalists' rag sellers' had grown critical of the excessive reaction of the Dundee magistrates, with the Tory *Courier* claiming that the charges of mobbing and rioting were an 'abuse of terms'. The Liberal *Advertiser* stated that the 'terms ought to be protested against for the good name of the city', and regretted that the authorities had 'allowed their natural inclinations to get the better of their judgement.' Further afield, the *London Star* reported that there was 'an old-world ring of witch-hunting' about the charge of 'shouting and making use of violent, threatening, abusive and profane language,' opining that 'surely the folk of Dundee are not so weak in the nerve as to be afraid of strong language.' Suitably embarrassed, the magistrates quietly substituted the charge of mobbing and rioting to one of obstruction, of which the three were later pronounced guilty and released on payment of Hutcheson's and Connor's fines – father-of seven Robertson was let off with a caution – which the socialists' heavily-promoted defence fund duly covered.[101]

The defiance of the ban, and the arrest of the main protagonists, did much to advance the socialist cause in Dundee and beyond. The *Advertiser* credited the authorities' actions with providing 'a very effective advertisement [for the socialists] from Land's End to John O'Groats', adding, that while dwindling audiences had threatened to leave the socialists 'wailing like the deserted pastors of the non-church going… if [they] were now to appear and hold forth on Sunday in the High Street or other busy thoroughfare, they would not only break the law, but draw congregations so large that they would provide public nuisances as well'. The socialists in Dundee were reaping the benefits of the widespread publicity. On Sunday, 31 March, the SDF held meetings in Albert Square, Commercial Street, and a large protest demonstration in Barrack Park, where an estimated 3,000 people gathered around two platforms to hear speakers from Glasgow, Edinburgh and Dundee denounce the actions of the magistrates. It fell to Edward De Courcey, who presided over the first platform, to open the proceedings, and Dundee-Irishman Slane to present the key resolution protesting 'this attempt by the authorities to suppress free speech in Dundee'. This meeting, he continued, regards it as part of the general design of the privileged classes and their agents in Trafalgar Square, Mitchelstown, and elsewhere, to suppress the discussion of the labour problem and the advocacy of the claims of the worker; and [gives] every support to those who have been arrested when in the act of vindicating the time-honoured right of free and public meeting.

Here was an unequivocal reference to the scene of one the most notorious confrontations of the Land War, the 'Mitchelstown Massacre' of 9 September 1887, when police fired into a group of anti-eviction protestors, killing three. On 13 and 20 November 1887, protest demonstrations in Trafalgar Square, organised by English socialists and Irish nationalists, had been attacked by the police and the army, resulting in several injuries, arrests and the death of one protester under a police horse. The resolution, supported by John Leslie from Edinburgh and Bruce Glasier from Glasgow (later a significant leader of the Independent Labour Party), was carried with great enthusiasm, and a similar resolution from the second platform was passed unanimously. The *Courier* noted that the speeches 'were all of a thoroughly Socialistic nature' and 'frequently evoked applause'. Another meeting on Magdalen Green later that evening also attracted a large audience.[102]

Leslie claimed that it was at these meetings he observed 'a silent young man as a very interested and constant attender', accompanied by his uncle who he knew to be 'one of the Old Guard of the Fenian movement'.[103] The young man was twenty-year-old James Connolly, and the uncle may have been his paternal uncle, Peter Connolly or MacBride, whose reputation as an 'old Fenian' has been widely acknowledged, or possibly his mother's brother, James McGinn, with whose in-laws, Owen and Mary Boyle, Connolly was lodging at 9 St Mary Street, next to Barrack Park.[104] In a letter to his fiancée, Lillie Reynolds, apparently written on Sunday 31 March, Connolly wrote that 'the house is full of people' – some of whom may have been attending the rally – who were excitedly discussing a murder committed the day before by neighbouring Irish grocer, Joseph Redmond, who had stabbed his wife in the back in full view of his customers.[105] A point of interest to the commentators was the fact that Redmond had displayed symptoms of mental illness – police doctor Charles Templeman later testified that five years earlier he had examined a delusional Redmond who claimed his neighbours were conspiring to carry him off and do him harm' because he refused to join the Land League, and were sending people to take goods from his shop without paying. Templeman stated he 'was told this was untrue'.[106]

In the spring of 1889, Connolly was facing his own predicament, having recently gone AWOL from the British Army just short of seven years' service, most of which had been in Ireland where he had met Lillie. Penniless and looking for work, Connolly had come to Dundee via Perth, probably on the advice of his brother, John, who was working in the city. Within a few weeks of having arrived, Connolly had acquired some knowledge of the composition and character of its large working-class female workforce, to which he added his own observations. On 17 April he wrote to Lillie, 'This is the town where women rule the roost. According to the census there are supposed to be eleven women to every two men'. (A poetic exaggeration perhaps, as the female-male ratio was closer to 3:2, although within the textile workforce it was much higher.) He continued:

> And if you see the street beside the mills at dinner hour or any [dull] hours, just as the mills are coming out, you would believe it, women, women hardly anything but women and girls of all shapes, descriptions, and sizes, short and small, long and tall, as beautiful as angels and ugly as sin. And their talk, oh the tower of Babel was nothing to it. You can hear at once all the twangs of every district in Scotland and the brogue of every county in Ireland. For there isn't a county in the Emerald Isle but what has sent [its] representatives here. I think Dundee has, as proportion to its population a stronger Irish population than any other town in Great Britain. The children here also work at 6 years of age going half-time to school and half to work. In the majority of families, both husband and wife work, the wife often earning more than the husband. Women can work when men can't get it here, and so the spectacle is often presented of the wife working while the husband sits idle at home. How would you like that [treat], Lillie? It often made my teeth water when I looked at them with envy, moryah....[107]

That last playful quip glossed over the unromantic fact that the work was long, hard and unhealthy, and wages were low all round. In reality, there was 'no much pleeshir livin' affen ten an' nine', or nine and six, the figure James Robertson had quoted in his speech at the High School gates, from which Connolly possibly derived some of his information. Connolly was a quick learner, and although he did not mention it in his letters to Lillie, it is highly likely he was gathering information on the state of Irish affairs – as he undoubtedly was on trade union issues – locally and further afield, and matching it to the insight he had gained from his time in Ireland.

The overlap of socialist, Irish, and indeed, Scottish nationalist agitation had not gone unnoticed in Westminster. In the course of a parliamentary debate on Scottish Home Rule, the Chief Secretary of Ireland, Arthur Balfour, alerted Gladstone to the radical Liberal MP for Mid-Lanark, Robert Cunninghame Graham's socialistic reasons for supporting Home Rule, which Balfour admitted were gaining ground in 'certain parts of Scotland'.[108] Significantly, Cunninghame Graham had also attended the infamous Trafalgar Square demonstration on 13 November 1887 at which he had been arrested. Of perhaps greater significance, however, was the fact that, eight days after the Dundee Anti-Coercion/Free Speech demonstration made national news, Balfour was moved to opine that 'much of the Irish agitation was a Socialistic agitation', and that the 'infection' of Irish agitation was also 'Socialistic'.[109]

Amongst Dundee's Irish community, the intensification of the Land War had revived the spirit of the Land League. At the weekly meeting of the A M Sullivan branch of the INL on 17 March, President John McErlain observed that 'a large number of those who had hitherto been found indifferent were beginning to manifest a keen interest in the politics of the day', and that the branch was now in 'a very flourishing condition'. Six weeks later, the branch endorsed a resolution condemning 'the brutal and oppressive evictions of the tenants at Olphert' and the 'outrageous' sentence passed on English (Liberal) MP Charles Conybeare by 'Balfour's Coercion Magistrate' for 'the "crime" of succouring the starving peasants of Donegal'.[110] Alluding to the more conservative elements of the local Irish community, McErlain noted 'the lethargy which prevailed in some circles while the brutal laws of Balfour were running their course in Ireland, and

Balfour's supporters were holding meetings at their doors'. Encouraged by the socialists' protests against Dundee's 'Coercion Magistrates', McErlain suggested that 'Dundee might make a general protest against such meetings.' Later that evening, James Robertson addressed an open-air meeting in the West Port on that very matter. By the same token, while the socialists raised a fund to meet the cost of Robertson and Hutcheson's legal defence, the A M Sullivan branch set up a fund for the defence of 'the patriot priest of Gweedore', Father McFadden, and for the distressed peasantry of Donegal, which the Chairman trusted would have a generous reception, not only from the men of St Mary's, but from 'all the friends of the Irish in Dundee'.[111]

Despite the INL's repeated endorsements of Home Rule-supporting Liberals, the real 'friends of the Irish', in this case, were the socialists. The initial pitching of the 'Free Speech' campaign as an anti-coercion protest, and the correlation of principled practical socialism with the cause of the Land League, put the socialists in the vanguard of radical Irish protest in Dundee, as it did in the rest of Scotland, England and Wales. This fact was not lost on James Connolly who two decades later wrote:

> Among Irish exiles in Great Britain, the Land League had to depend entirely on the championship of poor labourers and English and Scottish socialists. In fact, the latter were, for years, the principal exponents and interpreters of Land League principles to the British masses, and they performed their task unflinchingly at a time when the 'respectable' moneyed men of the Irish communities in Great Britain cowered in dread and of the displeasure of their wealthy British neighbours.[112]

Later in his life, Connolly recalled devouring the publications of the Land League in his youth, and it is easy to see how, nursing a passionate interest in the politics of Irish resistance and having observed developments in Dundee, he was sufficiently inspired by the actions of the socialists, and particularly in their efforts to link the Irish Land League with the fight for socialism, to join the Socialist League in April 1889.

According to a second-hand account cited by labour historian C Desmond Greaves, Connolly recalled buying *Penny Readings for the Irish*

People, a miscellany of Irish prose, poetry and short articles on Irish history, compiled and occasionally written by the publishers of *The Nation*, T D Sullivan and his brother Alexander, in whose honour the Dundee East End branch of the INL had been named in 1884.[113] It is of some significance that Alexander's wife, Frances Donovan, was an executive committee member of the Ladies' Land League who acted as Michael Davitt's main contact when he was in Portland Prison, in 1881–2; and it is of even greater significance that, as the Ladies' Land League was formally dissolved, at 32 Sackville Street, Dublin, on 10 August 1882, the women present resolved to establish leagues throughout the country for the purpose of 'teaching the rising generation their country's history and encouraging the circulation of national literature'.[114] It was a quietly subversive move – ostensibly, it conformed to the acceptably feminine role of teachers and nurturers of a younger generation, and it was less controversial than their previous role of front-line participants in a semi-revolutionary campaign. Nevertheless, from the knowledge and experience gained from that campaign, particularly of the spirit demonstrated by young adolescents in the under-credited Children's Land League, the women were acutely aware of the potential of, as the author of that final resolution, Mrs Burke, presciently phrased it, 'the rising generation'.[115]

Although the Land League campaign of 1879–82 was short-lived, it left a long legacy. Amongst the many legacies of the Ladies' Land League then, was the Irish cultural movement which aimed to inculcate a knowledge of Irish history and heritage, to revive cultural traditions, and promote the expression of Irish identity. Organised on a grassroots model based on the Land League, the Gaelic League, founded in 1893, was the first organisation since the dissolution of the Ladies' Land League in which women could participate fully, and take on a role equal to men. The Gaelic League proved to be a school for the 'Rising' generation – notably Maud Gonne, who joined it when every other nationalist organisation was closed to her, and Patrick Pearse (*as Gaeilge*, Pádraig Mac Piarais) who joined in 1896 at the age of sixteen. Even the self-educated socialist, James Connolly, who initially pointed out its limitations, came to recognise its revolutionary potential.[116]

For Connolly, the Land League was a seminal influence in the construction of a socialist world view, providing an Irish model for a wider international working-class solidarity. For all its shortcomings, the Land League campaign exposed essential truths about the economic structure of society and provided an object lesson on organisation and strategy which could be applied to future campaigns. In the events of Easter Week, Connolly lived to see the results of a previous generation's labour, for which, despite the prospect of military defeat, he considered himself lucky.

Although the Land League left many orphans, it also left many ghosts – notably, the women of the Ladies' Land League, and particularly Anna Parnell, whose resolute sense of justice and tireless propagandising throughout the most intense phase of the Land War emboldened countless women and working-class men to step up and join the Land League, from where they helped sustain a semi-revolutionary campaign which, due to political and class divisions, was closed down before it reached its goal. It was a hard lesson, epitomised in Anna's own tragic story of withstanding years of intensive work, prejudice and misogynistic abuse to be betrayed by her own brother. Succumbing to a physical and mental breakdown, she dropped out of public life, changed her name in an effort to maintain anonymity, and eventually drowned in a swimming accident off the North Devon coast in September 1911. However, Davitt's 1904 account of the Land League campaign, *The Fall of Feudalism in Ireland*, motivated Anna to write her own, *The Tale of a Great Sham*, completed in 1907. Unfortunately, despite all her labours (and the endeavours of younger sister Theodosia), Anna's manuscript failed to find a publisher. It was not until 1986, thanks to the efforts of Dana Hearne, that it finally did.[117] In her final analysis, Anna considered what would happen twenty years' hence, concluding significantly, that 'in spite of its poor prospects, armed rebellion seems to be the next thing tried, or played out, here'.[118] How right she was. Unfortunately, she did not live to see it.

Endnotes to Chapter 4

1. Fanny Parnell, 'Hold the Harvest' [third verse], as printed in *The Nation*, 4 September 1880.
2. Circular by the Ladies' Land League, printed in the *Dundee Weekly News*, 31 December 1881.
3. The Landlord and Tenant (Ireland) Act of 1870 recognised the customary right (in the areas where it existed, mainly in Ulster) to compensation for improvements made to a farm by tenants surrendering their leases. However, the Act was rendered ineffectual by a complicated claims procedure (which placed the onus of proof on the tenant applying), and the fact that the majority of Ireland's tenant farmers were not party to the custom.
4. *Dundee Evening Telegraph*, 28 November 1879.
5. Hannah disappeared off the record altogether after his public dissociation from the Home Rule Association in February 1872. By 1873, his wife and children were living in the Poor House, where his six-year-old daughter, Eliza, died of a brain tumour in May 1873. By 1881, his wife Eliza was working as a domestic servant and lodging with jute workers in the Scouringburn, while 17-year-old daughter, Jane, and nine-year-old son, Stephen, were in Smyllum Orphanage, Lanark. Eldest son, Philip, a calender worker, died of tuberculosis in Dundee Royal Infirmary in May 1886 aged 26, seven weeks after his 25-year-old brother, Francis, died of an epileptic seizure in Dundee Royal Lunatic Asylum. The fate of daughter Agnes, born c1869, is unknown. Census of Scotland, 1871, 1881; Death records for Philip and Francis Hannah.
6. 'The New Departure' aimed to realign the IRB within a broader coalition of physical force and advanced constitutional nationalists, in the belief that this would hasten the achievement of Irish national independence.
7. *Dundee Advertiser*, 29 November 1879.
8. *The Irishman*, 6 March 1880.
9. *People's Journal*, 20 March 1880.
10. *Dundee Courier*, 22 March 1880.
11. *Dundee Courier*, 15 February 1881.
12. See Chapter 2.
13. *The Nation*, 12, 19 February 1881.
14. *Dundee Courier*, 7 February 1881.
15. The New Departure aimed to realign the IRB within a broader coalition of physical force and advanced constitutional nationalists in the belief that this would hasten the achievement of Irish national independence.

16 Likewise, they continued to keep a keen eye on political developments. For example, a few days after the Land League meeting, the Dundee '98 Club met to debate whether the Irish MPs 'should...return to parliament after the ignominious way in which they were treated'. *The Nation*, 19 February 1881.
17 *Dundee Courier*, 7 February 1881.
18 *Dundee Advertiser*, 10 December 1880.
19 *Dundee Courier*, 14 March 1881, *Dundee Courier*, April 1881.
20 Ruth P Forbes, 'Patterns of cultural production and reception in Dundee, 1850–1900' (Unpublished PhD thesis, University of Dundee, 2003), pp95–96.
21 *Dundee Courier*, 10 May 1881.
22 *Dundee Courier*, 11 May 1881.
23 *Dundee Courier*, 13 May 1881.
24 *Dundee Courier*, 14 May 1881.
25 Census of Scotland, 1881.
26 Ó Catháin, *Irish Republicanism in Scotland*, p116.
27 *Dundee Courier*, 22 August 1881.
28 Devoy, *Recollections*, p113.
29 Davitt, *The Fall of Feudalism*, p299.
30 Fanny originally solicited support for the idea in a letter to the *Irish World* in August 1880.
31 Patricia Groves, *Petticoat Rebellion: the Anna Parnell Story* (Cork: Mercier Press, 2009), pp143–46, 164.
32 *Dundee Courier*, 2 March 1881; Ó Catháin, *Irish Republicanism in Scotland*, p117.
33 Even after the Third Reform Act of 1884, 61 per cent of adult males remained disenfranchised compared to 58 per cent in Glasgow, 51 per cent in Edinburgh and 35 per cent in Aberdeen, and at municipal level, over half were ineligible to vote.
34 Paul Bew, *Land and the National Question in Ireland, 1858–82* (Dublin: Gill & Macmillan, 1979), pp170–71.
35 NLI, Correspondence of Anna Parnell, MS 17 701.
36 *Dundee Evening Telegraph*, 6 August 1881. For detail on the profile of Ladies' Land League members in Dundee and Lochee, see Niall Whelehan 'Saving Ireland in Juteopolis: Gender, Class and Diaspora in the Ladies' Land League', *History Workshop Journal*, 2021, pp81–83.
37 *Dundee Courier*, 12 August 1881; *Dundee Evening Telegraph*, 23 August 1881.
38 *Dundee Courier*, 12 August 1881.
39 *Dundee Courier*, 16 August 1881.
40 The half-time system was, essentially, a 'loophole' in the Education Acts of 1871

and 1872, in England and Scotland respectively, which permitted children from 10 up to the legal school-leaving age of 12 to spend half a day in school and half a day in work (or alternate days in one then the other). Generally practised in areas of low-waged employment, by 1891, Dundee had the highest percentage of half-timers of any Scottish industrial centre (18per cent of the total textile workforce). For a discussion of the half-time system, see Anthony Cox, *Empire and Industry: the imperial nexus of jute, 1840–1940* (Abingdon: Routledge, 2013), pp68–71, 193.

41   *North British Daily Mail*, 20 August 1881; Ó Catháin, *Irish Republicanism in Scotland*, p117.

42   *Edinburgh Evening News*, 1 September 1881; *Edinburgh Daily Review*, 1 September 1881.

43   *Dundee Courier*, 6 September 1881.

44   *Dundee Courier*, 30 August 1881; *Edinburgh Daily News*, 1 September 1881; Dundee Courier, 6 September 1881.

45   *Greenock Advertiser*, 30 August 1881.

46   Resident Magistrates Charles Clifford Lloyd, Richard Eaton, Thomas Oliver Plunkett and Thomas Hamilton, and County Inspector of Clare constabulary, Henry Smith. As Resident Magistrate of Limerick, Lloyd jailed the entire committees of the Kilmalock and Kilfinan Land Leagues, including the radical Land League priest, Father Eugene Sheehy, the first priest to be imprisoned in the current phase of the Land War. Along with the Chief Secretary of Ireland, W E Forster, and Earl Spencer (the former and future Lord Lieutenant), Lloyd went on to set up the Special Magistrate system under which Ireland was divided into six areas within which divisional RMs collaborated with the police and troops in their area to repress the Land League. On 13 July 1881, County Inspector Smith, gave his men free rein to use firearms without fear of sanction when enforcing evictions. (Richard Hawkins, 'Lloyd, Charles Dalton Clifford' and 'Forster, William Edward', *Dictionary of Irish Biography*).

47   *Dundee Advertiser*, 25 October, 5, 29 November 1881; *Dundee Evening Telegraph*, 28 October 1881.

48   *Dundee Courier*, 28 October, 1 November 1881, 3 December 1881.

49   Margaret Ward, *Unmanageable Revolutionaries* (London: Pluto Press,1989), p24.

50   Ward, *Unmanageable Revolutionaries*, p25.

51   *Dundee Evening Telegraph*, 8,9 September 1881.

52   Sheehy Skeffington, *Michael Davitt*, p106; *Freeman's Journal*, 24 October 1881.

53   *Dundee Courier*, 28 October 1881.

54   Letters to Anna Parnell from: unidentified Boys' Land League branch; P. K. Kennedy of the Cashel Boys' Land League; and C Mathias, Eton College, NLI, MS 17 701. For more on the Children's Land League, see Riona Nic Congail, 'Young Ireland and *The Nation*: Nationalist Children's Culture in the Late Nineteenth Century', *Eire-Ireland*, 46:4 (2011), pp37–62.

55 *Freeman's Journal*, 15 November 1881; *Leeds Mercury*, 19 December 1881; *Belfast Telegraph*, 19 December 1881.
56 *Dundee Courier*, January 1881.
57 *The Nation*, 21 December 1881.
58 As one of the Ladies' Land League's most combative front-line activists and outspoken speakers, Marguerite Moore had defiantly faced off a police invasion of a Ladies' Land League meeting with the words, 'the law which takes the men's arms could not touch the women's tongues.' (*The Nation*, 12 November 1881). For more on Marguerite Moore, see Niall Whelehan, *Changing Land: Diaspora Activism and the Irish Land War* (New York: New York University Press, 2021), pp45–68.
59 *Dundee Courier*, 22 December 1881.
60 *Dundee Evening Telegraph*, 14 March 1882.
61 *Dundee Courier*, 12 April 1882.
62 *Dundee Courier*, 9 May 1882.
63 Carey was shot dead by another Invincible, Patrick O'Donnell, whilst emigrating to South Africa on 29 July 1883. O'Donnell, who was travelling on the same ship purely by chance, was executed for Carey's murder on 17 December. For detail, see Shane Kenna, *The Invincibles: The Phoenix Park Assassinations and the Conspiracy that Shook and Empire* (Dublin: O'Brien Press, 2019).
64 Sheehy Skeffington, *Michael Davitt*, p108. John Denvir cites anti-Irish riots in Brighouse, Yorkshire (where Cavendish was the local MP); Stalybridge, near Manchester; and Tredegar, South Wales. (Denvir, *The Irish in Britain*, pp296–7).
65 See also Chapter 3. Coyne's youngest son's birth record places the family at Francis Street in the Liberties district of Dublin in early 1882. Coyne died in Barnet, London, in January 1888. His family subsequently returned to Dundee where they remained for the rest of their lives as keen pro-Irish Republican sympathisers. According to local Sinn Féin organiser, Cathal Duthie, eldest son John, who carried the family tradition, was an active supporter of the movement in the 1919–23 gunrunning campaign. Eamonn Mooney Papers [hereafter EMP], letter from Cathal Duthie to Eamon Mooney, March 1955, EMP/3/A/31; Census of Scotland, 1881, 1891, 1901, 1911, 1921; birth register for Patrick Edward Coyne, 16 March 1882; death register for Edward Fox Coyne, January – March 1888; death register for John Coyne, 27 February 1955. Genealogical information accessed via Irish Civil Records; England and Wales Civil Registration Death Index, 1837–1915.
66 The final sum of six pounds was handed over to Marguerite Moore, when she returned to Dundee in September 1882 (Whelehan,' Saving Ireland in Juteopolis', p91).
67 *Dundee Advertiser*, 20 October 1882.
68 *Dundee Courier*, 2 November 1882.
69 *Dundee Courier*, 26 October 1882.

70 *Dundee Courier*, 23 September 1884.

71 The Dundee Parliament was formed in January 1880 with the aim of encouraging local politicians to develop their debating skills and possibly progress to a higher level of political leadership. It also provided a forum in which other non-elected members could discuss the social and political issues of the day. (*Dundee Courier,* 16 January 1880).

72 *Dundee Courier*, 13 April 1898; *People's Journal*, 10 March 1917.

73 For detail, see Andrew Newby, *Ireland, Radicalism and the Scottish Highlands, c1870–1912* (Edinburgh: EUP, 2019).

74 *Dundee Evening Telegraph*, 1 February 1882; *Dundee Courier*, 26 February, 19 March 1882. A branch was mooted, but failed to take off. This is possibly due, in part, to the relatively small number of Highlanders in the town (between 1851–91, around 1 per cent of Dundee's population were of Highland birth, most of whom were from Perthshire). (Charles W J Withers, *Highland Communities in Dundee and Perth, 1787–1891* (Abertay Historical Society: Dundee, 1996), pp15–16.

75 *Dundee Courier*, 16 April 1885.

76 Macrae went on, with John Stuart Blackie and others, to found the Scottish Home Rule Association in 1886, which fell into abeyance during the First World War, was revived afterwards, and subsequently merged with the separatist Scottish National League in 1928 to become the National Party of Scotland, and ultimately, in 1934, the Scottish National Party. (Nathan Kane, *A Study of the Debate on Scottish Home Rule, 1886*–1914, (unpublished PhD thesis, University of Edinburgh, 2015), pp118–9; Richard J Finlay, *Independent and Free: Scottish Politics: The Origins of the Scottish National Party, 1918–45* (Edinburgh: John Donald, 1994).

77 Karl Marx, letter to friend, 20 June 1881, reprinted in *The People*, 5 June 1892.

78 In August 1881, Leslie had chaired the Anna Parnell meeting in St Mary's Hall in the Cowgate, Edinburgh, on which occasion he described Anna as the advocate of 'a degraded and brutalised nation'. *Edinburgh Evening News*, 1 September 1881; *Edinburgh Daily Review*, 1 September 1881.

79 *Dundee Courier*, 15 June 1886.

80 The naming of the latter was likely prompted by the upcoming Parnell Commission, i.e., judicial enquiry (which opened on 22 October) into a series of articles published in the Tory-supporting *Times*, centring on a letter purportedly signed by Parnell in which he was demonstrated to have condoned the Phoenix Park assassinations. In February 1889, Richard Piggot, the former proprietor of *The Irishman* and the *Flag of Ireland*, crumbled under cross-examination and admitted to having forged the incriminating letter whereupon he fled to Madrid and, apparently, shot himself. The Commission finally reported in March 1890 when Parnell was fully exonerated. For a full discussion of the circumstances and proceedings of the Parnell Commission, see Davitt, *The Fall of Feudalism*, pp531–608. It is unclear whether the William O'Brien

Chapter 4 – The Land For The People 1879-89

branch was named after the fiery nationalist MP or the Young Ireland leader, William Smith O'Brien. Given the timing, the former seems more likely. However, it may have been a deliberately ambiguous choice designed to cut across generations, political traditions and draw in a wider base of support. The Father Mathew branch, named after the Cork-based founder of the Irish temperance movement, was possibly a reflection of the priorities of its leading members; Edward Roche, for example, was a devout Catholic and staunch advocate of temperance.

81   *Dundee Evening Telegraph*, 22 February 1884; *Dundee Courier*, 18 March 1885; *Dundee Advertiser*, 28 November 1887; *Dundee Courier*, 28 April 1888; *Dundee Courier*, 4 September 1888.

82   *Dundee Courier*, March 1885; *Dundee Courier*, 17 September 1888.

83   *Dundee Courier*, 28 April 1888.

84   Conceived and promoted by Timothy Harrington, John Dillon and William O'Brien, the Plan of Campaign aimed at securing reduced rents relative to agricultural prices, failing which all tenants would go on rent strike, and pay instead into a campaign fund towards assisting those who were evicted.

85   *Dundee Courier*, 13 August 1888; *The Scotsman*, 13 August 1888.

86   *Dundee Courier*, 13 January 1889; *Dundee Courier*, 5 March 1889; Scrapbook of the Dundee Radical Association, 1888–1889, Dundee City Archives [hereafter DCA], GD/X455.

87   *Commonweal*, 7 April 1888.

88   David Lowe, *Souvenirs of Scottish Labour* (W & R Holmes: Glasgow, 1919), p60.

89   *Dundee Courier*, 15 June 1886.

90   *Dundee Advertiser*, 28 March 1888.

91   Lowe, *Souvenirs of Scottish Labour*, pp58–60.

92   McCulloch had possibly come to Dundee through an arrangement between Bruce Glasier of the Glasgow Socialist League and William Cameron, Secretary of the Dundee Central branch of the SDF.

93   *Dundee Courier*, 11 March 1889.

94   This is likely a disparaging reference to the anarchist tendency in the Socialist League, of which Cameron was a leading exponent

95   *Dundee Courier*, 13 March 1889. The *Courier*'s strategically placed headline suggests that the letter was somehow connected to John Leslie, who may have instigated it in his capacity as Secretary of the Scottish Socialist Federation (the unifying socialist body in Edinburgh which he was hoping to replicate in Dundee) and James Robertson. Whatever their identity, the author's perspective was undoubtedly conditioned by contemporary socialist perceptions of the Molly Maguires in North America who arose out of the brutal conditions of Irish immigrants in the Pennsylvania coalfields, and whose attacks on perceived enemies targeted organisers and socialistic speakers as well as exploitative mine

owners. However, the Mollies were an evolving multi-faceted organisation, and it is hard to imagine ex-radical Land Leaguer and self-identified Irishman John Leslie – who David Lowe claimed had been the 'secretary' of a 'Ribbon League' aged seventeen (Lowe, *Souvenirs of Scottish Labour*, p261) – condoning such a superficial comparison. Kevin Kenny, *Making Sense of the Mollie Maguires* (Oxford: OUP, 1998. For links with the AOH, see Hughes and MacRaild, *Ribbon Societies in Nineteenth-Century Ireland and its Diaspora*, pp307–9). For more on Leslie's Irish allegiances, see J D Young, 'John Leslie, 1856–1921: A Scottish-Irishman as Internationalist', *Saothar*, 18 (1993), pp55–61; C Desmond Greaves, *The Life and Times of James Connolly* [1961] (Manifesto Press: Croydon, 2018), p20.

96 *Dundee Advertiser*, 18 March 1889.
97 *Dundee Courier*, 25 March 1889.
98 *Dundee Advertiser*, 26 March 1889.
99 *Dundee Courier*, 25 March 1889.
100 Walker, *Juteopolis*, p536.
101 *Dundee Advertiser*, 25 March 1889, *Dundee Courier*, 26 March 1889; *London Star*, 2 April 1889; *Dundee Advertiser*, 28 May 1889.
102 *Dundee Courier*, 1 April 1889; *Dundee Advertiser*, 1 April 1889.
103 NLI, William O'Brien papers, MS 13,933.
104 A James McGinn was the Secretary of the IRB-dominated Dundee '98 Club in 1881, although whether this was James Connolly's uncle is uncertain. *The Nation*, 19 February 1881. It is known that McGinn was a gas fitter in Dundee at the time, and that his wife Bridget, née Boyle, kept a women's lodging house in Albert Street, Lochee, while her sister-in-law, Mary Boyle, kept a mixed-sex lodging house in St Mary Street. Greaves, *Life and Times*, pp4,7. For more on Peter Connolly or MacBride, see Irish Military Archives [hereafter IMA] Bureau of Military History [hereafter BMH], witness statement of Ina Connolly-Heron, WS 919, p2; John O'Neill, 'The 1872 Edinburgh Lamplighters' Strike: creating James Connolly', The Treason Felony Blog,

https://treasonfelony.wordpress.com/2020/05/09/the-1872-edinburgh-lamplighters-strike-creating-james-connolly/, accessed 19 May 2023.

105 NLI, William O'Brien papers, MS 13,911.
106 *Dundee Advertiser*, 30 April 1889.
107 NLI, William O'Brien papers, MS 13,911.
108 An early convert to socialism and a co-founder of the Scottish Home Rule Association, Robert Bontine Cunninghame Graham, had stood as a Liberal Party candidate on a radical socialist programme which included Home Rule for Scotland; nationalisation of the land, the mines and other major industries; an eight-hour working day; and universal suffrage. In August 1888, he co-founded the Scottish Labour Party, of which he became President alongside Keir Hardie as Secretary.

109 *Dundee Courier*, 12 April 1889.

110 The Cornish barrister and radical Liberal MP, Conybeare, was sentenced under the Criminal Law and Procedure Act to three months in Derry Gaol for distributing bread to evicted tenants at Falcarragh, County Donegal.

111 *Dundee Advertiser*, 18 March, 19 April, 6 May 1889; *Dundee Courier*, 6 May 1889.

112 *Labour in Irish History*, 1910, reproduced in Shaun Harkin (ed), *The James Connolly Reader* (Chicago: Haymarket Books, 2018), p209.

113 Greaves, *Life and Times*, p90.

114 *Freeman's Journal*, 11 August 1882.

115 *Freeman's Journal*, 11 August 1882.

116 'The Gaelic Revival', *Worker's Republic*, 1 October 1898; 'Sinn Fein and the Language Movement', *The Harp*, April 1908.

117 At the time of commencing this study, it was once more out of print. Thankfully, due to the efforts of Dana Hearne, Margaret Ward and others, it has since been republished (by UCD Press in 2020). For the story of Anna's manuscript, see Ward, *Unmanageable Revolutionaries*, p264, n2.

118 Parnell, *Tale of a Great Sham*, p175.

CHAPTER 5

Celtic Twilight, Socialist Dawn 1890–1908

> The man that gets drunk is little else than a fool,
> And is in the habit, no doubt, of advocating for Home Rule;
> But the best Home Rule for him, as far as I can understand,
> Is the abolition of strong drink from the land.[1]

> Ah! come cast off all fooling, for this at last we know,
> That the Dawn and the Day is coming, and forth the banners go.[2]

CONNOLLY came to Dundee at an opportune moment for a budding political activist, when the Dundee socialists were in the midst of, what Greaves has termed 'their great free speech campaign' – a view derived from John Leslie's account, which was itself coloured by the socialists' response to a wider, more complex series of events. This version has been repeated in successive historical accounts since the publication of Greaves' influential biography of Connolly in 1961. Greaves, however, gave little consideration to the Irish political scene in Dundee.[3] If he had, he may have discerned that the Free Speech campaign was influenced by the ongoing anti-coercion campaign initiated by the INL and other Irish kindred organisations, to which the socialists, in a manner worthy of the Fenians, hitched their own banner and brought their own arguments. In those early spring weeks of 1889, the spontaneous alliance between the socialists and Irish nationalists set the tone for political activism in the spaces where the poorer working-class population were more likely to encounter it – the streets and parks of the city. The impoverished Connolly – who had absconded from the army in February and settled in the town a month later – was one of them.[4] The socialists were more confident than ever, the INL was enjoying its widest support since its formation in 1883, and the town's Liberals appeared to be reading from the same script. A proposal by the local INL that Dundee be persuaded to follow Edinburgh's example and grant Parnell the freedom of the city (Dundee was granted city status in January 1889) was readily supported by the Dundee Radical Association, who anticipated the reluctance of the Liberal Council, but pledged to campaign for it anyway. The Radicals also sent representatives to the Edinburgh investiture ceremony, where the congratulatory address presented by John Ogilvy and Joseph Carr outdid that of the INL's Daniel Logue in Irish nationalist hyperbole:

> The Dundee Radical Association heartily joins in welcoming Mr Charles Stuart [sic] Parnell MP, the trusted leader of the Irish race, to Edinburgh. The capital of Scotland has, in honouring him in this unprecedented political crisis, maintained its lofty pre-eminence of characteristic independence and irreproachable integrity. This Association congratulates Mr Parnell on his triumphant victory over the malignant and base attempts of the *Times* irredeemably to blast his reputation, and extinguish by infamous means the imperishable patriotic aspirations of the Irish nation.... It is convinced he has won the entire sympathy of the majority of the Scottish people, and the love of three-fourths, if not the whole, of the Irish nation.... It requires not the mantle of the prophet to predict that the name of Charles Stuart Parnell shall deservedly rank in the roll-fame of those illustrious patriots – Brindley Sheridan and Wolfe Tone, Curran and Grattan, William Smith O'Brien and Dan O'Connell. The touching language of an Irish poet is probably more applicable to Mr Parnell than to any statesman of the Emerald Isle during the latter half of the nineteenth century –
>
> 'I too shall be gone and my name shall be spoken
> When Erin awakes and her fetters are broken'.[5]

While Dundee did not grant the freedom of the city to Parnell, it conferred the honour on Gladstone a year later, on which occasion the attempts of the local magistrates to impose order on the streets were unceremoniously disregarded by crowds of 'urchins' who covered barricades and occupied lamp posts, factory workers who 'abandoned their spinning frames and looms' to go and see 'the Grand Old Man', and gangs of youths who paraded the streets chanting the improvised ditty, 'Home Rule for Ever O'. The atmosphere was one of friendly cooperation, with the staunchly Liberal *Dundee Advertiser* reporting that 'the greatest good humour and tolerance prevailed'.[6] The mood of tolerance and friendly cooperation was not to last. Two weeks after Gladstone's visit, the citing of Parnell as co-respondent in the uncontested divorce action of Captain William O'Shea, on grounds of his adulterous relationship with O'Shea's wife, Katharine, proved the cue for the 'Grand Old Man' to manoeuvre Parnell from leadership of the Irish Parliamentary Party on pain of abandoning the Liberal-Home Rule alliance if he remained. As the majority of Irish MPs moved against Parnell, the ensuing rift extended to the national movement and to the Irish people. The Edinburgh INL debated the matter vociferously, but voted with the parliamentary majority. In Dundee, all three branches voted against Parnell's continued leadership. However, an amendment tabled by members of the Michael Davitt branch (which paralleled the C S Parnell Irish National Foresters) that they delay judgement 'until such time as Gladstone gives the electorate a draft of this Home Rule Bill', elicited impassioned speeches of up to half an hour, at the end of which the original motion calling for Parnell's resignation was carried by a slim majority of three.[7] While some may have taken their lead from parliamentarians and priests, others may have been influenced by the fact that the ex-Fenian and socially progressive Michael Davitt opposed Parnell on the grounds that he had betrayed a historic trust and was no longer fit to lead the Irish people.[8] In a town where acknowledgement of local support was rewarded with enduring loyalty, the fact that Parnell, unlike Davitt or his sister Anna, had failed to visit Dundee, may also have worked against him.

Thus the 'uncrowned King of Ireland' was deposed, and the Irish movement split into Parnellite and anti-Parnellite factions, headed at parliamentary level by Justin McCarthy (who was elected leader), John Dillon, William O'Brien and Tim Healy for the anti-Parnellite majority, and John Redmond who led the Parnellite rump. The sudden death of Parnell from hypertension in October 1891 elicited sympathy but the divisions remained. The *Dundee Advertiser* acknowledged that 'considerable difference of opinion' existed in the Irish community concerning Parnell's

Chapter 5 – Celtic Twilight, Socialist Dawn 1890–1908

death. Notably, it also reported that 'neither address, wreath or any other offering will be forwarded by any section or party in Dundee, and the following of Mr Parnell in the city being so insignificant, the feeling is the late Chief will doubtless be allowed to pass without any recognition whatsoever'.[9] That the *Advertiser* appeared to be paraphrasing the official anti-Parnellite line, was borne out by its 'prediction' that the INL would present resolutions on the matter at their next branch meetings.

As predicted, the following day, Edward Bell[10] of the St Andrew's branch referred to Parnell's death briefly, but 'in feeling terms', and Patrick Brannigan of the A M Sullivan branch stated that the 'majority of Irishmen were opposed to Parnell's continued leadership but believed 'he had done a great service for Ireland'. Edward De Courcey and Thomas Morrison of the Michael Davitt branch stuck to the same script but sounded a more regretful tone, declaring that while they disapproved of 'the methods adopted by Parnell which caused so much disunion in the struggle since November, [they were] heartily sorry so grand a career ended under such painful circumstances, which must excite pity in the heart of every Irishman'.[11] Had it not been for the words, 'since November', the statement could have applied to Parnell's actions in scuppering the Land League nine years earlier. The views of the Lochee branch were not reported. Given the influence of local priests and devout Catholic, Edward Roche, on the committee, we can assume they were much the same.

Parnell's last-ditch appeal to the 'men of the hillside', his rapprochement with the socialists (who had consistently supported him, though he hadn't always reciprocated) and his adoption of a more radical programme, drew Fenian supporters to his side and closer to the socialist movement.[12] For the moment, however, their first loyalty remained with Irish kinship organisations. As the moderate nationalists who dominated the INL moved in an increasingly conservative direction, the Fenian and working-class supporters who had swollen their ranks during the anti-coercion agitation transferred their attention to the Irish National Foresters and the AOH whose memberships increased as the INL's dwindled. While the AOH's status as a secret society confounds an accurate assessment of its membership, between 1888 and 1892, the overall membership of the INF increased from 6,018 to 17,000, and the annual report of 1892 noted that twenty new branches had been formed in the past year, making a total of 210. The report also noted that fifteen old branches had ceased to exist, including, possibly, the Dundee C S Parnell whose former Financial Secretary, James McMahon attended the annual convention in Strabane that August.[13] Given the unsettled state of Irish politics, many nationalists were undoubtedly attracted by the Foresters' non-partisan image, an image it struggled to maintain when the defeat of a proposal to change the names of the Michael Davitt and John Dillon Dublin branches to the 'Independent' and 'Avondale' respectively (after the Parnellite policy of independent opposition and the Parnell family residence) led to complaints of 'rampant coercion' and vote-rigging from the secretary of the Michael Davitt branch, John Dowling.[14] McMahon's proposal to hold the next annual convention in Dundee was passed unanimously – it being the one place the delegates were agreed upon – and the following August, delegates from various parts of Great Britain and Ireland, and Melbourne, Australia, converged on the city to be greeted by an unprecedented show of civic hospitality which lasted the duration of the visit. Whereas the extra-curricular activity at Strabane had consisted of the customary procession and a banquet in the Town Hall attended by the local Catholic clergy, the hospitality laid on at Dundee was distinctly more 'high end' and included two orientation jaunts around the east and west sides of the city, an excursion to Perth on the 'Fifeshire' steamer, during which the visiting INF party was attended by civic dignitaries and serenaded by the Industrial Schools' band; an evening's music and dancing in Lochee Park, courtesy of the Camperdown Works' Band; an official photograph taken by J D Brown of Reform Street; and a banquet in the City Assembly Rooms hosted by Lord Provost Alexander Mathewson, and attended by several magistrates and councillors, the Dean of Guild and his predecessor, Henry McGrady (the first Irish Catholic to hold the position and that of Lord Provost three years later), and Chief Constable David Dewar. The presence of Dewar at the table was deliciously ironic, given that, as Ó Catháin notes, the police and secret service had the INF 'marked down as a Fenian infiltrated, anti-government and thoroughly disaffected group', and that, amongst others, no doubt, the delegate from Wishaw, James Moore of Dundalk, was under surveillance.[15]

General Secretary Joseph Hutchinson of Dublin stated that he had attended many INF conventions, but Dundee was the first municipal body to receive delegates of the Order in such a practical, warm and friendly manner. Next to this, the business of the convention, conducted in St Patrick's Hall, Tay Square, was of secondary importance. Indeed, Grand High Chief Ranger (INF president), Dr Charles O'Neill, noted that there were few proposals on the agenda, as 'the rules were now so perfect that they required few alterations or amendments', and the Order was growing in financial and numerical strength 'from one side of the world to the other'. The annual report indicated that that for the first time in its history, the accumulation of pounds exceeded members, and Ireland was the highest in funds with Scotland coming 'a good second'. At 411 out of 5,515, Ireland also had the highest number of honorary members – the honour having been conferred on prominent nationalists and public figures such as the Lord Mayor of Dublin who travelled to Dundee especially for the civic banquet and returned home the following day. While Scotland and Ireland had an equal number of branches, at 7,286, Scotland was far ahead in membership with the lowest percentage of honorary members. At 55 out of 660, however, Dundee had a higher percentage of honorary members, who included Catholic clergymen throughout the diocese and prominent (and affluent) Dundee Irishmen.[16]

At the civic banquet two days later, O'Neill expressed the gratitude with which he had observed the 'extremely fraternal feeling' that existed between his countrymen in Dundee and the native citizens of it. The objects of their order were 'distinctly National', he stated, and the fact that they found kindred organisations represented (a possible reference to the Irish National League), alongside Scottish gentlemen who openly sympathised with them and others 'who were not supposed to', augured well for the realisation of 'Ireland a Nation'. The Lord Mayor of Dublin, James Shanks, declared the occasion 'a red letter day' in the order's history, and an example which he hoped would be followed by other municipalities.[17]

The fact that Dundee's city fathers went out of their way to accommodate the convention belied a more complex agenda on their part, which the INF bought into and exploited in equal measure. Firstly, was the idea of civic pride and image building. Still buoyant from the attainment of city status and Gladstone's visit, the international nature of the INF convention provided another opportunity for the Town Council to present the city in a positive light and engage in inter-civic networking – an idea which the local INF likely encouraged with the assurance that the Lord Mayor of

Dublin would attend, and possibly the Lord Mayor of London.[18] To the Lord Provost and his cohorts, the prospect of networking with such high-ranking figures as the Lord Mayors of the Irish and English capitals was perhaps too good to resist. The concept of the city as the locus of civic power civil authority was a powerful one which was shared by Unionist-Nationalists, such as the Lord Mayor of Dublin, James Shanks, on the one hand, and the Home Rule-supporting Liberals of Dundee City Council on the other. Such was evidenced by the cries of acclamation which met Shanks's statement that 'the Lord Provost and the Corporation [of Dundee] had set their seal of approval on the Foresters' movement', and by inference, legitimised their aspirations to Irish self-government 'consistent with the desire to preserve the Union [and] serve and benefit the Empire of which they were all proud'. What those INF delegates who were sworn Fenians made of this can only be imagined. The IRB had their own agenda, and as the convention provided an effective cover for networking and organisation, we can assume they played it to their advantage. Indeed, while there is no evidence of IRB circles operating in the city, given the secret nature of the organisation, providing a safe front may well have been Dundee's prime role in the matter.

Then there was the wider political agenda. In July 1892, the Liberals were returned to government with Irish Party support, leading to the belief that Home Rule for Ireland was inevitable and imminent. These hopes were dashed in September 1893 when the Second Home Rule Bill was defeated in the House of Lords, precipitating Gladstone's retirement, and the return of a Tory Unionist government in 1895. The Dundee Liberals were acutely aware of the ability of the local Irish Party machine – some of whose representatives were on public boards – to turn the powerful Irish vote in their favour.

While the Town Council succeeded in convincing the Lord Mayor of the Irish capital that Dundee was 'one of the best managed, most progressive cities in the U.K.', behind the civic spin there was another more prosaic reason for fostering the Foresters. A depression in the jute trade had created an unemployment crisis, to which the cash-strapped authorities had responded by employing a charitable organisation to inquire into the distress, which had in turn triggered protests from the unemployed led by local socialist activists who had seized upon the opportunity to spread the class message. As able-bodied men were denied the right to poor relief under Scottish law, the INF's model of an independent self-supporting

Chapter 5 – Celtic Twilight, Socialist Dawn 1890–1908

benefit agency conducted by Irish working men, appeared to offer a partial solution which was consistent with Gladstonian principles of self-help and social advancement, and more palatable than charity.

However, the 660 benefit members of the INF were a minority amongst Dundee's large Irish workforce, and the Liberal concept of the typical citizen as a self-respecting aspirational working man making provision for himself, his wife and family in the event of future hardship, did not reflect the demographic structure of, and the experience of the many women and children employed within it. Indeed, a Scottish contributor to the SDF journal *Justice*, by the name of 'Sandy McFarlane', advised any comrade doubting the 'iron law of wages' (by which wages are stripped to the minimum required for subsistence) to go to Dundee where 'it requires the work of father, mother and the whole family to earn a decent future for one' [and] in which 'he will find the mother and all the children, legally or illegally entitled to work in factories &c, and the husband at home, rocking the cradle with one hand and holding a baby's sucking-bottle in the other, with one eye on the timepiece and the other on the kettle'.[19] Thus the majority of Dundee's Irish textile workforce remained locked in a cycle of low-waged, insecure employment and chronic poverty, and while many families undoubtedly sympathised with the principles of the INF and appreciated the need to put money by, immediate needs determined their actions. Most were not members of the INF and claimed no benefit from it. Moreover, the fact that experience of the Irish worker was more likely to be a female one, served to exclude (and inhibit) that female majority from participating fully in self-help institutions such as the INF and political power structures as the Irish National League. It was not until 1903 that the Lochee branch of the INF split from the central body and admitted women to its ranks, and despite the attempts of the INL to establish a local women's branch in the early 1890s, the organisation had been floundering since the Parnell split.

Irrespective of their gender, even fewer members of the Dundee-Irish working class were members of the INL. Most had little time for politics, and Ireland's historic struggle was of little relevance compared to their own present-day travails. While the Liberal Council and press painted a picture of commercial progress, industrial achievement and social harmony, *Justice*'s Scottish correspondent (most likely the aforementioned

Sandy McFarlane) dubbed Dundee 'the city of jute and sucking bottles', and vented his frustration at how the dominant jute economy (which had, in his earlier-stated view, skewed wages and perverted the family structure) had, for the most part, rendered the working population refractory to organisational discipline. 'If all cities were like Dundee' he moaned, 'it would make one despair', adding, 'I have often thought that the only way the labour question can be settled in Dundee would be for one of these occasional earthquake shocks which visit Comrie to visit this town with force sufficient and swallow it up'.[20]

Nevertheless, in the summer of 1893, the socialists were up and organising after a three-year hiatus. On 12 August, *Justice*'s 'Scottish Notes' announced the formation of a new branch in Dundee, 'in which important town one of the best branches used to exist, but which was destroyed by local circumstances into which we need not enter' – a cryptic reference, perhaps, to the individualistic personality of James Robertson whose desire to hog the limelight had alienated fellow-socialists in and out of the city but more generally, to the anarchistic tendency which had split the socialist movement in Dundee and elsewhere.[21] While the reporter stated that Dundee had been 'unfortunate' territory for the SDF, the same fate had also befallen branches in Paisley, Greenock and Coatbridge (incidentally, all areas of high Irish settlement), which he trusted could 'be reformed with some energetic comrades on the spot'.[22]

Two weeks later, Sandy McFarlane credited one particular comrade for rallying the Dundee crowd:

> Comrade Connolly has been assisting our comrades in Dundee, and that to the extent of making the crowds cheer him. Your hand, Connolly. I don't want to say hard things about the people of Dundee but I cannot help saying this, that the last time I saw a crowd in that city they seemed so crushed as to be incapable of laughing or cheering. I don't believe you can make much of a man that can neither laugh nor cheer. Hence my reason for saying Connolly is a brick in showing that the people of Dundee are beginning to "arouse from their slumbers" and make the attempt to abolish the father and the best friend of death, "Poverty".[23]

Chapter 5 – Celtic Twilight, Socialist Dawn 1890–1908

What Connolly was saying to cheer the downtrodden Dundonians was not recorded; nevertheless, their new enthusiasm came hard on the heels of a strike in the jute industry, which was all the more remarkable for coming at a time when unemployment threatened and, as local Labour Party activist David Lowe observed, 'rent was nearly due and summer duds required'.[24] The desire to maintain a sharp appearance in terms of holiday attire (albeit cheap, bright and flimsy) as distinct from drab work clothing, was an important source of self-esteem, especially to the young female millworkers, and cannot be underestimated. On 21 July, around fifty such 'girls', the bulk of whom were not 'organised', walked out of Queen Victoria Works after the manager refused to pay their due wages for two 'lie days'.

Despite the recommendation of the Reverend Henry Williamson, founder and President of the conciliatory Dundee and District Mill and Factory Operatives' Union, that they return to work, the strikers refused to do so, and spent the course of the day parading the city streets.[25] *Justice*'s 'Scottish Notes' noted with approval the new Dundee SDF branch's policy of 'tackling on to local grievances', and trusted it would prove more effective in in spreading the message rather than lecturing world-weary workers on socialist doctrine alone. Connolly, who had identified the need for such outdoor propagandists, reported that the Edinburgh SSF, of which he had succeeded his brother John as Secretary, had started a class in such and invited suggestions as to how it could be conducted.[26] Connolly had grown in confidence since the day he had, by John Leslie's account, 'saved the situation' when the latter was being bested by hecklers in the city four years earlier. Even then Connolly was aware of Dundee's large female working population – which was reflected in the crowd at open-air meetings – and was attuned to the loud-voiced mill lassies who doubtless appreciated his ready wit and ability to inject humour into the socialist message.

Connolly was also familiar with Dundee's large Irish population, and, given his deep interest in Irish affairs and the presence of the INF convention in the city that August, he may also have been keeping his ear to the ground with the possibility of drawing progressive nationalists into the socialist camp. In Edinburgh, John Leslie had long been preoccupied with winning over progressive elements of the national movement to revolutionary socialism, and it was around this time that he began giving a series of lectures on the Irish Question to the Edinburgh SSF which met in James and Lillie's' flat on the Lothian Road.

Leslie's lectures were subsequently turned into a series of newspaper articles, and latterly reproduced in a pamphlet entitled *The Present Position of the Irish Question*. The content of Leslie's one and only political publication has been considered amply by Connolly biographers, primarily due to its influence on Connolly's own writings.[27] While Greaves claims that Leslie's articles were written with an eye on the inaugural meeting of the Irish TUC which met in May 1894, Leslie also appealed to the hearts and minds of the wider constituency of working-class Irish immigrants and physical force Republicans who were otherwise alienated from Home Rule nationalism and outside the sphere of constitutional politics. Leslie, who despite his Scottish birth and paternal heritage, wrote under the by-line of 'one of the Wild Irishrie', (a term used by Ireland's Anglo-Norman colonisers to describe those 'outside the King's peace' or 'beyond the pale'[28]) and described himself as 'an Irish wage-worker, and an unskilled one at that; as one interested in the well-being of the class to which I belong, and which constitutes the bulk of the Irish as of all other nations; and therefore as one who does not believe that the Alpha and Omega of the Irish Question consists in the hoisting of the green and gold banner over the Old Parliament House in Dublin.' Leslie drew from his own experience of the 'brave old Land League', which 'refusing to recognise any side issues, went straight for the throat of Irish Landlordism', and which, from a nationalist perspective alone, did more than any other organisation 'to raise Ireland to a place among the nations of the earth than either of the great British Parties'. The story of how the revolutionary potential of the Land League had been diverted into 'the mere political channel' by Parnell and Gladstone had been thoroughly impressed on Leslie's mind. 'It ought to be', he asserted, 'engraven in letters of fire on the heart of every working class Irishman'. From Parnell – one of a long line of gentleman leaders who had 'always and ever betrayed them' – Leslie turned his attention to the forgotten figure of Fintan Lalor, 'who pointed out the class nature of the Irish movement and who laid down as the essential basis of a successful insurrectionary movement in Ireland, resistance by any and every method' – to eviction, in this case, 'by retaining the harvest and non-payment of rent'.[29] The final quotation of Leslie's first article, drawn from an old copy of the *Irish World* – 'Talk not of revolution, think not of the rifle or the pike until first the great truth of Man's Natural Rights is in engraved on all our hearts. Then prepare for the artillery.' – had originally dictated the course of action for physical force republicans. However, it might as well have mapped out the course of Connolly's life over the next twenty years.

Meantime, the priority was to propagate the socialist message and build the movement for workers' rights. Winning over the Irish movement to socialism was an uphill struggle, especially in Dundee where the socialists were presented with the challenge of, not only cultivating an apathetic and dispirited population, but of countering the massed ranks of the Liberal-supporting INL and other kindred groups, some members of which went to great lengths to discredit them. One such incident came to light during the course of a lecture by Labour Party propagandist, Henry Hyde Champion, in the Gilfillan Hall on 26 September 1893. The lecture, billed 'The Labour Party – what it is and what it should be', attracted an attendance of over a hundred people, primarily members of the Scottish Labour Party (SLP) and the SDF from Dundee, Glasgow and Edinburgh, some Liberals, various radicals and a significant Irish contingent. Given the composition of his audience, Champion concluded his speech, deftly, by insisting that the Labourists, when in Parliament, 'act on the principles dictated to them by Messrs Parnell and Biggar' while emphasising that the party 'first of all, be a Labour Party operating on the Socialist principle'. Questions were then invited from the audience, at which point a member of the Irish contingent, shoemaker Francis Dailly, proceeded to 'animadvert' against the socialist leaders in Dundee and criticise Keir Hardie's conduct in Parliament, giving rise to cries of 'Sit down, Francie' from Dailly's associates and general uproar. A diplomatic answer from Champion calmed the situation. However, after a series of questions from a cross-section of the audience, Labour Party member, Andrew Bremner, drew their attention back to the accusation made by Dailly regarding the 'moral character' of the leaders of the Labour Party in Dundee, and called on 'that man' to submit his proof publicly, which Dailly stated he would only do to a committee in private. The chairman, deeming Dailly had declined the opportunities given him, declared him 'a liar' to which Dailly repeated his original accusation and claimed to have been referring to the 'Socialist Party', whereupon Bremner called him a liar, Dailly reciprocated, and amidst escalating pandemonium, made his way to the platform while the exasperated chairman, SLP President, John Watson, begged the audience to help him out. Order was restored, and Dailly barred from further comment. Nevertheless, James Morton, the SDF's leading activist in Dundee, demanded that he 'divulge the names of the individuals he declaims as having rotten moral character'. This precipitated calls of 'enough', to which Morton responded:

> There has not been half enough...My character has been impugned, as a Socialist I have been tampered with, and even my bread and butter has been tampered with. Now here is perhaps a clue to that tampering. (Laughter) It is all very well to laugh, but if some of you had [received] the anonymous letters and postcards in regard to the movement that I have... you would take it very hotly.[30]

Dailly was again called to prove his claims and again refused, whereupon Morton pronounced him a coward, eliciting uproarious cries of outrage from one half of the room, and affirmation from the other, above which Morton yelled at the top of his voice, 'What do you tell me I am?!' By this time, Dailly and Morton were standing face to face, at which point, according to a *Courier* reporter, Morton 'drew back and "got in his left on the claret cup"' of the exuberant 'Hibernian', who prepared to retaliate but was hustled out the door. The meeting continued with some moderate heckling. Despite the chairman's advice to put it behind them, the dispute continued outside where Dailly, who had waited over an hour for Morton to emerge, threatened to 'spread his spectacles over [his] countenance'.[31]

While Dailly may have been regarded as a loose cannon by his compatriots, he succeeded in discomposing the socialists, and Morton, the main target of his verbal abuse and (possibly) poison pen, was buckling under the strain. Just three days earlier, a contributor to *Justice*'s 'Scottish Notes' revealed that he had received a note from Morton pleading for 'some speaker to go through and give him a rest'.[32] 'There is no doubt that Dundee wants a deal of working up, and all our spare forces should be thrown into that town,' the report continued, to which end, possibly, a conference of Scottish Socialists was arranged for Dundee on 14–15 July 1894, presided over by Léo Meillet, with delegates from Aberdeen, Dundee, Edinburgh, Falkirk and Glasgow, including lead organisers William Diack of the Aberdeen Socialist Society, and James Connolly of the Edinburgh SSF and SLP, both of whom spoke at well-attended meetings in Barrack Park and Magdalen Green.[33]

While some Edinburgh socialists, notably Leslie and Connolly, were endeavouring to win over the Irish movement, in Dundee they were encountering bitter opposition from key elements within it. On 12 May 1894, the *Labour Leader*, the organ of the recently-formed Independent Labour Party, disclosed that, at the Irish National League of Great Britain's annual convention, held in Liverpool that day, one of the Dundee delegates would table a motion 'condemning the ILP and all its works', and noted that, if carried, it would 'mark one more stage in the development of the movement.'[34] The agency behind this was most likely President of the A M Sullivan INL branch, Patrick Brannigan, also known to Dundee Labourists as President of the Dundee Operative Bakers' Union and a longstanding member of Dundee Trades Council. Brannigan, who used his position in all three bodies to propound the view that the ILP was a divisive faction on the fringes of the Liberal Party, was also the 'chief objector' to an invitation to the Trades Council to attend a meeting addressed by James MacDonald, the ILP's candidate in the 1895 General Election – on which occasion Brannigan swore he would 'never put his foot inside the door of the Labour Party meeting room' – and later led the opposing vote on a motion to endorse him.[35]

While Brannigan and his dwindling number of INL associates attempted to steer a new generation of enfranchised Irish working men away from the ILP and into the Liberal fold, it would be wrong to assume that the wider Irish movement, much less the Irish community, was unsupportive of the ILP or unsympathetic to socialism. Indeed, as the INL cranked up the party machine, the *Labour Leader* noted:

> Men who promised us their bitterest opposition are coming forth and joining the committee. [MacDonald's] meeting in Lochee proved by far the largest and most enthusiastic that had been held by any of the candidates, the sitting [Liberal]

members included. The same can be said of his Dundee meeting in the Gilfillan Memorial, only more so.... We were promised opposition at his meetings; but I am confident now that if any came forth with that intention, Mac converted them, for not one could be found in the hall bold enough to say the slightest word against him or the ideas he propounded.[36]

While the source of the 'promised opposition' was not identified, the reporter was almost certainly Labour activist, David Lowe, who recalled that, initially, 'otherwise friendly Irishmen were united against me for helping to build up a Labour Party because... they thought nothing should happen until Home Rule was passed'.[37] Given that the most prominent hecklers at election meetings from the 1870s onwards came from the Irish community, their silence on this occasion seems significant, particularly in the light of the belligerent intervention at the Champion meeting sixteen months earlier. Indeed, while the INL operated on the dubious assumption that all Irish electors followed their instructions and voted for the Liberal candidate, it is equally likely that a number of recently-enfranchised young voters and Fenian elements delighted in exercising the little power they had by voting for the Home Rule-supporting Socialist underdog.[38] At any rate, in the run up to the election, it appears that the Irish saved their loudest heckling for the Unionists.[39] In the outcome, the two Liberal candidates, Edmund Robertson and John Leng, emerged victorious with 7,602 and 7,592 votes respectively – a combined drop of 1,481 from their 1892 result, while MacDonald, who came last with 1,313 votes, practically quadrupled his 1892 result of 354 votes.

It seems that a younger generation of Dundee Irishmen were slowly warming to the idea of supporting a party which better represented their class interests as well as recognising their national aspirations. Among these Labour-supporting Irish nationalists was twenty-year-old jute worker Nicholas Marra who was not yet old enough to vote in the election, but became acquainted with the ILP, and subsequently joined it, and also the reconstituted United Irish League when it was launched in 1900. Nevertheless, at a post-election meeting of the A M Sullivan branch of the INL, Pat Brannigan continued to insist that, 'despite opposition from other parties', Irish electors were 'as faithful and loyal to Liberal principles as ever'.[40]

Chapter 5 – Celtic Twilight, Socialist Dawn 1890–1908

The Parish Council elections of April 1895 also saw the emergence of Edwin (Neddy) Scrymgeour as one of two ILP candidates who gained a seat, in Scrymgeour's case, polling second to veteran Home Ruler, Matthew McKenna, in the First Ward.[41] Over the next three decades, Scrymgeour, who went on to stand in municipal and parliamentary elections on a temperance ticket, proved to be a consistent supporter of workers' rights, women's suffrage and Irish claims to self-determination, and it was his record as 'a friend of Labour and a friend of Ireland' that ultimately helped procure him one of the most significant electoral victories in history.

For the moment, while the socialists conducted a vigorous election campaign in which they managed to win the support, and possibly the votes, of some members of the Irish working class, they struggled to gain their loyalty. Unlike their Edinburgh comrades, notably James Connolly, who used his platform as a candidate in local elections, to draw a comparison between tyranny in Ireland and poverty in the Cowgate, the Dundee socialists failed to apply the same energy to establishing a meaningful connection between socialism and radical Irish nationalism. Undoubtedly, their task was complicated by the negative campaigning of Brannigan and his INL colleagues in which they were influenced and supported by members of the Catholic clergy. However, given that the majority of Dundee's working-class Irish population remained stuck in chronically low-waged, insecure employment and squalid living conditions a generation or more after their ancestors had been compelled to emigrate, one can argue that there were fewer places more in need of a dedicated socialist propagandist from a similar class and cultural background who had the knowledge, ability and incentive to do it. A lack of financial resources may partially explain why the Dundee socialists failed to respond to John Leslie's plea, in the 14 December edition of *Justice*, for some 'comrade in Glasgow, Dundee, or anywhere else for that matter' to 'secure such situation' for James Connolly, who was presently unemployed and on the verge of emigrating to Chile. 'My pen is poor and my ink is pale', lamented the poet Leslie – a metaphor for his fading spirit as he contemplated the loss of 'the most able propagandist, in every sense of the word, that Scotland has yet turned out'.[42] While no Scottish comrade obliged, within five months Connolly secured a situation as a full-time organiser of the Dublin Socialist Society, a task which he undertook with relish by transforming the Society (originally the Dublin branch of the British ILP) into the Irish Socialist Republican Party, whereafter Leslie, deprived of his closest collaborator, gave up on his mission to work the Scots-Irish working class and the Irish national movement around to a socialist republican perspective.

With regards to the latter, the INL was in a sorry state. Special Branch records of 1897 note that attendance at the National Convention of the INLGB in Manchester on 5-6 June was the lowest in all the fifteen years of its existence.[43] The INL in Dundee had 'hardly the semblance of a branch' and was, in effect, little more than an electoral registration committee. In late April, the Chief Organiser of the INLGB, John Denvir, visited the city in a desperate bid to regenerate the local League, and possibly stop the drift towards the Home Rule-supporting Labour Party, by reassuring Irish voters that the Home Rule Bill was not, as many perceived, dead in the water and the Liberals set to drop it.[44] 'The Irish vote influenced too many constituencies for that to happen', Denvir insisted, as he begged the League to 'keep up its organisation to meet any emergency'. It fell to the Chairman, Matthew McKenna, to suggest, unenthusiastically, that they 'might form one branch to meet in a central hall on a week night instead of Sunday afternoon'.[45] Despite Denvir's bravado and a temporary show of willingness on the part of the 'fairly large' audience, many of whom were undoubtedly drawn by Denvir's celebrity status and former Fenian credentials, the INL in Dundee fell into abeyance shortly afterwards.

Ó Catháin points to senior IRB figures in Scotland such as Bernard Havilan and James Ward who were heavily involved in Labour and working-class politics throughout the 1890s and early 1900s – trade unionist Havilan entering the field of local electoral politics, while Ward remained firmly and discreetly focused, in line with his Fenian principles and tactics, on grassroots organisation. Simultaneously, both were pivotal members of various interlinked organisations which complemented and covered their IRB activity.[46] While the activities of Ward, Havilan, and other IRB figures operating in and around Glasgow in this period have come to light via British Secret Service files, there is no definitive record of similar activity in Dundee or the East of Scotland. There are a number of possible reasons for this. First, is the limited resources and reach of the security forces. Most information was obtained via a network of police spies and informants masterminded by Major Nicholas Gosselin, a network which did not extend, and therefore did not penetrate, beyond Glasgow and the West. The suspects on file appear not to have travelled north, or if they did, no-one pursued them. Second, there was no strategic threat from Dundee, the presumption being that any traffic in arms or explosives would likely be channelled through Glasgow. Third, while the city's large Irish population may have once posed an existential threat, the fact that the Dundee's Police Commissioners had dismissed the idea at the height of the Fenian scares in the 1860s, suggests that they were hardly likely to accept it in the relatively tranquil 1890s. Fourth and finally, is the strong possibility that the IRB in Dundee had been cut off by the Supreme Council or imploded due to apathy, economics and isolation. In the course of a talk to his Glasgow brethren in April 1904, IRB leader P T Daly threatened to cut off a circle for not having subscribed for three months, and the cripplingly low economic status of the Dundee-Irish working class, from which the Fenians had traditionally drawn their support, further mitigated against their subscribing to an organisation which was already fractured, militarily inactive and politically disengaged. The situation was not helped by an increasingly pervasive drink culture, and the fact that Irishmen often met in places where drink was available.[47] Indeed, the high concentration of public houses and illicit drinking in the Scouringburn appears to have contributed to the view, articulated in the Dundee press, that Irishmen were as much in the pockets of publicans and shebeen keepers as they were dictated to by priests, and that their votes could be bought for a few barrels of beer.[48] How much money donated towards 'another rifle for Ireland' went back into the publican's or shebeen keeper's pocket or into paying off personal debts, is impossible to say. Pilfering of funds was a problem, and for those in dire financial straits, a sore temptation.[49] In July 1904, a convention of the IRB in Scotland yielded six months' worth of subscriptions ranging from £3 to a few shillings remitted by fifteen Centres; as the word came from one of Gosselin's informants, 'the honesty of some of [them] was doubted'.[50]

By the turn of the century, an older generation of Dundee Fenians or otherwise advanced and influential nationalists had died, succumbed to ill health or turned their attention elsewhere. Thomas Morrison, the key link from the proto-Fenian National Brotherhood of St Patrick of the early

1860s through the Amnesty Association, the Home Rule Confederation and the '82 and '98 Clubs to the Land League, moved, temporarily, to Rattray in Perthshire shortly after the establishment of the latter, and – beyond a brief stint on the committee of the Michael Davitt INL in the early 1890s – had no discernible involvement in the national movement thereafter. The garrulous Thomas Flanagan, who ran the gamut of Irish political organisations in Dundee from the mid-1870s to the late 1880s, scaled down his activities after he took on his father's grocer's-spirit dealer's shop in the early 1890s. Consequently, he retreated from political life due to declining health and died in 1898 at the age of 42.[51] His contemporary J P Casey suffered a paralytic stroke in 1899 and died three years later aged 48, by which time Edward Roche of Lochee had put aside his nationalist politics to focus on his faith, family, community and business interests.[52] Former radical Land Leaguer and East Scotland INF chief, James Ward, died of presenile dementia in 1903 at the age of 61, while Edward De Courcey, the INL organiser and socialist who presided over the Free Speech/Anti-Coercion rally in 1889, also died of tuberculosis in the parochial hospital aged 49.[53]

The United Irish League

While the Fenian organisation in Dundee was dormant, the dawning of the century saw two new developments which revived and regenerated Irish political and cultural life in the city. The reunification of the Irish Parliamentary Party under John Redmond in February 1900 was followed by the rolling out of a reconstituted party machine ahead of the 'khaki election' of September-October 1900, so named because of the predominating concern with the South African 'Second Boer' War. (1899-1902). The United Irish League of Great Britain (UILGB) was launched in Dundee on 2 September following a meeting in Tay Square Hall addressed by UIL executive member and MP for South Louth, Robert McGhie, and chaired by Owen Kiernan of Glasgow, former Scottish organiser of the INLGB, and now of the UILGB, a role which he combined with high office in the AOH to the advantage, possibly, of both. Kiernan, who had spoken on an INL platform in the city in 1886, when he emphasised the importance of maintaining continuity of struggle, was instrumental in recruiting members of the AOH into the UIL, and McGhie's speech, which stressed that the new League was organised 'on the same principles of the old Land League...Irish nationalism and the abolition of Irish landlordism', and that 'nine out of ten Irishmen would rather contribute their £7 million [in taxation] to Boer armaments than to Britain', seemed calculated to appeal to residual Ribbon and pre-existing radical Land League elements.[54]

Thus encouraged, around fifty joined on the spot from which a large committee was appointed with Glasgow-born journalist, James O'Donnell Derrick as President, James McDaniel of Dundee as Secretary, and James Murray of Lochee as Treasurer. Much of the credit for establishing and expanding the UIL in Dundee, and subsequently the rest of Scotland, was down to O'Donnell Derrick, who came to the city to manage the *Dundee Catholic Herald*, the syndicated sister of Charles Diamond's *Glasgow Catholic Observer*, around the time of its launch in 1896. Born in the Calton area of Glasgow in 1870 to Sarah O'Donnell (whose name he later took) and Irish labourer, Anthony Derrick, the young James O'Donnell Derrick was steeped in the politics of radical land reform, possibly due to the formative influence of the Land League and his father's Mayo origins. While his second-generation Irish contemporary, James Connolly, followed the path of revolutionary socialism, O'Donnell Derrick placed his faith in the political doctrine of land reformer, Henry George. Spurning the INL and the Scottish Labour Party, in 1893, he joined the Scottish League for the Taxation of Land Values, the last of two organisations to emerge from the disintegrating Scottish Land Restoration League (the other being the Scottish Land Restoration Union), for which he conceived and helped found the journal, *The Single Tax*, in June 1894.[55] On his arrival in Dundee, O'Donnell threw himself into political life – weighing in on political meetings, gaining a place on the Parish Council for the Eighth Ward in 1898, and narrowly missing out on a Town Council seat the following year. In 1900, O'Donnell Derrick, who had already set up a local branch of the Scottish Single Tax League, of which he was President and Secretary, seized on the UIL as a popular vehicle through which to promote the allied aims of Irish self-determination and land emancipation, and quickly placed himself at the forefront of it.[56] In his inaugural address to the Dundee branch, O'Donnell Derrick made a play for non-Irish support by noting that contrasting opinions on the Boer War had not alienated Scottish favour for Home Rule nor in the right of nations to govern their own affairs, from which responsibility, he added, Britain should 'stay at home and civilise its Overgates and Scouringburns'.[57] As with the INL before it, however, the immediate object of the UIL was to mobilise the Irish vote for the two Home Rule-supporting Liberal candidates, in this case, John Leng and Edmund Robertson, following their endorsement by the UIL executive.[58] On this occasion, the Labour Party did not stand a candidate, hence there was no conflict of interests on the part of voters with socialist leanings, and predictably, Leng and Robertson retained their seats with an increased majority.

28 April 1901 saw the Dundee UIL hold its largest branch meeting to date when over 500 people passed a resolution congratulating the owner of the *Sligo Champion* and MP for North Leitrim, P A McHugh, on 'the signal mark of distinction...conferred on him' by his imprisonment for seditious libel, which, was deemed, in the long tradition of Irish political prisoners, as proof of 'a sturdy fight' against British injustice.[59] This was followed on 2 June by a capacity meeting in the Peoples' Palace in the Nethergate, addressed by William Redmond MP, the brother of the Irish Party leader, who was joined on the platform by representatives of the Catholic clergy, various members of the Dundee UIL executive, and, in a last-minute addition to the programme, Keir Hardie.

The presence of Hardie on the platform, and his comments – that Home Rule would only be achieved when 'the democracy of Britain united in strength with the democracy of Ireland and became the dominant power in the government', gave rise to talk in local political circles of a 'coalition in Dundee between the Irish and the Labour Parties' which one 'Irish correspondent' to the Liberal Evening Telegraph sought to disprove:

> It is true that amongst Dundee Catholics [*sic*] there are a number of men who hold advanced views on political and social questions, as there are a number who are Conservative in politics, even amongst the clergy. The Conservative section have no influence as politicians with the Irish vote. Amongst the advanced men, there are many who are Home Rulers first, though there are a few of no influence who are violent Socialists. The ILP in Dundee number some of the latter in their ranks,

hence the reason why [they] are pleased to find Keir Hardie on Sunday's Irish platform. Their pleasure will be short-lived when they get to know that Mr Hardie's presence has caused some trouble locally. Dundee Irish Nationalism is sound to the core... and while [it will] not allow Home Rule to be sidetracked by a Tory device[60] neither will socialist or labour tricks manage the same game.[61]

Amongst the flurry of protest the letter provoked, UIL committee member, James Murray, claimed its publication was 'calculated to cause irretrievable harm by alienating the only true supporters of the Irish cause in Dundee'. 'Irishmen of all shades of opinion have temporarily withdrawn into the background all personal predilections', he noted; however:

> a gentleman like Mr Keir Hardie, whose consistency and honesty of purpose command respect, is a more welcome guest than any number of guests who emphatically call themselves Liberals, or Imperial Liberals or advanced Liberals. It may unfortunately be true that some present on Sunday looked askance at the presence of so sterling an ally of the Irish people, but it is equally true that the same class view with dislike the growing popularity of the local branch.[62]

The same undercurrent of class tension was present in a letter from 'VP' (undoubtedly Nicholas Marra, the 26-year-old Vice President of the Dundee UIL) which contrasted 'the bad taste of a few gentlemen on the platform' with that of the UIL membership, who, at the last branch elections, had voted several socialists on to the Committee, and one (himself) to the Executive 'in the full knowledge of their politics'.[63]

Indeed, a number of young Dundee Irishmen, who in an earlier era may have been drawn to physical force republicanism and radical Land League activism, had found an outlet for their political energies in socialist politics which informed and encouraged their involvement in the Irish national movement. Moreover, while IRB organiser, P T Daly, discouraged members in Glasgow from joining the UIL, the lack of an active Fenian organisation in Dundee meant that there was no suggestion of betraying

Republican leaders or principles, but rather a greater sense of seizing an opportunity to promote the latter. This was identified by O'Donnell Derrick who, later that August, invoked the memory of the Lochee Land League to induce local nationalists to 'come to the front in line with their countrymen in Dundee' and form a branch of the UIL, whereupon a branch was duly established with former Lochee Land Leaguer and leading member of the Irish National Foresters, John Paterson as President, James Murray as Secretary and George Steel (also of the INF) as Treasurer.[64]

Within less than a year, O'Donnell Derrick had turned the UIL into the strongest Irish political organisation in the city since the Land League, which achievement led to him being appointed national organiser for the UIL in Scotland, a position he held until the UILGB was dissolved around 1918. With his departure to Glasgow, the UIL in Dundee lost a key cohering influence, and the political tensions inherent in the organisation rose to the fore. In late December, the suspiciously well-informed correspondent of the *Evening Telegraph*'s 'Here and There' column intimated that some members of the Dundee branch appeared concerned 'over the development of Socialism within the ranks' and were 'inclined to resent the policy of a comrade who seizes any and every opportunity of exploiting Socialism at League meetings'. The titbit concluded by flagging up the next branch meeting where a resolution calling for the resignation of 'an office-bearer understood to be a member of the ILP' would be discussed.[65] The following day, branch Secretary J Fagan moved that Marra be called to stand down as Vice President, as his position as President of the Dundee ILP constituted a conflict of interest in the likely event of Labour contesting the next Parliamentary election. President J McDaniel, seconding, explained that they were anxious to avoid a repetition of the North East Lanarkshire by-election the previous September when the UIL Executive's recommendation to vote for the Belfast-born socialist, Bob Smillie, over the aristocratic Liberal candidate, Cecil Bishopp Harmsworth, resulted in the Liberal Unionist, William Henry Rattigan, gaining the former Liberal seat. This had precipitated a return to the Liberal fold by the UIL's London Executive, upon whose instructions O'Donnell Derrick advised it was 'undesirable that any member of their organisation should hold office in any other political association'. Arguing against, Marra pointed out that the Irish Party and the ILP were 'fighting side by side

Chapter 5 – Celtic Twilight, Socialist Dawn 1890–1908

inside and outside Parliament' against the Boer War, and ridiculed the Imperialist stance of the Liberal Party which had no greater exemplar than Sir John Leng MP and his 'so-called Liberal newspaper', as McDaniel had previously termed it.[66]

Despite strong support from the membership, Marra was defeated by 54 to 49 votes. Resigning from his post a fortnight later, he urged his aggrieved supporters to 'Stick to the League and remedy wrong, if such there be'. It fell to prominent local nationalist, James Kelly, to offer a tactical way forward, and 'put in a welcome word for Socialism'.

> Let us work together; and so say we all. Let the Dundee Irish Party and the I.L.P go hand-in-hand, outstripping each other in strenuous efforts for the masses.... Mr John Redmond M. and Mr Keir Hardie, MP are working together amicably. Why not their respective provincial supporters? There are at least thirty ILPers in the League. They have been caught young. They are unsurpassed in enthusiasm and courage, and they are a power. In view of the imminent retirement of Sir John Leng, both parties should strive their utmost to unite, so that a representative will be got first who will vote first and always for Ireland, while going solid for Labour questions when they arise. Their interests do not conflict in Parliament; nor should they do in the provinces.[67]

Nevertheless, Marra remained a vociferous member of the UIL and, along with his Socialist allies, re-doubled his efforts to promote the cause of Ireland within the ILP. A week later, the Dundee branch of the ILP (which, conveniently, met on alternate Sundays to the UIL), led by President Marra, Vice President Charles Docherty, Assistant Secretary John Green, and John Ogilvy, resolved to request that the Free Library Committee obtain copies of T W Russell's *Ireland and the Empire* for the central and branch libraries. Proposing the motion, Ogilvy observed that while 'Irishmen were well-acquainted with the past history and present disturbed affairs of their own country [and] many Scots were not', the latter were willing to learn, and he believed, 'would profit greatly by reading such a valuable work.' Born in Cupar, Fife, in 1841, Thomas

William Russell had moved to Tyrone aged eighteen, for which constituency (South Tyrone) he was elected Liberal Unionist MP in 1886. Initially opposed to Home Rule, around 1899 Russell underwent a conversion, and, as Ogilvy claimed, 'now frankly acknowledged that the Irish Parliamentary leaders were men of intellectual distinction [who] were earnestly striving to accomplish a noble work for Ireland.[68] A report in the *Labour Leader* also intimated that the branch had invited John Ferguson, the radical Home Rule and Land League leader of decades past, now a senior Labour councillor in Glasgow, to address a future meeting.[69]

Progressive as they were, the reformist politics of the ILP and its UIL cohort were a far cry from the socialist republicanism of James Connolly who visited Dundee in July 1901 in the course of a tour facilitated by the SDF, with the joint purpose of reversing the reformist drift in the British socialist movement and to raise funds for the publication of the ISRP's newspaper, *The Worker's Republic*. Unfortunately, due to the disorganised state of the Dundee branch, whose former Secretary had left the city having failed to pass on correspondence, the branch was unaware of Connolly's visit until he turned up, leaving them with no time to promote his meetings. As a result, attendance was poor, collections low, and Connolly received a mere fraction of his expenses, obliging him to seek a loan from the Secretary of the Edinburgh SDF to pay his train fare to England for the next leg of his tour.[70] Such botched organisation meant that an opportunity to influence the reformists and steer a broader working-class Irish audience towards revolutionary ideas was lost, which, with especial regard to the latter, left the field open to the Labourites operating within the UIL.

1901-2 was successful year for the UIL in Dundee, which brought in over £48 in subscriptions, mainly on the back of several well-publicised meetings involving Irish MPs. However, despite talk of conciliation and unanimity, many of its members harboured doubts about the national leadership, which were reinforced by the 'bungled' visit of John Redmond, who had promised to visit Dundee after Edinburgh in January 1903. As the date drew nigh, the People's Palace was booked, but still nothing was heard. Finally, after several frantic attempts to wire him, Redmond replied that he 'couldn't do it', leading President, James Fagan, to comment that 'It was hard to understand why he could visit Edinburgh and so abruptly

Chapter 5 – Celtic Twilight, Socialist Dawn 1890–1908

cut off Dundee'. In a bid to apportion blame, Marra (possibly harbouring resentment at having been forced out of office earlier) pointed the finger at 'the Scottish Organiser' for having blundered, stating, somewhat cryptically, that a past member of the Executive had declared unofficially that 'no member of Parliament would visit Dundee, and he knew why'.[71] While the branch equivocated amicably over the matter, the ordinary 'Irishmen of Dundee', who, according to Fagan, had been 'in a ferment of excitement', were left feeling that they had been left out in the cold by the leader of the Irish Party whose actions echoed those of Parnell fourteen years earlier. To radical physical force nationalists, whose support for the Home Rule movement was conditional and tentative, the incident merely confirmed their doubts about the UIL and its remote gentlemen leaders. The same could not be said for Michael Davitt, the former high-ranking Fenian, radical Land League leader and ex-Honorary President of Dundee INL, now of the UIL's spirited Dundee branch, who visited the city on 7 April to address a meeting, ostensibly under the auspices of the UIL, but with strong INF involvement.

The meeting, which was held in the Foresters' Hall in Rattray Street, got under way with the passing of an all-encompassing resolution expressing confidence in the Irish Party under Redmond's leadership, and asserting demands for an Irish Parliament and the abolition of landlordism. Davitt, who was received with rapturous applause, reaffirmed the single unifying goal of the Irish people, and the right of all peoples 'to rule themselves and their country in accordance with their own ideas instead of being ruled by a stupid nation'. While his calculated aside that he was 'not referring to Scotland' met the approval of the diverse audience, a further reference to Home Rule provoked a cry of 'It's dead', to which Davitt retorted that 'there was nothing so living as a dead Irish Question', before going on to assure them that a satisfactory settlement to the land bill would help pave the way towards 'a final and, possibly, a lasting solution'.[72] It was to be Davitt's last meeting in Dundee. He died, prematurely, from septicaemia arising from a tooth extraction on 6 May two years later.

While the Dundee Irish remained loyal to Davitt, they did less so to the UIL. Indeed, while the organisation was expanding elsewhere, the reverse was true in Dundee. The Annual Report of 1902-3 noted that subscriptions were down almost half from the previous year, which was accounted by the fact that half of the proceeds of the Davitt meeting were sent to the '98 Memorial Fund Committee in Cork, possibly by a mutual arrangement with the Foresters. The somewhat partisan reporter of the *Evening Telegraph* also explained the anomaly of the lagging UIL membership with the show of enthusiasm at the Davitt meeting by speculating that 'Irishmen in Dundee, while ever ready to lend their aid in any matter of national urgency, [seem] inclined to take things easy when the sun is shining on the League'.[73]

Although the first half of the statement may have been true, clouds were gathering. They had first appeared in Lochee, whose UIL branch had a particularly strong overlap with the Father Mathew branch of the INF, which was larger, longer established and, with the obvious exception of women, more representative of Lochee's large textile workforce than the similarly male-dominated UIL with its preponderance of small businessmen. (Nicholas Marra, a jute worker, was a notable exception). Interestingly, one of the last reported meetings of the Lochee branch of the UIL, in May 1902, focused around an address by Marra on 'Nationality' in which he regretted that Scottish people were 'slowly but surely losing their distinct individuality as a nation', and contended that that their 'most important work' as Irish Scots, was 'to maintain intact their distinct nationality and realise those rights and inspirations which, more than anything else, would fit [Ireland] to become a nation once again'.[74] While Marra's address reflected the growing preoccupation with cultural nationalism, his contention that the preservation of national identity was a critical factor in the achievement of Irish independence, and of a broader anti-imperialist attitude, spoke to the pervasive notions of kinship and cultural expression underpinning the INF to whose members it was possibly directed. It is perhaps significant that shortly after Marra's lecture, the Lochee INF withdrew from the Dundee District, citing a desire to control their own funds. In a small city like Dundee, the limited income of the large but low-waged Irish population determined that 'in matters of national urgency', the coordination of resources across the committees of Irish organisations was a necessary means of maximising the benefits. This was an accepted way of doing things, and instances of 'creative accounting' were often overlooked. In this case, what was presented as a territorial split over the question of levies may have disguised class antagonisms and underlying political differences. At any rate, despite the attempts of District Treasurer, Peter Welsh, to pull the errant branch back into line via an appeal to the National Executive (which by 1902 had been extensively infiltrated by the IRB), the latter refused to intervene.[75] Thus vindicated, the Lochee branch later reaffiliated to the Dundee District following a change of personnel when Lochee Branch Secretary, Thomas Callan, was appointed District Secretary and Lochee Chief Ranger, James Vaughan, became a trustee.

Callan, Vaughan, and their like-minded colleagues, were well aware that there was financial strength in the high numbers of working women managing their own small earnings and, in many cases, the income of an entire household. The ability of women to come up with prodigious sums of money had been the success story of the Land League in Dundee and nowhere more so than in the Lochee Ladies' branch, to whose founding President, Lochee's leading Forester, John Paterson, was possibly related.[76]

In November 1903, the Father Mathew branch opened its ranks to all women between the ages of sixteen and forty, when Paterson, Vaughan (who was also former President of the Dundee branch of the UIL) and Callan addressed an audience of over a hundred women on the advantages of membership, i.e., the liberal allowances for sickness and death, and the sliding scale of rates to suit the limited income of those the Foresters wished to reach. The majority of those present enrolled on the spot, and it was predicted that another hundred would join within the week.[77] The speed with which women were recruited into the Foresters contrasted with the UIL's simultaneous endeavour to encourage women to join its ranks. Nevertheless, by December 1904, eighteen months after procuring its first woman member, 68 women out of a total of 201 UIL branch members had paid their shilling's membership fee.[78]

Throughout this period the Foresters and the League continued to collaborate over events such as the centenary commemorations of the 1803 Rising and Emmet's execution. On 29 August 1903, a delegation of 'Dundee Irishmen' participated in the main Irish nationalist event in Scotland that year, a 20,000-strong parade through the streets of Glasgow. Despite the presence of several flute and brass bands, the atmosphere was muted, owing, as Ó Catháin notes, to the untimely death of Hugh Murphy, the popular leader of Glasgow's Home Government branch of the UILGB, but possibly also to the passing, on 14 August, of the Land Purchase Act 1903 (Landlord Relief Act) without a single objection from Irish MPs. For those loyal nationalists who had placed their faith in Davitt's words, it was a sore disappointment which was compounded on 8 September by the UIL Directory's approval of a new national policy of class conciliation.[79] To radical physical force Republicans, this provided incontrovertible evidence that constitutional policy had failed and that the leaders of the Home Rule movement had sold out the mass of the Irish people. In his account of the Land League, published the following year, Davitt opined that the IPP/UIL's unqualified acceptance of the government's constraining terms 'successfully spoiled a radical and final settlement of the Irish land question'.[80]

Others were more forthright in their opinions. In her own blistering account completed three years later, Anna Parnell asserted that '33 years of Home Rule propaganda, real and pretended [had] resulted in surrender all along the line to the whole of England's claims and pretensions regarding Ireland, and in a virtual repudiation of [Ireland's] claim to independence as a right'.[81]

Despite this protestation, 'The Irishmen of Dundee'[82] lapsed into their ill-famed apathy. In an address to the Dundee UIL on the topic of 'Irish Ideals' on 15 October, Nicholas Marra (or O'Mara, as he was designated) lamented 'the tendency which now prevailed in towns such as Dundee for Irishmen to lose their nationality'. P J Russell, proposing thanks, testified that 'the national spirit was growing very low in Dundee', hence the need to encourage it. As part of the endeavour to do so, the meeting was punctuated by the singing of national songs by various members of the League, of which it was noted on this occasion, a number were women.[83]

The Cultural Movement and the Gaelic League

The movement for cultural nationalism was altogether more amenable to those excluded or otherwise alienated from constitutional nationalism and its political power structures. From the outset, the Gaelic League/Conradh na Gaeilge was fertile territory for physical force Republicans – the Dundee press later termed it 'the cradle of Sinn Féin and the Volunteers'.[84]

Mary Trotter describes it as 'the most heterogenous of nationalist groups in the period' – it was also the ground on which Fenians, feminists and radical cultural activists met, and nowhere more so than in the person of Maud Gonne, who, seeking to play a full part in the national struggle and finding all male-dominated organisations closed to her, joined the only one to accept women on equal terms, the Gaelic League, when it was formed in 1893.[85] She also became involved with the Celtic Literary Society, which officially did not, but adopted a more inclusive attitude in practice. (It also provided meeting rooms for Inghinidhe na hÉireann formed in October 1900 by Maud, Jennie Wyse Power, Anna Johnson and several other Republican-minded women.)[86] Indeed, a Special Branch agent who infiltrated a meeting of the Celtic Society that November, reported that 'there were ladies, Scotchmen and Welshmen present. They are mostly faddists and schemers'. Of Maud herself, he noted, 'She is shunned by P O'Brien [and] W Fields MPs and Dr Sigerson.[87] She is in poor health, her associates are of a poor class and she is drinking'.[88] Such a testimonial might well have endeared her and her 'associates' to a good number of marginalised Scottish cultural nationalists and Dundee's disproportionately large number of Irish working-class women'.[89] Yet, while Maud visited Glasgow a few days later where she concluded her address to a Manchester Martyrs commemoration in the Albion Hall with an appeal to the large number of women present to form a branch of Inghinidhe na hÉireann, she did not at any point visit Dundee.[90]

Where Conradh na Gaeilge in Glasgow was a natural haven for members of the IRB who infiltrated and controlled several of its branches, the dearth of an active Fenian organisation in Dundee diminished that possibility. The main catalyst in Dundee was Father Patrick Casey from Ballynoe, County Cork, who came to the city in 1897 to take up the position of senior curate at St Mary's Forebank. Significantly, Casey made his first public appearance on a platform of priests at the inauguration of Blackness Hall, which venue was to provide a key role in future Irish Republican activity in the city.[91] Casey landed in a sympathetic environment. His superior at St Mary's, Canon Michael Phelan, was a fluent Irish speaker, and junior curate, Father John Roche, was the eldest son of Edward Roche of Lochee, ex-Fenian and former President of the Lochee Land and Irish National Leagues. Described as a 'a shrewd observer of matters political' as well as an enthusiastic sportsman and an 'ideal priest', Father Casey was chosen by the Dundee UIL to chair the Willie Redmond meeting of 2 June 1901, in the course of which his comment that the Union of 1800 had been 'brought about by bribery, corruption and fraudulency' and his final salvo of Irish-Gaelic verse had the building 'rattling with applause'.[92] While Casey was attributed with founding the Dundee branch of Conradh na Gaeilge shortly afterwards, it is significant that the branch sprouted at the precise moment that former Conradh activist and Glasgow-based Fenian, Daniel Cronin, moved to the city in search of employment.[93] It is not unlikely that the experienced Gaelic activist Cronin, whose connections and name suggests was a Cork native, would have hooked up with fellow Corkonian and Irish language enthusiast with a view to forming a craobh (branch) in Dundee. At any rate, Casey took on the role of president, and for the next two years, as a contemporary commentator noted, 'wrought enthusiastically and successfully for its advancement'.[94]

Conradh na Gaeilge also had a vigorous propagandist in one local journalist who contributed a series of articles and titbits of information on the subject to the 'Day by Day' column of *Dundee Evening Post* and its sister publications from late 1901 to early 1905. The unnamed reporter, who was possibly a member of the UIL – he was, at any rate, extremely well-informed of the affairs of both organisations and attuned to the mood of the Irish community in general – endeavoured to impress the relevance of the Irish language movement upon a wider community of Scottish readers and influence them in its favour.[95] In February 1902, he seized upon the publication of the 1901 census, which had recorded a decline in the number of Scottish Gaelic speakers, to conduct an inquiry into the progress of the Irish Gaelic Movement. 'He did so', he claimed, for the following reasons:

> It really has the same yearning of hopes...of the Celtic race as its basis, although conducted by a distinctive branch of the family; [and] being a newer movement, and in the full glory of youthful enthusiasm, it might be reasonably expected to show examples of vigour and steady prosecution of its aims not at the moment associated with the cry for the preservation of [Scots Gaelic].

Chapter 5 – Celtic Twilight, Socialist Dawn 1890–1908

On the adoption of the Gaelic League amongst the Irish diaspora, he boasted, 'Nowhere outside the shores of Ireland has this development been taken up with more zest than Glasgow and the West, citing the seven branches in Glasgow with their estimated 600 members, and numerous others stretching from Dumbarton to Ayr, before heaping praise on Denis Brogan, President of the Glasgow central branch and 'an excellent Gaelic scholar' (Brogan was also President of the Glasgow UIL and an IRB man). He described his experience of a typical Conradh 'kaly' [sic]:

> Bhoys and girls gather together as if at a crossroads on the sea-barren coast of Donegal or Connemara… English is regarded as a foreign contestable. Should one of the vocalists elect to sing, say 'Kitty of Coleraine', it is announced somewhat after this fashion (translation) – "Mr Brian Boru will sing the English song entitled 'Kitty of Coleraine'"… as if [he] were about to sing in a language as unknown as Choctaw… Everything is Irish – aggressively so. There is order and yet no order – a curious contradiction which no race seems capable of harmonising except the Milesian of Innisfail. [96]

While over fifteen craobhacha were established up and down the west of Scotland at this time, Dundee was the only one in the east, and also the furthest north. On 3 June 1903, after almost two years of conducting its affairs in 'semi-private', the craobh held its first public event in the Vault, High Street – a lecture by J P Dalton, Secretary of Conradh na Gaeilge in Scotland, on Early Irish Literature, The event, which Father Casey proclaimed 'the first of its kind since the Reformation or, for that matter, since Creation', and the *Courier* interpreted as being of 'a unique manner as it [was] the first of its kind ever held in Dundee', was well attended, and featured songs sung in Irish by several members.[97] While the emerging Gaelic activist, Pádraig Mac Piarais, addressed the Glasgow central branch on the contemporary topic of 'The Irish Language in Scotland' in June 1902, however, there is no record of his ever having visited Dundee. It appears, perhaps as with Maud Gonne and other noted Irish Republicans, it was seen as too small, remote and undistinguished to merit the effort and expense.

Just as the Dundee craobh appeared to be gaining in strength, Father

Casey was recalled to his native Diocese of Cloyne, County Cork.[98] While this inhibited the functioning of Conradh na Gaeilge in Dundee, it failed to sap the enthusiasm of the aforementioned newspaper columnist who had had already begun looking to Ireland for cultural inspiration. Earlier in March, he hailed the fact that St Patrick's Day was now a legal holiday in Ireland, and cited the example of one civic-minded manufacturer who, 'deploring that his firm had used so many trees for making boxes', had planted 20,000 young firs to be ready for St Patrick's Day 1905 (declared an Arbour Day) thus making the urban landscape green in more ways than one. Noting the difficulty in carrying out such a scheme in Dundee, which was 'not yet a garden city',[99] he noted another rich resource in the preponderance of 'sweet singers and skilful accomplished instrumentalists amongst our Irish friends', and proposed instead an Irish 'Mod', to be held on St Patrick's Day and every St Patrick's Day thereafter, which would be anticipated eagerly by 'all classes of the community'. His appeal to 'a few of the local clergymen and the Gaelic League' to take it up appears to have been directed primarily at Casey, who, as fate would have it, was denied the opportunity to carry it through. Nevertheless, the idea was supported by the *Dundee Catholic Herald*, which, six months after Casey's departure, regretted that the local Gaelic League had 'thrown up the sponge'.[100]

The *Herald*'s columnist was possibly Lanarkshire-born Michael T Hannigan, who had taken over from O'Donnell Derrick as the paper's editor-manager, and who was also Treasurer of the Dundee UIL from 1904 up until the First World War. Indeed, the *Herald*'s enthusiasm for an Irish cultural festival mirrored the UIL's changing focus from Home Rule politics and electoral organisation to cultural and social events. A fortnight later, on 3 April 1904, the branch hosted a lecture by O'Donnell Derrick entitled 'A Tour in Ireland', illustrated with 'limelight views', which took the large audience, which had crammed into the Plumbers' Hall, Wellgate, on a journey 'in fancy' from Dundee to Dublin via Belfast, Derry, Donegal, Sligo, Roscommon, Mayo, Galway, Clare and Limerick, interspersed with portraits of Irish patriots and pictures of eviction scenes, incidents from the Land War, and commentary thereupon. The evening concluded with the customary singing of patriotic songs.[101]

While the entertaining presentation and its underlying political message appealed to a broad range of Irish nationalist opinion, the simulated tour of Ireland was also a good deal more affordable to the majority of Dundee-Irish population than a real one organised by the branch a year earlier. Such events were also more accessible to, and indeed pivotal in attracting, an increasing number of women members. Other social events were geared towards a wider, including non-Irish 'market' – in August, Hannigan's organisation of an excursion to Newport-on-Tay on the appropriately named pleasure steamers, the Thistle and the Shamrock, attracted 800 day-trippers, which, along with other social events, enabled the branch to wipe off a considerable amount of debt and end the year in credit.[102]

Meanwhile, it remained to the *Evening Post*'s 'Day by Day' columnist to champion the Gaelic League and remind the Irish community of their linguistic obligations. An appeal to Canon Phelan to 'stir up the dry bones of the [Gaelic League] for the sake of the old tongue and its associations', appears to have roused a number of 'Dundee Irishmen' (and presumably women) to renew their study of the Irish language, albeit on a 'semi-private' basis. On 11 September 1904, 'Day by Day' enquired, 'How are Dundee Irishmen getting on with their native tongue? Still enthusiastic, I hope, in view of the proposed "Irish Mod" – beg pardon Feis!' Noting that 'sermons in Irish [were] now being preached regularly in Ireland [and] in some of the Dublin churches the Rosary has been recited in Irish', he enquired: 'When will the local Gaelic League justify a similar innovation in Dundee? Why not the Very Rev. Canon Phelan?'[103]

All the while, he continued to report on the doings of the Gaelic League in Ireland. In January 1904, he announced 'Another victory for the League! On a postcard from Ulster, the words "Post card – the address to be written on this side" appear in Gaelic'.[104] 'Have the Gaelic League declared war on the Post Office?', he speculated on 11 March 1905, ahead of 'Language Week' when the League was set to 'redouble its efforts. 'The term has a double significance', he added, given the 'irritation of postal officers', who had resorted to returning Irish-addressed letters and parcels posted in Dublin to the Gaelic League's office for translation, triggering questions in Parliament from John Pius Boland, a zealous advocate of the Irish language, and John Redmond.[105] 'Should the flood of mysteriously-addressed missives continue', he opined, 'the Post Office servants will have a strong argument for increased remuneration'.[106] His next and final report on the subject, on 25 May 1905, was uncharacteristically brief but revealing: 'It is alleged the Irish Gaelic League has developed revolutionary tendencies, and the police are active in watching its doings'.[107] And that was the end of the matter.

While the cultural movement was pivotal in nurturing a new generation of militant Irish nationalists elsewhere in Scotland, in Dundee, where the IRB had little input, the task of reviving the Irish language was perhaps too esoteric for even a significant minority to pursue with any real energy, focus and sense of advancement. For the majority of second- and third-generation Irish, it diminished into insignificance compared to the daily task of procuring food and shelter on a subsistence wage, a way of life which had so long consumed their physical and mental energy that it had become a mindset. It was a predicament with which James Connolly was familiar. His words:

> You cannot teach a starving man Gaelic, and the treasure of our national literature will and must remain lost forever to the poor wage slaves who are contented by our society to toil from early morn to late at night for a mere starvation wage… an accursed social system which lowers the ideals of our people to such a degree that the most priceless manuscript of Celtic lore would hold but a secondary place in their esteem than a rasher of bacon.[108]

were especially apposite to Dundee and its large poorly paid Irish textile workforce. As depression in the jute industry took its hold in the second half of the decade, benefit societies such as the INF and AOH, which had been outlets for national expression and covers for militant republicanism, were more concerned with the legitimate and necessary business of dispensing benefits to victims of the 'accursed social system' rather than encouraging them to overthrow it.

The UIL, which some advanced nationalists had resigned themselves to supporting at the outset, had little to offer the majority of working-class men and especially women in the way of political or financial benefits, and while its occasional lectures and social events were well-supported, they alone were not sufficient to attract or retain members. By 1904, attendance at meetings had fallen off, and by 1905, Dundee's Michael Davitt branch had shrunk to the usual core of small businessmen, professionals and atypical upwardly mobile members of the working class such as Bernard McLaughlin, who held the post of Branch Secretary from 1904 until the organisation's demise around 1921 – a position he later held in tandem with that of Secretary of the William O'Brien lodge of the INF.[109] McLaughlin appeared on a political platform at a meeting nine days prior to the 1906 general election, espousing the advice of John Redmond and the UIL Executive to vote for the two Liberal candidates, Edmund Robertson and Henry Robson, on the basis that 'nothing they recommended would be detrimental to the cause of Ireland'.[110] It fell to James Kelly, who had spoken up for Marra and the socialists in 1902, to argue against giving the Liberals 'too large a majority' as Prime Minister Campbell-Bannerman had four anti-Home Rule 'Imperial' Liberals in his cabinet. In the event, enough voters agreed with him to ensure that Alexander Wilkie pipped Robson to become Dundee's first Labour MP, albeit far in the train of Robertson, who polled 9,276 votes against Wilkie's 6,833 and Robson's 6,112.[111]

By this point, Marra had put aside the UIL to focus on labour and trade union politics. On 13 March 1906, he became the first Secretary of the Dundee and District Jute and Flax Workers Union (JFWU), which was formed in the heat of a six-week long jute strike arising out of the 'unauthorised' grassroots action of poorly paid, mostly female spinners, many of whom were of Irish extraction.[112] While much of the work in initiating the union was done by Mary Macarthur of the Women's Trade Union League and National Federation of Women Workers, it is also likely that Marra's Irish nationalist affiliations helped to solidify the trust and support of the Irish-Catholic jute workers of Lochee, earning the JFWU many of its members.

The formation of the JFWU established the right of unskilled, mainly women workers to organise in a trade union to fight for better pay and conditions. Such elements might be expected to sympathise with the poorly paid Belfast dockers who, upholding that same right, banded together with the city's precariously employed carters in a four-month strike (which also arose out of a spontaneous, 'unauthorised' strike – in this case, by the newly unionised dock workers who refused to work with non-union men in April 1907). The Belfast strike was significant in that it saw the arrival in Ireland of Jim Larkin, who effected an alliance between the Labour Representation Committee, Irish Republicans and the working-class Loyalists of the Independent Orange Order to secure a broad cross-community support which bridged the old sectarian divisions. As clashes between strikers and scabs escalated into citywide rioting, on 27 July, the overwhelmed Royal Irish Constabulary, nursing their own grievances over pay and conditions, finally threw their lot in with the strikers, whereupon the British government sent in 2,550 extra troops to 'restore order'. The deployment of the British Army had the predictable result of ramping up resistance, all of which came to a head when troops opened fire on a group of protestors on the Falls Road on 10–11 August, killing two and wounding five others. [113]

The incident led to strong words in Parliament from Irish MPs and protest demonstrations in centres of large Irish population, including Dundee where, on the evening of Monday, 19 August, an enthusiastic crowd of 1,500–2,000 gathered in Albert Square to cheer on vigorous speeches by socialists, James Reid, James Duncan and Nicholas Marra, and endorse a resolution condemning the introduction of the military into a labour dispute.[114] The response of the Dundee labour movement, however, contrasted with that of the British leadership who, fearful that Larkin was fomenting revolution, had already seized upon the opportunity of his return to Liverpool for his mother's funeral to intervene and undermine the strike.[115]

The demonstration in Albert Square had strong echoes of the past. Both Reid and Duncan were veterans of the early socialist movement in Dundee. Duncan in particular had been a prominent street orator at the time of the Anti-Coercion/Free Speech campaign in 1889, that key manifestation of political solidarity which precipitated James Connolly's entry into the movement. More pointedly, the Belfast strike was a portent of what was to come in the Dundee carters' and dockers' strike of December 1911 which saw, for the first time in Scotland, the introduction of the military into an industrial dispute. Even more significantly, however, it was a precursor to the great Dublin Lockout of 1913, when savage attacks against strikers by the semi-militarised Dublin police gave rise to the creation of a workers' defence force which was subsequently moulded by James Connolly into the revolutionary Irish Citizen Army.

Chapter 5 – Celtic Twilight, Socialist Dawn 1890–1908

1908 saw the debut on the electoral stage of Sinn Féin, which unsuccessfully contested the North Leitrim by-election on 21 February but won eleven seats in local elections in Dublin. While the foundation of a Coiste Ceanntair Albainn (Scottish Executive) kindled a growing number of Sinn Féin cumainn in Glasgow and the West, Irish politics in Dundee remained firmly in the grasp of the UIL.[116]

The Dundee by-election of May 1908 also saw the entrance on to the scene of a future key player in the Anglo-Irish conflict, Winston Churchill. In the run up to the election, the UIL Executive issued a manifesto 'advising all the Irish electors of Dundee to support Mr Churchill wholeheartedly, as his declarations in respect to Home Rule are entirely satisfactory and have been pronounced by Mr Asquith to be the policy of the government'.[117] In a staunchly working-class community, the rejection of two practical socialists (Prohibitionist Neddy Scrymgeour and Labour trade unionist, G H Stuart) in favour of an upper-class English Liberal was motivated by the belief that consolidating the Liberal vote would render the Tories powerless to obstruct Home Rule legislation.

At a UIL meeting in the city, James O'Donnell Derrick commented that 'both Stuart and Scrymgeour were warm friends of Ireland, and in other circumstances both their Executive and [himself] would have been disposed to support either of [them]'.[118] At a crowded meeting in Lochee, Bernard McLaughlin, a future Labour councillor in the city, stated that 'only by acting up to the recommendation could they advance the cause of Ireland and prove the efficacy of the Irish vote'.[119] Churchill, who spoke on UIL platforms in the city, quickly caught on to the need to placate Irish voters. Home Rule promptly replaced tariff reform as the main topic of his election speeches, and his rallying cry, 'Let my victory in Dundee be a victory in Ireland', received a standing ovation.[120] The efficacy of the Irish vote was duly proved on Saturday, 9 May 1908 when Churchill cruised home to victory, and again in 1922, when his belligerent approach towards Ireland was a major factor in his humiliating defeat at the hands of a bitter, contemptuous electorate.

Endnotes to Chapter 5

1. William McGonagall, 'The Demon Drink' [verse nine], 1887, *Last Poetic Gems* (Dundee: David Winter, 1968).
2. John Leslie, adaptation of 'The Day is Coming' by William Morris [last verse], *Justice*, 5 May 1894.
3. Greaves, *Life and Times*, p14.
4. For more on Connolly's military service and the circumstances of his desertion, see Greaves, *Life and Times*, pp11–12; and John O'Neill, 'Where, oh where, is our James Connolly: #Connolly150', The Treason Felony Blog, https://treasonfelony.wordpress.com/2018/06/05/where-oh-where-is-our-james-connolly-connolly150/, accessed 19 May 2023.
5. *Dundee Courier*, 22 April, 26 June 1889.
6. *Dundee Advertiser*, 30 October 1890.
7. Their reservations were justified. When Gladstone revealed his second Home Rule Bill in 1893, it contained major flaws and was arguably less radical than the first.
8. *Dundee Courier*, 9 December 1889; Sheehy Skeffington, *Michael Davitt*, pp150–51.
9. *Dundee Advertiser*, 10 October 1891.
10. Despite the name, it is extremely unlikely that the Edward Bell named here, an Irish-born baker who emigrated to Dundee with his young family in the mid-1870s, was the same Edward Bell (Ivory), who was involved in the dynamite plot of May 1896 which aimed to target Queen Victoria and Czar Nicholas at a location between Leith Docks and Balmoral Castle. Ó Catháin, *Irish Republicanism in Scotland*, p182.
11. *Dundee Courier*, 12 October 1891.
12. Ó Broin, *Revolutionary Brotherhood*, pp44–45.
13. *Derry Journal*, 5 August 1892. McMahon is listed as the delegate from Dundee District, with no mention of branch. However, the C S Parnell branch, which was one of the strongest and most active Dundee branches prior to the split, may simply have dropped its name.
14. While the majority of the IRB took Parnell's side, a minority went anti-Parnellite, as did the Belfast branch of the Fenian-dominated Young Ireland Society from which Belfast-born Dowling may have defected. Ó Broin, *Revolutionary Brotherhood*, p49–50. Invitations to attend the convention were extended to Anti-Parnellite MPs Davitt, Dillon, T D Sullivan, Thomas Sexton and W N Kenny, who politely declined. *Irish Independent*, 20 August 1892; *Freeman's Journal* 6 August 1892.
15. *Dundee Courier*, 3 August 1893; *Dundee Advertiser*, 3 August 1893; Ó Catháin, *Irish Republicanism in Scotland*, p145.
16. *Dundee Courier*, 2 August 1893; *Dundee Evening Telegraph*, 31 July 1893.

Chapter 5 – Celtic Twilight, Socialist Dawn 1890–1908

17   *Dundee Evening Telegraph,* 2 August 1893; *Irish News and Belfast Morning News,* 10 August 1893.

18   *Dundee Evening Telegraph,* 31 July 1893.

19   *Justice,* 29 July 1893.

20   *Justice,* 29 July 1893.

21   Robertson left the city under a cloud in May 1890, having been charged with stealing a hired piano from the SDF's meeting room in the Overgate Hall, leading the Secretary of the Edinburgh SSF, John Connolly, to write to the Dundee papers that 'the well-known Socialist orator' they had thus characterised had been expelled from the SDF and was 'not likely recognised in Dundee by any of the Socialist branches there'. *Dundee Evening Telegraph,* 15 May 1890. The same year William Cameron of the Dundee SDF left the organisation to form the first anarchist group in the city. In July 1893, James Connolly, who had taken on his brother's office, reported that the Edinburgh SSF were sending a delegate to the International Workers' Congress in Zurich with explicit instructions to vote against the participation of 'Anarchists as such', as 'it would be scarcely less than idiotic, were they to admit to their council's men whose philosophy of life is but an 'exaggerated form of the individualism we are in revolt against'. *Justice,* 22 July 1893.

22   *Justice,* 12 August 1893.

23   *Justice,* 26 August 1893.

24   Lowe, *Souvenirs of Scottish Labour,* p108.

25   *Dundee Advertiser,* 22 July 1893.

26   *Justice,* 22 July 1893.

27   See, for example, Greaves, *Life and Times,* pp28–30; Donal Nevin, *James Connolly: A Full Life,* (Dublin: Gill & Macmillan, 2005), pp42–46; Lorcan Collins, *16 Lives: James Connolly,* (Dublin: The O'Brien Press, 2012), pp55–59. The articles were published in *Justice* between 24 March and May 1894, under the heading 'Passing Thoughts on the Irish Question'.

28   In *History and Antiquities of the County of Carlow,* 1833, Irish antiquarian Father John Ryan described the 'wild Irishry' as 'the mortal and natural enemies to the kings of England, and English dominion'. Quoted in Ivor Jennings, *Party Politics: Volume 3, The Stuff of Politics* (Cambridge: Cambridge University Press, 1962), p300.

29   *Justice,* 14 March 1894.

30   *Dundee Advertiser,* 27 September 1893.

31   *Dundee Courier,* 27 September 1893.

32   *Justice,* 23 September 1893.

33   *Labour Leader,* 14 July 1894; *Dundee Advertiser,* 16 July 1894; *Justice,* 21 July 1894. The Dundee venue may also have been chosen to counter the damaging impact of a Labour Congress held in the city in late 1893 in an apparent attempt

by Champion to revive the Scottish Trades Council's Labour Party as an electoral rival to the ILP, to which idea a number of the delegates, including all of the Dundee SLP, strongly objected. *Justice*, 30 September, 7 October, 14 October 1893. Champion, a founder member of the SDF and ILP, was also denounced for his opportunistic attempts to finance a party machine by soliciting donations from, amongst others, members of the Tory and Liberal Parties. Piqued at the criticism, he emigrated to Australia in 1894, where he failed to establish himself politically and returned to his original profession of journalism. Geoffrey Searle, 'Champion, Henry Hyde (1859–1928)', *Australian Dictionary of National Biography, Volume 7* (1979); 'Henry Hyde Champion', Spartacus Educational, https://spartacus-educational.com/TUchampion.htm, accessed 19 May 2023.

34 *Labour Leader*, 12 May 1894.
35 *Labour Leader*, 9 February 1895; *Dundee Courier*, 4 July 1895. Brannigan's reputation extended beyond Dundee. At a demonstration for the eight-hour day in May 1894, Keir Hardie made light of his views, observing that while 'Mr Brannigan, who he believed was present, did not admit the existence of the ILP, Lord Rosebery did, and he preferred to pit [the Prime Minister] against Brannigan [unless] it were a matter of making loaves'. *Dundee Courier*, 7 May 1894.
36 *Labour Leader*, 9 February 1895.
37 Lowe, *Souvenirs of Scottish Labour*, p61.
38 Walker notes that the local press also complained (or assumed) that the 'Irish voted as the priests instructed', a view which Walker himself appears to have accepted. *Juteopolis*, pp188, 268–69.
39 Walker, *Juteopolis*, p268.
40 *Dundee Courier*, 22 July 1895.
41 *Dundee Advertiser*, 4 April 1895.
42 *Justice*, 14 December 1895.
43 NAI, CBS, Precis Box 4, 13877 S.
44 A number of radical Home Rulers in Scotland, notably John Ferguson, had joined the Scottish Labour Party at its inception.
45 *Dundee Advertiser*, 27 April 1897.
46 Ó Catháin, *Irish Republicanism in Scotland*, pp172, 194. Havilan, who Special Branch files described as 'a bad class of suspect', and suspected of having links with dynamitards, stood as a Scottish Labour Party candidate in the Glasgow School Board elections in the spring of 1891. He was also secretary of the National Union of Dock Labourers. Both Havilan and Ward were key members of the Anderston Workers' Association, the Glasgow Young Ireland Society, the Glasgow Literary Society and the Derry Defence Fund. Ward was also Secretary of the Glasgow and West of Scotland '98 Centenary Committee, Vice President of Cumann na nGaedheal, and a member of the Gaelic League, from whose members he formed an IRB circle at Partick in 1904. NAI, Criminal Branch

Special (CBS) files, Precis Box 4, 261/15284, 7 January 1896, NAI, CBS, Precis Box 4, 29594 S, 25 June 1904.

47 In February 1904, the Irish National Club in Glasgow was refused registration owing to illegal whisky trading in the streets by some of its members. NAI, CBS, Precis Box 4, 29449 S, February 1904.

48 *Dundee Advertiser,* 6 May 1896; *Dundee Courier,* 22 October 1897.

49 In May 1895, Thomas Flanagan, who had previously appeared in court for defaulting on aliment payments to his estranged wife (who left him because of his violent drunken behaviour), was prosecuted for selling alcohol for consumption in his grocer's/spirit dealer's shop and lost his licence as a result. *Dundee Advertiser,* 9 January 1895; *Dundee Courier,* 22 May 1895.

50 In April 1904, P T Daly warned the Glasgow IRB against John Brawley of Glasgow Cumann na nGaedheal, who was under investigation by the IRB Supreme Council for pilfering funds, and castigated the Irishmen of Glasgow for letting him 'walk the streets unmolested'. NLI, CBS, Precis Box 4, 40822, 18 May 1904.

51 Flanagan's last appearances in public were at municipal election meetings where his increasingly erratic behaviour was noted. *Dundee Courier,* 22 October, 28 October 1897.

52 Roche owned a number of grocer's shops and residential properties in the Lochee and Hilltown areas. A leading parishioner of St Mary's Lochee, four of his six sons – John, Joseph, Alphonsus and Aloysius – went on to become priests, and one of his two daughters, Margaret Mary, became a nun. Unlike his fellow grocer, Flanagan, Roche was a staunch advocate of temperance and clashed with Flanagan over the latter's allegations of anti-Irish bias on the part of the Licensing Board for refusing to grant a sprit dealer's licence to former INL colleague, Joseph Duffy. *Dundee Courier,* 2 November 1895. Initially, Roche's devotion to his faith, parish and local community complemented his devotion to the Irish national movement; by the time of his death in March 1917 at the approximate age of 73, he had retired from political life.

53 Death records for Thomas Flanagan, 7 April 1898; J P Casey, 20 April 1902; Edward Roche, 3 March 1917, James Ward, 23 March 1903; and Edward De Courcey, 23 April 1905; *Dundee Courier,* 13 April 1898; *Dundee Courier,* 21 April 1902; *Dundee Evening Telegraph,* 21 April 1902; *People's Journal,* 10 March 1917. The death record for De Courcey gives his age as 39, however, the record of his marriage to Mary Hutton on 3 May 1886 gives it as 30. Given his obvious political experience at the time, I have taken the latter to be more likely. There is no record of James Connolly's Dundee-domiciled uncle, James McGinn, another possible Fenian (see Chapter 2). However, the death of McGinn's brother-in-law, Owen Boyle, in June 1904 was registered by his daughter, (Boyle's niece) Mary McGinn of 17 Albert Street, Lochee. Death record for Owen Boyle, 6 October 1904.

54 *Dundee Courier*, 3 September 1900. Whether Kiernan succeeded in recruiting in the opposite direction is harder to ascertain, given that AOH remained a secret society proscribed by the Catholic church. Kiernan was elected National Vice President of the AOH in Derry in June 1904, by which time he was also organiser of the UILGB in the North of England where he attempted to recruit from the former into the latter. Kiernan went on to forge a strong alliance between the AOH and the UIL in Armagh, and by the end of the decade, the AOH had replaced the UIL in several districts of Ireland. NLI, CBS files, Precis Box 4, 29640, 29753S; Anthony C Hepburn, *A Past Apart: Histories in the Study of Catholic Belfast, 1850–1950*, Belfast: Ulster Historical Foundation, 1996, p162, n28.

55 In 1894, the Scottish League for the Taxation of Land Values changed its name to the Scottish Single Tax League. *The Single Tax* was re-named *Land Values* in 1902, then *Land and Liberty* in 1919, which title it retains to this day.

56 *Land and Liberty*, March–April 1933, p195; *Irish Weekly and Ulster Examiner*, 18 February 1933.

57 *Dundee Courier*, 10 September 1900.

58 *Dundee Courier*, 1 October 1900.

59 *Dundee Courier*, 29 April 1901. McHugh was sentenced to six months' imprisonment for publishing an article on jury packing.

60 A reference to the Conservative Party's plans to establish a state-aided Catholic University in Ireland rather than open up Trinity College Dublin to Catholics.

61 *Dundee Evening Telegraph*, 6 June 1901.

62 *Dundee Evening Telegraph*, 10 June 1901.

63 *Dundee Evening Telegraph*, 10 June 1901.

64 *Dundee Evening Post*, 25 August 1901.

65 *Dundee Evening Telegraph*, 28 December 1901

66 *Labour Leader*, 4 January 1902.

67 *Labour Leader*, 25 January 1902.

68 Russell's book, *Ireland and the Empire*, published in 1901, was a piercing critique of Unionist policy in Ireland, and particularly of the Irish agrarian system. Isolated by most of his Liberal Unionist colleagues, he subsequently stood as an Independent Unionist, and ultimately as a Liberal Home Ruler for North Tyrone in 1911, which seat he retained until his retirement in July 1918.

69 *Labour Leader*, 2 February 1902. Interestingly, Marra's name is represented here in its more authentic Irish form O'Mara.

70 Greaves, *Life and Times*, p86; Nevin, *James Connolly: A Full Life*, p179.

71 *Dundee Evening Telegraph*, 6 January 1903.

72 *Dundee Evening Telegraph*, 8 April 1903.

73 *Dundee Evening Telegraph*, 19 May 1903.

CHAPTER 5 – CELTIC TWILIGHT, SOCIALIST DAWN 1890–1908

74 *Dundee Evening Telegraph*, 19 May 1902.
75 *Dundee Evening Post*, 5 August 1902.
76 See Chapter 4. The 1871 census indicates that Lucy Paterson, who emigrated to America with her two sisters in 1884, had a younger brother John. Census of Scotland, 1871; Whelehan, 'Saving Ireland in Juteopolis', p83.
77 *Dundee Advertiser*, 1 December 1903.
78 *Dundee Courier*, 18 December 1904.
79 Ó Catháin, *Irish Republicanism*, pp203–4; Philip Bull, *Land and Nationalism, Land, Politics and Nationalism, 1850–1938: A Study of the Irish Land Question* (Dublin: Gill & Macmillan, 1996), p164.
80 Davitt, *Fall of Feudalism*, p29.
81 Parnell, *Tale of a Great Sham*, p38.
82 Throughout the nineteenth century and first two decades of the twentieth, 'The Irishmen of Dundee', was often used as metonym for a group which included men and women, second and third generation Irish, including those of mixed Scots-Irish ancestry. The term was also used to describe audiences at Irish meetings, which may have contained a significant non-Irish element.
83 *Dundee Evening Telegraph*, 16 October 1903.
84 *Dundee Evening Telegraph*, 18 May 1922.
85 Mary Trotter, *Irish National Theaters: Political Performance and the Origins of the Irish Dramatic Movement* (New York: Syracuse University Press, 2001), p78.
86 Margaret Ward, *Unmanageable Revolutionaries*, p50.
87 George Sigerson, President of the Irish Literary Society and Maud's physician.
88 NAI, CBS, 23834/S, 7 December 1900.
89 In an address to the Dundee branch of the UIL in November 1903, Neddy Scrymgeour, a staunch advocate of Irish Home Rule and temperance, concluded that 'although they were anxious for many reforms in Ireland, they must first of all tackle the drink problem'. *Dundee Advertiser*, 6 November 1903.
90 Ó Catháin, *Irish Republicanism in Scotland*, p201.
91 *Dundee Advertiser*, 19 November 1897. Blackness Hall, which was on the site of the former Larch Street Hall, was located between Blackness Road and Larch Street at the Urquhart Street junction. It was the main venue for Sinn Féin meetings between 1919 and 1923, and was colloquially known as 'the Shinners' for many years after. It was demolished in the 1990s to make way for a new housing development.
92 *Dundee Evening Post*, 11 September 1903; *Dundee Evening Telegraph*, 3 June 1901.
93 Ó Catháin notes that Cronin was one of two (likely) Cork-born 'link-men' between the Glasgow Fenians of the Irish National Club and the Gaelic movement up until early-mid 1901. Ó Catháin, *Irish Republicanism in Scotland*, p203.
94 *Dundee Evening Post*, 11 September 1903.

95   At a meeting of the Dundee UIL in on 18 January 1903, the main speaker, veteran Home Ruler Michael Farrell supported by President Fagan, requested that all reporters from the Dundee daily press be excluded, citing his concern that their candid reporting of branch meetings left the UIL open to ridicule. This was challenged by several members, including Cooney and Marra, who pointed out that one of the reporters was also a member, whereupon it was agreed that he could stay in the latter capacity only. *Dundee Advertiser,* 19 January 1903.

96   *Dundee Evening Post,* 1 February 1902.

97   *An Claildheamh Soluis,* 20 June 1903; *Dundee Courier,* 4 June 1903.

98   *Dundee Courier,* 11 September 1903; *DEP,* 11 September 1903. Casey went on to become Bishop of the Diocese of Ross, County Cork, in 1935.

99   A reference to the ideas of Patrick Geddes, Professor of Botany at Queen's College and innovative town planner, whose Ramsay Garden project in Edinburgh was completed around this time. Geddes's proposal for a botanic garden to the east of Magdalen Green was rejected by the Town Council in 1906 on grounds of cost. Murdo Macdonald, 'The Patron, The Professor and the painter: cultural activity in Dundee ant the end of the nineteenth century', in Miskell, Whatley and Harris, *Victorian Dundee, Image and Realities,* pp143–44.

100 *Evening Post,* 11 March 1903; *Dundee Catholic Herald,* quoted in the *Evening Telegraph and Post,* 19 March 1904.

101 *Dundee Evening Post,* 4 April 1904.

102 *Dundee Evening Post,* 17 August, 22 August 1904; *Dundee Courier,* 19 December 1904.

103 *Dundee Evening Post,* 28 September 1904.

104 *Dundee Evening Telegraph,* 12 January 1904.

105 Boland, who was MP for South Kerry from 1900 to 1918 (when he lost his seat to Sinn Féin) occasionally addressed the House of Commons in Irish. Renowned as the first ever Irish Olympic gold medallist (for tennis in Athens in 1896), Boland had requested an Irish flag at the medal ceremony, but as none were available a Union Jack was used. The experience of having his achievement portrayed as an English victory spurred him to a greater awareness of his Irish identity and to take up the causes of the Irish language and Home Rule. Cyril M White, 'John Pius Boland's Olympic tennis diploma', *History Ireland,* 20:4 (July/August 2012).

106 *Dundee Evening Post,* 11 March 1905.

107 *Dundee Evening Telegraph and Post,* 25 May 1905.

108 James Connolly, 'The Gaelic Revival', *The Workers' Republic,* 1 October 1898, reproduced in Harkin, *The Connolly Reader* (Chicago: Haymarket Books, 2018), pp106–7.

109 McLaughlin, who was born and raised in the Dens/Hilltown area, was the youngest child of Irish immigrants – Bernard, a labourer, who died young, and

Christina, a flax weaver. With the benefit of a secondary education enabled by his older working siblings, McLaughlin became a proof-reader for the *Dundee Catholic Herald* under its editor-manager, Michael T Hannigan, Treasurer of the Dundee UIL from 1904 to 1914. Census of Scotland, 1891; death record for Bernard Mclaughlin, 1948; Dundee Trade Directories, 1906–1921.

110 *Dundee Courier* 8 January 1906.

111 Wilkie, MP for Dundee from 1906 to 1908 and 1910 to 1922, was a moderate reformist, and did not distinguish himself as a supporter of Ireland. Despite supporting Home Rule, his only Parliamentary intervention on an Irish-related topic was to complain about the importation of young men from Ireland to work on the building of aerodromes, when other, presumably non-Irish, men with the requisite skills were being conscripted into the army. Hansard, Aerodromes (Irish Labourers) HC [House of Commons] Debate, 7 July 1918, Volume 108, cc1041-2.

112 Walker, *Juteopolis* pp171, 199–207.

113 For detail on the Belfast Strike, see John Gray, *City in Revolt, James Larkin and the Belfast Dock Strike of 1907* (Belfast: Blackstaff Press, 1985); Emmet O'Connor, *Big Jim Larkin, Hero or Wrecker*, (Dublin: UCD Press, 2015).

114 *Labour Leader*, 23 August 1907.

115 The carters returned to work on the 15 August and the dockers on the 28 August. Gray, *City in Revolt*, p173.

116 Ó Catháin, *Irish Republicanism in Scotland*, p220.

117 *Dundee Advertiser*, 1 May 1908.

118 *Dundee Advertiser*, 4 May 1908.

119 *Dundee Advertiser*, 4 May 1908.

120 *Dundee Advertiser*, 7 May 1908.

CHAPTER 6

A New Militancy
1909–16

Let the great truth be fixed on your mind that the struggle for the conquest of the political state of the capitalist is not the battle, it is only the echo of the battle. The real battle is being fought out, and will be fought out, on the industrial field.[1]

> Come all ye scholars, saints and bards,
> Says the grand old dame Britannia.
> Will ye come and join the Irish Guards,
> Says the grand old dame Britannia.
> Every man that treads on a German's feet,
> Will be given a parcel tied up neat,
> A Home Rule badge and a winding sheet,
> Say the grand old dame Britannia.[2]

1908 SAW a sharp downturn in the jute industry, and a growth in the number of unemployed workers who, in their distress, were forced to fall back on charity. Interestingly, future Communist leader, Bob Stewart, then a full-time organiser for Neddy Scrymgeour's Scottish Prohibition Party, recalled the actions of one particular Catholic priest who worked 'like a Trojan…day and night' to deliver help, discreetly and without prejudice, to all who needed it, putting the prevaricating charitable authorities, employers and politicians to shame.[3] The priest was Canon John Turner of St Andrew's Cathedral, who, as the former parish priest of St John the Baptist's in Perth, had conducted the marriage of James Connolly and Lillie Reynolds on 30 April 1889.[4] A Perth-based publication of the time had noted that Dean Turner was 'known to all classes of the community' and that 'his familiar form [was] seen at all times and in all seasons, flitting in and out of the houses in the poorer parts of the city… ministering with untiring zeal to the manifold needs of his flock'.[5] Greaves posits the view that Connolly chose to marry in Perth to escape the constraining influence of the Catholic Archbishop of St Andrew's (Edinburgh), William Smith, who had pronounced defence of the Plan of Campaign to be 'a grievous sin', and whose attempt to depose one such defender Michael Flanagan, President of the Edinburgh St Mary's (Cowgate) branch of the INL, from the presidency of the Edinburgh Catholic Young Men's Society, was challenged by progressive nationalists and socialist republicans alike, including Flanagan's former INL colleague John Leslie.[6] The fact that the neighbouring Diocese of Dunkeld was 'between bishops' may have made things easier. Whatever the reason for the couple's decision, it is certain that the apprehensive Lillie – a Protestant, who James had advised to 'speak to the priest' in order to receive a dispensation to marry in the Catholic Church – would have found a sympathetic ear in Turner, described as 'shy and retiring in public', but whose 'kindly disposition and great earnestness of purpose' were evident to all 'those who came in touch with him'.[7] Significantly, during his seventeen-year tenure at Perth (1885-1902), Turner's parish had active branches of the INL and the INF.[8]

Although trade picked up in the second half of 1909, the experience of being dependent on charity created a lingering resentment amongst the poorer working class which resurfaced years later in the unemployed agitation of the early 1920s but, more immediately, fed into a new wave of militant trade unionism and industrial unrest. Between December 1908 and December 1911, membership of the JFWU increased from 3,724 to 5,524.[9] On 24 February 1911, around 1,000 recently-unionised spinners at Camperdown Works, Lochee, struck over plans to reduce the numbers working a frame from ten to eight, to which the employers responded by locking out the entire 5,000-strong workforce. Whether these spinners were Irish, as William [Billy] Kenefick presumes them to be, their actions contained many hallmarks of Irish nationalist activity, not least the spirit of self-reliance and economic solidarity, which motivated the women to raise money for non-union members not in receipt of strike benefit in the midst of their own straitened circumstances, and in the independent female leadership, which harked back to the Ladies' Land League.[10] Processions of strikers through Lochee and into the city centre, led by local marching bands, also evoked the parading tradition of the INF of which, it was noted earlier, a large number of Lochee women were members. Walker notes that 'for reasons which are not clear', a young woman wearing a green felt hat, who assumed a prominent part in the demonstrations, 'captured the imagination of those who supported the strike, and evoked the derision of those who opposed it'.[11] One suspects the reasons were clear enough – for many of the strikers and their supporters, green, not red, was the colour of rebellion and liberation. The woman in question was 27-year-old Susan Devine, a single mother of one and the head of a multi-generational all-female household, which included her mother, thirteen-year-old sister and two-year-old daughter.[12] The 'Girl in the Green Felt Hat' also travelled to Parkhead to take a collection at the Scotland-Ireland match the day after St Patrick's Day, on which significant day the strike was called off, when one of the striking women offered Lord Provost James Urquhart a small sprig of shamrock. It was at best a dubious compromise – with the strikers agreeing to work eight-woman squads on the condition that if it entailed overwork or hardship, the number would increase to ten. JFWU Secretary John Sime regretted that they had been driven back by 'the misery that existed in Lochee, especially among non-union members'. He, nevertheless, insisted, the strike had provided 'opportunity and good reason for joining' and 'in future disputes, no consideration would be given to non-union members'. Another negotiator, Alexander Eliot, concurred that 'it had been a serious struggle between labour and capital, and labour in Lochee had got the best of it'.[13] Despite the interplay of Irish resistance and class and worker solidarity, however (the strikers received support from the calenders' and tenters' unions, the Dundee Trades Council, the ILP and the SDF), it was a long way from the syndicalist strategising being promoted by Larkin and Connolly.

That all changed with the Dundee carters' and dockers' strike of December 1911 which, like the 1907 Belfast dockers' and carters' strike and the Liverpool general transport strike earlier that summer, had its origins in the low and inconsistent wages paid to those key links in the transport chain, the carters. On 18 December, around 1,200 carters and dockers struck over the demand for a minimum wage of 23 shillings a week, bringing trade in the city to a standstill as jute-laden ships clogged up the harbour, and mills, factories and other centres of production were forced to close through lack of coal. When the contractors imported scab labour from Aberdeen, thousands of 'idle' textile workers descended on the city centre, and violent clashes with baton-wielding police, many of whom had been drafted in from other parts of Scotland, ensued.[14] While the strike was led by the syndicalist-leaning Peter Gillespie of the North of Scotland Horse & Motormen's Association and Marra and Sime of the JFWU, much of the physical force action was instigated by strike-seasoned women and girls, who, amongst other things, encouraged the men to throw a lorry into the King William VI Dock, and also children, who had engaged in their own school strike in September.[15] Amidst the escalating disorder and the inability to procure more police from other cities, the magistrates telegraphed the War, Home and Scottish Offices, requesting urgent military assistance. Within twelve hours, 300 troops of the Black Watch, complete with service rifles and a plentiful supply of cartridges, poured into the city on three trains. Amongst the first detachment were troops who, at the behest of Home Secretary, Winston Churchill, had suppressed the Liverpool strike and shot dead two strikers, four months earlier. The response was fast and furious as dock workers up and down the coast resolved to block incoming Dundee steamers, and the Glasgow dockers, sailors and firemen poised themselves to walk out at the first whiff of blackleg recruitment or military deployment.

Tom Mann, the syndicalist leader of the Liverpool strike committee, hastened to Dundee, where, along with Gillespie and Joseph Houghton of the Scottish Union of Dock Labourers, he wired a telegram to the War, Home and Scottish Secretaries and local MPs Wilkie and Churchill (who had been promoted to First Lord of the Admiralty in October) stating that the strike was under complete control and the presence of the military was calculated to incite disorder. Marra and Sime did likewise on behalf of the JFWU. In the City Chambers, Councillor Neddy Scrymgeour accused the magistrates of 'throwing their influence on the side of the employers' by calling in the military'.[16] The following day saw a monster rally of around 4,000 people on Shore Terrace, chaired by Sime and addressed by Gillespie, Houghton, and James O'Connor Kessack, who had been involved in the Belfast strike and had replaced Larkin as national organiser of the NUDL in 1909.[17] O'Connor Kessack, who affirmed that he was there to see that no steamers left Dundee for any port in Scotland or England without his knowledge, proceeded to tell the strikers their demands were 'too moderate' and to criticise Dundee's continued support for 'Dear Winnie', who, 'if he came along, would be told he was a great man whereas he [O'Connor Kessack, who had stood unsuccessfully as a Labour candidate in Glasgow Camlachie in 1910] was asked why the hell he wanted to get into Parliament'. O'Connor Kessack, it seems, failed to appreciate the strong streak of Irish nationalism which led a large section of the Dundee working class to vote strategically for a candidate who, they believed, would help deliver Irish Home Rule.[18] Messages of support were also read from Ben Tillet of the London dockers deploring the 'military outrage', the Greenock dockers, and from Robert Cunninghame Graham, who stated that he would have been there were he not 'laid up ill'. It was down to Tom Mann to drive home the syndicalist message:

> The campaign now was only at the beginning, and that settlement when made, would only pave the way for something more effective later on. There was more than a fight in Dundee going on. They were organising all over the country to get rid of that cursed poverty. They did not go out to strike for fun, and they meant to see to it to have all the unions working in harmony, the skilled and the skilled and unskilled men [sic] making common cause. They were out for a fight with the ruling classes, and industrial solidarity was to be their motto.

It was not all riots and rowdyism. The picketers succeeded in making 'a number of converts' – the arguments of Houghton and Gillespie proving particularly persuasive, while other prospective scabs 'fled from the scene, awed by the demonstrations directed against them'. On 22 December, the fifth day of the strike, the *Evening Telegraph* reported that 'the ranks of imported labour are thinning gradually'. Finally, on the seventh day, the employers conceded to the workers' demands, whereupon the troops, who had remained in their temporary barracks in the Drill Hall in Parker Street, returned to Edinburgh the same day.[19] It was a victory for the strikers and a vindication of the power of combined strike action, working-class solidarity and political argument allied with physical force.

While there is little reference to the Dundee strike in annals of Irish labour history, it is hard to belief that Larkin or Connolly would have been unaware of it or not have taken an interest in the tactics adopted, as they had with the Rhondda miners' (the Tonypandy Riots) and the Liverpool strikes. The 'Dundee Labour War' was reported widely in the Irish press. In Belfast, where Connolly was organiser of the ITGWU, the local dailies carried reports on riots, demonstrations and deputations protesting against military intervention, and the success of the strikers in winning over 'free', i.e. blackleg labour to their cause and obtaining a satisfactory settlement.[20] On 29 December, the *Belfast Newsletter* reported how the Dundee strike had perturbed the defenders of capitalism in the Trade Disputes Act Reform League who cited the instances of intimidation and destruction of property as evidence that the Trades Disputes Act of 1906 gave trade union officials 'carte blanche to do whatever they chose in furtherance of a strike in the full knowledge that the law cannot touch their unions'.[21] There are other reasons why Connolly especially would have taken an interest in the Dundee strike, not least as his first involvement in organised labour occurred in the city where, in August-September 1889, he had compiled a file of newspaper articles on the London Dock Strike in which Mann had first come to prominence. Indeed, Connolly may well have participated in a demonstration of over 2,000 'bona fide workmen' and women in support of the strike in Albert Square on 5 September 1889, chaired by Cunninghame Graham, and addressed by Edward Aveling, Keir Hardie and Clementina Black (the organiser of the 1888 Bryant and May match girls' strike in London) all of whom were in the city for the Annual meeting of the TUC.[22]

It was in Dundee too that Connolly first referred to his involvement as a potential strike leader. In April 1890, he wrote to Lillie:

> If we get married next week I shall be unable to go to Dundee as promised as my fellow workers on the job are preparing to strike at the end of the month for a reduction in the hours of labour. As my brother and I are ringleaders in the matter it is necessary we should be on the ground. If we are not we should be looked on as blacklegs, which the Lord forbid...[23]

The proposed strike concerned the scavengers, of which overworked, underpaid fraternity the Connolly brothers were part. At that point, the scaffies in Dundee worked longer hours than those in any other Scottish town, and received only three days' holiday a year – New Year's, midsummer, and the Sanitary Committee's annual outing to Monikie when the scaffies were taken along. A letter to the Convener of the Sanitary Committee from the Dundee Labour Federation – which incorporated members of the SDF and the SLP, including John and James Connolly – claiming a holiday of 24 hours a week 'as a right... not a privilege', appears to have had some effect. On 16 April, the Committee instructed the Cleansing Department to 'readjust' the employees' holidays accordingly; thus, the six-month long dispute appears to have been resolved (or at least progressed) without a strike, and James and Lillie were married on 30 April.[24]

Connolly had met Mann in Edinburgh in the mid-1890s, and the two had later corresponded, with Mann recalling that Connolly's views on industrial unionism chimed with his own.[25] Connolly also appears to have been corresponding with O'Connor Kessack in 1911 although there is no reference in any surviving correspondence to the Dundee strike, which, if it was dramatic, was also short. Moreover, while Belfast's large workforce of women textile operatives and poorly paid dockers and carters had many parallels with Dundee's recently-unionised and mobilised strike activists, Connolly had his work cut out for him in a city which remained dogged by sectarian tensions, and where his efforts to organise the hitherto unorganised female spinners into a women's section of the ITGWU were condemned by the Catholic clergy on the one hand, and by the 'skilled' weavers of the predominantly Protestant Textile Operatives Society, on the other. It was, as Greaves notes, 'a hard nut which [even he, despite his success in other parts of Ireland] failed to crack'.[26] Dundee, at least, had no such problems.

The carters' and dockers' strike was followed by a protracted jute strike, which began on 9 January 1912 when around 40 weavers in one section of Grimond's Bowbridge Jute Works struck over a drop in wage rates. As weavers in other sections followed suit, on 1 March the number increased to 600, then 1,000, paralysing production and forcing the mill, which employed around 2,500 people, to close. As workers in other establishments asserted their own demands, the JFWU, called a strike of the entire textile workforce. Messages of support came from Tom Mann in Liverpool, Ben Tillet in London, and Joe Houghton and Manny Shinwell in Glasgow, who pledged to block supplies bound for Dundee. Within the city, the carters reciprocated the support received during their own strike, Indeed the jute workers also adopted the same tactics of intimidation and attacks on property and the police who protected it.[27]

One such incident at Camperdown Works, which became known as the Lochee Conspiracy Case, is worth examining in more detail. The incident, which occurred on 22 March, after the Joint Committee representing four textile unions had voted to return to work, involved three middle-aged women and two young girls who were charged under the 1875 Conspiracy and Protection of Property Act for 'assembling with a number of persons, thus forming a large crowd' at the south gate of Camperdown Works in Burnside Street and intimidating ten people 'by making a great noise, shouting, bawling, hissing at them, using threatening and abusive language to them, and threatening them with bodily violence and injury if they did not abstain from working'. All five women – Elizabeth Docherty or Ferrie (the ringleader), Catherine Rooney or Murphy, Jessie Ann Tosh or Mochan, Mary Brownlie and Mary Ann Grimond, were of Whorterbank (arguably, the most deprived part of Lochee), with the exception of Mary Ann Grimond, who lived in nearby Cobden Street. The case attracted much interest when it came to trial, not least because the celebrated figure of the 1911 Lochee millworkers strike, Susan Devine, appeared as a friendly witness attired in a long green coat and her iconic felt hat. Unlike other witnesses, who appeared uneasy and were contradictory in their evidence – one claimed her shawl was torn from her back, but couldn't say who did it, another that she 'thought it was a bit of fun', but also that she was 'terrified' – Susan gave her evidence in a calm and easy manner, stating authoritatively that the crowd 'did not meddle' with her, and that they were singing a 'war song', but there was no 'bad language'. The reasons for this most identifiably 'Irish' of strike activists crossing a picket line are uncertain – the accusation of 'blackleg' was tantamount to that of informer in working-class Irish circles; nevertheless, the previous day, the JFWU had advised its members to return to work as they had exhausted their funds.[28] By the time of the case came to trial on 11 April, practically all of Dundee's 30,000 textile workers were in the same position of having been locked out by employers who had thus responded to the refusal of the majority to return to work. Indeed, Susan's appearance in court may have been a tactic to undermine the two police witnesses and spare her fellow workers any further hardship. If that was the case, it failed. The Sheriff chose to favour the testimony of the police, and all five women were found guilty of intimidation and fined ten shillings each, which was paid by their agent.[29]

The strike ended three days later, following negotiations brokered by local MP Alexander Wilkie and W A Appleton of the General Federation of Trade Unions with agreements being reached on union recognition and collective bargaining. In the end, the workers were forced back through increasing distress and the spectre of their own starving children – in the last days of the lockout, the *Evening Telegraph* reported that a local religious charity had issued 10,000 tickets for free breakfasts to children in Dundee and Lochee in the past few weeks and that the Dundee ILP Holiday Home Committee had provided 600 hot suppers for children of locked out workers in two nights.[30]

While Kenefick notes that 'the strike and lockout of millworkers was the single biggest strike to affect one area in 1912 [and] the single most significant strike of its type to affect Scotland between 1910 and 1914'[31], unlike the carters' and dockers' dispute, there was little talk of class war or of transforming the political system. The nearest thing to a syndicalist statement came, not from the labour and trade union movement, but from Prohibitionist Neddy Scrymgeour, who advocated that the dispute be developed into a movement for a 'National Strike…to compel the Parliamentary representatives to demand a general election on the issue of state ownership', and criticised the union representatives who 'continue to drift along without commanding the political forces'.[32] Here, Scrymgeour recognised the strong sense of worker solidarity in the strikers, who had a conception of their collective power but lacked the leadership of a Connolly or Larkin to harness and channel it in a revolutionary direction.[33]

Incidentally, the Lochee Conspiracy trial took place on the same day that the Third Home Rule Bill was introduced to Parliament – its passage virtually assured due to the removal of the House of Lords' veto the previous August. On 10 March 1912, the Dundee UIL hosted a meeting by the author of *The Case for Home Rule*, Stephen Gwynn, and the Irish Party whip, Captain A J C Donelan, who were conducting a tour to prepare the ground. There was a polite but muted response to Gwynn's speech, which talked up Ireland's expanding trade and the benefits for Britain, and claimed that 'the ascendancy party in Ulster' was 'losing its power to influence' as 'Orangemen did not respond to the tap of the

Orange drums as they once did' – a highly ironic comment given that the forces of Unionist reaction were already rallying to block Home Rule.³⁴ Later that September, encouraged by the incendiary exhortations of Ulster Unionist Party leader, Sir Edward Carson, and marshalled by his mentor, Sir James Craig, 471,414 people lined up to sign – in many cases, in their own blood – the 'Solemn League and Covenant', pledging to use 'all means which may be found necessary; to defeat 'the present conspiracy to set up a Home Rule Parliament in Ireland', out of which number Carson and Craig formed the Ulster Volunteer Force (UVF), to arm and fight against it, on 13 January 1913.³⁵

The Dublin Lockout

Meanwhile, 1913 saw a growing number of wage disputes and wildcat strikes. Many of the workers involved, and particularly those labour activists of Irish extraction, took a special interest in the overtly syndicalist Dublin transport strike which was more immediately relevant to their experience and aspirations than the progression of the Home Rule Bill. The Dublin strike, which began on 26 August, exploded into the headlines on Monday 1 September, the day after 'Bloody Sunday' when the Dublin Metropolitan Police launched a brutal attack on a proclaimed strike rally in O'Connell Street killing two and injuring around 400 more. The Dundee press, which carried the now iconic photograph of the police baton charge on its front pages, filled in the details as 'old ladies and gentlemen, even children on their way home from church' were targeted, and a 'continuous procession of ambulances' ferried the injured to four different hospitals. ³⁶

The following Wednesday, Dundee Trades Council passed a resolution, circulated by the British trade union movement, 'protesting against the manner in which citizens were treated by the police, and call[ing] on the Chief Secretary for Ireland to once again establish the right of public meeting and conduct a very rigid enquiry into the conduct of the police'. Nicholas Marra, who pronounced the resolution 'a very mild one', reminded his fellow trade unionists of a lesson derived from his Irish nationalist grounding, 'If they wanted to make a movement in Ireland popular... they had only got to set the police against it', before going on to demand 'the release of Larkin and his fellow trade unionists [Connolly, who had received a three-month jail sentence for incitement to disorder, and William Partridge] until such time as Sir Edward Carson is arrested for saying exactly the same thing as Larkin did'.[37] The statement of the carters' leader, Peter Gillespie, that 'trade unionism in Ireland had been backward, and the workers were now trying to come in line with Scotland and England', revealed a patronising attitude to, or a limited understanding of Irish trade unionism. However, while some trade unionists, such as Gillespie, focused on the economic aspects of the strike, others with a basic knowledge of Irish history understood that 'repression breeds resistance', and were as attuned to the lightning rod effect of a martyred hero in building popular support for a movement, as the new generation of Irish revolutionaries were to the propaganda value of a well-managed funeral.

The funerals of the two strike martyrs, James Nolan and John Byrne, were cases in point. On 4 September, Francis Sheehy Skeffington wrote to the *Irish Independent*, owned by the anti-union transport boss, William Martin Murphy – who, earlier that week, had used his considerable influence over Dublin's employers to secure their involvement in a sympathetic lockout affecting 20,000 workers and their dependants – that the funeral of Nolan would 'rank in Irish history with that of Terence Bellew McManus as the beginning of a new era – the era of Irish labour militant and triumphant'.[38]

Earlier that day, over 20,000 people, many of whom wore the Red Hand badge of the Transport Union, followed Nolan's cortege as it made its way from Liberty Hall to Glasnevin Cemetery. The funeral of Byrne, the following Sunday, also bore the hallmarks of the funerals of Fenians, McManus and John O'Mahoney, and of Parnell, all of which had been organised to military perfection by the IRB. The following Tuesday, the front page of the *Evening Telegraph* carried a full report by 'A Special Correspondent' who described the scenes as Byrne's coffin was borne, on the shoulders of 'brother transport men', from St Mary's Pro-Cathedral through Byrne's neighbourhood to Liberty Hall, on which frontage was displayed a large black banner reading 'In Memory of Our Murdered Brothers'; then along to O'Connell Street from where the hearse wended its way north to Glasnevin followed by a cab containing a number of weeping women and 'a little kiddie of six to eight years, whose head was covered in bandages – injured', the reporter was informed, 'in the baton charge'.³⁹ Behind marched the 'transport men' – the incipient Irish Citizen Army – in ranks of four, all wearing the Red Hand badge, as did the scores of dejected transport workers who followed in their train, followed by the band of the Irish National Foresters. All along the route, sympathisers joined the procession in ever-increasing numbers, interspersed between the long stream of cabs and carriages.

Two hours later, the reporter was back in O'Connell Street as the crowds gathered again for a mass meeting addressed by leaders of the British labour and trade union movement who submitted the same 'mild' resolution put to the Dundee Trades Council earlier that week. The *Tele*'s correspondent observed that 'compared to the speeches of Larkin and other Irish leaders', theirs were 'orderly and conciliatory' – indeed, the Lochee-born Labour MP for Glasgow Blackfriars, George Barnes, sympathised with the strikers and deplored the actions of the police, but swore he would oppose Larkinism if it meant breaking agreements, anarchism in trade unionism and appeals to 'racial', i.e. national, sentiment.⁴⁰ The aim of this intervention was to settle the strike and to prevent 'Larkinism' (sympathetic strike action) from spreading across the Irish Sea. On 11 September, however, Larkin was released from prison and embarked on a tour of England and Scotland precisely to encourage it. As the Liverpool-born son of an Irish immigrant, Larkin was aware of the deep seam of Irish nationalism running through the working-class diaspora and had no hesitation in placing himself and the ITGWU within the tradition of militant Irish republicanism. The following Sunday, he told a meeting in Manchester that he was the son of a Fenian, and 'the Fenians were the outcome of certain conditions just as he and his friends were today, only we have a broader gospel, a wider gospel, a clearer gospel than they had'.⁴¹ At the end of a heated meeting in St Andrew's Hall, Glasgow, he urged the largely Irish audience to support Home Rule 'as a means to an end…whereby they would obtain better conditions for Irishmen'.⁴² He did not, however, bring his message further east.

Despite the ambivalence of the British trade union leadership, the campaign for sympathetic industrial action gained support from the Liverpool dockers and English and Welsh railwaymen who came out on strike amidst the general atmosphere of industrial unrest across the country.⁴³ Following on from a commentary on the dangers of the sympathetic strike, an editorial in the *Evening Telegraph* entitled 'Strike Fever', bemoaned 'the reckless spirit in which strikes appear to be entered upon. All over the country disputes exist. Dublin is perhaps the most outstanding case [and] the consequent restless movement... appears to be affecting all classes'.[44] The headline recalled the 'Fenian Fever' of the 1860s and the longstanding fear of the British establishment that unrest in Ireland would spread to the Irish diaspora and ultimately infect the British working class. The same day the *Dundee Courier* reported that a number of 'youthful workers' (sixty female spinners) at Camperdown Works had struck over a general demand for a 5 per cent increase in wages, bringing operations to a standstill. The *Courier* warned that 'given the large amount of unrest in the trade [this] may be the beginning of a serious dislocation'.[45] In a parallel development, which hints at a co-ordinated strategy, 60 female double spinners at the Constable Works of Malcolm, Ogilvie & Co. Ltd in the Dens area struck in an attempt to force up wages, causing the firm to temporarily shut down. Although Dundee's textile manufacturers were accustomed to spontaneous short-lived strikes, when the double spinners refused to return, the firm called on the protection of the Dundee and District Spinners' and Manufacturers' Association, who, taking their cue from the Dublin employers, advised shutting down all works of which their members were owners (which included most of the mills in the city) in an attempt to force a crisis and drive the strikers back. While some manufacturers were anxious to avoid this, fearing the loss of business which would result, others were not – the price of jute was 'prohibitively high', and a general lockout would create a delay in buying until it came down as well as removing the obligation to pay their workers. The strikers' demands were modest – an advance of 9d on their 17-shilling wage; nevertheless, the employers feared that giving into them would create a general demand all over the city.[46]

In an attempt to forestall a crisis, the Joint Committee, represented by Sime, Williamson and Reid of the JFWU, MFOU and Tenters' Union respectively, opened up negotiations with the employers' federation. As the employers closed ranks, the workers responded in kind. In addition to the 1,000 at the Constable Works, 500–600 workers at the neighbouring firm of James Scott & Sons' Dura Works came out, as did half the workforce at Victoria Works, Brook Street (the Scouringburn). At South Mill in nearby

Guthrie Street, 300 workers walked out, closing down production.[47]

On Tuesday, 30 September, the employers gave a final ultimatum to the double spinners – return to work, or there would be a general lockout affecting 30,000 workers. The *Evening Telegraph* proclaimed, 'The eyes of the Dundee textile world are turned upon the sixty double spinners who were the cause of the shutting down of Constable Works. It is theirs to decide whether there will be a general lockout or not'. The *Courier* deemed their actions 'callous and inexplicable'.[48] Attempts to undermine the strikers also came from their union representatives as the Joint Committee promised the employers they would do 'all in their power' to induce the disaffected workers to return.[49] Still the double spinners held out. Attendance at a meeting between the union representatives and the strikers was so poor that the meeting was rescheduled until the following Thursday, when, in the face of psychological pressure, the strikers finally agreed to return to work the following Tuesday (Monday being a public holiday), 'trusting that Mr Williamson will endeavour to deal with [their] complaint on as early a date as possible'. Nevertheless, the women made it clear that they did not accept responsibility for being the cause of any distress which would result from even a short-term stoppage of work, least of all a general lockout. Thirty of the 60 disaffected workers at Camperdown Works also agreed to return.[50]

As all 'seemed sorted', however, the appearance of lockout notices on the gates of federated works precipitated a second strike. At the Craigie Works of William Halley & Sons, 'the feeling ran very high' and, after a meeting at the mill gates, the spinners resolved to remain out as long as the notice remained up, bringing the establishment, which employed 400 people, to a standstill. At the Mid Wynd Works of James Scott & Sons, the calender workers also walked out in protest. That morning, the local press carried two photographs from the Dublin Lockout – of a crowd of strikers' families outside Liberty Hall waiting for the daily distribution of food, and of the selfless and charitable noblewoman, Constance Markievicz, standing over a stove, preparing stew. The overall picture was one of acute distress with 100,000 people reported to be on the verge of starvation, the plight of the children being especially pitiable. As well as evoking memories of the Dundee strike and lockout of 1912, this served to remind much of the textile workforce that they were part of a bigger fight. At any rate, the posting of lockout notices was perceived as a threat and a challenge from the employers, to which they, the workers, were compelled to respond. Indeed, the calenders' union, who had stood firm throughout the jute strike of 1912, had already resolved that a general lockout would be followed by a general strike, and made preparations to feed the workers' children. The lockout notices were removed the following Wednesday, and while 250 'obdurate' workers remained out for another day, most had drifted back by the end of the week. The 'peace' was short-lived, however, as one week later, 500 female hecklers and male batchers at the Lower Dens Works of Baxter Brothers & Co Ltd struck to enforce a demand for higher wages.[51] The following day, a hundred spinners came out in sympathy, declaring that they refused to be blacklegs. By Monday, the strike had spread to the Upper Works, affecting around 1,200, mostly female workers.

Into this scenario stepped James Connolly, in the course of a tour of Scotland and the North of England to raise funds in support of the Dublin strike. Connolly began his tour on Sunday, 19 October in the Meadows, Edinburgh, with a broadly appealing speech that charted the progress of the ITGWU up to its involvement in the strike' – which, he explained, was 'a fight not only for the workers of Dublin, but of Great Britain' and flagged up a significant political development – that 'the literary, artistic and professional people of Ireland were of one mind and on the side of the workers'. 'The old party cries had lost their meaning', he declared, and 'they cared not for either the Carsons or the Redmonds, for if the workers were to be sweated, then it didn't matter really whether it was under a green flag or a yellow flag'.[52] Later that evening in Leith, he railed against the appalling working and living conditions in Dublin, which they had resolved, for the sake of their children, to bring to an end 'if they had to tear society down to do so', and concluded with a pointed reminder that the sympathetic strike was the most effective expression of working-class unity.[53]

Connolly's speech in Dundee the following evening was not reported in any of the local newspapers, but as was the Scottish socialists' strategy of 'tackling on to local issues', it is likely that he touched on the strike at Baxter's and the recent threatened general lockout (or left it for local speakers to do so), drew parallels with Dublin, and ended with a call for practical support. Unlike Larkin, who appealed to supporters in Liverpool to supply 'the only ammunition which could kill Murphy – bread bullets', Connolly continued to stress the need for 'ready cash' and urge that all monies be sent directly to the Dublin strike fund:

> You cannot expect the thousands of strikers who are in lodgings to rub along with food in the shape of rations. The face of a landlady [to] whom a man has offered rations instead of lodging money would deserve to be reproduced in the best cinematograph in existence.

While Connolly excoriated slum-owning landlords, he was mindful that many Irish households supplemented their meagre income by taking in lodgers as his two Dundee-domiciled aunts, Bridget McGinn and Mary Boyle, had done.

Connolly continued his tour with meetings in Greenock, Clydebank and Falkirk, ending the week in Glasgow where he paused to reflect, in a piece for the *Forward* newspaper:

> The spirit of the workers of Great Britain is absolutely marvellous. We see old men and women, young boys and girls of all sorts and conditions lending a hand to the task. In Dundee, a mill town, and therefore a poorly paid centre, where women labour principally dominates, the local comrades collected over £22 in the streets on Saturday and Sunday, and at my meeting on Monday, held amidst a shower of rain, the amount collected was over £5. In addition to this, money was collected especially for taking care of the children should it be thought well in Dublin to send any of the children of the strikers to Scotland until the battle is over. When you know that one of the biggest mills in Dundee (Baxter's) is just now out on strike, and that the strike affects over 1200 women and girls, it must be admitted that this is a great achievement for Dundee, and speaks volumes for the spirit and zeal of the local Socialists. I was also glad to see that the local leader of the Prohibitionist Party was on the platform and gave an excellent fighting speech.[54]

Connolly was well-acquainted with the conditions endured by Dundee's large female workforce who had provided the subject of his first recorded observations on social and economic matters in a letter to Lillie in 1889. Lillie, it appears, was the sounding board for many of his ideas. Given his more recent experience of organising female mill workers in Belfast, Connolly was in no doubt as to how their sisters in Dundee had been poorly served by the trade union movement – in 1913, his cousin and last surviving relative in the city, 57-year-old Mary McGinn, had been working at Camperdown Works for nigh on three decades and was still illiterate and living in relative poverty.[55] Connolly was keenly aware that the lot of working-class women was to be doubly oppressed – economically, by employers who paid women lower rates than men who did the same job, and by social attitudes that consigned women to a life of unpaid, undervalued domestic drudgery. It was also their misfortune to be ignored and let down by the British trade union movement whose sectional nature and conciliatory leadership rendered it ineffective against wealthy and influential employers. Denied the opportunity to fight on by hamstrung trade union officials, they expressed their solidarity vicariously by supporting the Dublin workers in their fight.[56] Interestingly, such expressions of economic solidarity recall the large sums of money raised by the lowest ranks of the workforce, Irish immigrants, for resistance campaigns in decades past. Connolly was aware that money raised in such straitened circumstances bespoke an immense capacity for political solidarity, hence he singled out the workers of Dundee for special attention. Significantly, while some of his old comrades in the Scottish socialist movement had disparaged Dundee as 'the city of jute and sucking bottles', Connolly never did, but rather approached the crowd with empathy and humour. On that dreich October evening, his brother John had rocked up in the uniform of the Edinburgh Artillery and, as Greaves notes, was 'denounced in fine style' from the platform.[57] Knowing how much the Dundee crowd appreciated a free comic turn, one suspects that James had hatched it up and John was a willing foil. The prohibitionist with whom Connolly was so impressed was, of course, Neddy Scrymgeour, defender of syndicalism, critic of compliant union officials, supporter of Irish self-determination, and a strong proponent of women's suffrage.

The Suffrage and Suffragette Movements

Connolly was accompanied to Dundee by Charlotte Despard, President of the Women's Freedom League (WFL), who had joined him on the platform at the Meadows the previous day.[58] In a neat piece of synergy, while Connolly was addressing the crowd in Albert Square, Madame Despard was giving a talk in the YMCA, Constitution Road, chaired by Agnes Husband, on the topic of 'The New Crusade', in which she explained that the women's movement was a revolutionary movement with the same economic and spiritual force as other great movements – an allusion, possibly, to the industrial and national movements. She spoke too of their male allies, and noted how their recent campaign on the police courts had awakened them to the different kinds of justice that was dealt to the rich and the poor'. The 'crusade', she said, would not cease when they got the vote, but continue until they had 'eradicated the evils which deteriorated the human race', and made the world a different place, where their 'children would be safe' – her words echoing those of Connolly in Leith.[59]

In the week prior to Connolly's and Despard's visit, the WFL held a series of dinner hour meetings at factory gates, as well as evening meetings in Lochee High Street, the Hilltown and the Greenmarket, speaking and distributing leaflets to large numbers of working-class women who gave them a 'very sympathetic hearing'.[60] A meeting in Albert Square on the afternoon of Saturday, 18 October, addressed by the WFL's Scottish secretary, Anna Munro, also drew a large and appreciative audience which boosted the street collection for the Dublin strike, indicating that a considerable measure of sympathy and collaboration existed between the suffrage and socialist movements. Indeed, Anna later recalled that as 'latchkey' schoolgirls in Edinburgh in the 1890s, she and her sister had chanced upon an open-air meeting addressed by James Connolly and had been so impressed by the message of 'no more poverty' that they subsequently 'joined' the SDF and later helped Connolly in his campaign to stand for Edinburgh City Council in 1894.[61] That October, the Dundee branch of the WFL, under the presidency of Agnes Husband (who was also Vice President of the local Labour Party), also come together with their male allies to protest against the forcible feeding of hunger-striking suffragettes in Dundee Jail, and on the evening of Saturday, 18 October, nine male and female suffrage protestors were forcibly ejected from a meeting of the National Brotherhood Council, a benign evangelical organisation which was targeted as its President, and the principal speaker, Liberal MP for Ipswich, Charles Silvester Horne, had voted for the Prisoners (Temporary Discharge for Ill Health) Act 1913 (commonly known as the Cat and Mouse Act).[62]

Nine days earlier, a number of militant suffragettes had been similarly ejected from a meeting of Dundee women Liberals addressed by Winston Churchill, whose opposition to female suffrage made him a prime target for suffrage activists all over the country.[63] Churchill had his first real taste of suffragette opposition, in the Dundee by-election of 1908, at the bell-ringing hands of Irish WFL activist, Mary Maloney, who had pursued him across the city wrecking his meetings after he alleged that she had been carried drunk on the shoulders of dock workers during the recent Peckham by-election campaign. Leading organiser in the Women's Social and Political Union (WSPU), Annie Kenney, later wrote that such demonstrations 'helped to keep the suffragette cause before the people of Scotland'.[64] There was another important reason for Mary visiting Dundee. At a WFL organising meeting in the Gilfillan Hall on 28 April, she alluded to the political influence of 'the large section of the Irish population', and noted that they had hitherto been handicapped by the fact that 'the Dundee section were not pure Irish people'. 'I am', she stated, to loud applause, 'Irish to the backbone'.[65] Mary's famous bell went missing in the mêlée preceding an open-air meeting at the Gasworks on Friday, 8 May, whereupon she proceeded to challenge Churchill verbally, extracting a grudging half-apology for having impugned her morality. Churchill subsequently curtailed his outdoor meetings and endeavoured to screen his indoor (ticketed) ones.[66]

On 22 January 1914, around a dozen male and female suffragists were ejected from a meeting in the Gilfillan Hall at which Labour Party leader Ramsay MacDonald addressed the three burning issues of the moment – Home Rule, trade unionism and (briefly) women's suffrage. MacDonald assured the audience that they would do everything possible to get Home Rule through the House of Commons, which institution he prided the Labour Party in using 'to make life sweeter and better' for hundreds of thousands of their fellow human beings. Ironically, after having sat passively as they were turned out, he swore the Labour Party would 'stand by the suffragettes'. Turning his attention to industrial labour, he stated they had formed unions which negotiated with employers, submitted their cases to arbitration, and only came out on strike as a last resort. Labour had its case for force, he admitted, but he had never counselled it. Larkin, he granted, had done an 'admirable piece of work in Dublin' but 'made a mistake when he went beyond that and copied Carson in his consequential campaign' – an allusion to the formation of the Irish Citizen Army in November 1913, ten months after the UVF. Having marked out his reformist policy, he warned against involvement in revolutionary trade unionism.

> Trade Unionism is not going to succeed in this country by methods of sympathetic strike – by methods of tearing up contracts and by following the policy of Syndicalism... All this Syndicalism, this cry, this propaganda, and allurement, is a sort of Delilah in the pay of the Philistine capitalism, trying to shear off the locks of the Samson of Trade Unionism.[67]

His choice of metaphor is revealing. Couching his counsel in the form of a Biblical parable, he depicted syndicalism as female – the wily and deceitful seductress, the trade union movement as male – the archetypal brawny hero, and capitalism as the philistine paymaster lurking in the shadows. Earlier in the meeting, the Chairman, Alex Wilkie, had claimed that 'certain organisations', which he failed to name, were paying people to wreck their meetings, and that 'the men and women had earned their money'. Amongst those ejected were Lila Clunas, founding Secretary of the Dundee WFL, and May Grant of the WSPU, whose brother was arrested for punching one of eight stewards manhandling her out of the hall. Their treatment at the meeting led to the local suffragists breaking their alliance with the Dundee Labour Party, although not with socialism.[68] In the course of his speech, MacDonald also equated 'Larkinism' with 'militant suffragettism, burning houses and so on'.

Frustration at the failure of political leaders to 'get women's suffrage through' had led to a change in tactics. By 1914, the suffragette movement had progressed from ringing bells and throwing organic matter at prominent politicians to smashing windows and digging up golf courses to arson and bomb attacks. Scottish suffragettes, and those with Dundee connections, were particularly active in this regard.[69]

Ethel Moorhead

Tracing the movements of those involved, however, is complicated by the widespread use of pseudonyms, the peripatetic existence of many suffragettes, and the fact that the adoption of a civil disobedience campaign led many to boycott the 1911 census. Even Ethel Moorhead, arguably the most prolific of the Scottish militants, operated under at least four different aliases.[70] The English-born daughter of Irish parents from Counties Kildare and Offaly, Ethel had moved with her family to Edinburgh, and eventually to Dundee, where, early in 1910, she joined the WSPU. Ethel's first experience of direct action came on 7 December when she heckled and threw an egg at Winston Churchill, a day after Charlotte Despard had urged her supporters in Dundee 'to attend [his election] meetings and let him know that they did not intend to take such strife any longer'.[71] Despard was referring to the events of 18 November, dubbed 'Black Friday' due to the violence meted out by police and male bystanders to the 300 women who marched on Westminster following the government's decision to dissolve Parliament ahead of passing the Conciliation Bill which would have given the vote to a million women £10-property owners. Churchill, then Home Secretary, had rejected numerous calls for a public inquiry.

Ethel's initiation into a more organised form of political violence came in a mass window-smashing raid in London, by a flying column of Scottish suffragettes, on 3–4 March 1912, on which occasion she appeared in court alongside another Dundee-based activist, Florence McFarlane, and Janie Allan of Glasgow, all of whom had targeted Kensington High Street. Her first act of political violence in Scotland was, symbolically, to smash a glass case containing the sword of William Wallace at the eponymous monument in Stirling on 28 August 1912, with a stone wrapped in a piece of paper bearing the message:

> Your liberties were won by the sword.
> Release the women who are fighting for their liberty.
> A protest from Dublin

This was most certainly a reference to the three English suffragettes imprisoned in Mountjoy Jail for setting fire to the Theatre Royal, Dublin, in the midst of a performance attended by Prime Minister Herbert Asquith, who was in the Irish capital with IPP leader, John Redmond, to promote the Home Rule Bill. The exclusion of the women's franchise from the Bill had inspired the Irish Women's Franchise League (IFWL), led by Hanna Sheehy Skeffington, to their first act of political violence, a window-smashing raid on government offices at Dublin Castle on 13 June. At her trial, Hanna denounced Redmond – who had 'led them to believe they would get votes for women under Home Rule' but recanted – and declared her readiness to go to prison, where she would 'resist any attempt to treat her otherwise than as a political prisoner'.[72] Hanna also took care to flag up Asquith's upcoming visit in July, and urge her supporters not to let it pass. She and three of her comrades, Margaret Palmer and sisters Mary and Jane Murphy, were sentenced to a month in Mountjoy, plus another for failing to pay fines. Political Status was granted. It was denied, however, to the three English suffragettes who had, on their own initiative, answered Hanna's call. Gladys Evans, WSPU organiser from London, and Mary Leigh, were sentenced to five-years' penal servitude, and Lizzie Baker (alias Jennie Baines), to seven months with hard labour. The women embarked on a hunger strike and, for the first time ever in Ireland, forcible feeding was employed, to which Hanna responded by declining her political privileges – 'as long as English suffragettes in the same prison were treated as ordinary criminals' – and, along with her three Irish comrades, conducting a sympathetic hunger strike.[73] Over in Scotland, Ethel Moorhead would have been aware of the situation, which appears to have inspired her own symbolic act of solidarity. The following day, she appeared in Stirling Sheriff Court bearing a cut on her hand and the name Edith Johnston, in which she denied having smashed the glass, and claimed it was the act of an unknown woman who had, apparently, disappeared down three narrow flights of stairs without being apprehended. For expressing her wholehearted approval of the act and the written message, however, she was sentenced to seven days in Perth Prison.

A day after her release, 'Edith' appeared, in a visibly exhausted state, on the platform of an open-air meeting at the Corn Exchange, Edinburgh, carefully maintaining her cover while expressing her 'complete agreement' with the act and the written protest. Nevertheless, when one questioner continued to pry, 'Why did you break the glass at the Wallace Monument?', the chairperson, WSPU organiser, Elizabeth Finlayson Gauld, responded on her behalf:

> The Wallace monument was 'desecrated', in the ordinary sense, to remind all Scottish people, and the people of the world, that the daughters of that brave man, the daughters of this great nation had still an overwhelming desire for liberty. This sword of Wallace was valued as one of the great treasures in this country (cheers) and the suffragettes came there and smashed the glass (disturbance) in order to draw attention to the people that their liberty was won by fighting.[74]

It is significant that Ethel, a second-generation Irishwoman and adopted Scot, chose the most potent symbol of national liberation, and of the physical force by which it was obtained, to make her point. The symbolism of the sword also had a common resonance in the Celtic myth of the warrior hero, Fionn Mac Cumhaill, sleeping in a cave alongside his sword, Mac an Luin (Son of the Waves), and his faithful Fianna, from whom the Fenians derived their name and inspiration; and in the legend of Excalibur, the magical sword with which another mythological hero, Arthur, defended sub-Roman Britain against Anglo-Saxon invaders, after having lifted it out of a stone. Whether it was Ethel's intention to lift Wallace's sword out of the broken glass case was never revealed.

On the occasion of Asquith's visit to Leven in January 1913, Ethel was again arrested and charged (under the pseudonym of Margaret Morrison) with smashing twelve windows at Leven Police Office and blinding a police officer with pepper. She was remanded in Dundee Jail, from where she was released after four days on hunger strike.[75] Over the next few months, the militant suffragettes became steadily more experienced and proficient in their use of political violence. In May 1913, they did a thorough job in torching Farington Hall – a large mansion in the West End of Dundee, recently leased by property developer, Henry McGrady – causing £20,000 worth of damage.[76] The perpetrators were never caught, though a witness claimed to have seen two women dressed in black, carrying a suspicious-looking package and an umbrella – which item was later found at the scene, along with empty canisters and a rag – surveying large houses in the district. There is a fair chance that Ethel, whose family home was just along the road, was one of them.[77]

In the early hours of 5 June 1914, an attempt was made to blow up Dudhope Castle in Barrack Park by placing a bomb in the doorway. The bomb – in the form of a piece of lead piping filled with gunpowder and attached to a time fuse – was described as 'the real thing', and the entire operation pointed to careful planning. In the dungeon of the castle were stores of gunpowder which, if ignited, would have blown the castle to smithereens, damaged surrounding property, and possibly resulted in injury or death.[78] Suspicion immediately fell upon the militant suffragettes, but while the police made extensive enquiries, no one was arrested. The modus operandi appears to point to Ethel and her comrade Fanny Parker. The symbolic targeting of Scottish historical landmarks was one of Ethel's trademarks,[79] and as the ancient seat of the Constables of Dundee (most notably the Earl of Claverhouse – 'Bonnie Dundee' or 'Bluidy Clavers', depending on one's political perspective) and a former military barracks, the tenth-century castle also fulfilled the feminist criteria of being a citadel of male authority. If it had succeeded it would have trumped anything the suffragettes had previously achieved. However, the fuse, which had almost burnt down to the bomb, was extinguished by a gust of wind. Interestingly, the operation closely resembles the Fenian-inspired attempt to blow up the town's powder magazine in March 1868, which failed for similar reasons. As a second-generation Irishwoman, Ethel would have been familiar with the Irish tradition of revolutionary violence and self-sacrifice, and may have believed, like other militant Irish suffragettes, that it was in her DNA. Her biographer, Mary Henderson, states that she was 'always Irish at heart'.[80] At any rate, such methods owed a debt to the Fenians. Likewise, the tactics adopted by the suffragettes went on to influence a new generation of militant Irish nationalists. The resistance shown by the suffragettes gained the respect of James Connolly, who became one of the first men in Ireland (or indeed North West Europe) to adopt the tactic of hunger strike as a political weapon during his imprisonment in September 1913. His daughter Ina recalled that Connolly was quick to acknowledge the source of his inspiration, stating, 'what was good enough for the suffragettes to use is good enough for us'.[81] As prison became the field of war in years to come, Irish Republicans also adopted the tactic, and continued to use it to the extent that it is synonymous with Irish political imprisonment.[82]

The links between Scottish suffragettes and the Irish political conflict were more than just tangential. The relations between the progressive political movements of the time – radical socialism, Irish nationalism and militant suffragism – were complex and dynamic. Mary McAuliffe has shown how the suffragette movement in Glasgow was the entry point for young Coatbridge schoolteacher Margaret Skinnider to militant suffragism, then physical force Irish republicanism, thereon to a lifetime's involvement in feminist, nationalist and trade union politics.[83]

Florence McFarlane

With the exception of Margaret Skinnider, it is fair to say that most studies of Scottish-born or Scottish-based suffragettes have focused on their activity in Scotland rather than elsewhere.[84] Thus, while Ethel Moorhead has received her due share of attention, Florence McFarlane cuts a more shadowy figure – an indication of her competence and professionalism as a militant activist, as she was doubtless aware that maintaining anonymity was key to operational success. Born in Leith on 5 October 1867, Florence Geraldine McFarlane was the fourth of fourteen children and the second of eight daughters born to Marion Elizabeth McFarlane, née Newton, and John McFarlane, a wire cloth manufacturer. When Florence was fifteen years old, her mother died of heart failure, nineteen days after giving birth to her fourteenth child in twenty years. The experience of losing her mother as a consequence of years of relentless childbearing may have led Florence to bridle against the quiet life of domestic self-sacrifice to which women were socially conditioned, and to question the position of women in society in general. Her father's Liberal politics may also have been influencing factor: conversely, they may have served as evidence of political hypocrisy.

In 1886, John McFarlane sunk £20,000 of his own money, and a further £5,000 borrowed from his uncle, into founding a daily Liberal newspaper, the *Scottish Leader*. In May 1890, McFarlane dismissed all his unionised compositors after they struck over his introduction of a new labour-saving linotype printing machine, and his imposition of a system of 'payment by results' at less than half the rates received for hand labour before they had had a chance to learn what the machine could do. If that wasn't enough to blot his 'Liberal copybook', McFarlane called in the police to have all 70 of them forcibly evicted. One of the evicted 'comps', James Fleming, later stated that 'Donnybrook had nothing on it'.[85] The *Scottish Leader* dispute proved to be something of a test case for the Edinburgh Trades Council to which the compositors now turned for assistance. Just two weeks before, the Trades Council had refused to support a demonstration in support of the eight-hour day, and had instead organised a disastrous meeting with a 'Labour' speaker from London who was opposed, not only to the eight-hour day, but also to Home Rule and the disestablishment of the Church – views which were dramatically out of tune with those of the growing number of trade unionists in the city.[86] Tensions between the pro-Liberal 'old guard' and the socialist element were at an all-time high, and the decision of the Trades Council to support the compositors and to host a protest meeting on their behalf in St Mary's Hall, in the heart of Edinburgh's Little Ireland, seems to have been an attempt to forestall any further damage. Indeed, James Blair, who presided, warned that if the Trades Council did not support the compositors now, they would be 'in danger of losing any support they received from trade unionists'.[87] It is possible that James Connolly, who had recently returned to the area following his marriage, was in the audience. Connolly was now heavily involved in socialist and trade union politics, moreover, his first paid job, at the age of eleven, had been as a 'printers' devil' for the *Edinburgh Evening News*, tasked with oiling the machines and running errands for the compositors whose interests, in this instance, were especially close to his heart.[88]

Ringing loud and clear through all the rhetoric, however, was the universal indignation at the self-styled Liberal McFarlane's high-handed hypocrisy, which was laid out in a handbill produced by the Edinburgh typographers proclaiming that McFarlane, an avowed anti-coercionist and Home Ruler, had behaved no better than a tyrannical Irish landlord. A speaker from the Glasgow Typographical Association also noted how McFarlane had urged the railway workers to combine to press their employers for better conditions of labour, but had dismissed his own employees when they resisted his attempts to reduce theirs. James Battersby of the Scottish Typographical Association also noted that McFarlane had resisted the union's attempts to negotiate with him, and stated that if this was how Liberalism treated Labour, it deserved to perish. The meeting concluded by agreeing to send copies of all its resolutions to all Liberal MPs, and broke up amidst cheers at a final resolution, shouted from the gallery, 'for the social revolution'.

The compositors also had the ear of Robert Cunninghame Graham, who raised the issue in Parliament, much to the embarrassment of his Gladstonian colleagues. When ruled out of order by the Speaker, Cunninghame Graham maintained it was his public duty to question the sincerity of a newspaper which supports 'one policy in Ireland', viz. 'the union of agricultural labourers and the Plan of Campaign', but 'dismisses its own men for joining a union'.[89] In July, the Edinburgh compositors took their message to the home of the Liberal press in Dundee, where, at a meeting hosted by Dundee Trades Council, arch-Liberal President of the INL, Patrick Brannigan, stated that 'as a trade unionist, a working man and a Liberal' – and, no doubt, a confirmed anti-coercionist – he could come to no other conclusion than that the proprietor of the *Scottish Leader* was 'insincere and grossly inconsistent'. Robert Bruce, presiding, also observed that the paper 'was not selling in Dundee at all'.[90] The negative publicity from the case resulted in other newspapers refusing material, advertisers withdrawing revenue, and trade unionists, Liberals and Home Rulers boycotting it. The *Scottish Leader* limped along for another two years until, unable to continue at such a heavy loss, John McFarlane sold it to his former editor, Thomas Carlaw Martin, for the paltry sum of £2,500 in August 1892, having pumped £60,000 into it, £40,000 of it his own money. In November 1893, McFarlane was taken to court by his uncle, James McMurray, for failing to repay the initial £5,000 loan. After hearing evidence of the *Leader*'s bad printing, bad reporting, bad intelligence and huge financial loss, the judge declared the enterprise to be 'not only a failure, but a disastrous failure', and as McFarlane was clearly unable to repay, acquitted him.[91]

What Florence thought of this debacle is unknown. By this time, she had left the family home at Oswald Road to train as a nurse. By 1896, she was matron of a private hospital at 2 Archibald Street, Edinburgh, and the 1901 census finds her heading an all-female household of twelve containing four nursing, two auxiliary and three domestic staff, and two of her younger sisters, Adelaide and Elaine. In December 1909, she took 'a brave stand for justice' when she resigned from her post rather than dismiss one of her nurses who had taken part in a militant suffrage protest. A woman of 'deeds not words', Florence joined the WSPU alongside her older sister Edith Begbie, becoming Honorary Secretary of the Dundee branch, a post through which she came to know fellow militant, Ethel Moorhead, who joined the organisation in early 1910. In November, Florence and Edith were amongst 150 suffragettes arrested on Black Friday following the government's decision to dissolve Parliament ahead of the final reading of the Conciliation Bill. While Ethel was sentenced to fourteen days for smashing the windows of Winston Churchill's Eccleston Square home, Florence, along with the majority of protesters, was released the following day.[92] By 1912, she was a seasoned WSPU organiser, operating out of 61 Nethergate, Dundee, from where she travelled with Ethel Moorhead, to join a mass window-smashing raid in London on 3-4 March 1912. Florence was arrested, hammer in hand, having smashed the window of a jeweller's shop in Kensington High Street. Her statement from the dock speaks of her conversion to physical force and her belief in its efficacy:

> I wilfully broke the window of my own accord and I should like to say I haven't been spending my life smashing windows. Seventeen years of my life I have spent as a hospital nurse binding up wounds [but] I think my action will have more effect with the Government than any quiet going on.[93]

Florence was sentenced to four months in Winson Green Prison, Birmingham, where, along with her sister Edith and Gertrude Wilkinson, she refused food, earning her the title of 'Dundee's hunger striker'.[94] Florence may not have been related, but was almost certainly a mentor to another Dundee hunger striker, 24-year-old Margaret Macfarlane, who succeeded her as Honorary Secretary of the WSPU in Dundee and East Fife. Margaret was also a nurse, and was also sentenced to four months, which she served in Holloway Prison, for smashing one of the biggest and most expensive windows in London in the same raid.[95] Margaret also embarked on a hunger strike, and her account of being forcibly fed gives testimony as to the callous brutality of the procedure:

I was lifted into a chair and tied with a strong sheet to the back of the chair. As far as I can remember my arms were held on each side on the arms of the chair. There was a wardress with a feeding cup and one behind my chair, making a gag for the mouth with her fingers. Another held my knees. I told them that I would not swallow a drop of gruel voluntarily. When they found that I did not retain any of the food, the one who was gagging me egged the others on to tickle me, to hold my nose to make me swallow, and to grip me on the throat, which to me is most cruel. The pressing of the throat to make one swallow gives a fearful feeling of suffocation. When they got my feet up, my head was hanging right over the back of the chair, which added to the choking sensation.[96]

A surveillance photograph taken at Holloway Prison shows Margaret staring defiantly across the exercise yard, while a photograph of Florence, taken in the more sympathetic environment of Dorset Hall, the London home of suffragette lawyer, Rose Lamartine Yates, captures her sitting pensively in the garden as she recovers from her hunger strike a month or so later.[97] Meanwhile Ethel Moorhead, who was been acquitted through lack of evidence, had returned to Dundee from where she went on to instigate numerous acts of political vandalism.

While Ethel operated on Scottish soil, Florence found greater scope for her militant activism in Ireland, specifically Belfast, where she resurfaced in the spring of 1914 – after a period of discreet organisation in Birmingham – under the pseudonym of Madge Muir, working alongside English suffragette and Secretary of the Ulster WSPU, Dorothy Evans. In the midst of the developing Home Rule crisis, the WSPU had come to the province to extract a promise from Edward Carson that his Ulster Unionist Party would grant votes for women in an Ulster Parliament, as Redmond and the Liberals had dashed their hopes of obtaining them in a British or Irish one. While it seems politically naïve to think that the most reactionary political formation in the British Isles would grant equal rights to women when the Ulster Convention did nothing to suggest it, there was a measure of expediency and opportunism on both sides. The Irish Proclamation, which granted equal rights to all citizens of an Irish Republic, had yet to be written. Dorothy Evans admitted that she didn't know what to expect, and the Irish suffragettes themselves were divided on the issue.[98] While many resented the interference of the English and Scottish suffragettes of the WSPU, others saw their militant approach as entirely compatible with the Irish physical force tradition. For example, the Irish Women's Suffrage Society, with whom the WSPU held joint meetings, contained a strong militant strand who believed that self-sacrifice was in their Irish blood, and it is possible that some may have been pushing the situation to the brink of revolution.[99] For his part, Carson had no intention of supporting women's rights, but was simply manipulating the suffragettes in attempt to shore up power against his opponents.[100] In October, Dorothy was compelled to write to the *Irish Citizen*, the paper of the IFWL, that the words, 'we will take sides and fight against Home Rule' attributed to her in an interview with the *Belfast Telegraph* were not hers.[101] In September, she had received an assurance from the secretary of the Ulster Unionist Council that, in 'a separate Provisional Government, women should take part on equal terms with men'. Nevertheless, on 9 March 1914, Carson announced to a crowd of suffragettes who had laid siege to his London home, that it was 'ridiculous' to think that the franchise in Ulster should differ from any other part the United Kingdom.

The WSPU responded by issuing a 'declaration of war upon [Carson] and the Ulster Unionist Parliamentary Committee', and embarking on a campaign of unprecedented militancy. Between 14 and 20 March, twenty pillar boxes in Belfast were targeted in acid attacks, and on 27 March, one week after the Curragh Mutiny, when British army officers threatened to resign rather than take action against the UVF who were preparing to resist Home Rule by force of arms, Abbeylands, the residence of Sir Hugh McCalmont, in which grounds the UVF drilled, was burnt to the ground, causing £20,000 worth of damage.[102] A copy of the WSPU's newspaper, the *Suffragette* was found 40 yards from the building.

On the night of 31 March/1 April, an attempt to fire Lisburn Castle was averted by a caretaker who discovered the shutters and windows forced open, and the floor strewn with an array of candles, canisters and time fuses, paraffin-saturated newspapers and sticks of wood, and a piece of paper on which was written, 'Ulster suffragists set up militant policy'. Two days later, police raided the house shared by Dorothy Evans and 'Madge

Muir' at 13 University Gardens and found test tubes, candles, plasticine, cotton wool and chemicals, a coil of live fuse, a revolver and ammunition, cutting pliers and an electric flash lamp.[103] On 8 April, the two women appeared in court, charged jointly under the Explosives Substances Act of 1883 (brought in to deal with the Fenian dynamitards) on two counts of possession of explosives and intent to commit malicious injury to property. Alluding the first charge, Dorothy pointed out that Carson and his men were in illegal possession of explosives, yet no action was being taken against them, and to the second, Florence exclaimed, 'Your God is property', and threw her handbag, a book and a stick at the magistrate. After attempting to rush from the court, the women were remanded in Crumlin Road Jail until 20 April, but were released under the Cat and Mouse Act after four days on hunger and thirst strike.[104] The following day, an attempt to burn down Bangor railway station was discovered by a night watchman who found a burning candle in a box lined with paraffin-soaked cotton wool, the floor strewn with a miscellaneous collection of flammable material, the woodwork saturated with oil, and, fastened to the steps of the guard's cabin, a series of written messages, stating: 'No bluff here', 'Deeds not drill, for Suffragettes' (a variation on the WSPU's motto of 'Deeds Not Words'), 'Militant men go free, why imprison women?', 'Apply to Carson for damage by arson', and 'A message to Carson from a fighter for liberty'.[105]

Unsurprisingly, Dorothy and Florence failed to turn up at court for their committal, and were rearrested at noon the following day while walking to their office in College Square – it was noted that, in the case of 'Miss Muir', 'a certain amount of force was used' – formally charged, and conveyed to Belfast Police Court. Florence, who appeared first, proceeded to challenge the Crown Prosecutor, J R Moorhead, who asked for the court to be cleared, to which Florence called all those true Irishwomen present to remain and resist. Finally, tiring from the verbal onslaught, Moorhead asked that the press also be excluded, pointing specifically to the reporter of the *Irish Citizen* (presumably Elizabeth Priestley McCracken, whose solicitor husband, George was in court 'on a watching brief' for the WSPU). Along with other women journalists, she resisted attempts to bundle her out, whereupon Florence threw a small parcel at Moorhead. The women were the last to leave the court. Once outside the building, they continued their protest – one of them mounting a chair and giving a speech, which, the assembled press reported, drew a large crowd.[106]

The magistrate's decision to exclude both the public and the press, and the treatment of the women, attracted a weighty protest from the *Northern Whig*, which stated, 'the right of journalists to report all cases heard in court is too valuable a privilege to be abrogated simply because their presence may encourage a prisoner in noisy outbreaks', while the *Irish News* opined:

> the fact that the lady's vocal powers were exercised to the discomfort of the stipendiary magistrate and the representatives of the Crown, did not, in our view, justify turning the Public Court into a 'Star Chamber'... Miss Muir was entitled to a public trial and she did not get it.[107]

The hearing was adjourned, and the following day Florence was carried into court on a stretcher in an exhausted state, having resumed her hunger and thirst strike. A range of witnesses including postal officers, policemen, gardeners, caretakers and the city's chemical analyst, gave evidence of 300 letters destroyed in post boxes, the burning of Abbeylands, the attempt on Lisburn Castle, and the discovery of explosives at 13 University Street. Head Constable, William Baird stated that an increased number of recently reported 'outrages' corresponded with the accused's residence in the area, to which Moorhead added that these 'outrages' had been committed with materials exactly the same as those found in the defendant's bedroom.[108] Florence, who refused to take part in the proceedings, lay at full length throughout. Eventually she was released on bail, having been committed for trial in July, as was Dorothy, who appeared in court the following day.

Although Dorothy and Florence operated together, evidence points to the latter as being primarily the physical force activist, whose role, as suggested by her pseudonym, was to remain in the background – as she had for the past two years – while Dorothy, who continued to use her real name, was the political organiser, and the public face of the WSPU's Ulster campaign.

On 4 June, Florence appeared in court again, charged, alongside Mary Larmour of Glasgow, with 'wilfully and maliciously' setting fire to Ardmillan, a vacant property at Fortwilliam Park, North Belfast, owned by linen manufacturer, George Herbert Ewart. The women were arrested fleeing the burning building, having been witnessed in the act of lighting fires by patrolling policeman investigating the open gate. Florence refused to recognise the court, stating that there was no justice shown to women by the law, and declared [their] intention to 'always keep by Edward Carson and make life hot for all the men'. Mary Larmour, who also dissociated herself from the proceedings, asked the magistrate if he understood 'the absurdity of having us here while Sir Edward Carson is free', to which her solicitor, George McCracken, interjected knowingly, 'He is too strong for you', which she agreed was 'quite true'.[109] On 24–25 April, Ulster Unionists had landed a consignment of 24,000 rifles and three million rounds of ammunition at Larne, Bangor and Donaghadee, which was distributed to the UVF across Ulster, under the watchful command of Sir James Craig and with the full support of Edward Carson. The operation was covered in extensive detail by the Belfast unionist press, who heralded it as a 'political coup', and noted that while commander of British forces in Belfast district, Major-General Macready had met with the local military and police authorities with a view to implementing military law, no action was deemed necessary.[110] The treatment of the authorities and local press towards the militant unionists was in marked contrast with that of the militant suffragettes, who had been mocked, manhandled, arrested, imprisoned and, worst of all, criminalised. Incidentally, on the day prior to the burning of Ardmillan, the editors of the *Belfast Telegraph* and the *Belfast Newsletter* had been ambushed in their offices by two 'well-dressed women' who had landed a hefty punch on both men to the extent that the former was knocked to the floor and the latter was confined to his bed under medical supervision.[111]

Florence and Mary were supported in court by Dorothy and her new collaborator, Lisburn militant, Lillian Metge, with whom she went on to bomb Lisburn Cathedral on 31 July. Evidence was given of traces of five separate fires being started, and of the fact that, at the time of her arrest, Florence had been dressed in male attire, with a copy of the *Suffragette* in her coat pocket to which was pinned the message, 'For damages apply to the King and those who differentiate between men and women militants'.[112]

While the fact that Florence was dressed in men's clothing added an extra measure of spice to the newspaper headlines, it was also cited by J Stewart, the Medical Officer at Belfast Prison, as evidence of mental instability to discredit Florence's allegations of ill-treatment. Following their arrest, the women had embarked on the customary hunger and thirst strike, and a day later, Florence had made a written complaint – possibly concerning Stewart's attempts to force-feed her – to the Lord Lieutenant, Lord Aberdeen, who had previously proscribed against the practice.[113] The wearing of male clothing also has a later parallel with suffragette turned Irish revolutionary Margaret Skinnider, who in the Easter Rising changed outfits according to the roles she was performing: as a sniper at the College of Surgeons on Stephen's Green, she wore her soldier's uniform of knee breeches, belted jacket and puttees, whereas, as a despatch carrier and scout, she changed into a dress.[114] Indeed, otherwise impractical women's clothing, the voluminous long skirts and fancy hats, were particularly useful for concealing and transporting items whether it be dispatches, detonators, ammunition or other incendiary materials. It is reasonable to assume that Florence would have chosen to wear the less hampering 'male attire' of trousers when setting fire bombs – as an experienced incendiary, she would have been aware of the hazards posed by her long skirt, which she wrapped around her waist in readiness for a discreet getaway.

Florence and Mary were committed for trial – adding another item to Florence's charge sheet – and remanded in custody. After six days on hunger and thirst strike, however, the prison medical officials sought their temporary release under the Cat and Mouse Act. Florence's health especially, had been weakened by two hunger and thirst strikes in two months, and while an otherwise fit and healthy person could survive on hunger strike for around eight to ten weeks, a combined hunger and thirst strike could result in death within ten days. Having learned from previous experience, however, the women refused to accept anything other than an unconditional release, at which the authorities, noting their rapid deterioration and fearing a death on their hands, bundled them into an ambulance which was driven straight to the WSPU's offices. At the last minute, Florence and Mary were handed a sealed envelope containing the terms of their release: that they surrender to their trial at the assizes, that they notify the police of their address, that they do not leave that address for more than twelve hours and that they abstain from any further violations of the law. The *Suffragette* noted that as 'these conditions cannot be reinforced [they are] no conditions at all', and both women were taken to a safe house to recuperate.[115] Neither Madge Muir nor Larmour were seen or heard from again.

The trial date was set for 21 July, when the names of Dorothy Evans, Madge Muir and Mary Larmour were called in the halls of the court and from the steps of the courthouse to no reply. Dorothy was later dragged into court, subsequently remanded in custody, and then released on medical grounds due to hunger and thirst strike. On 2 August, she was rearrested (with Lillian Metge, Maud Wickham and Dorothy Carson) for the bombing of Lisburn Cathedral, by which time, Florence had been spirited out of the country. Throughout her time in Ireland, the authorities remained unaware of Florence's real identity. That said, a grainy photograph of Evans and Muir being driven through the streets of Belfast in a hired car decorated with suffragette flags, reveals the latter to be the same 'Dundee Hunger Striker' who was photographed recuperating in the garden of Dorset Hall two years earlier.[116]

The outbreak of war on 4 August brought an end to the WSPU's militant campaign as Christabel Pankhurst ordered the closure of all offices to support the war effort, effecting an amnesty for suffragette prisoners and triggering a split between pro- and anti-war activists. While Dorothy Evans took the pacifist line, Florence appears to have dissociated herself from the movement altogether, perhaps as a result of a physical and mental breakdown triggered by her prison experiences. She appears to have found solace in the New Thought movement, a school of metaphysical philosophy which pioneered techniques to develop mental powers and aid physical healing. In May 1915, she emigrated to California, where in addition to working as Librarian of the San Francisco Metaphysical Library, she wrote articles for metaphysical journals and gave lectures for the Home of Truth, a branch of the New Thought movement founded by Annie Rix Militz in 1905. It is likely Florence found a strong support network in its predominantly female membership whose sympathetic philosophy helped her to rebuild her broken health and regain her enthusiasm for feminist politics. In 1923, she returned to London where, alongside Dorothy Evans, she became involved in the Six Point Group, formed in 1921 by Lady Rhondda (ex-suffragette hunger striker, Margaret

Haig, née Thomas, to campaign for total equality between men and women in the six key areas of politics, economics, law, social and moral issues and work. In due course, Florence become Honorary International Secretary, and in October 1932, wrote to Irish Prime Minister, Éamon De Valera, in his capacity as acting President of the League of Nations, and his legal advisor, J Rhonda Hearne, thanking them for their assistance in helping to draft progressive legislation on married women's rights, particularly with regards to the amended Canadian constitution.[117] (Canada, like the Irish Free State, had obtained full legislative independence from Britain, under the Statute of Westminster, in December 1931). Given her earlier talent for militant action, however, the laborious task of lobbying ex-militant heads of state and other figures of male authority on women's rights doubtless stuck in her craw and contributed to an increasing sense of frustration and restlessness. In February 1939, she returned to the United States, via British Columbia, Canada, where amongst documents produced to gain entry was a doctor's certificate which described her as showing 'extreme nervousness and restlessness' – a characteristic 'affliction' she appears to have shared with former militant colleague, Ethel Moorhead, in the final years of her life in Dublin. The documents also testified to her clean police record. 'Madge Muir' had taken care of all that. Florence died in Los Angeles on 28 October 1944 at the age of 77.[118]

As an exiled Scot in America, Florence was happy to advertise her Edinburgh origins. She was, however, essentially an international feminist to whom national rights were only important if women were granted full equality. While Hanna Sheehy Skeffington's criticism that the 'English' suffragettes of the WSPU didn't always appreciate the nuances of the Irish political situation, was valid, the situation was complex and dynamic. As Sylvia Pankhurst recognised, the Irish conflict incited a particularly strong form of feminist militancy, which fed into the Irish national struggle. IRA Intelligence Officer for Cavan Town, Seamus McDermott, later recalled that 'suffragette threats to burn churches provided an excellent excuse for the Loyal Orange Lodge to arm their section of the Ulster Volunteers', which, in turn, precipitated the formation of the Irish Volunteers in every parish.[119] The suffragettes' war against unionism also served to expose the hypocrisy of the British government who responded to the Ulster unionists' threats of violence by giving in to their demands for partition yet dragged the suffragettes into court and threw them in jail where their verbal protestations and hunger strikes were treated less as a serious political challenge than a behavioural problem. The fact remains that the most intense challenge to Ulster unionism in the early months of the Home Rule crisis came from an alliance forged between the WSPU and the militant Ulster suffragettes in which Florence McFarlane played a pivotal role. Such was the contribution of 'Dundee's hunger striker' to the Irish political conflict, it was hugely significant.

As the outbreak of war closed the chapter on the most intense period of suffragette militancy, it opened a new one on physical force Irish republicanism. The formation of the Irish Volunteers in Dublin on 25 November 1913 was followed by the launching of a Scottish section in Glasgow on 11 January 1914. It appears to have been a West of Scotland affair only for while there were around twenty Volunteer companies in and around Glasgow by August, there is no record of any being formed in Dundee, possibly because the IRB and Sinn Féin, who were largely responsible for initiating the Volunteers, did not have an organisational presence there.[120] Nevertheless, the UIL and the AOH, which did, were fully behind the Volunteers, and it is perhaps significant that, just over two weeks after the Glasgow launch, the Dundee branch of the UIL called a meeting in the Foresters' Hall, which, the *Courier* noted, was 'one of the largest gatherings ever held under [its] auspices'. If there was any suggestion of a Dundee company being mooted, President Frank O'Rourke's announcement that there might be opportunities for Irishmen to meet in a social capacity now that their political work was drawing to a close, was perhaps not what some of the more militant nationalists were hoping to hear.[121]

Thus, while Dundee's Irish nationalists remained unaffected by the split in the Volunteers (prompted in September by John Redmond's call to enlist in the British Army's Irish Regiments in the belief that this would guarantee Home Rule) they were, nevertheless, caught up in the IPP's recruitment campaign. Amongst the delegates attending a UILGB meeting in London on 3 October, Dundee branch Secretary, Bernard McLaughlin, reported that 1,000 Irish recruits had gone from the city, and Fife mining villages (such as Methil, where a branch of the UIL had been formed in 1909), had been 'left depleted'.[122] James O'Donnell Derrick, who spoke

Chapter 6 – A New Militancy 1909–16

for the West of Scotland, added that at least 5,000, nearer 10,000, had joined the colours. At the close of 1914, the *Dundee Evening Telegraph* reported that over 2,000 Dundee Roman Catholics (which were generally considered as Irish) had enlisted, and that, according to Redmond, a total of 140,000 Irishmen were serving in the British Army, 16,442 of whom were in the National (Redmondite) Volunteers. At a meeting of the Dundee UIL on 31 January 1915, O'Donnell Derrick claimed that a total of 35,000 Irishmen from Scotland, and 15,000 Scottish Catholics were 'in the service of the government defending its war policy', citing the 2,000 from Dundee, plus 140 from Perth, 47 from Alloa, 40 from Crieff, 31 from Dunblane, 25 from Arbroath, 15 from St Andrews, 14 from Alva, three from Montrose, and another 800 from Rosyth – the massed recruits from the Fife mining villages, as proof that the Irish in the East of Scotland were 'doing their bit'.[23] While the UILGB's figures were undoubtedly exaggerated for political propaganda purposes, their recruitment drive was nevertheless proving effective.[124]

In the meantime, the wider propaganda campaign continued. The fate of Ireland was ever conflated with that of 'plucky little Belgium', in whose aid Saturday, 6 February 1915 was declared Irish Flag Day in Scotland. While the event was promoted by the AOH, most of the work in Dundee was undertaken by a female-led committee and a corps of volunteers comprising mostly young women, the Catholic Boys' Brigade and the St Mary's Cadets, who covered railway stations, football grounds, street corners and entertainment venues, buttonholing all passers-by until there were few who did not wear the green and gold flaglet.[125] Servicemen, it was noted, were liberal givers. At the end of the day, Dundee's contribution to Irish Flag Day raised £401, which added to the £480 from Edinburgh, £150 from Coatbridge, and accumulated smaller sums from other Scottish towns and villages, procured a total of around £5,000 for the Belgian Relief Fund.[126]

If there was any dissent to the IPP's position on the war it did not come to the fore at public meetings of the Irish national movement in Dundee. On 6 December, IPP MP for West Belfast, Joe Devlin, addressed a conference of 'nationalists' in the Kinnaird Hall which, given the numbers who had enlisted in the army, was 'practically a private gathering'. Still, Devlin's popularity within the Irish community (due in large part to his status as leader of the AOH) ensured that the hall was 'well-filled' with representatives from Perth, Blairgowrie, Arbroath, Tayport and Dundee, all of whom passed resolutions expressing their continued confidence in the IPP and endorsing its war policy.[127] The passing of the Military Service Act on 1 January 1916, however, threatened to bring dissenters out into the open and into direct conflict with the authorities. Ireland was excluded, on the counsel of Redmond, in order not to upset the fragile consensus. When conscription was introduced on 2 March, the Dundee branch of the UIL visited the local head of recruitment, Major Thomas Cappon, to offer their support and seek an assurance that any Dundee man wishing to join a regiment in Ireland would be afforded every facility. Cappon happily complied, affirming that every man, whether recruited under the Military Service Act or the Derby Scheme would be entitled to the same 'privileges'.[128]

By this time, most advanced Irish Republicans on Scottish, English and Welsh soil, including the IRB's Scottish representative on the Supreme Council, Glasgow-born Charles Carrigan, and Glasgow Fianna Éireann leader, Seumas Robinson, had made their way to Ireland to escape the draft and prepare for rebellion.[129] For those Dundee Irishmen who did not follow the official Irish Party line, most bowed to social pressure and to the financial inducement of the Separation Allowance – an important consideration given the chronically low wages in Dundee's staple industry.[130] While Dundee had the second highest percentage of conscientious objectors in Scotland (ranking second only to Glasgow), few took their stand openly on Irish political beliefs, or if they did, it was rarely reported. Most cited socialist principles which were, nevertheless, compatible with advanced Irish republican ones.

On Thursday, 20 April 1916, David Nairn, a calender worker of 151 Victoria Road, became the first person in Dundee to be prosecuted under the Military Service Act for failing to report for duty by 25 March. Taking his stand in the dock, he declared:

> For fifteen years my ideal has been the emancipation of the working class throughout the world. For fifteen years I have striven to see that realised. It is the only cause – the solidarity of labour – for which I could fight for and that is the cause for which I am prepared to die.[131]

Nairn, who stated that he wished to give evidence on his own behalf, entered the witness box and proceeded to criticise the government, the Military Service Act, and was just referring to 'the Irish people', when the Sheriff intervened and ordered him back into the dock where he was fined £2 and handed over to the military authorities. While little more is known of Nairn, his international socialist views and Irish sympathies chime with the syndicalism of the Industrial Workers of the World (IWW) and the socialist republicanism of James Connolly – indeed, the Dundee calender workers had demonstrated their support for the sympathetic strike when they voted to hold out during the protracted jute strike of 1912, unlike the three other unions involved. Nairn was taken to Perth Barracks, and subsequently transferred to Wandsworth Prison in South London where he found himself detained alongside soldiers of the Irish Revolution who had been shipped out of Dublin and interned in British jails in the weeks following the Easter Rising.

Just four days after Nairn's trial, the Easter Rising got under way. News of the rebellion was met with a hostile reaction from Dundee's moderate Home Rulers whose combined forces met the following Monday to condemn it as an 'act of treachery not only to the Empire but also to Ireland', and to express the hope that the 'Sinn Feiners and those associated with them...in their mad, motiveless and meaningless work [are] compelled to give way'. The meeting also pledged their continued confidence in the Irish Party and its policy on the war. Copies of the resolution, signed by the office bearers of the UIL, the INF and the AOH, were sent to John Redmond, T P O'Connor, the British and Scottish secretaries of the UILGB, and to the local press to which latter agency Dundee's established middle-class, middle-aged, moderate Irish Home Rulers were at pains to point out that, while Sinn Féin had a 'small branch' in Glasgow, 'no countenance had ever been given to it in Dundee'.[132]

On Friday, 28 April, Charles Carrigan became the first Scottish-born martyr of the Irish Revolution when he was killed in The O'Rahilly's charge on a British barricade in Moore Street while retreating from the burning GPO. While an estimated twenty Scottish, mainly Glasgow-based, republicans saw active service in the rising, the typical Dundee soldier of Irish descent fighting in Dublin in Easter Week was more likely to be on the side of the Crown.[133] On Saturday, 6 May, the *People's Journal* published a 'thrilling pen picture' of 'the Dublin front' from the hand of one such Dundee rifleman in an Irish regiment (probably the Royal Irish Rifles) in which he described his experience of combing the streets of the city for the last remaining insurgents:

> In the vicinity of our barracks, they are practically all Sinn Feiners. Many are middle class people. Well, we made our way under a heavy fire into a street only five minutes' walk from the barracks. We had to take shelter behind garden walls etc. for a while, but at the same time, we kept all the surrounding windows covered with one rifle. When the rebel fire slackened we raided a self-contained house. Bang went the door and a gentleman opened [it] with a smile. Our officer cheerily explained that he had come to search the house. The officer and sergeant began a thorough search, accompanied by an obliging young lady – the daughter, I presume. Meanwhile, I was downstairs in the kitchen. The occupants of the house were three young fellows, the father, the mother, and another old woman who sat by the fire and never spoke the whole time. The others kept up a strained conversation – trying to draw my leg. The gist of their conversation was that they wished the Sinn Feiners would be beaten, and that they had friends fighting in France. The old man volunteered the information that he had done some twenty years in the artillery. They asked me if I smoked, and I said 'Yes'. The officer, after an absence of about an hour, came down the stairs – he had found nothing. By this time the whole family were smiling, and even let us [look] in the tea canisters, coal cellar and so on. I could see our officer was not satisfied. He called one of the young fellows into the yard, and meanwhile I stood with my bayonet at his chest. The officer ordered him to get a spade and dig up the contents of the garden. 'Just as I thought', he remarked. We secured two Mauser rifles, a hundred rounds of ammunition, three Colt revolvers and even daggers, equipment &c. We went back to the kitchen. The two sentries we had left at the door came in, and so we had the whole family covered with our rifles. The young lady burst into tears. The smiles had left them and they were trembling like

leaves. 'Will they shoot the men, do you think?', queried the old lady. I candidly told the woman I would not be in their shoes for £1000. We took two sons away. The other fellow, seemingly was a lodger, but I suppose he was arrested later...

If there was any concern at the woman's distress and the men's fate, it was quickly put aside. 'Raiding has its good side too', he continued. 'The loyal people, after we have searched their homes, give us tea, and by Jove! we need it, because we have been living off hard biscuits and 'bully' all last week.' As the previous incident indicates, such 'loyalty' was often tenuous and deceptive; still, given the circumstances, it appears he was happy to be deceived. He continued:

> We have lost a number of our officers and men, killed and wounded. When the row started our regiment was the first out, and we got a hot reception from the Sinn Feiners. They were firing from all quarters... It was dreadful to hear all the women and children in the streets screaming, and several were hit crossing the zone of fire.

Still, he comforted himself, 'I have my old Hilltown pal here. We have been fighting side by side since this started. He and myself as Dundee men have only done our duty for King and country'.[134]

The anonymous serviceman's letter was likely written at the beginning of the week. In it he claimed: 'We captured Jacob's biscuit factory on Monday night. In fact, the undefeated rebel garrison, led by Thomas MacDonagh, had reluctantly surrendered the day before in line with the orders of the Provisional Government issued by Pearse at Moore Street on Saturday, 29 April. By the time the 'pen picture' appeared in print, Pearse and MacDonagh, along with two of their fellow signatories of the Republican Proclamation, Thomas Clarke and Joseph Plunkett, and another three rebel commanders,[135] had been imprisoned, court-martialled and executed.

Endnotes to Chapter 6

1. James Connolly, 'Sinn Fein and the Language Movement', *The Harp*, April 1908.
2. 'The Grand Old Dame Britannia' [fourth verse], published in *The Workers' Republic*, 15 January 1916.
3. Robert Stewart, *Breaking the Fetters* (London: Lawrence and Wishart, 1967), p45.
4. Born the son of a farmer in Glenlivet, Banffshire in 1853, Turner entered Blair's Seminary at the age of fourteen and continued his education at St Sulpice in Paris. He was ordained at the Seminary of Foreign Missions in Burma in 1878, after which he returned to Scotland as curate of St Mary's Forebank from 1878–1883, then Doune until 1885 when he was appointed parish priest of St John the Baptist's in Perth. In 1902, he was appointed Administrator of St Andrew's Pro-Cathedral, Dundee, which post he held until his death in November 1938. He was appointed Vicar-General of Dunkeld Diocese in 1917. *Scottish Catholic Directory*, 1879 and 1938.
5. *The Perthshire Critic*, 12 January 1894.
6. Greaves, *Life and Times*, pp20–21; *Freeman's Journal*, 28 May 1888.
7. Letter from James Connolly to Lillie Reynolds, 6 April 1890, NLI, William O'Brien Papers, MS13911; *The Perthshire Critic*, 12 January 1894.
8. *Dundee Advertiser*, 5 October 1889; *The Perthshire Advertiser*, 23 May 1898, 20 March 1901.
9. Walker, *Juteopolis*, p290.
10. William Kenefick, 'Locality, Regionality and Gender: Revisiting Industrial Protest among Women Workers in Scotland, 1910 to 1913', *Journal of Irish Studies*, 8:2 (Spring 2015), p41.
11. Walker, *Juteopolis*, p145.
12. Susan, who was born in Lochee on 13 February 1884, was also brought up in an all-female household headed by her Lochee-born mother, Mary Ann (née Gunning), also a spinner. Her Lochee-born father, William, an itinerant labourer, appears to have been absent from the family home for much of Susan's younger life, reappearing as head of the household in Campbell Street in 1921. While Mary Brooksbank later recalled (mistakenly) that she emigrated to America shortly after the 1912 strike, Susan in fact remained in Dundee, going on to have another child in 1913, and marrying 50-year-old widower, James Reilly, in 1925. She died in Wellburn Home, Lochee, in 1967 at the age of 83. Census of Scotland, 1891; 1911, 1921; marriage and death records for Susan Devine Reilly; Mary Brooksbank, interviewed by Hamish Henderson, October 1964, School of Scottish Studies, SA1968.317, accessed via Tobar an Dualchais, https://www.tobarandualchais.co.uk/. Thanks to Billy Kenefick for initially alerting me to Susan's identity.
13. *Dundee Advertiser*, 18 March 1911; *Dundee Courier*, 18 March 1911.

CHAPTER 6 – A NEW MILITANCY 1909–16

14 *Dundee Evening Telegraph*, 18 December 1911; *Aberdeen Press and Journal*, 20 December 1911. Police were drawn from Glasgow, Lanarkshire, Edinburgh, Aberdeen, Stirlingshire, Fife and Forfarshire to the cost of £1000. *Belfast Newsletter*, 25 January 1912.

15 'The *Courier* reported an incident where a merry band of 'young marksmen' in the north end of the town launched 'missiles of all descriptions' at a suspected scab lorry and the police, seriously injuring a police constable and reducing all the plate glass windows in the vicinity to smithereens, whilst evading all attempts to capture them. *Dundee Courier*, 20 December 1911.

16 *Dundee Courier*, 20 December 1911.

17 Larkin was suspended in December 1908, on the pretext of misappropriating funds, by a reformist element within the NUDL who balked at Larkin's revolutionary designs. He immediately went on to form the overtly syndicalist Irish Transport and General Workers Union.

18 James O'Connor Kessack was born in Aberdeen and later moved to Glasgow where he worked as an unskilled labourer while studying to become a lawyer. A devout Catholic, he was converted to socialism in 1901, joined the Socialist Labour Party, the Industrial Workers of the World (IWW), and helped form the Advocates of Industrial Unionism, the British propaganda arm of the IWW, in 1906–7. A sceptic regarding Irish and Scottish nationalism, he berated Connolly and Larkin for 'ranting' about the latter. When the First War broke out, he joined the British Army and was killed at the Battle of Ancre in November 1916. Eric Taplin, in Joyce M Bellamy and John Saville (eds), *Dictionary of Labour Biography*, Volume VI (London: Palgrave Macmillan, 1982), pp150–1; Nevin, *James Connolly, A Full Life*, p421.

19 *Dundee Evening Telegraph*, 21 December 1911; *Dundee Evening Telegraph*, 22 December 1911; *The Scotsman*, 25 December 1911; *Belfast Newsletter*, 25 December 1911.

20 *Belfast Newsletter, Irish and Belfast Morning News*, 20–23, 25 December 1911.

21 *Belfast Newsletter*, 29 December 1911.

22 *Dundee Advertiser*, 6 September 1889, *Dundee Courier*, 2 September 1889.

23 Letter from James Connolly to Lillie Reynolds, undated, William O'Brien papers, NLI, MS139111.

24 *Dundee Evening Telegraph*, 4 April 1890; *Dundee Advertiser*, 17 April 1890. The Dundee Labour Federation, formed on 24 September 1889, was a short-lived socialist labour grouping which appears to have been organised along similar lines to the Scottish Socialist Federation in Edinburgh, with a similar membership, albeit with a less theoretical focus and a more practical purpose. Executive members included James Aimer (President), Joseph Carr (Secretary), James Duncan and Edward De Courcey. Its first and most pressing task, four weeks after its formation, was to compile information on and seek redress to the scavengers' grievances – six complaints centring around wages (which had only increased by 6d in 11 years, now stood at 19 to 20 shillings ,and were not

consistent across the board); working conditions (they were expected to handle toxic bedding from infection-ridden homes, and, unlike the police, received no wet weather clothing); and holidays (they were expected to work five hours on Sunday morning, for which they received to extra pay, and were liable to be dismissed or fined 6d, sometimes 1s, if they absented themselves. By contrast, as one scaffie rep (possibly John or James Connolly) stated, their colleagues in Edinburgh received 22 shillings a week, worked alternate Sundays, and received fourteen days holiday a year, which arrangement they urged be adopted. The DLF was superseded, to an extent, by the Dundee branch of the Scottish Labour Party, formed in March 1892. *Dundee Courier,* 25 September 1889; *Dundee Courier,* 23 October 1889; *Dundee Courier,* 16 December 1889.

25   Nevin, *James Connolly, A Full Life*, p414.
26   Greaves, pp185; Nevin, pp399–400.
27   Kenefick, 'Locality, Regionality and Gender', p49.
28   Nicolas Marra, as the public face of the JFWU, was accused of being a blackleg, from which 'dastardly attack' James Reid, the leader of the Calenders' Union, defended him, as the decision was not his, but taken by a meeting of the Joint Committee representing the four unions involved in the strike: the JFWU, the Mill and Flax Operatives' Union, the Calenders' Union, and the Powerloom Tenters Society. *Dundee Courier,* 23 March 1912.
29   *Dundee Evening Telegraph,* 11 April 1912.
30   *Dundee Evening Telegraph,* 9 April, 10 April, 13 April 1912.
31   William Kenefick, *Red Scotland!: The Rise and Fall of the Radical Left, c.1872–1932* (Edinburgh: EUP, 2007), p133.
32   *Scottish Prohibitionist,* 23 March 1912.
33   On such example of worker solidarity occurred on 8 March 1912, when 400 women workers rejected a 5 per cent wage increase from Scott Sons of North Dudhope Works, and opted to remain on strike rather than scab on their fellow workers. *Dundee Courier,* 9 March 1912; Kenefick, 'Locality, Regionality and Gender', p50.
34   *Dundee Courier,* 11 March 1912.
35   Iain E Johnston, 'Edward Carson: Ulster Unionist of Irish Patriot', *History Ireland,* 3 (May/June 2012).
36   *Dundee Evening Telegraph,* 1 September 1913; *Dundee Advertiser,* 2 September 1913; *Dundee Evening Telegraph,* 2 September 1913.
37   *Dundee Courier,* 4 September 1913.
38   *Irish Independent,* 5 September 1913.
39   *Dundee Evening Telegraph,* 9 September 1913.
40   *Aberdeen Press and Journal,* 8 September 1913. Barnes was born in Lochee, where his father was a mechanic at Camperdown Works. The family moved to England in 1866, and returned to Dundee in 1872, where, after completing his apprenticeship, Barnes moved to Burness and then London where he became

General Secretary of the Amalgamated Society of Engineers. In 1893, joined the ILP, and in 1906, he and Alexander Wilkie became first Labour MPs to be elected in Scotland. A moderate who moved steadily rightwards, Barnes resigned from the Labour Party in 1918, after it withdrew from Lloyd George's coalition government in which he was Minister of Pensions, and subsequently set up the short-lived National Democratic and Labour Party. At the time, the Irish national press, which noted Barnes' long association with the UILGB's Glasgow Home Government branch, and his self-proclaimed Irish heritage, pronounced him a 'recreant'. He resigned from politics for good in 1922. *Irish Opinion*, 18 May 1918.

41 *Derry Journal*, 15 September 1913.
42 *Dundee Advertiser*, 22 September 1912.
43 Greaves, *Life and Times*, p213; *The Scotsman*, 22 September 1913.
44 *Dundee Evening Telegraph*, 15 September 1913.
45 *Dundee Courier*, 15 September 1913.
46 *Dundee Advertiser*, 25 September 1913.
47 *Dundee Advertiser*, 27 September 1913.
48 *Dundee Evening Telegraph*, 30 September 1913; *Dundee Courier*, 2 October 1913.
49 Joint Committee Minute Book, 29 September 1913, cited in Walker, *Juteopolis*, p316.
50 *Dundee Courier*, 3 October 1913.
51 *Dundee Advertiser*, 3 October 1913: *Dundee Advertiser*, 4 October 1913: *Dundee Evening Telegraph*, 8 October 1913; *Dundee Evening Telegraph*, 16 October 1913.
52 *The Scotsman*, 20 October 1913. At the Ulster Covenant rally of 27 September 1912, Carson and his followers had marched behind the faded yellow flag carried by the troops of William of Orange at the Battle of the Boyne.
53 *Leith Observer*, 25 October 1913.
54 *Forward*, 25 October 1913.
55 Mary McGinn was the daughter of Connolly's maternal uncle, James McGinn, and his wife, Bridget. In 1913, Mary was living at 3a Atholl Street (formerly Albert Street), Lochee. She died in Wellburn Home for the Aged Poor in 1931, aged 74. Her younger brother, Thomas, a seaman, appears to have left the city in the 1890s.
56 The strike at Baxter's came to an end on Wednesday, 22 October after the Conciliation Board, which included representatives of the firm and the trade unions, reached an agreement whereby the male batchers were granted the one shilling wage increase they had asked for, and the management gave an 'undertaking to investigate 'other complaints of a secondary nature'. In short, the demands of the female hecklers were put on the back burner. *Dundee Evening Telegraph*, 22 October 1913.
57 Greaves, *Life and Times*, p218.
58 Charlotte Despard, née French, was the English-born daughter of an Irish naval

commander, who took up charity work after the death of her husband, Anglo-Irish businessman Maximilian Despard, and had become steadily more radical ever since. An early member the SDF and the ILP, she become friends with George Lansbury, Eleanor Marx and Keir Hardie, and was a delegate to the Second International in 1893. She initially joined the National Union of Women's Suffrage Societies, then the more militant Women's Social and Political Union which she left in 1907 (due to Emmeline and Christabel Pankhursts' autocratic control) to co-found the WFL. The same year, she met Mahatma Gandhi, who informed her views on passive resistance and the tactic of the hunger strike. She was invited to Ireland where she hooked up with Hanna Sheehy Skeffington and others in the newly formed Irish Women's Franchise League, which actively supported the workers of Dublin throughout the Lockout. A firm supporter of the Irish Republican movement, she joined Sinn Féin during the War of Independence, took the Republican side in the Civil War and, alongside Maud Gonne MacBride and Hanna Sheehy Skeffington, set up the Women's Prisoners' Defence League, of which she was President, in 1922. In 1926, she left Sinn Féin to join the Workers' Party of Ireland, formed by Roddy Connolly and Nora Connolly O'Brien. She also joined the Communist Party of Great Britain and in 1930 toured the Soviet Union with Hanna Sheehy Skeffington.

59 *Dundee Courier,* 21 October 1913; *Scottish Prohibitionist,* 25 October 1913.

60 *The Vote,* 24 October 1913.

61 Journal of C Desmond Greaves, Volume 12, 1956–57, 18 May 1957. Desmond Greaves archive, http://www.desmondgreavesarchive.com/journal/desmond-greaves-journal-vol-12-1956-57/, accessed 29 May 2023.

62 The Prisoners (Temporary Discharge for Ill Health) Act 1913, which allowed for the release of prisoners weakened by hunger strike and their re-imprisonment on recovery. Elizabeth Crawford, *The Women's Suffrage Movement in Britain and Ireland: A Regional Survey* (London; Routledge, 2006), p239; *Dundee Courier,* 20 October 1913.

63 *Dundee Advertiser,* 10 October 1913. Churchill was in Dundee to shore up support for the Home Rule Bill, thus to secure and maintain the British Imperial State. Revealingly, the previous evening he had told a large, almost exclusively male audience in the Kinnaird Hall (ladies were admitted by invitation only) that he 'had not the slightest doubt about the power of the government to carry the policy through... still less... about the power of the State as a State... to maintain itself, and to maintain by law, and to put down disorder by whomsoever it is threatened and fomented'. As the majority of Home Rule supporters in the audience assumed that this State power would invariably be directed at Carson's Ulster Volunteers and not Irish nationalists, the response was overwhelmingly positive. Four weeks after Churchill's visit, Edward Carson made a flying visit to the city, addressing a meeting of Unionists in the King's Theatre, chaired by Dundee's most prominent Unionist, textile baron(et), Sir George Baxter. The meeting made little impact on wider public

opinion, however, with Carson himself acknowledging that nationalists, in Dundee at least, were in the majority. *Dundee Courier*, 8 November 1913.

64 *Sunday Post*, 9 October 1921.
65 *Dundee Courier*, 29 April 1908.
66 *Dundee Courier*, 9 May 1908.
67 *Dundee Courier*, 23 January 1914.
68 Lila Clunas eventually became a Labour councillor, as did Agnes Husband. Elizabeth Ewan, Sue Innes, Sian Reynolds, *The Biographical Dictionary of Scottish Women from the Earliest Times to 2004* (Edinburgh; EUP, 2006,), pp77, 175.
69 Norman Watson, *Dundee's Suffragettes: Their Remarkable Struggle to Win Votes for Women* (Perth: Percy Johnstone Publishing, 2018), pp43–44.
70 Ethel Moorhead's aliases included Margaret Morrison, Edith Johnston, Mary Humphries (her mother's name) and Mrs Marshall.
71 *Dundee Courier*, 8 December 1910; *Dundee Evening Telegraph*, 6 December 1910.
72 *The Irish Citizen*, 29 June 1912.
73 *Dundee Evening Telegraph*, 9 August 1912; *Irish Citizen*, 17 August 1912.
74 *Votes for Women*, 20 September 1912.
75 *Dundee Courier*, 4 February 1913.
76 *Forfar Herald*, 16 May 1913.
77 McGrady was Lord Provost of Dundee from 1896 to 1899, and the first Irishman to hold the position. Farington Hall, however, appears to have been chosen as it was lying empty whilst being renovated. It was built, in 1854, for Allan Edwards, whose family owned Logie Spinning Works in the Scouringburn, where nineteen workers, mostly women and girls, were killed in a horrific boiler explosion in 1859. There is a poignant irony in that the magnificent gothic mansion built on the backs of these and many other workers was reduced to a pile of ashes by two women with a few cans of petrol.
78 *Dundee Evening Telegraph*, 5 June 1914.
79 Ethel's last known operation was an attempt, with Fanny Parker, to blow up Burns' cottage in Alloway in July 1914.
80 Ethel spent two years in Ireland (1918–1920), then moved to Europe to pursue a career as an artist and co-edit the art and literary journal, *This Quarter*. She eventually retired to Blackrock, Dublin, where she died in 1955 aged 86. Mary Henderson, *Ethel Moorhead*, 2020.
81 IMA, BMH, Ina Connolly-Heron, WS 919, p79. The first was Dublin strike activist, James Byrne, who died from health complications arising from the experience on 2 November 1913.
82 William Murphy, *Political Imprisonment and the Irish, 1912–1921* (Oxford: OUP, 2014), p32.
83 Mary McAuliffe, *Margaret Skinnider*. (Dublin: UCD Press, 2020).

84 See, for example, Leah Leneman, *A Guid Cause: The Women's Suffrage Movement in Scotland* (Edinburgh: Mercat Press, 1995); Sarah Pederson, *The Scottish Suffragettes and the Press* (London: Palgrave Macmillan, 2017); Esther Breitenbach and Eleanor Gordon (eds), *Out of Bound: Women in Scottish Society, 1800–1945* (Edinburgh: EUP, 1992).
85 *Edinburgh Evening News*, 20 May 1890.
86 Greaves, *Life and Times*, p24.
87 *Edinburgh Evening News*, 27 May 1890.
88 Greaves, *Life and Times*, p32.
89 *Aberdeen Evening Express*, 21 June 1890; HC [House of Commons] Debate, June 1890, cc1479.
90 *Dundee Advertiser*, 24 July 1890.
91 *Aberdeen Evening Express*, 4 December 1893.
92 *Votes for Women*, 24 November 1910.
93 *Dundee Courier*, 7 March 1912.
94 *West London Observer*, 8 March 1912.
95 *The Suffragette*, 28 February 1913; *Votes for Women*, 28 March 1913.
96 *Votes for Women*, 5 July 1912.
97 'Suffragettes under surveillance: police mugshots of the militant women who won the vote', *The Telegraph*, 6 February 2018; 'Suffragettes relaxing in the grounds of Dorset Hall', 1912, Merton Memories Photographic Archive, https:// cis. photoarchive.merton.gov.uk/places-of-interest/places-of-interest-miscellaneous/ 760430-suffragettes-relaxing-in-the-garden-of-dorset-hall, accessed 19 May 2023.
98 Diane Urquhart, 'An articulate and definite cry for political freedom': The Ulster Suffrage Movement', *Women's History Review*, 11:2 (2002), pp278–81.
99 The Irish Women's Suffrage Society was the most dynamic and socially progressive suffrage organisation in Ulster at the time. Most of its members went over to the WSPU in March/April 1914 at the start of the latter's militant campaign against Carson and the Unionists.
100 Redmond later stated that if he had played his cards as well as Carson, he might have had the suffragettes behind him. Jason Burke, 'Carson's Betrayal of Women? Unionist attitudes to female suffrage, 1912–1914', Lecture, Public Records Office Northern Ireland, 8 August 2018.
101 *Irish Citizen*, 18 October 1913.
102 Sir Hugh McCalmont was a Major-General in the British Army, an ex-Unionist Party MP, and the grandson of Hugh McCalmont, who bought Abbeylands in 1803 from proceeds of the slave trade, which fortune passed on to his sons, of whom James inherited his Whiteabbey mansion, which he in turn left to his son Hugh. 'Hugh McCalmont of Abbeylands', Centre for the Study of the Legacies of British Slave Ownership, https://www.ucl.ac.uk/lbs/person/view/8582,

accessed 19 May 2023.

103　*Dublin Daily Express*, 23 April 1914.
104　*Northern Whig*, 15 April 1914.
105　*Belfast Newsletter*, 15 April 1914.
106　*Irish Citizen*, 25 April 1914; *Suffragette*, 24 April 1914; *Freeman's Journal*, 22 April 1914.
107　*Northern Whig*, 22 April 1914; *Irish Citizen*, 25 April 1914.
108　*Dublin Daily Express*, 23 April 1914.
109　*Northern Whig*, 4 June 1914.
110　*Belfast Newsletter*, 28 April 1914; *Belfast Telegraph*, 28 April 1914.
111　*Belfast Telegraph*, 4 June 1914.
112　*Belfast Newsletter*, 4 June 1914.
113　Letter from Madge Muir to Lord Aberdeen; minute by J Stewart, 4 June 1914, cited in Murphy, *Political Imprisonment and the Irish*, p28, n124.
114　McAuliffe, *Margaret Skinnider*, p30.
115　*Suffragette*, 19 June 1914.
116　*Suffragette*, 24 April 1914. Also, a photograph of Florence MacFarland [*sic*] at the centre of a protest by the Six Point Group in London in 1932 shows Florence and Madge to be the same person. 'Miss Florence McFarlane', The Dinner Puzzle, https://thedinnerpuzzle.com/portfolio/miss-florence-mcfarlane/, accessed 19 May 2023.
117　Mary E Daly, 'Wives, Mothers and Citizens: The Treatment of Women in the 1935 Nationality and Citizenship Act', *Eire-Ireland*, 38: 3 & 4, (2003), pp257–58. Despite their show of advancing the principle of gender equality, De Valera's government went on to curtail the rights of Irish women to work in industry and outside the home after marriage. Karen M Offen, *European Feminisms, 1700–1950: A Political History* (Stanford; Stanford U.P, 2000), pp318–19.
118　Full text of 'News Notes of California Libraries', Volume 12, January–October 1917, https://archive.org/stream/newsnotesof calif12cali/newsnotesofcalif12cali_djvu.txt, accessed 19 May 2023; *Sacramento Union*, 8 November 1919; *Occult Press Review*, July 1923; 'Miss Florence McFarlane', The Dinner Puzzle.
119　IMA, BMH, Seamus McDermott, WS 768, p1.
120　Ó Catháin, *Irish Republicanism in Scotland*, p273.
121　*Dundee Courier*, 31 January 1914.
122　*Dundee Courier*, 5 October 1914.
123　*Dundee Courier*, 1 February 1915.
124　Elaine McFarland, How the Irish Paid Their Debt: Irish Catholics in Scotland and Volunteer Enlistment, Aug 1914–Jul 1915', *Scottish Historical Review*, 82:214: October 2003, pp261–84.

125 The demise of the Fenian organisation in Dundee meant that the city did not have a slua (troop) of the militant republican youth group, Na Fianna Éireann (unlike Glasgow, where a slua was formed in 1910). The formation of the Catholic Boys' Brigade and the St Mary's cadets appears to have been an attempt by the Catholic Church in Dundee to discourage seepage to the semi-military, predominantly Protestant, Boys' Brigade. The former was also regarded as a preparation for the Catholic Young Men's Society. The organisation did not survive the war.

126 *Dundee Courier*, 8 February 1915; *Edinburgh Evening News*, 13 February 1915.

127 *Dundee Courier*, 7 December 1915; *People's Journal*, 11 December 1915. On a previous visit to the city, in 1911, Devlin predicted that Churchill would 'play as large and as vital and as historic a part in the settlement for the claim of Irish self-government as he so splendidly played in the solution of Home Rule in the Transvaal'. Churchill did, of course, go on to play such a part but not in the way that Devlin may have hoped. *Dundee Courier*, 11 April 1911. Churchill's role in sending in the military to quell the Welsh miners' strike of 1910 was also overlooked.

128 *Dundee Courier*, 18 March 1916. The Derby Scheme – introduced by the Director-General of Recruitment, Lord Derby, in October 1915 as a last-ditch effort to avoid conscription – had urged all men between the ages of eighteen and 41 to voluntarily register for military service pending call-up, only if necessary, and in stages according to marital status and age.

129 Carrigan, who was also a committed socialist, resigned from his post on the Supreme Council at the end of 1915. Ó Catháin *Irish Republicanism in Scotland*, pp235–36, 238). The exodus also included Michael Collins who resigned from his civil service post in London and moved to Dublin.

130 For example, the wife of a private or corporal received a weekly payment of 12s 6d, a wife and one child received 17s 6d, a wife and two children received 21s, and 2s was granted for each additional child.

131 *Dundee Evening Telegraph*, 20 April 1916.

132 *Dundee Courier*, 2 May 1916.

133 Stephen Coyle, Confused Counsels', in Stephen Coyle and Máirtín Ó Catháin (eds), *We Will Rise Again: Ireland, Scotland and the Easter Rising* (Glasgow: 1916 Rising Centenary Committee (Scotland), 2018), pp34–35.

134 *Peoples' Journal*, 6 May 1916.

135 Sean MacBride, Michael O'Hanrahan (MacDonagh's second-in-command) and Willie Pearse. Pearse, however, held no senior command, and is generally considered to have been targeted because of his connection to his brother Patrick, to whom he was aide-de-camp.

CHAPTER 7

Revolution 1916–23

The Irish militant movement in Scotland is not a growth following upon the National Awakening of 1916, but a continuation of that part which the Irish here have always played in the struggle for their country's freedom. The service rendered during the years of necessity was in many ways unique. It was an effort as tremendous was the situation that called it forth.[1]

I

ON WEDNESDAY, 3 MAY 1916, the executions of the leaders of the Rising began. The *Dundee Courier*'s London correspondent wrote:

> The Government have made short work of three of the ringleaders of the Irish revolt, Pearse, Clarke and MacDonagh – three of the signatories of the Provisional Government's proclamation. Of this misguided trio, it may be said at once that they all deserved their fate.[2]

Over the course of the next ten days, perspectives changed, from blustering condemnations of the executed leaders to a reserved sympathy for them, and, in the case of Dundee's Irish community, a simmering resentment at the forces who had ordered them to be shot.

On 8 May, the local military tribunal heard the appeal of an Irish gardener who, had initially sought an absolute exemption on the grounds of his domestic situation as the sole support of his mother, but now declared a conscientious objection on 'social and moral grounds', which he had 'honourably kept in the background until now'. The hearing took place after the fourth round of executions in Dublin, by which time twelve leaders had been shot, and only two signatories of the Proclamation, Seán

MacDiarmada and James Connolly, remained. Whether the events of the Rising gave the unnamed Irishman – who, it was stated at the outset, was not liable for military service in Ireland – the courage to voice his objection is unknown. Incidentally, sitting on the tribunal that day was Nicholas Marra, a long-term supporter of Irish independence, whose official role, as representative of the Dundee Trades Council, was to negotiate conditional exemptions for key workers in reserved occupations. Marra, however, was only one of a panel which included the hardline Sheriff, Edward Neish, who presided, and local industrialist and Honorary Sheriff, J C Buist, whose youngest son had deferred a place at Oxford to join the British Army, and had just departed for the front line.[3] Sympathy was limited, and the Irish gardener's appeal was rejected.[4]

As more information about the Rising came to light, the Dundee press began to present its main actors in a more sympathetic light. The midnight wedding of Grace Gifford to Joseph Plunkett was grist to the mill for the *People's Journal* which, specialising as it did in dramatic human narrative, carried the story centre front page beneath an illustration of the heads of Grace, Joseph, and Count Plunkett, framed by a garland of shamrocks and a rifle. The story contained all the elements of a tragic romance in which style it was narrated:

> 'Goodbye, darling wife. In another far happier world we shall meet again!' One last clinging kiss. Then a man in uniform, coughing to hide emotion, declared that the period of grace was ended. Out from the little bare room which had witnessed the tragic honeymoon, out into the bare chill of the coming dawn, passed a slip of a girl with a face like the face of a beautiful corpse. With automatic steps she made her way across the damp, scrunching gravel of the Dublin barrack square – the most touching figure of the Irish rebellion. A bride of three hours, and to be a widow at the time when the birds raise their morning love song! For, at midnight, in his cell at Richmond Barracks [*sic*], this girl, who had been Grace Gifford, had married Joseph Plunkett, the Irish rebel leader. And he was to die at sunrise.[5]

The story was followed by personal details on the executed leaders – Thomas MacDonagh, the husband of Grace's sister Muriel, a father of two, a professor at University College Dublin and a distinguished author; and Sean MacBride, the father of a young son by his 'beautiful rebel wife', Maud Gonne, 'the Irish Joan of Arc'. As the story went to press, a communiqué from Irish command headquarters in Dublin, elicited the sharp headline – 'Connolly shot', followed by the brief statement: 'All the signatories to the Republican Proclamation are now dead'.

If the story of Grace Gifford and Joseph Plunkett was calculated to tug at the heartstrings of the *Journal*'s large female readership, the news of the execution of James Connolly reduced hardened union men to tears. Fifty-four years later, the Dundee poet and political activist, Mary Brooksbank, recalled how her father, Sandy Soutar, wept openly, and that she, who 'didna ken anything', asked him why he was crying for a traitor. At the time Mary was a practising Catholic and relatively non-political, and her views were undoubtedly influenced by the condemnations of the Rising reported in the local press and expressed by the self-appointed representatives of Dundee's Irish-Catholic community. Sandy Soutar, however, who had met Connolly in the early 1890s through his trade union work, knew what he had really been fighting for. As Mary recalled, 'he made me sit down and he sensed me into things'.[6]

A week later, the Royal Commission into the causes of, and responsibility for the Rising revealed that 'the conduct of [it] showed greater organising power and more military skill than had been previously attributed to the Volunteers', who, it was reported, had 'acted with great courage' throughout. Far from it being a case of 'lions led by donkeys' – the phrase later used to contrast the bravery of the British Army foot soldiers who fought in the Imperialist 'Great' War with the incompetency of the military strategists who conducted it – it was a tale of heroism all along the chain of command, as the leaders of the Rising placed themselves on the front lines, for which they paid the ultimate price. Indeed, the inquiry acknowledged that the 'high character' and political idealism of the leaders 'accounted for the sympathy which they excited in a large number of people in Dublin and, in many cases, the country'. Underpinning it all were the 'deeper grounds of passionate national feeling for Ireland and long hatred for England'.[7] The findings of the inquiry, whose proceedings were reported in the local and national press, had a chastening effect on those moderate Irish nationalists who had initially condemned the Rising, and served to encourage their admiration and sympathy, if not overt support, for the 'Sinn Féiners'. On 19 May, the *Courier* reported another unacknowledged fact of the Irish Rebellion, i.e., 'the very prominent part taken in it by women and girls', from the pen of 'a lady who had acted as a Red Cross nurse'.[8] Her apparent knowledge of the Volunteers' manoeuvres, and the detailed information provided on Cumann na mBan (League of Women) activity, however, hints at a close involvement with the latter.

> On Easter Sunday, which was the day first appointed for the Volunteer manoeuvres, the women were also mobilised and ordered to bring rations for a certain period. It was only at the last moment, and for sufficiently dramatic reasons, that the mobilisation of both men and women was cancelled. Those Irish women, who did their work with a cool and reckless courage unsurpassed by any man, were in the firing line from the first to the last day of the rebellion. They were women of all ranks, from titled ladies to shop assistants, and they worked on terms of easy equality, caring nothing, apparently, but for the success of the movement. Many of the women were snipers, and both in the Post Office and in the Imperial Hotel, the present writer, who was a Red Cross nurse, saw women on guard with rifles relieving worn-out Volunteers. Cumann na mBan girls did practically all the despatch carrying…On one occasion on O'Connell Street, I heard a Volunteer captain call for volunteers to take a despatch to Commandant James Connolly under heavy machine gun fire. Every man and woman present sprang forward, and he chose a young Dublin woman, a well-known writer….She shook hands with her commander, and stepped coolly out amid a perfect cross rain of bullets from Trinity College and from the Rotunda end of O'Connell Street. She reached the GPO safely, and I saw Count Plunkett's son, who was the officer on guard, and who has since been shot, come to the front door and wish her good luck, and he shook hands with her before she dashed back to her own

headquarters. This was only one instance, but typical of hundreds that I saw of the part played by women during the fighting week. They did Red Cross work – I saw them going out under the heaviest of fire to bring in wounded Volunteers – they cooked, catered, and brought in supplies; they took food to men under fire at barricades; they visited every Volunteer's home to tell their people of his progress. These women could throw grenades, they understood the use of bombs; in fact, they seemed to understand as much of the business of warfare as men. The girl I have already referred to, and several others who were lucky enough to escape arrest, have shown, I hear, great courage and daring in helping rebels out of the country, destroying papers, and disposing of ammunition in churches. Many girls have been disowned by their families, the majority have lost their work, but the unexpected severity of the sentences…is so inflaming public opinion that men and women who never before would allow even the name of a Sinn Féiner to be mentioned in their presence are openly avowing their sympathy with the Volunteers… Sixty girls were released from Kilmainham prison a few days ago, but others are still imprisoned. Meanwhile, feeling is growing more and more bitter among the working women here in Dublin – they are beginning to make no secret at all of their opinions in spite of threats and cautions…[9]

The account concluded by drawing attention to another unreported feature of the fighting, the involvement of priests 'who rushed to the buildings held by the Volunteers, under the heaviest of fire' to administer to the spiritual needs of the insurgents. If the Red Cross nurse's testimony to the ability of women to participate in the rebellion at every level, and to openly express their opinions, 'in spite of threats or cautions', did anything to inspire women and girls of Irish extraction, the final image of a 'body of bare-headed Volunteers, with Cumann na mBan girls by their sides, kneeling in the firing line while the priest gave them the last absolution of the Roman Catholic Church', was calculated to put the seal of moral approval upon the Rising. Such accounts of self-sacrifice, courage and, in the latter case, piety in the face of brutal repression, served to generate support for physical force Irish nationalism amongst a new generation of Dundee Irishmen and women.

Around this time, hundreds of imprisoned Volunteers were being shipped out from Ireland's overcrowded jails to detention centres in England and Scotland. Of the 197 deported to Scotland on 19 May, the majority had fought under Liam Mellows in Galway from where they were transported, via Dublin, to Glasgow, and split into two batches – one bound for Barlinnie, and the other for Perth. Michael Kelly of the Clarenbridge Volunteer Company, who was in the latter, recalled that, unlike Glasgow, where they were given a good reception, the people at Perth railway station 'thought we were deserters from the British Army and booed us. We returned the boos with a vengeance'.[10] Support was soon forthcoming, however, as visits to the prisoners were being facilitated by local Irish nationalists through the columns of the *Dundee Catholic Herald*.[11]

Unlike Glasgow, where Irish nationalists of all stripes came together to form a branch of the Irish Prisoners' Aid Committee, which maintained contact with the prisoners' friends and relatives at home, there is no record of a similar structure being formed in Dundee.[12] There was little time to forge relationships, anyway. Indeed, a network of sympathetic Irish nationalists linking up with imprisoned Irish rebels was the last thing the government wanted. Moreover, the existence of large numbers of Irish prisoners who had agitated for Political Status and obtained it, gave the lie to the claim that 'only an insignificant fraction of Ireland favoured the Rising', and undermined the attempts of the British government to justify its continuing repression.[13] Thus, one month into their imprisonment, a number of prisoners were released – Daniel Kearns of the Kilcornan Irish Volunteer Company, County Galway, recalled he was released from Perth without questioning of any kind, and was back home by the end of June.[14] The remainder were transferred to the isolated setting of Frongoch internment camp in North Wales, where the number was further whittled down, by the Sankey Committee, from 2,000 to around 500 men, who, if not hardened revolutionary soldiers when they arrived, were, by the time they were released in December.[15] On the whole, the Irish prisoners in Perth and most other Scottish and English prisons, with the exception of Knutsford in Cheshire, testified to being 'reasonably well-treated', and contrasted their treatment with that of conscientious objectors for whom they had a genuine sympathy.[16] Of his experience at Wandsworth Detention Barracks, where a large percentage of conscientious objectors, including the aforementioned Dundee socialist David Nairn, were incarcerated, Joseph Lawless, Lieutenant of the Swords Company, Dublin, recalled:

> We heard the Conshies...being put through a gruelling course of squad drill in the exercise yard outside our cells, the NCOs in charge fairly revelling in the sadistic joy of making lives an "appropriate hell" for those poor beggars...On the other hand, we found the prison staff of Wandsworth quite decent to us, perhaps because they looked upon us as fighters, however misguided; and, as such, superior to 'conscientious objectors', who professing repugnance to fighting in any shape or form, they looked upon and spoke of with contempt.[17]

Frank Hardiman of Galway recalled, 'we were getting very concerned with the brutal treatment they were getting...we could hear their cries and moans every night, and we were determined to make the matter known outside'. Finally, when some of his comrades reported seeing a conscientious objector 'stretched on the floor of his cell apparently dead', Hardiman arranged to have a witness statement smuggled out of the prison which led to the matter being raised in Parliament, and to the commander responsible, Lieutenant-Colonel Reginald Brooke, being removed from his post.[18]

While the witness statements given to the Bureau of Military History reveal much about the Irish prisoners' impressions of the conscientious objectors, little information survives of the attitudes of the conscientious objectors towards the Irish POWS or the rebellion in Ireland.[19] Even Bob Stewart, who alongside Ewan Geddes Carr was the most frequently imprisoned of Dundee's conscientious objectors, failed to mention the subject in his memoirs. Arguably, by the time Stewart commenced his first period of detention in July 1916, the Irish prisoners had already been transferred to Frongoch.[20]

On 7 July, 24-year-old calender worker, Edward Clarke, of 7 Annfield Row, Dundee, appeared before the local military tribunal in the same batch of conscientious objectors which included Bob Stewart, then

Secretary of the Scottish Horse and Motormen's Association, trade union organiser Alexander 'Sandy' Ross and Ewan Carr of the ILP – all established socialists and anti-conscription campaigners. Clarke's anti-war stance, however, was of a more recent standing.[21] As a calender worker, Clarke may have been influenced by the open-air Sunday meetings of the Joint Committee Against Conscription, which was supported by all sections of the labour movement. However, as a possible descendant of the Cavan Clarkes who had helped to found the National Brotherhood of St Patrick in Dundee, or of James Clarke who had participated in the aborted Fenian rising in January 1866, it may be that reports of the Easter Rising, the accounts of the courage and idealism of its protagonists, and the executions of its leaders, had stirred his patriotic conscience and inspired to him to commit his own individual act of principle.[22] After his case was dismissed, Clarke appealed, judiciously, on grounds that he was a socialist and a Roman Catholic with which latter argument he had better luck – the tribunal deemed his conscientious objections to be genuine and granted him a conditional exemption.[23] It is also possible that one of the members of the tribunal, Nicholas Marra, himself a devout Catholic who had chosen the path of labour politics over the conservative nationalism of the UIL, and whose wife, Mary, was a descendant of the Cavan Clarkes, may have helped influence the result by coaching Clarke in a winning defence.[24]

Whether support for the Rising was an unspoken factor is unknown. Although a number of people in the socialist and labour movement, particularly those of Irish extraction, privately expressed support for the Rising, they were wary of doing so publicly.[25] The Dundee Irish were regarded as an integral part of the local community – from the middle of the nineteenth century the city's industrial economy had been dependent on a large Irish labour force, and the town's employers, politicians and press had been careful to promote a civic ethos of religious tolerance and cultural harmony. Nevertheless, while the Irish in Dundee enjoyed a greater level of acceptance than their compatriots in other Scottish cities, they were also aware that anti-Irish prejudice was an intrinsic part of Scottish society, and that attitudes could sharply shift in times of crisis. Public opinion could be manipulated to political ends, and, in the midst of engaging the population in a world war to protect its imperial interests, it was in the interests of the British establishment to portray the protagonists of the Easter Rising as a misguided minority who – as the ongoing trial of Roger Casement endeavoured to prove – had actively colluded with the German 'enemy'. Unless forced to question it (as the young Mary Soutar was), it was a line of propaganda the majority of the population were inclined to accept. Thus, while Irish-Catholic socialists such as Edward Clarke may have deemed it expedient to defer to Papal authority to escape fighting in England's war, they may have thought twice about declaring openly for Ireland's one.

The formation of a new coalition government in December 1916 saw the release of the Irish internees, which apparent act of 'good faith' led the Irish Parliamentary Party to believe that the government would support their vote to implement the Home Rule Act. Their hopes were dashed on 7 March 1917 when Lloyd George declared that any 'attempt to settle a question which would provoke civil disturbance in one part of the United Kingdom, and rend in twain, perhaps, the whole of the United Kingdom into two warring factions [was] unthinkable in the middle of a great war', to which the Irish MPs responded by walking out amidst a bitter exchange of words.[26] The mood was equally bitter at a protest meeting called by the Dundee UIL, whose President Frank O'Rourke refuted Lloyd George's proviso that before Home Rule could be implemented 'the Irish people would have to be as one, without one discordant note'. Such a case never existed in the case of any nation struggling for freedom,' O'Rourke declared, 'and if such conditions had to exist before freedom was granted, then all the blood shed over the world today would be in vain'. Despite the failure of the IPP to force the government's hand, the meeting pledged their 'continued and increased support' for them 'in whatever action they think necessary' until Home Rule was established.[27]

While the UIL did not speak for the breadth of Irish political opinion, at this stage most people were oblivious to the growing support for physical force nationalism in Ireland, which escalated after the East Clare by-election in July 1917, when Sinn Féin candidate Éamon de Valera trounced his IPP rival, and intensified after the death of Thomas Ashe on 25 September as a result of force-feeding on hunger strike. 1917 was also a period of extensive military reorganisation as the IRB was reconstituted, and the Volunteers regrouped, retrained and 'brought up to a pitch of enthusiasm'. There remained one major problem. Joseph Hood, a London-born Rising veteran who had returned to Ireland after his imprisonment to assist in the task, recalled, 'The few arms we had had been taken from us in 1916...We wanted arms first, last and all the time, and I think that only Mick Collins saw this clearly'.[28]

As the government poised themselves to impose conscription in Ireland in April 1918, the need to obtain the necessary material with which to mount a campaign of resistance if required, became urgent. At this stage, Collins was attempting to co-ordinate small streams of arms coming in from Scotland via various groups of Volunteers, IRB men, Cumann na mBan activists, and other sympathisers. While such operations were proving to be a valuable source of much-needed arms, their organisation was loose and chaotic. Some members of the Republican movement, it seems, were still uncomfortable with handling guns and explosives. Jean Quinn, the then sixteen-year-old Treasurer of the James Connolly Sinn Féin cumann, Glasgow, recalled how she first became involved in the business of gunrunning in the autumn of 1916:

> A number of young men [brought] a quantity of explosives into the hall. Certain members of the cumann who professed to be opposed to physical force objected, and I offered to keep it as I had a [furniture] store quite near. After that it became quite common for stuff to be sent to me.[29]

It was into this store that stepped Dundee's most prolific gunrunner, Lena McDonald, in the company of Irish Volunteer officer, Sean O'Doherty, in the late spring of 1918. By this time, the anti-conscription campaign in Ireland had given way to the 'German Plot', as the British government, forced to back down on compulsory enlistment in the face of mass opposition, ordered the arrest and imprisonment of leading Republicans on spurious allegations of conspiring with the German military to initiate another insurrection. The conscription crisis marked a turning point in the Irish struggle for independence as the desire for active resistance was manifested in a dramatic surge in membership for the Irish Volunteers and Sinn Féin. This had a motivating effect on Irish Republicans in Scotland – in Glasgow, a second branch of the Cumann na mBan (the Ethna Carbery) was formed in April. It was also around this time that a new, younger generation of Dundee-based activists came to the fore.

While Lena came from a longstanding Republican family, little is known of O'Doherty's background beyond the fact that he was born in January/February 1900 in Clara, County Offaly, and at the time of his arrest in April 1921, he was living at 101 Rosebery Street, Lochee, with his mother Mary, and working as a clerk for the Irish National Insurance Company. Three of his brothers had enlisted in the British Army at some point – possibly in Ireland – two of whom were killed in the war. Whether they had been encouraged by Redmond's call to patriotic Irishmen to show their loyalty by supporting the British war effort, and whether their deaths informed their younger brother's Irish Republican turn is not known.

The IPP's policy came back to haunt them at the end of the war when it was revealed that, from August 1914 to the signing of the Armistice on 11 November 1918, more than 8,000 Dundee Irishmen had joined the colours, at least 1,500 of whom had given up their lives.[30] Even taking Dundee's high recruitment rate into account – figures provided by Chief Recruitment Officer Major Cappon stated that a total of 35,500 men from the district had enlisted, 4,000 of whom had 'made the supreme sacrifice' – the disproportionately high number of 'Irish' casualties may have served to heighten the sense of guilt within the Irish community, in addition to their having misjudged the Easter Rising, at having supported the wrong war.[31]

The painful reality hit home as soldiers returning from the war, and the grieving relatives of others who didn't, were confronted with the fact that all their suffering and sacrifice had brought Ireland no closer to achieving self-government. In the run up to the General Election on 14 December, even Dundee's Irish Party Loyalists were spurning their old allies in the Liberal Party for non-Coupon, i.e., coalition government-endorsed, candidates. At a specially convened meeting of the Dundee UIL in the Forester's Hall, Neddy Scrymgeour, who was standing on a Prohibitionist/Labour ticket, stated that sitting MP Winston Churchill 'had been identified with a Home Rule scheme which was to operate in all parts of the country' (including Scotland), but had now 'withered up', then proceeded to dismiss Churchill's running mate, Alexander Wilkie – 'something of a Coalition and something of a Labour candidate' – as a fraud – 'they couldn't have much confidence in a party which adopted such a man'.[32] Scrymgeour was duly endorsed along with local trade unionist and unequivocal Labour candidate, James Sunney Brown, who, at an open meeting in the YMCA called by the UIL, pronounced it a 'scandal that Ireland hadn't had Home Rule many years ago', adding, pointedly, 'There were persons who had interests, and their interests were to keep the Irish people separate'.[33] These interests were, of course, British economic and imperial ones – and, at two meetings the previous night, Churchill had added Scotland to the mix when he put it to his audience:

> Is it not a pity that Ireland had not been able to throw in her lot, squarely and wholeheartedly, with the British Empire in the same way as Scotland, which had taken a leading and prominent part, had?

He continued:

> Six months before the war, the Liberal administration had reached an agreement with the leaders of the Nationalist Party that Ulster would not be forced into a Home Rule Parliament until she was ready and ripe for it. It was on that basis alone that [the government] had said [it] would force the Home Rule Bill through the House of Commons. In the middle of the war a disastrous rebellion [had broken] out in Dublin, a wild Sinn Féin movement [had] swept over Ireland and the demands they made went far beyond anything the British Government had ever been invited seriously to consider.[34]

Maintaining that it was 'only the disputes of Irishmen that prevented an effective solution to the question', Churchill concluded by inviting his audience to 'hope and pray that they [Irishmen] would endeavour to prepare the way so that Ireland was no longer the sick child of the Empire'.[35]

The Irish people did exactly that but not in the way that Churchill had hoped. While his appeals to British patriotic sentiment, aided by a supportive press, helped Churchill to retain his seat for the fourth and final time, and Wilkie for the third, the General Election saw the IPP swept aside in a landslide victory for Sinn Féin, giving a popular mandate to the ideals of the Republican Proclamation of Easter 1916, which was ratified at the inaugural meeting of Dáil Éireann on 21 January 1919. On the same day, the shooting dead of two RIC officers escorting a consignment of explosives at Soloheadbeg, South Tipperary, by Volunteers of the 3rd Tipperary Brigade set in course a chain of events which developed into a full-scale guerrilla war against British rule in Ireland.[36] In turn, this stimulated a new wave of activity across the Irish diaspora, and, in Dundee especially, the most energetic involvement in physical force republicanism since the Fenian campaign of 1860s, and the greatest manifestation of Irish solidarity since the Land League.

II

If the Rising of 1916 served its purpose of awakening the national consciousness of the Irish in Ireland, it also served to reinvigorate the national movement and its supporters abroad to the extent that passive support quickly developed into a desire for active involvement. However, as historian of the Irish in modern Scotland, James E Handley noted, 'it was not until guerrilla fighting broke out in Ireland that sympathisers in Scotland had the opportunity of rendering active service'.[37] Nevertheless, while the most committed of sympathisers were prepared 'to go to Ireland if called upon', orders dictated that 'Arms and Money – not men, were the pressing need'.[38] With this in mind, the IRA Executive, with Michael Collins at the helm, imposed an organisational structure on the Republican movement in Scotland in which the political and military worked sympathetically towards the same goal.

Sinn Féin

On the political front, Sinn Féin provided an open and legal network through which to rally support, conduct political propaganda, raise funds, and recruit for the IRA. In 1918, Sean (Jack) O'Sheehan, of the Sinn Féin Ard Comhairle was appointed organiser for Scotland. Under his energetic stewardship, Sinn Féin in Scotland expanded from one central club, the James Connolly in Glasgow, to 75 by the end of 1919. O'Sheehan eventually turned up in Dundee on 18 July 1920 to find a 2,000-strong audience, including a large delegation from Lochgelly, Kelty and Lochore, waiting expectantly in the Savoy Picture House in the Nethergate. The *Dundee Advertiser*, which described the meeting as one of the largest meetings of the Dundee Irish in recent years, noted that several hundreds were turned away. Despite the preponderance of flag waving, O'Sheehan announced his intention to forego the customary patriotic speech for 'dry facts', and reeled off examples of atrocities committed by the Black and Tans, Sinn Féin's achievements in the local government elections, and statistics on the National Loan (which was oversubscribed by £50,000) and the Land Bank (which enabled people to buy the small patches of land they farmed).[39] O'Sheehan stated that Sinn Féin had one aim – the international recognition of an independent Republic, after which it would cease to exist and the people would decide. There should also be, he added, self-determination for Scotland. Application forms were then handed round, a large number of which were returned signed.[40]

The Dundee Sinn Féin cumann was duly established, in the name of The O'Rahilly, who had been killed leading the evacuation of the GPO in Dublin on 28 April 1916. The choice was significant for more than one reason. As well as being Director of Arms of the Irish Volunteers, which he had helped to found, and co-ordinator of the Howth gunrunning operation of 1914, Michael Joseph O'Rahilly was also an enthusiastic genealogist who had traced his ancestors back to County Cavan and to the medieval Irish kingdom of East Breifne of which the Ó Rathailles were overlords. It was from here and from the surrounding counties of South West Ulster and North East Connacht that the majority of the Dundee's Irish population also originated.[41] Whether this influenced the decision to name the O'Rahilly cumann thus is unknown; regardless, within two months of its establishment, membership of it had reached 900, making it the second largest Sinn Féin cumann in Scotland after the Roger Casement in Greenock.[42]

By contrast, the UIL had shrunk to a rump. The Sarsfield and Father Matthew branches of the Irish National Foresters had disappeared altogether, and one person, Bernard McLaughlin, straddled the post of Secretary in the one surviving (William O'Brien) INF branch and the UIL. The Ancient Order of Hibernians continued to hold regular meetings. However, there had been little change in its office bearers since the start of the war. While some may have gone over to Sinn Féin, the majority of the cumann's members and supporters were of a new generation, and a large number of them were women.

On 19 September, a follow up meeting hosted by the O'Rahilly cumann attracted well over 2,000 people who filled the banner-bedecked Foresters' Hall and another smaller hall, leaving a large overspill on the street. The speakers were Sean O'Sheehan and Sinn Féin executive member Sean Milroy, to whom the *Advertiser* gave the distinction of having been a fellow-prisoner of the President of the Irish Republic, Éamon de Valera (in Lincoln Jail). O'Sheehan stated he was there to set the record straight about 'the campaign of tyranny, terrorism, murder and misrepresentation [by which the British government] meant to crush the national spirit'. 'The Irish nation will never be crushed', he added, predicting that if the hunger-striking Lord Mayor of Cork, Terence MacSwiney, was allowed to die it would create 'at least 100,000 more supporters of Sinn Féin in Ireland'. 'Sinn Féin', he declared, was simply 'fighting for what Lloyd George declared Britain went to war for – freedom of self-determination for all nations'. The audience clearly agreed – the *Advertiser* reported that all of O'Sheehan's points were 'loudly applauded and at times the proceedings were wildly enthusiastic'. On behalf of the branch, Chairman, Edward Fletcher, handed over £100 to go to Sinn Féin Head Quarters in Dublin, plus another £50 to prisoners' dependants, whereupon O'Sheehan and Milroy moved out into the street and, from the top of a taxi cab, repeated their message to a large, predominantly female, crowd.[43]

Around this time, the condition of MacSwiney, who had been on hunger strike in Brixton Prison since 13 August, was attracting international attention and eliciting widespread condemnation of the British government's refusal to grant any concessions. Issues concerning the morality of the hunger strike were also stimulating debate in theological circles. Early in September, celebrity theologian Father Bernard Vaughan, who had secured himself a reputation as a spiritual advisor to the English Catholic elite, opined, 'I should not feel entitled to administer the last rites of the Church to anyone, no matter what his nationality, who was deliberately dying of hunger-striking'.[44] When Vaughan admitted that 'other theologians far more learned [could] reverse my opinion', the young curate of St Andrew's Pro-Cathedral, Dundee, Father John Fahy, grasped the opportunity to bring him to task:

Father Vaughan S.J., at this opportune time, has done his bit to salve the conscience of the British Government by his condemnation of the morality of hunger-striking. I hereby challenge him to meet me in any place to apply the principles to the practical case of the moment, that of the Lord Mayor of Cork. I hold that the action of the Lord Mayor of Cork is not only moral but heroically moral.[45]

A 27-year-old curate barely a year into his first post was probably not the theological mind Father Vaughan had envisioned. However, the views expressed by Father Fahy were more representative of the working-class community he served, and, as MacSwiney's hunger strike progressed, of wider popular opinion.

The death of MacSwiney on Monday, 25 October, after a 74-day hunger strike, produced a huge surge in support for the Irish cause as demonstrations of public sympathy were held in every centre of Irish population across the world. Dundee Sinn Féin immediately fired off a telegram to Lloyd George, branding him and his government 'murderers and arrant cowards [who had] earned the disgust of all Dundee lovers of freedom' and pledging that 'MacSwiney shall be avenged'.[46] The following Wednesday, a delegation from the O'Rahilly Sinn Féin cumann was granted permission to hold a public procession to pay tribute to their fallen comrade on the understanding that there would be no banners bearing political sentiments and no 'party airs'.[47] Shortly before noon on Friday, 29 October, a crowd of 2,000 (a conservative estimate by the local press) gathered at Albert Square and marched solemnly, to the sombre accompaniment of the St Joseph's brass band playing 'The Dead March' from Saul and 'The Flo'ers o' the Forest', up Blackness Road to St Joseph's Church in Wilkie's Lane where a Requiem Mass was celebrated. Both the *Advertiser* and the *Courier* noted that a significant feature of the procession was that the vast majority (approximately three-quarters) were women.[48] The Mass was celebrated by the 26-year-old curate of St Joseph's, Father Richard Durand of County Waterford, assisted by deacons Father Thomas O'Shea and Father Patrick Donagher. Overseeing it all, as Master of Ceremonies, was Father John Fahy.[49]

Father John Fahy

John Fahy was born on 14 June 1893 in Loughrea, County Galway, a part of Ireland that had been at the forefront of resistance during the Land War. His father had been active in the Land League, and Fahy's biographer notes that 'land, religion and nationalism... were woven into almost every facet of his daily existence [that] he considered them to be so inextricably linked as to be indivisible'.[50] The link between religion and nationalism was much in evidence at Maynooth College where the young John Fahy encouraged his fellow seminarians to take an active part in the insurrection of Easter Week of 1916. By the time he took up his first post, at St Joseph's Church in the Diocese of Dunkeld in the autumn of 1919, Father Fahy was already fully committed to the ideals of the Irish Republic. It is of fundamental significance to the history of Irish republicanism in Dundee that Fahy's two years in the city coincided with the most intense period of political resistance in modern Irish history.

The parish of St Joseph's covered the Scouringburn (re-named Brook Street in 1907)/Hawkhill/Blackness area, which, more than half a century after the post-famine immigration of the mid-nineteenth century, remained one of the most densely packed 'Irish' neighbourhoods in the city. Indeed, conditions were amongst the worst in the country, with Dundee having the highest percentage of one- and two-roomed houses in Scotland, several cases of multiple families living in one dwelling, and persistently high rates of infant mortality – a situation that prevailed up until the 1930s.[51] In 1920, Father Fahy was appointed curate of St Andrew's Pro-Cathedral, half a mile down the road, which took in much of the same community, a large percentage of whom were low-waged textile workers employed in an industry which was in terminal decline and beset by growing post-war unemployment.

Father Fahy's affinity with the dispossessed had its origins in his native Galway; nevertheless, while the rural experience of rentier landlordism and evictions may have differed slightly from that of the urban slum dweller, the issue of land ownership and living conditions was one to which he was keenly attuned. Moreover, his intimate knowledge of the economic hardships and domestic tribulations of his parishioners, and his position of trust in the wider Catholic community, put him in an ideal position to motivate and organise a diffuse Irish immigrant population of up to three generations' remove.

Father Fahy, however, wore many other hats in addition to his priest's biretta. His oratorical and organisational skills, as well as his commitment to the Irish Republican cause, ably qualified him as a propagandist for Sinn Féin. He was also a member of the IRA, in which he performed the dual roles of chaplain and captain of the 4th Battalion (Dundee) Company of the Scottish Brigade. Fahy also established links with sympathetic groups and individuals, including Communist Bob Stewart, who had served four jail sentences for refusing military service in the First World War. Stewart later recounted his version of a 'famous Dundee story' where Father Fahy upbraided a group of Black Watch soldiers in his congregation for serving in the British Imperial Army and advised them to be true patriots and fight for Ireland. Stewart claimed that Fahy was later 'carpeted' by his Bishop for the incident.[52]

While there is little evidence of droves of Dundonians, or Scots in general, queuing up to join either the British Army or the more financially lucrative Black and Tans or Auxiliaries, high unemployment, short time and low wages prompted a number of young Dundee men, including those from the Irish-Catholic community, to take the King's shilling.[53] Here the story of one St Andrew's parishioners is illustrative. Peter Taylor, who lived in Session Street in the West Port, joined the British Army in 1919 when he was around eighteen years old. He was stationed in Dublin where, on one of his regular perambulations around the city, he stopped to ask some barrow-women why the buildings were in such a ruinous state, whereupon they told him about the events of Easter 1916, of which he was barely aware. After being invalided out of the army shortly afterwards – for a non-combative injury caused by tripping over a tent peg – he returned to his home parish of St Andrew's in Dundee, joining Sinn Féin shortly after. Whether Father Fahy's influence was a factor in his realignment is unclear but, given that Taylor was aware of events in Ireland and susceptible to priestly influence, it is not unlikely.

While Father Fahy's active involvement in Irish Republican politics may have vexed his Bishop, the Glasgow-born prelate, John Toner, was not altogether unsympathetic to the nationalist ideals which motivated it.[54] In March 1921, Bishop Toner was happy to welcome the controversial Archbishop of Melbourne, Daniel Mannix, to the city, and to host him at his house at 29 Roseangle. However, Fahy's immediate superior and

CHAPTER 7 – REVOLUTION 1916–23

Toner's right-hand man, the similarly named Vicar-General of the Diocese, John Turner, appears to have been a more effective ally. Indeed, when it came to supporting the beleaguered Irish (and Scottish) working class, Turner had no mean record himself. In April 1890, he had celebrated the marriage of James Connolly and Lillie Reynolds when the Archbishop of Edinburgh threatened to deny the sacraments to radical Irish activists. Bob Stewart also recalled how Turner's indefatigability and even-handedness in distributing relief during the unemployment crisis of 1908 had put the mealy-mouthed administrators of the local relief fund to shame.[55] Monsignor Turner appears to have recognised similar traits in the young Father Fahy, and to have identified his political beliefs, as well as his religious faith, as a driving factor. Indeed, at a function to mark Fahy's farewell to Dundee in June 1922, Turner described him as 'a holy and saintly priest' and 'a great patriot' comparable to Archbishop Daniel Mannix.[56]

Indeed, Father Fahy's role in the visit of the Cork-born Irish Republican Archbishop of Melbourne to Dundee in March 1921 brought considerable kudos to the Catholic Church and undoubtedly increased its standing in the city. Banned from Ireland and blocked from Glasgow, it fell to Sinn Féin organisational genius Sean O'Sheehan to direct a Scottish tour which circumvented the Glasgow ban by diverting supporters to the Coatbridge suburb of Whifflet, where 50,000 supporters poured in from all parts of the Clyde Valley, and brought huge numbers of people to Dalmuir, Dumbarton, Greenock, and Cowdenbeath, where 4,000 people gathered in and around the main hall which the authorities had given over for the occasion.[57] The authorities of Edinburgh and especially Dundee, where the tour concluded, proved to be equally hospitable.

The final meeting in Dundee was, arguably, the most dramatic and politically significant one. In the late afternoon of Tuesday, 8 March 1921, Archbishop Mannix detrained at the village of Longforgan, six miles west of Dundee, where he was met by a fleet of eight cars containing members of the Catholic clergy and Dundee Sinn Féin. The welcoming procession was choreographed to maximum effect. Shortly after 6 pm, the cars set off for Dundee, where an enthusiastic crowd had been gathering for over an hour in the cold March evening. The Archbishop's car, which contained his secretary, Father Moylan, Bishop William Cotter of Portsmouth, and Father Fahy, rolled up at the foot of Blackness Avenue to be greeted by 400 torchbearers and a crowd, the magnitude of which confounded the *Dundee Courier* who settled for the safe but ambiguous estimate of 'several thousands'. However, the reporter was in no doubt that the majority were women, hundreds of whom carried the flag of the Irish Republic. A brass band led off, followed by a hundred of the torchbearers, then the convoy of cars, followed by the main body of the march, accompanied by the remaining 300 torchbearers. The procession snaked through the streets of St Joseph's and St Andrew's parishes – along Hawkhill, up Peddie Street, down Blackness Road, along Brook Street and the West Port, through North Tay Street, Reform Street and the Nethergate in the city centre, then up the Perth Road, and down Roseangle, coming to a halt at the Bishop's residence by the corner of Westfield Place. The procession was ten miles in length, and the *Courier*, not renowned for its sympathy for Irish republicanism or the Catholic faith, noted that it took a full hour to pass. Crowds of four to five feet deep lined the entire route, and every window and vantage point was occupied. In hundreds of these windows, rows of candles had been placed. A snow storm, rather than dampening the enthusiasm of the spectators, added to the picturesqueness of the scene. The *Courier* noted 'the spontaneous goodwill of the enthusiastic crowd as they surged through the streets', and even the arch-Republican Archbishop – who by this time was undoubtedly accustomed to extreme responses – seemed taken aback. At Westfield Place, Mannix alighted to massive cheers and proceeded to bless the O'Rahilly cumann's banner, which 'came within an ace of being burnt' as the enthusiastic torchbearers surged forward to witness the act.[58]

The event was a propaganda coup for Sinn Féin, helping to consolidate existing support and transform faint hearts into rebel ones. Sinn Féin may also have drawn some financial benefit from the admission charges to two well-attended public meetings at the Foresters' Hall (2s 6d) and the Marist Brothers' grounds in Forebank Road (1s). The following evening, over 2,000 people packed into the grounds of the latter which, according to the *Dundee Advertiser*, took on a 'fairy-like' aspect, as long lines of electric light bulbs illuminated Irish Republican flags that floated from the glistening trees, the surrounding buildings, and above the audience, along with several shamrock-decorated banners bearing the words 'Ceud Mile Failte'. After a 'great ovation' and an appropriately politic introduction from Monsignor Turner, the Archbishop commenced his well-practised condemnation of the British government, which, he declared had gone to war against Germany on the pretext of freedom for all nations but had responded to Irish aspirations for freedom by sending in the Black and Tans who better befitted the epithet of 'murder gang' than the Honourable Member for Dundee was wont to apply to the IRA. On the latter point, Mannix deployed his considerable rhetorical powers to remind his audience of their political obligations. While thanking 'Juteland' for the magnificent reception it had accorded him, he continued:

> Unfortunately, Dundee has a large measure of responsibility for the ban that was put upon movements[59]. Dundee has not merely a Parliamentary representative, but it has the honour or the dishonour of having its representative in the present Black and Tan Coalition Government. Dundee ought to have a very different type of representative. If the people of Dundee consult their own interests and the interests of Dundee, they would find somebody who would be in closer touch with the people of Dundee.[60]

By conflating the Parliamentary constituency with the community of Dundee, which he named no less than six times, Mannix drove his message home – the electorate of Dundee were in a key position in to score a direct hit at the British government by taking out one of its key players, the progenitor of the Black and Tans himself, Winston Churchill.

While Mannix has been credited with turning Dundee-Irish opinion against Churchill, opinion in the city had been turning long before. A significant number of communists in the city had always been opposed to Churchill's politics, as had the Labour movement, who were now in a better position to field a candidate against him. By 1921, Dundee City councillors deemed Churchill to be 'foreign', i.e., a non-local, upper-class carpetbagger who had calculatedly used his Dundee constituency as a launching pad for his lofty political ambitions. In many of these aspects, the opinions of Dundonians were the opinions of the Dundee-Irish. Moreover, the executions of the 1916 leaders, the Liberal Coalition's backsliding on Home Rule, and the deployment of the Black and Tans, had already transformed Dundee-Irish opinion, added to which Archbishop Mannix's moral counsel to vote him out, served to provide the imprimatur of Catholic Church.

The death of MacSwiney, followed on 1 November by the execution of 18-year-old student, Kevin Barry, after earnest hopes of a last-minute reprieve, had already put paid to any notions that the British government might respond to moral persuasion. Earlier in September Sean O'Sheehan had predicted that if MacSwiney died, the result would be 'at least 100,000 more supporters of Sinn Féin in Ireland.' Within two days of MacSwiney's death, the membership of Dundee Sinn Féin Club was reported to have risen to 1,500.[61]

The Irish Republican Army

As noted earlier, the Sinn Féin Clubs were the key conduit through which the IRA in Scotland recruited, and the stark increase in membership in both organisations, was largely motivated by a growing support for physical force republicanism in the wake of MacSwiney's death. In Dublin, Michael Collins, Adjutant-General and Director of Intelligence, understood the need to prepare for all eventualities, hence the importance of establishing a military command structure should the need arise for back-up. To this end, Joe Vize had been dispatched from Dublin in 1919 to tighten up the military organisation, much as O'Sheehan had built up the Sinn Féin Clubs. By 1920, the Scottish Brigade of the IRA was organised into five battalions which comprised 24 companies. Dundee, in the 4th Battalion, was amongst the last areas to be integrated into the newly restructured Scottish command, although, as evidence of existing volunteer activity and the speed of recruitment indicates, the organisation was substantially in place. The 4th Battalion area also covered Fife, which was also allotted to the 3rd (Edinburgh) Battalion.

While many young rebel hearts may have possessed a desire to join the fighting in Ireland, the primary role of the IRA in Scotland remained, as stipulated by Collins, the procurement and trafficking of arms, and it was here that most energy was directed. In spite of the formal structure, however, the practicalities of arms trafficking often involved members of different battalions and companies working across divisional areas with the cooperation of individuals outside the army command.

It has been frequently acknowledged that in the period between 1919 and 1921, Scotland contributed more in the way of material aid to the Irish liberation struggle than any other country.[62] It has also been suggested (though less widely acknowledged) that, per head of population, Dundee procured more arms than any other town in Scotland.[63] Appropriately, given its reputation as a 'woman's' town, the most prolific gun runner in the city was a woman operating with other women. Her story, their story, is both illustrative and illuminating.

The McDonald Women

In terms of ethnicity, class and gender, Mary Helen McDonald fits the profile of a typical early twentieth-century Dundonian. Lena, as she later became known, was born on 11 November 1897 at 8 East Henderson's Wynd, the home of her maternal grandmother. Her mother, Helen, born in 1869, was the eighth and youngest child of Bridget Higgins (née Tighe), the daughter of Sligo stonemason Thomas Tighe, and Margaret Collins; her carpet weaver husband, Patrick, was the son of Donegal farmer, John Higgins, and Agnes Golden. In the wake of An Gorta Mór, Bridget and Patrick emigrated to Dundee, where they met, married and set up home in East Henderson's Wynd in the heart of the rapidly-growing Irish community. The address is significant. As demonstrated in Chapter 2, 8 East Henderson's Wynd had been the headquarters of the West Port branch of the National Brotherhood of St Patrick in the early 1860s, which organisation was a recruiting ground for the IRB, and there is strong evidence that Patrick was involved from the start.

As the youngest of the eight siblings, Helen appears to have inherited her father's advanced nationalist views, which she in turn transmitted to her two daughters. Patrick died of chronic bronchitis in 1890, at the approximate age of 61.[64] Two years later, in November 1893, Helen married Peter McDonald, a groom/coach driver of Irish-Scots parentage – Edward McDonald of King's County (County Offaly) and Mary Mitchell of Dundee. Their first child, Catherine Ann (later known as Cathy), was born on 13 September 1893, followed by Lena just over four years later. The marriage did not last, and by 1901 Helen was back living with her elderly mother and two middle-aged sisters, Margaret and Mary, at 8 East Henderson's Wynd.[65] It was here that Cathy and Lena were brought up in an all-female household headed by Bridget, who looked after the girls while their mother and aunts went out to work as a charwoman and jute winders respectively. Cathy and Lena later attributed their Republican ideals to the influence of their grandfather. However, as Patrick died before they were born, the influence was more likely a posthumous one filtered through Bridget's reminiscences of her husband's Fenian past and Ireland's troubled history, reinforced by Helen and her sisters. In the final years of her life, Bridget suffered from dementia, and Helen, by then a midwife, appears to have acted as her primary carer, assisted by the girls, which possibly influenced their decision to become nurses and, ultimately, to specialise in midwifery. Bridget died in 1915, at the (under) estimated age of 83, by which time Cathy and Lena had acquired a strong sense of duty and Irish identity.[66] A 'family holiday' to Ireland followed from which they appear to have returned fully committed rebels, for not long afterwards, they aligned themselves with the Irish Volunteers.[67]

Little is known of the Irish Volunteers in Dundee at this time. However, by early 1918, a small Company existed actively engaged in the procurement and transportation of arms. By now, the McDonalds had moved to a property at 31 Brook Street owned by pawnbroker, James Farrell, who also owned the shop below which Helen and Cathy managed, possibly in lieu of rent. Helen also took on a greengrocer's business opposite managed by Lena. From these premises the three women formed a cottage industry which incorporated the funding, procurement, storage and transportation of arms and ammunition.

The operation had another more covert source of funding which came to light some years later when one Thomas Dempsey appeared in Dundee Sheriff Court on longstanding charges of illicit stilling. Dempsey, who, despite his obvious Irish identity and Glasgow base, was described characteristically in the local press as a Dundee labourer, had been arrested in Glasgow on the night of 12-13 June 1926, fifteen months after the discovery, at his former address at 58 Brook Street, Dundee, of three stills, several gallons of 'wash', a recipe for making whisky, and various receptacles containing spirits, low wines and spirit colouring. He pled guilty, citing in mitigation his circumstances at the time – he had broken his collarbone, was unemployed, and had four children and a pregnant wife to support. Things were 'very bad', and had it not been for 'a certain lady and her two daughters' coming to his aid, he did not know what he would have done. Dempsey was ordered to pay £30 (which he was unable to to) or serve 60 days in prison. Fifty days later, Dempsey again appeared in court this time charged with illegal possession of a rifle, three revolvers and 31 rounds of ammunition which investigating customs officers had found in a deeper search of the flat. Dempsey – who, unbeknownst to his interrogators, was Commanding Officer of the No 2 Scottish Brigade of the IRA and of the 1st (Dundee and Fife) Battalion during the Civil War – 'speculated' that the firearms had likely been gathered for the purpose of going to Ireland when 'the trouble was on', and had been dumped at his house as it was 'convenient'. He, however, stated that had not been living there at the time and was unaware of their presence. At any rate, he had no use for them now. In view of Dempsey's previous time in prison and the explanation given, Sheriff-Substitute W H Blyth-Martin took a 'lenient view' and imposed a fine of £5 (which Dempsey still couldn't pay) or another twenty days in jail. On this occasion he did not mention the lady and her daughters, but one suspects the authorities had already made the connection.[68]

With money provided by Helen's businesses, Cathy and Lena began purchasing munitions, initially from pawnbrokers, second-hand shops and private individuals. Later, their sources expanded to include soldiers stationed at the nearby Dudhope Barracks, Broughty Castle, and the army camp at Barry Buddon. Lena proved particularly adept at locating material, identifying sympathetic contacts and, subsequently, as a student nurse, gaining the trust of people across social and professional barriers. One of her most useful contacts, a medical doctor who was also a Major in the British Army, freely supplied her with large quantities of guns and ammunition from the stores of the Officers' Club, as well as signing her off nightshift duty when it clashed with military operations.

The initiative, productivity and discretion of the McDonald women was quickly noted by senior officers in Dundee and Glasgow who appear to have incorporated them into more than one supply chain. Initially, the sisters passed the arms to the Commanding Officer (O/C) of the Dundee Volunteers, Thomas McNiffe, of 58 Brook Street, and Captain Sean O'Doherty. Around May 1918, Lena accompanied O'Doherty on an arms drop to 49 Kent Street, Glasgow, where she was introduced to Jean Quinn, Lieutenant of the Ethna

Carbery branch of the Cumann na mBan, and told that, from now on, she would be delivering the goods in person. Lena and Jean had much in common – both managed shops owned or leased by their mothers, whose homes and adjacent business premises functioned as unofficial meeting places and arms dumps. Both women were discreet, resourceful and quick-thinking, and both showed a maturity beyond their years.

The furniture store was a perfect front for arms trafficking. Jean recalled: 'There was nothing unusual about goods continually coming and being dispatched. I had numerous opportunities of buying rifles and revolvers'. Jean went on to receive material from amongst other places, Maryhill Barracks and as far afield as Shetland. Her most reliable supplier, however, was Lena McDonald of Dundee who, for over a year from her first visit, made a weekly trip to Glasgow, often accompanied by Cathy, carrying quantities of arms and ammunition in Gladstone bags, golf caddies and egg crates. Jean then packed up the material in packages and boxes, concealed it in items of furniture, and, making 'good use of [her] trade with furniture dealers in Ireland', sent it on to Belfast and Dublin where it was picked up for transportation and distribution.[69]

In July 1919, Lena was ordered by McNiffe to make her deliveries to 74 Abercromby Street, Glasgow. She claims she did not know the reason, but as the change coincided with the arrival of Joe Vize in Scotland, one can assume that GHQ were attempting to exert control over the supply chain. By 1920, Lena was travelling through to Glasgow two or three times a week dropping material with Vincent Campbell at Abercromby Street and with Frank McKenna at the Ivanhoe Hotel in Buchanan Street. GHQ Vice-Quartermaster, D P Walshe (alias James Mitchell alias Joseph Dunne), and Senior Purchasing Officer, Joe Booker, also made regular trips to Dundee to pick up munitions.[70]

Father John Fahy later testified that Lena McDonald 'was instrumental in procuring more arms (rifles, revolvers, ammunition etc.) than any other member of the IRA in Scotland'.[71] It is difficult, if not altogether impossible to estimate the precise amount and the financial outlay, suffice to say in 1919, the McDonalds brought in well over a hundred rifles for which they paid 10s to £1 each, and between 10 to 24 revolvers a week at around 15s each, most of which was paid out of Helen's funds. These prices were considerably less than those paid by the Purchasing Committee in

1919–20, which was around £4 for a rifle and £2 10s for a .45 revolver.[72] By 1920–1, the McDonalds were bringing in between seven and fourteen rifles a week, and many more revolvers besides, that were so 'easy to get' that Lena failed to recall a figure. The quantity of ammunition is even less calculable, as bullets were often secreted into the shop in small quantities.

November 1920 saw the largest single haul of weapons in the city, thanks to an audacious operation in which Tom McNiffe walked into the army barracks in Barrack Park with four other Volunteers and a British Army officer, and walked out again with 500–600 rounds of ammunition, fourteen rifles and several dozen revolvers. The material was then packed into waiting cars and driven, by Lena and Father Fahy, to Stirling, where the rifles were passed on to Brigade Transport Officer James Quinn, and then on to Glasgow, where the small arms were dropped at the Ivanhoe Hotel.

Early in 1920, a message was relayed, via Constance Markievicz, to Seamus Reader, Vice Commanding Officer of the Scottish Brigade, complaining that GHQ in Dublin was not distributing material 'fairly', i.e., to meet the needs of the most hard-pressed areas.[73] For example, Cork was experiencing some of the most brutal and systematic repression to which the IRA were mounting a vigorous resistance despite being grossly outnumbered by British military forces. Tom Barry, Commandant of the 3rd Cork Brigade, later claimed that the three Cork Brigades combined had only 310 riflemen as that was the total number of rifles in the entire county.[74] The Scottish Brigade leadership responded by agreeing to allow individual brigades to augment their supplies independently, providing they did not cut in on GHQ sources or push up prices by paying more than the Purchasing Committee. To this end, Henry Coyle of the Mayo and Sligo Brigades and Sean Healy, Purchasing Officer for the 1st Cork Brigade, travelled to Dundee to conduct transactions at the Brook Street dump.[75] Father Fahy later testified to 'unofficial' consignments of arms procured by Lena and brought to Ireland from this period. For example, over the next twelve months, Healy made several trips to Dundee, lodging with Sean O'Doherty at Rosebery Street, or at the McDonald family home, which functioned as a safe house.[76]

At this point, the reasons why Dundee may have become a centre for 'independent' purchases merit some attention. Dundee's position on the periphery of the Scottish Brigade area and of the organisation itself, made it easier to escape unwanted attention from GHQ or at least to mollify any concerns. Outside of the Glasgow conurbation, GHQ appears to have had a relatively low opinion of the capabilities of the other Scottish units, and consequently, less to do with them. Unlike the West Coast battalions, which were well disciplined and clearly structured with all the responsibility accountability this entailed. Dundee was, as Seamus Reader enigmatically described, 'an area of its own'.[77] From the perspective of the Scottish leadership, it was more practical and expedient for the Purchasing Committee to refer independent agents to Dundee (and also Edinburgh) as appears to have been the case with Coyle and Healy. The equation worked both ways, however, with independent agents such as Healy introducing GHQ purchasers, D P Walshe, Joe Booker and possibly Liam Mellows, to the Dundee sources.

There is another reason why Dundee may also have attracted independent purchasers. As noted earlier, the prices the McDonalds paid for munitions (often out of Helen's funds) were significantly less than those paid by the Purchasing Committee. Whether this was reflected in the prices passed on to IRA purchasing agents is not recorded – however, it appears that the open-handedness of the McDonalds would brook no material reward – Father Fahy later claimed that 'because of [their] work for Ireland [the family] lost much financially'. Suffice to say that, years later, Healy and Booker were generous in their praise of Lena and her management of the Brook Street dump.

While Lena generally confined her purchases to guns and ammunition in the Dundee area, purchasing missions occasionally extended to other areas. Within the Fife mining communities there was a high degree of mutual sympathy between Irish republicans and militant socialists. John McArthur, a radical socialist miner from Buckhaven, recalled how the latter 'took a close interest in the Irish troubles' and were strongly influenced by the politics of Connolly and Larkin. McArthur also recalled Constance Markievicz being invited to speak at a packed-out Methil Co-operative Hall where she was given a rapturous reception.[78] With their pro-Irish revolutionary politics, antipathy toward the British Establishment, and previous experience of gunrunning – an attempt had been made to ship arms from Methil docks to Russian revolutionary forces in 1906-7[79] – the Fife radicals were ready recruits into the IRA's Scottish operations. When the aforementioned anonymous doctor referred Lena to a source amongst the Methil miners, the resulting haul – four tins of powder explosives, a large quantity of fuse, plus a tea chest full of revolvers and ammunition – was so large that it required Lena to draft in the McLean brothers from the Glasgow Battalion's 'flying transportation column' to convey it back.

The Dundee Gunrunning Case of 1921

By late 1920, the British security forces, spurred by the start of the IRA's campaign in England, had stepped up their intelligence war on Irish republicans in Scotland through a range of methods including surveillance, infiltration, interception of communications and the use of informants. They were also assisted, consciously or otherwise, by the press, as newspaper reports which portrayed the Irish 'troubles' as criminal, hence an anathema to law-abiding citizens, undoubtedly encouraged some people to pass on information to the police. In December 1920, the *Dundee Courier* noted:

> The recent outrages that have taken place in Ireland have created a great impression on the minds of Dundee folks, and all classes from the highest to the lowest have allotted to themselves the task of spotting likely 'desperados'. Even the slightest departure from normal behaviour attracts a small army of suspicious ones.

The *Courier* went on to report a recent incident where a number of workers at Dundee docks had observed a well-dressed middle-aged man making 'exhaustive enquiries regarding harbour affairs'. While some of them kept him talking, others ran for the police who wasted no time in dragging the suspect off for questioning, during the course of which he claimed to be a government agent. A medical examination subsequently concluded that he was 'of low intellect' and 'not wholly responsible for his actions'.[80]

If eccentric behaviour and mental debility invited unwarranted attention, the McDonald women constituted perfect models of normalcy and respectability. By all appearances they were what they seemed to be – two dutiful daughters helping out in the family shop while they trained to be nurses, a credit to their hardworking mother, who had herself worked her way up from charwoman to certified midwife and shopkeeper without a man at her back but with the support of her two millworker sisters and elderly mother. While contemporary attitudes to women were perhaps a key factor in helping them to retain their cover, their poise, geniality and willingness to help encouraged the trust of IRA comrades and neighbours alike. So much so that the latter were prepared to dismiss the former turning up in the dead of the night to load crates of material into awaiting motor vehicles.[81]

This was not to last, however. The application of improved police intelligence had already led to around twenty arrests that December, including those of Scottish Brigade Transport Officer, Henry Coyle, and Charles Strickland who had been arrested at Alloa transporting a quantity of explosives from Lochgelly to Glasgow; and Jean Quinn, who had been pulled in for further questioning after a police raid at her home at 49 Kent Street had found Sinn Féin membership cards, a Cumann na mBan uniform and balance sheets from the James Connolly Sinn Féin cumann in her bedroom.[82]

In the early hours of Thursday, 28 April 1921, D P Walshe and Sean Healy, who were in Dundee to oversee the latest consignment, were packing the munitions into a crate (with the assistance of Lena, Father John Fahy, Sean O'Doherty and three other men) when two policemen, alerted by the light, knocked at the door to investigate. As the men crouched behind the counter, Lena approached the door and assured the policemen that all was well, and – apparently satisfied with her explanation that she was catching up on some stocktaking, and the gift of a free orange – they departed. Healy later claimed that Lena's quick-thinking and composure averted a shoot-out as 'these guns weren't going to be taken without a fight'.[83] Walshe then concluded the arrangements and instructed O'Doherty to dispatch the material later that morning. As the usual transport was unavailable – the lorry having been captured along with Coyle and Strickland at Alloa – it was decided to send the crate by rail, and hire a local carrier to deliver it to the station. O'Doherty drafted in the strong arms of James Devaney, James Kimmet and James Malloy to help with the heavy lifting.

Lena, who remained highly critical of O'Doherty, recalled that the men turned up dressed like stereotypical IRA men, in soft hats and great coats, and insisted on sitting in a highly-visible position on the back of the lorry as they accompanied the load to the station. They seemed intent on drawing attention to themselves. Lena later recalled that there had been talk of money going missing and the finger of suspicion was pointing at O'Doherty, who was Secretary of the O'Rahilly Sinn Féin cumann, and Devaney, who was President. This may have been part of a bigger problem with an innocent explanation – it has been suggested that the discrepancies in the Scottish IRA accounts, which had resulted in Vize's recall to Dublin and the despatch of Liam Mellows to Scotland to conduct an investigation, arose from the necessity of protecting hidden supply chains.[84] Indeed, Mellows is recorded as having visited Dundee in April, although whether this was related to the investigation or some other issue relating to arms supply is unclear.[85] Whatever the reason, O'Doherty and Devaney were feeling the heat (Healy recalled that O'Doherty was in a 'highly anxious state'), and possibly fearing army discipline and loss of position in the organisation, may have engineered their own arrests as a distraction and a means of saving their reputations. Significantly, as Secretary of Dundee Sinn Féin, O'Doherty had placed prominent announcements in the death notices of the *Evening Telegraph* twice in the previous two months requesting members to attend the funerals of comrades.[86] That the police authorities might be watching and that he was providing information which would enable them to observe and identify Sinn Féin activists in the district, suggests that O'Doherty was either careless, stupid, over-confident or acting deliberately.

What transpired over the next few hours has been recounted several times from different perspectives, often at second hand and several years later. Healy claimed the lorry was followed by the police – evidently still observing the building after the previous night's visit – who recognised the men on board. Lena held that, once the crate had been deposited at the station, O'Doherty and Devaney entered the guard's van and attempted to remove it, provoking the censure of the railway porter and drawing his attention to the crate. The *Courier* reported that, on securing the packing of the case, which was marked 'Fragile – Eggs' the porter slipped his hand through the sparred lid, traced the outlines of a revolver, and went to the office to report it, where the consigner of the case (presumably O'Doherty), on overhearing the conversation, made a run for it.[87] According to the *Advertiser*, the two carters, suspecting the case was too heavy for eggs, had already called the police, who duly arrived and opened it to discover the assorted weaponry within. The crate was then repacked, sent on, and the Glasgow CID notified.[88]

The *Advertiser* reported that that 'the first point of enquiry' led to 'a round-up of Sinn Féiners', on whom the police already had information – O'Doherty, Kimmet, Devaney and Malloy were arrested later that night. Lena recalled that she turned up at Mass on Friday morning, where Father Fahy told her to hurry home, pack some things and head for Glasgow. She had just got in the door when the police came in after her. That same day, the police in Glasgow arrested provisions merchant, James McGlinchey, after he accepted delivery of the case at his shop in 73 Ingram Street.[89] The Dundee arrests were subsequently overshadowed by events in Glasgow, when a bid to rescue recaptured IRA fugitive, Frank Carty, from a police van on Wednesday 4 May, resulted in the death of a police officer and the arrests of twenty people, including D P Walshe, who had co-ordinated the operation. This was followed by a further wave of arrests in the city over the next few weeks.[90]

Meanwhile, back in Dundee, Malloy had been released and the remaining prisoners remanded in police custody pending trial arrangements. On 17 May, McGlinchey was granted bail after his solicitor, Bernard Caulfield, produced references from such pillars of society as the Chairman of Govan Parish Council, who described McGlinchey as 'straightforward and industrious', referred to his work on the Blackfriars War Committee and the Parish Council, and offered to pay £1,000 towards bail; and Professor of Latin at Glasgow University, John Phillimore, who testified to McGlinchey's high moral character and cited his involvement in charitable non-political societies. Caulfield further stated that his 47-year-old client, who was married with two children, had four extensive businesses and employed twenty people. James Devaney, who had five young children and a small hairdresser's business, could not count on such illustrious support, and the sheriff rejected both his and Lena's bail applications. O'Doherty and Kimmet appear not to have applied. McGlinchey's award was successfully appealed by the Crown, who had him transferred to Glasgow 'to facilitate [their] investigations' there. The charge was later dropped and McGlinchey was released on 22 July along with eighteen of the prisoners who had been arrested in relation to the Glasgow prison van ambush.[91]

The pleading diet took place in Dundee Sheriff Court on Friday, 29 July, amidst scenes which the *Dundee Advertiser's* court reporter deemed 'extraordinary'. A large number of spectators, the majority of whom were women, had gathered in the public gallery. On entering the dock, the accused at once turned towards them and shouted words of welcome, whereupon the crowd stood up, waved their hands and offered loud cries of encouragement. Sheriff Malcolm threatened to clear the court if there were any more demonstrations, and quietness was quickly restored. The accused were named as Sean O'Doherty, insurance agent, 101 Rosebery Street; James Devaney, hairdresser, 3 St Matthew Street; James Kimmet, caulker; 28 Crescent Lane; and Lena McDonald, housekeeper, 31 Brook Street. John Ross was the solicitor for Lena, and A F Burke for the other three. The charges, which took several minutes to read out, can be broadly summarised as follows:

> conspiracy to further the objects of an [unnamed] organisation by the unlawful use of violence, especially by the means of explosives, firearms etc.; trafficking weapons for the aforesaid purpose; possession of seven rifles (three with slings), two rifle slings, one rifle cover, two oil bottles for rifles, one rifle pull-through, one rifle sling swiver, four revolvers (three in leather holsters), seven bayonets (five with scabbards, one with scabbard and frog and one without scabbard), two clips and ten rifle cartridges (loaded); and attempting to transport these by rail to Glasgow.

Each tendered a plea of not guilty in loud tones and the trial date was set for 8 August at the High Court in Edinburgh. As the prisoners left the dock, The *Advertiser* noted that O'Doherty, who had been 'wreathed in smiles throughout the whole proceedings', shouted 'God Save Ireland' in Irish at which the spectators rose to their feet, waved, shouted 'Goodbye Sean' and urged Lena, who was clearly displaying a more solemn demeanour, to 'Cheer up'.[92]

On Monday, 8 August, the four duly appeared before Lord Justice-Clerk Scott Dickson at the High Court of Justiciary in Edinburgh, amidst an atmosphere of intense public interest occasioned by the Glasgow prison van trial which opened the same day. Unlike the 'Van' trial, which lasted for three weeks, the 'Egg Box' trial was brief. On behalf of O'Doherty and Kimmet, Morrice MacKay, KC, who also represented D P Walshe in the Glasgow case, tendered pleas of guilty to the whole charge. Devaney pleaded guilty to the charge of attempting to transport weapons to Glasgow on 28 April only, and Lena pleaded not guilty to all charges. The Crown's Counsel accepted the pleas and Scott Dickson ordered that Lena be discharged, whereupon she turned to O'Doherty and kissed him before standing down.

In attempting to mitigate for O'Doherty, MacKay stated that he was the sole support of his widowed mother as two of his brothers had been killed in the war while another was serving in the British Army. He was an exceptionally moral young man who, like many other young men in Ireland and this country, had naively succumbed to a 'mistaken patriotism'. O'Doherty, he uttered, 'took full responsibility for having introduced the other two prisoners to conveying the arms to the station'. Kimmet did not appear to merit much of a defence, the only comment being that he was 'only 23' (he was 25) and 'in steady work as a riveter'. As the most proletarian of the four, and a single man, he had less to lose and, arguably, more to gain. Indeed, 'Dode' Kimmet eventually returned to his work in the politically sympathetic environment of Dundee's Caledon Shipyard where he did gain a measure of prestige due to his role in the Dundee gunrunning incident. MacKay played up Devaney's respectable lower middle-class status and family man image as the hard-working proprietor of a hairdresser's business and the father of five young children. As a native Irishman (in fact, Devaney, like Kimmet and Lena, was third generation Irish), he had naively offered, when asked by other Irishmen, to help convey the stuff to the station. He admitted that he had thought 'something not quite legal was going on'.

O'Doherty and Kimmet were sentenced to three years' penal servitude. The Lord Justice-Clerk conceded that Devaney 'was in a rather different position' but nevertheless sentenced him to eighteen months imprisonment. On leaving the dock, O'Doherty, displaying his penchant for playing to the gallery, shouted 'God Save Ireland'. The prisoners then shook each other's hands and saluted the bench as they were taken down.[93] Devaney was incarcerated in Dundee Jail – a concession, no doubt, to his lesser culpability and domestic circumstances (his youngest child, Terence McSwiney Devaney, was only ten months old), and O'Doherty and Kimmet found themselves in Peterhead alongside Henry Coyle and around 30 other IRA men.

Lena emerged from the court to be greeted by a group of female friends, who presented her with a bouquet of flowers intertwined with tri-coloured ribbons, and a large crowd who blocked the High Street, obliging the police to 'usher' them along to the Tron Church. This, however, was nothing compared to the welcome Lena received on her return to Dundee, which was masterfully choreographed by Sinn Féin in the manner of Archbishop Mannix's reception five months earlier. Long before Lena's train was due to arrive at 8.45 pm on Thursday, 11 August, a crowd of several thousand had lined the pavements of Union Street and crammed into the space between the adjacent West and Tay Bridge Stations, causing considerable difficulty to the police who struggled to keep order. As the train steamed into the station, cheers were raised, whilst the retinue of young male attendants who had accompanied Lena from Edinburgh waved Irish Republican flags from the windows. In what read like a parodical account of a Royal visit, the *Dundee Courier* reported that Lena, 'an attractive young lady... attired in a navy blue costume', stepped down from the train to be greeted by 'a number of friends' who had been granted admittance to the platform.[94] After being presented with another bouquet of flowers by Mary Devaney, the daughter of James, Lena stepped outside the station entrance to another outburst of cheering, a banner bearing the sign 'Welcome' and Irish flags *gu leor*. On entering an awaiting car, Lena stood up in the rear and threw her flowers into the crowd, following which the car proceeded slowly up the street, followed by a number of young men, to continued cheering, singing and shouts of 'God Save Ireland'. The convoy wended its way along the Nethergate and up the West Port, through an ever-increasing crowd, to Brook Street and Blackness Hall where Lena was accorded an official reception. The *Dundee Catholic Herald* described the event as 'one of the most remarkable ever held in Dundee' and 'evidence of the feeling prevailing for Irish independence, apart altogether from', the *Herald* attempted anxiously to deny, 'the original motive which brought [it] about'.[95]

The jubilation was short lived, as a few days later, Lena was rearrested, held for trial and released again in October due to lack of evidence. After Lena's first arrest in April, Cathy, who helped to manage the pawnbroker's shop, continued to receive and put aside quantities of weapons. Cathy kept a lower profile than her sister but remained equally committed and performed an important role in the supply chain. At four years older than Lena, however, and further advanced in her nursing career, she also had other demands on her time. The family may also have relied on her professional wage.

While Lena's detention curtailed her ability to purchase arms, the Truce in July halted it for a considerable time longer. Lena recalled 'she was not asked to buy anything' during this period; moreover, aware that she may have been under observation, she was reluctant to approach suppliers for fear of 'pulling them in'. Still, she continued to receive weapons free of charge, courtesy of the sympathetic pawnbroker, and to run them through to Glasgow, occasionally Edinburgh, once or twice a week. At the outbreak of the Civil War, Lena resumed purchasing on a smaller scale. By this time, the post-war sources of weapons were drying up, and she was now relying primarily on the pawnbroker and a cousin in the British Army who gave her equipment he purloined from the Officers' Club for nothing.

It is significant that Lena later blamed Sean O'Doherty for her arrest, as she did not appear to have done so at the time of the trial. In an interview before the Military Pensions Board in Dublin in 1938, Lena maintained that not only had O'Doherty and Devaney (no mention of Kimmet), 'told where [they] got the stuff from', but that they had revealed that D P Walshe had been operating in Dundee under the alias of Joseph Dunne.[96] The reasons for this damning indictment can perhaps be found in the different positions Lena and O'Doherty took after the signing of the Anglo-Irish Treaty where O'Doherty's actions may have led Lena to review his past behaviour. After his release from prison in February 1922 (as part of the pardon for Irish political prisoners), O'Doherty, and his old Sinn Féin sidekick Devaney, became enthusiastic proponents of the Treaty and Michael Collins's biggest cheerleaders.

While the fact that she kissed him at the trial hints at a romantic element to their relationship, it may also have been an expression of the close comradeship that arose from their membership of a small tight-knit

Chapter 7 – Revolution 1916–23

unit engaged in hazardous operations. On the surface, they had much in common – both were of a similar age, working-class background and educational attainment, both were in 'respectable' jobs, and both had a profound sense of their common Irish identity and, so it seemed, common goal. As a young girl, Lena may have viewed O'Doherty as a kindred spirit, as a more mature woman who had had seventeen years to reflect, these superficial factors disguised fundamental differences in attitude and ideology. In retrospect, the attention-seeking behaviour, the courtroom melodramatics and the apparent financial mismanagement, had already signified the ineffectual superficial patriot he was, and signposted to the status-seeking renegade he would become.

A key factor in reinforcing this negative image was Father Fahy, who had also been in same active service unit as Lena, and had also sided against the Treaty. Fahy remained a vociferous critic of the Free State government throughout the 1920s and 1930s, (and of Irish governments thereafter) and his frequent clashes with the authorities often exasperated his otherwise sympathetic Bishop. He also accompanied Lena to her interview and undoubtedly coached her in preparation for it.

Indeed, Lena appears to have had far more in common with Father Fahy, who had come to Dundee with a highly developed political consciousness and an acute awareness of the gravity of the situation in Ireland. Unlike most of his Dundee comrades, Fahy had a direct connection to the falling victims of Black and Tan violence which was particularly severe in his native Galway. When ex-Maynooth confrere and fellow Republican, Father Michael Griffin, was abducted, shot, and his body dumped in a bog at Cloghscoltia, South Galway, on 14 November 1920 – the modus operandi of the Auxiliaries, who had shot dead the heavily pregnant Eileen Quinn 13 days earlier and went on to kill brothers Pat and Harry Loughnane 12 days later[97] – Father Fahy had hurried to Galway to stand all-night vigil at his coffin. On his return to Dundee, he set up a Sinn Féin cumann named in Griffin's honour, under the chaplaincy of Father Durand of St Joseph's, and taking in many of latter's parishioners. Moreover, he had a genuinely inclusive attitude, and knew the strategic value of befriending progressive political elements and encouraging involvement at all levels and in many ways. Indeed, at St Andrew's Cathedral, he established a sports committee (of which Lena was a member) which not only allowed him to indulge his passion for Gaelic sports, but provided a cover for Volunteer activity, and the means to instil the requisite team spirit, group discipline, physical fitness and Irish cultural identity.

As stated earlier, Father Fahy's position as a priest gave him a deeper insight into the conditions of the largely working-class community he served and strengthened his resolve to work towards the just and equal society enshrined in the Proclamation of the Irish Republic. As a trainee nurse and prospective midwife, whose large extended family was embedded in that community, Lena encountered the same people in the same difficult situations. The Proclamation of the Irish Republic guaranteed equal rights and opportunities to all of its citizens, including women. Father Fahy, her comrade and confidante, with whom she shared the same political outlook, was her real kindred spirit.

By contrast, O'Doherty, Devaney, and other members of Dundee Sinn Féin, appeared to inhabit an increasingly narrow, self-selected social circle which resembled the clannish, predominantly male societies of the pro-Home Rule days. With the recall of Father Fahy to his native Diocese of Galway in June 1921, the organisation lost an important radicalising influence. Barely three weeks after Fahy's departure, Dundee Sinn Féin voted to form a new separate club for men only – yet a separate club for women was not even discussed.[98] By autumn, Dundee Sinn Féin was becoming increasingly territorial, politically myopic, and hostile to any other group that threatened to steal their clothes.

It can be argued that Sinn Féin in Dundee, distanced from the Scottish leadership in Glasgow, and even further removed from Dublin, remained relatively ignorant of GHQ strategy, which was not always clear to begin with. Moreover, the implementation of a military strategy, and the focus on arms procurement and basic military training, i.e., drilling, in Scotland, was not accompanied by a programme of political education. Gifted organiser though he was, Collins was no Connolly. Granted, it was never Sinn Féin's intention to become a political force in Scotland, the fact that the organisation in Scotland remained detached from domestic politics and problems meant that it did not seize the opportunity to fully exploit the rich potential in its midst.

Nevertheless, while procurement of arms was the primary role designated to the IRA in Scotland, another part of GHQ operational strategy, conceived principally by Cathal Brugha and directed by Rory O'Connor, aimed to undermine the British State by cultivating links with sympathetic elements in Great Britain, mainly in England, who would be prepared to supply arms and carry out acts of sabotage against factories, ports and farm supplies. The extent and success of the latter is difficult to ascertain as acts of sabotage were harder to identify, incidents occurred outside IRA command, and the courts were possibly wary of ascribing political motives to 'criminal' offences, particularly around the time of the miner's dispute of 1921. Indeed, while the sabotage campaign was never officially extended to Scotland (in order to protect the arms supply), individual units, particularly in the Fife mining communities, where organisation was looser, may have acted on initiative.

The Fife Farm Fires Incident

On 14 September 1921, miners William Reid and John Turner, and ex-soldier Edward Joseph McAuley appeared before Lord Blackburn at Perth Circuit Court charged with having had, 'in concert with various others', set fire to seven farms in the Lochgelly district on 15 May, destroying quantities of hay, turnips, oats and straw. Reid and McAuley were also charged with illegal possession of explosives and a revolver. Police subsequently found a Sinn Féin membership card and an empty detonator box in the home of Reid, who was arrested along with Turner in the vicinity of Westerton Farm on the morning of the fires. McAuley was arrested leaving his house at 2.15 am the same morning, on his way, he claimed, 'to see a man, McGuire', who it also transpired was President of the local Sinn Féin club. When questioned as to what he was doing visiting the President of Lochgelly Sinn Féin at two in the morning with an unlicensed revolver in his pocket, McAuley, who proved to be a comedian in the witness box, replied 'for nothing', denied all knowledge of McGuire's political affiliations and of Sinn Féin in Lochgelly, and claimed that he had taken the revolver when he left the army for shooting ducks on Lochgelly Loch. Crown Prosecutor, D P Fleming, then questioned McAuley's wife who failed to recall him ever bringing any ducks home, and Police Sergeant David Wilson, who claimed to have witnessed McAuley in a local pub the night before his arrest striking himself on the chest and proclaiming, 'I'm a Sinn Féiner and proud of it'. However, when

Fleming asked Wilson if the police had any knowledge of McAuley drilling, Lord Blackburn upheld the Defence Counsel's objection that the accused had not been previously informed of the questions. Fleming's attempt to introduce the 'expert' testimony of Detective Inspector Louis Noble of the City of Glasgow Police, who had been conducting investigations into the aims and membership of Sinn Féin in Scotland and had been instrumental in procuring the convictions of several Glasgow activists, including Jean Quinn, was similarly dismissed. Lord Blackburn did, nevertheless, admit the testimony of Superintendent Peter Morton of the Fifeshire Constabulary, who confirmed that explosives had been disappearing from mines 'on a pretty large scale'.[99]

In his summing up, Lord Blackburn advised the jury that Reid's professed and proven membership of Sinn Féin 'gave rise to suspicion', but only because he was found with explosives which many Sinn Féiners were 'prone to use'. Lord Blackburn also spoke of the difficulty of detection in the case: 'at the time Fife had been packed with police and military, patrolling roads in every direction within a short radius, yet they were only able to bring before the Court three men'. (An indication, it appears, of the sympathy which existed in the community for the recent miners' strike.) After the evidence of 59 witnesses, including people who had seen all seven fires and found gelignite cartridges at various places afterwards, only two of the men were convicted of causing one fire at Westerton Farm. Reid was also found guilty of possession of explosives and sentenced to eight years' penal servitude. The *Courier* reported that he smiled, and turned to the gallery with the words, 'Cheer up, we will soon be back. God Save Ireland', at which a number of women began to weep hysterically and had to be told to be quiet. Twenty-one-year-old Turner, who Lord Blackburn described as a young fellow who had been made a puppet by 'extreme elderly men', was found guilty of fire-raising, and sentenced to a salutary twelve months' imprisonment without penal servitude. Father of three McAuley, who had been awarded the Croix de Guerre in the war where he had served as a Sergeant in the Royal Engineers until he was discharged after being gassed, was found not guilty on all charges.[100]

The Fife farm fires case shows clear evidence of Irish Republican involvement, however tenuous, and certainly of the Irish Republican sympathies of two of the men involved. Nevertheless, the fact that the case was also described in the press as 'a belated echo of the recent miners' strike', indicates that there was little or nothing to distinguish acts of sabotage carried out by disaffected members of the Scottish working class from those commissioned or inspired by the IRA, possibly because the lines had already been crossed, and for many of the perpetrators, the ultimate objective, i.e., the destabilisation of the British State, was the same.

A central part of GHQ strategy was to generate political support for Irish republicanism amongst disaffected sections of British society – to make common cause with the labour movement and unemployed workers through infiltrating groups, attending public meetings, rallies, protests etc.

At this point, an examination of one of the most important exponents of this strategy, Sean McLoughlin, is in order.

Sean McLoughlin

Despite being acknowledged as 'the boy commandant of the Easter Rising', McLoughlin's role in Irish and socialist history has, until recently, been underplayed and overlooked.[101] Sean McLoughlin was born in Dublin in June 1895 to a trade unionist father, whose socialist ideals he appears to have imbibed, and an 'extreme nationalist' mother who appears also to have influenced his decision to join the Gaelic League in his mid-teens and Na Fianna Éireann shortly after. In November 1913, he joined the Irish Volunteers – siding with the minority faction when the organisation split over Redmond's call to support England in the war – and in 1915 he was sworn into the IRB by Thomas Clarke.[102]

On Easter Monday 1916, McLoughlin's company (under the command of Seán Heuston) was dispatched to the Mendicity Institute, by the Royal Barracks and the Four Courts, to hold off the approach of British troops until the main garrisons were established. After holding out for two days, during which time he acted as courier, McLoughlin took up base at the GPO, where James Connolly, who identified his leadership qualities, ordered him to take possession of the offices of the *Irish Independent*. McLoughlin duly did, returning the following day to find Connolly lying wounded on a stretcher and the garrison attempting to withdraw into the bullet-swept side streets as the building threatened to combust around them. Amidst the panic and confusion, McLoughlin diverted the tired and disorientated party out through Henry Place into Moore Street, at which point, Connolly, Clarke, MacDiarmada, Pearse and Plunkett agreed to transfer Connolly's military command to him. McLoughlin gave the order to burrow through the buildings, and was on the point of deploying a 'Death or Glory' squad to deflect British fire from the leaders of the Provisional Government, when he was informed of the decision to surrender. McLoughlin recalled that his bitterness at the decision was only assuaged by the consoling words of Tom Clarke, and candid advice of James Connolly, who predicted that the British would attempt to decapitate the revolution by executing the leaders, and urged McLoughlin to keep his head down as there would be 'plenty to do in the future'.[103]

It has been speculated that McLoughlin owed his life to a British Army officer, who out of curiosity or sympathy, removed the distinctive orange commandant's tabs from his uniform prior to his interrogation by Castle detectives. Thus, McLoughlin escaped execution, and after a period of internment at Frongoch, returned to action as a full-time military organiser until he was felled by the Spanish flu pandemic in 1918. Around this time, he became more deeply involved in the socialist movement, joining the Socialist Labour Party of Great Britain and the Socialist Party of Ireland (which became the Communist Party of Ireland in October 1921). At some point, he appears to have visited Glasgow (with James Connolly's son, Roddy), where he made contact with 'A' Company of the 1st Glasgow Battalion of the IRA – formerly 'A' company of the Irish Volunteers – which was being reorganised on strong ideological lines by Joe Robinson, possibly with McLoughlin and Connolly's input.[104] Subsequently, 'A' Company gained a reputation for being one of the most uncompromising, politically advanced and independently minded units in existence, a situation that eventually led to the entire company being dismissed by Michael Collins. McLoughlin also made contact with sympathetic socialists, including John Maclean and Willie Gallacher of the Clyde Workers' Committee.

At the end of 1919, McLoughlin embarked on a protracted speaking tour of Scotland which concluded in July 1920 with a week of successful political activity in Dundee. McLoughlin also found time to get married, to Isabella Barr of Glasgow, on 7 January, with Roddy Connolly and Edward Grant Carr – the socialist organiser and Sinn Féiner with whom he was lodging – acting as witnesses.[105] It was while he was in Dublin, where he had returned with his pregnant wife, that he was approached by Michael Collins and Minister of Defence in Dáil Éireann, Cathal Brugha, who proposed that McLoughlin return to his socialist politicking on the British mainland with the dual mission of recruiting 'all likely elements who would be prepared to supply arms and carry out sabotage work', and attending public meetings 'to produce a favourable atmosphere for the Irish cause'. MacLoughlin recalled that he was 'very hostile' to the proposal as the Tan War was heating up and he was anxious to return to military command. However, he felt he had little alternative as he was finding it increasingly difficult to operate in Ireland as the Special Branch were on his tail following a shooting affray and were raiding his house up to twenty times a day. Collins also insisted that no-one else was equal to the task.[106]

On 24 November 1920, McLoughlin left Dublin, travelling firstly to Sheffield, where he contacted members of the local Irish Club, (affiliated to the Irish Self-Determination League, the badge of convenience by which Sinn Féin operated in England), and then north to Dundee. Significantly, once back in Dundee, McLoughlin did not team up with the Irish Republican movement, probably as the arms operation was already under control. Rather he picked up where he had left off in July, by renewing his activity with the Socialist Labour Party, and particularly with the Unemployed Workers' Movement, which had emerged that summer as a response to the escalating unemployment crisis.

By 1920, the short post-war boom had gone into sharp reverse, impacting severely on industry in general, and the declining Dundee jute trade in particular. By the end of that year, hundreds of families were facing cold, starvation and eviction. On 29 December, a broad section of concerned parties, including members of the Town Council, various clergymen, a deputation of ex-servicemen, and a large body of unemployed workers, crowded into the Town Hall to discuss how to best alleviate the crisis. No sooner had Councillor John Ogilvie (the Secretary of the Dundee Labour Party) advocated setting up a relief fund similar to that of the trade depression of 1908 than two of the unemployed workers rose to challenge him. The first and elder of the two – most likely unemployed labourer, Jock Thomson[107] – stated that he had been a 'victim' of that crisis and would not agree to the same methods now. The second – who the *Advertiser* identified as the 'chief spokesman, Mr Sean McLoughlin, [from] Glasgow', and the *Courier* claimed it had learned 'on enquiry' was a member of Sinn Féin – explained the reason why. 'Changes had taken place in the working classes' who may have been satisfied with 'a small dole' twelve years ago; now, however, the very concept of charity 'got up the back of any decent working man'. To repeated bursts of applause from his cohorts, McLoughlin declared that he wished to make the following 'revolutionary' proposals: first, that the municipality take responsibility for meeting the rent payments of the unemployed; second, that municipal restaurants be opened free of charge; third, that the municipality find work at once for all those unemployed; and finally, that all trade with Communist Russia be resumed. To the consternation of the officials on the platform, McLoughlin declared that some of them were not in touch with the working classes; he, however, was speaking for the unemployed and they, he insisted categorically, 'did not want and would not accept charity'.

By contrast, the representative of the ex-servicemen, J R Soutar, stated that they would be willing to settle for 'half a loaf when they could not get the whole', and would consider it a contribution from the general community to men, who 'either in khaki or blue, had served their country'. If the notion of 'half a loaf' was objectionable to the unemployed workers, the mere mention of 'khaki and blue' in the context of British ex-servicemen, must have provoked McLoughlin, who longed to return to the armed struggle, even further. As Lord Provost Alexander Spence called for volunteers to set up a relief fund, McLoughlin urged the meeting to have nothing to do with it and, with a unanimous show of hands and a 'considerable amount of cheering', the unemployed workers filed out of the hall, returning two weeks later to present a letter to the Lord Provost demanding an emergency meeting, calling for the use of a hall in the Town House where they could meet, and for the Council to pay the rents of the unemployed.[108]

McLoughlin's performance at Dundee Town Hall was not empty rhetoric or political posturing. He was now a committed revolutionary socialist with a clear international perspective. McLoughlin firmly believed that the establishment of socialism in Ireland would trigger uprisings throughout the British Empire and, ultimately, precipitate the destruction of capitalism in Britain itself. His directive from Collins and Brugha was not only compatible with his philosophy, but indivisible from it. In

McLoughlin's view, the triumph of socialism in Britain was critical to the survival of an Irish Socialist Republic. Thus, the importance of inducing the Scottish and English working class to support Irish independence, and the working class in all countries to support socialism.

Nor were the unemployed workers unwitting pawns in a plan masterminded by Collins and Brugha in a Dublin backroom. McLoughlin was not fomenting discontent against the British state where it did not already exist. The Communist Party, with which several members of the Unemployed Workers' Movement, including Jock Thomson, became associated, was (unlike the Labour Party) unequivocal in its support for the Irish Republic.[109] However, many more of its participants were alive to the potential of an Irish Socialist Republic, which was perhaps closer to their own cultural experience and more imaginable than revolutionary Russia. For Dundonians of Irish extraction, it was also their inheritance. Not surprising then, that the unemployed workers in the city chose to carry the flag of the Irish Republic at protest meetings – to them it was, like the red flag, a revolutionary symbol. And not surprising then, that McLoughlin would have easily recruited, as he later claimed, the Dundee unemployed to break up a Council Meeting which planned to pass a resolution condemning the 'terrorist activities of the IRA'.[110]

Shortly after this intervention, McLoughlin moved on to Motherwell, Dunfermline, Edinburgh, Glasgow and the west Scotland, and then back to Fife where, over the course of four weeks in March–April, he addressed several meetings in which he related the struggle for socialism in Britain to the revolutionary struggle in Ireland. Significantly, McLoughlin is recorded as having received his greatest support in the mining towns of Dunfermline and Cowdenbeath just prior to the aforementioned farm fires.[111]

In Dundee, McLoughlin left behind an increasingly militant unemployed movement in which local activists, and a growing number of women, took the initiative in a growing number of angry protests.[112] One prominent activist was 23-year-old Mary Soutar, having been thus encouraged by Jock Thomson, who recognised a genuine home-grown revolutionary when he saw one.[113] On 26 September 1921, Mary was arrested for sedition for inciting participants at an open-air meeting to break shop windows and take food rather than let their children starve. Twenty days before, the failure of the Parish Council to respond swiftly to urgent demands for relief had precipitated three consecutive days of rioting and looting throughout the City Centre, the West End and Lochee, in which skirmishes between missile-throwing protesters and baton-wielding police resulted in numerous casualties and arrests.[114] The following weeks saw more demonstrations and riots, and a police crackdown on the movement as prominent speakers were routinely arrested and imprisoned on sedition charges. Indeed, Mary's arrest (the first of three) came a few days after the fifth arrest and imprisonment of John Maclean, whose 'seditious remarks' she had consciously repeated.[115]

Being on the receiving end of repressive police tactics and vindictive sentencing quickly led to the conclusion that civil resistance was not enough. On 24 October, a visiting 'unemployed leader' from Glasgow, who the Dundee press identified (possibly erroneously) as John McShane[116], addressed an open-air meeting in Albert Square:

> We will make it bloody hot for the police, and we will have a revolution very shortly, and don't you forget it, the men with the notebooks. They are doing the same to us as they are doing to Sinn Féin leaders in Ireland. They are arresting our leaders. We must adopt Sinn Féin tactics here.[117]

At which the crowd cheered approvingly and proceeded to march through the city streets. While the term 'Sinn Féin' was applied to all manifestations of Irish republicanism at this time, there was no doubt that McShane was referring to the guerrilla tactics of the IRA. He was later arrested for sedition.[118]

On 14 October, a letter appeared in the *Evening Telegraph* from 'An Irishman', stating:

> There appears to be a great misunderstanding in the public mind at present regarding the unemployed movement in Dundee. I have heard it repeatedly said that it is in alliance with the Sinn Fein Movement. The origin of this idea must have arisen from the fact that Irish Republican flags were carried by the unemployed. I want to make it clear to those people that the Sinn Fein organisation in Dundee has no

connection with the unemployed movement. I would also wish to draw the attention of those leaders of the Dundee unemployed that members displaying Irish Republican colours during their parades in the city have no authority to do so from the Sinn Fein organisation.[119]

He concluded by advising the leaders of the Dundee unemployed to 'take steps to prevent a repetition of this thing'. The identity of 'Irishman', and how much weight he carried in Dundee Sinn Féin is difficult to determine. The irony was, that in his talk of misunderstandings, and his preoccupation with directing authority at an organisation which was intrinsically inimical to 'that sort of thing', he was oblivious to the fact the highest-ranking survivor of the Insurrection of Easter 1916, had already visited Dundee, (on the directions of arguably the two most powerful men in the Republican movement), to help facilitate the links between Irish Republicans and left-wing elements which the local Sinn Féin 'leadership' was apparently anxious to curtail. By this time, McLoughlin was once again involved with the unemployed workers movement in the north of England, all the while continuing to report back to Cathal Brugha in Ireland.[120] It is also worth noting that, as a military organiser, McLoughlin was opposed to conferring high rank on any individual as he believed it militated against effective action by creating dissension and weakness.[121]

While 'Irishman' used the columns of the local press to engage in proscriptive pettifogging over the exclusive rights of Sinn Féin to carry Irish Republican colours, those members of the unemployed movement who did had a better handle on Sinn Féin policy, whether they were aware of it or not. Out of large numbers of people who participated in the events organised by Sinn Féin, a significant number undoubtedly participated in the activities of the National Unemployed Workers' Movement (NUWM), which, despite being established by the Communist Party, accommodated different organisations and members of none. By the autumn of 1921, the objectives of the NUWM were more immediately relevant to their economic circumstances, and certainly livelier than the predominantly fund-raising organisation that Sinn Féin had become over the past few months. With the exception of Lena McDonald's welcome reception in August, throughout the Truce period, the Republican movement in

Dundee did not appear to mobilise its supporters to a significant degree. Denied the opportunity for military action in the IRA, many rank-and-file members may have perceived another outlet for their energies in the socialist and unemployed movements. Amongst the ubiquitous crowds of women who turned out at Irish Republican events, many may also have relished the opportunity for minor acts of rebellion that the street demonstrations afforded.

Ironically, while women appear to have formed the majority of Sinn Féin's grassroots supporters in Dundee, this vast source of radical energy remained woefully unorganised and underdeveloped. By 1920, there were fourteen active branches of Cumann na mBan in Scotland, mainly in Glasgow and Edinburgh.[122] Incredibly, despite the fact that the Irish immigrant experience in Dundee was predominantly female, there is no record of a branch of Cumann na mBan being established in this period, which begs further examination.

The failure of the Irish Republican movement in Dundee to spawn a separate women's section can be partially explained by a weakness in the organisational structure of the movement itself. This possibly had its roots in Michael Collins' perceptions of Scotland, a country with which he had few connections and comparatively little interest in. If, as Ó Catháin claims, Collins' early working life in London led him to reflect a metropolitan view of Scotland as a 'grey, desolate and cold northern "other"'[123], his Glasgow-based intermediaries may also have initially perceived Dundee – which was slow off the mark in establishing its support for physical force republicanism after the Easter Rising, and the last district in the Scottish Brigade area to become integrated into the reorganised national structure – as an unimportant peripheral backwater compared to the west coast and to Edinburgh and Leith, with their strategic links to Ireland and Europe respectively.

Arguably, this marginality was later turned to the IRA's advantage. On an official level, however, while Sara O'Kane, Captain of the Anne Devlin branch, Glasgow, reorganised Cumann na mBan in that city in 1917, Cumann na mBan in Scotland did not have a national organiser of the stature of Sean O'Sheehan (Sinn Féin) and Joe Vize (IRA) after Collins became Director of Organisation in 1919.

Nevertheless, the lack of a formal branch does not rule out the existence of an informal one which mobilised as the need arose, reflecting the *ad hoc* nature of grassroots, often female-driven, political and industrial action in the city. Unlike the Anne Devlin or Ethna Carbery branches, it may have had no name or command structure. Regardless of their official status, however, women activists attached to the Republican movement in Dundee did much the same work as Cumann na mBan elsewhere, and were subsequently perceived, and retrospectively claimed, to be members of it. In 1955, former President of the Dundee Kevin Barry Sinn Féin cumann, Cathal Duthie, identified around a dozen women Irish activists, two of whom, Annie Agnew and Annie Barrett, he described as having been members of 'Dundee's Cumann na mBan'. (The fact that Duthie's perspective may have been influenced by intervening events and the desire to create a narrative which conformed to the historical record, will be considered in the next chapter.) Five other women were listed as having been members of the O'Rahilly Sinn Féin cumann: Maggie Steel, who performed the role of Literary Secretary, and Mrs Alf Wilson, Mrs Grattan and Mrs John Kelly, who were listed alongside their husbands. Four others were identified as having been members of the IRA: Mary Ann Boyle, Christina Clarke, Mrs Alf (Mary Ann) Wilson and Lena and Catherine McDonald.[124] As the only other Dundee-based woman besides Lena to receive a military service medal – but not the only one to be involved in gunrunning – Catherine McDonald also claimed on her application form to have been a member of 'Cumann na mBan attached to the Dundee 'A' Company of the IRA'. In the absence of a record of a Dundee branch ever having existed, evidence of Lena's pension application in 1938, and a supporting reference from Jean Gillespie, née Quinn, former Lieutenant of the Ethna Carbery Cumann na mBan, testifying to Catherine's membership, was accepted as sufficient verification of 'activity in Dundee' to merit the award of a medal. However, her claim to be a member of Cumann na mBan continued to be queried.[125]

As in other places, the character of this activity was shaped by local conditions and culture. In Dundee especially, class as well as gender was a major issue. Stephen Coyle notes how Cumann na mBan in Scotland was composed mainly of young single professional women, with a large percentage of schoolteachers (as were Margaret Skinnider and Sara O'Kane).[126] The McDonald sisters were nurses. Unlike most Dundee-Irish women, they were socially and geographically mobile. The fact that they had access to and could drive a car, rare for a woman in the early 1920s, enabled them to move small quantities of arms across the country. While a small minority of women had advanced up the socio-economic scale in jobs which served their community, such as nursing and teaching, the majority in employment were semi-skilled, low-paid textile workers. The limited opportunities intrinsic to a single industry town militated against social mobility. This, of course, also applied to men. However, while the IRA may have been more hospitable to working-class men, working-class women were rarely admitted on the same terms. According to Margaret Skinnider, the Cumann na mBan in Glasgow worked more closely with the IRA than they did in Ireland, participating in arms raids and organising dumps.[127] Still, while individual women within Cumann na mBan undoubtedly possessed competence, skill and courage equal to any man, and occasionally got the chance to prove it, Cumann na mBan remained essentially an auxiliary force whose main activities of first aid and fund-raising, with a little less drilling and gunrunning, may not have held sufficient appeal to the typical Dundee-Irish mill worker.

Here, the McDonald sisters remained exceptions. As noted earlier, by the end of 1918, they had aligned themselves with the IRA, by which time they had established firm contacts outside of Dundee, particularly with 'B' Company of the IRA in Glasgow. Yet, while Lena McDonald worked alongside members of Cumann na mBan, such as Jean Quinn, she herself never joined and remained unequivocally a member of the IRA throughout her involvement.

The reasons why women offered such unequivocal support to the Irish Republican movement are perhaps easier to identify. The large numbers of women who emigrated from Ireland to Dundee in the nineteenth century, carried the knowledge, memories and traditions of 'the old country'. They in turn became the role models for the generations of women who followed. The experience of the majority of these women was one of poverty, industrial discipline and domestic responsibility, of being excluded, alienated or inhibited from entering political structures and male-dominated cultural networks. Walker concluded his study of Dundee's jute workers in this period with a definition of 'a class which was normally too burdened by present anxieties to pursue politics beyond their own domestic situation – an 'anxious adult view [which] was unable to contemplate risk beyond the family' and sought relief in entertainment not agitation.[128] While this may have some substance, Walker appears to a take a narrow view of politics which diminishes the importance of the domestic sphere and role of entertainment in propagating political opinions. For many second and third generation Irish Dundonians, the first knowledge and understanding of what it meant to be Irish was acquired at their mother's or grandmother's knee, often expressed in the entertaining form of stories, poems and songs. The fact that music and song provided one of the most potent and durable forms of popular consciousness was not lost on James Connolly who wrote several revolutionary songs set to old tunes, and asserted that 'Until the movement is marked by the joyous, defiant singing of revolutionary song, it lacks one of the most distinctive marks of a popular revolutionary movement, it is the dogma of a few, and not the faith of the multitude'.[129] And while collective consciousness of the Irish Republican tradition may have been receding into the past under layers of nostalgia, the Easter Rising and ensuing War of Independence had brought it back up to the surface with a vengeance.

Given the socio-economic circumstances of most Dundee women, particularly those of Irish extraction, the freedoms inherent in the Proclamation of the Irish Republic were, not only entirely compatible with their class and gender interests, they were also their cultural inheritance. Such factors may have affected how the Irish in Dundee viewed the Anglo-Irish Treaty and the positions they subsequently took.

III

The period of Treaty and the ensuing Civil War was a difficult one in which many were forced to re-evaluate their views and review their position. For some, it was too traumatic and complicated. For others it strengthened their resolve, and made them even more committed. While the number of public meetings promoting the Treaty dwindled, by contrast, Republican speakers continued to fill halls with supportive audiences. And while the 'soft' support fell away, support came from other political allies. Communists, who were acquainted with the logic behind Connolly's Marxist-inspired maxim, believed that imperialists, hoisting green flags or dressed in green uniforms, were still imperialists. Likewise with radical Scottish nationalists such as Seumas Mac Garaidh of Arbroath, whose pan-Celtic philosophy presupposed a fundamental antipathy to the British imperialist state and a deep sense of kinship with the Irish Republican cause.

Seumas Mac Garaidh

Born James Carr MacDonald Hay into a poor working-class background in Arbroath in February 1885, Mac Garaidh transcended his limited formal education by immersing himself in the history and culture of Scotland from his early teens onwards. Within a few years, he was fluent in the Gaelic language, and in 1911, he helped to organise the first recorded Gaelic class in his native Arbroath. Around this time, Mac Garaidh – who had by now Gaelicised his name – became involved in the Gaelic nationalist and wider Pan-Celtic movement whose principal crusaders, the London-based Gaels, Ruaraidh Erskine of Marr – and William Gillies a.k.a. Liam Mac Gille Iosa, advocated solidarity, cooperation and collaboration between the six Celtic nations, and particularly, given their historic and linguistic links, between Scotland and Ireland. Despite the opposition to English Imperialism this position entailed, in 1915, Mac Garaidh fell for the British government line that the First World War was being waged to uphold the rights and freedoms of small nations, and enlisted in the British Army. After nearly four years soldiering in Mesopotamia, Mac Garaidh returned to Scotland with a changed perspective and, in the light of the actions of Easter Week 1916, a renewed respect for the Irish people in their long unbroken resistance to English rule.[130]

After attending the third Pan-Celtic Congress in Edinburgh in June 1920, Mac Garaidh reported that 'never was the spirit of fraternity and sympathy with the mutual aspirations of the Celtic countries more urgent than at this period', and expressed the hope that discarding the 'merely spectacular' aspects of Celtic nationalism was 'a sign of earnestness of the present Congress that it will work towards something more practical in the world of things Celtic'.[131] 1920 also saw the founding of Comunn na Albannach/the Scots National League (SNL) by Erskine and Gillies, with the object of securing full Scottish independence. On 17 August, following a promotional meeting by SNL Secretary and editor of the pro-Sinn Féin journal 'Liberty', John McArthur, Mac Garaidh and a number of supporters formed a branch in Arbroath. The *Arbroath Herald* reported that a branch had also been formed in Aberdeen the previous night and others were 'in the course of promotion in Edinburgh, Dundee, Paisley, Greenock and Dumfries'.[132]

Despite getting off to an enthusiastic and promisingly radical start – the revolutionary socialist John Maclean chaired a meeting in Arbroath in September 1920, and President of the Miners' Federation, Bob Smillie, sent a message of endorsement to the inaugural meeting of the London branch in March 1921 – the SNL's failure to attract popular support and members of a sufficiently radical persuasion was a source of increasing frustration to Mac Garaidh.[133] Far from being the political mechanism which would attract wider support and participation, and bridge cultural nationalism to a militant nationalist resistance – which Erskine and Gillies had anticipated in the creation of Fianna na h'Alba – the SNL still resembled a cultural movement composed predominantly of Gaelic romanticists content to linger in the Celtic twilight. By 1922, Mac Garaidh was growing impatient with the SNL's insular turn and its failure to appeal to the Scottish masses. On 15 February, he reported on the inaugural meeting of the Dundee branch, by informing readers of the *Dundee Courier* that:

> Scotland is on the verge of becoming an extinct nationality. Language is being neglected; national sentiment is practically dead Scotland is, in fact, thoroughly Anglicised. It would be interesting to learn what methods this SNL propose to remedy this state of affairs [given that] 'most Scotsmen whom I meet [are] quite unconcerned [and] pleased to give their votes to any old English "carpet-bagger" who comes along.[134]

The trite response from Branch Secretary, H Mac Gille Phadraig (Harry Kirkpatrick), that 'there is but one remedy – to secure the restoration of Scottish independence, and with that we have our remedy', in Mac Garaidh's view '[left] much to be desired', as no attempt was made to define what Scottish independence actually meant, how it was to be secured, hence 'what the League really [stood] for'.[135]

In the absence of a clear political philosophy and practical strategy for achieving independence, Mac Garaidh took to the correspondence columns of the local press to discuss, criticise and promote anything related to the issue of national self-determination. If he was ambivalent in his support for the SNL, Mac Garaidh had no such reservations about Sinn Féin, on whose behalf he picked up his pen to propagandize for a week later.

> We all regret recent happenings in Ireland but we are not deluded into placing the onus of blame on Sinn Fein, which stands for nationality. Sinn Fein has always recognised a very important point of its propaganda, and one which I would seek to impress upon your correspondents, namely that the greatest danger to the peace of Europe and the world is not the race of little peoples demanding the recognition of their national aspirations, but is, has ever been, and always will be, the policy of "might is right", practised by the Imperial Powers in their campaign of aggression and oppression. Sinn Fein in Scotland, as in Ireland, is the expression of the public disapproval of [the] orgy of Imperial war and bloodshed, and aims at the peaceful establishment of a non-imperial Government in these respective countries. Sinn Fein repudiates war, and it repudiates the Imperial spirit as a war-maker. Sinn Fein stands for the nation as an independent entity, and the nation as such is the most powerful factor for the enduring peace of the world. [136]

At the turn of 1921-22, Mac Garaidh turned his attention to the plight of the Irish Republican prisoners in Perth prison.

The Perth Prison Protest

As noted earlier, Irish Republicans had been transported to Scotland following the Easter Rising in May 1916. With the escalation of the Tan War, the British government once again chose to deal with the increasing number of IRA prisoners by periodically transporting batches from different parts of Ireland to Scottish prisons. By the end of 1921, around 50 to 60 Irish Republican prisoners were incarcerated in Perth Prison.

Once inside British gaols, the IRA continued to prosecute the war against the British Empire, albeit along different lines from the military campaign. Having succeeded in obtaining Political Status following the death of hunger striker, Thomas Ashe, in September 1917, Republican prisoners had continued to assert their status as soldiers of the Irish Republic. This involved defying the British state at every turn, by refusing to comply with the rules and regulations of its prisons, and, unsurprisingly, attempting to break out of them. Indeed, the *Dundee Courier* prefaced the report of one such attempt with some background information on the 'Sinn Feiners' who, 'while in prison [have shown] the spirit which characterises the movement', noting that a batch recently transferred from Peterhead Prison had been particularly turbulent.[137]

On Friday 2 December 1921, the Scottish Prison Commissioners in Edinburgh received information from Dublin about a planned escape from Perth Prison scheduled for the following weekend. On the evening of Friday, 9 December, the prison was placed on lockdown. The IRA prisoners were moved to the penitentiary block in the south side of the prison where, from a central tower, they could be kept under constant observation, while an augmented force of police and prison warders guarded the precinct at every port. Staff were forbidden from leaving, and the gate to married quarters was locked. Meanwhile, unaware that the plan had been leaked, an IRA unit from Dundee, led by Captain Patrick O'Neill, in which Lena McDonald was assigned the role of getaway driver, waited on the other side of the wall in anticipation of the men shinning over it. They departed three hours later after they failed to appear.[138]

Two weeks after the foiled jailbreak, the prisoners were still confined to the penitentiary block. The early release of untried political internees in Ireland, which began on 8 December, two days after the signing of the Anglo-Irish Treaty, had already been denied to sentenced prisoners. When, on Christmas Eve, the men were further deprived of the 'cheer of Christmastide' to which they had been accustomed in previous years in Ireland, they began a hunger strike and smashed the windows of their cells. They then dismantled the furniture, using the tables to barricade the doors, and the iron bars from the bedsteads to pierce the two-feet-thick cell walls all along the wing until communication had been established between all the prisoners, and a ready arsenal of stones and iron bars had been accumulated. Through information obtained from a source inside the prison, a reporter from the *Dundee Courier* reconstructed a vivid and detailed account of the events of the following five days. As the prisoners fended off a forced entrance by the prison warders, the authorities drafted in a twenty-strong detachment of the Black Watch from Perth Barracks, 'who marched into the prison wearing steel helmets and all the paraphernalia of active service'. Meanwhile, warders placed the prison's fire hose into a hastily constructed hole on the top level of the four-storey penitentiary block, and directed water onto the flats below. Still the prisoners held out. After another two days without having moved them, the high-pressure hose of the City Fire Department was drafted in and, from then on, the situation deteriorated. As 'water poured from the cells like mountain torrents', the last defiant half a dozen prisoners were herded into one cell and blasted with jets of water until half-starved, half-drowned and with 'all the fight knocked out of them', they were finally overcome.[139]

As 'the curtain fell on the final act', Seumas Mac Garaidh, writing in his own name, and possibly under the pseudonym of 'Oglach',[140] expressed a debt of gratitude to the *Courier* for publishing particulars of the treatment meted out to the 'Sinn Féin' prisoners, which, he observed, 'contrasts strangely with what we would naturally imagine to be the lot of political prisoners'. Both letters stated that the Irishmen were being held on the 'false pretext of committing a "crime"', and maintained that the only 'crime' they were guilty of was patriotism, which, Oglach asserted, was 'so deeply engrained in the heart of every Irishman that all the conceivable methods of torture for the past two years have failed to eradicate it'. Oglach also speculated that the continued detention of the prisoners in Scotland, unlike their recently released comrades in Ireland, belied an attempt by the British government to blackmail Dáil Éireann into voting for the Treaty by using the prisoners as political hostages.[141] Mac Garaidh, who equated the criminalisation of the Irish liberation struggle, and the attendant persecution of the Irishmen with the atrocities visited upon William Wallace, was outraged that 'the British government chooses a Scottish prison for such a purpose', and urged Dundee Sinn Féin to 'lose no time in drawing attention to the matter'.[142]

Despite this episode of gross prison brutality, Patrick McCabe, O/C of the Mullingar Brigade of the IRA, who was serving out a four-year sentence in Perth at the time, recalled conditions there were 'not too bad on the whole'.¹⁴³ Irish Republicans, it appears, were accustomed to worse. Moreover, the filtering out of information about the incident (which spread quickly throughout Perth), followed by the leaking of every damning detail to the press, suggests the presence of sympathetic prison staff who undermined the efforts of military and prison officials to sweep it under the carpet. Indeed, the leaking of information may have motivated the prison authorities to release the prisoners earlier than planned, at 30 minutes' notice on 13 January, much to the annoyance of local Sinn Féiners who had asked to be informed in advance that they might arrange a welcoming reception and provide them with supplies for the journey home.¹⁴⁴

If Mac Garaidh was attempting to engineer a show of Celtic solidarity between local Irish Republicans and the mass of the Scottish population whose national consciousness he sought to arouse, he was almost a century ahead of his time. Not that Dundee Sinn Féin did not share his concerns – besides the involvement of local IRA volunteers in the escape attempt, the welfare of prisoners and their dependants was one of the most enduring aspects of the movement's work. Nevertheless, after the departure of Father Fahy, Dundee Sinn Féin appear to have shown little enthusiasm for domestic political alliances or propaganda campaigns on social, economic or humanitarian issues. The claim of Father Fahy's biographers that he was involved with the Scottish Nationalists (probably the Scots National League) and attended Communist meetings, is perfectly consistent with Fahy's policy of forming alliances with sympathetic groups, his family and community roots in the Irish Land League, and the initial left-wing trajectory of his populist politics.¹⁴⁵ However, as stated earlier, the insular turn taken by Dundee Sinn Féin – indicated by the distancing of its leading members, if not its grassroots supporters, from the Unemployed Workers' Movement – and the relatively weak position of the SNL, suggests that any tentative links with Scottish Nationalists were never fully developed.¹⁴⁶ At any rate, the release of the last Irish Republican prisoners from Scottish jails in February 1922 put an end to any prospects of a joint campaign on that particular issue.

For all his efforts in attempting to foster a Celtic resistance, Mac Garaidh found himself in a similar position to many Irish Republicans – classed as a potential troublemaker by prospective employers and subject to suspicion by the police authorities. After taking a realistic appraisal of his personal circumstances and the political situation, Mac Garaidh took the route a number of Scottish IRA veterans later followed and sought his fortunes elsewhere. In 1923, he left for the US, settling in San Francisco where he went on to publish his poetry, establish Gaelic classes, and inaugurate the San Francisco Mod. Mac Garaidh died on 9 January 1966, a month short of his 81st birthday, perhaps never having achieved his dream of a free independent Gaelic Scotland, but with his reputation as a true patriot and pan-Celt intact.[147]

The signing of the Treaty on 6 December 1921, rapidly brought the differences in the Irish Republican movement to light, and marked the beginning of a propaganda war which divided supporters into increasingly hostile camps. Most of the key organisers in Scotland were opposed to the Treaty, which fell far short of Republican aspirations, and the anti-Treaty forces were the first to rally.

On 29 December 1921, an enthusiastic audience of around 2,000 people, again predominantly women, gathered in the Caird Hall to hear Vice-President of Sinn Féin in Scotland, Thomas Wilson, and founding President, Thomas McDonnell, present the Republican line. Wilson, who expressed the hope that 'those who did not like the Treaty would be bound in their consciences to it', stated that 'if the Irish people accepted it [it], they would do so under duress'. Citing international law expert, Erskine Holland's definition of a nation as 'an entity that is absolutely and entirely free', he added that the Sinn Féin movement in Scotland were 'not acting as dictators', 'but if the Irish people chose to accept the Treaty 'they would tell them that they in Scotland would not support the Government that would come into existence' as a result. To prolonged cheers, he affirmed that they continued to support the ideal of a Republic, and 'willingly [give] acclaim to President de Valera'. They honoured 'the men and women who had conducted the Irish barque through the troublous waters that had led her to the port of comparative liberty', but they would not accept the Treaty until it was considered irrefutably as nothing more than 'a means to an end'.[148]

On 9 January 1922, a letter in the *Dundee Advertiser*, from a 'leading Irishman', claimed – rather unconvincingly, given the large numbers at the Republican rally eleven days before – that 95 per cent of the Irish people, and an equivalent percentage of the Irish people in Dundee, supported the

Treaty. How he arrived at this figure, and who he considered to be 'the Irish people in Dundee', was not revealed.[149]

There were some influential Irish-Catholic voices raised in favour of the Treaty in the city. The Catholic Church in Ireland had taken the pro-Treaty line and had many platforms on which to promote it. The annual celebration of the feast of St Patrick, with its entertaining mix of patriotic songs and speeches, music, recitations and dancing, was one of the most popular events in the Dundee-Irish calendar. On 16 March 1922, the guest speaker, Bishop Joseph (later Cardinal) MacRory of Down and Connor, made full use of the opportunity to bring the audience into the Treaty camp: firstly, by affirming that he was a Republican at heart; secondly, by assuring them that accepting the Treaty did not mean 'renouncing Ireland's natural birthright of freedom'; and finally, by warning that 'If the Treaty settlement was rejected, Ireland would be largely destroyed by lack of sympathy abroad and division at home'.[150] Significantly, while the *Courier* recorded every burst of applause and shout of approval for MacRory's various points, the *Evening Telegraph* noted that the loudest cheers were reserved for references to the Republican movement.[151]

Whether MacRory succeeded in converting any wavering Republicans to the 'stepping stone' approach to Irish independence is uncertain. The Republican movement in Scotland, however, remained firmly anti-Treaty. By the end of March, Sinn Féin and the IRA had regrouped and reorganised. There were now 33 Sinn Féin cumainn in Scotland.

After some initial tension between key figures, namely former office bearers James Devaney and Sean O'Doherty, and current Secretary Patrick O'Neill, the original O'Rahilly club was re-organised, and partially absorbed into the new Kevin Barry cumann. Both were eventually incorporated, at the end of 1922, into Cumann Poblacht na h'Eireann in Albain, the Scottish equivalent to de Valera's Cumann na Poblachta in Ireland and Art O'Briain's Irish Self-Determination League in England.[152]

The IRA was reorganised, under Scottish Divisional Commander, Joe Robinson, into two brigades covering the west and east of the country. Commanding the former (No 1 Brigade) was Seamus Reader, who was to succeed Robinson in the latter stages of the Civil War. Commanding the latter (No 2) was Thomas Dempsey, formerly of 'G' (Glasgow Central and Anderston) Company of the 1st Glasgow Battalion, and a member the

IRB's Clydebank circle.[153] Beyond this, little is known of Dempsey's background. It is possible he was a relative of peripatetic Belfast Republican, Seamus Dempsey, a long-standing comrade of Robinson with whom he had helped to organise Na Fianna Éireann, and subsequently the Irish Volunteers in Glasgow in the early 1910s. By 1916, the prodigious Dempsey was also chief organiser of the Belfast Fianna, and reputedly, Centre of the Belfast circle of the IRB, for which organisation he was obliged to act as a transatlantic courier in January–February, frustrating James Connolly's plans that he work with the pro-socialist Volunteers of Glasgow 'A' Company in the run up to the Rising. Of that event itself, Dempsey endeavoured to mobilise the Northern Volunteers, but was thwarted by the confusion surrounding Eoin MacNeill's countermanding order. In 1918, he resurfaced in the company of his old Belfast and Glasgow comrades, Nora Connolly, Margaret Skinnider and Eamonn Mooney, on a fund-raising/propaganda (and possibly arms smuggling) tour of the United States.[154]

Here, the dearth of evidence and gaps in existing records present a challenge to historical interpretation. An inventory of Scottish IRA membership and operations submitted to the Board of Military Pensions in 1935-8 contains extensive data on the west of Scotland but scant information on the east. Dundee on the northernmost fringes of the Scottish Divisional area, was, arguably, of less importance strategically, and less familiar to the Glasgow-centred Scottish command. Lena McDonald's application for a military service pension states that she had 'no personal contact' with Seamus Reader, Scottish Division O/C at the latter end of the Civil War, who supplied much of the information. Moreover, paper commands did not always tally with personnel and operations on the ground. While Cathal Duthie and Eamonn Mooney later endeavoured to fill some of the gaps, the record was doubly handicapped by being compiled over three decades retrospectively and without the input of No 2 Brigade Commandant Thomas Dempsey.[155]

Thus, while much information exists on No 1 Brigade, namely, an extensive record of membership rolls and details of some of its operations, less is known of No 2, besides the fact that it was divided into two battalions: the 1st Battalion, which covered the North of Forth district (Dundee, Fife and Perth), contained an estimated 600 Volunteers, ostensibly under the command of Dempsey, assisted by battalion officers,

Patrick O'Neill, John Boyle, James Chaplin, W Connachie, James Reilly, Thomas Robbins and Alf Wilson (Dundee), and Phillip Cullen, W Kelly, and McCabe (Buckhaven/Lochgelly, Fife). The 2nd Battalion, which covered Edinburgh, Leith, the Lothians and the east central belt, contained an estimated 300 officers and men under the command of Scottish Divisional Transport Officer, Paddy Hyland of Winchburgh.

The battle for hearts and minds, however, continued to be the main area of combat and by April the Republicans were winning. On 19 April 1922, Sinn Féin Scotland organised a rally in the Caird Hall, addressed by Mary MacSwiney, sister of the late hunger striker and Lord Mayor of Cork, Terence, and Margaret Pearse, mother of Patrick and Willie, who had been executed by the British for their part in the insurrection of 1916. By this time all three men had acquired the status of martyrs for the Irish Republic.

Mary MacSwiney, an uncompromising Republican whose propaganda skills had been honed by a lengthy US speaking tour, led off by disputing the myth that Michael Collins, who had signed the Treaty, 'could not make a mistake'. Collins, she stated, 'certainly has a good reputation. He has done a great deal for Ireland, but he is not infallible'. Mary went on to state her belief that 'if the Irish people accept the Treaty, it will be through fear of war with England', but that the fear of Civil War in Ireland was so much greater that this was unlikely. Referring to the conditions for negotiation laid down in a statement by anti-Treaty forces, she explained that the Republican Army were not acting as military dictators, but rather demanding an assurance that the people could vote freely without the threat of war hanging over their heads.[156] Mrs Pearse, in the black-veiled dress of mourning, then threw in the killer emotional punch. 'Two of her sons', she said, 'had fallen in the Republican cause, and the spirit which led them to make the supreme sacrifice was stronger in the land than ever'.[157]

It was master class in audience manipulation By following a blunt explanation of the Republican position with a direct appeal to the heart, the speakers could reach members of the audience who were irresponsive to rational arguments, or alienated from politics altogether. Indeed, many people were still unsure of the machinations surrounding of the signing of the Treaty. Yet, while Mary MacSwiney and Margaret Pearse were also members of Dáil Éireann, many more people, especially women, could identify with, and were more inclined to trust the words and instincts of a bereaved mother or sister than a mere politician. Unsurprisingly, resolutions in favour of the Irish Republican position were carried overwhelmingly and enthusiastically. The meeting was a coup for the anti-Treatyites, who also provided a photo opportunity on the steps of the Caird Hall – complete with the children of local Republicans bearing baskets of flowers and fruit – that even the pro-Treaty *Dundee Courier* couldn't resist.

By late April, Sean O'Doherty, out of jail and out of kilter with the Scottish leadership, joined his old comrade James Devaney in promoting the Treaty, a task in which they were assisted by a supportive Dundee press which obligingly provided them with ample inches of column space. Within days of the Republican rally, the *Courier* announced that 'Dundee may soon have the opportunity of hearing Mr Michael Collins speak on the Irish settlement', as a committee headed by O'Doherty, Devaney and Kimmet, 'who share an episode with a recent period of Ireland's "strange and eventful history"', had written to Collins, Minister of Defence Richard Mulcahy and Sean Milroy TD, inviting them to visit the city. The *Courier* quoted from a letter written by Devaney to the President of the Kevin Barry cumann, Charles 'Cathal' Duthie, suggesting that he inaugurate a debate on 'The Irish Free State or Republic' so that 'the other side of the question be heard' and 'your members will be able to judge matters for themselves'. Devaney added that he would take the position of Collins, who, he noted, 'was accorded a high compliment by an opponent at a recent meeting in Dundee, when the audience was told "he had played a man's part in Ireland". So far', the *Courier* wrote, 'the challenge has not been accepted'.[158]

A meeting of 'various Irish bodies' (which the press failed to name), called by O'Doherty and Devaney to discuss a prospective visit by Collins, followed, at which the Republicans in the audience made their opposition abundantly clear, not least to Devaney's suggestion that that 'eight or nine individuals in Glasgow' were attempting 'to dictate to the rest of Scotland whether they were to hear Collins or not'. Consequently, it was agreed at a follow-up meeting, by a majority vote, to exclude Dundee Sinn Féin from all further discussions on the subject.[159]

On 8 May, Devaney presented the Dundee press with Collins' reply to the committee's invitation. 'Unfortunately', Collins wrote, 'matters requiring urgent attention here in Ireland make it impossible for me to come to Dundee at present', but 'I will be very happy indeed to come in the near future'. Citing the problems of widespread unemployment and industrial stagnation, Collins claimed that the Treaty had 'placed power in [their] hands when it was urgently necessary', and that he was 'willing and anxious to submit the issue... before the people who, he maintained, were 'overwhelmingly in [its] favour.' Although he accused the anti-Treatyites of waging a wrecking campaign, he was confident that the differences were 'temporary' and 'already being overcome'. 'Ireland suffers a little from war fever', he conceded, 'but less than any other country in similar circumstances'. He concluded optimistically, however, by assuring 'our friends in Dundee... that Ireland now ceases to be the Cinderella among the nations, and is about to take her place as the first of the small nations of the world'.[160]

There is something of the standard reply about Collins' promise. However, the sentiments appear to have been genuine. Collins would have been aware of the need to shore up support in the Scottish pro-Treaty camp, yet, as his efforts were directed into attempting to avert civil war in Ireland, the propaganda war in Scotland was put on the back burner. In eager anticipation of a future visit, however, Collins' supporters set about organising a series of fund-raising concerts to defray the costs of a reception and presentation, beginning with two concerts in the Oxford Picture House in Lochee. A few days later, O'Doherty announced that, in the absence of 'the accepted leader of the Irish nation', three members of Dáil Eireann – Kevin O'Higgins, Sean Milroy and Sean Nolan – would be welcomed to Dundee by a mass demonstration on Saturday, 20 May.[161] In the event, only Milroy, former Sinn Féin propagandist and now a prominent pro-Treaty one, showed up, accompanied by Richard Purcell and J P Connolly, former Tyneside IRA officers, new pro-Treaty election funds managers for Scotland and the North of England. Significantly, the Republican Organiser for Scotland, Joe Robinson, counselled Patrick O'Neill against holding a counter-demonstration on the day of Milroy's talk as 'everyone should have the opportunity of hearing both sides' – a decision that was approved by the leadership in Ireland. Nevertheless, Robinson, who declined an invitation to talk at such a demonstration, advised having 'several of our men in the hall to ask questions', sent 4,000 handbills for distribution before and after the meeting, and visited the city the night before to discuss tactics with the Dundee Republicans.¹⁶²

The following day, Milroy addressed a crowded meeting in the Foresters' Hall. Mindful of the underlying tension, he admitted that 'those who lived out of Ireland, whether friendly or otherwise, had been bewildered of late by events', that 'some of Ireland's best friends [were] despairing [at] the curious attitude adopted by some opponents of the Treaty'. Milroy endeavoured to put these doubts to rest, by stating that 'the men who had won the Treaty had got them nearer to [a higher] ideal than anything that had been accomplished in the last 700 years'. With unconscious irony, he continued, 'it was not a winning cause that had to resort to the argument of a revolver', predicting hopefully, that 'Saturday's agreement' would mean 'the end of that kind of argument'. Here, Milroy was referring to the previous day's signing of the electoral pact between Collins and de Valera which, in agreeing to an interim coalition Parliament of pro- and anti-Treaty members, paved the way for a reconciliation of the two political parties. Tentative efforts to unify the two sections of the Army, however, had been unsuccessful.¹⁶³ The accompanying speakers bolstered Milroy's bid to convert sceptics to the 'stepping stone' thesis; with Connolly describing the Treaty as 'a great onward step', and Purcell stating that 'to say it was the final settlement was to say that this was the final generation of Irishmen'.¹⁶⁴ Purcell's concluding announcement, that Collins would visit Dundee after the election, was received with loud applause, and no doubt contributed to the £15 collection raised at the end of the meeting.

Away from the buoyant atmosphere of the Foresters' Hall, however, Milroy expressed his reservations to a *Courier* reporter. The Pact, he stated, contained 'the same basic terms as put forward before and not accepted', and would require 'some new articles to meet the wishes of those who had [previously] rejected it'. Nevertheless, he believed it would 'have a good effect in stabilising the nation' and would, he hoped, 'put an end to differences of opinion'.¹⁶⁵

Amidst the press hype surrounding the prospective visit of Collins, plans were advancing in the anti-Treaty camp to bring de Valera to Dundee as part of a wider Scottish speaking tour. While it has been often contended, with little supporting evidence, that de Valera once stayed in the city undercover, correspondence between Joe Robinson, Pat O'Neill and de Valera (via the pen of Eamonn Donnelly), indicates his desire to do so openly.¹⁶⁶ Nevertheless, the Republican leadership also advised, in the same vein as Collins, that the situation in Ireland was too volatile and unpredictable to make any firm arrangements.

Predictably, the British Cabinet deemed the Pact to be a direct violation of the Treaty. The draft Constitution of the Irish Free State, which may have been just Republican enough to avert civil war, was similarly rejected. Colonial Secretary Churchill, who was incandescent at Collins' attempts to outfox the British, summoned Collins and Dáil President, Arthur Griffith, to London where they caved in to pressure to redraft a Constitution more favourable to British imperial interests. [167] Thus, while a date was eventually set for de Valera to speak in Dundee on Monday, 19 June, the publication of the dramatically revised Constitution on the morning of polling day on Thursday, 15 June, before many voters had had a chance to read it, scuppered the arrangements. The *Courier* reported that de Valera '[is] in consultation with his lieutenants. Things are moving fast and an unexpected situation may develop out of affairs as they stand at this minute'. [168]

In the North of Ireland, things had already reached a crisis point. On 17 June, the *Dundee Catholic Herald* reported the story of a young Belfast Catholic who had turned up at their offices in Bell Street having 'fled for his life' from Loyalist violence, and who had been wandering around Scotland for several weeks in a fruitless attempt to find work. The *Herald*, who may have scented a police agent, sought and obtained further evidence in the form of a letter from the lad's mother from which it quoted:

> All the men are gone [and] our own friends are scattered all over Scotland, not one of them having got a job. We are in starvation here. We had to stay in the felt works[169] all night on Saturday as the Loyalist snipers were shooting at the back of the house. The British soldiers came into the house and retaliated. One of your aunts has had to sell all her furniture, while two of your cousins had to seek lodgings in another quarter.[170]

The young man went on to inform them that the new civilian police force, the Ulster Specials, were composed of 'the scum of the earth', and related how he had witnessed one of their number shoot a Catholic man, and use his bayonet to cut the representation of a cross on the wounded man's foot. 'What have the British loyalists to say to this? And what does the *Dundee Advertiser* think?', blasted the *Herald*, which five months previously had accused the *Advertiser* of 'bolster[ing] up the Black and Tan methods' and promulgating crude Irish stereotypes.[171] The *Herald* concluded that their staff had provided for the young man's immediate needs and directed him to a quarter where he could find food and shelter.

Until this point, much debate on the Articles of Agreement had focused on the question of sovereignty and the oath of allegiance. Such first-hand accounts of the suffering and brutality endured by the besieged Catholic population of Belfast were a timely reminder of the consequences of Partition, and may have served to dampen support for the Treaty.

Ironically, in the same week that the young Belfast refugee appeared on the *Herald*'s doorstep, a farewell function for Dundee Sinn Féin's most ardent Treatyite, Sean O'Doherty, proved to be the proverbial damp squib. The *Herald* noted that the event, which was held in the Forester's Hall on Sunday, 11 June, 'was not too well attended', which it attributed to 'the weather and the unfortunate hour of the proceedings' – an appropriate metaphor given that Ireland was on the brink of civil war.[172] O'Doherty left for Ireland the following day. His decision to leave Scotland at this point, when his political allies were still holding out for a visit by Michael Collins, is unclear. It is possible he was following in the footsteps of Henry Coyle, with whom he had spent six months in Peterhead Prison. O'Doherty had been a key link in the arms supply chains operated by Coyle and Strickland up until their arrest in December 1920, and had likely fallen under the former's command, or at least his influence, while in prison. Within a week of his release on 13 February, Coyle had returned to Ireland and joined the National (Free State) Army. O'Doherty had clearly maintained contact and the pair were quick to hook up. On 26 June, O'Doherty attended Coyle's wedding at St Mary's Church, Abercromby Street, Glasgow, presenting him with a silver teapot on behalf of the officers and men of Dundee Company of the IRA. However, while Coyle's involvement in the Civil War and his career thereafter has been well documented,[173] nothing more was heard of O'Doherty, who died before 1938.[174] The circumstances remain unknown.

As O'Doherty left Dundee, Father John Fahy returned, ostensibly to attend two belated farewell functions – which coincided with his 29th birthday on 14 June – an afternoon reception in the Queen's Hotel, presided over by Monsignor Turner and attended by the priests of his former parishes, including Father Durand, and an evening celebration in the Foresters' Hall. Unlike O'Doherty's function, the Foresters' Hall was crowded with an enthusiastic throng of supporters who gave Fahy a standing ovation and presented him with the receipt for a five-seater motor car, which awaited him in Dublin, and a 'handsome hand-painted address'. Amongst the nine-person concert party who contributed to a musical programme was Annie Glover, who had performed at O'Doherty's 'do', and Lena McDonald, who hadn't. The fragile political situation in Ireland was, judiciously, not mentioned.[175] Nevertheless, it is significant that Fahy's flying visit to Dundee occurred as preparations were being made by the IRA in Scotland to send an expeditionary force to Ireland in the event of an escalation to armed conflict.[176]

If the war of independence against the centuries-old oppressor had been a cause to glorify, then the prospect of former comrades-in-arms laying each other to waste was too depressing for many to contemplate. Despite the bitter political clashes which had followed the signing of the Treaty, the outbreak of physical hostilities in late June still came as a blow to most Dundee activists and sympathisers. The fatal shooting of Collins at Béal na Bláth by Republican forces on 22 August stunned many people within and outwith the movement. Despite the divisions, Collins was highly regarded by many Republicans, who subsequently chose to remember him as the organisational genius who brought Ireland to the brink of freedom but fell at the last hurdle.

The Treatyites now had a martyr who they could enlist into the continuing propaganda campaign. On 24 September, Sean McFergus of Glasgow, addressed a gathering in the Masonic Temple, under the auspices of the Dundee branch of the pro-Treaty Irish Liberty Club. McFergus appealed to Irishmen to rally behind the newly established club and finish the work of Collins and Griffith (who had died of a cerebral haemorrhage on 12 August). McFergus, who had recently returned from Ireland, stated that 'the National Forces were gradually assuming control' and 'the back of the rebellion [was] broken'. He predicted that the question of the Ulster counties would be soon be settled as 'the hard-headed businessmen of Belfast would realise that only by throwing their lot in with the rest of the country could they hope to maintain their position'.[177] A flag was then unfurled bearing the portrait of Michael Collins.

The Treaty had already obtained the support of the Catholic hierarchy in Ireland. However, McFergus's view that all that was required to finish the job was the approval of the business class in the North fell far short of the revolutionary Republican ideal. On 13 September, a large number of supporters gathered in the Foresters' Hall to hear pro-Republican priest, Father Torley, urge them 'not to follow politically the Irish bishops who were willing to accept the so-called freedom of the Free State'. His appeal to them to be 'out-and-out Republicans' and to 'teach their children that they were foreigners in a foreign land' who followed 'no King but only a President, the President of the Irish Republic' drew cheers of affirmation.[178]

Torley also advised them 'to take no part in elections [unless] their religion was involved', possibly an allusion to the continued state maintenance of Catholic schools – a major concern of the Catholic Church in Scotland at the time.[179] In the run up to the General Election in November, the issue formed two of five questions submitted to the six candidates for the two-seat Dundee constituency by Monsignor Turner on behalf of the Catholic Church. The fifth question, 'Will you give your vote and influence with your party in helping Ireland towards national unity and facilitating the establishment of an Irish Free State' was answered affirmatively by four of the candidates – Neddy Scrymgeour (Prohibitionist), E D Morel (Labour), D J MacDonald (Coalition Liberal) and R R Pilkington (Liberal). Churchill did not respond.[180] Willie Gallacher, the Communist candidate, took the opportunity to espouse his Irish Republican credentials:

> I have been not only interested, but closely identified with the Irish struggle throughout its various phases. I was the one man more than any other outside the Sinn Féin Movement who was trusted by Irish leaders. My earnest and continued support will be given to Irish Republicans, and whatever I can do to buck the power of Ireland's imperial enemies will be done with my whole heart.[181]

Gallacher's words were also mindful of his campaign team, a prominent section of which was 'a small group of lads who were heart and soul with the IRA'.[182] This element made their opinions abundantly clear at an eve of poll meeting at the Drill Hall in Bell Street, where Winston Churchill was interrogated on his part in 'giving the Black and Tans a free hand to beat the men, women and children of Ireland down, and called to acknowledge the fact that, in 1918, the Irish people had voted for freedom and hadn't got it. Churchill's response, that 'our' soldiers and policemen '[have] every right to defend themselves', and 'Haven't they got [freedom] now?' were met with roars of indignation from the red-green alliance whose relentless hissing, heckling and singing of 'The Red Flag' drove Churchill from the platform after 40 minutes.[83] It had not been a good day for Churchill as, at the close of an earlier meeting, a woman had thrown a bag of excrement at him.[184]

In an echo of earlier comments on the carrying of the Irish flag at unemployed rallies, the strident interventions of the Irish element at Churchill's election meetings were deemed, by the *Dundee Catholic Herald*, to be the work of Communist agitators:

> ...at some critical point someone unfurls a flag or displays an Irish emblem to the accompaniment of an Irish song. Then the buzz amongst the Churchill cronies – 'The Irish again' – and the impression is allowed to spread that the disturbances are caused by Irishmen and women.

As was the case with the unemployed protests, the fact that a number of Dundee Irishmen and Irishwomen were as equally well-versed in 'The Red Flag' as in 'God Save Ireland', and were only too willing to join with the 'Communist element' in holding Churchill to account for his crimes against the Irish people, and indeed for the British government's attacks against the working class, was a fact that this self-appointed spokesman for the Irish community seemed unable to countenance.

While, in his view, associations with hooliganism did nothing 'to further the cause', Irish anger at Churchill was nevertheless righteous. Indeed, even the temperate *Dundee Catholic Herald* bristled at the 'impudence, ignorance and treachery' of O'Kelly, McLoughlin, Maloney, Murphy and May, the signatories of a polling day notice which appeared in the local press urging Irish voters to support the Treaty by keeping Churchill in the British Parliament.[185] This was possibly at the behest of Richard Purcell, J P Connolly and other English-based, pro-Treaty campaigners, who canvassed Irish electors in Dundee to vote for Churchill, and appear to have been totally oblivious to the hostility towards him within, and beyond, the Irish community.[186] The main priority of Irish electors was, as Archbishop Mannix had earlier counselled, to kick Churchill out and replace him with someone who better represented their interests.

It was not to be Gallacher. In the event, he came last, polling 5,906 votes – a respectable outcome nevertheless given that it was the Communist Party's first parliamentary contest in Dundee. According to Bob Stewart, Gallacher and his supporters had no illusions about winning, their main aim being 'to expose Churchill and to contribute to his final defeat'.[187] While a significant number of the Dundee Irish campaigned for, and may indeed have voted for Gallacher, the majority threw their electoral weight behind Scrymgeour who had already paved the ground, particularly amongst a new generation of women voters. 'Ladies especially [are] invited', read the announcement of a talk on 'the Irish Question' in Blackness Hall on 9 November 1921, in which Scrymgeour had gone on to denounce the British government's 'despicable scrapping of the Home Rule Act, and its face-saving offer of Dominion Home Rule status (which he attributed to international pressure), and to lambast the Ulsterites who 'were being left to suck their Orange dry'. 'It would be interesting,' he noted, 'to see how many in Dundee would deign to pick up the pieces'.[188] Indeed, despite Scrymgeour's colourful food metaphor, as noted earlier, the consequences of the Treaty had proved to be a lot less savoury for the artificially created Catholic-nationalist minority in the new northern 'statelet' who were suffering disproportionately in terms of discrimination, displacement and sectarian violence.[189]

Although the Civil War saw a tailing off in the large support previously enjoyed by the Republican movement in Dundee, a number of committed activists maintained their allegiance to the Republic and continued in their efforts to realise it. Their activities rarely met with opposition – Irish sympathisers in Dundee appear to have remained ambivalent in their perspectives. There was, however, the occasional exception. On 16 January 1923, the *Courier* reported that a well-attended meeting of Irish Republican supporters who had gathered in the Masonic Temple to hear reports on the situation in Ireland, was disrupted by 'a number of young women who were evidently Free Staters'. The meeting, which was chaired by Thomas Dempsey, heard addresses from Glasgow-based organiser, Joseph Browne, who overstated the military strength of the IRA, and disparaged the Free State forces as a 'pantomime army'; and from socialist republican and 1916 veteran, Dr Kathleen Lynn, who, more practically, appealed to the audience to do all they could to support the Republican Army. In the midst of Browne's concluding remarks, the Free Staters left the hall, shouting vigorously, at which point the hitherto silent majority retaliated, 'pitting their vocal efforts against the anti-Republicans' who lingered in the street 'pouring ridicule on the Republicans' before drifting away.[190]

There were no dissenting voices, however, when Constance Markievicz addressed a 400-strong audience which packed into Blackness Hall two weeks later. The *Courier* reported that 'unrestrained enthusiasm prevailed throughout the whole proceedings, the cry "Up, de Valera!" being time and again raised with the greatest exclamation'. After the customary rendition of 'The Soldier's Song', Madame Markievicz got down to the business of galvanising support for the Republican cause. After a vivid evocation of the state of Ireland during the Tan 'Terror', she disclosed that, in contrast with the high salaries of British Cabinet Ministers, her salary as Minister of Labour in the Republican government never exceeded £500 a year. Referring to the Irish Catholic hierarchy's attempts to ostracise the IRA, she reassured the predominantly Catholic audience that 'it was "bunkum" to say [the Republicans] were trying to start a new religion.' They remained 'true to the Catholic faith'; indeed, many who had, reputedly, been excommunicated, 'lived the lives and died the deaths of saints.' She concluded by making a strong financial appeal for the moral and financial support of those in Dundee 'for those who are now on the hills'. A resolution, pledging support 'to the Government of the Irish Republic and to President de Valera and those associated with him in the fight for Freedom', and calling upon 'Irish exiles the world over to unite behind the Republic', was then passed unanimously to great cheering.[191]

Up until that point, Constance Markievicz was the best-known Irish Republican figure, and certainly the highest-ranking woman, to have openly visited Dundee. Her long public involvement in the Irish independence movement had been documented widely in the local press – from the Dublin Lockout in 1913, through to her part in the Easter Rising of 1916, where she had, reputedly, escaped execution on account of her gender. Her visit to Dundee provided a much-needed morale boost to the Republican movement in the city, and may have succeeded in drawing some drifting supporters back into the Republican fold.

The call for moral and financial support from Irish expatriates came at a critical point. While Republican activists in Scotland continued in their efforts to propagandize and procure arms, the situation in Ireland was unfavourable. The Republican campaign was desperately short of funds and, despite Browne's inflated statistics and Markievicz's fighting talk, the IRA was vastly under-resourced in terms of weaponry, hence effective combatants. Former Adjutant/Intelligence Officer of the First Southern Division IRA, Florrie O'Donoghue, who remained neutral in the Civil War, estimated a relative strength of five Free Staters to one IRA Volunteer, added to which the Free State forces held the barracks, armoured cars and artillery.[192] More importantly, the steady stream of popular support which had sustained the guerrilla campaign throughout the Tan War was drying up.

In the early hours of Sunday, 11 March, the Republican movement in Scotland and England received a critical blow when around 110 activists were effectively kidnapped in a series of raids carried out at the behest of the Free State authorities with the sanction and support of the British government. Of the 37 people rounded up in Scotland, the sole Dundee operative was Patrick O'Neill, who was arrested by the Dundee police at his lodgings at 32 South Tay Street on charges of 'acting or being about to act in a manner prejudicial to the restoration of law and order in Ireland', put in a police car and conveyed directly to Glasgow, from where, alongside the other 36 prisoners, he was placed on the torpedo-boat destroyer HMS Wolfhound, shipped to Dublin and interned in Mountjoy Jail.[193]

Here was a concerted manoeuvre by the Free State and British governments to wipe out the Irish Republican movement in Scotland, England and Wales by taking out the key players, the identities of whom were passed on to British intelligence services by Free State agents. Indeed, an unidentified high-ranking Republican who had evaded arrest in Glasgow disclosed to a press reporter that 'the leaders had been taken'.[194] The high number of prisoners from Glasgow was a measure of the status and the relative strength of the Republican movement in the city at the time – it also indicates a high level of penetration and local knowledge on the part of intelligence agents. Among those arrested were Commandant-General Joe Robinson, O/C of the 1st Scottish Brigade, PR chief Joe

Browne, and Paddy Hyland, O/C of No 2 Battalion, 2nd Scottish Brigade.

Patrick O'Neill

Patrick Joseph O'Neill was born in the parish of Ballinderry, County Tyrone, in 1898, to John O'Neill, a farmer, and his wife Rose Ann. As the second son of eight children, and therefore not in line to inherit the farm, Patrick trained as a teacher, qualifying in June 1920. In September, he obtained his first teaching post, which, as jobs were scarce in Ireland, was a temporary one in Middlesborough; and his first permanent one as an assistant teacher at St Mary's Boys' School, Forebank Road, Dundee, the following February. In May-June 1921, he joined the O'Rahilly Sinn Féin cumann, later taking on the position of Secretary, a post he held until the organisation was restructured on a Republican footing in October 1922. He also helped set up the Kevin Barry cumann which, thanks to his organising and recruiting skills, incorporated some of the O'Rahilly's, and possibly the Father Michael Griffin's, membership.[195] In the autumn of 1922, O'Neill was appointed regional (North of Forth) organiser of the newly formed Cumann Poblacht na h'Eireann in Albain, the sister body of Cumann na Poblachta in Ireland and the Irish Self-Determination League in England, in which capacity he organised successful meetings in Fife and, admittedly, less fruitful ones in Perth.[196] As a captain in the Dundee Battalion of the IRA, O'Neill was also responsible for arms procurement in the district, all the more so after Lena McDonald stood down from purchasing following her release from jail in 1921.

As with Lena, the Dundee police had been tracking O'Neill's movements and intercepting his mail. Prior to his arrest in 1923, the Chief Constable of Dundee, John Carmichael, had noted, later reporting to Scotland Yard that, during a visit to Ireland in April 1922, O'Neill was sent a package from a 'Miss Ford [sic] of Dundee' containing four revolver cartridges concealed in a newspaper. (Mayo-born Catherine Forde, of 106 Annfield Street, was a teacher at St Joseph's Primary, Blackness Road, and an 'intimate friend' of O'Neill.) A report from Detective-Inspector Andrew Oliphant states there had been insufficient evidence to prosecute her, or to charge O'Neill, who had been questioned by police and denied all knowledge, although, as Oliphant opined, his demeanour suggested otherwise. Carmichael also cited correspondence from Joe Robinson, John

Slaven of the Thomas Whelan Republican Club, Methil, and receipts from a Mrs O'Connor of the Irish Republican Treasury in Dublin, found at O'Neill's address at the time of his arrest.[197]

The scale of the arrests, which were carried out under the nullified Restoration of Order in Ireland Act of 1920, not to mention the blatant collusion between the Free State and British authorities, served to disrupt Republican operations and discompose British-based supporters, as was the undoubted intention. The discovery, in mid-April, of a box of 200 cartridges on a piece of ground adjoining 'a large textile establishment in the northern district of Dundee', led police to speculate that it 'may have some connection with Irish Republican activities in Britain', and that the prospect of more police raids may have prompted the custodian to ditch any incriminating material.[198]

On the 19 April, a meeting of the serried ranks of the Dundee Irish movement fired off an angry missal to the Secretary of State for Scotland, Lord Novar, condemning 'the kidnapping and continued detention in Free State prisons of Irishmen resident in England and Scotland and, in particular, the deportation of P J O'Neill of Dundee'. The message, which accompanied other written protests from Labour Party branches in Glasgow and Edinburgh, and from the National Unemployed Workers' Movement, was signed on behalf of the meeting, by P Connor, J Kelly and T Dempsey.[199]

Meanwhile, in Mountjoy Jail, as the Scottish deportees appealed against their arrests and deportation through appointed lawyer E Rosslyn Mitchell of Rosslyn Mitchell and Tullis Cochrane, O'Neill applied to present his own case before the Advisory Committee in London. The Committee, which had been set up by the Home Secretary to examine and report on the cases of the 'Irish Deportees', consisted of three senior members of the British legal profession, all of whom had been chosen because of their legal experience and loyalty to the British establishment. Chairman Lord Trevethin (Alfred Lawrence) was former Lord Chief Justice for England and Wales and a member of the Privy Council. Sir Henry Mather Jackson had been Chair of the Appeal Tribunals during the War and was Chairman of the Monmouthshire Quarter Sessions and of several railway, dock and coal companies. Sir Matthew Wallace CBE had been a member of the Defence of the Realm (Losses) War Compensation

Court and was an ex-President of the Scottish Chamber of Agriculture. H R Scott acted as Secretary.

O'Neill's request was granted, and his case was heard, along with that of Glasgow shopkeeper James Hickey, at Brixton Prison on 4 May. Unlike Hickey, who denied all involvement in the Republican movement beyond being 'pulled in' inadvertently by Joe Robinson because he had a licence to sell firearms, however, O'Neill affirmed his allegiance to Cumann Poblacht na h'Eireann in Albain which he maintained was purely political and perfectly legal. Here an examination of his interview is pertinent and illuminating.[200] The Committee began by establishing O'Neill's identity, his place of origin, the date he left Ireland and the date he came to Dundee – February 1921. The interrogation proceeded:

LORD TREVETHIN: And then the Treaty came along?
O'NEILL: December the same year.
Q: And then you took up a position of opposition?
O'NEILL: At that time I belonged to an organisation which decided on the Treaty.
Q: Yes, but you did not continue on that side?
O'NEILL: No, I did not.
Q: You rebelled, so to speak?
O'NEILL: No, I have a statement in my pocket which I will read if you like.
Q: I do not want your written statement. Can you answer the question? I will read the statement. *O'Neill hands it over.*

O'Neill's Statement

At the time of my arrest I was ignorant of why I should have been deported, but on reaching Mountjoy, I was informed that I was suspected of being complicated [sic] in the traffic of arms and ammunition to Ireland for the use of the Irregulars there. Mr Bridgeman [William Bridgeman, the Home Secretary], I am led to believe, stated that there was a conspiracy existing to destroy public property in Britain. I wish to leave a statement of my case before you. I do not belong to any militant body in Britain, or never have, nor have I been engaged actively, passively, or in any way whatsoever in the traffic of arms in Britain, or never have, nor have I been engaged actively, passively, or in any way whatsoever with the traffic of arms between this country and Ireland, nor have I any knowledge (whatsoever) of any movement for the destruction of public or private property in Britain, nor would I associate myself with such a movement. I have been a member of the Poblacht na h'Eireann in Albain organisation in Dundee and acted as Secretary to a branch there. I was aware that this organisation was legal and constitutional in Britain as it never has been suppressed or declared illegal, hence I was right to infer that so long as I acted constitutionally as the laws of the country permitted, I couldn't be guilty of any offence. I acted as Irish history lecturer at the weekly meetings of the Gaelic League branch here and this so far constitutes my connection with Irish movements. Any statements which may have been made against me in contrary to this I declare as false and without foundation.

Q: When did you write this?
O'NEILL: In prison this morning. It is known as Poblacht na h'Eireann in Albain. It is the equivalent of the Self-Determination League in England. It has never been suppressed or declared illegal.
Q: Where did you get this information?
O'NEILL: I was always told that. It has never been suppressed.
Q: But you do know the lady in Dundee who sent you some revolvers?
O'NEILL: No, I know of no lady.
SIR H.M. JACKSON: Only cartridges?
O'NEILL: I know of no-one who sent me these. The Detective Inspector called at the school afterwards and asked me for a list of names of all the people who had written to me during the time I was in Ireland. I gave him a list of three, and he interviewed all of these.
CHAIRMAN: And he showed you an address and asked you if

you knew the writing?

O'NEILL: Yes, he asked if I knew the writing, and I said I could not recognise it, as I did not know it. He showed me a paper parcel.

Q: You organised things, did you not, in Dundee?

O'NEILL: No, sir.

Q: There was no organisation until you came?

O'NEILL: Yes, there was, long before I came.

Q: Was there this Poblacht?

O'NEILL: Yes, there was an organisation.

Q: And you became an officer of it?

O'NEILL: No, I did not become an officer, but only a member of it. It is a purely political body.

Q: "Purely political" is a curious expression. It is clearly a body devoted to upsetting the government of this country.

O'NEILL: No, it has nothing to do with the government of this country otherwise I would not be in it.

Q: But these are the things found in your house?

O'NEILL: May I see them?

Q: Yes, of course you may. What did you do with the money you collected?

O'NEILL: These were receipts. I had nothing to do with those: they were handed over to me when I became Secretary.

Q: You did become Secretary. I thought you said you did not become an officer.

O'NEILL: I think I mention that in the statement – Secretary of a branch of this organisation.

O'NEILL: My position is this, I wished the Irish people to decide for themselves, as soon as they did I was done with it. In other words, to secure for the Irish people to self-determine it for themselves.

Q: This was not so much self-determination for themselves when you in Dundee were collecting money for it. That is not self-determination if it was somebody else.

O'NEILL: We were not collecting money for it.

Q: Did you not send money to Ireland? There is a receipt for

£50 here.

O'NEILL: That receipt was for money that went to the Dependents' Committee – the White Cross Society in Ireland.

Q: There is nothing about that on it.

O'NEILL: That is where it went to... At least it that is what the money was sent for.

Q: [What] it was sent for, but there is nothing about dependents there, is there?...This is the translation of it: 'Treasury of the Republic, Dublin. I hereby acknowledge having received from P. O'Neill, 32 South Tay Street, Dundee, the sum of £50. On behalf of the Treasurer, Mrs O'Callaghan – J.J. O'Kelly, for C & F." [There] is a really long letter complimenting you upon the contribution of £50, saying that it makes £90 in all since E. [Eamonn] Donnelly visited Dundee in November, and "I think this will take first place amongst the Clubs, proving their loyalty to the Republic.' That is what the letter says?

O'NEILL: Yes, who is the writer, please?

Q: S. Duggan, written from Bank Street. [Seamus Duggan, Secretary of Cumann Poblacht na h'Éireann in Albain, lived at 26 Bank Street, Cambuslang.]

SIR MATTHEW WALLACE: Do you know him?

O'NEILL: Yes

CHAIRMAN: It is signed S. something. You change your names so absurdly that nobody can read them. Very few of them can read Gaelic. Are you a Gaelic scholar?

O'NEILL: No, not a Gaelic scholar, but I have an elementary knowledge of Gaelic.

Q: That is the extent most of them seem to have. They can just about write it very slightly, but you could not write it as you could ordinary language?

O'NEILL: No, I am only able to say a few phrases. I could not write a letter, for instance.

Q: Just enough to make people shout when you are on a platform.

O'NEILL: No, I never use it.

Q: This is collecting money for the establishment of a Republic in Ireland. That is what you call an innocent political operation, do you?

O'NEILL: It is constitutional.

Q: Why constitutional?

O'NEILL: Because the people of Ireland elect to govern themselves.

Q: They did have government and they have been killing themselves ever since. Do you call that innocent?

O'NEILL: The position is this: what you all know. There was a pact signed by the two opponents – the Anti-Treaty Party and the Treaty Party, and the object of this Pact was to have an election of the people to elect a common Parliament called Dáil Éireann to unite for the time being until such times as something could be offered to the Irish People to put things straight for them. The last election in Ireland was held on that basis. It was temporary until such time as the people could be educated on the different sides of the question; until that time, until the case was properly before the people to give them an opportunity of deciding which they would have – Republic or a Treaty, and that has not been done yet.

Q: But how in the world could you they do it: supposing they said they would have a Republic, that means war?

O'NEILL: Yes, possibly.

Q: That is what you vote for?

O'NEILL: If the Irish people say they want a Republic, I agree that the Irish people are entitled to their own government... It possibly means war but I have sent no money or arms for that purpose.

Q: You are receiving British money as a schoolteacher in Britain and organising or endeavouring to organise a Republic in Ireland.'

O'NEILL: 'I simply want the Irish people to choose for themselves.'

Q: It is no good going back on that phrase. That is nothing. You do not want that at all. What you want them to do is to constitute a Republic.

O'NEILL: I was aware that the Republican Organisation, Poblacht na h'Eireann in Albain was a legal organisation.

Q: You are collecting money – your organisation in England and Scotland – and sending that money over to supply the armed forces of the Republic in Ireland with the power to fight.

O'NEILL: So far as I am aware no money went for armed forces in Ireland.

Q: There is no power on your part to prevent that money supplying them with bombs, pistols or anything else.

Q: You are a schoolmaster teaching others.

O'NEILL: We all have liberty of opinion though.

[Here O'Neill, who was a devout Catholic, anticipates a speech made by Archbishop Mannix in Dublin in October 1925: 'When a man becomes a priest, he does not cease to be a citizen, and, being a citizen, he has a right to his own opinions like other citizens'.[201]]

Q: This is more than opinion, this is action.

O'NEILL: It cannot be action. There is nothing to implicate that I have been connected with army rebellion in Ireland.

Q: Who came to address [these] meetings for you in Dundee?

O'NEILL: The Countess Markievicz and Dr Kathleen Lynn on another occasion.

Q: Did Joe Robinson come?

O'NEILL: I remember him at one meeting. That was before I had anything to do with the secretaryship. That was in 1922, I think it was.

Q: You know that the Countess was actually engaged in hostilities, fighting?

O'NEILL: No. At Least she never said, as I knew nothing of it. She never proclaimed it from the platform where I heard her speak.

Q: Do you mean to say that you heard her speak and she did not proclaim the armed fighting and advocate it?

O'NEILL: Yes, she advocated it.

Q: Of course she did.

O'NEILL: I do not remember her saying she took part in it. Of course she advocated it.

Q: She not only advocated it, but she took part in it herself.

O'NEILL: She may have, for all I know.

SIR MATTHEW WALLACE: That was what she was there for.

CHAIRMAN: To urge you to form branches or Companies of the Irish Republican Army in Scotland.

O'NEILL: No.

Q: Do you mean to say that you did not hear her advocate the formation of Companies of the IRA in Scotland?

O'NEILL: Yes Sir. I mean to say I never heard her advocate such a thing. She simply came at the request of the Irish residents of Dundee to lay the Irish case before them, and I never heard her advocate the establishment of a Republican Army in Scotland.

Q: Companies of the Republican Army?

O'NEILL: Companies either.

Q: Were you a member of a Company?

O'NEILL I was not – at no time.

Q: Were there not Companies known to you?

O'NEILL: There were no Companies known to me, neither in Dundee nor outside.

Q: Have you been to Glasgow?

P. O'Neill: Yes.

Q: Do you know that they have Companies in Glasgow?

O'NEILL: No, I know nothing about the military body, whether established in Scotland or Ireland. I know nothing about the military part which is known as the IRA.

Q: How did you manage to keep your mind from any knowledge of it? It was buzzing around you, you know. They were drilling and doing all sorts of things.

O'NEILL: I never saw drilling while I was in Dundee, and since I came from Ireland I never saw any company of the IRA drilling, nor have I belonged to such an organisation as the IRA.

Q: You have never seen a Company of the IRA in Scotland?
O'NEILL: No.
Q: You know this man [Joe] Robinson was the O/C. Scotland, did you not?
O'NEILL: No, I knew nothing about the IRA in Scotland.
Q: How did you manage to avoid knowing that? You saw him and knew him?
O'NEILL: A man like that possibly would not tell me seeing that I was not a member.
[There] are two distinct bodies. The political [one] I belonged to has no connection with the military part known as the IRA. As I said before, I never have belonged to the IRA...
Q: And yet you were sending them money?
O'NEILL: As I said before, for propaganda purposes.
Q: They are distinctions that are unreal, you know. Is there anything more you wish to say to us?
O'NEILL: I want to make it clear that I do not belong to the military body in Scotland. I belong to the organisation I have already mentioned, and I understood it to be purely constitutional and legal in Britain. That is why I belonged to it, and that is all I have to say. I have not in any way assisted armed rebellion in Ireland either by sending arms or munitions or war materials whatsoever.

And so, O'Neill refused to be drawn on his military involvement or to implicate anyone else. At the end of a gruelling interrogation, the Advisory Committee had nothing on him, yet the fact that the two parties represented ideological forces that were fundamentally antagonistic to each other became more apparent as the interview wore on. O'Neill had banked on the fact that his knowledge of the law would be enough to secure his liberty – in Mountjoy he had taken legal advice from Rosslyn Mitchell who had, no doubt, considered him capable of advocating for himself and advised accordingly. Nevertheless, O'Neill's defence that Cumann Poblacht na Eireann n'Albain had 'not been suppressed', and Trevethin's response: 'you are intelligent enough to know that you cannot suppress everything', suggests that when British imperial interests, including the Dominion status of the new Irish Free State, were at stake, the law could be disregarded. Trevethin's final comment: 'You have not actually conveyed guns...You have only done the indirect propaganda for the purpose of getting money and supplying them with money', indicates that O'Neill's opinions alone were sufficient to make him an existential threat. Scottish Brigade records show that he was a captain in the IRA, although, at this point his interrogators had no way of proving it.[202] Still, O'Neill's vigorous defence of the right of the Irish people to wage war in the pursuit of a Republic stuck in the craw of these scions of the British establishment. Consequently, O'Neill's appeal was rejected on the grounds that 'it would be injurious to the restoration and maintenance of law and order in Ireland to set at liberty at present a youth which hold and acts on such opinions'.[203]

This undoubtedly came as a blow. However, the damage had already been done. The day after his appeal, (before he knew the outcome), O'Neill wrote to his guarantor, Brother Liguori, the Head Teacher of St Mary's, that he had altered his views 'and when I get back I will be able to tell you why'.[204] He mentioned how he was sustained by the daily visits of a priest, by Mass on Sundays, Benediction, Rosary and hymn practice four times a week, and the privilege, as a political prisoner, of being allowed to use his books for study. The letter concluded with a request to remember him to his friends and 'say a prayer for me'.[205]

Alone and isolated in the 'Belly of the Beast', O'Neill would have had plenty of time to reflect upon his position. The fact that the Free State authorities had used the IRA intelligence network built up by Michael Collins to bring down their former comrades was bad enough, the fact that they had got the British government to do their dirty work was the ultimate betrayal. O'Neill may have maintained his Republican ideals in the hope that they would one day prevail. For the moment, his role had been rendered redundant, and he may have considered it was time to direct his energy elsewhere.

His faith in the law was not totally misplaced, however. Twelve days later, the majority of the deportees, O'Neill included, were released amidst charges of illegal suspension of *habeas corpus* by the British government and allegations of torture against the Free State prison guards.[206] Of the various abuses reported by the ex-prisoners, being held in handcuffs for several days and forced to eat food off the floor recalled the degrading treatment meted out to the legendary Fenian, O'Donovan Rossa, in nineteenth-century British jails; and the experience of one deportee who was thrown against a wall and suspended by the hands for several hours, anticipated the interrogation techniques used by the British Army in the mass internment of Northern nationalists in August 1971.

On 17 May, the Scottish deportees returned to an enthusiastic welcome at Glasgow Central Station before departing to their respective homes. O'Neill was back in Dundee by evening. Two weeks later, he applied to the Education Authority to be reinstated in his post. After some initial opposition and a further meeting, his request was eventually approved by a majority vote of eleven to five.[207] In 1925, he returned to Ireland, along with his most trusted collaborator, Catherine Forde. The two were married and settled in the border village of Middletown, County Armagh, where Patrick was appointed Principal Teacher of St John's Boys' School, a position he held until his retirement in the early 1960s. Between rearing five children, Catherine, (commonly known as 'Red Kate' on account of her hair rather than her politics), also taught in the same school while 'P J' found a less controversial outlet for his nationalist ideals and organisational talents in the Gaelic Athletic Association, of which he was Secretary, then Chairman of the Armagh County Board for over 30 years.[208]

On 24 May, the issuing of a ceasefire order to Republican forces, followed by de Valera's 'Legion of the Rearguard' statement, marked the end of the Civil War. With the military campaign suspended for the foreseeable future, it fell to Dev's Lieutenant, Constance Markievicz, assisted by Joseph Browne, to console Dundee's Irish Republicans and their allies. On Friday, 29 June, Markievicz addressed two large meetings in the AOH and the ILP halls, held under the auspices of the O'Rahilly and Kevin Barry Sinn Féin cumainn. In contrast to her previous bombastic rhetoric, Madame was uncharacteristically reflective. The Republican movement in Ireland, she conceded, 'may not appear very strong at present', yet it was 'growing and developing' and would 'never be blotted out'.[209] The audience, however, remained typically enthusiastic. 'When question time arrived', another report stated: 'it was quite clear that the glamour which existed for a while regarding the Irish "Free State" is fast disappearing. The Irish of Dundee, who have the real interests of Ireland at heart are again rallying to the cause'.[210]

As was the custom with visiting Irish Republicans, Markievicz stayed at the McDonalds at 31 Brook Street. The hospitality was reciprocated in September when Lena delivered a small quantity of munitions to her home in Dublin en route to a 'holiday' in Galway (to see Father Fahy, no doubt). The 'unofficial' delivery was made at the request of Jean Quinn who, in the wake of successive police raids and having already served one prison sentence for arms possession, was worried about hoarding weapons in her house. Throughout 1923, Lena continued to carry munitions to Glasgow. At this point, it was primarily to get rid of material which her pawnbroker supplier wished to offload. Lena made her last delivery to Glasgow a week before Christmas in 1923.[211]

The activity did not end with the military campaign, however. The Irish Republican movement in Dundee now turned its attention to the plight of the many thousands of Republican prisoners held in Free State prisons and internment camps, the most prominent being de Valera, who was arrested while addressing an election meeting in his East Clare constituency in August 1923. Immediately, the Kevin Barry Sinn Féin cumann issued a statement declaring that the election – the first to be held under the Free State constitution – could not, under the circumstances, 'be regarded as a reflex of the Irish people'. Correspondingly, as the Republican prisoners embarked on a mass hunger strike on 13 October, the O'Rahilly cumann castigated the Free State for their 'inhuman and uncivilised treatment' and called for their immediate release.[212] Throughout 1923 and 1924, the two Dundee cumainn and their supporters organised collections, held fundraising concerts and made individual contributions towards the Irish Republican Prisoner Dependants' Fund (IRPDF). The donors and sums raised were acknowledged in the columns of *Eire: The Irish Nation* – the official mouthpiece of the Irish Republican movement in Scotland, England, Wales [213] – now available from 58 Brook Street, the residence of O/C of the Dundee IRA, Thomas Dempsey, and from the Literary Secretary of the O'Rahilly cumann, Maggie Steel.[214] The last IRPDF event, a concert by 'The Dark Town Minstrels' of St Patrick's parish, organised by the Kevin Barry cumann in the ILP hall on 30 March 1924, was reported to have attracted a 'crowded house'.[215] By the time the last few Republican prisoners were released in 16-17 July 1924, however, the campaign was drawing to a close. The O'Rahilly cumann had ceased operating, its most stalwart members falling in with the Kevin Barry.[216] It fell to Annie Barrett, Secretary of the latter, to send a telegram to de Valera offering their congratulations and expressing their confidence that 'Ireland's freedom is in safe-keeping'.[217] On 17 August, President of the cumann, Charles Duthie, addressed the weekly branch meeting in the ILP hall. At the end of a two-hour long speech in which he traced the different phases of the Irish struggle since 1916, Duthie urged those all who had been 'luke-warm since the Treaty' to 'rally to the standard of complete independence and help President de Valera attain what he set out to accomplish'.[218] Unlike reports of previous meetings which invariably boasted the large attendance and positive feedback, there was no mention of either. Duthie was preaching to the converted, but even here it seems, they had little enthusiasm for constitutional politics.

In December 1926, de Valera visited the city, where he addressed a large meeting in the YMCA hall in the appropriately named Constitution Road. Declaring that the present division in Ireland was 'not with the will of the Irish people', and that the 'pretended Treaty' had been 'put over' by force and fraud, Dev then deployed his singular talent for wrapping constitutional strategy in military and populist language to drum up moral and financial support for his new political party, Fianna Fáil. The aim, he said, was 'to reorganise the shattered national forces', 'clear the ground', and put 'the people's representatives' in the Free State Parliament from where they would 'make it clear that Ireland did not want to subject itself to British or any other power'.[219] While many of his listeners may have appreciated the rhetoric, Dev's attempts to proselytise for the constitutional path to full Irish independence failed to convince either the diehards or the wider Irish community. Furthermore, while the Kevin Barry Sinn Féin Club continued to exist, it was within a wider Scottish network which lumbered on with an ever-diminishing membership over the next decade. Moreover, it was with a perspective which became increasingly inward looking, backward looking and estranged from political developments in Ireland, Scotland or anywhere else.[220] It would be another 50 years before Dundee saw its next significant engagement with insurrectionary Irish republicanism.

In conclusion, the years between 1916 and 1923 saw a significant growth in support for physical force Irish republicanism in Dundee.

Initially, this started as a slow-burning response to the 1916 insurrection and executions, and reached its height during the Tan War when Sinn Féin, in alliance with the Catholic Church, succeeded in mobilising huge numbers for the visit of Archbishop Mannix in March 1921. This sympathy extended beyond the Irish-Catholic community to a significant section of Dundee's large working-class population. Given the resentment at the British government for having led them into a bloody war to uphold the right of small nations to self-determination only to deny Ireland that same right; and the revelations of British brutality in Ireland – and the role in it of Winston Churchill, who had already alienated a wide section of the Dundee electorate – the issue was a straightforward one of common decency and justice. Unsurprisingly, Dundee's large working-class population, so long victims of an unfair economic system that the epithet 'underdog' could have been invented for them, took the side of the victims of injustice.

However, it is tempting to overplay the degree of support for physical force Irish republicanism and forget that Irish activists in Dundee and the rest of Scotland were operating in a relatively hostile environment. While Irish Republicans in Scotland were rarely subject to direct physical repression – the cutting edge of British state violence being reserved for their comrades in Ireland and the largely friendly native population there, the Scottish-based authorities favoured a 'softly, softly' approach that employed increasingly sophisticated intelligence-gathering techniques, including an extensive network of paid and unpaid informants, the latter of which were motivated by petty resentments and jealousies, desire for favourable attention from the authorities, and, occasionally, political enmity. The long arm of the British state extended from the corridors of Whitehall down to the local police office, as was clearly exemplified in the mass arrests and deportations to the Free State in March 1923, which, though subsequently ruled illegal, succeeded in incapacitating the Republican movement in Scotland.

With the exception of avowed Scottish nationalists and the Communist movement, the majority of Dundonians outside the Irish community were, if not hostile, then largely ignorant or indifferent. Many were anxious to be seen as law-abiding, if only through an anxious self-preservation and a desire to keep trouble from their door. This also applied to the Irish community where a reputation as a known Sinn Féiner could be a double-edged sword as Lena McDonald found out after she returned home from prison and her triumphant welcoming reception to face the wrath of neighbours who told her that she should have been executed.[221]

Thus, while an assessment of militant Irish republicanism in Dundee does not exactly conform to Eamonn Mooney's claim that the Scottish Division of the IRA were 'working in the midst of a hostile people', the fact that many IRA veterans later faced difficulties in finding work because of their association with the Movement, resulted in a number of them leaving Scotland altogether.[222] The factors which contributed to this, particularly in the next two decades, will be considered in the next chapter.

Endnotes to Chapter 7

1. Statement relative to the work of the IRA in Scotland from Thomas J Wilson, Battalion Commandant, Scottish Brigade, IRA, to Éamon de Valera. IMA, Military Service Pensions Collection [hereafter MSPC], RO/603, p149.
2. *Dundee Courier*, 4 May 1916.
3. As an example of Sheriff Neish's lack of compassion, in November 1915, he sent a young Lochee woman, Bridget Devlin (or Keenan), to prison for bigamy. Bridget had married serviceman, Hugh Rafferty, in December 1914 after a long separation from her first husband, John Keenan, who had declared himself single when he joined the army in August 1914. Keenan was killed on 9 May 1915, and had been dead for six months by the time the case came to court. *Dundee Evening Telegraph*, 13 November 1915. Buist's son, Charles, a captain in the Royal Artillery, was killed in action in Belgium in October 1917.
4. *Dundee Courier*, 9 May 1916.
5. *People's Journal*, 13 May 1916.
6. Mary Brooksbank, interviewed by Hamish Henderson, June 1970, School of Scottish Studies, SA1970.375.
7. *Dundee Courier*, 19 May 1916.
8. Unacknowledged by the British government or press, that is. James Connolly had already acknowledged the role of women in the Rising in his last despatch from the GPO on 28 April, and his last statement to his court martial, on 9 May, and smuggled out of Kilmainham Jail by his daughter Nora on the eve of his execution.
9. *Dundee Courier*, 19 May 1916.
10. IMA, BMH, Michael Kelly, WS 1564.
11. R McCready, 'Mad, Meaningless and Motiveless'? The Dundee Irish and the Easter Rising,' in Lusk and Maley, *Scotland and the Easter Rising* (Edinburgh: Luath Press, 2016), p177.
12. Stephen Coyle, 'Irish Internees in Scottish Prisons', in Coyle and Ó Catháin, *We Will Rise Again*, p73.
13. IMA, BMH, Joseph Lawless, WS 1043, p182.
14. IMA, BMH, Daniel Kearns, WS 1124, p6.
15. The Advisory Committee chaired by Justice (later Lord) Sankey, met in London in August 1916 to review the prisoners' cases by conducting interviews with them to establish their 'innocence or complicity in the Rising'. The prisoners perceived it as a cynical move by the British government to get them to plead that they had been duped into participating in the Rising by their leaders, so as to justify the executions. IMA, BMH, Joseph Lawless, WS 1043, pp 82–183; Joseph Furlong, WS 335, p12.
16. IMA, BMH, Patrick McCabe, WS 1551, p14; Michael Lynch, WS 511, p13.

17 IMA, BMH, Joseph Lawless, WS 1043, p187.

18 The conscientious objector involved, C H Norman, a religious pacifist, had been confined in an undersized straitjacket after attempting suicide, had fainted in agony, and been left unconscious on the floor, after which he was taken to hospital. Norman returned a week later when he was subjected to more brutality by Brooke. The publicity given to the Norman case led to a review of the treatment of consciousness objectors in British prisons. IMA, BMH, Frank Hardiman, WS 406, p13; *Daily Herald*, 1 July 1916; *Dundee Courier*, 5 July 1916.

19 The Bureau of Military History was established in 1947 by the Irish Minister of Defence, Oscar Traynor, with the purpose of giving people who had been actively involved in the independence movement from 1913 (the formation of the Irish Volunteers) to 1921 (the end of the War of Independence) a chance to record their experiences; and assembling and coordinating material which would ultimately form the basis for a history of the movement. Over the course of the next ten years, 1,773 witness statements were collected by a staff of interviewing officers under the direction of a twelve-strong Advisory Committee, headed by historians Robert Dudley Edwards and T W Moody, Director of the National Library and Second World War codebreaker, Richard Hayes, and historian and Assistant Keeper at the National Museum of Ireland, G A Hayes-McCoy. In 1959, the archive was locked away in a government storeroom for 44 years, until after the last witness to receive a military pension had died, when it was transferred to Cathal Brugha Barracks and made available to the public. It was subsequently digitised and made available online in 2012. For an evaluation of the Bureau of Military History and its flaws, see Fearghal McGarry. 'Too Many Histories?' The Bureau of Military History', *History Ireland*, 6, November/December 2011.

20 *Dundee Evening Telegraph*, 7 July 1916.

21 *Dundee Courier*, 8 July 1916.

22 Clarke had walked out of his job when he was forced to work on making armaments.

23 *DC* 25 July 1916. Clarke cited the authority of Pope Benedict XV, to wit, that 'all Roman Catholics taking part in the war were doing so in defiance of the Pope's wishes'.

24 On 21 June, Marra had advised a meeting of Dundee Trades Council, that any tradesman wishing to get an exemption from war work 'must *appear* as if he is a conscientious objector'. *Dundee Courier*, 22 June 1916.

25 John McLean, who was imprisoned in Edinburgh Castle for sedition, was a notable exception.

26 *Dundee Courier*, 8 March 1917.

27 *People's Journal*, 17 March 1917.

28 IMA, BMH, Joseph Good, WS 776, pp33–37.

29 IMA, MSPC, pension application of Jean Gillespie, MSP34REF83.
30 *Dundee Evening Telegraph*, 10 December 1918.
31 Walker, *Juteopolis*, p452.
32 *Dundee Advertiser*, 2 December 1918.
33 *Dundee Courier*, 12 December 1918.
34 *Dundee Courier*, 11 December 1918, *Daily Record*, 11 December 1918
35 *The Scotsman*, 11 December 1918.
36 The Soloheadbeg ambush is often held up as the first act of the War of Independence. In truth, there was no such signal moment (the Easter Rising can lay claim to that, and there had been minor skirmishes in the interim). However, it did produce the first Crown force fatalities since Easter week. J Bowyer Bell, *The Secret Army* (London: Sphere, 1972), p32.
37 Handley, *The Irish in Modern Scotland*, p297.
38 IMA, MSPC, RO/603, p149.
39 The Black and Tans were a force of police constables devised by Winston Churchill and other members of the British Cabinet to assist the overstretched RIC in combatting the IRA. Recruited largely from ex-British Army servicemen, they derived their name from their makeshift uniforms which combined dark green ('black') police, and khaki ('tan') military clothing. For detail, see Richard Bennett, *The Black and Tans* (London: Four Square Books, 1959), and D M Leeson, *The Black and Tans: British Police and Auxiliaries in the First Irish War of Independence, 1920–21* (Oxford: OUP, 2011).
40 *Dundee Advertiser*, 19 July 1920.
41 Interestingly, one of the units of the Cavan Irish Volunteers, which O'Rahilly inspected in in the summer of 1914, was known as the Briefne Regiment. NLI, MS10, 547/4/2, letter from O'Rahilly to Colonel Maurice Moore, 9 July 1914.
42 Eamonn Mooney Papers, quoted by Shaun Kavanagh, 'Sinn Fein and the Irish Republican Movement in Greenock', in Lusk and Maley, *Scotland and the Easter Rising*, p97.
43 *Dundee Advertiser*, 20 September 1920.
44 *Dundee Evening Telegraph*, 1 September 1920. Father Bernard Vaughan, whose London parish took in the fashionable Mayfair area, made his name as a popular lecturer on aspects of Catholicism, including a series of sermons on 'the Sins of Society' in 1906. He also had the ear of Edward VII and was Spiritual Advisor to the English Catholic Women's League, which mainly comprised wealthy noblewomen and middle-class professionals, many of whom had converted from Anglicanism. Paula M Kane, 'The Willing Captive of Home?': The English Catholic Women's League', *Church History*, 60:3, 1991, pp331–55. James Joyce also based the character of Father Purdon (named after a street in Dublin's brothel district) in *Dubliners* (1914) on him. M C Rintoul, *Dictionary of Real People and Places in Fiction* (London: Routledge, 1993), p915.

45 *Dundee Evening Telegraph*, 6 September 1920.

46 *Dundee Courier*, 26 October 1920.

47 *Dundee Evening Telegraph*, 27 October 1920; *Dundee Courier*, 28 October 1920.

48 *Dundee Advertiser*, 30 October 1920.

49 In the background, was sympathetic parish priest, Canon John McDonald, who unlike his predecessor, the autocratic Monsignor Joseph Holder, was popular within his working-class parish, and had a thorough knowledge of Irish and Scottish history. *Arbroath Herald*, 11 January 1929.

50 Jim Madden, *Father John Fahy, Radical Republican and Agrarian Activist* (Dublin: The Columba Press, 2012), p17.

51 Cox, *Empire, Industry and Class*, pp72–73, 179–80.

52 Stewart puts the incident as having occurred during the Great War, which conflicts with Father Fahy's period in Dundee. Stewart, *Breaking the Fetters*, p154. Alternative versions of the story hint at the right date, and claim that Fahy was addressing the Black and Tans.

53 The majority of Black and Tans and Auxiliaries were drawn disproportionately from London and the Home Counties. See Leeson, *The Black and Tans: British Police and Auxiliaries in the First Irish War of Independence, 1920–21*, pp87, 122, 127.

54 Toner, who was appointed Bishop of Dunkeld in 1914, was also the brother-in-law of Denis Brogan, former President of the Glasgow branches of Conradh na Gaeilge and the United Irish League, and member of the IRB, to whom his sister, Elizabeth, was married.

55 See Chapter 6.

56 Madden, *Father John Fahy*, p25.

57 *Dundee Catholic Herald*, 12 March 1921.

58 *Dundee Courier*, 9 March 1921; *Dundee Catholic Herald*, 12 Mar 1921.

59 The Liberal government's proscription of Dáil Éireann, Sinn Féin and other nationalist organisations in September 1919.

60 *Dundee Advertiser*, 9 March 1921.

61 *Dundee Evening Telegraph*, 27 October 1920.

62 De Valera stated that 'The financial contribution to the Irish struggle among the Scottish communities was in excess of funds from any other country, including Ireland'. Tom Gallagher, *Glasgow: The Uneasy Peace, Religious Tension in Modern Scotland, 1819–1914* (Manchester: Manchester University Press, 1987), p94; Iain D Patterson, 'The Activities of Irish Republican Physical Force Organisations in Scotland, 1919–1921', *The Scottish Historical Review*, 72:1 (1993), p40.

63 IMA, MSPC, Lena McDonald, MSP34REF56954.

64 Death record of Patrick Higgins, 1 November 1890. Neither Patrick, Bridget nor their family appear to have been sure of their exact dates of birth, as their ages vary across census and death records.

Chapter 7 – Revolution 1916–23

65 The couple remained married and Peter McDonald continued to live and work in the town. At the time of his death in 1942, he was living in Commercial Street in the city centre. Death record of Peter McDonald, 3 September 1942.
66 Death record of Bridget Higgins, 21 January 1915.
67 *Dundee Evening Telegraph*, 24 April 1966.
68 *Dundee Evening Telegraph*, 14 June 1926; *Dundee Courier*, 15 June, 4. August, 11 August 1926.
69 IMA, MSPC, pension application of Jean Gillespie, MSP34REF83.
70 IMA, MSPC, pension application of Lena McDonald, MSP34REF56964.
71 IMA, MSPC, pension application of Lena McDonald, MSP34REF56964, letter from Father John Fahy to the Pensions Board.
72 IMA, BMH, Seamus Reader, WS 933, p5.
73 IMA, BMH, Seamus Reader, WS 933, p7.
74 Tom Barry, *Guerrilla Days in Ireland* [1949] (Dublin: Anvil Books, 1989), pp157–58.
75 Healy's Brigade Commandant, Sean O'Hegarty, was largely responsible for devising the aggressive and militant tactics which other brigades copied. Like Tom Barry, firmly believed that more weapons meant more men in the field and increased the odds in their favour.
76 IMA, MSPC, Lena McDonald, MSP34REF56964.
77 IMA, BMH, Seamus Reader, WS 933, p7.
78 Ian MacDougall (ed), *Militant Miners: Recollections of John McArthur, Buckhaven, and letters of David Proudfoot, Methil to G. Allen* (Polygon Books, 1981), p18.
79 Kenefick, *Red Scotland*, pp73, 164.
80 *Dundee Courier*, 10 December 1920.
81 *Dundee Evening Telegraph*, 24 April 1966.
82 *Dundee Catholic Herald*, 19 March 1921. After a lengthy interrogation, in which she was pressurised to implicate other named persons, Jean reputedly uttered, 'These people have nothing to do with it. I alone am responsible'. She was subsequently sentenced to a year's detention in March 1921.
83 Sean Healy, 'From Boyhood to Manhood: In the Service of Ireland', *The Kerryman*, 20 January 1968.
84 Ó Catháin describes a 'virtual hole' in the Scottish accounts 'created by the necessity of disguising the multiple supply lines, protecting the IRB channels [and] protecting civilian contractors'. Ó Catháir, 'Michael Collins and Scotland', in F Ferguson and J McConnell (eds), *Ireland and Scotland in the Nineteenth Century* (Dublin: Four Courts Press, 2009), pp160–75.
85 C Desmond Greaves, *Liam Mellows and the Irish Revolution* [1971] (Belfast: An Ghlór Gafa, 2004), p232.

86 *Dundee Evening Telegraph*, 17 February 1921; *Dundee Evening Telegraph*, 21 March 1921.
87 *Dundee Courier*, 30 April 1921.
88 *Dundee Advertiser*, 30 April 1921.
89 *Sunday Post*, 8 May 1921.
90 For a full account of the Glasgow prison van incident, see Coyle, *High Noon on High Street*.
91 *Dundee Advertiser*, 23 July 1921.
92 *Dundee Advertiser*, 30 July 1921. 'God Save Ireland' was the *Advertiser*'s translation, but it is more likely to have been 'A Dia Saor Eire' – 'God Free Ireland', which slogan O'Doherty had included in a recent Sinn Féin press announcement. *Dundee Evening Telegraph*, 20 April 1921.
93 *Dundee Courier*, 9 August 1921.
94 *Dundee Courier*, 12 August 1921.
95 *Dundee Catholic Herald*, 13 August 1921.
96 This did come up in the 'Van' trial at the High Court (where Walshe aka Thomas Mitchell was on trial for conspiracy), eliciting the evidence of a Dublin witness, and a handwriting expert who concluded that Dunne was probably Walshe. However, Walshe was found not guilty, released and subsequently rearrested in relation to his escape from Strangeways Prison in 1919.
97 The murder of Pat and Harry Loughnane, who were active in the South Galway IRA, is considered to be one of the most shocking incidents of the Tan War. The brothers were arrested on 26 November 1920, taken to Gort Barracks where they were beaten for hours, then tied to the back of a lorry and dragged for miles along the roads before being shot. Their charred and mutilated bodies were found in a pond ten days later.
98 *Dundee Catholic Herald*, 9 July 1921.
99 *Dundee Courier*, 15 September 1921; *Dundee Evening Telegraph*, 15 September 1921.
100 *Dundee Courier*, 16 September 1921.
101 For a full discussion of the life and politics of Sean McLoughlin, see Charlie McGuire, *Sean McLoughlin, Ireland's Forgotten Revolutionary* (Pontypool: Merlin Press, 2011).
102 McGuire, *Sean McLoughlin*, pp12–13.
103 IMA, BMH, Sean McLoughlin, WS 290, p29.
104 Robinson had missed out on the Rising due to his being confined in Edinburgh Castle (initially), then Reading Jail, along with Seamus Reader, on charges of arms raiding.
105 McGuire, *Sean McLoughlin*, pp54, 66; Jim Friel, 'Irish Radical Links with Garngad and Springburn', in Coyle and Ó Catháin, *We Will Rise Again*, p144.
106 IMA, BMH, Sean McLoughlin, WS 290, p46.

CHAPTER 7 – REVOLUTION 1916–23

107 John 'Jock' Thomson was born in Castle Street, Montrose on 30 October 1875 to Ann Thomson, an unmarried flax worker and a Protestant – although he was baptised a Catholic by the Reverend Patrick Gray of St Thomas', Arbroath on 16 January 1876. Little is known of his early life beyond the fact that he appears to have raised by his grandparents, Helen (née Anderson), a jute preparer, and Jock Thomson, a harbour labourer, and the time of his marriage, to Isabella Dolan in November 1899, he was working as a jute preparer and living in the east Dudhope area of Dundee. The couple already had two daughters – their decision to marry in nearby St Mary Magdalen's (Scottish Episcopal) Church, may have been a concession to their mixed heritage (Isabella had an Irish father and a Dundee-born mother of Aberdonian stock). In turn, it may simply have been the most convenient and accommodating option. Shortly after, Jock joined the British Army, in which he served throughout the South African 'Second Boer' War, returning – as a gap of around seven years between the birth of the fourth and fifth of their eight children suggests – to civilian life around 1908 just as Dundee was entering a deep trade depression. The experience of unemployment and of eking out an existence on a meagre army pension and charity handouts appears to have radicalised him. As a 40-year-old father of seven (four of whom were under working age) when the Military Service Act came into operation, he avoided conscription, possibly being assigned to war work. By 1920, however, he was unemployed again. Despite his early association with the fledgling Communist Party, he held off from joining it, preferring to maintain his status as an independent spokesman for the unemployed workers' movement until late 1921, when he was persuaded to stand as the Communist Party candidate for Lochee in the council elections of November 1921, in which he polled 501 votes against 749 for the Labour candidate, James Rooney, and 2,545 for the sitting candidate, Bailie David Neave. Thomson died of pneumonia on 8 July 1923 at the age of 47. Mary Brooksbank, who described him as 'a real man of the people', recalled that around 10,000 people followed his coffin from his home at 14 Cochrane Street to Eastern Cemetery three days later. A pivotal figure in revolutionary working-class politics in Dundee in the 1920–1923 period, today he remains largely forgotten. Birth, baptism, marriage and death records for John Thomson; Census of Scotland, 1881, 1891, 1911, 1921; *Evening Telegraph*, 2 November 1921; Mary Brooksbank, *No Sae Lang Syne: A Tale of This City*, Dundee, 1968, p31.

108 *Dundee Courier*, 30 December 1920; *Dundee Advertiser*, 30 December 1920; *Dundee Courier*, 14 January 1921.

109 Matt Treacy, *The Communist Party of Ireland 1921–2011* (Dublin: Brocaire Books, 2012), pp9–10.

110 IMA, BMH, Sean McLoughlin, WS 290, pp46–47.

111 McGuire, *Sean McLoughlin*, p77, 80; *The Socialist*, 14 April 1921.

112 For example, on 21 July 1921, 100–200 married women led a raid on the unemployment bureau, then marched on the Town House and the offices of the JFWU, of which many of them were members, to demand intervention on a new regulation which prevented both members of a married couple from drawing unemployment benefit at the same time. *Dundee Courier*, 22 July 1921.

385

113 Mary accredited Jock Thomson with speaking in her defence when both appeared in court charged with disrupting the two-minutes' silence at the Armistice Day commemoration (in November 1921), and acting as her sponsor when she joined the Communist Party (shortly after he did), which she recalls as occurring in 1922. Mary Brooksbank, interviewed by Hamish Henderson, 22 May 1968 and June 1970, School of Scottish Studies, SA1968.317, and SA1970.375.

114 *Dundee Advertiser,* 7, 8 and 9 September 1921.

115 Mary was subsequently convicted, ordered to find £5 and cautioned to be of good behaviour for six months or go to jail for twenty days. *Dundee Courier,* 14 October 1921.

116 Most likely Harry McShane, as no other 'unemployed leader' of that surname appears anywhere else in this context. For whatever reason, there is no reference to this incident in *No Mean Fighter* (1978), McShane's biography, which was constructed from a series of recorded interviews. However, three undisputed facts – McShane's membership of the Tramp Trust Unlimited (the group of five touring socialist propagandists headed by John Maclean, to whose arrest 'John' McShane referred); the Tramp Trust's two main areas of concern (the Irish struggle and unemployment); and McShane's role as chief organiser of the Unemployed Workers' Movement in Scotland from 1921 through to the 1930s – would appear to corroborate this.

117 *Dundee Courier,* 4 November 1921.

118 Despite the testimony of several friendly witnesses, Sheriff Malcolm chose to believe 'the men with the notebooks' and sentenced McShane to 60 days in prison, a £5 fine and caution for twelve months good behaviour or another 30 days in prison. *Dundee Courier,* 4 November 1921.

119 *Dundee Courier,* 14 October 1921.

120 McGuire, *Sean McLoughlin,* p89.

121 MA, BMH, Sean McLoughlin, WS 290, p45.

122 Stephen Coyle, 'No Ordinary Women – the Untold Story of Cumann na mBan in Scotland', talk, Glasgow, April 2014.

123 Ó Catháin, 'Michael Collins and Scotland', p169–70.

124 EMP/3/A/31, letter from Cathal Duthie to Eamonn Mooney, March 1955; EMP/3/C/13, IRA membership roll, 4th Battalion 'D' (Dundee and District) Coy, 1919–23, compiled 30 March 1955. Annie Barrett, who Duthie states was Treasurer of Cumann na mBan in Dundee, was Secretary of the Kevin Barry Sinn Féin cumann, as Annie Steel was Treasurer of The O'Rahilly cumann, in the post-Civil war period. *Eire, The Irish Nation,* 3 November 1923, 22 March 1924.

125 Catherine was awarded a military service medal on 4 October 1956. However, the award of a certificate was deferred until 9 September 1970, prior to which the note, 'No C na mBan record for Dundee', was written on her application file. IMA, MSPC, medal application of Catherine McDonald, MD 58417.

126 Coyle, 'No Ordinary Women'.

CHAPTER 7 – REVOLUTION 1916–23

127 IMA, MSPC, pension application of Margaret Skinnider, MSP34REF19910.
128 Walker, *Juteopolis*, p536.
129 James Connolly, *Songs of Freedom* (1907).
130 Steve Jackson, 'Seumas Mac Garaidh: Neach-iol Ghàidhlig agus Fìor 'Pan-Celt'', *Carn*, 147 (August 2010), pp2–3.
131 *Arbroath Herald*, 4 June 1920.
132 *Arbroath Herald*, 19 August 1921.
133 *Dundee Evening Telegraph*, 2 March 1921.
134 A reference, no doubt, to Churchill, who was, at that point, still MP for Dundee, although not for much longer. *Dundee Courier*, 15 February 1922.
135 *Dundee Courier*, 16 February 1922; 18 February 1922.
136 *Dundee Courier*, 20 February 1922.
137 *Dundee Courier*, 12 December 1921.
138 Lena later estimated the date of the escape attempt as December 1920. However, contemporary records indicate that it occurred in December 1921. IMA, MSPC, Lena McDonald, MSP34REF56964.
139 *Dundee Courier*, 12 December 1921; 28 December 1921; 30 December 1921. The likelihood that both letters were written by the same person is indicated by commonly repeated words and phrases. The main difference is that Mac Garaidh, writing as 'we', speaks from a broader Scottish nationalist perspective which appeals for solidarity on the basis of a common Celtic identity. Oglach writing as 'I' expresses a more personal, overtly pro-Irish Republican viewpoint. The tactic of adopting different identities to compensate for the shortcomings of the Scottish nationalist movement is consistent with late-twentieth century Pan-Celt, Seumas Mac a' Ghobhainn's assessment of Mac Garaidh as a 'one man nationalist movement'. Seumas Mac a'Ghobhainn, *Irish Weekly and Ulster Examiner*, 21 March 1970.
141 *Dundee Courier*, 31 December 1921.
142 *Dundee Courier*, 2 January 1922.
143 IMA, EMH, Patrick McCabe, WS 155, p13. McCabe was sentenced to four years for conspiracy, a planned attack on Castlepollard RIC Barracks, and his part in the kidnapping of British magistrates, Maxwell Moore and G R Hyde, in October 1921.
144 *Dundee Catholic Herald*, 28 January 1922.
145 *Scottish Catholic Observer*, 8 August 1969, quoted in Madden, *Father John Fahy*, p229; Brian S Murphy, 'The Stone of Destiny: Father John Fahy (1894 [*sic*]–1969, Lia Fail and Smallholder Radicalism in Modern Irish Society', in G Moran (ed), *Radical Irish Priests, 1660–1970* (Dublin: Four Courts Press, 1998), p88.
146 It is worth noting, however, that a number of high-ranking anti-Treaty IRA veterans in Scotland from the 1st Scottish (West of Scotland) Brigade, including Seamus Reader (who also joined Fianna na h'Alba), and H W Hutchinson, became involved in the 'Scottish Nationalist Party', probably the National Party

of Scotland (formed 1928), although, as Hutchinson later recalled, they resigned when the Secretary 'turned out to be a bitter anti-Catholic'. IMA, BMH, H W Hutchinson, WS 853. John McCormick, National Secretary of the Nationalist Party of Scotland, and subsequently, the Scottish National Party (1934), promoted the anti-Irish Catholicism of right-wing influencers, Andrew Dewar Gibb and George Malcolm Thomson, in policy documents and election speeches. (See, for example, Tom Gallacher, *Glasgow, the Uneasy Peace*, pp171–2; and Michael Rosie, *The Sectarian Myth in Scotland*, ((Basingstoke: Palgrave Macmillan, 2004), p104.

147 Jackson, 'Seumas Mac Garaidh: Neach-ioí Ghaidhlig agus Fíor 'Pan Celt'', p2.

148 *Dundee Courier*, 30 December 1921.

149 *Dundee Advertiser*, 9 January 1922.

150 *Dundee Courier*, 17 March 1922.

151 *Dundee Courier*, 17 March 1922; *Dundee Evening Telegraph*, 17 March 1922. How much of a 'Republican' MacRory really was, was ultimately proven in 1936 when, after being approached by Spanish Count Ramirez de Allerano, a Carlist who aimed at restoring the Bourbon monarchy, MacRory encouraged Irish fascist leader, Eoin O'Duffy, to form an Irish Brigade to support Franco's anti-Republican Nationalist forces in the Spanish Civil War.

152 National Archives of Ireland (NAI), Joseph Robinson Papers [hereafter JRP], list of Scottish Sinn Féin cumainn, MS1094/14/1; letter to unnamed from 'S', 10 December 1922, MS1094/15/5.

153 IMA, MSPC, R0/106, membership rolls of the Scottish Brigade of the IRA.

154 IMA, BMH, Seamus Reader, WS 627, p4, and WS 1727, p7; Dan Branniff, WS 222, p4; John Southwell, WS 230, p2; Gerry Holchon, WS 328, pp24–5; Nora Connolly O'Brien, WS 285, p42; Edmund O'Brien, WS 697, p50; photograph of Nora Connolly, Margaret Skinnider, Peter Murray, Eamonn Mooney, Mickey Lawlor, Seamus Dempsey and Tommy O'Connor, taken at Coney Island, May 1918, in McAuliffe, *Margaret Skinnider*, pp8–79, plate 2. Tommy O'Connor of Liverpool was also a trans-Atlantic courier for the IRB before the Rising and an arms smuggler for the IRA after.

155 The whereabouts of Thomas Dempsey, who emigrated to North America, were unknown in 1935–38. By the time one of his children was located in Dublin in the 1950s, Dempsey was dead. Mooney, who alongside Seamus Reader, H W Hutchinson and others, had relocated to Ireland, cited the wide dispersion of Scottish IRA veterans as an obstacle to constructing a full and accurate record of the 1916–23 period. (IMA, MSPC RO/603, pp24, 27.)

156 The statement, issued on 13 April 1922, presented the conditions on which the anti-Treaty forces headquartered in the Four Courts in Dublin would negotiate with the pro-Treaty forces in the Dáil. Other conditions included maintaining 'the existing Republic', placing the pro- and anti-Treaty Army under the control of an elected independent executive, disbanding the police, and handing policing over to the IRA. Dorothy Macardle, *The Irish Republic* [1937] (Dublin: Irish Press, 1951), p723.

CHAPTER 7 – REVOLUTION 1916–23

157 *Dundee Courier,* 20 April 1922.
158 *Dundee Courier,* 26 April 1922.
159 *Dundee Courier,* 1 May 1922; *Dundee Courier,* 15 May 1922.
160 *Dundee Courier,* 9 May 1922.
161 *Dundee Courier,* 13 May 1922; *Dundee Courier,* 20 May 1922.
162 NAI, JRP, 1094/14/3, letters from Joseph Robinson to P O'Neill, 14 May 1922, and Eamon Donnelly to Joseph Robinson, 20 May 1922.
163 Macardle, *The Irish Republic,* pp738, 741.
164 *Dundee Courier,* 22 May 1922.
165 *Dundee Courier,* 22 May 1922.
166 NAI, JRP, 1094. Donnelly was the Director of Organisation of Cumann na Poblachta, the anti-Treaty party led by de Valera.
167 Macardle, *The Irish Republic,* pp743–46, 750.
168 *Dundee Courier,* 19 June 1922.
169 Probably Erskine's Felt Works, which was situated on the Shore Road in the Whiteabbey area of north-east Belfast.
170 *Dundee Catholic Herald,* 17 June 1922.
171 The *Dundee Catholic Herald* attributed the *Advertiser*'s unsympathetic treatment of Ireland from it having 'turned Tory'. *Dundee Catholic Herald,* 14 January 1922. In 1905, the proprietor of the *Advertiser,* John Leng, who was also a Liberal MP for Dundee from 1886 to 1906, and an early supporter of Home Rule, had sold the majority of his firm's shares to D C Thomson and Co, publishers of the Tory *Dundee Courier,* under whose control the *Advertiser* gradually shed its strong pro-Liberal slant. The two newspapers eventually merged, becoming the *Dundee Courier and Advertiser,* during the General Strike of May 1926.
172 *Dundee Catholic Herald,* 17 June 1922.
173 Coyle, who attained the rank of Commandant in the Free State Army, stated that he joined on 20 February 1922 (following which he was arrested twice by the IRA), and was attested at the beginning of May. He resigned his commission on 16 June 1923, at the end of the Civil War. In 1924, while a member of Dáil Éireann, he was arrested on a charge of embezzlement and sentenced to three years' imprisonment due to which he forfeited his right to a military pension. It is possible that the practicalities of arms trafficking in Scotland, i.e., the need to juggle multiple arms channels and disguise the identity of suppliers, had habituated Coyle to 'creative accounting'. Nevertheless, he eventually managed to salvage his reputation, and his pension rights, which were restored in 1951. IMA, MSPC, Henry Coyle, 24SP9346, 24C822. See also Gerry Coyle, *Henry Coyle: A Forgotten Freedom Fighter* (Ballina, 2022).
174 In a reference letter to the Military Pensions Board in October 1938, Lena McDonald refers to 'the late Sean Doherty'. IMA MSPC, Jean Gillespie, MSP34REF83.

175 *Dundee Catholic Herald*, 17 June 1922.

176 Scottish Brigade records state that an expeditionary force left for Ireland after the Four Courts were attacked by Free State forces on 28 June. It contained an estimated 25 IRA and Cumann na mBan volunteers, the majority of whom were from the Glasgow district. According to Charles Duthie, two members of the IRA/Sinn Féin in Dundee, Matthew Boyle and John Clarke, fought in the Four Courts. IMA, RO/603; EMP/3/A/31.

177 *Dundee Courier*, 25 September 1922.

178 *Dundee Courier*, 14 September 1922.

179 Catholic schools were incorporated into the state sector under the 1918 (Scotland) Education Act, a decision that continued to be opposed by sections of Scottish society.

180 *Dundee Courier*, 11 November 1922.

181 *Dundee Courier*, 11 November 1922.

182 W Gallacher, *The Last Memoirs of William Gallacher* (London: Lawrence and Wishart, 1966), p170.

183 The meeting was preceded by a police baton charge against thousands of people who struggled to gain admittance.

184 *Dundee Advertiser*, 14 November 1922; *Dundee Courier*, 14 November 1922.

185 *Dundee Catholic Herald*, 18 November 1922.

186 This faction also canvassed electors in Birmingham to vote for sitting MP, Austin Chamberlain, for the same reason. Gerard Noonan, *The IRA in Britain 1919–1923: 'In the heart of enemy lines'* (Liverpool: LUP, 2014), p245); *Dundee Advertiser*, 15 November 1922; *Dundee Courier*, 15 November 1922.

187 Stewart, *Breaking the Fetters*, p130. Churchill dropped to fourth place, behind Scrymgeour and Morel (who were both elected), and his running mate MacDonald.

188 *Dundee Catholic Herald*, 5 and 12 November 1921.

189 The months following the Treaty saw a spike in violence (peaking in May 1922, with an estimated 83 fatalities) and hundreds of expulsions. Niall Cunningham, *The Social Geography of Violence during the Belfast Troubles*, CRESC, University of Manchester, March 2013), p7; G B Kenna, *Facts and Figures on the Belfast Pogroms, 1920–1922* (Dublin: O'Connell Publishing Co, 1922).

190 *Dundee Courier*, 16 January 1923.

191 *Dundee Advertiser*, 2 February 1923; *Dundee Courier*, 2 February 1923.

192 Florence O'Donoghue, *No Other Law*, 1954 (Dublin: Anvil Books, 1986), p300.

193 *Larne Times and Weekly Telegraph*, 17 March 1923.

194 *Larne Times and Weekly Telegraph*, 17 March 1923.

195 The Father Michael Griffin cumann did not survive Father Durand's departure from the city later in 1922. Some members, such as Gaelgeoir Peter McNulty,

CHAPTER 7 – REVOLUTION 1916–23

(who became a prolific supporter of the Irish Republican Prisoners' Dependants' Fund) remained individually active. Some may have been recruited into the new Kevin Barry cumann while others may have drifted away altogether.

196 NAI, JRP, letter from S (Duggan) to unnamed (probably Eamonn Donnelly), 10 December 1922, 1094/15/5; National Records Office of Scotland [hereafter NRS], Irish Disturbances, HH55/72, Report to the Advisory Committee on Patrick Joseph O'Neill.

197 NRS, Irish Disturbances. HH55/72, memos from J Carmichael to the Commissioner of Police, New Scotland Yard, and A Oliphant to J Carmichael, 3 and 5 May 1923. Carmichael already had form here. Patrick Moylett, former Justice of the Sinn Féin courts, later claimed to have been in Dundee in 1923 when a meeting of the Town Council called him to account for the release of Thomas 'Jock' Burke, who had been incarcerated in Dundee Jail pending trial for murder earlier in 1920. Ex-British Army officer, Burke, had gone on to command the notorious Auxiliaries in Galway where, in November 1920, he was implicated in the murder of the Loughnane brothers. Carmichael's 'defence' was that had he been following the orders of a higher authority in London. BMH, Patrick Moylett, WS 767, p36; BMH, Pádraig Ó Fathaigh, WS 1717, p2.

198 *Dundee Advertiser,* 17 April 1923.

199 NRS, Irish Disturbances, HH55/71.

200 NRS, Irish Disturbances, HH55/72, Report to the Advisory Committee on Patrick Joseph O'Neill.

201 Speeches of His Grace the Most Reverend Dr Mannix, Archbishop of Melbourne, in the Rotunda, Dublin, 22 and 29 October 1925 (Dublin, 1925), p16. He also echoes the position of the early Fenians, i.e., the right of an individual to hold an independent political opinion without fear of sanction from the Church or any other authority.

202 IMA, RO/106, p56.

203 NRS, Irish Disturbances, HH55/72, File on Patrick Joseph O'Neill.

204 The Free State Authorities required all internees appealing to the Advisory Committee to sign an undertaking that they 'had not acted and were not about to act in any manner prejudicial to the restoration of order in Ireland', and to supply the names of two guarantors to vouch for their future conduct. O'Neill nominated Father Thomas O'Shea (the curate of St Andrew's Pro-Cathedral, who had succeeded Father Fahy), and Brother Liguori, the Head Teacher of St Mary's. Brother Liguori went on to become the first Head Teacher of St John's High School, Dundee, in 1931, and Provincial of the Marist order in Scotland, Ireland and England in 1934. He retired in 1953 after 45 years of teaching.

205 NRS, Irish Disturbances, HH55/72, P J O'Neill to Brother Liguori, 5 May 1923.

206 On 24 April, the Court of Appeal ruled that the Restoration of Order (Ireland) Act 1920 had been effectively repealed by creation of the Irish Free State. A hurriedly passed Indemnity Act limited but nevertheless obliged the British

government to pay up £43,000 to the deportees. Ray Wilson and Ian Adams, *Special Branch: A History: 1883–2006* (London: Biteback Press, 2015), p130. Six deportees, including leader of the Irish Self-Determination League, Art O'Briain, were rearrested on conspiracy charges.

207 *Dundee Courier*, 2 June 1923.

208 O'Neill played an instrumental role in establishing and organising Gaelic sports in the mid-Armagh area in the 1920s to 1950s. Under his direction, Armagh became the first senior Gaelic football team from the Six Counties to reach an All-Ireland final (against Kerry in 1953). His eldest son, Gerry, who succeeded him as Principal Teacher of St John's Boys' School in 1963, and as a GAA coach and official, was a member of the team. O'Neill died in his home at Westport House, Middletown, on 8 July 1966. In 1984, the Middletown Gaelic Athletic Club, Eoghan Rua's, ground was named O'Neill Park/Pairc Uí Néill in his honour. Interview with Eithne O'Hare, née O'Neill, by Joe Jordan, 7 February 2011, GAA 125: A Peoples' History, AR/1/41; interview with Gerry Mellon by Joe Jordan, 10 February 2011, GAA 125: A Peoples' History, AR/1/51; *Irish Press*, 9 July 1966.

209 *Dundee Courier*, 30 June 1923.

210 *Eire, The Irish Nation*, 7 July 1923.

211 IMA, MSPC, Lena McDonald, MSP34 REF56964, letter from Jean Gillespie to the Pensions Board, 30 October 1938; letter from Lena McDonald to the Pensions Board, 7 November 1938; Jean Gillespie, MSP34REF83.

212 *Sinn Fein*, 17 August 1923; *Eire: The Irish Nation*, 3 November 1923.

213 Published in Glasgow by editor, P J Little, *Eire* was conceived as an alternative to the pro-Free State anti-Republican press of Charles Diamond the (publisher of the *Glasgow Catholic Observer* and the *Dundee Catholic Herald*). Assiduously anti-imperialist and pro-Republican, its format and content can be summarised roughly as follows: a section on the doings of the Irish Republican movement in Scotland and England (and presumably Wales); a section on 'England's difficulty' – exposing Britain's colonial difficulties, and looking at who else was taking England/the British Empire on; and a section on Free State atrocities and the war in Ireland, including eye-witness accounts of IRA Volunteers and critiques from, for example, Mary MacSwiney on the British Labour Party. The paper ran from 20 January 1923 to 25 October 1924. NLI, Art O'Briain papers, letter from PJ Little to Art O'Briain, 9 January 1923, MS8432/16.

214 *Eire, The Irish Nation*, 20 January 1923, 22 March 1924, 12 April 1924.

215 *Sinn Fein*, 13 April 1924.

216 The O'Rahilly cumann's banner was later presented to the O'Rahilly Republican Brass and Reed (flute) Band, Dublin, In January 1934, it formed the centrepiece of an exhibition to mark the band's second reunion at Sinn Féin headquarters, 41 Parnell Square. *An Phoblacht*, 13 January 1934.

217 *Eire, The Irish Nation*, 5 August 1924.

218 *Sinn Fein*, 23 August 1924.
219 *Dundee Courier*, 9 December 1926.
220 Máirtín Ó Catháin, 'A Winnowing Spirit: Sinn Féin in Scotland, 1905–1938', in (ed) Martin Mitchell, *New Perspectives on the Irish in Scotland* (Edinburgh: John Donald, 2008), pp114–26.
221 *Dundee Evening Telegraph*, 25 April 1966.
222 IMA, MSPC 5O/603, pp24, 27.

CHAPTER 8

A Partitioned Politics 1923–69

The sectarian issue clouded everything.[1]
There's not a man of all our land
Our country now can spare
The strong man with his sinewy hand,
The weak man with his prayer.[2]

THE RELEASE of the bulk of Irish political prisoners in 1924 brought to an end the most vigorous and productive phase of Irish republican activity in Scottish history.[3] And while a minority of committed supporters continued to rally round the cause, the political climate of the next two decades conspired against any attempts to win favour for it.

The 1920s and 1930s saw a surge in anti-Irish-Catholic sentiment, which has been described as 'the most intense phase of sectarian bitterness in Scotland since the seventeenth century'.[4] This was largely stimulated by the publication, in April 1923, of a report, commissioned by the Church of Scotland, on 'The Menace of the Irish Race to Our Scottish Nationality', which accused the Irish population in Scotland of being the main source of criminal behaviour and, in a time of high unemployment, taking jobs from native Scots.[5] The report informed debate within the Church of Scotland for the next twenty years and continued to shape popular attitudes in much of Scotland for decades afterwards. These intensely anti-Irish attitudes also served to inhibit public expressions of cultural identity by sections of the Irish community itself. For example, in October 1923, the board of Dundee Hibernian Football Club – founded in 1909 by local businessman, Pat Reilly, with 'Irish capital to the value of £1000' – agreed to change the club's name to Dundee United. The name 'United' was chosen after the original suggestion of Dundee City was opposed by the city's other senior football club, Dundee. This was happily accommodated, the chairman of Dundee Hibernian, James Dickson, stating that 'they were willing to adopt any name so long as the word Hibs went out'.⁶ The timing of the name change, which was proposed three months after the publication of the Church of Scotland's report, suggests that it was motivated by a desire to attract wider popular support and appeal to the pockets of non-Irish business sponsors by ditching the Hibernian signifier. A statement that the change of name would not be regretted, however, was contested by club founder, Pat 'O'Reilly', who stated that the memory of Dundee Hibs would remain 'forever green'.⁷

The Dundee press, now in the hands of D C Thomson, was quick to endorse the report's findings. Other members of the Church of Scotland were less enthusiastic, however. On 7 October 1924, the chief propagandist for the report, the Reverend Duncan Cameron of Kilsyth, addressed a meeting in the Foresters' Hall in which he complained that ministers and members of the Church of Scotland and United Free Churches were failing to 'rise to a sense of the gravity of the situation'. Cameron declared he was in the city to warn them of the dangers of Irish immigration and build a campaign to obtain legislation to stem it. The meeting, which was held under the auspices of the Scottish Reformation Society, was packed with an invited audience of ministers, elders and other prominent members of various Protestant denominations, but predominantly the United Free Church. It also attracted an organised group of hecklers, most likely rallied by Dundee Sinn Féin, who the *Courier* presumed to be 'Roman Catholics'.⁸

In rhetoric thick with xenophobic paranoia, Cameron endeavoured to alert 'the people of Dundee' to 'the growing menace of the Irish race to their Scottish home'. 'In the west of Scotland', he opined, 'one-third of the population was Irish, and the Scottish race was disappearing like the mist off the Highland hills'. Through persistent interruptions, the Reverend James Weatherhead of St Paul's United Free Church, declared that he did not deny the right of the Catholic Church to exist in Scotland, although 'as a child of the Reformation' he was fundamentally opposed to its doctrines. He did, however, resent the presence of 'a great body of people, poor, thriftless and ignorant, who were great burden on the community' and received a disproportionate share of attention and money from the Parish Council, the charities and the jails. Significantly, Weatherhead's comment that 'as a member of a free and independent community whose fathers had fought for freedom and independence through the ages [he] resented this element acting in such a way as to destroy the freedom of his country', provoked – not surprisingly, coming as it did in the wake of an unresolved war of Irish liberation in which Irish-Scots Dundonians had played a vital role – the loudest, most spirited protests of the evening and a demand for questions that persisted until the hecklers were threatened with expulsion.

At the close of the meeting, a resolution was passed bemoaning 'the displacing of Scottish workers by Irish immigrants from the Free State [and] urging upon the Government to enact such laws as will regulate immigration of people outside the United Kingdom to this country'. A local committee was formed consisting of fourteen ministers of various Protestant churches and eighteen members of the Protestant 'community', including ex-Bailie J H Martin, an elder and session clerk of St Cuthbert's Church for over forty years; Thomas Watson of Balgowan; Alex Scott of the jute manufacturing firm of H & S Scott, and his sisters, the Misses Scott of Riversdale (all of whom were active members of St Mark's Church); and the Misses Lindsay of Dudhope Terrace, the daughters of the late minister of Tay Square UF Church. Most were drawn from the affluent middle classes, an untypical demographic in Dundee but a powerful and influential one nevertheless – for example, the Scotts were the owners of Tayfield Works, a major employer of labour in the city, and Martin and Watson served on the boards of several charities and institutions.

Over the next few years, the Thomson press continued to promote anti-Irish opinion in its editorial and letters columns. On 22 February 1928, a letter from the unambiguously named 'Scotland for the Scots' – the title of a lecture by the Reverend Duncan Cameron, who was still touring the country reminding the people how they were being 'menaced' – claimed that 'the greatest calamity throughout all the ages is the presence at the present of so many alien, illiterate and degenerate Irish Roman Catholics in our beloved land'. The writer went on to paint a picture of the Irish Free State as a penurious tin pot entity that had descended into a state of lawlessness where juries were rendered 'dumb' though fear of assassination, and 'murderers', including the killers of Minister of Justice, Kevin O'Higgins, who had been assassinated by the IRA the previous September, 'escaped the rope'. 'Where are those cowardly brutes now?', he ranted. 'Possibly in Glasgow or even Dundee filling jobs while our young men are searching in vain for work'.[9]

The letter provoked a slew of correspondence of which the *Courier* printed a subjectively 'balanced' selection. 'Anon.' of the Hilltown, agreed that 'something effective must be done' to rid Scotland of the Irish menace. Directing his ire at the bugbear of many Protestant bigots, the Education (Scotland) Act 1918, which brought Catholic schools under the realms of the state, he urged his fellow-thinkers in Dundee to do their utmost to repeal it by 'taking an interest' in the Education Authority elections.[10] James Bell of Cupar, Fife, vented his rage at the new Irish Free State which, despite having attained a measure of control over its own affairs, continued to drain the coffers of the British treasury which was now proposing to hand over one million pounds to compensate the southern Loyalists. Alternatively, one Irishman of the pen-name 'Munster', pronounced 'Scotland for the Scots" letter 'a gem and a jewel, brimful of wit and humour (whether conscious or unconscious)', and, congenially, offered 'a bottle of the best "Irish" [whiskey] to the crankiest letter [he] could find'. Frank Boyle of Dundee was less good humoured. Pointing an excoriating finger at 'those valiant heroes who, generally under the safety of a nom de plume, are ever ready to defend [Scotland] against menaces which do not exist', he suggested that the pathological hatred of Ireland, the Irish, and Irish-Roman Catholics was symptomatic of a deeper crisis within the Church of Scotland which would surely find another scapegoat if every Irish Roman Catholic were to leave Scotland tomorrow.[11]

In an editorial of 24 February 1928, the *Courier* claimed that 'the Irish vote was now dominant in Scottish politics and held the balance of power in the populous midland district'.[12] The *Courier* had already bemoaned the growing power of the trade unions which inhibited employers from using cheap imported labour but, also removed their justification for employing Irishmen over Scotsmen in the first place. Female labour, it appears, was not 'the problem' as it remained cheaper across the board. Interestingly, D C Thomson's reputation for not employing Catholics stems from shortly after this – when the government failed to give in to pressure from the Church of Scotland to restrict immigration – although whether this was a deliberate policy of the firm, or a reflection of the prejudices of certain individuals working within it is unclear. D C Thomson did in fact employ a number of Irish Catholics from the 1940s onwards; still, these were mainly young women in junior positions on non-superannuated salaries.

Most had not attended Catholic schools – a key signifier of ethno-religious identity but not an infallible one.

Behind the anxieties about the Irish menace, however, there lurked a fear of the red one. On 18 October 1927, the *Courier* proclaimed that 'every Socialist Member of Parliament from the west and centre of Scotland owes his position to the Irish vote', without which 'reinforcement' Scottish Labour voters 'would be in the minority'. Five weeks before, it also stated that: 'In Britain's far-flung Empire, with its many coloured races, and in our trading interests, Moscow has tried to find vulnerable points of attack and fruitful soil for the seeds of revolution'.[13] Throughout the Irish Revolutionary War – which continued to be a source of inspiration to the Indian independence movement – Sinn Féin had been termed 'Irish Bolsheviks'.[14] Now, having been denied a Republic but granted Dominion status within the British Empire, the new Irish Free State was seen as the open door through which Soviet agents, as well as radical Irish republicans, could plot to undermine it from within.[15]

With the exception of the local press, these anti-Irish, anti-socialist views were less pervasive in Dundee, particularly in its dominant industries of textiles and shipbuilding, with their long tradition of worker solidarity. This protected known Irish Republicans such as James 'Dode' Kimmet – who made lifelong friends in the Caledon Shipyard in the Stannergate, where he worked for much of the 1920s through to the 1940s, and in the adjacent gas works in Dock Street where he subsequently worked until his retirement in 1961 – from the prejudice experienced by many Irish Catholics in the west and central belt of Scotland. His former accomplice, Jim Devaney, who had a barber's shop in the district, likely drew his customers from the same demographic.

Nevertheless, the bigots had their abettors amongst sections of the upper working class as the McDonald women soon found out. Unlike many Irish sympathisers in Dundee and the majority of the working class, Lena worked in neither of the above industries, nor could she hide her former involvement from neighbours or employers. Around 1934, Lena and her mother Helen moved from Brook Street to Glenagnes Road on the prestigious Logie Housing estate, the first public housing scheme to be built in Scotland on the back of Lloyd George's promise to create 'homes fit for heroes'.[16] Tenancies were allocated to people in secure employment, i.e., council clerks, teachers, nurses, postal workers and members of the police force – the presence of the latter possibly heightening the feeling that she was being watched. By this time, Helen had lost her business and Lena was finding it increasingly difficult to get work in her chosen profession of nursing.

Long before this, however, the Republican movement in Scotland had been beset by problems of apathy and lack of finance which the climate of prejudice only served to compound. This was demonstrated by the predicament of the former O/C of the 2nd Scottish Brigade, Thomas Dempsey, who appeared in Dundee Sherriff Court on 4 and 11 August 1926 on deferred charges of arms possession at 58 Brook Street. Dempsey, who had just served nigh on 50 days in jail for illicit stilling at the same address, 'speculated' that the arms had been dumped there by the Irish movement for the purpose of going to Ireland when the 'trouble was on'.[17] The movement had been 'popular' then, but was, it seemed, no longer, as he had been unable to procure £5 bail from those whom he 'thought were his friends in Dundee'. Abandoned by his former comrades and his own solicitor (who failed to appear on both occasions), the hard-pressed Dempsey was found guilty, and obliged to spend another twenty days in jail.[18] He emigrated to North America shortly afterwards.

The Ancient Order of Hibernians Revived

By the late 1920s, what remained of the Irish Republican movement in Dundee had turned inwards and assumed an increasingly non-political role. By contrast, the Ancient Order of Hibernians, which had ceased operating after its ill-judged condemnation of the Easter Rising, experienced a something of a revival. While the AOH in the west of Scotland was regarded as a bulwark against growing anti-Irish sectarianism and Orange violence, the Order in Dundee cultivated a benign, more 'community friendly' role, whilst maintaining its function as a Friendly Society for the Irish-Catholic community and a fund-raising body for Catholic charities, causes and institutions. The main event from 1924 was the organisation of an annual excursion to the Carfin Grotto, 'the Scottish Lourdes', inaugurated two years earlier. The first trip in October 1924, attracted around 1,500 excursionists who travelled in three special trains. A report, garnered by a *Courier* reporter on the Dundee pilgrims' return, spoke of 'affecting sights' as 'the invalids, some three or four in number, bedridden for years and suffering from paralysis' were borne across the railway tracks to spare them the pain of being hulked over the bridge, and 'the entire party walked along the road four abreast saying the Rosary and singing hymns'. 'The village of Carfin', it noted, 'has witnessed many processions, but the one from Dundee yesterday was probably outstanding for the reverential demeanour of the whole assembly', who, notwithstanding the heavy rain, 'knelt on the ground supplicating Our Lady' and singing hymns, including 'Ave Maria', with 'beautiful effect.' According to AOH Secretary, Sam Devine, who may have been engaging in some Dundee exceptionalism which the *Courier* was always happy to promote, 'the trip [was] the largest which had ever visited the grotto from any part of the country'.[19] Over the next few years, the event grew even more popular. The trip in May 1928 attracted 2,000 people – the biggest number ever, and more positive headlines when it was reported that an eight-year-old girl, deaf since birth, had recovered her hearing.[20]

Against the weight of anti-Catholic propaganda, the popularity of the Carfin trips and the positive publicity these engendered, served to enhance the standing of the AOH in Dundee and no doubt brought it several new members and supporters. However, its fortunes soon unravelled when founding member, Thomas McGovern, who had been entrusted with holding the funds from the May 1928 excursion, appeared in court charged with embezzling £100 earmarked for the building of a new church, St Peter and Paul's, in Byron Street. Evidence from a range of witnesses not only revealed McGovern to be a fraudster and a cheat, but also exposed a history of financial mismanagement and poor organisation by the Dundee AOH Executive, whose attempts to distance themselves from McGovern's misdoings failed to wash with the Sheriff, who sentenced McGovern to a month in jail. Nor did it wash with the Irish-Catholic community.[21] The incident put an end to the Carfin trips, or at least to the Hibernians' organisation of them, and destroyed the trust of the Irish-Catholic community in the AOH, which was never totally regained. The AOH resumed its organisation of excursions some years later, though on a much smaller scale – for example, an excursion on the Tay Ferries in the summer of 1937 attracted around 400 passengers and another unfavourable headline when one of them fell overboard.[22] The AOH's last public appearance as an identifiably Irish organisation was at a civic pageant to mark the Silver Jubilee of George V, presenting a 'tableau' on the founding of the Irish Free State – one of 22 scenes representing the developments of the British monarch's 25-year reign.[23] While the AOH may have attracted some pro-Treaty and non-aligned Irish nationalists, it is likely that the most radical and progressive of Irish republicans balked at their brand of conservative Catholic nationalism and had little to do with them in the first place.

The Spanish Civil War

While one generation of Irish republican activists shored up their memories of past involvement, from the mid- to late 1930s, the impulse to a more active form of radical republicanism focused on Spain, as the attempt by right-wing forces led by General Franco to overthrow the democratically-elected government of the Spanish Republic, and the consequent fight to defend it, commonly known as the Spanish Civil War, had clear echoes of the Irish one. Interestingly, Peter Taylor, former member of Sinn Féin and the IRA in Dundee, adhered to the Catholic hierarchy's advice to support Franco's Nationalists, on the grounds that the Spanish Republic and its supporters were anti-Catholic.[24]

There is a certain irony in the fact that, following the establishment of the Irish Free State, Taylor's former political and spiritual mentor, Father John Fahy, collaborated with Peadar O'Donnell, one of the most prominent 'Reds' in Ireland, in the campaign against the payment of land annuities to the Cumann na Gaedheal government (who collected them on behalf of the British), and on various other popular radical issues throughout the 1920s and 1930s. Father Fahy supported O'Donnell to the hilt and counted him as one of his greatest friends; correspondingly, O'Donnell described Fahy as a 'fine propagandist' with a gift for leadership that his 'occasional incoherence', like Jim Larkin, only served to emphasise.[25] After O'Donnell founded the Republican Congress – also known as 'The Red IRA' – in 1934, Fahy defended him against attacks from the Church (and State):

> In the past we faced the foul music of Imperialism openly and fearlessly, and now that I am retired from the conflict, I am quite certain that my comrade Peadar O'Donnell will continue his fight for the dispossessed and noblest element of nation openly,

honestly and fearlessly as long the Good God leaves him his terrestrial existence. Peadar O'Donnell is as good a Catholic as I am and as long as he remains such and is true to the Land of his Fathers, I shall be honoured to have association with him.[26]

In 1936, O'Donnell was one of the first Irishmen to join the Spanish Republican forces and subsequently encouraged other Irish republicans, including Frank Ryan, who would go on to lead the Irish contingent in the International Brigades, to do the same.[27]

A large number of volunteers also came from Scotland, and Dundee in particular.[28] Whether considerations of an Irish Republic played a major part in their support for the Spanish one is uncertain. Although a number of Dundee's International Brigaders had Irish surnames – Boyle, Cassidy, Curran, Galligan, Maguire, McCabe, Sullivan – by the 1930s, many Dundonians were the products of mixed marriages extending back three or four generations. Moreover, given the large percentage of Irish women marrying Scottish men, the focus on Irish surnames as an indicator of inherited political tradition overlooks the essential point that the Church of Scotland's claim, in its notoriously racist report, that the 'fusion of the Scottish and Irish races in Scotland...will remain an impossibility' as the Irish are 'obedient children of the Church of Rome' and the Scots 'stubbornly adhere to the principles of the Reformed Faith',[29] had long been disproven in Dundee. For example, the parents of Lochee-born International Brigaders Allan and Charles Craig, Peter Craig and Mary Connor, were married in St Luke's Presbyterian Church while their two younger sons were baptised in St Mary's RC.[30] Indeed, this 'fusion' of Irish and Scots, had created a new generation of working-class Dundonians whose political inheritance was the radical traditions of both nations, and which, in the context of the Spanish Civil War, likely strengthened the impulse to international solidarity.

Like most Dundee Brigaders, the Craig brothers were too young to have been actively involved in the Republican movement during the Revolutionary War but old enough to have been aware of it. Like the majority of International Brigaders, however, most Dundee volunteers described themselves as communists or anti-fascists, and the connection to Irish republicanism was tangential. There were exceptions, however: for example, William McDade, who was 39 when he joined the International Brigade, was also born in Lochee (at 43 Coupar Street), but identified as Irish, a conception which his commanding officer at the Battle of Jarama, Tom Wintringham – who described him as 'a diminutive Belfast man' – was inclined to believe. McDade was in fact third-generation Irish, the son of Linlithgow-born William Joseph McDade and Lochee-born Mary Ann Trail who were married in the Church of Scotland at 13 High Street, Lochee, on 11 January 1897. McDade, who had served in the Irish Guards (possibly joining around 1915 at the time of John Redmond's recruitment campaign), also claimed to have been in the IRA, and to have spent time in the French Foreign Legion before returning to Dundee where he took up the trade of carpentry until December 1936 when he enlisted his considerable military expertise in the service of the Spanish Republic.[31]

Republican principles and military ardour were, however, insufficient to overcome the superior weaponry of the Nazi-backed Nationalist forces. As the last volunteers made their way home and the Spanish Civil War drew to an unsatisfactory close, back in Ireland, the IRA, now in the control of militant social conservatives under the leadership of Sean Russell, were preparing to launch a new campaign of incendiary sabotage – dubbed 'S-Plan' – against the British State. On 15 January 1939, following the failure of the British government to respond to their ultimatum to withdraw British troops from the occupied north, the IRA issued a declaration of war, which they followed up a day later with the first in a series of bomb attacks on the national power grid and the communications network across England. A proverbial 'net' was 'thrown around the coast' as one of the biggest roundups of 'suspects' since 1923 got under way with 'practically every (Irish) colony' and port being visited by detectives.[32] Although all the explosions occurred in England, across Scotland guards were placed on power stations, gasworks, reservoirs and docks – measures which the police stressed were 'precautionary', as they had 'not the slightest reason' to expect bomb attacks outside England. The view that Scotland was not a target for IRA saboteurs was verified four weeks later by Scottish Nationalist Wendy Wood, who – following an anti-republican meeting of John Cormack's Protestant Action Society in the Usher Hall, Edinburgh, which she and her fellow pro-republican nationalists had been bravely leafleting – announced to the assembled press reporters that she, as leader of Comunn airson Saorsa na h'Alba (the League for the Freedom of Scotland)[33] had received 'a definite guarantee' from the IRA that they had no intention of damaging property in Scotland as 'they did not consider Scotland to be party to the dispute'.[34] When pressed by a reporter that this 'presumed knowledge on her part of the IRA's responsibility in outrages elsewhere', Wendy responded that 'the guarantee had been communicated to her verbally, and that she had in turn passed [it] to the Scottish police', and pointed to 'the fact that in spite of the vulnerability of many items in Scotland, nothing had been touched by IRA agents. Agents provocateurs,' she added, 'may try it on, but the guarantee will prove itself'.[35] As indeed it did.

While no acts of IRA sabotage occurred on Scottish soil, as in the Tan and Civil Wars, Republican operators and sympathisers in Scotland were instrumental in procuring the explosives and, in some cases, constructing the bombs. For example, on 7 June, three Irish republicans and one Scottish nationalist appeared at Stirling High Court charged with conspiring to steal 200 pounds of gelignite and 300 detonators from Barleyside Colliery, Falkirk. The trial was interesting for the appearance of two witnesses – colliery employees William Anderson and Arthur Lynch Scobbie – who, in an apparent deal with the authorities had agreed to turn Crown's evidence in exchange for a lighter sentence,[36] and two others, Wendy Wood and Amhlaidh MacAindreis, who spoke in defence of the Scottish nationalist, Matthew Somerville.[37] The Crown, however, needed little encouragement to play down any suggestion of collaboration between Scottish nationalists and the IRA. Indeed, the Crown Prosecutor instructed the jury, that at no point in his dealings with Anderson, had Somerville – who had been visiting Anderson to collect hire purchase payments – 'raised the question of Scottish Nationalism'. Somerville received eighteen months ordinary imprisonment, reflecting, Lord Wark emphasised, 'the small part [he] had played in the charges'.[38] The others received sentences ranging from ten years (for the ringleader, Terence McSherry) to five years' penal servitude. In a final dramatic address to the jury, McSherry, who alone of the accused had refused to recognise the court or appoint a lawyer in his defence, declared himself 'a citizen of the Irish Republic and a soldier of the IRA', irrespective of which, he maintained the charges against himself and the other men to be a 'complete fabrication'.[39] Addressing the attacks in England, he maintained that the British government were responsible for the explosions that had taken place and would continue to do until the demands in the ultimatum were granted. For this he made no apology. Through repeated warnings from the judge, he declared that as long as Ireland remained partitioned, it was the duty of all Irishmen to treat English rule with contempt wherever it existed. And, standing by the Proclamation of the Irish Republic, he concluded, pointedly that 'Ireland's only enemy is England, and in every generation since the conquest of Ireland the Irish State [sic] has resisted by force. The entire forces of Scotland are subject and humble servants of their imperial masters in England'.[40]

On 8 August, three men appeared in the High Court of Justiciary Glasgow, charged with possession of explosives and, in the case of one Edward McGill, the theft of 100 sticks of gelignite and detonator nippers from the Garngad Brick and Sand Company Co Ltd. It was noted that the explosives in McGill's possession had been found in a drawer at his house in Beechgrove Street alongside a selection of republican artifacts and literature including 'photographs [sic] of Wolfe Tone and Liam Mellows and 21 copies of the *Wolfe Tone Weekly*.[41] The other two men, Michael James O'Hara and John Carson, were charged with possession of 467 sticks of gelignite, an electric cable and an alarm clock on which was pencilled a circle that 'appeared to indicate' the point at which in which an electric cable could be attached to cause an explosion'. All three men had been arrested three months earlier at the hall at 132 Trongate occupied by the Celtic Literary Society and the Wolfe Tone Club – fronts for the IRA in Glasgow, which, it appears, had been penetrated by police agents. All declared they were 'soldiers of the IRA' and refused to plead or accept legal counsel. The jury took less than twenty minutes to find them guilty on all counts, and all were sentenced to ten years' penal servitude.[42]

While there is substantial evidence of explosives being procured and possibly of bombs being manufactured in Scotland, given the nature of the material, most activity took place in the industrial west and centre of the country, and there is little to suggest that participation in the IRA's bombing campaign extended further. By all accounts, Scotland remained 'off the map.' Nevertheless, the north-east Tory press continued to speculate. In May, the *Aberdeen Press and Journal* opined that 'Scotland, so far, is immune, 'but if the outrages continue and increase then the public temper may rise against Ireland and Irishmen...there may be a demand for an investigation into the life and affairs of all Irish people in this country and for the deportation of all suspects'.[43]

On 31 July, the *Evening Telegraph* offered another reason as to why Scotland had not been included in the campaign:

> the leaders in the conspiracy recognised – or were warned – that to adventure to terrorism in Scotland would involve warfare against the Irish people and Irish interests in Scotland... Although the IRA terrorists have not engaged in warfare in Scotland there is a possibility that some of those who have had a part in the conspiracy may seek shelter in Scotland.[44]...In this war against the community, the sheltering of trouble makers might lead to complications...there can be no easygoing disregard of the danger in aiding and abetting criminal conspirators who are menacing the lives of English, Scottish and Welsh people.[45]

In the existing climate of anti-Irish prejudice engendered by the Church of Scotland's report on the 'Menace of the Irish Race to Our Scottish Nation' from which the last words conspicuously borrowed, the *Evening Telegraph*, which, as opposed to the *Courier*, was aimed at the Dundee working class, added fuel to the fire. *The Press and Journal* had already noted that 'German nationals [were] being deported for behaviour less harmful'. Significantly, it was around this time that Lena and Helen McDonald made the decision to uproot themselves from the one square mile in which they their family had lived for the best part of a century and move to Ireland, despite the fact that they had no home or job to go to – factors which undoubtedly drove Lena in her pursuit of a military pension.[46] It fell to the redoubtable Father Fahy, ensconced in his parish in Loughrea, County Galway, and Honorary Secretary of the Old IRA (Scottish Division) Association, Eamonn Mooney, tasked with coordinating the applications of Scottish IRA veterans, to track down potential referees, including Joe Robinson, D P Walshe, Henry Coyle, Joe Booker and Sean Healy, all of whom had visited Dundee and could verify Lena's involvement. The glowing testimonies of Booker, Healy, Fahy and Jean Gillespie (all of whom took the Republican side in the Civil War), bore witness to her prolific contribution. In 1940, Lena wrote from her temporary lodgings in Belfast to Taoiseach Éamon de Valera and Tánaiste Seán T O'Kelly with a reminder that they had availed of her hospitality in Dundee, and prevailing on them to expedite her application. The pension was granted in 1941.[47]

The Coventry bombing of 25 August 1939, which resulted in the death of five people and the injury of 72 more, was an unmitigated disaster which seriously undermined the IRA's support base and precipitated the end of its English campaign.[48] Although the bombings continued until the spring of 1940, by the outbreak of the Second World War on 3 September 1939, the campaign was effectively over. In October, IRA Chief of Staff Sean Russell attempted to rally the dwindling number of activists (hundreds of whom had already been interned or deported in a raft of Emergency Powers legislation on both sides of the Irish Sea) with the following statement:

> 'England's difficulty is Ireland's opportunity' has ever been the watchword of the Gael. Now is the time take up arms and strike a blow for the Ulster people.[49]

Nevertheless, Russell's tired repetition of the 'England's difficulty' mantra rang hollow when that 'difficulty' was Nazism, the horrific consequences of which right-wing supremacist ideology – the annihilation or exclusion of ethnic, social and political groups deemed 'sub-standard' or deviant to the Aryan ideal – were becoming more widely known. Unlike the First World War, which was conducted in the furtherance of imperial interests, and therefore opposed on such grounds by anti-imperialists, the Second World War was, in many respects, a 'popular' one. Indeed, for some who had fought on the side of the Republic in the Spanish Civil War, it provided a chance to resume the fight and, hopefully, finish the job.

Overall, neither the IRA's English campaign of 1939–40 nor its Northern Campaign of 1942–4 made much of an impact in Scotland. By the end of the Second World War, the IRA was at the lowest ebb – a combination of imprisonment, poor organisation and demoralisation having decimated its membership and weakened its support base.

The Irish Anti-Partition League

A number of those sympathetic to the IRA's ideals now turned their attention to pursuing a united Ireland by other means. For most in the diaspora, this meant supporting the Irish Anti-Partition League (APL), founded in November 1945 by members of the Six County Nationalist Party, including Glasgow-born James McSparran, and Coatbridge-born Eddie McAteer, the brother of former IRA Chief of Staff and commander of the Northern Campaign, Hugh McAteer, who was currently serving a fifteen-year prison sentence in Crumlin Road Jail. Despite its moderate founders, the IAPL was conceived as a 'united front' whose purpose, similar to the United Irish League in the Home Rule campaign, was to rally the Irish vote, place pressure on political candidates and raise money to fund a campaign which would 'broadcast to the world our claim [and] expose the injustice of partition'.[50] The APL also gained the support of nationalist politicians in the Twenty-Six counties, members of the British Labour Party – notably the MP for Manchester Platting, Hugh Delargy, who was appointed Chairman of a British, later English, Council, and Scottish nationalists such as Oliver Brown, a zealous advocate of pacifism, socialist republicanism and the founder of the Scottish Socialist Party in 1942. A Scottish Council was formed in early 1947 with Frank O'Neill of Glasgow as Chairman and Sean McCann as National Organiser. By July, several branches had been formed in Glasgow, Paisley and Coatbridge with plans under way for one in Dundee under the direction of the District Organiser, Daniel Skelton.[51]

Skelton, who originally hailed from Greenock/Port Glasgow, was a veteran Irish republican of some standing, due in part to his having been one of the few members of the Scottish Brigade presently living in Dundee to have seen active service in Ireland.[52] Skelton had joined the IRA in 1919 at the age of sixteen, possibly lying about his age in order to do so. Indeed, such was his eagerness to join the fight that he later travelled to Ireland where he attached himself to the Dungannon Company of the 2nd Battalion, 1st Tyrone Brigade, under the command of Joseph Donaghy – at least he claimed, and was believed to have done so. Intriguingly, Brigade records have no Daniel Skelton on the rolls of the Dungannon Company at the two 'critical dates' (pre-Truce 1921 and post-June 1922) – the only identifiably Scottish Volunteers[53] amongst the 42–67 members listed being Joseph Finn of Merklands, and Henry McHugh of Clare Terrace, Glasgow.[54] There was however, a John Skelton, living in Dungannon, and it is possible that Skelton was operating under a different forename.[55] Charles McGleenan, O/C of the IRA in Armagh, recalled an operation on the Armagh-Monaghan border early in 1922 which was aborted after 'a man named Skelton, who had come to Castleshane [the camp in County Monaghan from where the IRA had been launching attacks on enemy forces] from the Dungannon area' opened fire prematurely, alerting the targets, a party of B Specials, to their presence. McGlennan states that he was later told the man was an unreliable type'.[56] The Volunteer's behaviour could also be attributed to a nervous skittishness on the part of an over-eager and undisciplined youth lacking experience in the field – and a possible reflection of the low level of military training in Scotland. Alternatively, Dan's Skelton's involvement may have come at a time when, as McGlennan's statement suggests, the IRA was engaging in 'off the record' operations in the immediate post-Treaty period prior to the official resumption of hostilities in June 1922.

Whatever the truth of the matter, Skelton eventually returned to Scotland. In the mid-1930s, possibly viewing Dundee as a more sympathetic environment in which to operate economically and socially, he moved to 87 King Street in the city centre, later opening a confectioner's shop in Kerr's Lane, Lochee. However, Skelton, who remained unmarried, found his real vocation, and also a paternal role, as a key organiser of Irish nationalist activity. Over the next few years, he built up an extensive network of contacts in Irish circles across Dundee and the surrounding district, all the while maintaining his west coast connections. Consequently, he found himself in the position of being the Dundee link for the Republican movement in Scotland and the fulcrum of Irish republican activity in the area for the next three decades.

The Dundee Brothers Pearse branch was duly formed in August with Peter Docherty as Chairman, a role in which he was assisted by General Secretary of the JFWU, John Joseph Duffy. In due course, the job of Social Secretary – arguably, the most important and enduring in terms of raising funds for the Irish national cause in all its aspects and permutations – was taken on by twenty-year-old Agnes Innes supported by her female relatives.

The naming of the branch after Pearse – not Connolly, despite the latter's connections with the city – merits some consideration. In the Cold War years of the late 1940s and early 1950s, it may have reflected an uneasiness about Connolly's espousal of a socialist republic and an ignorance of Pearse's support for it. In 1919, Irish republican and communist Sean McLoughlin had written:

> If the 'Rising' had succeeded there is no possible doubt that it would have been the first victory in the world for a Socialist Republic. In this [Connolly] was ably supported by Pearse, who was much more a practical idealist than people seem to think – witness the 'Proclamation'.[57]

McLoughlin was well placed to make such a claim. After all, in the last critical moments of the Rising, he had come to know both men and to understand their motives. Three decades on, however, Connolly's reputation as the leader whose 'practical ideals' exemplified the Irish Republic had been eclipsed by that of Pearse, the one-dimensional image of whom – as a 'pure idealist' and the personification of 'Irish Ireland' – had become fixed in Irish popular consciousness.

In this context, the naming of the Dundee branch in his honour may also have been a reflection of the anti-communist sentiment prevalent in the Catholic Church. For example, in March 1949, the Dundee Education Authority voted to exclude communist candidates standing in the municipal elections from holding meetings in Catholic schools as, according to Vicar-General of the Diocese, Joseph McGhee, 'it was impossible to join the interests of the Catholic community [with] the Communist Party'.[58] Interestingly, one of the candidates seeking re-election on this occasion was APL member, John J Duffy, who, although a socialist was hardly a radical one, and may have feared the communists cutting in on his vote.[59] Suffice to say, Labour candidates were not subject to the same exclusions. Indeed, while the APL in Dundee was politically left of centre, it was also socially conservative. Most of its members were part of the 'Catholic community' although the Church itself neither endorsed nor condemned it. Others, such as Dan Skelton, remained committed Irish republicans. All things considered, then, and given Pearse's prime status in the pantheon of Irish martyrs, the choice of name may simply have been the most popular one.

Meanwhile, the campaign continued to gain in scale and importance as de Valera, who was voted out of power on 4 February 1948, seized the opportunity to recover his republican credentials by responding, albeit belatedly, to a challenge from the Anti-Partition League in Dublin to use his influence, if not his political office, to induce the British government to act on partition. The following March, de Valera embarked on a worldwide anti-partition tour which covered all parts of the Irish diaspora. Despite his earlier acknowledgement of the key role played by the IRA in Scotland during the Tan and Civil Wars, he could only manage one visit there – to Glasgow in October 1948. An earlier tour schedule, which included visits to Dundee and Paisley, was pulled six weeks before; consequently, the mass meeting in St Andrew's Hall, Glasgow, on 17 October, sold out many weeks in advance and drew supporters, as the Chair of the Scottish Council of the APL, P Lennon boasted, 'from Dundee to Dumfries, and Ayrshire to the Lothians'. Dev began, somewhat predictably, by recalling the close relationship between Ireland and Scotland', before proceeding to talk up his 'past record' on partition: i.e., his endeavours to prevent Lloyd George 'from pursuing the course which would lead to the cutting up of Ireland'; his sixteen years as head of government during which he had never failed to press every British Prime Minister and Foreign Secretary to end the injustice of partition; and his refusal to bring Ireland into the Second World War, despite the suggestion it would bring about Irish unity – 'My answer was', he claimed, 'we have been fooled before by that'.[60]

The visit of de Valera to Glasgow has often been portrayed as the high-water mark of the anti-partition agitation in Scotland, certainly in Glasgow. However, for all the grandstanding rhetoric, neither the meeting nor the tour succeeded in shifting the British government's position on partition or in impressing the issue on the wider non-Irish population. Dev was effectively preaching to the converted, a fact of which he appears to have been aware as his response the question: 'Do you think the British people are sympathetic?' indicates. His answer? 'The British people very largely do not know about it'.[61]

The highest point of the anti-partition campaign in Dundee, however, was a meeting organised by the Brothers Pearse APL branch in the Marryat Hall on 25 September 1949. At the last minute, the scheduled speaker,

Jack Beattie, the Westminster Labour MP and recently-unseated Stormont one for West Belfast, pulled out – not an unusual experience for Dundee's Irish nationalists, as over the past 85 years O'Donovan Rossa, Charles Stewart Parnell, John Redmond, Michael Collins and, most recently, Éamon de Valera, had cancelled engagements in, or declined invitations to visit the city.[62] Beattie was replaced by R H (Roddy) O'Connor, who, as well as being the newly elected Nationalist Member for West Tyrone in the Stormont Parliament, was also a director of the *Ulster Herald*, whose 'Special Correspondent' (possibly O'Connor himself) provided a detailed report of the proceedings. While there was a lot less hype and clamour than the de Valera meeting, the audience in the Marryat Hall was 'large and attentive', enthusiastic and engaged, and the debate was more proactive and far-sighted. O'Connor was joined on the platform by Dundee branch president, Peter Docherty, and representatives of the Scottish Council, including Dan Skelton of Dundee and James Feeley of Paisley – the latter a 'well-known and vigorous worker in the cause of Irish freedom' who had addressed previous meetings in the city. O'Connor, who had not, pronounced himself 'amazed and delighted to find so much manifest enthusiasm for the Irish cause'. He had been aware that 'there was interest in the cause of Irish unity and independence'; until he came to Dundee, however, he had never thought it had 'so many people [who] were prepared to join in this, the final effort of the struggle'.[63]

O'Connor went on to condemn the Six-County Parliament – the 'shameless repudiation of democracy' that was 'in existence against the wishes of the vast majority of the Irish population', and through which the manufactured unionist majority maintained its dominance and privilege via the abolition of proportional representation and the gerrymandering of Parliamentary and local government constituencies. A solicitor by profession, O'Connor cited the litany of injustices exacted upon the nationalist 'minority', who 'never succeeded in getting any public appointment of importance and seldom succeeded in getting one at a lower grade', and backed it all up with hard facts and detailed examples from his own, predominantly nationalist, constituency.[64] The main focus of the meeting, however, and the reason for calling it, was the Ireland Act 1949, passed by the Attlee government on 2 June in retaliation for Ireland having declared itself a Republic the previous April. The Act, which guaranteed the 'constitutional integrity of Northern Ireland' subject to the consent of the Six-County Parliament, effectively copper-fastened the unionist veto and reinforced partition.[65]

Not surprisingly, the anti-partitionists were furious. Peter Docherty, presiding, informed the meeting that, following the passing of the Act, he and two other members of the Brothers Pearse branch had called on Dundee's two Labour MPs, John Strachey and Tom Cook, to remind them that 50,000 of Dundee's 200,000 population were Irish sympathisers, and to seek their reasons for having voted for the Act. The explanation they were given, he stated, was 'not satisfactory', and they had 'clearly expressed' their indignation. In a typically forthright speech, James Feeley, a Labour activist of twenty years standing, warned the British Labour Party that it could 'no longer afford to disregard and flout the substantial voting element that stood for justice in Ireland'. For his part, he was so disappointed at the Labour MPs who had reneged on their election promises that he had 'completely severed' his connections with the party. And, having demonstrated how he had stood by his principles, he urged the people of Dundee to be as 'firm in their determination to see Irish unity', trusting that 'independence [would] be established before long'.

It fell to O'Connor to assure them that:

> The present generation of Irishmen were just as determined as their fathers and ancestors had been to complete the struggle for the absolute freedom of the Irish Nation. The country had been invaded many hundreds of years ago, but at no time had it been conquered. There had always been from the first day the invader landed a continuous struggle against foreign domination and that struggle would continue to go on as long as would be necessary and until absolute freedom was procured for the whole nation.[66]

Prophetic words, but neither the APL nor O'Connor's constitutional nationalists would be at the forefront. Besides exposing the complicity of the British Labour Party in the continuing oppression of Ireland, the passing of the Ireland Act revealed the ineffectiveness of the existing anti-partition campaign. As angry protests in Ireland gave way to a new impetus to armed struggle, the IRA gradually regrouped, recruited and reorganised. In Scotland, and Dundee especially, where that was not an option, it led to frustration, disillusionment and a tailing-off in popular support for the APL. The meeting in the Marryat Hall was the Dundee's APL's last hurrah – the Brothers Pearse branch ceased operating shortly afterwards, its chief organiser Skelton having returned to the republican fold.

In a working-class town where the majority of Irish sympathisers had long lived at the thin end of the wedge, the recommendation by Feeley to boycott the Labour Party was not realistic – to vote Tory was an anathema; to abstain and fail to exercise a hard-won democratic right, was even more so. The Communist Party candidate, David Bowman, may have picked up a number of votes. However, the anti-communism of the Catholic clergy – not to mention the APL, and indeed of the Republican movement itself – may have discouraged others. Such counsel also tested the loyalty of many Labour Party members. The following month, the Chair of the APL in England, Hugh Delargy, who had vigorously opposed the Ireland Bill, quit the League altogether complaining that it had become 'too political' and was dictating to people how they should vote.[67]

While Dundee's Irish sympathisers were undoubtedly disappointed at the actions of their MPs, the majority continued to vote for them. By the mid-twentieth century, class loyalties, plus concerns about their own economic situation, had come to override any loyalty to Ireland or concern about its condition, however sincere this was; the concept of the 'Irish community' had all but disappeared as successive generations of intermarriage, common working culture and class cooperation had produced a distinctive Dundee identity which incorporated the Irish one but also diluted it. Moreover, and somewhat ironically, the low-level prejudice of the interwar years proved far more effective in undermining Irish identity than did the blatant sectarianism and virulent anti-Irish racism experienced by Irish Catholics in Glasgow and the West, which had served to keep Ireland and their Irish identity at the forefront of their consciousness. For the majority of younger fourth- and fifth-generation Irish-Dundonians however, it had been edged out to the periphery.

The APL's existence in Dundee was brief (two to three years at most). Elsewhere, the APL continued to operate until the early 1960s. In England and Wales, for example, where society had not been subject to the same onslaught of anti-Irish sectarianism, it provided a focus for Irish identity, and, in some instances, helped 'rejuvenate the Irish community' in large hubs of Irish immigration such as London and Newcastle.[68] Here, however, there was another motive – to steer Irish immigrant workers away from the 'communist-front' Connolly Association to which the APL feared it was losing support.[69] Interestingly, Hugh Delargy had been an enthusiastic supporter of the Connolly Association before aligning himself with the APL in 1946.[70]

The Connolly Association, formed in London in 1938 to campaign for the rights and freedoms of the Irish people on the foundation of Connolly's ideals, was well-placed to infuse some radical energy into the anti-partition campaign. Following the passing of the Ireland Act 1949, the Association shifted the thrust of its campaigning work from the economic problems of Irish immigrants to the condition of Ireland, gaining several new members and supporters in the process. In the early 1950s, the Connolly Association came north to Scotland where, given its appeal to republicans, communists, labour activists and more recent Irish immigrants looking for a focus for their patriotism, it would seem to be assured of winning over a large section of the working class, particularly the distinct admixture of Irish-sympathising socialist-supporting Dundonians who had formed the bulk of the Irish republican and unemployed worker movements of the early 1920s. The Scotland of the early 1950s, however, was a very different place. Although the anti-Irish influencers in the Church of Scotland had been superseded by a more moderating force, the 1923 report (of which the Connolly Association seemed entirely ignorant) cast a long shadow. Leading Connolly Association activist, C Desmond Greaves, recalled that while '[the Connolly Association] had very successful meetings in Dundee, and won members in Edinburgh' – such as might be expected in the cities of Connolly's first foray into socialist politics, even more so of his birth – and 'sold 2,000 copies of our paper in one "Irish week"' in Glasgow, 'we could never establish an organisation'. Attempts to organise meetings in Glasgow brought the source of the problem into sharp focus. Within minutes of hoisting of a tricolour on a piece of waste ground in the Gallowgate, the police swooped, arresting the speakers on a series of 'bizarre' charges including 'causing a crowd to collect' and 'pulling a button off a policeman's uniform'. Greaves concluded: 'it was clear that

Scotland was a different place from England or the Twenty-Six counties. The arm of the authority was much harsher'. Meetings in Govan and Greenock were subsequently suppressed, as was the displaying of the Irish tricolour – on the express orders, Greaves was told, of the Secretary of State for Scotland. However, whereas in Ireland, state repression begat a more organised and militant resistance, in Scotland:

> The sectarian issue clouded everything. When we addressed meetings at factory gates, we were invariably asked about Celtic and Rangers. In this atmosphere no literate Irish leadership could come, and despite splendid meetings we never established ourselves. There was goodwill but nobody knew what we were talking about. The Labour Movement was terrified of the sectarian issue, and small blame to them.[71]

Thus, John J Duffy, Vice-Chair of the Dundee APL, Secretary of the JFWU and prospective socialist candidate in municipal elections, kept his Irish politics separate from his labour and trade union activity – a dichotomy that was also imposed on James Connolly's political legacy by the Scottish labour movement. Dundonians often credited their city with not being infected by the same aggressive sectarianism of Glasgow and the West. They were also anxious to keep it that way; to avoid stirring latent anti-Irish prejudice which – as known Irish republicans had found to their cost – existed amongst certain sections of the Scottish working class. Best then not to risk incurring class disunity but rather to commit intensive discussion of controversial Irish affairs (Irish affairs were always controversial) to Irish organisations and trusted friendship groups.

While there appears to have been more heat than light surrounding the Connolly Association's attempts to organise in some parts of Scotland, the heat had long gone out of the anti-partition movement. By the mid-1950s, the Scottish Council of the APL had shrunk to a core of moderate nationalists whose capitalist politics were unrepresentative of the Scoto-Irish working class and whose opposition to physical force was out of synch with the growing popular mood in Ireland. In June 1954, an IRA raid on Gough Barracks, Armagh – the most daring and lucrative in recent years – elicited congratulatory resolutions from town and county councils and Old IRA Associations across the Twenty-Six counties, and provided a further stimulus to IRA recruitment.[72] In the Six Counties, the Stormont government reacted by reintroducing the Special Powers Act, which, by granting extensive interrogation powers to the Royal Ulster Constabulary and its notoriously sectarian auxiliary force, the B Specials, fanned the flames of resistance. In December, a skirmish between ten customs officers and four IRA men on the Tyrone-Monaghan border ended in the shooting of one of the former as the latter abandoned their arms-laden vehicle and melted into the countryside while fighting a rearguard action.[73] On 5 March 1955, the B-Specials opened fire on a van driving down an 'undesignated' road near Keady, County Armagh, killing the driver, eighteen-year-old Arthur Leonard, and critically wounding his companion.[74] The response of the APL to these incidents is revealing. At a St Patrick's night dinner in Glasgow, Chair of the Scottish Council, William Coyle condemned 'the recent happenings in South Tyrone and South Armagh', which, he opined, were 'not in any way encouraging to any person or firm wishing to establish businesses in the Border area'. Interestingly, Coyle did not distinguish between the B-Specials or the IRA – all were equally condemned under the sobriquet of 'trigger-happy men'.[75]

The revival of the Republican movement in Ireland – and particularly the re-emergence of the IRA – gave a new impetus to the movement in Scotland. In Dundee, the recruitment drive was directed by Dan Skelton who, from February to October 1955, placed a notice in the monthly Sinn Féin newspaper, the *United Irishman*, inviting interested parties in the Dundee area to 'Join the Republican Movement', with his address as point of contact.[76] Whereas in Ireland, this standard notice was the entry point into the IRA for a new generation of eager young republicans, in Dundee it was as much about remobilising old members as recruiting new ones. A new Sinn Féin cumann, named, appropriately, after the most senior of the Easter Proclamation's signatories, 58-year-old Thomas Clarke, was the outcome. No record remains of the membership which seems to have been composed of veterans of the 1919-23 campaign, most of whom were, like Clarke, in their fifties and sixties, and selected members of Irish kinship groups. Indeed, the rehabilitation of Sinn Fein in Dundee was preceded and paralleled by a concerted effort by the Old IRA (Scottish Division) Association to reclaim and reassert their role in the past and continuing fight for a full Irish Republic. The early to mid-1950s saw a number of belated applications to the Irish government for military service medals from Scottish Tan War veterans, including Dundee-born James Kimmett, James Devaney and Dundee-domiciled Daniel Skelton. Though the deadline for applications had closed on 30 January 1950, Kimmet appealed that he had been 'unaware that such a scheme existed' until Seamus Reader – who was now living in Dublin and working at Leinster House – informed him while he was visiting Ireland 'on holiday' in 1951.[77]

This period also saw an attempt to fill the gaps in the 2nd IRA Brigade records resulting from the emigration to America of the now-deceased Thomas Dempsey, former O/C of the 2nd (East Scotland) Brigade and its 1st (North of Forth) Battalion. As with the initial endeavour to procure pensions for hard-pressed and ignored Scottish-based IRA veterans, the task was largely undertaken by the Honorary Secretary of the Old IRA (Scottish Division) Association, Eamonn Mooney, who was, in this instance, assisted by the former President of the Dundee Kevin Barry Sinn Féin cumann, Cathal Duthie.

Charles 'Cathal' Duthie was born at 30 Rosebank Road, in the Hilltown area of Dundee, on 9 November 1885, the only child of William Malloch Duthie, a Kirriemuir-born baker, and Eliza Short (or Hunter), a Dundee mill worker, both of whom had Irish mothers and largely absent or missing Scottish fathers. The young Charles spent his formative years in the care of his maternal grandmother, Elizabeth Short, the daughter of 'famine' immigrants, John and Alice Short, before moving to Glasgow, where his parents set up a joint baker-pawnbroker business in Camlachie, before returning again to Dundee after William died of a heart attack in 1906. Charles possibly found his way into Irish cultural, and subsequently political, nationalism through his wife, Catherine Kelly, the Glasgow-born daughter of Irish immigrants, or possibly through the priest who married them, Canon Michael Phelan of County Kilkenny, a fluent Irish speaker, influential educationalist and supporter of the Gaelic League. It is equally likely that Duthie was radicalised by the tight-knit working-class Irish community into which he was born, and in which, with the exception of the Glasgow years, he lived most of his life – a near neighbour was John Fox Coyne, the son of Fenian, radical Land Leaguer, and militant physical force Irish republican, Edward Fox Coyne, who had settled in the area in the late nineteenth century.

Duthie, who was also known as Charles Duffy in his capacity as a Volunteer in the Dundee Company, 4th Battalion of the Scottish Brigade of the IRA, came to the fore in the post-Treaty period as President of the Kevin Barry Sinn Féin cumann, alongside Secretary Patrick O'Neill, a position he held until the organisation faded into oblivion in the mid- to late 1920s. It is likely that he was involved in the APL, although, unlike Skelton, he held no office in it. Following the demise of the APL in Dundee, Duthie re-emerged on the scene as a key member of the local Labour Party. The early 1950s saw him chairing election and other public meetings – at which, as noted earlier, the topic of Ireland was rarely mentioned – and proposing candidates for municipal elections, although he never stood as a candidate himself.[78] By 1955, he had returned to the Irish republican fold, from where, as Eamonn Mooney likely figured, his local knowledge, organisational experience, and – unlike his peripatetic or deceased ex-comrades – known location and availability, made him the logical candidate to help fill the gaps in the historical record.

In March 1955, Duthie wrote to Mooney at the latter's request, with information on personnel and activity in Dundee, Perth and Fife during the Tan and Civil Wars. The resulting record identified around four dozen activists – a long way short of the estimated 600 IRA Volunteers recorded in the Scottish Brigade records at the time of the Civil War.[79] Duthie made no distinction between the Tan and Civil Wars, adopting the conciliatory term 'the momentous years of the struggle'. Staunch republican Duthie also credited 'the late Sean O'Doherty', latterly a Free Stater, with being 'the pivot on which Sinn Fein and the IRA [in Dundee] rested', and acknowledged the involvement of the pro-Treaty Canon Michael Fahy, also deceased, in the O'Rahilly cumann. Duthie also took the opportunity to inquire after the status of the military service medal applications of James Devaney (Free Stater) and Dan Skelton (republican) – which not been acknowledged by the Pensions Board – and to update Mooney on the status of former comrades upon whose behalf he extended greetings to the Honorary President of the Old IRA Scottish Brigade, Father John Fahy, 'ever remembered in Dundee', and Lena McDonald.[80] However, the patriotic tone of Duthie's letter and his contact with Skelton and other old comrades indicates that the 'struggle' was still a priority, and that he remained committed to it, most likely as one of the initiators of the Thomas Clarke cumann.

On 24 September 1955, members of the cumann travelled through to the AOH Hall, Royston, for a Cois Tine (literally, 'fire side', i.e., a meeting combining business and pleasure) with the Glasgow James Connolly cumann, to 'strengthen east-west links', thus to effect a smooth-running Scottish network through which to co-ordinate activity and maximise resources.[81] The main activity was raising funds; ostensibly, for An Cumann Cabhrach (the Republican Aid Association), formed in November 1953 to support the dependants and provide for the needs of republican prisoners following the imprisonment of three IRA men for an arms raid on an Officer Training Corps base in Felstead, Essex. There was, however, an unwritten agenda: funds were channelled into procuring material for a future planned military campaign. Here, the Dundee link in the chain was Dan Skelton, who, from the council semi- in St Mary's housing scheme that he shared with his substitute family, Margaret Innes, née Duffy, and her adult daughters, Margaret and Agnes – all experienced fundraisers for the Irish cause – directed the local effort.

The arms raids and other 'border incidents' of 1953-5 were, of course, the prelude to the IRA's Border Campaign of 1956-62, Codenamed 'Operation Harvest. The campaign aimed – by means of attacking strategic military and administrative strongholds, sabotaging the communications network, and directing propaganda at the local population in the occupied border counties – to consolidate rebel forces and create large 'liberated areas' from which to launch further attacks, thus rendering the six-county statelet ungovernable and, ultimately, driving the British out of Ireland altogether.[82]

While the Border Campaign enjoyed initial success and popular sympathy in the South – with one epic failure inspiring two classic rebel songs, and eliciting numerous messages of support from Old IRA Associations, including one from the Old Scottish Brigade – it failed to absorb the nationalist population in the North.[83] On the other side of the Irish Sea, the Border Campaign had even less of an impact. Supporters in Scotland did endeavour to send much-needed explosives in late 1959. However, despite the growth of the mass media – by this time, most households had televisions and radios – the dearth of reportage on the situation in Ireland meant that few people outside of Irish circles were aware of it.[84] In his address to the APL's annual conference in Manchester in October 1959, the General Secretary for Ireland, Maurice Roche, noted that 'with a few notable exceptions, the national press and the BBC are noticeably silent and, in some cases, unfavourably disposed where Ireland is concerned'. Roche urged the delegates to double their efforts 'to drive home to the British Government and people of Britain by every legitimate means at our disposal their grave responsibility to help find a solution'.[85] Hampered by an unsympathetic media, however, they were running out of options. While the 'people of Britain' remained for the most part ignorant, their government was more intransigent than ever. On 7 March 1959, the same day that the Chairman of the APL in England, Tadgh Feehan, sent a telegram to the Prime Minister, Harold Macmillan, urging him, on behalf of the 'Irish in Britain', to 'initiate discussions towards bringing about a united Ireland', Macmillan was in Belfast assuring the Ulster Unionist Party of his own (British Conservative) Party's belief that 'the link with Ulster under the Crown must be permanent' and congratulating the RUC and the B Specials for their 'outstanding efforts' in putting down the IRA.[86]

By 1959, the Border Campaign was effectively over, having failed in military terms, and in its objective of stimulating resistance amongst a largely sympathetic but vulnerable nationalist population. Interestingly, while the IRA blew up a BBC transmitter in Derry on the first day of the campaign on 12 December 1956, little effort was made to establish an alternative medium through which to 'direct propaganda at the inhabitants' as per plan.[87] Indeed, unlike the contemporary liberation fighters in Batista's Cuba, with whose socialist objectives the IRA of the time had little ideological affinity, there was no 'rebel radio' in border country.[88] Nor was there any political strategy to speak of beyond the removal of the British presence and the achievement of a united Ireland, regardless of the form it might take.[89] As some in the Republican movement eventually came to see it, it was only by engaging directly with the social and economic concerns of the population on both sides of the border, and offering a radical alternative to the model of the Twenty-Six county state, that the movement would gain the grassroots support that would energise the struggle and set them on the course to victory. At any rate, without that crucial popular support the campaign was doomed to failure. The realisation of that fact had already resulted in the Cork units withdrawing from the campaign in 1958, over three years before it was officially called off in February 1962.[90] Moreover, as far as most people in Scotland, England and Wales were concerned, a campaign focused exclusively on the Irish border did not generate the media attention that may have led even a small minority of them to examine the reasons behind it – a fact that later drew many Irish republicans to the candid conclusion that one bomb in England was worth ten in Belfast. Nevertheless, like the ill-fated English and Northern campaigns of 1939-40 and 1942-4 respectively, the Border Campaign validated the principle of continuous struggle against foreign domination in every generation since the conquest of Ireland, affirmed in the Proclamation of the Irish Republic, invoked by physical force republican Terence McSherry at Stirling High Court in June 1939, and by constitutional nationalist Roddy O'Connor in Dundee's Marryat Hall in September 1949.[91]

While the torch of resistance passed to a new generation of young Irishmen and Irishwomen, the Irish republican tradition in Scotland largely remained in the hands of an older generation of activists, many of whom could trace their involvement back to the Tan War. This was especially the case in Dundee; for example, when Clann na hÉireann was formed in 1964 in an effort to regenerate the staid Sinn Féin organisation in Scotland, England and Wales, Glasgow become one of its most active branches, thanks in part to the dynamic input of a new breed of organisers headed by Persis and Val Renehan, who emigrated to the city from County Limerick in 1961.[92] In Dundee, it fell once again to Dan Skelton, now in his seventh decade, to set up a branch, which, in essence, consisted of a handful of passive supporters who did little to develop a deeper understanding of Irish republicanism beyond its traditional support base. Indeed, Clann na hÉireann, such as it existed in Dundee, performed much the same function of the former Thomas Clarke cumann, i.e., the maintenance of links with Irish republicans in other parts of the country, and a medium through which to recall and celebrate the Irish resistance tradition.

Still, remembrance and memorialisation also had the potential to rejuvenate and revitalise, a fact nobody knew better than the IRA, who set about organising a series of commemorations; for example, of the hitherto neglected United Irishmen, William Orr and Jemmy Hope, long before the 50th anniversary of the Easter Rising in 1966. The anniversary of the

Rising also inspired the biggest and most extensive commemoration in the Southern state's history, as well as stimulating an abundance of television documentaries, memoirs, exhibitions and newspaper articles.[93] Amongst the widespread press coverage, an article in the *Dundee Evening Telegraph*, entitled 'They were gun runners for the IRA', carried an interview with Lena and Cathy McDonald in which they recounted, with an air of couthy nostalgia, the methods by which they armed 'IRA rebels fighting the British forces in Ireland' down to the typically prosaic Dundee detail of 'customers' smuggling in bullets in fish and chip paper.[94] The sisters were in Dublin for the 50th anniversary celebrations, where they joined their Old Scottish Brigade comrades in laying a wreath at the memorial to the Overseas Units of the IRA at St Fintan's Cemetery in Howth, and receiving medals from the Lord Mayor of Dublin in recognition of 'their bravery, nobility and sacrifice during the independence struggle'.[95] The fact that, as the *Evening Telegraph* noted, the numerous 'men with prices on their heads' who had stayed in their home included current and former Presidents, Éamon de Valera and Seán T O'Kelly, that the sisters were given places of honour at official state ceremonies, and 'feted and praised by the leaders of the nation they helped to found', appeared to acknowledge that these methods had been, at least partially, successful.

Implicit in the story and the presentation of it, was a sense – possibly influenced by the apparent thawing in relations between the Southern, Northern and British governments, as denoted by the historic talks between Taoiseach Seán Lemass and Northern Ireland Prime Minister Terence O'Neill, and the repatriation of Roger Casement's remains – authorised by Prime Minister Harold Wilson after years of Tory denial – that the days of recourse to physical force were over. The fact that the staunch Tory Unionist firm of D C Thomson were prepared to publish an article that spoke of the IRA in such congenial terms also suggests that it was no longer considered a threat. That perspective would soon change.

In contrast with the blaze of publicity which attended the 50th anniversary celebrations of the Easter Rising in Dublin, the centenary of the birth of James Connolly, marked by the unveiling of a commemorative plaque in Edinburgh's Cowgate, on Saturday, 8 June 1968, was an altogether more low-key affair. Although widely reported in Ireland, where Connolly had been elevated to the status of national icon, the event received little coverage in the Scottish press – a consequence, perhaps, of the establishment's indifference to working-class politics, but more likely, to a deep uneasiness about the subject's involvement in revolutionary physical force Irish republicanism.[96] Connolly, it seems, was still dangerous.

The plaque, which was erected by Edinburgh Trades Council after a fifteen-year long battle with Edinburgh Town Council – and Heriot Watt College, which occupied the site of Connolly's birth, six yards from where the plaque was erected – who declined the invitation to attend. They did, however, deign to provide a platform for the guests. These included Connolly's daughters, Nora and Fiona, Dr Edward Brennan of the Irish Embassy in London, representatives from the Irish Congress of Trade Unions, the Scottish Trades Union Congress, the New Zealand Federation of Labour and the Irish Transport and General Workers Union, as well as the Secretary of the Connolly Association, Sean Redmond, and, as a nod to the local Irish community, the President of the Edinburgh United Ireland Association.[97] Clann na hÉireann and Dundee Trades Council were also represented, as were the trades councils of Aberdeen, Glasgow, Kirkcaldy, Perth and Belfast.

Despite initial plans to hold a commemoration in Dundee – in December 1967, Dundee Trades Council formed a committee to organise it – for some reason, whether it be hesitancy, incompetence, apathy or a combination of all three, the event failed to take place.[98] Nevertheless, the decision of Edinburgh Trades Council to honour James Connolly in the form of a bronze plaque, which likely originated in the Connolly Association's meetings in the city in the early 1950s, may have encouraged their counterparts in Dundee to acquire a bronze-painted bust of Connolly – the work of an apprentice welder in the Caledon Shipyard. Unlike the Edinburgh plaque, the Dundee bust remained intact, admired and 'unmolested' – despite the covetous intentions of local Irish republicans – in the relatively secure environment of the Trades Council Club in Rattray Street until the premises were vacated in 1997.

While the majority of the platform party were drawn from the trade union movement, the attendant crowd, which, according to various estimates, ranged from over 200 to around 500, was a more eclectic mix, comprising members of Connolly's family, 'veteran Scottish socialists', cultural figures, university lecturers, students, workers and curious passers-by. Whether any of the latter were also Irish republicans is unknown. In central Scotland of the 1960s, most working-class Irish sympathisers were wary of expressing their views publicly for fear of jeopardising their employment prospects or incurring anti-Irish prejudice. One confirmed Dundonian Connollyite who had no fear of doing this, however, was the independently minded radical communist and poet-musician, Mary Brooksbank – an 'old rebel', if not strictly an 'Irish' one.

The unveiling was performed by Edward Brennan – an up-and-coming diplomat who later became Ireland's first ambassador to the Soviet Union – who acknowledged that while 'Connolly had various claims to international recognition…in Ireland, his name would remain indissolubly linked with the Easter Rising of 1916…which marked the first stage of the final struggle for Ireland's independence'. Connolly had not baulked at revolutionary violence, or as Brennan termed it, in poetic Pearseian terms, 'blood sacrifice', but rather, like Pearse and the other leaders, had believed it 'would rekindle among the Irish people the flames of patriotism'. It was, Brennan concluded, 'a measure of his patriotism that he was prepared to lay down his life in that cause'.[99]

'The Soldier's Song' was sung, then 'The Red Flag', following which Mary Brooksbank stepped forward, and proceeded to sing an unnamed song, which Scottish folklorist Hamish Henderson described as 'her Connolly song', and Irish historian Owen Dudley Edwards, as 'one of Connolly's own'. Whatever its origins, many of those present would have appreciated the musical and political narrative Mary was creating by appending the anthems of Irish national liberation and international socialism, both of which had been written by Irishmen,[100] with a song of the Scots-born Irishman who reconciled the two, whether he was its author or subject.[101] The crowd 'took up' the refrain, and, as Henderson recalled, it 'made the occasion'.[102] For Mary, it was also a chance to make amends for her insensitive and ignorant comments regarding Connolly's execution 52 years earlier, for which she had been 'sensed up' by her grieving socialist father. It only remained for a member of the Irish Transport and General Workers' Union band to play 'The Last Post' as the Starry Plough was lowered and, slowly and symbolically, raised again. 'Everyone seemed profoundly moved', wrote Dudley Edwards, who supported Nora's view that 'it is Scotland's triumph today'. The republican Labour MP for West

Belfast, Gerry Fitt, was less impressed, confiding that he was 'not optimistic' that the event would bring 'the Scottish and British working class' any closer to supporting 'Connolly's ideal [and purportedly his] of a 32-county Socialist Republic'.[103]

The plaque was barely up four days when it vanished, having been prised from the wall in the early hours of Wednesday morning. The Secretary of Edinburgh Trades Council, John Henry, proclaimed it a 'stupid and senseless act', doubtless perpetrated by 'someone opposed to Connolly's views as a socialist and an Irish patriot'.[104] The finger of suspicion pointed to supporters of Edinburgh Protestant Action who earlier on Sunday had picketed a meeting of Edinburgh Trades Council in the belief that Gerry Fitt was addressing it on the subject of Connolly's contribution to trade unionism.[105] Fitt, however, had returned to Belfast to attend another commemoration at MacRory Park – a stone's throw from Connolly's former home at Glenalina Terrace where a plaque was unveiled by his son Roddy. The event, which attracted 5,000 to 10,000 people, was coordinated by the Wolfe Tone Society and featured key addresses by spokesman for the Republican Clubs, Liam McMillen (Billy McMillen), the commander of the Belfast IRA, and twenty-year-old community activist, Joe McCann, also a seasoned IRA Volunteer.[106] Under the innocuous title of Secretary of the National Democratic Party, McCann called for the establishment of a 'united [left-leaning] political force' without which they would 'continue to be discriminated against, walked over and treated as second-class citizens'. Connolly, he claimed, would not have tolerated such injustices but would 'regard the division as a disgrace to the name of Irishmen'. In conclusion, he urged them to follow Connolly's example and 'walk proud in the righteousness of our cause'.[107]

The phrase was a prophetic one. Within a few months, the civil rights marchers had walked into a scenario whereby their well-chosen tactics of peaceful protest and civil disobedience were met with the predictable state-supported sectarian violence, setting in motion a chain of events which gave rise to the most intense and protracted phase of the war against British rule in Ireland since the War of Independence. The summer of 1969 was a turning point. As marches and demonstrations gave way to increasingly violent confrontations, hundreds of Catholics/nationalists were forced to flee their homes as Loyalist mobs set fire to entire streets of

Catholic homes – the biggest internal movement of refugees in Ireland since the pogroms of 1921–2, and the biggest movement of refugees in Western Europe since the Second World War. As the besieged nationalist people strove to defend their communities, they turned to the IRA for the means to do so. The imperative was to procure arms – of any type and from every source.

Across the Irish Sea, the task was delegated to Gerry Doherty, who was appointed National Organiser for Clann na hÉireann in the spring of 1969. Doherty, who was arrested in a police sting later that November, recalled receiving detonators from Dan Skelton of Dundee which, despite the immediate need for defensive weaponry, were gratefully received.[108] It was Skelton's last known act for the republican cause – and a fitting end to a career as an Irish activist which began at the start of the War of Independence exactly 50 years earlier. He appears to have retired from the movement shortly afterwards (possibly following the split in January 1970). At any rate, there was little left to 'mobilise'. Skelton was amongst the last of a dying breed of ex-Tan and Civil War activists who had maintained the republican tradition in Dundee for almost half a century. Cathal Duthie had died in 1966, Devaney in 1964. Meanwhile, Lena and Cathy McDonald remained in the United States from where they continued to maintain links with a dwindling number of old friends across the Atlantic. They did return to Dundee on occasion, but more often it was Ireland that drew them back. In 1972, the sisters retired to St Petersburg, Florida, where Lena died in Bay Hospital on 20 May 1982, and Cathy died nine months later in February 1983. Dode Kimmet, who remained well-known in local Irish circles due to his role in the famous gunrunning incident, lived on until 1985. Unlike Skelton, however, he was no organiser. Skelton himself died in 1982, and it is perhaps a testament to his discretion that, by that time, few young Irish activists in the city had ever heard of him. It also serves to illustrate how disengaged the preceding generation had become from the Irish liberation struggle and how much of Dundee's long Irish republican tradition had been lost and forgotten.

Endnotes to Chapter 8

1. C Desmond Greaves, *Reminiscences of the Connolly Association: An Emerald Jubilee Pamphlet 1938–1978.*, Desmond Greaves Archive, http://www.desmondgreavesarchive.com/pamphlets/reminiscences-of-the-connolly-association/, accessed 19 May 2023.
2. Daniel Skelton, Dundee, in *The Catholic Standard*, 14 September 1951.
3. Around 28 prisoners remained incarcerated in Peterhead Prison, the last ten of whom were released in January 1926.
4. T M Devine, *The Scottish Nation* (Penguin: London, 1999), p498.
5. The Committee was appointed in 1922 in response to a request by the Presbytery of Glasgow and the Synod of Glasgow and Ayr to consider the impact of Irish immigration on 'the unity and homogeneity of the Scottish people'; and of the Education (Scotland) Act of 1918, which granted state funding to Catholic Schools.
6. *Dundee Courier*, 18 October 1923.
7. *Dundee Evening Telegraph*, 31 October, 1 November 1923.
8. *Dundee Courier*, 8 October 1924.
9. *Dundee Courier*, 22 February 1928.
10. 'Scotland for the Scots' also noted the efforts being made in the west of Scotland to repeal the 'egregious' Act, and stated that 'If this can be done, we in Dundee should give all the assistance we can'. *Dundee Courier,* 22 February 1928.
11. *Dundee Courier*, 5 March 1928.
12. *Dundee Courier*, 24 February 1928.
13. *Dundee Courier*, 15 September 1927.
14. *London Morning Post*, 15 August 1921. In an anonymous publication compiled from a series of articles from *Blackwood's Magazine* in 1920–1, James Connolly was described as 'the Prince of Irish Bolsheviks'. *Tales of the RIC* (Edinburgh and London: William Blackwood, 1921), p80.
15. *Dundee Courier*, 30 May 1923.
16. The Logie Estate, built in 1920–1, was designed by City Architect, James Thomson, on the garden city model, it became the benchmark for council housing in Scotland and is a considered a milestone in Scottish planning history.
17. See Chapter 7.
18. *Dundee Courier*, 4 August, 11 August 1926.
19. *Dundee Courier*, 7 October 1924.
20. *Dundee Courier*, 14 May 1928.

21 *Dundee Evening Telegraph*, 12 October 1923; 22 November 1928. The matter came to light after Sam Devine and another AOH executive member, Leon Farrell, attempted to pass off a dud cheque to Canon Lavelle who was subsequently informed by his bank. At the end of the trial, the £100 was still unaccounted for.

22 *Dundee Courier*, 19 June 1937

23 'The Great War', presented by the Territorial Army, covered four years (1914–17) and comprised several different scenes. The INF also presented the tableau for 1924, 'Wembley Arena'. *Dundee Courier*, 29 April 1935.

24 Information courtesy of the family of Peter Taylor.

25 Peadar O'Donnell, *There Will Be Another Day* [1963] (Dublin: Red Sky Books, 2017), p87.

26 Letter from Father Fahy to Bishop Dignan, September 1934, quoted in Madden, *Father John Fahy*, p39.

27 Peadar O'Donnell, *Salud! An Irishman in Spain* [1937] (Dublin: Friends of the International Brigade in Ireland, 2020).

28 Daniel Gray claims 520 of the British Battalion were from Scotland, over a fifth of whom were from Dundee. Daniel Gray, *Homage to Caledonia: Scotland and the Spanish Civil War* (Edinburgh: Luath Press, 2009), pp19, 132.

29 *Dundee Courier*, 15 May 1923.

30 Marriage record of Peter Craig and Mary Connor, 22 July 1901; Baptismal records of Allan Craig, 11 December 1904 and Charles Craig, 22 May 1908.

31 Birth record of William McDade, 30 June 1897; Marriage record of William McDade and Mary Ann Trail, 11 January 1897; Tom Wintringham, *English Captain*, [1939] (London: Faber and Faber, 2011), p60; IBA Archives, Box D-7 File A/2, RGASPI 545/6/9. www.international-brigades.org.uk/the-volunteers. Another Brigader, James Farrell, listed as living at 46 Constable Street, Dundee, claimed to have been, at various points, a member of Na Fianna Éireann, a cadet in the British Army, a lieutenant in the IRA during the Civil War, and a member of the Communist Party of Ireland until 1934 when he moved to London. However, the identification of Farrell as a Dundee Brigader appears to be the result of an error in a list of 109 British and Irish POWs being held by Franco's Nationalists at Cardena concentration camp at Burgos, which was received by the British government and subsequently released to the press. *Dundee Courier, Dundee Evening Telegraph, The Scotsman*, 1 Jul 1938; Mike Arnott, *Dundee and the Spanish Civil War* (Dundee Trades Council, 2008).

32 *Dundee Evening Telegraph*, 17 January 1939.

33 This short-lived organisation was formed by Wendy and her political and romantic partner, Amhlaibh MacAindreis.

34 *Edinburgh Evening News*, 15 February 1939.

35 *Aberdeen Press & Journal*, 16 February 1939.

36 The two were released a month later after having served three and half months of a nine-month prison sentence for theft of explosives. *Falkirk Herald*, 15 July 1939.

37 *Dundee Courier*, 8 June 1939.

38 *Dundee Courier*, 10 June 1939. Somerville was released on appeal on 6 July, when his conviction was quashed. The appeals of two of the Irish Republicans, Francis McNeece and Samuel Kennedy, were dismissed. *Aberdeen Press & Journal*, 7 July 1939.

39 J I Mitchell, solicitor for Samuel Kennedy, also accused Anderson of concocting the story in order to get remission. *Falkirk Herald*, 19 June 1939.

40 *Falkirk Herald*, 10 June 1939.

41 The broadsheet of the Republican movement after *An Phoblacht* was suppressed in 1937.

42 *The Scotsman*, 9 August 1939.

43 *Aberdeen Press & Journal*, 5 May 1939.

44 As some undoubtedly did, including Harry White of Belfast, who – after a bomb he was preparing exploded prematurely in his Manchester digs – fled north from to his aunt's house in Glasgow to lie low until it was deemed safe to return to Ireland Danny Morrison, *All the Dead Voices* (Cork: Mercier Press, 2002), p34.

45 *Dundee Evening Telegraph*, 31 July 1939.

46 The 1934 Military Service Pensions Act, brought in by the first Fianna Fáil government on 13 September 1934, extended the terms of the original 1924 Act to include members of Cumann na mBan and operatives who had taken the Anti-Treaty side during the Civil War. This included the majority of Scottish veterans whose applications were expedited through the offices of the Old IRA (Scottish Division) formed in Dublin in November 1934. For background, see Máirtín Ó Catháin, 'The Old IRA and the 1916 Pensions', in Coyle and Ó Catháin, *We Will Rise Again*.

47 Father Fahy also cited financial loss and continuing police harassment as the motivating factor in Lena and Helen McDonald's relocation. After a period of ill-health, during which the women were forced to rely on the hospitality of friends and outdoor relief payments to survive, Lena resumed her nursing career, working mainly in Ireland with a brief interlude in Birmingham, before emigrating to New York along with sister Cathy in the early 1950s. IMA, MSPC, MSP34REF56964.

48 The IRA operative, Joby O'Sullivan, later recalled conveying the ticking bomb (which was concealed in the basket of a bicycle) to its intended target, a police station, when the wheels of the bicycle got stuck in tram tracks of a busy street, causing him to panic and abandon it. Two IRA men, James McCormick and Peter Barnes, who had not planted the bomb, were subsequently convicted and hanged at Winson Green Prison, Birmingham on 7 February 1940. Jenny

Scott, 'Coventry IRA bombing: the 'forgotten attack on a British City', https://www.bbc.co.uk/news/uk-england-coventry-warwickshire-28191501, accessed 19 May 2023.

49   M L R Smith, *Fighting for Ireland? The Military Strategy of the Irish Republican Movement* (London: Routledge, 1995), p64.

50   *Irish Press*, 24 December 1945.

51   *Irish Press*, 23 July 1947.

52   The others were Matthew Boyle, who fought in the Four Courts under Rory O'Connor at the beginning of the Civil War, and James Clarke who served in Ireland at the same time. Letter from Cathal Duthie to Eamonn Mooney, March 1955, EMP/3/A/31.

53   Those living at Scottish addresses when the rolls were compiled, retrospectively, in 1936.

54   IMA, MSPC, RO/383, Membership rolls of the 2nd Northern Division, 1st (Tyrone) Brigade, 2nd (Dungannon) Battalion, 1919–23.

55   This is unlikely to have been the same person; however, Skelton appears to have done this when he moved to Dundee: for example, on the Dundee Electoral Registers, he appears as 'David' from 1936–39', then as 'Daniel' from 1945 onwards.

56   IMA, BMH, Charles McGleenan, WS 829, pp29–30.

57   *The Socialist*, 13 March 1919.

58   *Irish Press*, 16 March 1949.

59   Duffy was elected councillor for the First Ward in 1945 but lost his seat to the centre-right 'Moderates' two years later.

60   *Irish Press*, 18 October 1949.

61   *Irish Press*, 18 October 1949. *Irish Press*, 18 October 1949 *Irish Press*, 18 October 1949.

62   John 'Jack' Beattie was a unique quantity in Six-County politics. Initially a member of the ILP and an active Home Ruler, he was the one member of the Unionist Northern Irish Labour Party in the Six-County Parliament to voice his support for Irish unity. In 1945, he left the NILP and formed the Federation of Labour under which name he was elected MP for West Belfast. Beattie was also the only member of the Stormont Parliament to simultaneously hold a seat in the Westminster Parliament which he retained until 1951. James Quinn, 'Beattie, John 'Jack'', *Dictionary of Irish Biography*, https://www.dib.ie/biography/beattie-john-jack-a0517, accessed 19 May 2023.

63   *Ulster Herald*, 1 October 1949.

64   O'Connor maintained his seat in the Northern Ireland Parliament until it was dissolved in 1972. In 1969, he gave evidence to the British government's (Cameron) Enquiry into the Causes of Disturbance in Northern Ireland (prompted by the Civil Rights marches of October 1968 and January 1969).

Examples of the many abnegations of civil rights such as those cited at the Dundee meeting likely formed the basis of his evidence.

65 The relevant part of the Act 'declare[d] that Northern Ireland remains part of His Majesty's dominion and of the United Kingdom' and' affirm[ed] that in no event will Northern Ireland or any part thereof cease to be part of His majesty's dominions and of the United Kingdom without the consent of the Parliament of Northern Ireland'.

66 *Ulster Herald*, 1 October 1949.

67 *Northern Whig*, 31 October 1949. In February 1948, the Paisley branch of the APL asked Irish voters to abstain from voting in the Paisley by-election due to the 'unsatisfactory' replies of the two candidates, Douglas Johnstone, (Labour) and John MacCormick (Scottish Nationalist) on the question of partition. *Irish Press*, 18 February 1948.

68 Jacob Murphy, 'A Four Nations Approach to the Irish Anti-Partition Campaigns of the 1940s and 1950s', https://fournationshistory.wordpress.com/2015/12/28/a-four-nations-approach-to-the-irish-anti-partition-campaigns-of-the-1940s-and-1950s/, accessed 19 May 2023.

69 In 1960, the Annual Report of the Anti-Partition League accused the Connolly Association of being 'utterly dishonest' in using Irish nationalism 'as a cloak to enlist young Irishmen to further the cause of international Communism.' *Western People*, 19 November 1960.

70 Greaves, 'Reminiscences of the Connolly Association'

71 Greaves, 'Reminiscences of the Connolly Association'.

72 *Ulster Herald*, 19 June 1954; *Irish Press*, 22 June 1954.

73 *Irish Press*, 8 December 1954.

74 *Irish Press*, 7 March 1955.

75 *Irish Press*, 18 March 1955.

76 *United Irishman*, Feabhra–Deireidh Fómhair 1955.

77 IMA, MSPC, military service medal application of James Kimmet, MD25955.

78 Information on Charles Duthie obtained, from Statuary Birth, Marriage and Death records, Scottish census of 1891, 1901, 1911; *Dundee Evening Telegraph*, 11 April 1950; *Dundee Courier*, 7 August, 13 October 1951; *Dundee Courier*, 5 May 1952; *Dundee Courier*, 30 April 1954.

79 IMA, MSPC, RO16.

80 In April 1953, Lena travelled from New York to Dublin to organise an honorary dinner for Father Fahy on behalf of the Scottish Brigade veterans: in turn, she was the recipient of one herself. *Irish Press*, 10 April 1953.

81 *United Irishman*, Samhain 1955.

82 J Bowyer Bell, *The Secret Army* (London: Sphere, 1972), p335.

Chapter 8 – A Partitioned Politics 1923–69

83 'Sean South of Garryowen' and 'The Patriot Game' (the latter written by Glasgow-domiciled Dominic Behan (the nephew of the composer of 'The Soldier's Song', Peadar Kearney)), the respective subjects of which, Seán South and Fergal O'Hanlon, were fatally wounded in a botched raid on Brookeborough RUC Barracks in County Fermanagh on New Year's Eve in 1956–7. The deaths of the two men aroused a huge wave of public sympathy – South's funeral cortege was attended by around 50,000 people across the length and breadth of Ireland. *Evening Herald*, 9 February 1957.

84 The consignment was discovered by the RUC, however, and GHQ officer Sean Garland, was arrested when he went to collect them at Victoria Station, Belfast. Brian Hanley and Scott Millar, *The Lost Revolution: The Story of the Official IRA and the Workers' Party* (London: Penguin, 2009), p18.

85 *Evening Echo*, 24 October 1959.

86 *Irish Press*, 7 March 1959.

87 IRA volunteer, Mick Ryan, recalls half-heartedly participating in one 'propaganda' exercise which involved postering large swathes of County Antrim with copies of a 'manifesto' commemorating the first anniversary of the 'Campaign of Resistance' and setting out its objectives. Michael Ryan, *My Life in the IRA: The Border Campaign* (Cork: Mercier Press, 2018), p144.

88 Radio Rebelde was set up by the Cuban revolutionary army's media wing, under the command of Che Guevara, in the Sierra Maestra in February 1958, to broadcast the aims of the revolutionary movement and report on the progress of the campaign. https://www.radiorebelde.cu/english/about-us/, accessed 19 May 2023.

89 Whether Sean South was, as has been widely claimed, politically and socially conservative, is open to debate. He was certainly motivated by a deep religious faith. However, the majority of young IRA volunteers appear to have been, much like Mick Ryan, 'abysmally ignorant' of politics. Ryan, *My Life in the IRA*, p52.

90 Hanley and Millar. *Lost Revolution*, p17.

91 'In every generation the Irish people have asserted their right to national freedom and sovereignty; six times in the past three hundred years they have asserted it in arms.'

92 Hanley and Millar, *Lost Revolution*, p49; 'Persis Renehan Remembered', oration by Stephen Coyle, 26 January 2019, reproduced in *The Irish Voice*, February 2019.

93 Hanley and Miller, pp51, 55.

94 *Dundee Evening Telegraph*, 25 April 1966. Chips are reputed to have been first sold in Scotland in Dundee's Greenmarket by Belgian immigrant, Edward de Gernier, in the 1870s.

95 *Irish Press*, 15 April 1966.

96 The anniversary also occurred in the aftermath of the assassination of US Senator Robert F Kennedy on 4 June 1966.

97 *Belfast Telegraph*, 10 June 1968; *Irish Examiner*, 10 June 1968; *Irish Democrat*, 15 June 1968. All newspaper reports, with the exception of Owen Dudley Edwards writing for the *Irish Times*, failed to credit Nora and Fiona with their respective professional titles of Senator and Doctor. The *Belfast Telegraph* also described Fiona as 'the wife of a London businessman'.

98 Journal of C Desmond Greaves, Volume 1967–68, 8 December 1967, Desmond Greaves Archive, http://www.desmond greavesarchive/journal-vol-191967-68/, accessed 19 May 2023.

99 *Irish Examiner*, 10 June 1968.

100 'The Soldier's Song' was written by Peadar Kearney in 1907, and 'The Red Flag' by socialist, Land Leaguer and one-time Fenian, Jim Connell, in 1889.

101 Much of Connolly's poetic output remained obscure until the publication of *The James Connolly Songbook* by the Cork Workers' Club in 1972 brought them into wider circulation. However, knowledge of his songs had long been transmitted orally. Moreover, while no 'Connolly song' appears in Mary's published anthology, *Sidlaw Breezes* (1952), much of her work never made it into print.

102 Timothy Neat, *Hamish Henderson: A Biography Volume 2: Poetry Becomes People (1952–2002)* (Edinburgh: Polygon, 2009), p217.

103 *Irish Times*, 10 June 1968. Ironically, as a growing number of the Scottish working class grew to support that ideal, Fitt became increasingly hostile to those who actively pursued it (i.e., the Republican movement), and to those who supported them. This provoked the taunt 'Gerry Fitt is a Brit', which was vindicated when he accepted a British peerage in October 1983.

104 *Irish Examiner*, 14 June 1968.

105 *Belfast Telegraph*, 10 June 1968.

106 Liam (Billy) McMillen joined the IRA in 1944 and was a veteran of the Border Campaign. After August 1969, he was blamed for failing to procure sufficient weapons to defend nationalist areas from loyalist attacks; a key factor in the Official-Provisional split of December 1969/January 1970. McMillen took the side of the Officials. He was killed in the Official IRA (OIRA)/Irish National Liberation Army (INLA) feud on 28 April 1975.

107 *Belfast Telegraph*, 10 June 1968; *Irish Examiner*, 10 June 1968. Joe McCann who joined the IRA in 1963 at the age of sixteen, proved to be one of its most prodigious and legendary guerrilla fighters. In the 1969/70 split, he sided with the Officials. Unlike the OIRA leadership, however, McCann was a staunch advocate of revolutionary violence and remained committed to physical force which took priority over his political activism. The most militant member of the OIRA by far, McCann's role in the defence of the Markets Area during the British Army internment incursions of August 1971 also won him the respect of the Provos, as well as giving rise to one of the most iconic photos of the conflict. McCann was shot dead by a member of the British Parachute Regiment on 15 April 1972, which killing was ruled 'unlawful' in 2020. McCann's legacy

remains a controversial one. Although claimed by the Officials as 'one of theirs', his commitment to physical force and his political trajectory up until his death, which preceded the OIRA ceasefire in May 1972 and the OIRA/INLA split in December 1974, suggests that he may have gone over to the Provisionals following the former, or to the INLA following the latter.

108 I am indebted to Stephen Coyle for this information. Doherty and his collaborator, Eamon Smullen, were sentenced to five and eight years respectively for attempting to buy rifles from an arms dealer in Huddersfield. Hanley and Millar, *Lost Revolution*, p141.

CHAPTER 9

A Legacy Reclaimed
1970–85

And if we stay silent we're guilty
While these men lie naked and cold
In H Block tonight remember the plight
Of those on the blanket.[1]

Nail your colours to the top of the flagpole,
slog on and fuck the consequences.[2]

WHEN it came to re-engaging with the war in Ireland, Dundee was relatively slow off the mark. While the split in the Republican movement spurred former Clann na hÉireann activists in Glasgow to set up the Provisional-supporting Pearse Sinn Féin cumann, which raised money for the dependants of the hundreds of Northern nationalists interned in August 1971 – and more discreetly for the IRA[3] – there was no parallel development in Dundee. It was not until the second half of the decade that a new generation of Irish republican activists began to emerge, the majority of whom were in their teens and early twenties with no prior involvement in Irish republicanism, and – with a few notable exceptions – little real knowledge of Irish history. Most found their way in through different intersecting and often conflicting traditions that can be broadly categorised as Irish cultural organisations and radical left-wing politics. Notwithstanding, the distinction between these two 'traditions' should not disguise the fact that, as in the past, many people who came to Irish republicanism via the socialist route were also part of the Irish diaspora who, more often than not, had a higher appreciation of radical republican ideas – the Edinburgh-born James Connolly being the definitive example.

Before examining the emergence of the modern Irish solidarity campaign in Dundee, it is necessary to look at the political and military situation in Ireland at the time. By the mid-1970s, the nature of the war had changed. The height of armed resistance of 1970–2, when bombings and shootings occurred on an almost daily basis, was over. In 1972 and 1974, the IRA had negotiated truces, which the British had been incapable of honouring, and which the latter had used to re-organise the RUC and Ulster Defence Regiment (UDR), retrain them in the use of sophisticated intelligence-gathering equipment, and improve their arsenal of weapons. The Provisional IRA had also used both truces to their advantage. Their volunteers were now better trained politically as well as militarily. Their arsenal had also been increased by RPG rocket launchers and M16 machine guns. As part of their re-organisation, the Provisionals had developed a dual strategy of military attacks on crown forces and bombing economic targets to cripple the Six County economy.

As the IRA waged a guerrilla war of attrition to weaken the will of the British State to remain in Ireland, there was another war of a different character going on. This was essentially a propaganda war centred around captured Republican prisoners. In 1972, Republicans in Long Kesh prison organised a campaign to be recognised as political prisoners, emphasising the political nature of their 'crime' and the basis for their being incarcerated in the first place. The resulting concession of 'Special Category Status' was 'Prisoner of War' status in everything but name, and was regarded as a significant step towards legitimising the national liberation struggle in Ireland. Indeed, the terms of Special Category Status conceded by the British government that year – the right to wear their own clothes; the right to be excused from prison work; the right to free association with other prisoners; the right to organise their own educational and recreational facilities; and the right to one visit, one letter and one parcel per week – had been afforded to prisoners of war since the Second World War.

On 1 March 1976, Special Category Status was withdrawn, and it is from this point that the struggle to win it back – which began in September, when newly sentenced prisoner, Kieran Nugent, refused to wear the prison uniform, and reached its height during the hunger strikes of 1980-1 – can be traced. The attempt to criminalise the armed struggle, which formed the basis of British strategy in Ireland in the late 1970s, was generally known as 'Ulsterisation' (also as 'Normalisation' or 'Criminalisation'). It was maintained that what was happening in the occupied Six Counties in the north of Ireland was not a political struggle against the British State but a regional crime wave. At the same time as Political Status was withdrawn, trial by jury was abolished and replaced by a single judge sitting in a private 'Diplock' court, so-named after the judge who conceived it. This was justified by the argument that widespread intimidation had made jury courts unworkable. The suggestion that it would equally prevent juries being packed with Loyalists – a valid criticism of local government bodies in the Six County state since its inception – fooled no-one: the object was to put Irish Republicans in jail.[4]

The prime military objective of Ulsterisation was to scale down the participation of the regular British Army to such a degree that its presence would be negligible. The responsibility for maintaining 'law and order' would be increasingly shifted to the locally-recruited UDR and Royal Ulster Constabulary (RUC). This attempt by the British to portray a legitimate national liberation struggle as a provincial crime wave was nothing new. The American government had deployed the same strategy in Vietnam with similar disastrous results. Long before that, the strategy of criminalisation had formed an essential part of British policy in its imperial governance of Ireland. In his account of the Tan War, Irish revolutionary leader, Ernie O'Malley, illustrates how, when even a militarised police force proved inadequate to the task, mercenary forces such as the Black and Tans and the Auxiliaries were brought in in order to allow Britain to demonstrate to the world that what was happening in Ireland was a policing operation and not a war.[5] The language of criminalisation was also deployed by the progenitor of the Black and Tans and master-manipulator of imperial management, Winston Churchill, in his reference to the IRA as 'the murder gang'.

By 1978, the struggle to have prisoner of war status restored was two years old. The prisoners were confined to their cells for 24 hours a day. Since they refused to wear a prison uniform, they remained naked except for a blanket. As attacks on prisoners on 'accompanied' visits to the showers and latrines grew increasingly brutal, in April 1978, the prisoners made the decision to remain in their cells where they were reluctantly forced to smear their own excrement on the walls. Thus, the blanket protest escalated to a 'no wash' protest, also described disparagingly by the British media as the 'dirty' protest. Meanwhile, the campaign was spreading to the wider community. Soon the international media was carrying interviews with

Sinn Féin representatives and prisoners' relatives explaining the background to the H-Block protest. At the same time, demonstrations organised by Sinn Féin and the Relatives' Action Committee were getting some coverage on British television. Regardless of how brief and slanted this was, it went some way to increasing peoples' awareness of the war in Ireland, and Britain's involvement in it.

This was all the more remarkable given the climate of censorship at the time. In the early 1970s, an alliance of Conservative MPs, former army officers and right-wing journalists was formed, which, in keeping with their beliefs, maintained that the majority of current affairs television programmes on the Irish 'troubles' served to legitimise the IRA and undermine the British State. A pattern thereby developed where these 'concerned individuals', most of whom were influential members of the British establishment, would place pressure on the government and the broadcasting authority to demand that all programmes relating to the Irish 'troubles' be vetted, whereupon programmes would be cut, censored or cancelled, and the journalists and technicians who had worked on them would demand their names be taken off the credits. Two important things emerged from this. First, as political journalist Peter Taylor noted, 'the banning of a programme not only drew attention to its content, but also threw into sharp relief the restrictions on reporting in Northern Ireland'.[6] Second, it revealed that not all sections of the British establishment (as represented by the Fourth Estate), were behind the war in Ireland: more specifically, it showed that there were a number of journalists who were prepared to challenge the British narrative of it. This gave rise to alternative information groups such as the London-based Information on Ireland Campaign, which produced pamphlets examining various aspects of Britain's intervention in Ireland (for example, on the use of plastic bullets, the history of the war in Ireland and the origins of the blanket protest), and the Campaign for Free Speech in Ireland, which documented instances of censorship on the reporting of it. In turn, this provided key source material for a developing network of Irish solidarity groups organising under the banner of the United Troops Out Movement (UTOM).

*

The Emergence of the Dundee Irish Solidarity Campaign

By the spring of 1978, there was a sense that events in Ireland were moving to a crisis. The escalating prison protest, and the reporting of it, had produced a greater awareness and understanding of the situation, which in turn had led some people, not only to sympathise with the prisoners on a humanitarian level, but also to support the political goals for which they had been fighting and which had led to their imprisonment. In addition, the mass campaign in Ireland, spearheaded by Sinn Féin and the Relatives Action Committee, to agitate for the prisoners' demands, provided the inspiration and incentive to a more active form of solidarity. By the end of 1977, there was already an *ad hoc* Irish solidarity group in existence in Dundee, comprising a handful of radical socialists and socialist republicans, most of whom had found their way into Irish political activism through membership of left-wing organisations.

Michael Taylor was a case in point. Like many Dundonians, he was of Irish extraction, although it is fair to say that, up until this point, like most Dundonians of his generation, he had little sense of it. For him, the route into Irish political activism came about during what was intended to be a 'gap year' between school and university, which, for a working-class youth from Fintry housing scheme, was a porter's job at Liff Hospital, where he was introduced, through nurses Linda Green and Una Turner, to the International Socialists (IS). Another Irish solidarity activist who joined the IS around this time described his reasons for doing so:

> The Labour Party came across to me like a family business – people joined because their parents were already committed to its ideas. At that time, if you were interested in politics at a grassroots agitational campaigning level you gravitated towards one of the student radical groups of the late 1960s [which had been] reconstituted as political parties.[7]

For all their flaws, the Trotskyist groups encouraged their members to explore a wide range of literature and ideas, often through the medium of left-wing book shops. As the most prominent radical left group organising in Dundee at the time, the IS, which had its local office/book shop at 3 Roseangle, was the obvious choice.

It was at one of IS's local hangouts, Willie Frew's bar in the West Port, that Taylor fell in with fellow-radicals, Frank Malone, a working-class labourer from Lochee, and through him, his brother, John – both of whom were 'recruited' – and Stuart Johnson, a young London-born student of English literature at Dundee University who was not. Like Michael Taylor, the Malone brothers were also of Irish extraction. Unlike Taylor, however, they had an acute sense of their Irish identity, which they attributed, partly, to their Irish-Catholic upbringing in Lochee. More importantly, they had a keen appreciation of the Irish Republican struggle which they had inherited from their father, John Malone senior, a hard-mouthed, hard-drinking millworker with a natural affinity with the Irish rebel tradition.[8] However, they were also sensitive to the fact that theirs was not the typical Dundee experience, that while Irish culture was a thriving part of many working-class communities that had attracted immigrants, 'in Dundee it [mostly] expressed itself in supporting Celtic'.[9]

The meeting in Willie Frew's, which proved to be a seminal one, came at a significant point in terms of international anti-imperialist struggle. The year 1976 saw the emergence of a mass popular resistance movement in Palestine (which defied the Israeli government's attempts to expropriate Palestinian land by staging a national 'Land Day' protest on 30 March), and the Soweto uprising (sparked by the South African government's imposition of the Afrikaans language in native African schools). Closer to home, September saw the beginning of the blanket protest in response to the British government's withdrawal of Special Category Status for Irish political prisoners on 1 March. Michael Taylor recalled. 'Some of us were beginning to question the IS's (or the Socialist Workers' Party's, as it became that year) focus on the economic concerns of a white, male British workforce – i.e., wages and working conditions, which differed little from the Labour and Communist Party's preoccupation with British trade unionism – and the lack of time devoted to anti-imperialist struggles in South Africa, Central America, Palestine and, especially, Ireland.[10] John Malone recalled, 'It seemed incredible that after eight years of renewed direct British involvement in Irish affairs there was nothing resembling a substantial solidarity movement on Ireland'.

Michael Taylor recalled that they asked for 'educationals' and were unceremoniously rebuffed. Realising that there was a 'theoretical gap' that the local leadership were unwilling or incapable of filling, they set about doing it themselves through a process of self-directed learning. For Malone:

> It was at this time that I developed an interest in the writings of Marx, Engels and Lenin on Ireland. The Marxist writings that fired my enthusiasm were those on imperialism, colonialism and the rights of nations to self-determination. They were always dismissed by the left as dated and irrelevant to contemporary political struggle. Central to the works of Marx and Engels is that they both observed the failure of the working class in Britain to support the Irish liberation struggle. Aside from the basic issue of class solidarity, it was in their own interests, for in collaborating with the national bourgeoisie in the suppression of the Irish liberation struggle they weakened their ability to defend themselves against attack. For me the issue of class solidarity with national liberation struggles was best summed up by Lenin in *The Rights of Nations to Self-Determination* [where he] repudiated the view that workers in oppressor (imperialist) nations should not support the national liberation struggles of oppressed nations (colonies), and reminded socialists of their duty towards the [latter]:
> 'The policy of Marx and Engels on the Irish Question serves as a splendid example of the attitude the proletariat should adopt towards national movements, an example which has lost none of its immense practical importance. It serves as a warning of that servile haste with which the Philistines of all countries, colours and languages hurry to label as Utopian the idea of altering the frontiers of states that were established by the violence and privileges of the landlords and bourgeoisie of one nation. If the Irish and English proletariat had not accepted Marx's policy and had not made the secession of Ireland their slogan, this would have been the worst sort of opportunism, a neglect of their duties as democrats and socialists and a concession to English reaction and the English bourgeoisie.' This, if anything, was to become the foundation of my personal philosophy.[11]

Chapter 9 – A Legacy Reclaimed 1970–85

Through the resources of John Malone senior, the small group of 'dissidents' also gained access to literature not obtained through the British left: Tim Pat Coogan's *The IRA* and J Bowyer Bell's *The Secret Army* – the first detailed histories of the IRA, both published in 1970; and classic works from the Irish revolutionary canon such as *Army Without Banners* (the American edition of Ernie O'Malley's *On an Another Man's Wound*, published in 1967), and Tom Barry's *Guerrilla Days in Ireland*. These well-thumbed paperbacks were passed around the group. Michael Taylor recalled, 'I was learning more about Ireland from an unskilled factory worker than I had ever learned from the British left'. Or indeed, it would seem, from any other source at that time. In the summer of 1978, the group sent off to Ireland for *An Phoblacht/Republican News*, which they read and sold, along with *Troops Out*, the monthly bulletin of the UTOM, which was obtained, initially, from Beano's, a wholefood store-cum-alternative-newspaper outlet on the Perth Road. Thus, they educated themselves and others, and from an Irish Republican perspective, which was deemed of major importance. Around this time, Taylor was approached by his great-uncle Peter, who mentioned his involvement in Dundee Sinn Féin in the early 1920s and invited him to peruse his extensive collection of Irish Republican literature. Meanwhile, the group persisted in its attempts to draw the SWP and the organised left into forming an Irish solidarity campaign, although, as John Malone recalled, it was evident that 'they didn't treat Ireland with the same priority as we did'. Ultimately, it was this indifferent attitude which spurred the group into action.

In the summer of 1978, Dundee hosted its first major civic festival since the opening of the Tay Road Bridge in 1966. A joint initiative of the Chamber of Commerce and the City Council, its main aim was to attract tourists and business investment, and to encourage the local population to play a greater part in the city's cultural, social and economic life. As such, it featured a week-long programme of activities and events beginning with a parade through the city centre on Saturday, 14 July. However, as John Malone recalled:

> It attracted our attention for different reasons. A company of Scottish soldiers in full military dress complete with rifles and fixed bayonets was to lead off the parade. This was a golden

opportunity – historically, the Scottish regiments have a reputation for brutality in Ireland. We were armed with placards highlighting the H Block issue, and leaflets which gave a background to the Irish struggle and history of the terrorist activities of Scottish regiments. The procession started, we waved placards, shouted about H Block etc. [Meanwhile] Mike Taylor and another were in the car park of a local shopping centre overlooking the festival. As the parade passed, they scattered leaflets over the crowd and addressed them through a megaphone.[12]

Besides a token scuffle with the police which lasted no more than a few minutes, the protestors encountered no opposition – the largely apolitical Dundee crowd, it appears, viewed them as harmless eccentrics who were well-meaning but misguided. Nevertheless, the fact that 'no one got lifted and we made our point' marked it down as a modest success. Thus encouraged, the group decided to form a branch of UTOM in Dundee, the logic being that the local press was more inclined to listen to a named organisation than a group of individuals – that said, it was understood that D C Thomson's were not the best friends of the Irish people, never mind the Republican movement. Moreover, if there were other people outside the group who identified with the Irish struggle, there would be an identifiable organisation into which they could pour their energies.

The next priority was to inform all like-minded groups and invite their participation. This included the SWP who, Malone detailed, 'informed us that they were already in the process of forming a branch' and 'as soon as the details were finalised, they would let us know'. After several weeks of prompting with no response, the *ad hoc* group took the initiative and called a public meeting on January 1979. Around fifty people turned up, most of whom, including a contingent from the AOH in Lochee, were unconnected with the British left. Michael Taylor opened the proceedings by stating that after ten years of British troops on the streets of Ireland it seemed strange that they had to hold the meeting in the first place. Mindful of the composition of his audience, he also emphasised Lochee's much-vaunted reputation as a hub of Irish tradition. The main speaker was the Chair of Clydeside UTOM and the organisation's main representative in Scotland, Martin O'Leary, who was – as were many UTOM organisers at the time – a member of the International Marxist Group (IMG). O'Leary, who had been involved in the original Troops Out Movement (TOM) in England in the early to mid-1970s, spoke of the circumstances which necessitated the UTOM's formation and its history from that point onward.

With a large and enthusiastic audience, the organisers were confident of some moderate success. There was, however, one incident which, momentarily, deflated their spirits – an interjection from a member of the SWP who stated that while his organisation supported the right of self-determination for the Irish people and gave 'unconditional but critical support' to the IRA, no group, however brave or determined, was a substitute for a mass movement rooted firmly in the working class. Moreover, he claimed, whenever the IRA 'killed civilians', it increased the difficulties of taking the argument of Irish self-determination into the British labour movement, and if the UTOM's demands were not taken into the labour movement, then the meeting, and anything that came out of it, would be meaningless.

As many of those present saw it, the SWP's interjection exposed all the prejudices of the British left, not least their inherent colonialism, which regarded IRA volunteers, not as guerrilla fighters rooted in the wider working-class community from which they drew sustenance and support, but as an isolated group of bombers and gunmen detached from it; and their contempt for anyone else who did not share their view of what constituted a revolutionary party or movement. Malone recalled that these words were all the more galling as the SWP had sponsored the meeting and given a commitment to support the activities of any branch that emerged from it.[13] That they had agreed to do this after having variously rejected, opposed and ignored the efforts of non-affiliated Irish solidarity activists to organise in the city suggests a cynical attempt to dictate the agenda of the incipient Dundee UTOM branch with a view gaining control of the national organisation – an organisation which was currently dominated by their political rivals, the IMG, whose representative was sitting on the platform. To the Dundee organisers, however, it simply demonstrated the gulf that existed between them, as pro-Republican solidarity activists, and the British left. By this stage, however, it was not considered to be a problem as the former were in the majority, their ranks having been swollen by the young Republican-minded affiliates of the AOH.

The Ancient Order of Hibernians

Besides the radical left, the other conduit to Irish solidarity activism was that of Irish ethno-cultural organisations, the main one of which in late 1970s Dundee was the Ancient Order of Hibernians. After the trials and tribulations of the late 1920s, the AOH in Dundee had limped on until the eve of the Second World War when it effectively ceased operating. By the late 1960s, however, the AOH in Scotland had undergone a revival, and as the early years of 'the Troubles' saw the AOH in the North of Ireland scale down and eventually suspend its marches, the AOH in Scotland took up the mantle.[14] Thus, in 1974, the newly formed Dundee and Lochee AOH divisions came to host the largest Irish march in the city for over fifty years. With the exception of its location, Dundee was an ideal choice for many reasons: it was one of the few areas in Scotland where the 'Troubles' had not penetrated; a large percentage of its population were of Irish-Catholic extraction; it had a strong tradition of working-class unity; Irish organisations were not the focus of prejudice or controversy; there was no threat of Loyalist opposition – for the most part, the Orange Order maintained a low profile and a 'respectable' image which discouraged the 'Billy Boy' tendency; and there had been no recent history of 'sectarian' violence. Indeed, probably the most commonly recounted experience of 'sectarian' confrontation in the middle years of the twentieth century involves the game of 'Scotch or Irish' played out by gangs of schoolchildren, usually on St Patrick's Day, in which the 'wrong' answer to the eponymous question would be met with a token shove or the pulling of a green or blue-ribboned pigtail. Significantly, the question 'Protestant or Catholic' was rarely asked, and many Scots-Protestant Dundonians also recall buying sprigs of shamrocks from their Irish-Catholic friends and neighbours.[15]

The march, which took place on the afternoon of Saturday, 29 June (the Feast of Saints Peter and Paul), attracted an estimated 4,000 people, including officers of the Board of Erin (the AOH's governing body), fourteen AOH divisions from the North of Ireland and West of Scotland, and eight bands, including the recently-formed John F Kennedy Flute Band from Perth. Once assembled at Camperdown Park, it proceeded, Irish tricolour at the head, across the Kingsway[16] – which was closed off to traffic – down Coupar Angus Road, through Lochee High Street, Logie Street and Lochee Road to a rally in Dudhope Park, where the young

James Connolly had attended his first major political demonstration – a Free Speech/Anti-Coercion rally organised by the Dundee socialists in collaboration with Irish nationalists – 85 years before. There was no evidence of political collaboration on this occasion however, most socialist organisations in Dundee were conspicuously quiet on Ireland, and, besides a nod to the principle of Irish unity, which the speakers maintained should be pursued through 'peaceful and constitutional means', the AOH made no reference to the armed struggle or to those prosecuting it. While the march passed without incident or opposition, however – and rather appears to have gathered even more supporters en route – it was played down in the local press, whose estimate of 1,500 participants was at odds with the AOH's own figures and the recollections of those present.[17]

The march gave a kick start to the AOH in Dundee and Lochee, which, from its newly acquired premises in Kirk Street, Lochee – the site of the old Lochee Bog Mission – set about drawing in a new generation of members and supporters. Central to the operation was Derek McGlone, who, as well as being President and co-founder of the AOH's most recent incarnation, was also a member (later Grand Knight) of the Knights of St Columba and an avid supporter of Glasgow Celtic. The founding of the Padraig Pearse Celtic Supporters' Club – an unconscious echo of the Dundee Anti-Partition League's Brothers' Pearse branch – followed, of which McGlone, the director of a Lochee-based taxi firm, took on the position of Treasurer.[18] Through McGlone's contacts in the local transport business, the AOH organised buses to Celtic games; and it was here, and at other social events, that many young supporters became acquainted with the Irish rebel tradition, often though the narrative of songs such as 'The Rising of the Moon (the 1798 Rebellion); 'The Foggy Dew' (the Easter Rising); 'The Boys of Kilmichael' (the Tan War); 'Take it Down From the Mast Irish Traitors (the Civil War); 'Sean South of Garryowen (the Border Campaign), and 'Say Hello to the Provos' (the formation of the Provisional IRA and ongoing military campaign).

At this point, most of them were oblivious to the AOH's dubious history: to the 'Ancient Order of Hooligans' epithet coined by James Connolly after a mob of shillelagh-wielding Hibernians attacked a socialist meeting in Cobh in 1911.[19] For the moment, they were too caught up in the process of reconnecting with their Irish heritage, and to a republican tradition which many Irish-Dundonians of their parents' generation had suppressed or sidelined. The process was an emotional and collective one, and not subject to rigorous criticism or deep intellectual analysis.

In Glasgow, however, some radically minded 'Hibees' were beginning to buck against the conservative Catholic nationalism of the AOH. In 1975–6, the enduring problem of bad organisation and financial mismanagement coupled with the failure of the AOH to support the armed struggle, led a number of like-minded individuals to form the James Connolly Republican Flute Band (RFB) which adopted a conspicuous and unequivocal pro-Republican stance. The AOH responded by refusing the band permission to march on its parades, whereupon the band nurtured links with Republicans in the North of Ireland. Invitations to attend the annual Easter and Anti-Internment marches in Derry and Belfast followed, setting the precedent for solidarity visits to other Republican marches and commemorations by other Scottish bands in the years to come.[20]

In Dundee the dynamic was different. Whereas in the west of Scotland, the conservative Catholic element was firmly rooted – in some districts, the AOH had been operating since the late 1950s – in the new Dundee and Lochee, the younger pro-Republican element were involved from the early stages. They were also in the majority, a fact that gave them greater scope to initiate and organise activities. McGlone, however, remained President and, as such, towed the Board of Erin line on Irish unity (which was also that of the Irish government), or at least paid lip service to it.[21] Notwithstanding, Dundee's isolation from the other Scottish divisions and its smaller size and population, meant that in order to maintain its existence, the AOH had to embrace a wide range of opinion. For the local leadership, such as it was represented by McGlone, this meant accommodating the growing number of young Hibernians who professed support for Irish republicanism and the IRA. Here, Dundee's distance from the west-central hub – a disadvantage in some other respects – gave them the confidence to diverge from the official line in the knowledge that it was likely to be overlooked or ignored. From the perspective of the younger Republican-minded Hibees, the AOH was still the main organisation through which they gained access to the Irish cultural world, to the circuit of parades with their marching bands, patriotic music, flags and banners, and to the sociability and camaraderie of the Celtic Supporters' bus.

Meanwhile, the escalation of the prison protest had rekindled the historic political differences in the global Hibernian movement. At its annual conference in Killarney in late June, the American AOH passed resolutions calling for a general amnesty for all Irish political prisoners, and an independent enquiry into the Amnesty Report on prison brutality, and supporting the 'ideals of Irish Republicanism'. Its President, John Deane, also criticised the Irish government for failing to take a sufficiently hard line with its British counterparts, and to advocate that it 'compel Britain to make a declaration of intent to withdraw [from the North] within ten to twenty years'. While it favoured a 'peaceful and legal' route to 'total and absolute independence', however, the conference also blocked a resolution endorsed by Irish America's most high-profile politician, Senator Edward Kennedy, calling on delegates to repudiate violence and those who advocate it.[22] Chairing the resolutions' committee was Fermanagh-born priest, Father Sean McManus, a longstanding Irish Republican and an unapologetic supporter of the Provisional IRA.[23] McManus, who was ordained in 1968 at the age of 24, had served his novitiate as a Redemptorist Father at St Mary's Monastery, Kinnoull, Perth, before returning to Fermanagh in the summer of 1971 where he was arrested at an anti-internment protest after he intervened to prevent the RUC from beating up a young protester. McManus, who was fined £20 for obstructing a police constable, refused to recognise the court, arguing that it had 'no legitimate authority'; moreover, that he did not, 'never [had] and never [would] recognise the Colonial State of British Occupied Ireland' as it was founded on 'a morally and politically criminal action… was illegally imposed by force [and] illegally maintained by force against the wishes of the Irish people. Therefore, its institutions, its laws, and its political expressions [were] invalid'.[24] As a result of his political activism, in 1972, McManus was removed to the United States where he quickly resumed his mission to evangelise for the cause of Irish unity and draw attention to British injustice in the occupied Six Counties, by founding the Irish National Caucus which aimed to rally Irish American opinion and lobby the US Congress on the matter. McManus was likely one of the instigators of a letter circulated to US companies by the American AOH, advising them not to invest in 'Northern Ireland' as 'Britain was maintaining the only concentration camp in Europe' there.[25]

While the American AOH threw its weight behind the campaign for political status, the Scottish divisions remained loyal to the Board of Erin who issued a terse statement emphasising that the two organisations were not connected; and that the letter, which would 'help no-one', was 'the last thing we would engage in'.[26] Many of the younger rank-and-file members, particularly those in Scotland, would have begged to differ. The year 1979 saw more Glasgow Republicans leaving the AOH, including the constituents of another four flute bands, who along with the James Connolly RFB, organised themselves into the Scottish Republican Band Alliance (RBA). At the same time, the young Republican-minded Hibees of Lochee entered into an alliance with the small band of radical socialists, socialist republicans and other Irish solidarity activists who were organising under the broad banner of the UTOM.

The United Troops Out Movement

As can be assumed from its name, the UTOM had its origins in the Troops Out Movement (TOM) which was formed in London in 1973 by a broad mix of left groups, trade unionists, pacifists and other social progressives, and had collapsed four years later under the dual pressure of organising in the heartland of British imperialism and the perpetual attempts of the various groups to exert organisational control over it. At the height of this internecine warfare the TOM had split into two separate factions, and the UTOM had evolved out of one of these after going through a process of realignment and reunification. Nevertheless, the threat of renewed factionalism was ever present. So much so that the UTOM leadership felt the need to emphasise the anti-sectarian, united-front nature of the movement by placing the following statement in every edition of its monthly bulletin:

> The UTOM is a national movement campaigning around the following demands:
> Troops Out Now
> Self-determination for the Irish People!
> We work in a non-sectarian way with trade unions, Labour Party branches, left groups, black and white anti-racist groups, students, women's groups, gay groups, and other sections of the community receptive to the argument that there is a war going

on in Ireland and no solution acceptable to the Irish people can be reached until Britain withdraws.

This served as a constant reminder of the persistent threat of sectarian warfare, and as a check upon the empire-building tendencies of certain groups, which – as evidenced by the SWP's intervention at the Dundee launch meeting – were already reasserting themselves.

Despite their differences on what constituted an Irish solidarity movement, most of the Dundee group agreed that the IRA was fighting a legitimate revolutionary war, and were staunch in their commitment to organise activities in support of it. The UTOM leadership's attitude to the war in Ireland, however, remained ambivalent. At the same time as carrying articles on the history of the conflict from the 1916 Rising, through the Tan and Civil Wars, the foundation of the Loyalist state to the Civil Rights Movement, the UTOM did not support the ongoing war of national liberation. At the same time as carrying articles documenting the history of British Army atrocities in Ireland, they published interviews, and produced a film in which former British soldiers talked candidly of joining the army to escape unemployment, and the downside of being members of an army of occupation, such as being confined to military barracks and unable to go out for a drink or to meet local girls.[27] At the heart of this strategy was the desire to build a movement that was based more on the anti-Vietnam War movement in the United States – the motto, 'Troops Out Now!' being a modification of 'Bring Our Boys Home' – than on any notion of supporting the forces waging a war of national liberation in Ireland.

At no point in its history did or could the TOM or UTOM claim to be a pro-Republican movement. So why did the IRA-supporting activists of Dundee choose to affiliate to it? Why did they not form an independent Irish solidarity group? According to Malone:

> We were less experienced politically then and the UTOM seemed to be the only organisation that wasn't built exclusively around party building or selling papers. The most practical advantage to affiliating was that, apart from being the only movement active on Ireland, they had a national profile and

seemed to be able to co-ordinate, mobilise and organise at a national level. To begin with we knew nothing about UTOM except what we read in the paper, Troops Out. I personally was impressed with what I'd heard, and when you consider the shabby record of most of the left towards Ireland my optimistic view seems understandable.[28]

It was also appreciated that the UTOM could not be expected to build a mass British-based movement on the basis of support for the armed struggle. However, this created no problems in Dundee as all branches were given organisational autonomy, and the activities of each branch were dictated by local circumstances and conditions.

The first branch of the UTOM was formed the following month. In keeping with their aversion to bureaucratic structures, office bearers were kept to a functional minimum: Michael Taylor took on the role of Secretary, and the post of Treasurer was filled by Stuart Johnson, who – unlike Taylor and the Malone brothers – had no prior affiliation to the British left. The first mobilisation followed a few weeks later.

In March, the branch got wind of a meeting, organised by the Dundee University students' group of the Monday Club, entitled 'Ireland – Target for International Subversion', to be addressed by Ulster Unionist MP for Londonderry [sic], Willie Ross, who, like several other leading Loyalist politicians – including founder of the Ulster Vanguard Movement, William Craig, and future UUP leader, James Molyneaux – was a prominent member of the Club, and was also Chairman of its Northern Ireland Policy Committee. The Monday Club, which had been formed by right-wing Tories in 1961 in response to the de-colonialist policies of the Macmillan government, well-known for its support for the South African apartheid state and the white supremacist government in Rhodesia. This loyalty naturally extended to – or possibly originated in – a support for the Northern Irish 'state', an opposition to direct [British] rule, and a fundamental antagonism to the idea of a united Ireland. Given the Monday Club's record on Southern Africa, the meeting also attracted around thirty members of the Zimbabwean Students' Association – in 1979, the war of Zimbabwean national liberation against white minority rule was in its final stages – who, once the Irish solidarity activists explained who Willie

Ross was and what he represented, immediately grasped the significance and entered into a united front against a common enemy:

> As soon as the [first] speaker started, he was drowned in a torrent of abuse... after repeated interruptions, the reactionaries sheepishly trooped out, surrendering the room, for which they had presumably paid money, to ourselves and the Zimbabweans. A spontaneous anti-imperialist rally was held in which stirring speeches were given, to rapturous applause, by Dundee UTOM and the Zimbabwean students... highlighting the common cause of the struggles in Zimbabwe and Ireland against the forces of bigotry, reaction and imperialism. [29]

The meeting concluded with a march through the city centre to the army recruiting office in Barrack Street where another impromptu rally was held. A report was sent to *Troops Out*, and to *AP/RN* who published it under the by-line of 'Dundee UTOM correspondent S Johnson', adding to the worries of the author who had just had a job interview with D C Thomson's and was anxiously awaiting the outcome.[30]

If the Monday Club affair made for a good starting point, such opportunities were few and far between. The branch continued to highlight the similarity between the struggle in Ireland and other liberation struggles. While exiled Africans, Palestinians and Chileans, however, were invariably sympathetic to their pro-Republican views, the local Labour establishment was generally not, and since most of these groups were dependent on the Labour establishment for material and political support, Dundee UTOM's attempts to establish meaningful links with other anti-imperialist elements were hampered. That said, the various groups were not insensitive to their predicament. For example, at an Irish meeting in early 1982, one exiled Chilean spoke candidly of his identification with the Irish liberation struggle, and of the Chilean refugees' unequal relationship with the 'blue eyed boys' of the Labour establishment; making it clear that he, as a communist, was aware of the paternalistic nature – not to mention the inherent colonialism – of the British left establishment of which the local Labour authority was an integral part; but also explaining that maintaining the relationship was an essential tactic in the wider strategy of rallying the international forces of social democracy to their side, thus to undermine the fascistic governments that were running his and other countries.

Probably the most forthright body of international supporters to lend its weight to the Irish solidarity campaign in Dundee in this period was that of the Iranian Students' Association. Unlike the Chileans, who were political refugees with prior involvement in communist or socialist organisations, the Iranian students – who had come to the city to study at Dundee University or Dundee Institute of Technology (renamed Abertay University in 1994) – were largely impelled to political action by the outbreak of the Iranian Revolution in January 1979. They consisted of two groups: the Islamic Socialists of the Peoples' Mujahedin of Iran, and the more radical, but numerically smaller, secular Marxists of the Organisation of Struggle for the Emancipation of the Working Class (aka Peykar). In the course of attending a showing of the documentary film, *The Patriot Game*, in the autumn of 1979, they met up with the activists of Dundee UTOM, and from then on, participated in most of its meetings, street protests and other activities, if only to read out messages of solidarity. The differences between the two groups required careful navigation when it came to offering reciprocal support, however. For example, on one occasion, the participation of one well-meaning Irish solidarity activist in a rally organised by the People's Mujahedin elicited a severe dressing down by a member of the Peykar who had been observing from the other side of the street.

Despite the diversity of ideologies within Dundee UTOM, most members were, in their various ways, united in their support for the Republican movement. However, as Malone observed:

> There was always one voice raised opposing the Republican slant of our agitation – that of the SWP. We would propose activities that would emphasise the justification for the struggle being waged by the Republican Movement. They would 'trot' out their line that the Brit troops were just proles in uniform and it was more important to win over the hearts and minds of rank-and-file soldiers etc. Although we were always conscious of the differences, they in no way inhibited our activities.[31]

Relations were becoming increasingly strained, however. In the spring of 1979, the branch decided to picket an army recruiting stall in Dundee City Centre:

> Most of us were selling AP/RN and Troops Out and distributing leaflets. Jim Barlow [of the SWP] was talking to an officer like he was an old mate, giving him the SWP line about trade union[isation] of the army, that soldiers were proles in uniform etc. I've as much sympathy for unemployed people who join the army as anyone, and there are circumstances in which such arguments are justified, but this was a member of the officer class, not a [formerly] unemployed person from Glasgow, London or Manchester. This cosy talk ended with the officer telling Barlow that, if he had his way, he would wrap an armoured car in barbed wire and drive it straight through an H Block march. After their conversation ended, Barlow told me he was winning him over. I replied, 'Was that before or after he ran over you with the 'pig' wrapped in barbed wire?[32]

By late March, the branch was finding itself hampered by the lack of funds and a venue in which to hold meetings. The Lochee Hibees came to the rescue, procuring the use of their hall for the latter, and for a fundraising social night which was held a week after the assassination of the Shadow Secretary of State for Northern Ireland, Airey Neave, by the Irish National Liberation Army (INLA), although, as one former activist was quick to point out, that was not the reason. Indeed, the event raised badly-needed funds, which went towards the cost of hiring a bus to the branch's next activity, participation in a Troops Out/Anti-H-Block demonstration in Glasgow on 21 April – the biggest event organised by UTOM in Scotland to that date. For many Irish solidarity activists in Scotland, it proved to be the most significant event of the year.

The demonstration, which included contingents from Sinn Féin, the SWP, the IMG and other left groups, as well as the James Connolly and other Republican flute bands, was intended to be the first Irish march into the city centre since 1972. No sooner had it departed the Queen's Park assembly point, however, than it was met with a hail of bottles, bricks, beer cans and sectarian abuse from Loyalist counter-demonstrators who broke through the police lines and attacked the marchers who fought to defend themselves as mounted police waded into the crowd making several indiscriminate arrests. A modicum of order was restored, and again the march proceeded. However, at various points along the route it was halted, for no other reason it seemed, than to allow pockets of waiting Loyalist protestors to choose their targets more selectively:

> So...off we marched, heartened by the bold skirl of the bands. We could take [the loyalists] on...but you were also taking on the police, eh? Next recall is up in the Gorbals, wi' the old tenements still standing. You could see masses of Union Jacks on the railway line at Gorbals Cross. [Then] it went around that the cops were abandoning us.[33]

Finally, the march was stopped at the request of the organisers, a mile short of its destination, and the demonstrators led by the police onto a patch of waste ground where they were dispersed in small groups, ostensibly, for greater security and safety.[34] This only served to leave the disorientated Dundee contingent stranded in unfamiliar territory and even more vulnerable. It fell to Frank Malone, who was better acquainted with the geography and, more pertinently, the 'sectarian boundaries' of Glasgow, to navigate the perilous route into the city centre. Michael Taylor described the journey:

> We crossed Gorbals Bridge...but it didn't stop there. [Our] unfamiliarity with the area was taken advantage of by wee squads of loyalists. We were heading for George Square. I mind in our flight wee shits pretending to want to help us...bottles appeared in their hands. Cannae mind where the bus was, maybe that's why we were heading for the square. Finally, a very serious post-mortem took place at the next UTOM meeting in Dundee.[35]

A resolution was passed condemning Clydeside UTOM for its poor stewarding. Martin O'Leary, who had been called to Dundee to account for the organisers' actions, 'took the full flak' which, in hindsight, Taylor believes was 'unfair' as he could not be held accountable for the behaviour of the 'leader' who had managed the affair – as noted earlier, the UTOM was in the midst of a power struggle – or of the Glasgow police, much less the Loyalists. In mitigation, the English-born and formerly based activist, O'Leary, had little knowledge or experience of the latter two, and was clearly out of his depth. Malone saw this as less of a mitigating factor but more of a fundamental flaw in the UTOM leadership itself:

> This march showed what a disaster it was for the middle class leadership of the UTOM to take the initiative where strong working class emotions and feelings of loyalty, both republican and loyalist, are involved. The petty bourgeois [such as those] that made up the leadership of UTOM have had a relatively prosperous life compared to their working class compatriots. They are brought up to believe that the police are there to serve and protect them, their property and their rights; whereas, from the cradle to the grave, the working class know that the police exist to defend certain 'interests' in society. They accept that at some time in their lives they will be intimidated or in some other way attract the attention of the State. It is the petty bourgeois with all their prejudices about 'all equal in the eyes of the law' and the neutrality of the courts that are traumatised when the police openly side with the forces that are hostile to their activities. Such as happened in Glasgow on April 21.
>
> It is taken for granted that as a result of the Irish emigration in the 19th century pride in either the Irish national identity or Orange bigotry was a way of keeping the native culture alive.[36] With the perpetual nationalist revolution in Ireland, for both sections of the community in Glasgow, 'cultural pride' became political loyalty. The middle class leadership of UTOM were unwilling or unable to see that when a demonstration is organised on Ireland, all sorts of scum slithers out of the sewers, and the only context [in which] they see it is in support for the IRA. Furthermore, the UTOM failed to consider that loyalists in Scotland have a reputation for neanderthal savagery and religious bigotry which is well deserved and is every bit the equal of Paisley and his ilk in Ireland.[37]

The naïve faith of the UTOM leadership in the Glasgow police to act impartially was borne out in their report in their bulletin, *Troops Out*, which bemoaned the lack of police protection as 'a thin red line – it couldn't be called a cordon – shambled between the marchers and the Orangies'.[38] Simultaneously, the leadership's failure to organise adequate stewarding, and their inability to take any responsibility for the debacle that ensued was glossed over in a veil of contradictory, self-delusional rhetoric. *Troops Out* defended the '[wise decision] not to try for the centre', yet proclaimed that 'the march had broken the myth that you can't march in Glasgow'. Likewise, the *Socialist Challenge*, the paper of the IMG – of which march organiser Chris Bambery, as well as Martin O'Leary, was a leading member – claimed that 'a successful march was organised in Glasgow, despite being followed by a few Loyalists throwing beer cans'. The fact that it had failed to reach its stated destination – the City Halls, where a mass rally was to take place – was not mentioned. The Dundee branch were no two minds about it – the march was an unmitigated disaster.

Valuable lessons were learned from it, nevertheless. Besides exposing the flaws in the UTOM leadership, the march showed that considerable support existed for a pro-Republican Irish solidarity movement in Scotland. For although the demonstration was organised by the British left /UTOM, the majority of the estimated 600-800 participants were not members of left-wing or pacifist groups, but working-class people, mainly of Irish-Catholic extraction, from the housing schemes of Glasgow. This was reflected in the slogans they shouted. John Malone recalled, 'It was all "Brits Out", "IRA" and "Political Status Now" not "End the War!"' It was also the first time the Dundee activists had been on a march with Republican flute bands in attendance, and, as Malone recalled: 'You didn't notice the bricks and bottles so much with the deafening sound of Irish revolutionary songs being hammered out by [their] massed [ranks]'.[39]

The Hibees also noticed the bands. Malone recalled, 'once back in Dundee they talked about nothing else but holding a march on any pretext so flute bands could parade through [the town]'. From this moment, the idea of Padraig Pearse RFB took root, although the band itself did not emerge fully formed and labelled until sometime later. The choice of name, which commemorated the revolutionary martyr and signatory of the Republican Proclamation, and mirrored that of the Lochee Celtic

Supporters' Club, was a logical and relatively uncontroversial one: the only quibble, that there was another AOH band of the same name elsewhere in Scotland, was sportingly dismissed. At the same time, the members' support for the IRA continued to be accommodated. However, for the time being, the band remained under the broad umbrella of the AOH, its members initially teaming up with the John F Kennedy Flute Band from Perth, now under the stewardship of Terry O'Donnell, a former founder member of the James Connolly RFB.[40]

Although most members of Dundee UTOM – from the radical socialists who supported the IRA on grounds of international revolutionary solidarity, to the Hibees whose solidarity stemmed from their Irish-Catholic background – were unequivocal in their support for the Republican movement, the alliance was not always without controversy. For example, the day after the Glasgow march, the Society for the Protection of the Unborn Child organised a rally in Dundee city centre in support of the Corrie amendment, i.e., the Parliamentary Bill introduced by the Conservative MP for Ayrshire, John Corrie, which aimed to restrict the abortion rights granted to women under the 1967 Abortion Act. Consequently, a debate on 'The Right to Choose' was initiated by Dundee UTOM activist, Susan Cross – who championed a variety of radical causes including involvement in the Women's movement – in which the socialist republican element and all the women in the branch supported it, and the Hibees opposed it on religious grounds. The debate ended with the branch agreeing on Ireland but agreeing to disagree on abortion.

The next mobilisation of the branch was at the annual Dundee May Day parade, which John Malone described as the one day in the year when 'the local labour establishment design to mingle with the masses whose interests they are supposed to protect':

> At least our participation in this traditional snail's crawl into the city centre shook it up. We were optimistic to start with considering the international, anti-imperialist theme. There were speakers from as far afield as Chile, Zimbabwe and South Africa. It was the day after Thatcher's election victory. In view of this, the leftists thought that slogans such as 'Tories Out' and 'Thatcher Out' should be the order of the day. Our contingent

began a barrage of 'Troops Out!', 'Political Status Now!' and 'Smash H Block!' Initially, there was no response but gradually we got a few dirty sneers from leftist paper sellers pimping their product – Christ, if looks could kill, I thought – then a voice shrieked, 'This is a day of international working class solidarity, nothing to do with Ireland'.[41]

This somewhat contradictory interjection merely served to reinforce the Irish solidarity activists' lack of faith in the British labour movement and the British left in general. Nevertheless, shortly after this, members of Dundee UTOM collared the Secretary of the Dundee Labour Party, George Galloway, who assured them that the Labour Party could be won around to supporting a United Ireland at its next conference. The branch, however, had few illusions, and continued to direct their energies elsewhere.

After the May Day parade, the branch settled into the grind of selling *Troops Out* and *An Phoblacht/Republican News* from their regular pitch at the Overgate corner, which, despite undergoing redevelopment in the 1960s, had been the stomping ground of socialist agitators since the Free Speech campaign of 1889. *AP/RN*, in particular, drew a regular stream of customers – a noteworthy point given the intensity of IRA activity at the time, which reached its height with the assassination of Lord Mountbatten at Mullaghmore Harbour, County Sligo, and the killing of eighteen British soldiers at Warrenpoint, County Down, on 27 August 1979. Indeed, it was noted that sales went especially well when a picture of an IRA volunteer appeared on the front page:

> There was a noticeable lack of ambivalence on the part of the local people. We would be selling *Republican News* with a picture of an armed Provo volunteer and a defiant headline such as 'Liberation War Goes on' or 'IRA Strikes Back'... people passed by, there would be two responses [along the lines of] 'Up the IRA' or 'IRA scum.' Of course, we always drew dirty looks from the cops but, at this time, they left us alone.[42]

One of the major advantages of campaigning in Dundee was that political loyalties were not as intense or toxic as in the west central belt.

As John Malone explained, 'Other UTOM branches couldn't believe it when we said we could sell *AP/RN* unmolested. Only now do I realise what a revelation [this was], for in certain parts of Glasgow you could get your throat cut for wearing a Celtic scarf'.

In the late summer the branch extended their sales of Irish Republican literature to include *The Starry Plough*, the paper of the Irish Republican Socialist Party (IRSP), for which Malone took responsibility:

> The Hibs weren't too keen on this for the basic reason that they saw the movement in Ireland as the exclusive property of the Provos. The initial reason for ordering it was to give local people access to a wider range of republican opinion, and since INLA members had been killed on active service, they were equally entitled to our solidarity. Personally, I always considered myself more of a follower of Connolly than Pearse. I pointed out the writings of Karl Marx on Ireland, his activities in warning the proletariat against national chauvinism over Ireland and, of course, his activities to campaign for an amnesty for O'Donovan Rossa and other captured Fenian leaders. I also felt that the final vindication that socialism and nationalism were not in opposing camps was the execution of James Connolly, the Irish Marxist, for his participation in the 1916 Rising. Also, that the Rising was carried out by the Irish Volunteers and the Irish Citizen Army – the ICA, which was formed by the Irish Transport and General Workers' Union as a workers' militia intended to protect workers from police but moulded into a revolutionary force under Connolly's direction. It was called by Lenin 'The first red army in Europe'. Despite these discussions with the Hibs, it was never a question of Provos vs. INLA, but solidarity with revolutionary movements in Ireland on the whole.[43]

Protesting Against the UDR

The Dundee UTOM branch carried on in this vein until the end of August, when it was learned that the UDR were due to undergo training at the Territorial Army base at Barry Buddon by Monifieth on the eastern outskirts of Dundee. The branch promptly set about organising a series of protest actions drawing attention to the history and nature of the regiment, including the high level of collusion with Loyalist paramilitary groups; and – as Barry Buddon was the only camp in Scotland to be used by the regiment – calling for the UDR to be withdrawn from the country altogether. A leaflet to that effect was drafted, and, as Stuart Johnson had left for London to take up a job at the *New Musical Express*, Michael Taylor wrote a piece for *Troops Out*. Letters were also submitted to the *Dundee Courier*, which did not print them, and to the *Dundee Standard* – the newly established newspaper promoted by, amongst others, George Galloway – which did.[44]

At the same time, the Dundee Labour Party, with which Dundee UTOM maintained a working relationship, approved a motion, introduced by its Monifieth branch, objecting to the presence of the UDR in the area and demanding that the 2,300 acres of Ministry of Defence land no longer be used for military training of any kind. This was supported by the Labour MP for Dundee West, Ernie Ross, who wrote to the Defence Secretary, Francis Pym, demanding the withdrawal of the UDR, which, he stated, was 'not regarded as a neutral body by Roman Catholics in Northern Ireland', nor, he implied, by the population of Dundee, which had 'a large Roman Catholic [element], many of [whom were of] Irish descent'. 'We don't have the community differences that sometimes occur', he added, and 'don't want to import [them] here'.[45] He also expressed concern that 'forces hostile to the regiment' would target the area, and cited an incident the previous Monday (3 September) when the Wellgate shopping centre was evacuated to allow an army bomb disposal unit – which was speedily dispatched from Edinburgh with a police escort – to detonate a suspicious package.[46] 'It was a hoax', he stated, 'but a very elaborate [one]. It worried me and it clearly worried the security forces'. The fact that the incident occurred exactly one week after the Mountbatten and Warrenpoint killings suggests that the security forces were not taking any chances.

News of the letter elicited a terse statement from the UDR headquarters in Lisburn, whose spokesman maintained that 'the UDR [was] a regiment of the [British] Army, and there [was] no reason why it shouldn't train at any army base in Britain'; adding that the UDR had held training camps in England and Wales with 'no complaints at all' from the local residents.[47]

Chapter 9 – A Legacy Reclaimed 1970–85

The camps, he added, were 'morale boosters' which provided a 'break from security duties' and a chance to socialise with the local population in a non-threatening environment. The Dundee MP's letter also roused the ire of Derek Peters, Secretary of the Belfast Ballynafeigh branch of the Northern Ireland Labour Party, who claimed that 'Mr Ross's remarks [were] an insult to the soldiers of the Highland regiments who had died defending democracy in Northern Ireland', adding that 'If Mr Ross really means that Ulster should be expelled from the United Kingdom then he should say so, leave the Labour Party and join the British branch of Provisional Sinn Féin'.[48] While this would have made for an interesting prospect for the constituents of Dundee West, Lochee included, and given an extra-controversial twist to the twinning with the Palestinian city of Nablus the following year, Ross remained steadfastly loyal to the British Labour Party for the rest of his life.

Predictably, amongst the first to rally to the defence of the UDR were the local Tory Unionist politicians and their allies in the press. Approached for comment by the *Courier*, the MP for Perth and East Perthshire, Bill Walker responded, 'These chaps need our support [and] once we commit them to any kind of campaign, they should have the whole-hearted support of Parliament'. Walker, an ardent Thatcherite, who was also a volunteer with the RAF Reserve and the Air Training Corps, added, 'These chaps are doing a volunteer job. It is just unfortunate they happen to be 'in a part of the United Kingdom where there is trouble', and stated that he would be arranging with their commanding officer 'to drop in to see them'.[49] The MP for South Angus, Tory Peter Fraser, commented that 'the fight against terrorism in Northern Ireland [was] far from over', and it was 'vitally important' that those prosecuting it had the opportunity to train.[50] The *Courier*'s letters page also gave full vent to a narrow range of opinion which belaboured the point that the UDR was a regiment of the British Army, who, as 'soldiers of the realm' were entitled to defend it. Interestingly, the SNP MP for Dundee East, party leader Gordon Wilson, was either not consulted or declined to comment.

Besides the Wellgate bomb hoax, no other suspicious incidents were reported, with the exception of one 'accident' on Friday, 14 September when seven women UDR soldiers from the 9th Antrim Battalion were admitted to Dundee Royal Infirmary after their Land Rover overturned when hitting a small mound on the main road out of the camp, although whether this was due to sabotage or incompetence is not known.[51] Shortly after this, Dundee UTOM organised a picket of the same road, which caught the UDR unawares – it was observed that the guards were noticeably unnerved. Besides attracting a large contingent from the AOH, the protest was well-supported by the local left, including the Labour Party, and received a sympathetic write-up in the *Dundee Standard*. The success of the protest generated enthusiasm for the next event – a march from Lochee into the city centre on Saturday, 13 October, which was conceived and promoted as a national (Scottish) UTOM demonstration. John Malone recalled, 'This was the first major demonstration launched on the back of Dundee UTOM, so it was as much a test of our abilities and confidence as individuals as well as collectively.' Despite the optimism of the Hibees, others admitted to feeling a certain ambivalence: it was the first demonstration in Dundee in recent memory exclusively on Ireland (non-political AOH marches excepted); on the other hand, UTOM activities in Scotland were never given the same prominence by the London-based leadership as those organised in England. These reservations proved to be justified. In the event, Dundee UTOM's hopes of attracting a projected 500 supporters from all over Scotland failed to materialise.[52] In the event, the march attracted around a hundred people, comprising members and of Dundee UTOM and a 'sprinkling' of UTOM branches from Glasgow. The Revolutionary Communist Group (RCG), although invited, withheld support 'on principle', citing their fundamental differences with the UTOM's Brit-left leadership and the organisation's reformist approach to the war in Ireland. Malone recalled, 'The Hibs [took] the view it was a pointless exercise when it was announced there'd be no flute band'. Michael Taylor had the task of negotiating the route with the local police: at the last minute, however, they refused to let it proceed up Lochee High Street and diverted it around empty streets of decaying, condemned tenements in the process of being demolished (to make way for the Lochee bypass), thus depriving the marchers the opportunity of taking their message to a potentially sympathetic audience. Hopes of procuring high-profile speakers – namely, veteran campaigner, Harry McShane, and Mary Nellis of the Derry Relatives' Action Committee – through the offices of the national UTOM organisation were also dashed, leaving Michael Taylor to speak for Dundee UTOM, Martin O'Leary for Glasgow/Clydeside UTOM, and Jim Barlow from the local SWP. It may have passed muster as a moderately successful local rally; as a national demonstration, however, it was a dismal flop.

Meanwhile, the British State propaganda machine had swung into full gear. Earlier that week, the Prime Minister, Margaret Thatcher, dismissed suggestions that the UDR were to be 'banned' from using the Scottish camp, stating in a letter to Independent Unionist MP for North Down, John Kilfedder, that '[the UDR] should have access to the most suitable training facilities available', and 'the government [had] every intention of ensuring that such training continues as long as is necessary'.[53] On Monday, 15 October, a day after the arrival of the UDR's 11th (Craigavon) Battalion at Barry Buddon, Secretary of State for Northern Ireland, Humphrey Atkins, was helicoptered in, whereafter being briefed by UDR chief, Brigadier David Miller, he proclaimed that 'Mr Ross's campaign [sic] to have the regiment shifted' had 'floundered', and cited the low numbers at the Dundee rally as evidence. He also stated that 'the people around here [were] delighted to see the UDR', to which a UDR spokesman added, 'there was no resentment amongst the locals [who had] gone out of their way to make us feel welcome'.[54] This, no doubt, included the aforementioned Bill Walker MP, the local (Tory) councillors, selected members of the Monifieth Community Council and other 'concerned' residents, who saw the presence of the UDR, or indeed any other regiment at the camp, as a means of stalling the equally controversial plans of the behemoth chemical company ICI to site a petrochemical plant on the peninsula.[55]

Underlying Atkins' visit, and Thatcher's letter, was the fear that the campaign to have the UDR removed would – in addition to a recent spate of IRA attacks on off-duty soldiers – serve to demotivate existing members of the UDR and scare off potential recruits, thus jeopardising the government's ability to 'manage' its Six-County toehold through its Ulsterisation strategy. That the visit was reported, not in the local Dundee, Scottish, or even British national press, but the *Belfast Telegraph*, suggests that the propaganda was directed primarily at an Ulster unionist audience with the intention of dispelling the notion that, as one Monifieth councillor stated he had been informed, 'the Scots were against them'.[56]

Atkins concluded his visit with an address to the ranks – preceded by a public call for more full-time and part-time members – in which he affirmed his belief that the 11th (Craigavon) Battalion would 'continue to give dedicated and impartial service to the whole of the people in Northern Ireland' – a highly disingenuous comment given the 11th Craigavon's past record of involvement with Loyalist murder gangs[57] – and concluded that 'no-one should be in any doubt about the government's determination to put down terrorism'. Compared to this, outmanoeuvring a small ragbag of troops out campaigners in Dundee was small beer; nevertheless, as the State's small intervention even at this level shows, the campaign was not without impact. Whether the tentacles of the British government extended to the UTOM in this period is unknown. Given the recent revelations of police infiltration in the original Troops Out Movement in the mid-1970s and the reconstituted TOM in the early 1980s, it may shed a new light on the national leadership's failure to mobilise support for the Dundee demonstration.[58] At the time, however, the Dundee branch attributed the poor turnout to the London-centric mentality of the UTOM leadership and the national chauvinism of the British left. In this respect, at least, they were partly right.

Meanwhile, the RCG's criticisms had given some of the group cause to ponder. Shortly after the march, Michael Taylor and John Malone approached the RCG's representative in Dundee, Ron Tuck:

> Mike made a remark which was intended as a tribute to their principles... It was the wrong thing to say to the RCG who took everything so seriously. Ron Tuck replied [with words to the effect]: 'The march has [demonstrated] that the Dundee UTOM is no more or less principled or opportunistic than the national leadership...when you're not pimping ex-British troops around the country [59] you say send the UDR back to Ireland. It further shows the contempt your national leadership has for you [that] a pathetic handful was the best [it] could do for a national mobilisation in Scotland'.[60]

Although his relationship with the RCG remained antagonistic, Malone admitted to having a grudging admiration for their 'iron commitment to principle'. Neither, it was observed, had they been idle in this period. Shortly after the UDR demonstration, the RCG arranged, under the banner of their alternative campaign, 'Hands off Ireland', a Dundee premiere of *The Patriot Game* in the Trades Council Club in Rattray Street.[61] This groundbreaking film, which documented the history of the Irish war of liberation from a Republican socialist perspective and featured 'in-house' footage of the IRA in action against a musical backdrop of Irish rebel songs, naturally attracted the Republican-minded members of the Dundee UTOM, as well a number of supporters from the international movement including, as stated earlier, the Iranian Students' Association.

The customary post-film discussion was followed by speeches from the organisers, including Gary Clapton of the Edinburgh RCG, who launched into a full-blown attack on the UTOM leadership and its middle-class left constituents who, he claimed, condemned the Republican movement while courting the most reactionary sections of the British Labour movement. By way of example, he cited two demonstrations occurring on Sunday, 12 August, both of which commemorated the tenth anniversary of the deployment of British troops in the north of Ireland. One, in Belfast, organised by the Republican movement, saw over 15,000 people march behind an IRA colour party in support of the armed struggle and the Blanketmen. The other, in London, organised by the Young Liberals and headed by prominent members of the British liberal/left establishment, – including Labour MP, Kevin McNamara, who had likened the IRA and INLA to 'rapists, burglars and murderers', and Liberal MP, Cyril Smith, who ironically, was later revealed to be a serial child abuser – saw around half that number rally around the slogan of 'End the War', which declaimed, on equal terms, the less savoury aspects (and the expense) of Britain's involvement in Ireland and the revolutionary violence of the IRA and INLA. While the RCG prided itself on being the only British contingent on the former march, the UTOM had chosen to align itself to the latter.[62]

However, Clapton reserved his most cutting comment until last. At the time of the Mountbatten and Warrenpoint killings, when 'the RCG stood with the Irish people', he stated accusingly – and somewhat presumptuously, given the upset their campaign had caused the regiment and its supporters – the UTOM were wanting to send 'the UDR back to Ireland to kill [them]'. Malone recalled:

It must be remembered that practically the whole of Dundee UTOM was in attendance. Not a single voice was raised by 'our branch' to defend [it]. It was as if the UTOM had been judged guilty and sentenced to death and no-one was prepared to offer any plea in mitigation. It was a position we always considered after our run in with the RCG. What the fuck were a bunch of 'Republicans' doing in the UTOM? Even the UDR demonstration…came across as a group of well-intentioned liberals fearful of the Irish 'troubles' being imported to Dundee. Furthermore, even if we did organise pro-Republican solidarity activities within the framework of UTOM, we were still a minority, and the Trotskyists and liberals who made up the majority were not too keen on [these] activities. The only occasion when pro-IRA rhetoric and positions were beyond doubt was at the marches we attended in Scotland [where] most of marchers were drawn from the local Irish communities and there was always a flute band in attendance. As can be guessed, it was from this point that the basis of our doubts about the UTOM emerged.[63]

These doubts were further vindicated at the semi-annual UTOM conference in London on 8–9 December when, it was decided to change the name back to the Troops Out Movement, on the assumption that 'there [was] now one national broad front movement'. The conference report cited 'the number of branches in attendance', which augured well for a series of national initiatives, including 'several national demonstrations, a Labour weekend to discuss and initiate work in the labour movement – seen by the conference as a major focus, and commitment to general propaganda work with other forces advocating withdrawal'.[64]

All the talk of a broad front movement and coordinated campaigning work cut little ice with the Republican-minded members of the Dundee branch who were of the opinion that the left groups that had destroyed the old TOM (in this case, the SWP and the IMG) were reasserting organisational control, the evidence being the decision to conduct work in the labour movement, and the defeat of a motion to adopt 'Political Status Now' as a third demand. As a concession to the large minority who voted for it, it was agreed to work towards winning support for the 'Political Status' demand at the next conference, while continuing to raise the two other demands wherever possible. In the meantime, the national leadership aimed to promote a campaign on humanitarian grounds, emphasising the undemocratic nature of the judicial process in the Six Counties.

Such developments led some members of Dundee TOM to question their relationship with the movement. Nevertheless, while groups such as the RCG had a position on Ireland that better reflected their own, the national TOM remained the most prolific Irish solidarity organisation covering the geographical span of England, Scotland and Wales, for which it had the approval of the Republican movement (mirroring, no doubt, the strategy of the Chilean and other liberation movements mentioned earlier). Affiliation to the larger movement also provided a badge of legitimacy to an otherwise unbranded and overlooked band of pro-Republican Irish solidarity campaigners operating in isolation in a small city in the east of Scotland. And it was for these reasons, that despite their cynicism, frustration and conflicted feelings about doing so, they stayed in the 'national' movement until it could 'no longer be justified on anything resembling principle'.[65]

The last, and possibly most bizarre act of Dundee TOM in 1979, occurred in the early hours of Christmas Day:

> Mike Taylor, myself and others decided to erect a H Block banner from an electricity pylon at the back of Whitfield [which] like most of the housing schemes in Dundee, was built on farm land purchased by the local council. [Behind it] were fields, hills and a network of electricity pylons on top The decision was arrived at spontaneously at a Christmas Eve party at Mike Taylor's, who, as can be guessed, lived in Whitfield at the time… As we drank more of Mike's bootleg wine/beer, as always, our thoughts turned to Ireland and to the diversity of tactics the H Block committees used to focus attention on the H Blocks. Although marches in support of the blanket men were progressively gathering support, they also used more unorthodox methods… including white line pickets, the occupation of local buildings festooned with H Block banners, the spraying of

'Political Status Now!' on hoardings and, presumably, on at least one occasion, erecting a H Block banner over an electricity pylon.

We decided to wait until after midnight before we embarked. I suppose the only thing worse than hill-climbing in absolute darkness is doing it when you're half-pissed. God knows how we managed it. There was a lot of throwing ourselves on the ground as cars passed – an exercise in futility when you think of it as the last thing any motorist would be focussed on is pitch-black high ground a hundred yards to the left of or right of them. I have absolutely no idea who climbed the pylon and erected the banner – it wasn't me that's for sure. When we returned to Mike's it was the cause of more celebration which meant more drinking. All our efforts were something of an anti-climax – when returning from my mother's on the Whitfield bus [the next day], the banner was barely visible... you'd have to be consciously looking for it to spot it. The problem arose because it was only three-four feet and the slogans on it were only legible if you were right up next to it.

At first glance, all this fucking about, getting drunk etc. seems to detract from the seriousness of the situationI mention it: first, because it was one of the many 'events' we organised, and it would be a very boring [campaign] if it consisted of an endless round of meetings and marches. Second, I've always been struck by the fact that the left groups took everything so totally seriously, and I see no contradiction between doing something on grounds of political principle while at the same time having a good time and a few laughs... Finally, it is [also] a reminder of the times we all thought along the same lines before the movement fragmented.[66]

The Bloody Sunday Demonstration, Birmingham, 1980

The year 1980 began optimistically enough with Dundee TOM participating in the eighth commemoration of Bloody Sunday, held that year, in parallel with the annual commemoration in Derry, in the English city of Birmingham.

CHAPTER 9 – A LEGACY RECLAIMED 1970–85

The following section, with minor stylistic alterations, draws on John Malone's appraisal of this march in particular, his perspective on Irish demonstrations in the 1970s and 1980s, and his experience, as a Dundee-based activist, in participating in them.

If anything, I have to admire the courage of the organisers [the English-based representatives of Sinn Féin] in selecting Birmingham as the location. First, I must explain why the decision to hold it in Birmingham was seen as a 'provocation', at least by reactionary forces. It is a long-established communist principle that communists support the right of oppressed nations unconditionally to wage war to liberate their country. On this principle, from 1972 onwards, the IRA, as is the right of any oppressed people waging an armed struggle against imperialist forces, extended the war to England. On 21 November 1974, five explosions occurred in Birmingham pubs resulting in the deaths of 21 civilians and the injury of a further 160. Following these explosions, five Irishmen living in Birmingham were arrested as they boarded the Heysham–Belfast ferry. A sixth was arrested in Birmingham. They were sentenced to life imprisonment on the basis of confessions they always maintained were extracted by torture, amidst a rabid wave of anti-Irish hysteria whipped up by the gutter press. In November–December 1987, their original life sentences were upheld by the court of appeal, and, as I write [1989], the case of the Birmingham Six is regarded as the most notorious miscarriage of 'British justice' in recent years.

The transport for the march was organised, not through Dundee but Glasgow. In order to get from Scotland to Brummie in time for the march an overnight journey was necessary. The bus was hired by a coalition of groups to pick up people from Dundee, Edinburgh, Glasgow and other areas en route. As well as ourselves and the SWP from Dundee, were the Glasgow and Edinburgh representatives of the TOM and the RCG .. It was the first contact we had with Mike Duffield and Kirstin Crosbie of the Glasgow RCG. Surprisingly, we had little communication with them. This was all the more strange considering how closely we worked with them during and after the second hunger strike. I put this down to the antagonism that existed between the TOM and the RCG at a national level. Despite this hostility, we all had a grudging admiration for the RCG over the more avowed or apparent 'pro-Republican' nature of their solidarity activities.[67]

The march itself took place on Sunday, 27 January with an estimated 2,000 people in attendance. The broad spectrum of speakers included representatives from Sinn Féin, the IRSP, the Relatives Action Committee, the Women in Ireland group, Women Against Imperialism, the Bradford Asian Youth Movement and the Iranian Students' Association, and Brendan Gallacher, father of Blanketman, Willie Gallacher. As *AP/RN* noted, Kevin Colfer of London Sinn Féin 'set the tone for others to follow' when he affirmed that 'no-one is going to prevent the Irish people and their socialist brothers from marching in support of the men in the H-Blocks and the women in Armagh'. (The women in Armagh Jail, who had the right to wear their own clothes, were engaged in a 'no work' protest and began a 'no wash' protest on 7 February.) It further stated that 'there was a genuine revolutionary content to all the speeches [which] in their various ways, called for support for the liberation struggle and Political Status. This also included the speech of the TOM speaker, Pat Arrowsmith – the independently minded activist and veteran peace campaigner who had fasted in sympathy with the hunger-striking IRA prisoners, Dolours and Marion Price in June 1974 – who called for the repatriation of Irish political prisoners in English jails.[68]

The report in *Troops Out* betrayed a more ambivalent perspective. Firstly, it emphasised that the demonstration did not 'consist of Sinn Féiners', presuming to suggest that while the many members of Birmingham's large Irish community were 'out on the streets, along with us, the growing number of British people who want the troops out', they were not members or supporters of the Republican movement. Secondly, seven weeks after the TOM conference had voted down a motion to adopt 'Political Status Now!' as a third demand, *Troops Out* carried a picture of a Political Status banner on the front page. It also gave prominence to a British soldier who made obscene gestures at the march from halfway up a lamppost. [69]

> As for the march itself, I see no reason to disagree with the AP/RN estimate of around 2,000. What I take issue with is the TOM appraisal... For to merely condemn reactionary terror doesn't go far enough. It is also necessary to support revolutionary violence. However, despite the negative aspects of some of the Troops Out article, the march was another magnificent indication and enormous vindication of the potential that existed for a principled, that is a pro-Republican, solidarity movement. Slogans such as 'Troops Out!' were thin on the ground. 'IRA! IRA!', 'Remember Bloody Sunday!' and 'No More Bloody Sundays!' were the order of the day...The 200 or so skinhead supporters of the fascist groups such as the National Front and the British Movement that followed the march intent on disrupting it weren't viewed as a serious threat, mainly, because some of us had seen it all before, and because this march appeared better organised and more disciplined than the debacle we had been on before, namely, the demo in Glasgow in April 1979 organised by the UTOM.
>
> I felt the increased number of Trotskyist groups was a much more serious problem. I can't remember before or since seeing a greater number of Trot groups on one demonstration. As well as the SWP, the IMG and the RCG, there was the Workers' Revolutionary Party, the Revolutionary Communist Tendency, the Spartacus League and the Revolutionary Communist League, to name but a few. This doesn't include the endless list of anarchist, Maoist groups etc...They all put out their own leaflets giving, not only a different analysis, but a different solution to the war in Ireland. However, they all had one thing in common – concealed in the most fraternal language possible was the message, 'if only the stupid Irish would listen to us "the troubles" would have ended years ago'. It was one thing to have the commemoration plagued by Trotskyists/Maoists/anarchists distributing more papers and leaflets than I can remember, it was another when their religious zeal interfered with the

speeches at the rally. There was also their personal gossip to contend with. Our group was near the back of the march and the rally had already started by the time we arrived. The sound of the speakers was barely audible. When an impassioned speech was being delivered honouring the murdered dead of Bloody Sunday, and asserting the determination of the Irish people to continue, our view was obscured and the speech drowned out by a reunion of what I took to be a bunch of middle class feminists who continued to talk through the minute's silence. I always felt it showed an atrocious lack of social breeding to interrupt a private conversation. Mick Taylor had no such scruples – he told them, 'We have come all the way from Dundee for this. Could you have the decency to shut up for one minute?'.

After that, the rest of the rally went ahead without incident; however, another problem soon arose. The drivers of the buses were overdue for some or other reason. As the march dispersed, the remainder of the demonstrators were stuck between a couple of hundred skinheads and a very unsympathetic looking line of cops who viewed us as no more than a gang of IRA scum. At one point someone made a joke about putting the wagons in a circle but as each wayward driver turned up and more buses departed, that idea seemed more remote. Looking back on it, although this situation seemed potentially dangerous, I feel that even from this something was gained, namely, the knowledge that the people on Irish marches could be put into two categories – 'middle class kiddies' and 'slum dwellers.' While the middle class kiddies were chain smoking like fuck and looking like they desperately needed a change of underwear, the slum dwellers were being practical and breaking up banner poles and commandeering the wooden staves from placards for clubs. As each driver turned up, and the number of besieged marchers decreased, and the number of skinheads seemed to increase, the marchers that remained were becoming increasingly apprehensive. You were conscious of an atmosphere of 'What are we going to do?' and 'How are we going to get out of here alive?' Fortunately, like the cavalry in the last reel of a John Wayne film, all the drivers arrived and everyone got away safely. On the bus home there was endless talk of what might have happened. This wasn't the first time we'd had a narrow escape.

Certainly, attending Irish marches regardless of the content, whether organised by TOM or Sinn Fein, was certainly more hazardous than the variety of causes supported by the Brit left on the parades they organised. As someone who has participated in a variety of demonstrations against unemployment, pro-abortion, trade union struggles, and in support of liberation struggles in Palestine, South Africa and Latin/Central America, there is no conceivable parallel with the hostility that accompanies Irish marches. Of course, the accompanying hostility is appropriately manufactured and engineered by what James Connolly summed up as perfectly as 'the prostitute pressmen'. For, despite the few petit bourgeois radical journalists who resist censorship, by and large, their loyalties have always been and always will be with their own national bourgeoisie. The hostility further flows from the view among the ruling class that any public activity critical of British policy in Ireland is/was sub-consciously pro-IRA and 'stabbing our boys in the back'. Alternatively, such demonstrations are accused of 'exporting the Irish sectarian troubles to the British mainland' – although, as noted on the first march we attended in Glasgow in April 1979, Orange reaction and bigotry in Scotland has never needed the excuse of 'IRA sympathisers' to give vent to their rabid and notorious sectarian hatred. The process by which the press set out to suppress democratic rights on the issue of Ireland, i.e., banning marches, is quite straightforward. As soon as permission for a march was applied for or approved, the gutter press launch a tirade of editorials accusing the organisers of importing sectarian strife to Britain. This soon evolves into 'Ban those evil people' and 'Keep IRA supporters off our streets'. In this, two things are clear. Firstly, none of them view this as freedom of dissent or expression. They all emphasise the amoral views of the organisers. Secondly, they give a kind of 'moral justification' to the forces opposed to such demonstrations. Then when the marches go ahead and are attacked by gangs of loyalists and other reactionary elements, they have the nerve to throw up their hands in horror, totally ignoring the anti-Irish racism for which they are responsible for encouraging in the first place.

The very act of participating in such a demonstration was a hazard in itself, the most obvious being the missiles – bottles, bricks, [and, on one occasion in Glasgow, razor-spiked potatoes] – that rained down on the march as it progressed. The most dangerous periods, however, were just before the march set off and after it ended. Finding the assembly point was dangerous if the march was held in a city you weren't familiar with. On most occasions, we arrived just as the march was taking off. As the rally dispersed, this was equally dangerous as roaming gangs of loyalists hung around the outskirts, preying on the stragglers. It goes without saying that security and discipline were the order of the day at such events. It's also the reason why when problems arose, such as at the Bloody Sunday march in Birmingham with the wayward bus drivers, we felt, with good reason, that one day our luck would run out.[70]

If returning to Dundee after participating in such adrenaline-fuelled events was something of an anti-climax, the group settled back into the grind of paper selling, street stalls and organising public meetings. On the afternoon of Saturday, 19 April, Dundee TOM hosted a meeting addressed by former civil rights leader and current anti-H Block campaigner, Bernadette Devlin McAliskey – which drew a large local audience, and a small group of Loyalist protesters headed by the arch-Protestant zealot, Pastor Jack Glass – in which she criticised the failure of the British labour movement to address the key areas of concern to Irish people in the Six Counties, namely, the presence of British troops on their streets and the torture going on in the prisons.[71] The following weeks also saw a thawing in the relationship with the RCG who accepted that, unlike the national leadership, the Dundee TOM were not apologists for imperialism; likewise, the branch affirmed that they had local autonomy and the day this was threatened they would leave.

Meanwhile, the reluctance of the Hibees to take part in street campaigning was proving something of a sore point for those who did.[72]

> They seemed to think that even selling *AP/RN* was the job for left-wing fanatics, certainly not the thing decent Catholic boys got up to… although they did come down to talk about the war and how great it would be to have a [Republican] flute band in Dundee. Resentment gradually built up [as] they didn't seem to mind sharing in the democratic process of TOM, and having a say in the activities we planned.[73]

Michael Taylor concurred:

> As for the Hibees joining street work, it never happened. They would drop down for their copy of *An Phoblacht*, maybe hang about for a bit, letting you know next week was an away game so they wouldn't be around.[74]

The women in the branch also had particular reason to be critical of the AOH. Besides their position on women's reproductive rights, the predominantly male environment and culture was not always congenial to female participation, although attitudes were changing.

In their defence, the Hibees saw their role differently, as perpetuating a traditional notion of Irish solidarity that was rooted in the practices of kinship organisations – the charitable/social function of the AOH, for example, was channelled to organising fund-raising socials for the Irish Republican Prisoners' Dependants' Fund. Likewise, the aspiration to form a flute band that emulated the more politically-advanced Glasgow Republican flute bands and ultimately the colour parties of the IRA, was rooted in the parading tradition of the INF and more recently, the revived AOH. The desire to create a pro-IRA image within the apolitical strictures of the AOH was also expressed in tokenistic acts of rebellion, such as the occasion when the fledgling Lochee Padraig Pearse Band participated, in conjunction with the John F Kennedy Band, in an Easter parade in Gweedore, County Donegal, sporting pin-on Easter lily badges – a mark of allegiance to the Provos – as opposed to the stick-on badges favoured by the Officials, or the 'Stickies' (then Sinn Féin, the Workers' Party).

Certainly, such activities, whether it be parades, fund-raising socials, not to mention travelling through to Celtic games on the supporters' bus, were more congenial than standing on street corners in all seasons trying to get the message across to the unpredictable or apathetic Dundee public. Moreover, campaigning in the city centre on a busy Saturday afternoon carried the risk of being targeted by visiting Rangers supporters, off-duty British soldiers or the relatives thereof, not to mention the implications of being spotted by an unsympathetic employer or challenged by the police. Dundee, although more tolerant, was not immune to sectarianism. Every neighbourhood had its anti-social elements, and most campaigners had the experience of running the gauntlet of sectarian abuse at some point. One campaigner remembered ducking into a local pub for safety after being spotted posting notices about an Irish meeting; another (woman) activist recalled being called a 'Fenian c-' and a 'Fenian b-' by a gang of local Loyalists. Unpleasant as such 'interactions' were, most committed activists learned to develop a thick skin and a sense of perspective – things, after all, were much worse in Glasgow and the Six Counties.

The Hibees were infinitely more comfortable in their own trusted social circle, on their own territory. Lochee was considered safer than other parts of Dundee – a perception that was rooted partly in fact but which gained strength over the next generation until it developed into a form of Lochee exceptionalism. Being part of a close-knit, like-minded group, combined with frequent visits to Parkhead and association with Glasgow-based Celtic supporters also served to reinforce and magnify perceptions about the nature and extent of sectarianism in Dundee (Lochee, of course, excepted). Another key factor affecting their aversion to street campaigning in the city centre was their relative youth and lack of political experience compared to the more independent, slightly older 'left' activists.

The branch soldiered on through the summer of 1980 in the same autonomous manner as they had for most of 1979. Thus, it was not until October that they became aware of the problems that had arisen at the national TOM conference in June which saw the SWP and the IMG reassert their organisational control over the movement. In a bulletin published by Camden and Islington TOM, the branch stated, 'the debate exemplified some of the worst methodological procedures employed by the left', to which the East London branch added, 'the conference was shamefully packed by IMG and SWP members, many of whom were not members of TOM' who went on 'to take over the movement for their own ends and change the emphasis from an anti-imperialist movement to a human rights campaign'.⁷⁵

The 'Political Status' motion was rejected on the basis that it would alienate potential support, mainly from the Labour Party. Instead, the conference agreed to sponsor the 'Charter 80' campaign, which invited support for the five demands of the prisoners 'irrespective of whether you support or not [their] actions, ideology or political affiliation'.⁷⁶ As the name implied, Charter 80 was modelled on Charter 77, the campaign initiated that year by a small group of Czech artists, intellectuals and other political dissidents – many of whom had lost their official positions in academic or public life following the Soviet invasion of 1968 – who criticised their government for violations of specific human rights, such as freedom of speech and freedom of conscience guaranteed under various international conventions. Charter 77 aimed to encourage a broad appeal: consequently, it was deliberately and expressly 'anti-political'.⁷⁷ Not surprisingly, the Socialist Republicans in Dundee TOM saw it as a counter-revolutionary move which, having the look of bourgeois democracy, gave the forces of western capitalism a launch pad from which to attack and undermine the communist states of East and Central Europe. 'I was opposed to being in any way associated with it', Malone affirmed. More pertinently, however, the name Charter 80 carried with it the implication that the imprisoned guerrilla fighters of the IRA and INLA were not revolutionaries waging a war of liberation against a foreign army of occupation, but dissidents. Representatives and supporters of the Republican movement came to a similar conclusion. Sinn Féin had little time for a campaign that denied the political nature of the prison struggle and the wider struggle that underpinned it. The London support group of the IRSP put it bluntly:

> In claiming that our prisoners are "dissidents", the campaign is guilty of a misnomer. They are prisoners of war. Its appeal for human rights is tacit acceptance of British colonial domination of our country. To reduce the struggle to a human rights issue is to evade the nature of the problem.⁷⁸

Hunger Strike

The changes within the organisational outlook of TOM again led the Dundee activists to reconsider their membership of it. All such considerations were put aside, however, with the announcement that, after four years of struggling to regain Political Status from an increasingly intransigent British government, the Blanketmen of Long Kesh were to embark on a hunger strike. In a long and detailed editorial, *AP/RN* traced the origins of the crisis from the withdrawal of Political Status in 1976 to the systematic efforts to break the struggle by torture, harassment and lengthy periods of solitary confinement. It concluded by calling on 'all those who do not want the prisoners to die to protest vigorously and at a level which will pale all past activities into insignificance, and to mobilise thousands on the streets in a force which will tear lumps out of British intransigence'.[79]

Of around 400 Blanketmen, seven, drawn from the Six Counties were chosen to lead the strike – Brendan Hughes, Tommy McKearney, Ray McCartney, Tom McFeeley, Sean McKenna, Leo Green and John Dixon – the number seven representing the seven signatories of the Easter proclamation. The hunger strike went ahead on Monday, 27 October – timed strategically to reach its critical point at Christmas; to increase the moral pressure on the British government to reach a settlement before one of the prisoners died. The pressure was ramped up on 1 December when three women in Armagh Jail – Mairead Farrell, Mary Doyle and Mairead Nugent – joined the strike, and in mid-December when they were joined by another thirty men in Long Kesh.

As time was literally a matter of life and death, a broad front approach was called for. In Ireland, this was organised under the banner of the National H-Block Committee, which included Sinn Féin, the IRSP and the Relatives Action Committee, as well as church and community groups. There was also a subtle shift in emphasis on the part of Sinn Féin and others in the prison campaign from winning Political Status to pressing for the five demands. Mass demonstrations were organised in Ireland, followed by similar demonstrations all over the world. In those early days, there was a feeling that there was everything to play for. John Malone recalled:

> We naively felt that the mass street mobilisations in Ireland and throughout the world would provide impetus and inspiration to

the Brit left. After all they weren't being asked to support "terrorism", i.e., revolutionary war, but to organise activities to win the demands of the hunger strikers and of equal importance save lives.

Indeed, the call to support the five demands was entirely compatible with the policy of TOM and of the Charter 80 campaign it sponsored, which had also been endorsed by Labour MPs, trade union leaders, cultural figures, and various other representatives of civil society.[80] The campaign got off to a promising start. In England, a 5,000-strong march in London on 15 November, was the largest Irish demonstration in the English metropolis for many years. The march, organised under the auspices of the Campaign for Withdrawal' to mark the sixtieth anniversary of partition, attracted a broad spectrum of liberal-left-Irish support. Understandably, for reasons of morale, propaganda and tactics, Sinn Féin-*AP/RN* chose to focus on the contingent rallying behind the 'Don't Let The Irish Prisoners Die' banner, and interpreted the large turnout as evidence of the improved political consciousness of the British population.[81] The event was also worthy of note as it included one of the last public appearances of the one surviving child of James Connolly, Nora Connolly O'Brien, a staunch defender of the POWs, prior to her death in June 1981.[82] In Dundee, the local TOM activists organised a number of activities around the hunger strike. Not all acts of Irish solidarity in this period can be attributed to the group. For example, in the early hours of Remembrance Sunday, a large pro-IRA slogan was painted on the war memorial on top of Dundee Law. According to the police who discovered it, the slogan, which was painted on the side of the memorial where the memorial wreaths were to be laid consisted of three rows of words covering an area of three to four feet and referred to IRA men killed by British troops. The Council's parks' manager, who was subsequently contacted by the police, later claimed that that he had anticipated 'something like this might happen' and 'had a painter on standby'. By the time the ceremonial party ascended the Law a few hours later the words had been well-covered; nevertheless, the Secretary of the local British Legion declared himself 'horrified', opining that such a 'stupid' and 'idiotic' act 'only succeeded in ridiculing the perpetrators and their cause'. Labour Lord Provost James Gowans cut a more diplomatic tone, stating that that he while he sympathised with 'the death of anyone anywhere and unnecessary death sickened [him]', 'these types of slogans didn't help' and 'certainly [weren't] necessary to remind [him] of what [was] happening in Ireland'.[83] Whatever the opinions of the ceremonial party, the graffiti was a conspicuous attempt by Republican sympathisers to drive home a political point about the presence of British troops in Ireland.

Earlier that week, the *Dundee Courier* carried a letter from Secretary of the Dundee Labour Party, George Galloway, in which he stated that the British government could avert an 'explosion of unparalleled violence' by 'recognising the obvious – that the republican prisoners in the Maze ARE in special category', and recommended that free association be granted in extension to the civilian-style clothing already promised. 'With the explosive and emotional issue of prison conditions out of the way', he concluded, 'the Government could then get down to finding agreement to the only possible long term solution – British military and political withdrawal from Ireland'.[84] The letter was a prelude to the unveiling, on 22 December 1980, of Dundee West Constituency Labour Party's plan – as discussed with Dundee TOM in the summer of 1979 – for an initiative on Northern Ireland, to be put to the Party's Scottish conference in Perth on 13–15 March.

> 'The Dundee Resolution', as it was termed, consisted of the following five points:
>
> 1. The introduction of a Bill of Rights on Northern Ireland as demanded by the 1971 Trades Union Congress.
>
> 2. The repeal of all repressive legislation, including the Emergency Provisions (Northern Ireland) Act.
>
> 3. The replacement of the RUC with a non-sectarian police force acceptable to people of both communities.
>
> 4. The withdrawal of British troops to barracks pending their complete withdrawal.
>
> 5. Recognition that the constitutional destiny of Ireland is the concern of the Irish people as a whole and that the

British Government should hand over power in Northern
Ireland to the United Nations so that the international
community can devise a means of ascertaining the wishes
of the entire Irish people.

Such an initiative, it was claimed, 'would open new possibilities for the Irish people to work towards an end to the partition of their country towards attaining their long-cherished goal of a united, democratic Ireland, free from all discrimination and sectarianism'.[85]

Meanwhile, as the hunger strike neared its critical stage in mid-December, Dundee TOM organised a demonstration from Charleston housing scheme through Lochee into the city centre. The march attracted over a hundred people, many of whom were from the local area – including the Padraig Pearse AOH/Celtic Supporters' group – plus members of the local left and other independently minded Irish sympathisers. If the numbers compared unfavourably with similar marches in Glasgow, the opposition was negligible – the handful of Loyalist hecklers who awaited in the city centre were also unarmed. Indeed, the police, who were drafted in from local sub-stations to escort the march, seemed resentful of their role as superannuated traffic wardens and were equally perplexed as to the relevance of the Irish issue to Dundee. Unsurprisingly, the demonstration failed to make the local press, which was preoccupied with the most controversial issue of the moment – Dundee's twinning with Nablus on 18 November, the first such link to be established with any Palestinian city by any municipality in the world since the emergence of the town twinning movement after the Second World War.

This relatively sedate affair contrasted with the demonstration in Glasgow the following week, less than two days after the hunger strike ended. The march, which was held under the auspices of the Glasgow H-Block/Armagh Committee, was unremarkable by Glasgow standards: Roystonhill in north-east Glasgow, where it took place, was an area of large Irish settlement, impromptu Irish marches were not unusual – indeed, one local resident commented that they happened every other weekend – and there were no plans to march into the city centre, hence little threat of Loyalist opposition. Nevertheless, for the Dundee contingent, the deployment of mounted police on a political demonstration – unknown in Dundee since the unemployment riots of the 1920s – remained an unfamiliar, unnerving experience.

The hunger strike was called off at 7.46 pm on Thursday, 18 December – quite literally at the last hour, with Sean McKenna on the brink of death – in anticipation of a deal contained within the pages of a 34-page document drawn up by the Northern Ireland Office and sent to Catholic churchmen in the Six Counties, one of whom had revealed its content to the hunger strikers. In addition to 'civilian-style clothes' already conceded, it made concessions on the other four demands; viz., eight letters, four parcels and four visits per month; free association at evenings and weekends, vocational and educational training, and a commitment to reinstate remission. Within hours of the prisoners calling off their strike, however, the government claimed that there had been no deal and the hunger strikers 'had been persuaded to give up because they finally accepted – something they had resisted until yesterday – that the government would not budge on political status'.[86] Moreover, the 'civilian-style clothes' amounted to the replacement of traditional British prison denims with US-style prison garb of oversized garishly-coloured trousers and tops.[87] It became obvious that the prisoners had been duped, leaving them little option but to continue their protest and deeming another hunger strike extremely likely.

If the commitment of their pro-Republican supporters was beyond question, the hopes raised by the broad-based London march were short-lived. In short, outside of Ireland, mass mobilisation did not occur. Any attempts to nurture popular support for the hunger strikers proved ineffective against the weight of British propaganda and the general lack of coverage in the British media. Recognition of this fact led Bobby Sands, contemplating a second hunger strike, which he as O/C of the IRA prisoners was destined to lead, to write to *Troops Out* that he felt 'uneasy at the Tory government's ability to detach the English people from the question of the H-Blocks during the first hunger strike'. Continuing to engage in optimum tactics, however, he added:

> The hope for change exists. TOM and our socialist brothers and sisters are that hope. I appeal to the people of England to listen to TOM so that their awareness of the Irish conflict may grow.[88]

If, as Ruan O'Donnell stated, 'the hunger strikes were a stringent test of the capacity of the British left and their ostensible allies', it was a test which – to many supporters of Irish insurrectionary republicanism, including those in Dundee – they failed to pass.[89] Malone recalled, 'If anything, the hunger strikes exposed the impotence not only of TOM but the Brit left generally'. In Scotland especially, experience of the first hunger strike served to widen the gulf that existed between the British left and the pro-Republican element.

In December 1980, the IMG walked out of a meeting of the *ad hoc* Scottish Hunger Strike Action Committee to mobilise support for the Glasgow march if it did not abandon the slogan 'Victory to the Hunger Strikers'.[90] This was particularly ironic given that, in the early 1970s, the IMG had adopted the slogan 'Victory to the IRA', the only British left group to do so.[91] Indeed, the IMG's more advanced position on Ireland had initially led John Malone and Michael Taylor to support it to the extent of selling its paper, *Socialist Challenge*, after leaving the SWP in 1977. Despite his reservations, Malone continued to do so until the summer of 1980. His assessment of the organisation is typically illuminating:

> The first thing I'll say about the IMG is they didn't share the SWP's crass populism and subservience to economic struggles... Much of the space in [their] paper was given over to the application of revolutionary Marxist theories to a diversity of ideas such as literature, art and similar subjects which most of the Brit left felt didn't bear much relevance to labour movement struggles. The IMG also enjoyed a good working relationship with autonomous movements such as the Black Liberation Movement active in some of the immigrant communities in England, and the Women's and Gay Liberation Movements. They were equally strong on anti-racism and anti-colonialism, which was deeply ingrained in the predominantly white militant working class as a legacy of England's imperial history. The IMG also enjoyed a better reputation on Ireland, flowing, no doubt, from their activism on black nationalism, and against colonialism, racism and discrimination.
>
> The difference between the IMG and the SWP was more to do with style and content than principle. The one significant

difference between them, however, was that, at one time, the IMG called for 'Victory to the IRA' and the SWP never has.

It has been said that the SWP were always in danger of getting their tongues rammed up the arse of anyone who they thought of in the vaguest of terms as a potential trade union militant. The IMG were equally obscene, but in another way. I have never before or since had such dealings with an organisation whose members were such abject slaves to bureaucratic planning. I once had the experience of participating in a Scottish conference – I believe aggregate was the term – held in the IMG's premises, a book shop in Queen Street, Glasgow. Most of the afternoon was spent listening to opposing factions inside the IMG arguing back and forth over various points in the minutest detail. I thought I was in danger of spending the rest of my life in that room. The chairman was on the point of winding up the discussion when a member of one of the factions put up his hand on a point of order and proceeded to bore everyone to death for the next 20–30 minutes. Everyone, that is, who was not of the 'form a committee, form a sub-committee faction' of Marxist-Leninism, if it isn't a perversion of the term Marxist-Leninism to describe those people as such. [Thus,] when my 'association' with the IMG ended, it wasn't a traumatic decision. Nor did it involve a lot of soul-searching.

It was this obsession with bureaucratic procedure that enabled the IMG, in alliance with the SWP, to manoeuvre their way into positions of leadership in the national TOM from where they could shape and control its policy.

The failure of the IMG to support the Glasgow march in December was exceeded by the actions of the SWP who pulled out of a meeting of the Glasgow H-Block/Armagh Action Committee to mobilise for a march from Roystonhill to the City Hall, Candleriggs, on 14 February, claiming that it was 'ill-timed', moreover, that the committee was controlled by Sinn Féin or, alternatively Sinn Féin and the RCG.[92] This was equally ironic given the SWP's own attempts to gain organisational control over the TOM. On this occasion, however, any plans to do the same with the Glasgow Committee were thwarted by the Republican majority who had remained wary of the British left since the ill-fated Troops Out march of 21 April 1979.⁹³ Despite calls to ban it by several local councillors, reinforced by a fear-mongering unionist press, the march went ahead. At various points along the route, the demonstrators were assailed by squads of Loyalists – many of whom been bussed in from Orange Lodges across west-central Scotland and the North of Ireland – culminating in a battle, appropriately, at John Knox Street.⁹⁴ Over the course of the demonstration, 157 arrests were made, mostly of Loyalists, including Pastor Jack Glass and two other Protestant ministers.⁹⁵ Still, the marchers pressed on through to the City Halls to become the first group of Irish political demonstrators to reach Glasgow city centre in ten years.

Unlike the Troops Out march of April 1979, it was an unequivocal success. For the small band of Dundee supporters in attendance, it was an affirmation of their pro-Republican position. It also threw into sharp relief the ideological differences that existed between pro-Republican Irish solidarity campaigners in Scotland and the British left. Indeed, the same day that the Glasgow march took place, the TOM held a conference in London which the SWP chose to attend, including those who were also members of Dundee TOM who claimed to represent the branch.⁹⁶ While this itself was of little concern to the pro-Republican majority, the attempts of the SWP to sabotage the Glasgow march (the IMG did, reluctantly, support it) was the final straw. At the end of February 1981, the Dundee branch finally called time on TOM, and formed an independent Irish solidarity committee, just as the second hunger strike was set to begin.

On 1 March, the fifth anniversary of the withdrawal of Special Category Status, Bobby Sands embarked on hunger strike, the first of a cohort of four Blanketmen to do so over the next three weeks. Unlike the first hunger strike, large shows of public support were slow to materialise. Inside the jail, the prisoners were aware of a 'definite lack of enthusiasm', that 'marches and demonstrations were not drawing the numbers needed to seriously worry the Brits', and their 'only hope was to mobilise national and international opinion, [which] didn't seem to be happening'.⁹⁷ In Scotland, plans to organise a national, i.e., all-Scotland march in Glasgow on Saturday, 4 April were beset by other problems. For the past years, the numbers on marches in support of the Republican prisoners, though undeniably smaller than those in Ireland, had been slowly growing. For example, the Bloody Sunday march in Blackhill in January 1979 attracted around 800 people, the Troops Out/anti-H-Block march in April 1979 drew a similar number, the post-hunger strike march in December 1980 an estimated 1,000, and the march in February 1981 around 1,500. As the hunger strike progressed, support continued to grow. Around 3,000 people were expected to attend the march in April, which would have made it the largest Irish political march in Scotland in the present phase of the war and the greatest show of support for the prisoners to date. Meanwhile, rallied by a visit from Iain Paisley – who had 'intervened' on behalf of his jailed brethren following the February march – the forces of Scottish Loyalism had vowed to 'stop or disrupt' it, or indeed any other activities in Scotland deemed conducive to the spread of 'Romanism and Republicanism'.[98]

Amidst warnings of 'escalating sectarianism', the Secretary of State for Scotland, advised by the convenor of Strathclyde Police, called a ban on all public processions in the Strathclyde region for the next three months, with the exception of traditional, non-political marches held regularly before 1971.[99] Thus the AOH and the Orange Order escaped the ban. The march organisers (Glasgow H-Block/Armagh Committee) responded by calling an open-air rally, which, lacking the colourful atmosphere of a parade and the presence of the Republican flute bands, did not draw the same numbers or have the same impact.

The election of Bobby Sands as MP for Fermanagh and South Tyrone provided a much-needed morale boost to the prisoners and their supporters everywhere. John Malone reflected:

> It made me think of a similar event in Ireland's past when Jeremiah O'Donovan Rossa, imprisoned Fenian leader, was elected Member of Parliament for Tipperary... At the time of his election, Marx wrote, 'The Irish have played a capital joke on the English Government by electing 'convict felon' O'Donovan Rossa'. More than a century later the nationalist electorate of Fermanagh and South Tyrone played a similar 'capital joke' on the Brits by electing a similar 'convict felon', Bobby Sands... It has to be said it was a victory, not only for the H Block prisoners and the political status battle, but for the Irish people and their

Chapter 9 – A Legacy Reclaimed 1970–85

legitimate war of liberation to determine the future of their nation. As this historical victory sent shock waves around the world, it occurs to me that a lot of shite went down the toilet with it. Most of this concerned the 'principle' that had guided Brit strategy for the past ten-twelve years... namely, that the IRA was and is a minority, and has no popular support... I'd lost count of how many times I had listened to Brit lackey politicians... all basically saying the same thing: 'if the IRA believe they have a mandate for their actions (I presumed they meant revolutionary guerrilla war) then let them put it to the test at the ballot box'... Well, the Irish people took them at their word and a mandate was sought and won...

The response of the Brits to Bobby Sands' victory was a salutary reminder that if you play the game by the rules laid down by the bourgeoisie then you haven't a fuckin hope... legislation was rushed through parliament barring 'convict felons' from standing in elections. This went hand-in-glove with speeches, statements and reactionary rhetoric from Brit politicians saying that that the parliamentary process does not exist to sanction 'murder', 'terrorism' and other 'outrages'.

The death of Bobby Sands in the early hours of Tuesday 5 May 1981 sent shock waves around the world. People who had previously been indifferent to the prisoners' struggle were genuinely shocked that the government had allowed an MP to die, as indeed were many seasoned Irish solidarity campaigners. Michael Taylor reflected, 'it was a lesson in how ruthless British imperialism could be'. Others were moved by the young Irishman's courage and bravery. A young future campaigner recalled sitting on a bus the five days after Sands' death: 'Three well-dressed older women were sitting in front of me, on their way home from church. "I see that Bobby Sands died", one of them said. "What a brave man", a second replied. And the third, "Yes, very brave". It seems a small thing now, but at the time, to have that affirmation after all the negative propaganda – I could have wept'.

Two days before, 100,000 people had followed Bobby Sands' coffin as it made its three-and-a-half-mile journey from his family home in Twinbrook to Milltown Cemetery:

As I watched Bobby Sands' funeral on TV and the long procession of mourners disappearing over the horizon... I was put in mind of the stories I had heard about the first Christians [who] were ripped apart [while] the Roman mob cheered. Their only defence was their Christian faith and moral principles... So it was with the hunger strikers... In the same way that the spectacle of the deaths in arena was [directed] by Roman imperialists, so British imperialism in Ireland [presided over] the massacre in the H Blocks. With each new death, the 'mobs' in the Brit lackey press 'cheered', backing their imperial British masters... In the Brit's war against the prisoners, all the tanks, guns and manpower were no match for the moral principles, not only of the prisoners themselves, but of the Irish people who demonstrated qualities of courage, determination and bravery that the Brits, with all their material superiority hadn't a snowball's chance in hell of matching... It's something I'll never forget. To see the support for the Republican POWs demonstrated on such a gigantic scale. The massive display of mourning that accompanied the funerals of Bobby Sands and the nine hunger strikers that followed him. Even the Brit press, servile and quisling as it is at its worst, could not ignore the colossal outpouring of grief that accompanied the funerals of the hunger strikers, both in Ireland and throughout the world.

Another thing was that seeing the Irish people as human beings, and each new death as a human tragedy, was discouraged by the British imperialist bourgeoisie, especially those sections of it that controlled the 'free press'. Whoever said that there is equality in death must have been holidaying on the moon during the hunger strikes. The Brits continued as they started. From the first death to the last, the hunger strikers were invariably referred to in such terms as 'hardened', 'dogmatic' and 'fanatical'... the lid was screwed down tight on any media coverage that was perceived as sympathetic for the suffering of their families [and] of those murdered by the Brits or 'indigenous' mercenaries as the RUC or UDR.[100]

The Dundee Hunger Strike Action Committee

As the death of Bobby Sands was followed by that of Francis Hughes, Raymond McCreesh and Patsy O'Hara, the campaign gathered momentum. The deaths of the hunger strikers also changed the nature of the campaign, as paper sales and leafletting sessions conducted by a handful of core supporters were augmented by black flag vigils and mass pickets of up to fifty people stretching the breadth the City Square. A Dundee Hunger Strike Action Committee was formed in alliance with the RCG, whose supporters in Glasgow had initiated the Glasgow Hunger Strike Action Committee (GHSAC) several months before. Its first public meeting, which included a showing of the film, 'Ireland's Hunger Strike', attracted an audience of around fifty people.[101]

One effect of the ban on political marches in Scotland's most populous region was to channel Republican energy into the legal parades of the AOH to which many young Irish-Catholics remained connected through its affiliated flute bands. Thus, the atmosphere at the annual AOH St Patrick's Day march, which took place in Coatbridge, was fraught with emotion when the platform speakers announced that they could not support the hunger strikers as their actions were akin to suicide. Interestingly, this recalls the hunger strike of Terence MacSwiney, when theologian Father Bernard Vaughan stated that he 'could not administer the last rites to anyone…deliberately dying of hunger striking', and was taken to task by young Dundee-based curate and IRA captain, Father John Fahy. Fahy's ascription of MacSwiney's actions as 'heroically moral' was as representative of the views of young Republican-minded Hibees in 1981 as it was of the community for whom he spoke in 1920.[102] A mass exodus from the AOH followed, as bands flocked to the Republican Band Alliance, including the Padraig Pearse band of Lochee, for whom – unlike many AOH bands named after Catholic saints and martyrs – a change of name was unnecessary.

The new 'Lochee Republicans', as they subsequently styled themselves, also overcame their aversion to street politics, as, motivated by a moral imperative, they participated enthusiastically – subject to football fixtures – in the Saturday afternoon pickets where they helped to provide safety in numbers. The upsurge in activity in support of the hunger strikers also attracted opposition from Loyalist counter-demonstrators. The squad of

Scottish Loyalists 'assigned' to the Dundee protests formed a motley crew; the author recalls standing close enough to one of them to see the inscription 'Remember 1906' – presumably a misspelling of 1690 – tattooed on his arm. On more than one occasion, Loyalist counter-demonstrators would lunge forth at the picketers who were forced to fight back to defend themselves. Malone recalled:

> The women who stood on the pickets...took their share of verbal abuse, being called Fenian/Papist/IRA sluts, whores [and worse] by people with accents certainly not indigenous to [Dundee]. They all displayed exemplary qualities of determination and guts[103].

Another consequence of taking up regular occupancy of the City Square was that the campaigners came up against the local byelaws – one of which required all parties organising an event in the City Square to apply for a licence – and the police who enforced them. This too had its comical moments, as, for example, when the Irish proprietor of a travelling carousel who had booked the square, stated he had no objections to sharing the space, whereupon he put on a tape of raucous rebel songs, picked up a placard and joined the protest. One campaigner recalled, initially the police 'pretty much left us alone', although they did warn them to keep their chants of 'Victory to the Hunger Strikers' down a few decibels lest they commit a breach of the peace. As time progressed, however, and particularly with the appearance of the Loyalists on the scene, the harassment stepped up as banners and newspapers were confiscated, bags were searched and protestors were charged with numerous breaches of the City Square byelaw.

On 29 August, seven days after the funeral of Micky Devine, the last of the ten hunger strikers to die, the DHSAC organised a march from Charleston into to the city centre which attracted around 200 people, mainly young supporters from the wider Lochee area, plus the Iranian students, the GHSAC, and the Edinburgh RCG (who also operated under the banner of the Edinburgh Irish Solidarity Committee). The SWP, however, refused to support it, or to print the publicity leaflets, on the assumption that the DHSAC was a front for the RCG – an assumption

Malone was quick to repudiate on behalf of the non-RCG majority.[104] Nevertheless, some members of the SWP, notably those from a working-class Dundee background, continued to support the pickets – the ties of friendship, community and class it seems, were more important than party loyalties – with one travelling to Belfast with another pro-Republican activist to attend the internment anniversary demonstration on 9 August.[105]

The Dundee demonstration concluded with two arrests arising from a scuffle in the City Square between one demonstrator and a Loyalist counter-demonstrator – the police also confiscated the papers of the former, on the pretext that they were 'large leaflets' for which he did not have the requisite licence.[106] With seven charges pending from breaches of the City Square byelaw, an investigation by those affected uncovered a loophole which exempted those holding political events from applying for permission, on the principle that the City Square was a protected area of 'Free Speech'. In an unconscious echo of the Dundee Socialists' 'Free Speech' campaign' of 1889, the DHSAC set about organising a defence campaign:

> The idea was floated that we appeal to the local labour movement for their assistance on the basis that 'an injustice to one was an injustice to all', and an attack on the democratic rights of the DHSAC was an attack on the democratic rights of the Dundee proletariat on the whole. I personally was never too confident of success, as I had no memory of the Dundee labour movement ever fighting to defend anything. Nevertheless, credit must be given where it's due and Mike Taylor did more than anyone to pressurise [them] into accepting that the attack on the principle of free speech in the City Square was an issue that couldn't be swept under the carpet. Mike was also an active trade union member, and the advantage of this is that he was seen by the Trades Council as one of their own, and not one of us pro-IRA 'fanatics'. As time passed and piles of petition sheets were returned filled, Mike was increasingly convinced that some form of support was on the agenda. I must confess I was infected with his optimism. At the very least I expected some symbolic gesture from the Trades Council that they were aware of what was going on in their city...

> The actual thing that got them off the hook was a notorious, and what I always felt was a hypothetical 'police dossier' shown to [the Secretary of] the Trades Council by the Chief Constable. According to Mike, the Trades Council were on the point of taking some action[107], when they saw the dossier, after which, they were, presumably, of the opinion that we deserved all we got. We were generally accused of making nuisances of ourselves; in particular, of being hostile and aggressive to passers-by. Allegations were made that women who were indifferent or hostile to our paper selling, leafletting or soliciting for petition signatures were subjected to verbal sectarian abuse and spat on. If there's one thing I can say with absolute certainly is that if such behaviour were true it would've been political suicide. Those pickets were, after all, basic propaganda exercises and the point of them was to bring to the attention of the people of Dundee the massacre unfolding in the H Blocks. We wanted [their] sympathy and, flowing from this, to win their support for the prisoners' demands, and, ultimately, the Dundee Irish Campaign. Also, it goes without saying that if you treat people like shite the last thing you'll get is their sympathy. Despite all the factionalism and feuding within the DHSAC, even when the bitterness and distrust was at its height, there was agreement on certain issues, the most common of which was, regardless of how things turned out; ultimately, whether we had success beyond our wildest imagination or the thing ended in absolute disaster, discretion was all. A balance had to be struck between our principles and offending the local people.

If Dundee Trades Council balked at defending the principle of Free Speech, a more practical and effective form of support came from the SNP MP for Dundee East, Gordon Wilson, who wrote a letter to the Chief Constable on his constituents' behalf, pointing out the letter of the law – namely, the exemption of political activity from the City Square byelaw – and respectfully bidding him to rein in his officers as they were acting extrajudicially.[108] By the time the matter was resolved several months later, however, the hunger strike was long over.

Meanwhile, tensions within the DHSAC were becoming apparent. The perception that the RCG was taking a controlling hand in affairs was alienating some and causing resentment in others. The unity of the group was slowly fragmenting, and the different priorities of the group were pulling it in different directions.

The young Lochee Republicans had no desire to get embroiled in a free speech war with the local police. Besides seeing it as a distraction from the main issue – the hunger strike in particular and the Irish struggle in general – they were, as noted earlier, anxious to keep trouble from their door. Unlike the two Edinburgh-based RCG members on the committee who were mature middle-class professionals in well-paid careers, they were, for the most part, young, working-class school leavers on traineeships, in insecure jobs, or looking for work in a time of high and growing unemployment. Moreover, they had a new focus for their energies in the Republican Band Alliance.

John Malone, who had less to lose in the material sense – being permanently unemployed due to chronic health problems – was prepared to go to the wall on the issue, and criticised 'the Hibs', as he continued to call them, for not doing so. He also continued to offer conditional support to the RCG on the basis of its support for pro-insurrectionary Irish republicanism. Nevertheless, after his experience with the SWP and the IMG, particularly with the Troops Out Movement, he ferociously resisted any attempts to turn the DHSAC into a 'creature' of the RCG. Like his working-class Lochee contemporaries, if not his ideological soulmates, he also resented the patronising attitude of middle-class RCG 'interlopers' who talked down their suggestions, and redrafted leaflets and letters in order to reflect their own political programme:[109]

> Generally, their 'strategy' consisted of long tirades, laying down the law...We were all of us a little insulted that we were viewed as so pig shit thick that we needed...to have the virtues of international solidarity amongst the oppressed classes taught to us in such a patronising manner. If anything was [gained] by being raised in Whitfield, Lochee or similar schemes, it was that we were ever conscious of the motivation and righteousness of those that adopt the strategy of armed struggle to combat the

> material and social deprivation [as well as political oppression] that is the lot of scheme dwellers in Dundee. In fact, we could more easily identify with such struggles as [we recognised] that their lot was a damn sight worse than ours...We all took it for granted that the IRA in Ireland were part of a more general worldwide liberation struggle against the same enemy...the international financial and political structure of imperialism.

On the other hand, Michael Taylor, as the most avowedly anti-imperialist member of the group, was increasingly won over by the RCG's anti-imperialist anti-racist rhetoric, and embraced its political programme so thoroughly and enthusiastically, that at the end of the hunger strike, he made the decision to join the group.

Underpinning it all was the long-drawn-out nature of the hunger strike itself. As the hunger strike dragged on with no resolution in sight, the campaigners became increasingly demoralised – not least at their own inability to influence events – their enthusiasm waned, and the mass pickets became less frequent. The hunger strike was eventually called off on 3 October, with the prisoners stating that they had been robbed of an effective weapon by the Catholic clergy, who had removed the political pressure on the British government to concede their demands by placing moral pressure on the relatives of the hunger strikers themselves.[110]

While Sinn Féin was quick to state that if anyone one suffered a setback it was the British, the Dundee campaigners viewed the ending of the hunger strikes as a massive defeat:[111] Malone recalled: 'The fact that the Irish people and their national liberation movement survived such a traumatic and serious setback [was] a testament to their resilience'. However, the most basic problem facing 'those of us involved in anti-imperialist propaganda in Scotland was that we didn't have revolutionary proletarian communities tempered by more than ten years of a guerrilla war of attrition to fall back on'. Some areas undoubtedly survived better than others. For example, Glasgow had maintained a sympathetic Irish movement for six decades, so the ending of the hunger strikes had little effect on the determination to carry on that existed amongst those of pro-Republican Irish stock. Dundee, on the other hand, suffered more than most – 'since it wasn't a "hot bed" of Republicanism at the time', Malone recalls, 'it was even less so after. This was in spite of the initial success of the mass pickets organised at the beginning, and intermittently, and admittedly in 'bastardised' forms towards the end'.

The Dundee Irish Republican Solidarity Campaign

It only remained for the DHSAC to be put to rest and given a decent burial. A march had been planned for 28 November, due largely to the enthusiasm of the young Lochee Republicans. The most pressing task, however, was to ensure that the Dundee Irish solidarity campaign survived in some shape or form. Michael Taylor recalled: 'Witnessing the massive defeat of the hunger strike made us determined not to lose the gains'. The first item on the agenda of the last business meeting of the DHSAC was a change of name. The one ultimately agreed upon, the Dundee Irish Republican Solidarity Campaign (DIRSC), was, as Malone explained:

> the logical conclusion of our activities over the last few years from the summer of '78. For despite the years of fluctuating, changing priorities, the Dundee Irish Campaign had always emphasised the pro-Republican nature of its solidarity activities and politics. It was obvious that the unyielding commitment to the struggle being waged by the IRA and INLA on behalf of the Irish people should be reflected in the name as well as the actions of the group. For me personally, the name had historical significance as inspired by the heritage and traditions of the Irish national liberation movement.

The DIRSC's first public meeting, a showing of the film, *Prisoner of War*, attracted around forty people, including a group of burly young men from the Dundee University football team who the organisers initially thought were Loyalists come to wreck the meeting. Consequently, the conversation turned to the need to defend public meetings from Loyalist attacks. While that situation never arose in Dundee, marches and street rallies were another matter, and a Free Speech rally in the City Square on 14 November was attacked by the usual squad of Loyalists, who shouted and spat at passers-by who stopped to take leaflets.[112] Such behaviour was repeated at the march on

28 November, which was, otherwise, something of an anti-climax. With the exception of the 30-40-strong flute band, the turn-out (around 150 in total) was lower than that at the march in August – the prime reason being that, since the hunger strike had ended, all sense of urgency had evaporated; correspondingly, the moral force used to appeal to the British left and other humanitarian-minded groups and individuals was considerably weakened. Nevertheless, for those who participated, it was an uplifting experience, and the young Lochee Republicans achieved their ambition of having a Republican flute band – the Bobby Sands RFB from Coatbridge – lead a march from Charleston into the city centre, where a scuffle between a Loyalist counter-demonstrator and a band steward resulted in the arrest of the latter and an ensuing court case which was resolved some months later.

The main speakers were, as at the August march, representatives from the former GHSAC – now the Glasgow Irish Freedom Action Committee (GIFAC), and the Edinburgh RCG. Messages of solidarity were read out by a member of the Iranian Students' Association, and on behalf of the James Connolly IRSP cumann in London. The SWP, although invited, refused to attend. Michael Taylor chaired the rally and John Malone spoke for the DIRSC:

> For the last few days before the march, I wracked my brains for something positive to say considering how morale had absolutely dive bombed since the end of the hunger strike. The best solution I found was in Irish heritage and history... in the character of the Irish people and the liberation movement [to which] they have committed themselves for centuries. On the surface, this heritage might seem, to someone unacquainted with it, an endless catalogue of massacres and outrages culminating in defeats and setbacks for the forces of radicalism, progress and liberation. Yet, remarkably the Irish people and the Republican Movement have shown tremendous resilience for turning events round and perplexing their enemies... So it was with the ending of the hunger strike – another 'difficulty' in the long list that litter the struggle for liberation.

The importance of this Irish resilience in overcoming apparently impossible difficulties has always been recognised by revolutionary theorists and ideologists. Friedrich Engels touched on this in his 'Notes for a History of Ireland':

> The English knew how to reconcile people of the most diverse races with their rule. The Welsh, who held so tenaciously to their nationality and language, have fused completely with the British Empire. The Scottish Celts, though rebellious until 1745, and since then almost completely exterminated first by the government and then by their own aristocracy, do not even think of rebellion.

Yet of the Irish he said:

> Only with the Irish the English could not cope. The reason for this is the enormous resilience of the Irish race. After the most savage repression, after every attempt to exterminate them, the Irish, following a short respite, stood stronger than ever before. It seemed they drew their main strength from the very foreign garrison forced on them in order to oppress them.[113]

Despite all the talk of a new beginning, for the first three months after the march, the DIRSC existed in name only. The young Lochee Republicans drifted back to their trusted social and cultural circles. Michael Taylor, who had joined the RCG after the hunger strike, threw himself into that organisation's campaigning activities with a newfound vigour. His old comrade John Malone also participated half-heartedly in its supporters' group.

In late February 1982, at the instigation of John Malone, the DIRSC was revived and reconstituted around a group of half a dozen core activists. That fact that, like Connolly's Irish Socialist Republican Party, it had more syllables than members, was not considered to be a disadvantage as the Dundee Irish solidarity campaign had never been a mass movement in the first place. The advantage was that they were committed to promoting a more aggressive pro-Republican solidarity. Conditions of membership stipulated that there would be 'no time-servers', i.e., everyone would be expected to pull their weight: correspondingly, all members' opinions would be given equal consideration. Accordingly, invitations were extended to all sympathetic parties, including the RCG, who accepted.

Once back into the routine of paper selling and distributing leaflets, it was evident that 'something had changed'. Malone lamented, 'The old unity had gone. It all seemed so fragmented'. Arguably, that 'unity' had always been transient. Indeed, in the four years of its existence, the broadly pro-Republican solidarity campaign had been held together by the exigencies of the struggle in Ireland, principally, the prison struggle culminating in the hunger strikes. Once that was over there was no critical issue of the same urgency and magnitude to campaign around. In the first few months, the DIRSC concerned itself with highlighting the British government's 'supergrass' strategy.[114] *AP/RN* and *The Starry Plough* continued to attract a steady stream of customers; the days of the mass pickets, however, were over. Consequently, the Scottish Loyalists – who mobilised when Irish Republicans, aka the 'forces of Romanism', appeared to be gaining ground, numerically, territorially or politically – retreated into the background. Despite perceptions of it having 'fragmented', the group reassembled – for example, a twenty-strong Dundee contingent attended a hunger strike commemoration in Glasgow on 15 May, for social and cultural events, and public meetings. General attendance at the latter, however, had dropped since the hunger strike – the bulk of the audience at a showing of *The Patriot Game* and a meeting on 'The British War in Ireland' consisted of half-a-dozen core campaigners and a smattering of Lochee Republicans. A larger number turned out in to hear Francie Molloy of Sinn Féin, fresh from his stint as a candidate in the recent Northern Ireland Assembly elections in October, address a meeting on the Republican movement's electoral strategy – a strategy which, he assured his inquiring audience, would continue to defend the IRA's right to wage war against the British presence in Ireland.[115]

Meanwhile, relations with the RCG, who saw themselves as being in the vanguard of the Irish solidarity movement in Britain, were becoming increasingly strained. At a conference in London on 20 November, entitled 'Building an Irish Solidarity Movement', the key speaker, the RCG's chief ideologue and strategist, David Yaffe (pen name Reed), conceived of a broad front overarching 'national', i.e., British, movement – a network of Irish Solidarity Committees across England, Scotland and Wales – to be 'built on the basis of the two core demands "Victory to the Irish People" and "Troops out Now!"' – a third demand of 'Repatriation of Irish Political Prisoners in English jails' was added later – which would 'reject all sectarianism and seek joint work and unity with any individual or organisation which would help to take the movement forward'.[116] As a corollary of this, support for the Republican movement would not be a condition of membership, as this would alienate potential supporters who could be drawn in on a variety of democratic or humanitarian demands such as the banning of plastic bullets, non-jury Diplock Courts and Repeal of the Prevention of Terrorism Act. Sinn Féin and the IRSP would be invited on marches but not to lead them. Similarly, with military-style Republican flute bands and Irish tri-colours and Starry Plough flags, as this implied support for the Republican movement.

As the RCG's representative in Dundee, Michael Taylor was put in the position of defending and promoting its policies with a view to incorporating the Dundee Irish campaign into the Irish Solidarity movement (ISM). Malone recalled: 'We were equally determined in asserting that the DIRSC was an independent, autonomous solidarity group'. The ensuing debate, in which the small pro-Republican majority prevailed, culminated in the RCG being 'shown the door'. 'This', Malone lamented, 'was the hardest thing to bear' as 'Mike was a friend as well as a comrade going back to the beginning of the whole campaign'.

By the summer of 1983, there were two Irish solidarity groups operating in Dundee: the overtly and unequivocally pro-Republican DIRSC, which focused exclusively on the Irish struggle, and sold Republican newspapers, and the ISM-led Irish Solidarity Committee (DISC), which functioned, in essence, as an off-shoot of the RCG's *FRFI* supporters' group, and sold its eponymously-named newspaper, *Fight Racism! Fight Imperialism*! On Saturday, 13 August, the similarly-fashioned Edinburgh Irish Solidarity Committee travelled through to Dundee to help drum up support for the DISC's launch meeting the following Tuesday. The ensuing meeting, which included a showing of the perennially popular *The Patriot Game*, drew an audience of around 25 people – including the DIRSC and their erstwhile Lochee Hibee confederates – twelve of whom 'pledged to support the Irish people' and to help set up an ISM-affiliated committee.[117] Signatures on a pledge sheet did not always extend to sympathetic action, however, and while the ISM gathered support in England – from Irish political prisoners in English jails,[118] a number of Sinn Féin cumainn, dissident TOM branches, and various left and civil rights groups – it failed to take off in Scotland. Many Scottish activists saw the ISM as a front for yet another British left group, with which they had fundamental differences. The predominantly working-class Republican Band Alliance had had their fill of being exploited and patronised by middle-class leftists. As a spokesperson for the James Connolly RFB later commented: 'We realised we could organise more effectively outside any particular party or grouping. We could be a political entity in our own right'.[119] Such was the reasoning that also led the DIRSC to guard and defend its autonomy with such ferocity.

Underpinning this were issues of class, culture and nationality, whereby overlapping working-class, Scots and Irish identities enhanced and strengthened others and begat a more radical, and distinctly Scottish form of pro-Republican solidarity. While this had a history stretching back to beyond the Tan and Civil Wars to the United Irishmen and United Scotsmen, it now led a new generation of young working-class Scots, who had been reawakened to their Irish identity and common Celtic heritage by the experience of the hunger strikes, to seek a new type of political and cultural engagement with the Irish liberation struggle. It also led many of them to identify strongly with Scottish republicanism and, particularly for those ranked in the bands, to participate in Scottish nationalist events. For example, in the early 1980s, the James Connolly RFB led the annual William Wallace commemoration in Elderslie under the sobriquet of 'The Spirit of Wallace', and the Lochee Padraig Pearse RFB participated in a Scottish Republican march in Stonehaven under the name of 'Misneach Dundeagh'.[120]

That this had implications for the role and nature of Irish solidarity in Scotland, and the type of movement required, was pointed out in a comradely manner in the correspondence columns of *FRFI*. In February 1983, the Organiser of the Scottish Republican Socialist Party (SRSP), Donald Anderson, advised the RCG that that their failure to understand the national struggles in Wales and Scotland was a 'fundamental error' that needed to be addressed if they were to 'understand the role and nature of British imperialism in Ireland and elsewhere'. 'Irish Republicans' he stated, 'can appreciate the Celtic break-up of the British State, for principled as well as tactical reasons, as the struggle is older than capitalism itself'.[121] The question was also taken up by Mike Duffield, co-founder of the GIFAC and member of the RCG, who stated that recognising Scotland's right to self-determination was 'a question of *principle*' which, if deviated from, would [put], English communists in the position of being part of the oppressing force against the Scottish people'. Citing the example of 'the greatest communist Scotland has produced' – John Maclean, who moved from espousing a British revolution to calling for a Scottish Republic within the space of a year on the basis of changed circumstances[122] and the belief that Scottish workers were more advanced than English ones – he concluded: 'There is no other position communists in England and Scotland can take without departing from a clear anti-imperialist position'.[123]

The failure of the RCG to acknowledge, let alone adopt this principle, was proving a sore point for many of its wavering Scottish supporters. The answer was implicit in the title of David Yaffe's' book, *Ireland, the Key to the British Revolution* – the exposition of the theory and strategy driving the formation of the Irish Solidarity movement in November 1982, and which had been developed and refined in the months thereafter. For many Scottish activists, the strategy had one central flaw: namely, it failed to take into account the different relationship of Scotland to the British State, the historic relationship between Scotland and Ireland, and by association, to the national liberation struggle and the Republican movement itself.

Matters came to a head at the ISM's launch conference in London on the weekend of 1–2 October 1983. The final session concerned the relationship between the ISM and the Republican movement. The leading motion, proposed by the RCG's 'Terry Marlowe' (aka Terry O'Halloran) and Michael Holden of Luton Sinn Féin, supported 'the right of self-determination and defended the right of the Irish people to pursue that demand by whatever means they choose'. An amended motion, moved by the GIFAC, together with the SRSP, DIRSC, Mosquito Press, and the Glasgow-based Kashmir Independence Movement, asserted that recognising that right carried with it 'a duty to support the movements chosen to lead the struggle, the methods they used to achieve it, and, consequently called on the ISM to 'give wholehearted, unconditional and uncritical support to all sections of the Republican Movement'. The motion – which was proposed by the Revolutionary Communist League (RCL) after the Glasgow contingent had departed for Scotland amidst accusations of gerrymandering by the organisers[124] – was defeated by a majority vote. In a subsequent statement in its newspaper, the RCG claimed that it 'obliterated the distinction between the movement in the oppressed nation (Ireland) and in the movement in the oppressor nation (Britain)... ignoring the fact... that they are separate and distinct movements with a common goal; the defeat of British imperialist rule in Ireland'. The statement continued: 'The Republican Movement formulates its tactics and strategy in the light of political conditions in Ireland', and the ISM 'must be free to formulate *its* tactics and strategy in the light of political conditions in Britain... to reach out to the widest possible forces and bring them into the anti-imperialist solidarity movement'. Thus, it concluded, 'the GIFAC [*sic*] motion, wrong in principle would be sectarian in practice'; all of which led John Malone to observe, 'What in previous years the RCG had insisted were principles, and we still [did], they now called sectarianism and cited as obstacles to building a solidarity movement'.[125]

On 27 November 1983, following a march to commemorate the sixtieth anniversary of the death of revolutionary republican socialist, John Maclean, GIFAC hosted a conference to initiate a Scottish-based Pro-Republican Irish Solidarity Movement (PRISM). In effect, this was a loose alliance of autonomous groups and organisations, including GIFAC, the SRSP and the DIRSC, plus support from Mosquito Press,[126] all of whom were represented. Support was also received from other quarters, namely, the Tyneside Action Committee on Ireland and the unequivocally pro-IRA Red Action, the Derry IRSP, and Irish (IRA), Welsh and Scottish political prisoners. In due course, the PRISM also drew support from the Republican Band Alliance and the Glasgow IRSP Support Group.

While GIFAC's association with the fervently Maoist Mosquito Press led it to accommodate the latter's views, and indeed some its members to later promote them,[127] at this point, its core group of supporters comprised a broad mix of communist and other independently minded Irish and Scottish Republicans, including one Spanish Civil War veteran. The common denominator, besides their indignation with the Anglocentric perspective of the RCG's Irish Solidarity Movement, was a strong socialist ethic and an unconditional support for insurrectionary Irish republicanism, all of which made them natural allies for the DIRSC, who had already added the GIFAC-produced *Ireland's War* to its list of pro-Republican publications sold in the city.

While the ISM claimed the support of the RCG-led Edinburgh and Dundee Irish Solidarity Committees and Irish Solidarity/Troops Out societies at Glasgow, Edinburgh and Stirling Universities, the latter societies proved to be short-lived. Attempts to establish an Irish Solidarity Society at Dundee University were also voted down by the Students' Association.[128] Elsewhere in Scotland, particularly in the largest centres of Irish population in the west central belt, the majority of Republican support groups, including the Republican Band Alliance and Glasgow Sinn Féin, rebuffed or distanced themselves from it.

Despite the undercurrent of tension, relations between the DIRSC and the RCG's Irish Solidarity Committee remained relatively comradely, a situation that was assisted by the fact that, after the initial push of the ISM in the summer of 1983, the RCG in Dundee prioritised its anti-apartheid activities over its Irish solidarity ones. Indeed, members of the DIRSC participated in some of these activities, including a 12-hour picket on 3–4 November 1983 in solidarity with the City of London Anti-Apartheid Group's non-stop picket of the South African Embassy in London. Still, conducting an Irish solidarity campaign remained an uphill struggle, particularly in Dundee, which unlike Glasgow, lacked the support network of a large and dynamic Irish-Catholic community, and the benefit of a regenerated Irish Republican tradition from which the majority of Dundee's fifth- and sixth-generation Irish population were still too estranged to relate.

The ex-Hibees, by contrast, inured by their experience of the hunger strikes, had come to embrace the Irish Republican tradition as part of their heritage. The bulk of their collective energy, however, was now directed towards social and cultural activities, such as fund-raising for Irish Republican prisoners, and membership of imitative military-style flute bands. The fact that such activities were conducted in a milieu which was by its nature, if not its intention, exclusionary – inextricably linked to Celtic Supporters' Clubs and a male-orientated culture originating in the AOH – served to discourage a large section of the wider community, not least those elements of the Dundee Irish diaspora whose mixed Scots-Irish heritage had blurred ethnic lines across the generations. For their part, the fact that this environment enabled them to link into a wider network of flute bands and Irish associational culture undoubtedly served to strengthen their identification with, and loyalty to the Republican movement. However, unlike the original (James Connolly) Republican Flute Band in the early days of the band alliance, the Padraig Pearse, along with a growing number of other new bands, had no real programme of political education; nor did their undoubted enthusiasm for militant Irish republicanism extend to proactive campaigning beyond their own social and cultural circle.

The ISM's Dundee committee, always secondary to the RCG's less contentious, less divisive and ultimately more successful anti-apartheid campaign, was eventually jettisoned in its favour. The Edinburgh Irish Solidarity Committee, the larger and more active of the RCG/ISM's two Scottish-based groups, was eventually beaten off the streets by Loyalist thugs in 1984. In Dundee, least of any other Scottish city, that was never a problem. The counter-side to this was that the absence of opposition and quietly tolerant attitude of the vast majority of the local population was not enough to sustain a vital proactive Irish solidarity campaign, especially one with a radical political perspective. And if an advanced understanding of radical Irish republicanism was rare, attempts to develop it were continually hampered by lack of money, resources and enthusiasm arising from the different perceptions of what constituted solidarity, and indeed, what constituted republicanism. Given the strength of opinion and the personalities involved, some fragmentation was perhaps inevitable. Unlike Glasgow, however, Dundee was not big enough to withstand it. By 1985, the drive to build on the gains of the hunger strike, which was most keenly felt in its immediate aftermath, had dissipated. The burden of shouldering such a campaign was taking its toll, mentally, physically and emotionally, on the small number of people doing it. In the early spring of that year, the DIRSC too was wound up.

Endnotes to Chapter 9

1. From 'On the Blanket' [chorus], Mick Hanly, 1880.
2. John Malone, unpublished memoirs [hereafter JM memoirs].
3. On 22 March 1973, Caroline Renehan, the daughter of Glasgow Sinn Féin Secretary, Persis, was arrested alongside brothers James and John Sweeney of County Donegal, in the act of delivering 630 sticks of gelignite and 150 detonators to the house of Father Bartholomew Burns at St Teresa's RC Church, Possilpark. James Sweeney was found to be carrying £1,768, a small amount of Irish currency and a cheque from the Internees' Dependants' Fund for £1, and a search of Caroline's handbag revealed her Sinn Féin membership card. Although both claimed they had been lured into the operation by the now-fugitive Father Burns – Caroline's lawyer claimed she had been an 'unwilling pawn' of 'other unscrupulous people – she and Sweeney were convicted and sentenced to five and seven years respectively. *Belfast Telegraph*, 3 & 4 May 1973; *Evening Herald* (Ireland), 18 May 1973.
4. Rules of evidence were also inverted, placing the onus on the defendant to prove that a statement had not been given voluntarily – a virtual impossibility in the circumstances, which further encouraged interrogators to use brutality in order to extract confessions.
5. Ernie O'Malley, *On Another Man's Wound* [1939] (Dublin: Anvil Press, 1979), p152.
6. Peter Taylor, 'Reporting Northern Ireland', in *The British Media in Ireland* (Campaign for Free Speech in Ireland, 1978).
7. JM memoirs.
8. A fellow pupil at St Mary's approved school, Glasgow, in the late 1960s, recalled how Frank Malone was widely admired for his knowledge of Irish history, of which the other boys – including himself, also a Lochee boy of Irish extraction – were largely ignorant. Conversation with Alex Cahill, 1991.
9. JM memoirs.
10. The IS's campaign slogan of the moment was 'No Deal with Healey', a summation of the TUC's rejection of the wage controls introduced by Chancellor of the Exchequer, Denis Healey, as a prerequisite to securing a £2.3 billion loan from the International Monetary Fund to help bring down inflation.
11. JM memoirs.
12. JM memoirs.
13. JM memoirs.
14. Joseph M Bradley, 'Wearing the Green: A History of Nationalist Demonstrations among the Diaspora in Scotland', in (T G Fraser (ed), *The Irish Parading Tradition: Following the Drum* (Basingstoke: Macmillan Press, 2000), pp111–28.

15   Dundee Oral History Project, reminiscence group discussions on 'Race, Religion and Politics', conducted 1988.
16   Built as a ring road (Scotland's first dual carriageway) in the 1930s, the Kingsway had since been surrounded by post-war housing schemes. However, it remained Dundee's main by-pass.
17   *Dundee Courier*, 29 June 1974; *Sporting Post*, 29 June 1974.
18   McGlone initially obtained the keys to the Bog Mission Hall, of which the AOH was granted planning permission for 'change of use', from Dundee City Council, a number of whose members in the 1970s and early 1980s were also in the Knights of Columba. For example, one ex-councillor and member of the latter order told the author that he inducted a well-known Lochee councillor who 'wasn't even a Catholic'.
19   *Forward*, 18 March 1911.
20   Bradley, 'Wearing the Green', p120.
21   At the Dundee rally in 1974, the Scottish divisions of the AOH had assured representatives of the Board of Erin of 'their support for the Order's aim of achieving Irish unity through peaceful and constitutional means'. *Belfast Telegraph*, 15 August 1974.
22   *Belfast Telegraph*, 29 and 30 June 1978.
23   In 1975, McManus told a British television reporter that had been 'on record' for supporting the Provisional IRA 'for quite a long time'. *New York Times*, 21 September 1979. McManus's eldest brother, Patrick, O/C of the South Fermanagh Brigade IRA, was killed in a premature explosion near Swanlibar on the Cavan-Fermanagh border on 15 July 1958. Another brother, Frank, was a Nationalist Unity MP for Fermanagh and South Tyrone from 1970 to 1974.
24   *Irish Times*, 7 September 1971. The fine was paid anonymously.
25   The letter also maintained that the British government gave into pressure from the Orange Order to partition Ireland in 1921 knowing that that it would allow the Orange Order' to impose its [own] brand of apartheid'. *Belfast Telegraph*, 1 July 1978.
26   *Belfast Telegraph*, 1 July 1978.
27   'Home Soldier Home', shown at the UTOM national conference in June 1978. (*Belfast Telegraph*, 1 June 1978).
28   JM memoirs.
29   JM memoirs.
30   *Troops Out*, April 1979; *An Phoblacht/Republican News* [hereafter *AP/RN*], 31 March 1979. Fortunately for Johnson, his interviewers appeared not to have read *AP/RN* and he got the job. Johnson remained a reporter with D C Thomson, and a 'correspondent' for Dundee UTOM until September 1979 when he moved to London to take up a position at the *New Musical Express*. Under the name of 'Brian Johnston', he also wrote to *AP/RN* on the subject of popular music and

CHAPTER 9 – A LEGACY RECLAIMED 1970–85

its ability to address the Irish liberation struggle. *AP/RN*, 22 November 1980. Johnson continued to be involved in Irish solidarity campaigns throughout the hunger strikes and thereafter, and remained in touch with his old comrades in Dundee until his death from cancer, in his mid-thirties, in 1988.

31 JM memoirs.
32 JM memoirs.
33 Interview with Michael Taylor, 29 October 2021.
34 In a BBC Scotland television documentary, *The War Next Door: Scotland and the Troubles*, Chris Bambery, who was also the IMG's full-time organiser in Glasgow at the time (although he left the following May and joined the SWP in December) – claimed that he was the organiser of the 21 April march, and had made the decision to stop it. *The War Next Door: Scotland and the Troubles* Episode 2, 19 November 2019.
35 *The War Next Door: Scotland and the Troubles* Episode 2, 19 November 2019.
36 More specifically, of the attitudes engendered by the Church of Scotland's sectarian report on the 'Irish Menace' in 1923.
37 JM memoirs.
38 *Troops Out*, May 1979.
39 JM memoirs.
40 Interview with Steve Keenan, 8 November 2021.
41 JM memoirs.
42 JM memoirs.
43 JM memoirs.
44 The *Dundee Standard*, which ran, intermittently, from 1979–8, was founded as a Labour alternative to the Tory Thomson press. It was edited by journalist Ron McKay, who Galloway had met while he was on a 'fact-finding visit', i.e., left-wing junket, to Beirut in 1978 where McKay was working as a stringer for the *Sunday Times*. Stephen Khan, 'How Scottish feuds were reignited in desert sands', *The Guardian*, 27 April 2003.
45 *Dundee Courier*, 8 September 1979.
46 *Dundee Courier*, 4 September 1979.
47 *Belfast Telegraph*, 11 September 1979.
48 *Belfast Telegraph*, 11 September 1979. Peters was initially a member of the Communist Party of Northern Ireland, and a staunch advocate of civil rights (he was a founding member and the first secretary of NICRA in 1967), until, according to fellow activist, Frank Gogarty, his business property (pub) was bombed by the PIRA. Peters then became a convert to the 'two nations theory', advocated by Unionists and some communist factions, which maintained that Ulster Protestants and Irish Catholics formed two distinct peoples, and effectively justified partition. 'The Founding of the Northern Ireland Civil Rights Association', Frank Gogarty, interviewed by Richard Deutsch, *Etudes*

Irelandes, June 1987, pp143–56. By 1980, Peters was arguing that the granting of any concessions to the hunger striking prisoners would be 'a cave-in to the terrorists', unless extended to prisons throughout the UK *Belfast Telegraph*, 25 October, 17 December 1980. In May 1981, he responded to Tony Benn's innocuous suggestion that British troops be withdrawn from the Six Counties and replaced with a UN peace-keeping force, by calling on the Parliamentary Labour Party to expel Benn for 'encouraging terrorism', and urging all trade unions in Northern Ireland to use the block vote against him in the depute leadership election. *Belfast Telegraph*, 15 May 1981.

49   Walker's old-school sexist language disregards the fact that a number of the 'chaps' were women. The UDR was the first regiment in the British Army to fully integrate women – albeit their duties on the ground were mostly confined to searching women and children, driving patrol vehicles and operating radios; and their training at Barry Buddon consisted of first aid, map reading and driving army vehicles – a move which can be viewed, synergistically, as an example of 'fem-washing' designed to promote a progressive image of the regiment, and a tactic to maximise recruitment. National Army Museum, https://www.nam.ac.uk/explore/ulster-defence-regiment, accessed 19 May 2023.

50   *Dundee Courier*, 10 September 1979.

51   *Dundee Courier*, 15 September 1979.

52   *Dundee Evening Telegraph*, 11 October 1979; *Dundee Evening Telegraph*, 13 October 1979.

53   *Belfast Telegraph*, 10 October 1979.

54   *Belfast Telegraph*, 16 October 1969.

55   *Dundee Courier*, 25 July 1979; *Dundee Courier*, 13 September 1979.

56   Councillor Ian Mortimer reported that he had been informed by BBC Northern Ireland that this was the case, and that he was 'trying to allay this feeling'. *Dundee Courier*, 13 September 1979.

57   Most notably the Glenanne gang, the members of whom were responsible in the planning and execution of a number of sectarian killings throughout the 1970s, the best known being the Miami Showband massacre on 31 July 1975, planned by Robin 'The Jackal' Jackson, a former member of the 11th (Craigavon Battalion) of the UDR and a commander in the UVF, and in which two members of the 11th (Craigavon)/UVF were blown up by their own bomb, and for which two others were later jailed. See, for example, Anne Cadwallader, *Lethal Allies: British Collusion in Ireland* (Cork: Mercier Press, 2013).

58   In 2021, an inquiry into undercover policing (in England and Wales) identified two agents of the Special Branch's Special Demonstration Squad, both of whom rose to high positions of office in the TOM – Richard Clark aka 'Rick Gibson' (1974–1976) and 'Michael James' (1980–1983). Another witness (MI5 Witness 2) also stated that the 'pressure to investigate often came from the Prime Minister and Whitehall'. For details, see Undercover Policing Inquiry Report, 23 April 2021, Campaign Opposing Police Surveillance; Written statement,

CHAPTER 9 – A LEGACY RECLAIMED 1970–85

'Michael James' HN 96, publication date, 16 December 2021, Undercover Policing Inquiry, https://www.ucpi.org.uk, accessed 19 May 2023.

59 A reference to a national speaking tour organised by the UTOM, in which former British soldiers, Lloyd Hayes and Brian Ashton spoke of their experience serving in the Six Counties.

60 JM memoirs.

61 The debut project of Irish-American film director Arthur MacCaig, who went on to make seven more films about Ireland and several about the Basque-Spanish conflict. Dónal Foreman, 'The Films of Arthur MacCaig', https://donal.foreman.com/arthurmaccaig/, accessed 19 May 2023.

62 Clapton's account closely echoes the report of Diane Fox, 'Aug 12: What it means', *Hands Off Ireland*, 9, November 1979, pp14–15.

63 JM memoirs.

64 *Troops Out*, February 1980.

65 JM memoirs.

66 JM memoirs.

67 JM memoirs.

68 *AP/RN*, 2 February 1980. Pat Arrowsmith had considerable experience of English jails, having served eleven sentences for political offences, and of having been – like the Price sisters – force-fed while on hunger strike (in Gateside Prison in 1961). At the time of the Bloody Sunday march, she had been in correspondence with Bobby Sands, who initially wrote to her on 17 August 1979. 'A tribute to Bobby Sands and Pat Arrowsmith: previously unpublished letter'. Public Reading Rooms, https://prruk.org/a-tribute-to-bobby-sands-and-pat-arrowsmith-previously-unpublished-letter/, accessed 19 May 2023.

69 *Troops Out*, March 1980.

70 JM memoirs.

71 *Dundee Standard*, 25 April 1980.

72 This is, of course, a generalisation. Despite their strong collective identity, the 'H bees' were composed of individuals with different levels of awareness and commitment, who were also at different stages of political development. The relative youth of most of them meant this was an ongoing process. Some members of the ACH group went on to became actively involved in campaigning work, while at least one member of the original Willie Frew's/SWP drinking set gravitated towards the Celtic one.

73 JM memoirs.

74 Interview with Michael Taylor, 29 October 2021.

75 Quoted in Interview with Michael Taylor, 29 October 2021.

76 Charter 80, 'Human Rights for Irish Political Prisoners', manifesto and application form.

77 Gregor Feindt, 'Prague, 77: Charter 77', Leibnitz Institute of European History, https://hhr-atlas.ieg-mainz.de/articles/feindt-prague, accessed 19 May 2023.

78 *Troops Out*, October 1980. The London IRSP group likely included London-based Irishman and IRSP member, Nick Mullen, who later joined the IRA, becoming Quartermaster in England, where he served nine years of a 30-year sentence for conspiring to cause explosions. Mullen was also critical of *The Morning Star* /Communist Party of Great Britain, which endorsed Charter 80. Ruan O'Donnell, *Special Category: the IRA in English Prisons, Volume 2, 1968–78* (Dublin: Irish Academic Press, 2015), pp83, 182.

79 *AP/RN*, 18 October 1980.

80 The wide selection of signatories included Labour MPs Tony Benn and Eric Heffer, as well as Mick McGahey of the Scottish National Union of Mineworkers, Ron Todd of the TGWU, playwrights, Margaretta D'Arcy and John Arden, singer, Christy Moore, Connolly biographer, C Desmond Greaves, and cultural theorist and leading member of the Communist Party of Great Britain, Stuart Hall.

81 O'Donnell, *Special Category, Volume 2*, p182.

82 *AP/RN*, 22 November 1980.

83 *Dundee Courier*, 10 November 1980.

84 *Dundee Courier*, 5 March 1980.

85 *Dundee Courier*, 23 December 1980.

86 *Dundee Courier*, 19 December 1980; *Dundee Evening Telegraph*, 19 December 1980.

87 O'Donnell, *Special Category, Volume 2*, p185.

88 *Troops Out*, February 1981.

89 O'Donnell, *Special Category, Volume 2*, p181.

90 *Fight Racism! Fight Imperialism!* [hereafter *FRFI*], January/February 1981.

91 The slogan was dropped in the wake of the IRA's English bombing campaign in 1974. David Reed, *Ireland: The Key to the British Revolution* (London: Larkin Publications, 1984), p267.

92 *FRFI*, March/April 1981. RCG members Kirstin Crosbie and Mike Duffield were deemed to have earned their Irish Republican spurs, having been twice arrested under the PTA in August and December 1980 – ostensibly for selling pro-Republican literature outside Celtic Park – losing their jobs as a result, whereupon they embarked on unpaid careers as full-time political activists focused specifically on Irish republican solidarity work. The Glasgow Two, as they were dubbed by the RCG's newspaper, *FRFI*, went on, with others, to form the Glasgow Hunger Strike Action Committee (GHSAC), and thereafter the Glasgow Irish Freedom Action Committee (GIFAC).

93 History of the James Connolly RFB, [author unknown], posted by Emmet Óg Mclean, 18 February 2020, http://facebook.com/emmet.mclean.5/posts/2584535481825717, accessed 19 May 2023.

94 At which symbolically-named street the mass of the loyalist counter-demonstrators had gathered. Earlier the police had, somewhat suspiciously, rerouted a bus containing the 57-strong Billy Reid RFB, who were travelling from Parkhead to Roystonhill, into the thick of the counter-demonstrators, then straight to Stewart Street police station where they were detained until the march was over.

95 *AP/RN*, 21 February 1981; *Belfast Telegraph*, 16 February 1981.

96 *Troops Out*, March 1981.

97 Richard O'Rawe, *Blanketmen: An Untold Story of the H Block Hunger Strike* (Dublin: New Island Books), pp108–9.

98 *Belfast Telegraph*, 16 February 1981.

99 *Belfast Telegraph*, 1 April 1981.

100 JM memoirs.

101 *FRFI*, July/August 1981.

102 See Chapter 7.

103 JM memoirs.

104 *FRFI*, October/November 1981.

105 The activist's most abiding memory of the visit is of her bewildered SWP companion asking for directions in Belfast City Centre. He approached, not a local resident, but a long-haired, bandana-wearing American-Indian (Wally Feather, a native-American land, civil and cultural rights campaigner) and a colourfully dressed, guitar-slinging African-American (the Reverend Fred Kirkpatrick, a longstanding Black civil rights activist, folk musician and former contemporary of Martin Luther King) who had come to Belfast to express the solidarity of their peoples with the Irish struggle. Conversations with Audrie Taylor; *AP/RN*, 22 August 1981.

106 *FRFI*, October/November 1981.

107 A resolution from the National Union of Public Employees, vowing 'to uphold the democratic right to free speech and civil liberty' had been unanimously passed and a letter to the Chief Constable written. The bulk of the allegations arose out of another march held in November 1981. See below.

108 Interview with Michael Taylor, 24 March 2022. Gordon Wilson, MP for Dundee East from 1979 to 1987, was acquainted with the Chief Constable, having been assigned police protection arising from his position as leader of the SNP at the time. He was also a lawyer by profession.

109 JM memoirs.

110 *AP/RN*, 10 October 1981.

111 '1981 – the year of the hunger strikes is no mere temporary setback for British policies in Ireland. Nationally and internationally, its effects will be felt as the struggle for Irish independence progresses in the months and years ahead.' Statement by Sinn Féin Vice-President Gerry Adams, *AP/RN*, 10 October 1981.

112 *FRFI*, December 1981.

113 Karl Marx and Friedrich Engels, *On Ireland and the Irish Question* [1848] (Moscow: Progress Publishers, 1974).

114 The strategy of the British government and the security forces whereby arrested paramilitaries or 'converted terrorists' were induced to testify against their alleged former colleagues in return for large sums of money, immunity from prosecution, and new identities outside of the Six Counties. Around 600 people from nationalist and unionist communities were convicted on the word of 'paid perjurers', many of which convictions were later overturned. The 'supergrass' system, which was widely condemned throughout the world, was ultimately terminated (in 1985) by the justiciary who were anxious to save the judicial system from further reputational damage. Steven Greer, *Supergrasses: A Study in Anti-Terrorist Law Enforcement in Northern Ireland* (Oxford: Clarendon Press, 1995).

115 Molloy had been the running mate of Owen Carron, one of five successful Sinn Féin candidates in the Assembly Elections of 20 October 1982, the party's first foray into electoral politics since the hunger strikes. 'The Ballot Bomb', *Iris*, November 1982.

116 *FRFI*, January 1983.

117 *RFI*, September 1983.

118 Notably the IRA prisoners in Albany Jail, two of whose spokesmen were careful to point out that 'no single body could assume the mantle of' 'claiming... the Republican imprimatur' in Britain. O'Donnell, *Special Category, Volume 2*, p288.

119 'Rebels with a Cause', in *Labour and Ireland*, 15, March/April 1987.

120 Misneach, from the Scots Gaelic/ Irish 'courage; or 'spirit'; described to the author as an improvised translation of 'Bonnie Dundee'.

121 *FRFI*, February 1983.

122 Chief of which was the struggle for national liberation in Ireland.

123 *FRFI*, April 1983.

124 Namely scheduling the debate at the end of the day, regardless of the travel arrangements/work commitments of the Scottish attendees. Alternatively, the RCG claimed GIFAC 'boycotted' the conference after their proposal that a preliminary march be headed by Irish Republican flags and organisations was rejected by the organisers. *Ireland's War*, 2, August 1983, and 3, November 1983; *FRFI*, October 1983.

125 *RFI*, October 1983; JM memoirs.

126 Mosquito Press were initially members of the Marxist-Leninist RCL, from which they split in late September 1983, taking their 'press' (the editor of the RCL's paper) with them. Ardent supporters of the Democratic People's Republic of Korea (DPRK), Mosquito Press also had links with the family of James Connolly, via Nora Connolly O'Brien, from whose recollections they compiled a short book, *We Shall Rise Again*, in 1981.

127 GIFAC were not the only group to engage with DPRK politics in this period. In April 1984 members of GIFAC and DIRSC attended an international conference in London, held under the auspices of the Friends of North Korea, which included a contribution from Sinn Féin's Gerry MacLochlainn, who argued that the Irish 'Sinn Féin' (We Ourselves) and related slogan 'Sinn Féin Amháin' (Ourselves Alone), and the Korean 'Juche' and 'Chajusong' (literally, 'self-reliance' and 'independence and freedom from external domination'), developed by the DPRK's founder, Kim Il-Sung, were the same concept. In 1986, MacLochlainn travelled to the DPRK with Sinn Féin councillors Sheena Campbell (who was assassinated by the UVF in 1992) and John Doyle, for an international youth conference in Pyongyang. *Ireland's War*, 18, June 1986.

128 *FRFI*, February 1984.

EPILOGUE

After a lull of around two years, an attempt was made to construct another politically-oriented Irish solidarity campaign in Dundee. Meanwhile, the political landscape was slowly changing. November 1986 saw Sinn Féin drop its abstentionist policy in the Twenty-Six counties, triggering another split in the Republican movement and the formation of the breakaway Republican Sinn Féin under the leadership of former President of Provisional Sinn Féin, Ruairí Ó Brádaigh. As the IRA continued to mount military operations, Sinn Féin, under the presidency of Gerry Adams, was engaging with friendly elements within the British left establishment. Already, in 1983, it had established contact with Labour Party politicians, including the leader of the Greater London Council, Ken Livingstone, and the newly elected MP for Islington North, Jeremy Corbyn, both of whom had made 'fact-finding' visits to the Six Counties. This stepped up considerably after January 1987 when the Labour Co-ordinating Committee's consultative conference on Ireland adopted a policy of British withdrawal, to be enacted, supposedly, within the lifetime of the next Labour government.

The formation of the Dundee Committee for a United Ireland (DCUI) at the beginning of 1987 can be viewed in this context; as stemming, in part, from an initiative of the Labour Committee on Ireland (LCI), whose Scottish area committee was reformed in February with a view to establishing a national committee to promote its aims.[1] This involved collaborating with the British left, and the Republican community in Scotland, which at this point was largely represented by the Republican Band Alliance in alliance with other smaller pro-Republican groups.[2] This was reflected in the structure of the DCUI, in which the role of chairperson was assumed by a member of the LCI, the role of secretary by a member of the Workers' Revolutionary Party – neither of whom had been involved in previous Irish campaigns in the city – and the role of treasurer by former members of the Padraig Pearse flute band and other veterans of the Dundee Hunger Strike campaign. The latter formed the largest group on the committee and, as the Labour Party subsequently backed off following the IRA's bombing of the Enniskillen war memorial in November 1987, ultimately came to dominate it. The initial Labour movement involvement, however, remained evident in the committee's meeting place – the Trades Council Social Club in Rattray Street, within sight of the bust of James Connolly.

Despite its large pro-Republican element, however, the DCUI was less politically radical than the previous campaign; it called for a united Ireland, not a Socialist Republic. Initially, its activities focused on humanitarian and social justice issues. In the first few months of its existence, members were roped into attending LCI-organised fringe meetings at the Scottish Trades Union Congress and Scottish Labour Party conferences calling for the banning of plastic bullets, the repeal of the Prevention of Terrorism Act, and justice for the Birmingham Six and the Guildford Four. As with every other Irish campaign in the city since the 1860s, however, prisoner solidarity remained an enduring area of activity. For example, on International Women's Day 1987, the DCUI participated in a Stop the Strip Searches demonstration at Durham Prison – the northernmost English prison to hold Irish Republican combatants (no IRA or INLA prisoners were incarcerated in Scottish prisons throughout this phase) – where IRA prisoners, Martina Anderson and Ella O'Dwyer, were being subjected to up to five strip searches a day.[3] As the Labour Party retreated to a safe distance and the left element became even more marginalised, the Dundee committee's activities focused more on rallying for demonstrations and organising fundraising social events. As in previous years, such occasions were enlivened by the presence of the Republican Band Alliance which now numbered around fourteen bands.[4], several members of whom joined with the DCUI and local left to counter-protest an Orange march through Dundee city centre on Saturday, 11 July 1987.[5] This period also saw several members of the DCUI take part in Easter commemorations in County Armagh under the banner of the Wishaw-based Crossmaglen Patriots RFB into which the Padraig Pearse had integrated.

However, despite the involvement of the ex-Lochee Hibees, the DCUI was no regrouping, much less regeneration, of the Troops Out and other pro-Republican Irish solidarity campaigns. It lacked the intensity and urgency of the Dundee Hunger Strike Action Committee and the advanced republican socialist perspective of the DIRSC. For a combination of reasons, both political and personal, the other key players in these campaigns failed to engage with it. It was also short-lived. By early 1989, it had ceased operating. Nevertheless, for all its shortcomings and limitations, the Dundee Committee for a United Ireland provided an important vehicle through which a new generation radicalised by the hunger strikes could demonstrate their support for the Irish liberation struggle whilst continuing to solidify and develop their new-found and revivified Irish cultural identity. The process was, and is, an ongoing one.

*

I have chosen to end here, aware that much remains unsaid, and much more remains to be written. For example, the long-term impact of the hunger strike in Scotland merits a deeper, more critical study which the exigencies of space and time preclude here. The extent to which the pro-Republican nature of the Irish solidarity movement in Scotland, and its deep-rooted allegiance to the Republican movement in Ireland rendered it vulnerable to weaknesses within that movement itself also raises important questions that would benefit from further investigation and analysis.

In his biography of Michael Davitt, published in 1908, Francis Sheehy Skeffington wrote that it was still 'too near to Fenianism to permit of its discussion with the desirable discretion'.[6] Writing at a similar distance from the post-hunger strike era of the 1980s, one feels that also may be the case. It is my hope that, in the course of time and as more information becomes available, other more capable hands will be better placed to carry this through. For the moment, my overriding hope is that, by shedding a light on some of the hidden and forgotten aspects of Irish Republican activity in Dundee, this contribution will fill some of the gaps in the broad story of Irish republicanism and weave some vibrant new Irish threads into the rich tapestry of Scottish radical history.

Endnotes to Epilogue

1. *Labour and Ireland*, 15, March/April 1987.
2. *Ireland's War*, 19, October 1986.
3. *Ireland's War*, 24, October 1987.
4. *Ireland's War*, 28, September 1988.
5. On this occasion, the protesters' attempt to stop the march was not successful. However, on 6 October 2001 a march by the City of Dundee branch of the Apprentice Boys of Derry, from Dudhope Terrace into the city centre, was curtailed by the police at Lochee Road in response to a counter-demonstration organised by ex-members of the DCUI. *Dundee Courier*, 8 October 2001.
6. Sheehy Skeffington, *Michael Davitt*, p30.

SELECT BIBLIOGRAPHY

ARCHIVAL SOURCES

NATIONAL LIBRARY OF IRELAND

Anna Parnell correspondence
Art O'Briain papers
Larcom papers
William O'Brien papers

NATIONAL ARCHIVES OF IRELAND

Criminal Branch Special Reports
Fenian files
Joseph Robinson papers

IRISH MILITARY ARCHIVES

Bureau of Military History Witness Statements
Military Service Pensions Collection

NATIONAL RECORDS OF SCOTLAND

Irish Disturbances files

DUNDEE CITY ARCHIVES

Liff and Benvie Poor Register, 1854–65
Log book of St Mary's School
Scrapbook of the Dundee Radical Association, 1888–1889

UNIVERSITY COLLEGE DUBLIN

Eamonn Mooney papers

SELECT BIBLIOGRAPHY
NEWSPAPERS AND JOURNALS

Aberdeen Evening Express
Aberdeen Press and Journal
An Claidheimh Soluis
An Phoblacht
An Phoblacht/Republican News
Belfast Morning News
Belfast Newsletter
Belfast Telegraph
Bradford Observer
Chartist Circular
Commonweal
Daily Herald
Daily Record
Derry Journal
Dublin Daily Express
Dublin Evening Post
Dundee Advertiser
Dundee Catholic Herald
Dundee Courier
Dundee Evening Telegraph
Dundee Standard
Dundee Warder
Edinburgh Daily News
Edinburgh Daily Review
Edinburgh Evening News
Éire, the Irish Nation
Evening Echo
Falkirk Herald
Fight Racism! Fight Imperialism!
Flag of Ireland
Forward
Freeman's Journal
The Guardian
Glasgow Free Press
Glasgow Herald
Greenock Advertiser
Hands Off Ireland!
Ireland's War
Iris
Irish Democrat
Irish Examiner
Irish Independent
The Irish Citizen
The Irishman
Irish News
Irish Press
Irish Times
The Irish Voice
Irish Weekly and Ulster Examiner
Justice
The Kerryman
Labour and Ireland
Labour Leader
Land and Liberty
Larne Times and Weekly Telegraph
Leith Observer
London Morning Post
London Star
The Nation
North British Daily Mail
Northern Star
Northern Warder
Northern Whig
Occult Press Review
The People
Northern Warder
People's Journal
Perthshire Advertiser Perthshire Critic

Sacramento Union
The Scotsman
Scottish Prohibitionist
Sinn Fein
Sligo Champion
Sligo Chronicle
The Socialist
Sporting Post (Dundee)
The Suffragette
Sunday Post
Troops Out
Ulster Herald
United Irishman
The Vote
Votes for Women
Weekly News
West London Observer
Western People

OFFICIAL AND SEMI-OFFICAL PUBLICATIONS

Census of Ireland, 1901, 1911

Census of Scotland, 1841–1921

Dundee Directories

Dundee Electoral Registers

England and Wales Civil Registration Death Index, 1837–1915

Hansard

Irish Civil Records

Register of Births, Marriages and Deaths, Scotland

Report of Royal Commission on Hand-loom weavers, 1841

Report of the General Board of Health on the epidemic cholera of 1848 and 1849

ONLINE ARTICLES AND BLOG POSTS

'A tribute to Bobby Sands and Pat Arrowsmith: previously unpublished letter', Public Reading Rooms, https://prruk.org/a-tribute-to-bobby-sands-and-pat-arrowsmith-previously-unpublished-letter/ Radio Rebelde, About us, https//www.radiorebelde.cu.english/aboutus/

Feindt, Gregor, 'Prague, 77: Charter 77', Leibnitz Institute of European History, http://hhr-atlas.ieg-mainz.de/articles/feindt-prague

Flags of Political Reform in 19th century Wales, https://www.crwflags.com/fotw/flags/gb_charw.html

Foreman, Dónal, 'The Films of Arthur MacCaig', https://donal.foreman.com/arthurmaccaig/

'Henry Hyde Champion', Spartacus Educational, https://spartacus-educational.com/TUchampion.htm

History of the James Connolly Republican Flute Band, posted by Emmet Óg McLean, 18 February 2020, http://facebook.com/emmet.mclean.5/posts/2584535431825717

'Hugh McCalmont of Abbeylands', Centre for the Study of the Legacies of British Slave Ownership, https://www.ucl.ac.uk/lbs/person/view/8582

'Miss Florence McFarlane', The Dinner Puzzle, https://thedinnerpuzzle.com/portfolio/miss-florence-mcfarlane/

Murphy, Jacob, 'A Four Nations Approach to the Irish Anti-Partition Campaigns of the 1940s and 1950s', https://fournationshistory.wordpress.com/2015/12/28/a-four-nations-approach-to-the-irish-anti-partition-campaigns-of-the-1940s-and-1950s/

O'Neill, John, 'Terminology: 'Tan War or 'War of Independence'?', The Treason Felony Blog, https://treasonfelony.wordpress.com/2025/11/29/terminology-tan-war-or-war-of-independence/

O'Neill, John, 'The 1872 Edinburgh Lamplighters' Strike: creating James Connolly', The Treason Felony Blog, https://treasonfelony.wordpress.com/2020/05/09/the-1872-edinburgh-lamplighters-strike-creating-james-connolly/

O'Neill, John, 'Where, oh where, is our James Connolly: #Connolly150', The Treason Felony Blog, https://treasonfelony.wordpress.com/2018/6/05/where-oh-where-is-our-james-connolly-connolly150/

Roob, Alexander, 'William James Linton: Art of Graphic Media', Melton Prior Institute, 2011, https://meltonpriorinstitut.org/pages/textarchive.php5?view=text&ID=99&language=English

Scott, Jenny, 'The Coventry IRA bombing: the 'forgotten' attack on a British City', https://www.bbc.c.uk/news/uk-england-coventry-warwickshire-28191501

OTHER ONLINE SOURCES

Desmond Greaves Archive, https://www.desmondgreavesarchive.com/

Dictionary of Irish Biography, https://dib.ie

GAA 125: A People's History, http://www.gaa.ie

International Brigade Archive, https://www.international-brigades.org.uk/the-volunteers

National Army Museum, https://nam.ac.uk/

Tobar an Dualchais, https://www.tobarandualchais.co.uk

Undercover Policing Inquiry, https://www.ucpi.org.uk

WORKS OF REFERENCE

Australian Dictionary of National Biography, Volume 7 (1979)

Bellamy, Joyce M and John Saville (eds), *Dictionary of Labour Biography*, Volume VI, (London: Palgrave MacMillan, 1982)

Ewan, Elizabeth; Innes, Sue; Reynolds, Sian, *The Biographical Dictionary of Scottish Women from the Earliest Times to 2004* (Edinburgh; EUP, 2006)

Rintoul, M C, *Dictionary of Real People and Places in Fiction* (London: Routledge, 1993)

PAMPHLETS

Arnott, Mike, *Dundee and the Spanish Civil War* (Dundee Trades Council, 2008)

Taylor, Peter, 'Reporting Northern Ireland', in *The British Media in Ireland* (Campaign for Free Speech in Ireland, 1978)

The Dundee Textile Industry, 1790–1885, from the papers of Peter Carmichael of Arthurstone (Scottish History Society, 1969)

Withers, Charles W J, *Highland Communities in Dundee and Perth 1787–1891* (Abertay Historical Society: Dundee, 1996)

RADIO AND TELEVISION BROADCASTS

The War Next Door: Scotland and the Troubles, BBC Scotland, broadcast 12 and 19 November 2019

TALKS AND PRESENTATIONS

Burke, Jason, 'Carson's Betrayal of Women? Unionist attitudes to female suffrage, 1912–1914', Public Records Office Northern Ireland, 8 August 2018

Coyle, Stephen, 'No Ordinary Women – the Untold Story of Cumann na mBan in Scotland', Glasgow, April 2014

Coyle, Stephen, 'Persis Renehan Remembered', Glasgow, 26 January 2019, reproduced in *The Irish Voice*, February 2019

JOURNAL ARTICLES

Challinor, R, 'Peter Murray McDouall and 'Physical Force Chartism'', *International Socialism*, 21:1 (1981)

Collins, Brenda, 'Proto-industrialisation and pre-Famine Emigration', *Social History*, 7:2 (1982), pp127–46

Daly, Mary E, 'Wives, Mothers and Citizens: The Treatment of Women in the 1935 Nationality and Citizenship Act', *Eire-Ireland*, 38:3 & 4 (2003), pp257–8

Deutsch, Richard, 'The Founding of the Northern Ireland Civil Rights Association', interview with Frank Gogarty, *Etudes Irelandes* (June 1987), pp143–56

Jackson, Steve, 'Seumas Mac Garaidh: Neach-iomairt Ghàidhlig agus Fior 'Pan-Celt', *Carn*, 147 (August 2010)

Johnston, Iain E, 'Edward Carson: Ulster Unionist of Irish Patriot', *History Ireland*, 20:3 (2012)

Kane, Paula M, 'The Willing Captive of Home?': The English Catholic Women's League', *Church History*, 60:3 (September 1991)

Kenefick, William, 'Locality, Regionality and Gender: Revisiting Industrial Protest among Women Workers in Scotland, 1910 to 1913', *Journal of Irish Studies*, 8:2 (2015)

McBride, Terence, 'Ribbonmen and Radicals: the cultivation of Irishness and the promotion of active citizenship in mid-Victorian Glasgow', *Irish Review*, 21:1 (2015), pp15–32

McFarland, Elaine, 'How the Irish Paid Their Debt': Irish Catholics in Scotland and Volunteer Enlistment, Aug 1914–Jul 1915', *Scottish Historical Review*, 2 (2003), pp261–84

Moody, T W, 'Michael Davitt and the 'Pen' Letter', *Irish Historical Studies*, 4:15 (1945)

Nic Congail, Riona, 'Young Ireland and *The Nation*: Nationalist Children's Culture in the Late Nineteenth Century', *Éire-Ireland*, 46:3 (2011), pp37–62

Patterson, Iain D, 'The Activities of Irish Republican Physical Force Organisations in Scotland, 1919-1921', *Scottish Historical Review*, 72:1 (April 1993), pp39–59

Urquhart, Diane, 'An articulate and definite cry for political freedom': The Ulster Suffrage Movement, *Women's History Review*, 11:2 (2002)

Walker, W M, 'Irish immigrants in Scotland: their priests, politics and parochial life', in *Historical Journal*, 15:4 (1972)

Whelehan, Niall, 'Saving Ireland in Juteopolis: Gender, Class and Diaspora in the Ladies' Land League', *History Workshop Journal* (2021)

White, Cyril, 'John Pius Boland's Olympic tennis diploma', *History Ireland*, 20:4 (2012)

Young, J D, 'John Leslie, 1856-1921: A Scottish-Irishman as Internationalist', *Saothar*, 18 (1993)

MEMOIRS

Barry, Tom, *Guerrilla Days in Ireland* [1949] (Dublin: Anvil Books, 1989)

Devoy, John, *Recollections of an Irish Rebel*, 1842-1928 (1929)

Gallacher, W, *The Last Memoirs of William Gallacher*, (London: Lawrence and Wishart, 1966)

Lowe, David, *Souvenirs of Scottish Labour* (Glasgow: W & R Holmes, 1919)

MacDougall, Ian (ed), *Militant Miners: Recollections of John McArthur, Buckhaven, and letters of David Proudfoot, Methil to G. Allen* (Edinburgh: Polygon, 1981)

McShane, Harry; Smith, Joan, *No Mean City* (London: Pluto Press, 1978)

Malone, John, unpublished memoirs

Myles, James, *Rambles in Forfarshire or Sketches of Town and Country* (Dundee, 1850)

O'Donnell, Peadar, *There Will be Another Day* [1963] (Dublin: Red Sky Books, 2017)

O'Donnell, Peadar, *Salud! An Irishman in Spain* [1937] (Dublin: Friends of the International Brigade in Ireland, 2020)

O'Malley, Ernie, *On Another Man's Wound* [1939] (Dublin: Anvil Press, 1979)

Ryan, Michael, *My Life in the IRA: The Border Campaign* (Cork: Mercier Press, 2018)

Stewart, Bob, *Breaking the Fetters* (London: Lawrence and Wishart, 1967)

Wintringham, Tom, *English Captain* [1939] (London: Faber and Faber, 2011)

BOOKS

Anon, *Tales of the RIC* (Edinburgh and London: William Blackwood, 1921)

Beiner, Guy, *Forgetful Remembrance: Social Forgetting and Vernacular Historiography of a Rebellion in Ulster* (Oxford: OUP, 2018)

Bennett, Richard, *The Black and Tans* (London: Four Square Books, 1959)

Bew, Paul, *Land and the National Question in Ireland, 1858–82* (Dublin: Gill & Macmillan, 1978)

Bull, Philip, *Land and Nationalism, Land, Politics and Nationalism, 1850–1938: A Study of the Irish Land Question* (Dublin: Gill & Macmillan, 1996)

Cadwallader, Anne, *Lethal Allies: British Collusion in Ireland* (Cork: Mercier Press, 2013)

Callahan, Matt (ed), *Songs of Freedom: The James Connolly Songbook* (Oakland: PM Press, 2013)

Chase, Malcolm, *Chartism: A New History* (Manchester: MUP, 1970)

Collins, Lorcan, *16 Lives: James Connolly* (Dublin: The O'Brien Press, 2012)

Cox, A J, *Empire and Industry: the imperial nexus of jute, 1840-1940*, (Edinburgh: Routledge, 2013)

Coyle, Stephen, *High Noon on the High Street* (Glasgow: Clydeside Press, 2008)

Coyle, Stephen, and Ó Catháin, Máirtín, (eds), *We Will Rise Again* (Glasgow: 1916 Rising Centenary Committee (Scotland), 2018)

Crawford, Elizabeth, *The Women's Suffrage Movement in Britain and Ireland: A Regional Survey* (London: Routledge, 2006)

Davitt, Michael, *The Fall of Feudalism in Ireland* (London and New York: Harper and Row, 1904)

Devine, T M (ed), *Irish Immigrants and Scottish Society in the Nineteenth and Twentieth Centuries* (Edinburgh: John Donald, 1991)

Devine, T M, *The Scottish Nation* (London: Penguin, 1999)

Denvir, John, *The Irish in Britain from the earliest times to the fall and death of Parnell* (London: Kegan Paul, Trench and Trübner, 1892)

Dillon, William, *Life of John Mitchel, Volume 1* (1888)

Ford, Robert, *Vagabond Songs and Ballads of Scotland* (Paisley: A Gardner, 1904)

Fraser, T G (ed), *The Irish Parading Tradition: Following the Drum* (Basingstoke: MacMillan Press, 2000)

Gallacher, Tom, *Glasgow, the Uneasy peace: Religious Tension in Modern Scotland, 1819-1914* (Manchester: MUP, 1987)

Goldstrom, J M and L Clarkson (eds), *Irish Population, Economy and Society* (Oxford: Clarendon Press, 1981)

Gray, John, *City in Revolt, James Larkin and the Belfast Dock Strike of 1907* (Belfast: Blackstaff Press, 1985)

Greer, Steven, *Supergrasses: A Study in Anti-Terrorist Law Enforcement in Northern Ireland* (Oxford: Clarendon Press, 1995)

Groves, Patricia, *Petticoat Rebellion: the Anna Parnell Story* (Cork: Mercier Press, 2009)

Ferguson, Frank and James McConnell (eds), *Ireland and Scotland in the Nineteenth Century* (Dublin: Four Courts Press, 2009)

Finlay, Richard J, *Independent and Free: Scottish Politics: The Origins of the Scottish National Party, 1918–45,* (Edinburgh: John Donald, 1994)

Gray, Daniel, *Homage to Caledonia: Scotland and the Spanish Civil War* (Edinburgh: Luath Press, 2019)

Greaves, C Desmond, *The Life and Times of James Connolly* [1961] (Croydon: Manifesto Press, 2018)

Greaves, C Desmond, *Liam Mellows and the Irish Revolution* [1971] (Belfast: An Ghlór Gafa, 2004)

Handley, J E, *The Irish in Scotland* (Cork: Cork University Press, 1943)

Handley, J E, *The Irish in Modern Scotland* (Cork: Cork University Press, 1947)

Hanley, Brian, and Scott Millar, *The Lost Revolution: The Story of the Official IRA and the Workers' Party* (London: Penguin, 2009)

Harkin, Shaun (ed), *The James Connolly Reader* (Haymarket Books: Chicago, 2018)

Henderson, Mary, *Ethel Moorhead* (2020)

Hepburn, Anthony C, *A Past Apart: Histories in the Study of Catholic Belfast, 1850–1950* Belfast: Ulster Historical Foundation)

Jennings, Ivor, *Party Politics: Volume 3, The Stuff of Politics* (Cambridge: CUP, 1962)

Johnson, Thomas, *History of the Working Classes in Scotland* [1920] (Glasgow: Unity Publishing, 1946)

Kenefick, William, *Red Scotland!: The Rise and Fall of the Radical Left, c1872–1932* (Edinburgh: EUP, 2007)

Kenna, G B, *Facts and Figures on the Belfast Pogroms, 1920–1922* [Dublin: O'Connell Publishing Co., 1922], independent reprint, 2019)

Kenna, Shane, *Jeremiah O'Donovan Rossa: Unrepentant Fenian* (Sallins, County Kildare: Merrion Press, 2015)

Leeson, D M, *The Black and Tans: British Police and Auxiliaries in the First Irish War of Independence, 1920-21* (Oxford: OUP, 2011)

Lenin, V I, *Imperialism, the Highest Stage of Capitalism* (1916)

Lusk, Kirsty, and Maley, Willy (eds), *Scotland and the Easter Rising: Fresh Perspectives on 1916* (Edinburgh: Luath Press, 2016)

Lyons, F S L, *Ireland Since the Famine* (London: Fontana Press, 1973)

Madden, Jim, *Father John Fahy, Radical Republican and Agrarian Activist* (Dublin: The Columba Press, 2012)

Macardle, Dorothy, *The Irish Republic* [1937] (Dublin: Irish Press, 1951)

Marx, Karl and Friedrich Engels, *Ireland and the Irish Question* [1848] (Moscow: Progress Publishers, 1974)

McAuliffe, Mary, *Margaret Skinnider* (Dublin: UCD Press, 2020)

McBride, Laurence W (ed), *Reading Irish Histories: Texts, Contexts and Memory* (Dublin: Four Courts Press, 2003)

McGuire, Charlie, *Sean McLoughlin, Ireland's Forgotten Revolutionary* (Pontypool: Merlin Press, 2011)

McNeill, Mary, *The Life and Times of Mary McCracken* (Belfast: Blackstaff Press, 1988)

Miskell, Louise, Christopher A Whatley and Bob Harris (eds), *Victorian Dundee, Image and Realities* (East Linton: Tuckwell Press, 2000)

Mitchell, Martin, *The Irish in the West of Scotland, 1797–1848: Trade Unions, Strikes and Political Movements* (Edinburgh: John Donald, 1998)

Mitchell, Martin (ed), *New Perspectives on the Irish in Scotland* (Edinburgh: John Donald, 2008)

Moran, Gerard (ed), *Radical Irish Priests, 1660–1970* (Dublin: Four Courts Press, 1998)

Morris, R J and Liam Kennedy (eds), *Ireland and Scotland: Order and Disorder* (Edinburgh: John Donald, 2005)

Morrison, Danny, *All the Dead Voices* (Cork: Mercier Press, 2002)

Murphy, William, *Political Imprisonment and the Irish, 1912–1921* (Oxford: OUP, 2014)

Neat, Timothy, *Hamish Henderson: A Biography Volume 2: Poetry Becomes People (1952-2002)* (Edinburgh: Polygon, 2009)

Nevin, Donal, *James Connolly: A Full Life* (Dublin: Gill & Macmillan, 2005)

Newby, Andrew, *Ireland, Radicalism and the Scottish Highlands, c.1870–1812* (Edinburgh: EUP, 2019)

Noonan, Gerard, *The IRA in Britain 1919–1923: 'In the heart of enemy lines'* (Liverpool: LUP, 2014)

O'Brien, William, and Ryan, Desmond, (eds), *Devoy's Post Bag*, Volume1 (Dublin: C J Fallon, 1948)

Ó Broin, León, *Revolutionary Underground: The Story of the Irish Republican Brotherhood*, 1858–1924 (Dublin: Gill & Macmillan, 1976)

Ó Catheoir, Eva, *Soldiers of Liberty: A Study of Fenianism, 1858–1908* (Dublin: The Lilliput Press, 2018)

Ó Catháin, Máirtín, *Irish Republicanism in Scotland, 1858–1916: Fenians in exile* (Dublin: Irish Academic Press, 2007)

O'Connor, Emmet, *Big Jim Larkin, Hero or Wrecker* (Dublin: UCD Press, 2015)

O'Donnell, Ruan, *Special Category: the IRA in English Prisons, Volume 2, 1968–78* (Dublin: Irish Academic Press, 2015)

O'Donoghue, Florence, *No Other Law* [1954] (Dublin: Anvil Books, 1986)

Offen, Karen M, *European Feminisms, 1700–1950: A Political History* (Stanford; Stanford University Press, 2000)

Ó Lúing, Seán, *Fremantle Mission* (Tralee, Co. Kerry: Anvil Books, 1965)

Ó Lúing, Seán, *Ó Donnobháin Rosa Volume 1* (Baile Átha Cliath [Dublin]: Sáirséal & Dill, 1969)

O'Rawe, Richard, *Blanketmen: An Untold Story of the H Block Hunger Strike* (Dublin: New Island, 2005)

Ó Tuathaigh, Gearóid, *Ireland Before the Famine, 1789–1848* (Dublin and London: Gill & Macmillan, 1972)

Parnell, Anna, *Tale of a Great Sham* [1907] and Hearne, Dana (ed) (Dublin: Arlen House, 1986)

Reed, David, *Ireland: The Key to the British Revolution*, (London: Larkin Publications, 1984)

Rosie, Michael, *The Sectarian Myth in Scotland* (Basingstoke: Palgrave MacMillan, 2004)

Sheehy Skeffington, Francis, *Michael Davitt* [1908] (London: McGibbon and McKee, 1967)

Smith, M L R, *Fighting for Ireland? The Military Strategy of the Irish Republican Movement* (London: Routledge, 1995)

Treacy, Matt, *The Communist Party of Ireland 1921–2011* (Dublin: Brocaire Books, 2012)

Trotter, Mary, *Ireland's National Theaters: Political Performance and the Origins of the Irish Dramatic Movement* (New York: Syracuse University Press, 2001)

Walker, William M, *Juteopolis: Dundee and its Textile Workers, 1885–1923* (Edinburgh: Scottish Academic Press, 1979)

Ward, Margaret, *Unmanageable Revolutionaries: Women and Irish Nationalism* (London: Pluto Press, 1989)

Watson, Norman, *Dundee's Suffragettes: Their Remarkable Struggle to Win Votes for Women* (Perth: Percy Johnstone Publishing, 2018)

Whelehan, Niall, *The Dynamiters: Irish Nationalism and Political Violence in the Wider World, 1867–1900* (Cambridge: CUP, 2012)

Wilson, Ray and Ian Adams, *Special Branch: A History: 1883–2006* (London: Biteback Publishing, 2015)

SELECT INDEX

'82 clubs 115–119, 126, 135, 212

'98 clubs 126–128, 134, 136, 187, 192, 212

A

Adams, Gerry 516

Adams, James 26

Agnew, Annie 339

Aimer, James 172, 283

Amnesty Association 83, 94–95, 106, 116–117, 120, 125, 128, 131, 135, 139, 212

An Conradh Gaelige. *See* Gaelic League

An Cumann Cabhrach (Republican Aid Association) 420

An Gorta Beag 98, 134

An Phoblacht/Republican News (AP/RN) 392, 430, 443, 453, 455, 460–461, 472–473, 477, 480–481, 500, 508–509, 511–513

Ancient Order of Hibernians (AOH) 168, 171, 175, 192, 197, 212, 228, 236, 276–279, 374, 399–401, 420, 429, 444–450, 459, 464, 477, 483, 488, 491, 505, 508, 511

Anderson, Donald 502

Anderson, Martina 517

Anderson, William 404, 430, 436

Anderston Workers' Association 234

Anglo-Irish Treaty (1922) 326, 341, 345

anti-coercion (Free Speech campaign) 146, 170, 182, 194, 197, 212, 230, 265–266, 447

Anti-Partition League (APL) 408–421, 432

Armitstead, George 137

Arrowsmith, Pat 472, 511

Ashe, Thomas 299, 345

Asquith, (Prime Minister) Herbert Henry 231, 261–262

Atkins, Humphrey 465–466

Auxiliaries. *See also* Black and Tans 304, 308, 311–312, 327, 358–359, 381–382, 391, 438

Aveling, Edward 245

B

B Specials (Ulster Specials) 355, 409, 417, 421

Bains, Jennie. *See* Lizzie Baker

Baker, Lizzie (Jennie Bains) 261

Balfour, Arthur 170, 176, 182–183

Bambery, Chris 458, 509

Barlow, Jim 455, 465

Barnes, George 251, 284–285

Barnes, Peter 430

Barr, Isabella 332

Barrett, Annie 339, 376, 386

Select Index

Barrett, Michael 93, 104
Barry, Kevin 312
Barry, Tom 317
Beattie, John 'Jack' 412, 431
Bell, Edward 197, 232
Bell, James 397
Bell, (Reverend) David 64
Biggar, Joseph 116, 123, 130, 165, 205
Birmingham Six 471–472, 517
Black and Tans. *See also* Auxiliaries
Black, Clementina 245
Blackburn, Lord 329–330
Blennerhasset MP, R P 112
Blyth-Martin, (Sheriff-Substitute) W H 315
Bobby Sands Republican Flute Band 498
Booker, Joe 316, 318, 406–407
Border Campaign 420–422, 434, 447
Bowman, David 414
Boyle, Bridget. *See* Bridget McGinn
Boyle, Frank 397
Boyle, John 351
Boyle, Mary 108, 192, 255
Boyle, Mary Ann 339
Boyle, Matthew 390, 431
Boyle, Owen 180, 235
Bradley, James 107
Brady, John 107

Brannigan, Patrick 197, 207–209, 234, 266
Breen, Helen 100
Bremner, Andrew 205
Brennan, (Dr) Edward (Irish diplomat) 424–425
Brennan, (Dr) Edward (Repealer) 18–20
Brennan, Thomas 134
Brian Boru 50, 61, 225
Brogan, Denis 225, 382
Brooksbank, Mary (Mary Soutar) 282, 293, 299, 335, 385–386, 425
Brown, James Sunney 302
Brown, Oliver 408
Browne, Joseph 360–363, 374
Brownlie, Mary 247
Brugha, Cathal 329, 333–335, 337, 380
Bureau of Military History 192, 297, 380
Burke, A F 323
Burke, Augustine 20, 25
Burke, Mrs 184
Burke, Ricard O'Sullivan 103
Burke, Thomas 'Jock' 391
Burnett, Robert 48
Burns, (Father) Bartholomew 507
Burns, Robert 66, 84, 287
Butt, Isaac 106, 113–114, 131, 134
Butti, (Father) Peter 148
Byrne, James 287

Byrne, John 250
Byrne, William 79

C

Callan, Thomas 221
Campbell, (Provost) D 152
Campbell, Duncan 229
Campbell, Sheena 515
Campbell, Vincent 316
Campbell-Bannerman, (Prime Minister) Henry 229
Cameron of Kilsyth, (Reverend) Duncan 395–396
Cameron, Richard 46
Cameron, William 191, 233
Cappon, (Major) Thomas 278, 301
Carmichael, (Chief Constable) John 363, 391
Carr, Edward Grant 332
Carr, Ewan Geddes 297–298
Carr, Joseph 172, 195, 283
Carrigan, Charles 278–279, 290
Carroll, (Dr) William 126, 132
Carron, Owen 514
Carson, (Sir) Edward 249–250, 254, 259, 268–270, 272, 285–286, 288
Carson, John 405
Carson, Dorothy 274
Carty, Frank 1, 322
Casement, Roger 299, 304, 423

Casey, James Peter (J P) 126, 135, 137, 169–170, 212
Casey, (Father) Patrick 223–226, 238
Catholic Church 41–42, 62–67, 89, 110–119, 138, 141, 236, 240–241, 290, 295, 305, 309–312, 349, 358, 377, 395–397, 401–402, 410, 414, 484
Catholic Young Men's Society (CYMS) 63–66, 94, 115, 117, 241, 290
Champion, Henry Hyde 205, 208, 234
Chaplin, James 351
Chartism 4, 6, 14–18, 26–27, 29, 30–34, 38, 44, 47–48, 55, 63
Chartist strikes 16–18, 26, 31
Children's Land League 184, 188
Chile/Chilean refugees 209, 453–454, 459, 469
Church of Scotland 8, 130, 394–395, 397, 402–403, 406, 415, 509
Churchill, Winston 7, 231, 243, 258, 260, 267, 286, 290, 301–302, 311, 355, 358–360, 377, 381, 387, 390, 438
Clann na hÉireann 422, 424, 427, 436
Clancy, Agnes 112
Clancy, Thaddeus 107–109, 112, 114–115, 118, 120–121, 129, 135
Clapperton, (Reverend) Robert 56–57, 115, 117, 138
Clapton, Gary 467, 511

Select Index

Clarenbridge Volunteer Company 296

Clarke, Christina 339

Clarke, Edward 297–299, 380

Clarke, James 70–73, 78–81, 83

Clarke, John 390

Clarke, Peter 54–56, 60–61, 100

Clarke, Philip 54–55, 100

Clarke, Thomas 76, 132, 281, 291, 331–332, 417

Clerkenwell explosion 88, 90, 104

Clunas, Lila 259, 287

Clyde Workers' Committee 332

Colfer, Kevin 472

Collins, Margaret 313

Collins, Michael 290, 300, 303, 312, 326, 328, 332–334, 338, 351–357, 373, 412

Communist Party of Great Britain (CPGB) 286, 337, 360, 385, 410, 414, 441, 512

Communist Party of Ireland (CPI) 332, 429

Communist Party of Northern Ireland (CPNI) 509

Comunn airson Saorsa na h'Alba (League for the Freedom of Scotland) 404

Comunn na Albannach. *See* Scots National League (SNL)

Conlon, Charles 79–80, 103

Connachie, W 351

Connolly Association 415–416, 424, 432

Connolly, J P 353–354, 359

Connolly, James 2, 7, 46, 168, 180–184, 192, 194, 202–205, 207, 209, 213, 218, 228, 230, 232, 235, 240–242, 244–246, 248, 254–257, 263, 265, 279, 283–285, 292–294, 300, 303, 309, 318, 320, 328, 331–332, 341, 350, 379, 409, 410, 415–416, 420, 423, 424–426, 428, 434, 436, 447, 461, 475, 481, 499, 514, 517

Connolly, Fiona 424, 434

Connolly, John 168, 203, 233

Connolly, Lillie. *See* Lillie Reynolds

Connolly O'Brien, Nora (Nora Connolly) 286, 350, 379, 424, 434, 481, 514

Connolly, Peter 180, 192

Connolly, Roddy 286, 332, 426

Connolly-Heron, Ina 286

Connor, James 178–179

Connor, Mary 402, 429

Connor, P 364

conscientious objectors

Conybeare MP, Charles 182, 193

Coogan, James 140

Coogan, John 20–21, 25, 45

Coogan, Tim Pat 443

Cook, Tom 413

Corbyn, Jeremy 516

Cormack, John 403

Costello, Mary 20

Coyle, Henry 317–318, 320, 325, 356, 389, 406

Coyle, Michael 107
Coyle, Stephen 10, 339, 435
Coyle, William 417
Coyne, Edward 72–73, 131, 189
Coyne, Edward Fox 125, 131–132, 162, 189, 418
Coyne, John Fox 189, 418
Craig, Allan 402, 429
Craig, Charles 402, 429
Craig, (Sir) James 249, 272
Craig, Peter 402, 429
Craig, William 452
Cronin, Daniel 224, 237
Crosbie, Kirstin 471, 512
Cross, Susan 459
Crossmaglen Republican Flute Band 517
Cullen, (Archbishop/Cardinal) Paul 54, 56, 64–65, 100
Cullen, Phillip 351
Cumann na mBan 294–295, 300, 316, 320, 338–340, 386, 390, 430
Cumann na Poblachta 349, 363, 389
Cumann Poblacht na h'Eireann in Albain 349, 363, 365, 372
Cumming, James 48
Cummings, James 26
Cunninghame Graham MP, Robert Bontine 182, 192, 244–245, 266

D

D C Thomson 389, 395, 397, 423, 444, 453, 508
Dailly, Francis 205–206
Dalton, J P 225
Daly, James 134–137
Daly, John 30, 122, 125–126, 132
Daly, P T 211, 215, 235
Daniel, Peter 107
Darcy, Annie 158
Daunt, William O'Neill 8, 21–23
Davidson, Father 68
Davidson, William 30
Davitt, Michael 46, 93–95, 105, 114, 133–140, 145–147, 156, 161–167, 184–185, 196, 219–220, 222, 232, 518
De Courcey, Edward 172–173, 179, 197, 212, 235, 283
Deasy, John 171
Deasy, Timothy 87
Delargy, Hugh 408, 414–415
Dempsey, Seamus 350, 388
Dempsey, Thomas (T) 314–315, 349–350, 360, 364, 375, 388, 399, 418
Denvir, John 210
Despard, Charlotte 257, 260, 285
de Valera, Éamon 275, 289, 299, 305, 348–349, 354–355, 361, 376, 382, 389, 407, 411–412, 423
Devaney, James 320–326, 328, 349, 352, 398, 418–419, 427

Select Index

Devine, Catherine 98

Devine, James 126–127

Devine, Micky 492

Devine, Sam 400, 429

Devine, Susan ('The Girl in the Green Felt Hat') 242, 247, 282

Devlin McAliskey, Bernadette 476

Devlin, Hugh 78

Devlin, Joe 277–278, 290

Devoy, John 53, 77, 79, 81, 85–86, 91, 126, 136, 138, 145

Dewar, (Chief Constable) David 198

Dillon, John Blake 44

Dillon MP, John 133, 156, 161, 170–171, 191, 196, 232

Docherty, Charles 217

Docherty, John 150

Docherty, Elizabeth/Elizabeth Ferrie 247

Docherty, (Father) John 150

Docherty, Peter 409, 412–413

Doherty, Gerry 427, 435

Dolan, Isabella 385

Donelan, (Captain) A J C 248

Donnelly, Eamonn 354, 368

Donovan, Dan 34

Donovan, Frances 184

Donovan, William 30

Doyle, John 515

Doyle, Mary 480

Doyle, William 169

Dublin Lockout 7, 230, 249–256, 286, 361

Dublin Socialist Society 209–210

Ducley Edwards, Owen 425, 434

Duffield, Mike 471, 503, 512

Duffy, Charles. *See* Charles 'Cathal' Duthie

Duffy, Charles Gavan 23–24, 44

Duffy, John Joseph (J) 235, 409–410, 416, 431

Duffy, Margaret. *See* Margaret Innes

Duffy, William 18

Duncan, James 230, 283

Duncan, John 15–16, 18, 27, 44, 173–174

Dundee and District Jute and Flaxworkers Union (JFWU) 229, 241–243, 246–247, 252, 284, 385, 409, 416

Dundee and District Mill and Factory Operatives' Union 203

Dundee Catholic Herald 213, 226, 239, 295, 325, 355, 359, 389, 392

Dundee Chartist Church 27

Dundee Chartist Council 16, 44

Dundee Committee for a United Ireland (DCUI) 516–518

Dundee Confederate Club/Dundee Confederates 24, 27, 29, 33

Dundee Hibernian Football Club 394

Dundee Hunger Strike Action Committee 491–497

Dundee Irish National Institute(DINI) 71–73, 102, 107, 109, 127

Dundee Irish Republican Solidarity Campaign (DIRSC) 497–506, 515, 517

Dundee Labour Federation 246, 283

Dundee Labour Party 257–259, 333, 460–464, 482

Dundee Operative Bakers' Union 207

Dundee Radical Association 172–173, 195

Dundee Standard 462, 464, 509

Dundee Trades Council 207, 242, 249, 251, 266, 292, 380, 424, 467, 493–494

Dundee Trades Democratic Suffrage Association 16

Dunne, Joseph *see* D P Walshe

Durand, (Father) Richard 306, 327, 357, 390

Duthie, Charles 'Cathal' (Charles Duffy) 189, 339, 350, 352, 376, 386, 390, 418–419, 427, 432

E

Easter Rising (1916) 1, 6, 105, 132, 273, 279, 291–311, 331, 337–338, 341–342, 344, 350, 361, 376, 379, 381, 399, 422–423, 425, 447, 451, 461

Edinburgh Irish Solidarity Committee 492, 501, 506

Edinburgh Trades Council 265, 424, 426

Edinburgh United Ireland Association 424

Éire The Irish Nation 375, 392

Emmett, Robert 32, 46, 126–128

Emmett Flute Band 134

Engels, Friedrich 442, 499

Erskine of Marr, Ruaraidh 342–343

Evans, Dorothy 268–269, 274

Evans, Gladys 261

F

Fahy, (Canon) John 305–309, 316–318, 320, 322, 327–328, 347, 356–357, 375, 382–383, 391, 401, 406–407, 419, 430, 432, 491

Fahy, (Canon) Michael 419

Farrell, James 314, 429

Farrell, Mairead 480

Farrell, Michael 114, 116, 140, 238

Feather, Wally 513

Feehan, Tadgh 421

Feeley, James 412–414

Fenian Brotherhood 47, 51, 54–55, 58, 73, 75, 83, 90, 92–93, 97, 102

Fenian Sisterhood 82

Ferguson, John 109–110, 112–113, 118, 121, 129, 135, 137, 146, 158–161, 218, 234

Ferrie, Elizabeth. *See* Elizabeth Docherty

Fianna Fáil 376, 430

Select Index

Fianna na h'Alba 343, 387

Fitt, Gerry 426, 434

Fitzgerald, Francis 61

Flanagan, Daniel 107–108, 139

Flanagan, Michael 241

Flanagan, Patrick 39–40

Flanagan, Thomas 'Tim' 120, 135–136, 139–140, 144, 150, 158–160, 165, 170–171, 212, 235

Flynn, Patrick 108

Forde, Catherine 363, 374

Forrester, Arthur 34

Forster, William Edward 'Buckshot' 149, 157–159, 161, 188

Forsyth, William 167

Free Church of Scotland 130

Free Speech campaign. *See* anti-coercion

G

Gaelic Athletic Association 374

Gaelic League (An Conradh Gaelige) 7, 184, 222–231, 234, 331, 366, 418

Galbraith, Joseph 110

Gallacher, Brendan 472

Gallacher, John 107

Gallacher, Willie (Blanketman) 472

Gallacher MP, Willie 332, 358, 360

Galloway, George 460, 462, 482, 509

Gaulc, Elizabeth Finlayson 262

Gavan Duffy, Charles 23–24, 44

George, Henry 166, 213

George V 401

Gibb, Andrew Dewar 388

Gifford, Grace 292–293

Gillan, (Reverend) John 18–19, 22

Gillespie, Peter 243–244, 250

Gillies, William (Liam Mac Gille Iosa) 342

Gillis, James (Vicar Apostolic) 56

Gladstone, (Prime Minister) William Ewart 112, 149, 153, 155, 158, 161, 168, 171–172, 174, 182, 195–196, 199–200, 204, 232

Glasier, Bruce 180, 191

Glass, (Pastor) Jock 476, 487

Glasgow Fianna Éireann 278, 290

Glasgow H-Block/Armagh Committee 483, 486, 489

Glasgow Hunger Strike Action Committee (GHASC) 491, 498, 512

Glasgow Irish Freedom Action Committee (GIFAC) 498, 503–504, 512, 514

Glasgow IRSP Support Group 504

Glover, Annie 357

Golden, Agnes 313

Golden Junior, Peter 25

Golden Senior, Peter 25

Gonne, Maud 184, 223, 225, 286, 293

Gordon, Reverend (Arbroath) 22–23

Gowans, (Lord Provost) James 481–482

Graham, James 18, 26, 31, 34, 46, 48

Grant, May 259

Grattan, Henry 195

Grattan, Mrs 339

Gray, Mary 158

Greaves, C Desmond 183, 194, 204, 240–241, 246, 256, 415–416

Green, John 63, 82, 94, 101, 112, 115, 135, 137, 217

Green, Leo 480

Green, Linda 440

Griffin, (Father) Michael 327, 363

Griffith, Arthur 355, 357

Grimond, Mary Ann 247

Gunning, Mary Ann. *See* Mary Ann Devine

Gwynn, Stephen 248

H

H-Blocks (Long Kesh Prison) 469, 472, 484, 490, 494

Hagan, Francis 107, 114

Hannah, Daniel 53–58, 60–61, 65, 67, 69, 80–82, 95, 98, 100, 104, 107–109, 115, 129, 135, 186

Hannah, Eliza (adult) 186

Hannah, Eliza (child) 186

Hannah, Francis 186

Hannah, Jane 186

Hannah, Philip 186

Hannah, Stephen 186

Hannigan, Michael T 226, 239

Hardie, Keir 192, 205, 214–215, 217, 234, 245

Hardiman, Frank 297

Harrington, Timothy 172, 191

Healy, Sean 317–318, 320–321, 383, 406

Healy, Tim 172, 196

Henderson, (Councillor) Frank 114, 137

Henderson, Hamish 282, 425

Henderson, Sheriff 17

Henderson, Thomas 16

Hennessy, James 71, 95, 107, 109–110, 114, 116, 118–120

Hennessy, Mary 112

Higgins, Andrew 107

Higgins, Bridget (Tighe) 313–314

Higgins, John 313

Higgins, Patrick 65, 69, 92, 104, 114, 382

Hoey, Christopher Clinton 63–64, 70, 101

Holder, (Father) Joseph 115, 117

Holder, (Monsignor) Joseph 382

Holland, Charles 100

Home Rule 7, 105–125, 130–131, 135, 137, 140, 146, 149–150, 160, 162, 165, 168, 170–171, 174–176, 183, 186, 190, 194, 196, 200, 204,

208–210, 212, 214–215, 218–219, 222, 226, 229, 231–232, 234, 236–240, 244, 248–249, 251, 258, 261, 263, 266, 268–269, 276, 279, 286, 299, 301–302, 311, 328, 360, 389, 408, 431

Home Rule Association (HRA). *See* Home Rule

Home Rule Confederation. *See* Home Rule

Hood, Joseph 299

Hope, Jemmy 29, 422

Hopper, Catherine 148, 158

Houghton, Joseph 'Joe' 243–244, 246

Hughes, Brendan 480

Hughes, Francis (hunger striker) 491

Hughes, Francis (Dundee Home Rule Association) 108

hunger strike (1912–1914 – suffragettes) 257, 261–263, 267–268, 270–271, 273–274, 276, 286, 299

hunger strike (1917–1923) 305–306, 345, 351, 375

hunger strike (1981) 4, 8, 437, 472, 480–500, 502, 505–506, 509–514, 516–518

Husband, Agnes 257, 287

Hutcheson, Robert 177–179, 183

Hutchinson, Joseph 198

Hutchinson, H W 387–388

Hyland, Paddy 351, 363

I

immigration (Irish immigration) 2, 6, 13, 98, 307, 395–397, 415, 428

Independent Labour Party (ILP) 180, 207

Independent Orange Order 230

Independent Unionist 236, 465

Industrial action. *See* Strikes (industrial)

Industrial Workers of the World (IWW) 279, 283

Inghinidhe na hÉireann 223

Innes, Agnes 409

Innes, Margaret (Margaret Duffy) 420

International Brigades 402–403, 429

International Marxist Group (IMG) 445, 455, 458, 468, 473, 478, 485–487, 486, 495, 509

International Socialists (IS) 440

Iranian Students Association 454, 467, 474, 498

Irish Anti-Partition League (IAPL) *see* Anti-Partition League

Irish Citizen Army 230, 251, 259, 461

Irish Confederation 24–34, 45, 47–48, 73

Irish immigration. *See* immigration

Irish Independent 250, 331

Irish Liberty Club 357

Irish National Association of Scotland (INA) 70

Irish National Caucus 449

Irish National Foresters (INF) 7, 168–171, 196–198, 200, 216, 220–221, 251, 304

Irish National Land League/Land League 7, 128, 133–171, 181–185, 189, 192, 197, 199, 201, 204, 212–222, 303, 307, 347

Irish National League/Irish National League of Great Britain 7, 124, 163–165, 171–172, 207

Irish National Liberation Army (INLA) 434, 455, 467, 479, 497, 517

Irish Parliamentary Party (IPP) 7, 112, 163, 165, 170, 196, 212, 218–219, 222, 261, 276, 278, 299, 301–302

Irish Prisoners' Aid Committee 296

Irish Protestant Association 70

Irish Proclamation of Independence 268, 281, 291, 293, 303, 328, 331–332, 335–336, 338–340, 405, 410, 417, 422, 458

Irish Republican Prisoners Dependents' Fund (IRPDF) 391

Irish Protestant Association 14

Irish Republican Army (IRA) 1, 4, 104, 275, 303, 308, 311–312, 315–322, 325, 328–329, 334–346, 348–350, 353, 356, 361–363, 371–372, 375–379, 381, 384, 386, 388–390, 392, 396, 401, 403–409, 411, 414, 416–423, 426–427, 429–431, 433–439, 443, 445, 447–449, 451, 457–460, 465, 467–468, 471–475, 477, 479–481, 484–486, 489, 491–493, 495–497, 500, 504, 508, 512, 514, 516–518

Irish Republican Brotherhood/ Irish Revolutionary Brotherhood (IRB) 5, 7, 51, 54, 63–65, 70–98, 101–105, 109, 111, 113, 116–118, 120, 124–126, 128, 130, 132, 135–136, 138–139, 143, 146, 169, 186, 192, 200, 210–211, 215, 221, 223, 225, 228, 232, 234–235, 250, 276, 278, 299–300, 313, 331, 350, 382, 388

Irish Republican Socialist Party (IRSP) 461, 472, 479–480, 501, 504, 512

Irish Self-Determination League 333, 349, 363, 392

Irish Socialist Republican Party 210, 499

Irish Solidarity Movement (ISM) 501–506, 518

Irish Transport and General Workers Union (ITGWU) 245–246, 251, 254, 283, 424, 461

Irish Volunteers 275–276, 300, 304, 314, 331–332, 350, 380–381, 461

Irish Women's Franchise League (IWFL) 261, 286

Irish World/Irish World and American Industrial Liberator 127, 132, 187, 205

Islamic Socialists of the Peoples' Mujahedin of Iran 454

J

Jackson, (Sir) Henry Mather 364, 366

Jackson, Robin 'The Jackal' 510

James Connolly Republican Flute Band 448, 450, 455, 459, 502, 506

Jenkins, Edward 114, 121

John F Kennedy Flute Band 446, 459

Johnson, Anna 223

Johnson, Stuart (S) 441, 452–453, 462, 508

Jute and Flaxworkers Union (JFWU). *See* Dundee and District Jute and Flaxworkers Union

K

Kane, Paul 170

Kashmir Independence Movement 503

Keane, Augustus Henry (A H) 64, 69–70

Kearns, Daniel 295

Keenan, Jane 150

Keenan, (Reverend) Stephen 19, 22

Kelly, Catherine 418

Kelly, James (Dundee Home Rule Association) 107

Kelly, James (pro-socialist nationalist) 217, 229

Kelly, Michael 296

Kelly, Mrs John 339

Kelly, Robert 106, 129

Kelly, Thomas J 86–87

Kelly, W 351

Kenefick, William (Billy) 241, 248, 282

Kennedy, (Senator) Edward 433, 449

Kennedy, John 160

Kennedy, Samuel 430

Kenny, C 67–69, 71, 73, 77, 92

Kenny MP, W N 232

Kessack, James O'Connor 243–244, 246, 283

Kettle, Andrew 134

Kiernan, Oliver 173, 212, 236

Kilfedder, John 465

Kilmainham Agreement/Treaty 161–162

Kilmainham Jail/Prison 295, 379

Kimmet, James 'Dode' 320, 322–326, 352, 398, 418, 427

King, Martin Luther 513

Kirkpatrick, (Reverend) Fred 513

Kirkpatrick, Harry. *See* H Mac Gille Phadruig

Kirwan, (Captain) John 116, 119, 121, 130

Knight, (Reverend) William 111, 130

L

Labour Committee on Ireland (LCI) 516

Labour Party 203, 205, 207–208, 210, 214, 234, 257–259, 285, 333, 335, 364, 392, 408, 413–414, 419, 440, 450, 460, 462–464, 479, 482, 510, 516–517

Ladies' Land League (LLL) 7, 113, 133, 144–163, 184–185

Lalor, James Fintan 26, 46, 204

Land League 4, 7, 70, 98, 113, 127–128, 133–151, 153–170, 181–189, 197, 204, 212–213, 215–216, 218–219, 221–222, 241, 303, 307, 347

Land War 7, 98, 119, 137, 144, 147, 153–154, 162, 170, 180, 182, 185, 188, 226, 307

Larkin, Jim 88, 135–136, 230, 239, 242–244, 248–254, 259, 283, 318, 401

Larmour, Mary 271–272, 274

Lavelle, (Father/Canon) Patrick 54, 60, 64–70, 92, 100–101, 127, 138, 429

Lawless, Joseph 297

Lawrence, Alfred (Lord Trevethin) 364

League for the Freedom of Scotland. *See* Comunn airson Saorsa na h'Alba

Leigh, Mary 261

Lemass, Seán 423

Leng MP, (Sir) John 99, 208, 214, 217, 389

Lenin, V I/Leninism 105, 442, 461, 486, 514

Leonard, Arthur 427

Leslie, John 168, 175, 178, 180, 190–192, 203–204, 207, 209–210

Letters, (Dr) Patrick 114, 123–124

Liberal Party 168, 174, 192, 207, 217, 301

Liguori, Brother 373, 391

Livingstone, Ken 516

Lloyd George, (Prime Minister) David 285, 299, 305–306, 398, 411

Logue, Daniel 136, 195

Long Kesh Prison. *See* H-Blocks

Loughnane, Harry 327, 384, 391

Loughnane, Pat 384, 391

Lowe, David 173, 192, 203, 208

Loyal National Repeal Association (LNRA). *See* National Repeal Association

Luby, Letitia 80–81

Luby, Thomas Clarke 76

Lynam, Edward (Ned) 126–127

Lynn, (Dr) Kathleen 361, 370

M

MacAindreis, Amhlaidh 404, 429

Macarthur, Mary 229

MacBride, Maud Gonne. *See* Maud Gonne

MacBride, Peter. *See* Peter Connolly

MacBride, Sean 290, 293

MacDiarmada, Seán 291–292, 332

MacDonagh, Thomas 281, 290–291, 293

Select Index

Macdonald, (Reverend) Archibald 56
MacDonald, Ramsay 258–259
Macfarlane, Margaret 267
Mac Garaidh, Seumas (James Carr MacDonald Hay) 342–344, 346–348
Mac Gille Iosa, Liam. *See* William Gillies
Mac Gille Phadruig, H (Harry Kirkpatrick) 343
Mackay, Brigadier-General 30
Mackay, (Reverend) James 22
MacKay, Morrice 324
Maclean, John 332, 336, 343, 386, 503–504,
MacMahon Sword 50–53, 127
Macmillan, Harold 421, 452
MacNeill, Eoin 350
MacPherson, John 20, 22
Macrae, (Reverend) David 166–167, 171, 190
MacRory, (Bishop/Cardinal) Joseph 349, 388
MacSwiney, Mary 351, 392
MacSwiney, Terence 305–306, 312, 491
Mahon, John Lincoln 168, 172
Malloy, James 320, 322
Malone, Frank 3–4, 8, 441–445, 451–452, 454–459, 461, 464, 466–467, 471, 479–481, 485, 488–489, 492–493, 495–501, 504
Maloney, Mary 258

Manchester Martyrs 88–89, 134, 136, 146, 223
Mann, Tom 243–246
Mannix, (Archbishop) Daniel 308–312, 360, 370, 377, 391
Markievicz, (Countess) Constance 253, 317–318, 361–362, 370, 374–375
Marlowe, Terry (Terry O'Halloran) 503
Marra, Nicolas 208, 215–217, 219–220, 222, 229–230, 236, 238, 243, 249, 284, 292, 298, 380
Martin, (Bailie) J H 396
Martin, James 142–143, 148
Martin, John 109
Martin, Peter 54–55
Martin, Thomas Carlaw 266
Marx, Karl 163, 167, 442, 461, 488
McAliskey, Bernadette Devlin 476
McArthur, John 318, 343
McAteer, Eddie 408
McAuley, Edward Joseph 329–330
McAuley, William 107
McAuliffe, Mary 264
McCaffrey, Hugh 108
McCann, Joe 426, 434
McCann, Patrick 124, 126–127
McCann, Sean 408
McCarron, Mary 148, 158
McCartney, Ray 480
McCheyne, John 138
McCormick, James 430

McCorry, Peter 73–75, 93, 101–102, 104

McCracken, Elizabeth Priestly 270

McCracken, George 272

McCracken, Henry Joy 46

McCrea, Emmet 28–29

McCrea, John 15, 27, 31–32, 34, 46, 48

McCulloch, David 174–176, 191

McDade, William 403

McDaniel, James 213, 216–217

McDermott, Seamus 275

McDonald (Reverend) Archibald 56–57, 59

McDonald, Catherine Ann 'Cathy' 104, 313–319, 323, 339–340, 386, 398–399, 423, 427

McDonald, Edward 313

McDonald, Helen (Higgins) 313–319, 406, 430

McDonald, (Canon) John 382

McDonald, Mary Helen 'Lena 100, 300, 313–319, 339–340, 350, 357, 363, 378, 385, 389, 398–399, 406, 423, 427, 430

McDonald, Michael 108

McDonald, Peter 313, 383

McDonnell, Thomas 348

McElroy, John 18, 54–55, 61–62, 67, 69, 71–72, 100

McErlain, John 182–183

McFarlane, Florence Geraldine (Madge Muir) 264–270, 274–275, 289

McFarlane, John 264–266

McFarlane, Marion Elizabeth 264

McFarlane, Sandy 201–202

McFeeley, Tom 480

McFergus, Sean 357–358

McGee, Thomas D'Arcy 33, 47

McGhee, Joseph 410

McGill, Edward 405

McGinn, Bridget (Bridget Boyle) 192, 255

McGinn, James 180, 192, 235, 285

McGinn, Mary 235, 256, 285

McGlinchey, James 322

McGlone, Derek 447–448, 508

McGrady, Henry (Lord Provost) 198, 262, 286

McGuigan, John 72, 78, 80–81

McHale, (Archbishop) John 65

McHugh, Edward 150

Mackay, (Reverend) James 22

McKearney, Tommy 480

McKenna, Frank 316

McKenna, Matthew 116, 119–120, 209–210

McKenna, Sean 480, 484

McKinney, Samuel 20, 27, 54, 65, 94, 100

McLaughlan, Alex 108

SELECT INDEX

McLaughlin, Bernard 229, 231, 238, 276, 304

McLaughlin, Michael 76–77, 79, 102

McLoughlin, Sean 331–335, 337, 359, 384, 410

McMahon, James 198, 232

McManus, (Father) Sean 449, 508

McManus, Terence Bellew 54–55, 69, 250

McMillen, Liam 'Billy' 426, 434

McNally, Patrick 50–52, 54, 65, 69, 100

McNeece, Francis 430

McNiffe, Thomas 315–317

McShane, Harry 386, 464

McShane, John 336, 386

McSherry, Terence 404, 422

McSparran, James 408

Meagher, Thomas 23, 27, 29–32, 47, 61

Meillet, Léo 168, 207

Mellows, Liam 296, 318, 321, 405

Metge, Lillian 272, 274

Milroy, Sean 305, 352–354

Mitchel (Young Irelander leader) John 29–30, 32, 48, 52, 116, 126, 135

Mitchell, E Rosslyn 364, 372

Mitchell, James. *See* D P Walshe

Mitchell, John (Chartist) 17, 44

Mitchell, Mary 313

Mitchell, Thomas. *See* D P Walshe

Mollie Maguires 45

Molloy, Francie 500, 514

Monday Club 452–453

Mooney, Eamonn 350, 378, 388, 406, 418–419

Moore, James 198

Moore, Marguerite 158–160, 189

Moorhead, Ethel 260–261, 264, 267–268, 270–271, 275

More, E D 358, 390

Morris, William 172–174, 232

Morrison, Thomas 54, 56, 60–61, 69, 71, 95, 100, 106–109, 116, 120, 124, 126, 131, 135–137, 197, 211

Morton, James 206

Mosquito Press 503–504, 514

Mountjoy Jail 261, 362, 364

Muir, Madge. *See* Florence Geraldine McFarlane

Mulcahy, Richard 352

Munro, Anna 257

Murphy, Captain James 86

Murray, James 213, 215–216

Myles, James 38, 44, 49

N

Na Fianna Éireann 290, 331, 350, 429

Nablus 463, 483

Nairn, David 278–279, 297

National Brotherhood of St Patrick (NBSP) 6, 53–64, 114, 135, 143, 211, 298, 313

National Charter Association 15

National Guard 29–33, 46

National Repeal Association (Loyal National Repeal Association (LNRA)) 18–21, 23, 35

National Unemployed Workers' Movement (NUWM) 337, 364

National Union of Public Employees (NUPE) 513

Neary, Bridget 100

Neave, Airey 455

Neave, (Bailie) David 385

Neely, Daniel 65

Neilson, Andrew 48

Nelson, (Reverend) Isaac 110–111

Nolan, James 250

Nolan, John 'Amnesty' 94–95, 542

Nolan, Sean 353

Northern Campaign 407

Northern Ireland Civil Rights Association (NICRA) 509

Nugent, Kieran 437

Nugent, Mairead 480

O

O'Briain, Art 349, 392

O'Brien, Mahon 50

O'Brien, Murtagh 50–51

O'Brien, William (MP) 170–171, 178, 190–191, 196, 229

O'Brien, William Smith (Young Ireland leader) 27, 29–30, 51–53, 190–191, 195

Ó Catháin, Máirtín 2, 76, 104, 130, 210, 221, 237, 338, 383

O'Connell, Daniel 14, 18–20

O'Connell, John 18

O'Connell, Maurice 20

O'Connor, Feargus 16–17, 44, 48

O'Connor, John 125

O'Connor, Mrs 364

O'Connor, R H 'Roddy' 412–413, 422, 431

O'Connor, Rory 329, 431

O'Connor, T P 139–140, 172, 279

O'Connor, Tommy 388

O'Connor Power, John 116, 122, 131, 223

O'Doherty, (Captain) Sean 300–301, 315, 317, 320–328, 349, 352–353, 356–357, 384, 419

O'Donnell Derrick J 213, 216, 226, 231, 276–277

O'Donnell, Frank Hugh 122

O'Donnell, James J 146

O'Donnell, Patrick 189

O'Donnell, Peadar 401–402

O'Donnell, Sarah 213

O'Donnell, Terry 459

O'Donoghue, Daniel 53, 122

O'Donoghue, Florrie 362

O'Donovan Rossa, Jeremiah 54–55, 70, 72, 76, 80, 101, 110, 128, 132, 136, 374, 412, 461, 488

O'Duffy, Eoin 388

O'Dwyer, Ella 517

O'Farrell, George 19, 21

Official IRA (OIRA) 433–435,

Ogilvy, John 172–173, 195, 217–218

O'Halloran, Terry. *See* Terry Marlowe

O'Hara, Michael Joseph 405

O'Hara, Patsy 491

O'Higgins, Kevin 353, 396

O'Kane, James 122, 160, 165–166

O'Kane, Sara 338–339

O'Kelly, Seán T 359, 407, 423

Old IRA Association (Scottish Division) 378, 406, 417–420, 423, 430

O'Leary, Martin 445–456, 458, 465

O'Mahoney, John 73, 75–76, 104, 250

O'Malley, Ernie 438, 443

O'Malley, Thaddeus 110–111

O'Neill, (Dr) Charles 199

O'Neill, Frank 408

O'Neill, Hugh 26–27, 45

O'Neill, Patrick (Repealer) 20, 25

O'Neill, (Captain) Patrick Joseph 345, 349, 352–354, 362–374, 391–392, 419

O'Neill, (Prime Minister) Terence 423

Operation Harvest 420

O'Rahilly, Michael Joseph 'The' 279, 381

O'Rahilly Brass and Reed Band 392

Orange Order/Orangeism 14–15, 21, 43, 61, 98, 108, 143, 230, 249, 275, 285, 399, 446, 457, 475, 488, 508, 517

O'Rourke, Michael 108

Orr, William 422

O'Sheehan, Sean (Jack) 303–305, 309, 312, 338

O'Sullivan, C P 154

O'Sullivan, Joby 430

P

Padraig Pearse Republican Flute Band 134, 477, 498, 516

Paisley, Ian 43, 488

Palestine 441, 475

Pankhurst, Christabel 274, 286

Pankhurst, Emmeline 286

Pankhurst, Sylvia 275

Parnell, Anna 7, 105, 147–160, 190, 222

Parnell, Charles Stewart 7, 122–123, 133–134, 139–140, 146, 161–165, 167, 169–172, 185, 190, 195–198, 201, 204–205, 219, 232, 250, 412

Parnell, Fanny 145–146

Paterson, John 169, 216, 221

Paterson, Lucy 148, 237

Pearse, (Mrs) Margaret 351

Pearse, Patrick (Pádraig Mac Piarais) 184, 385

Pearse, Willie 290, 351

Peel, Robert 19, 46

Perth 22, 40, 76–77, 85, 146, 181, 198, 240–241, 261, 277–279, 282, 296, 329, 344–347, 350, 419, 424, 446, 449, 459, 463, 382

Phelan, Michael 138, 223, 227, 418

Phin, Laurence 108, 140

Phoenix National and Literary Society 51, 55, 99, 101

Phoenix Park Assassinations 161, 189–190

Plan of Campaign 170, 173, 191, 241, 266

Plunkett, Joseph 64–65, 153, 188, 281, 292–294, 332

Price, Dolours 472, 511

Price, Marion 472, 511

Pro-Republican Irish Solidarity Movement (PRISM) 504

Protestant Action 403, 426

Provisional IRA 437, 447, 449, 508–509

Purcell, Richard 353–354, 359

Pym, Francis 462

Q

Quinn, Eileen 327

Quinn, Jean 300, 315–316, 320, 330, 339–340, 375, 407

Quinn, James 317

Quinn, John 25, 153

R

Rankin, Henry 48

Reader, Seamus 317–318, 349–350, 384, 387, 418

Red Action 504

Redding, Patrick 14, 108

Redmond, John 149, 196, 212, 217–219, 227, 229, 254, 261, 268, 276, 278–279, 288, 301, 331, 403, 412

Redmond, Joseph 180

Redmond, Sean 424

Redmond, Willie 214, 224

Reid, James 230, 252, 284

Reid, William 329–330

Reilly, Pat 394–395

Reilly, Patrick 40

Reilly, Philip 81

Relatives Action Committee 440, 472, 480

Renehan, Persis 422, 507

Republican Band Alliance. *See* Scottish Republican Band Alliance

Republican Congress 401

Revolutionary Communist Group (RCG) 464, 466–469, 471–473, 476, 486, 491–493, 495–496, 498–506, 512, 514

Revolutionary Communist League (RCL) 473, 503, 514

SELECT INDEX

Revolutionary Communist Tendency 473

Reynolds, Lillie (Lillie Connolly) 180, 240, 309

Reynolds, Thomas 101

Ribbon Societies/Ribbonism 13–14, 20–21, 23, 35, 40, 43, 57–59, 61, 92, 97, 114, 169, 175, 192, 213

Rigg, (Bishop) George 125

Robbins, Thomas 351

Robertson, Edmund 208, 214, 229, 233

Robertson, James 174–179, 182–183, 191, 202

Robertson, John 31

Robinson, Joe 332, 349–350, 353–354, 362–363, 365, 370, 372, 384, 406

Robinson, Seumas 278

Roche, Edward 119–120, 150, 152 158–160, 164–165, 169–170, 191, 197, 212, 235

Roche, (Father) John 223

Roche, Maurice 421

Rooney, Catherine 247, 385

Ross, Alexander 'Sandy' 298

Ross, Ernie 462–463, 465

Ross, John 323

Ross, Willie (Ulster Unionist MP) 452–453

Rowan, Edward 108

Royal Perthshire Rifle Militia 79, 103

Royal Ulster Constabulary (RUC) 417, 421, 433, 437–438, 449, 482, 490

Russell, (Prime Minister Lord) John 24, 31, 60

Russell, P J 222

Russell, Sean 403, 407

Russell, Thomas (United Irishmen) 46

Russell, Thomas William (T W) (MP) 217–218, 236

Russia 132, 334–335

Ryan, Frank 402

Ryan, Mick 433

Rylett, Harold 158

S

S-Plan 403

Sands, Bobby 484, 487–491, 498, 511

Sanna, Bridget 20

Saorsa na h'Alba. *See* Comunn airson Saorsa na h'Alba

Scheu, Andreas 167–168, 172

Scots National League (SNL) (Comunn na Albannach) 342–344, 347

Scottish Hunger Strike Action Committee 485

Scottish Labour Party (SLP) 192, 205, 213, 234, 246, 284, 517

Scottish Land Restoration League (SLRL) 165, 213

Scottish National Party (SNP) 190, 388, 463, 494, 513

Scottish Prohibition Party 231, 237, 240, 243, 248, 301, 358, 360, 390

Scottish Republican Band Alliance 450, 491, 495, 502, 504-505, 516-517.

Scrymgeour, Edwin (Neddy) 209, 231, 237, 240, 243, 248, 256, 301, 358, 360, 390

Sexton, Thomas 172, 232

Sheehy Skeffington, Francis 35, 250

Sheehy Skeffington, Hanna 261, 275, 286, 518

Shinwell, Manny 246

Sinn Féin 6, 189, 222, 231, 237-238, 276, 279-281, 286, 294-295, 299-306, 308-310, 312, 320-322, 325-330, 332-334, 336-339, 342-349, 351-353, 356, 358, 363, 378, 384, 390, 392, 395, 398, 401, 417, 422, 436, 439-440, 443, 455, 463, 471-472, 475, 478, 480, 486, 496, 500, 503, 505, 507, 514-516

Sinn Féin/The Workers' Party. *See* Workers' Party. *See also* Sinn Fein

Skelton, Daniel 'Dan' 408, 410, 412, 414, 417-420, 422, 427, 431

Skinnider, Margaret 1, 264, 273, 339-340, 350

Slaven, James 169

Slaven, John 363-364

Sligo (arrests of Dundee Fenians) 83, 136

Smillie, Bob 216, 343

Smith, Cyril 467

Smith, Graham 10

Smith, (County Inspector) Henry 153, 188

Smith, James 48

Smith, Thomas 158, 164

Social Democratic Federation (SDF) 167

Socialist League (SL) 172-174, 183, 191

Socialist Workers' Party (SWP) 441, 443-445, 451, 454-455, 465, 468, 471, 473, 478-479, 485-487, 492-492, 495, 498, 509, 511, 513

Solohedbeg 303, 381

Somerville, Matthew 404, 430

Soutar, J R 334

Soutar, Mary. *See* Mary Brooksbank

Soutar, Sandy 293

South Africa 189, 442, 459, 475

Spain 401

Spartacus League 473

St Mary's Flute Band 150

St Patrick's Flute Band 134, 150

Steel, Annie 386

Steel, George 216

Steel, Maggie 339

Stephens, James 54, 72, 76, 81

Stewart, Bob 240, 297, 308-309

Stewart, Ellen 158

Stewart, J 273

Stokes, (Sir) William 129

Strachey, John 413

Strickland, Charles 320, 356

strikes (industrial) 117, 203, 229–230, 241–255, 257, 259, 282, 284, 290, 330–331, 385

Sullivan, Police Constable 154

Sullivan, Alexander Martin (A M) 109, 171, 184

Sullivan, Timothy Daniel (T D) 172, 184, 232

Sweeney, James 507

Sweeney, John 71–72, 154, 507

Sweeney, William 20, 23–25, 27, 100

T

Taylor, Alex 172

Taylor, Michael 440–441, 443–444, 452, 456, 462, 464, 466, 469, 474, 477, 485, 489, 493, 496–499, 501

Taylor, Peter 308, 401, 429, 439,

Thatcher, (Prime Minister) Margaret 10, 459, 465

The Workers' Party. *See* Workers' Party

Thomson, Ann 385

Thomson, Helen (Anderson) 385

Thomson, James 428

Thomson, John 'Jock' 335, 385–386,

Tighe, Thomas 313

Tillet, Ben 244, 246

Toner, (Bishop) John 308–309, 382

Toner, John (Repealer) 20–21

Torley, Father 358

Torley, John 135–136

Tosh, Jessie Ann 247

Traynor, Oscar 380

Traynor, Patrick 108

Trevethin, Lord. *See* Alfred Lawrence

Troops Out Movement (TOM) 8, 445, 450, 466, 468, 495. *See also* United Troops Out Movement (UTOM)

Trotter, Mary 237

Tuck, Ron 466

Turner, John (Miner) 329–330

Turner, (Canon/Dean/Monsignor) John 240–241, 282, 309, 311, 357–358

Turner, Una 440

Tynan, (Dr) John 56

Tyneside Action Committee on Ireland 504

U

Ulster Defence Regiment (UDR) 437–438, 461–470, 490, 510

Ulster Specials. *See* B Specials

Ulster Volunteer Force (UVF) 249, 259, 269, 272, 510, 515

United Irish League (UIL) 7, 124, 140, 163, 208, 212–222, 224–226, 228–229, 231, 236–239, 248, 276–279, 298–302, 304–305, 382, 408

United Irish League of Great Britain (UILGB) 212, 216, 222, 236, 276–277, 279, 285

United Troops Out Movement (UTOM) 439, 443–445, 450–462, 464–468, 473, 508, 511

V

Vaughan, (Father) Bernard 305–306, 381, 491

Vaughan, James 221

Vincent, Arthur 69, 71, 316

Vize, Joe 312, 316, 321, 338

W

Walker, Archibald 48

Walker MP, Bill 463, 465, 510

Walker, William 2, 55, 76, 100, 178, 234, 242, 340

Wallace, (Sir) Matthew 364, 368, 371

Wallace, William 260, 262, 346, 502

Walsh, James 56

Walsh, Owen 54–55, 62–64, 67–76, 89, 93, 100, 102, 104, 135

Walshe, D P (James Mitchell/Thomas Mitchell/Joseph Dunne) 316, 318, 320, 322, 324, 326, 384, 406

Ward, James 141–143, 149, 169, 210, 212, 234

Ward, James (Glasgow) 98

Warrenpoint 460, 462, 467

Weatherhead, (Reverend) James 395

Wickham, Maud 274

Williamson, (Reverend) Henry 203, 252–253

Wilson, Alf 351

Wilson, Gordon 463, 494, 513

Wilson, (Prime Minister) Harold 423

Wilson, (Mrs Alf) Mary Ann 339

Wilson, Thomas J 348, 379

Women's Freedom League (WFL) 257–259, 286

Women's Social and Political Union (WSPU) 258–262, 267–271, 273–276, 286, 288

Wood, Wendy 403–404

Workers' Party (The Workers' Party) 286, 478. *See also* Sinn Fein

Workers' Revolutionary Party (WRP) 473, 516

Y

Yaffe, David (Reed) 500, 503

Yeaman MP, James 114, 121

Young Ireland 4, 6, 19, 23–24, 26, 32, 51–52, 54, 61, 94, 105, 127, 191, 232, 234

Z

Zimbabwe 452–453, 459

Zimbabwean Students' Association
see Zimbabwe

OTHER TITLES FROM TIPPERMUIR BOOKS

Spanish Thermopylae (2009)

Battleground Perthshire (2009)

Perth: Street by Street (2012)

Born in Perthshire (2012)

In Spain with Orwell (2013)

Trust (2014)

Perth: As Others Saw Us (2014)

Love All (2015)

A Chocolate Soldier (2016)

The Early Photographers of Perthshire (2016)

Taking Detective Novels Seriously: The Collected Crime Reviews of Dorothy L Sayers (2017)

Walking with Ghosts (2017)

No Fair City: Dark Tales from Perth's Past (2017)

The Tale o the Wee Mowdie that wantit tae ken wha keeched on his heid (2017)

Hunters: Wee Stories from the Crescent: A Reminiscence of Perth's Hunter Crescent (2017)

A Little Book of Carols (2018)

Flipstones (2018)

Perth: Scott's Fair City: The Fair Maid of Perth & Sir Walter Scott – A Celebration & Guided Tour (2018)

God, Hitler, and Lord Peter Wimsey: Selected Essays, Speeches and Articles by Dorothy L Sayers (2019)

Perth & Kinross: A Pocket Miscellany: A Companion for Visitors and Residents (2019)

The Piper of Tobruk: Pipe Major Robert Roy, MBE, DCM (2019)

The 'Gig Docter o Athole': Dr William Irvine & The Irvine Memorial Hospital (2019)

Afore the Highlands: The Jacobites in Perth, 1715–16 (2019)

'Where Sky and Summit Meet': Flight Over Perthshire – A History: Tales of Pilots, Airfields, Aeronautical Feats, & War (2019)

Diverted Traffic (2020)

Authentic Democracy: An Ethical Justification of Anarchism (2020)

'If Rivers Could Sing': A Scottish River Wildlife Journey. A Year in the Life of the River Devon as it flows through the Counties of Perthshire, Kinross-shire & Clackmannanshire (2020)

A Squatter o Bairnrhymes (2020)

In a Sma Room Songbook: From the Poems by William Soutar (2020)

The Nicht Afore Christmas: the much-loved yuletide tale in Scots (2020)

Ice Cold Blood (2021)

The Perth Riverside Nursery & Beyond: A Spirit of Enterprise and Improvement (2021)

Fatal Duty: The Scottish Police Force to 1952: Cop Killers, Killer Cops & More (2021)

The Shanter Legacy: The Search for the Grey Mare's Tail (2021)

'Dying to Live': The Story of Grant McIntyre, Covid's Sickest Patient (2021)

The Black Watch and the Great War (2021)

Beyond the Swelkie: A Collection of Poems & Writings to Mark the Centenary of George Mackay Brown (2021)

Sweet F.A. (2022)

A War of Two Halves (2022)

A Scottish Wildlife Odyssey (2022)

In the Shadow of Piper Alpha (2022)

Mind the Links: Golf Memories (2022)

Perthshire 101: A Poetic Gazetteer of the Big County (2022)

The Banes o the Turas: An Owersettin in Scots o the Poems bi Pino Mereu scrievit in Tribute tae Hamish Henderson (2022)

Wild Quest Britain: A Nature Journey of Discovery through England, Scotland & Wales – from Lizard Point to Dunnet Head (Keith Broomfield, 2023)

Guid Mornin! Guid Nicht! (Lawrence Schimel and Elīna Braslina, Scots translation by Matthew Mackie, 2023)

Madainn Mhath! Oidhche Mhath! (Lawrence Schimel and Elīna Braslina, Scottish Gaelic translation by Marcas mac Tuairneir, 2023)

FORTHCOMING

William Soutar: Collected Works, Volume 1, Published Poetry (1923–1946) (Paul S Philippou (Editor-in-Chief) & Kirsteen McCue and Philippa Osmond-Williams (editors), 2024)

William Soutar: Collected Works, Volume 2, Published Poetry (1948–2000) (Paul S Philippou (Editor-in-Chief) & Kirsteen McCue and Philippa Osmond-Williams (editors), 2023)

The Stone of Destiny & The Scots (John Hulbert, 2024)

The Mysterious Case of the Stone of Destiny: A Scottish Historical Detective Whodunnit! (David Maule, 2024)

The Whole Damn Town (Hannah Ballantyne, 2024)

Balkan Rhapsody (Maria Kassimova-Moisser, translated by Iliyana Nedkova Byrne, 2024)

The Black Watch from the Crimean War to the Second Boer War (Derek Patrick and Fraser Brown, 2024)

William Soutar: Collected Works, Volume 3 (Miscellaneous & Unpublished Poetry) (Paul S Philippou (Editor-in-Chief) & Kirsteen McCue and Philippa Osmond-Williams (editors), 2025)

William Soutar: Collected Works, Volume 4 (Prose Selections) (Paul S Philippou (Editor-in-Chief) & Kirsteen McCue and Philippa Osmond-Williams (editors), 2026)

All Tippermuir Books titles are available from bookshops and online booksellers. They can also be purchased directly (with free postage & packing (UK only) – minimum charges for overseas delivery) from www.tippermuirbooks.co.uk.

Tippermuir Books Ltd can be contacted at mail@tippermuirbooks.co.uk